SOCIAL PSYCHOLOGY

Daniel Perlman
University of Manitoba

P. Chris Cozby
California State University, Fullerton

Holt, Rinehart and Winston
New York / Chicago
San Francisco / Philadelphia
Montreal / Toronto / London / Sydney
Tokyo / Mexico City / Rio de Janeiro / Madrid

Published for the
Society for the Psychological
Study of Social Issues (SPSSI)

Publisher: John Michel
Acquisitions Editor: Marie Schappert
Senior Developmental Editor: Rosalind Sackoff
Senior Project Editor: Arlene Katz
Art Director and Cover Design: Bob Kopelman
Production Manager: Annette Mayeski
Photo Research: Joe Samodulski
Text Design: Beverly Haw Leung, / A Good Thing, Inc.
Managing Editor: Jeanette Johnson
Cover Photo: Reginald Wickham

Library of Congress Cataloging in Publication Data

Main entry under title:

Social psychology.

  Bibliography: p. 542
  Includes indexes.
  1. Social psychology. I. Perlman, Daniel. II. Cozby, Paul.
HM251.S6716   302   82-6237
ISBN 0-03-053766-5   AACR2

CBS COLLEGE PUBLISHING
Holt, Rinehart and Winston
The Dryden Press
Saunders College Publishing

Copyright Acknowledgments appear at the end of the indexes.

PREFACE

What now seems like a long time ago, the executive officers of the Society for the Psychological Study of Social Issues (SPSSI) decided to sponsor a text on social psychology—the study of how we influence and are influenced by others. Several senior members of SPSSI had ideas about the form the book might take. When we were approached to assume editorial responsibilities for the project, we were excited by the prospects of a SPSSI book and we enthusiastically agreed to serve. We began by assembling both an advisory board and a group of chapter authors. By 1979, our vision for the volume was beginning to become a reality.

In many ways, editing this book has been like directing a play or orchestrating a symphony. As co-editors, we have had the challenging task of coordinating the efforts of a number of very talented individuals. Like most directors, we have tried to produce a work that would be fresh, technically excellent, and interesting. Now, as the final manuscript is going to press, we want to preface the book by making a few remarks about why we and the other contributors wrote it, our goals, and the unique features of our approach.

One of the prime reasons for undertaking this project was to develop a book that would reflect the values of SPSSI as an organization. SPSSI has always stood for ideals such as social equality and the belief that social science knowledge can be of practical value. These ideals and values will be manifest throughout the book.

A second impetus for embarking on the project came from the biases manifest in other texts on the market in the late 1970s. At that time, the existing books (and, indeed, the field itself) primarily reflected a laboratory experimental approach. Along with this approach came the heavy reliance on college sophomores as subjects, the frequent use of deception in experiments, and concern over whether the field was providing solutions to pressing social problems. The laboratory approach came under criticism leading to a so-called "crisis" in the field. In thinking about the research SPSSI members had been doing for over forty years, we realized it provided an antidote to many of the problems facing social psychology in the 1970s. SPSSI members had always done research outside the laboratory using diverse populations and data collection techniques. There had never been any doubts about the social relevance of what SPSSI researchers were doing. We felt this research definitely strengthened the field and provided leads concerning how social psychology should develop in the future. Although we highly value the experimental approach, we wanted to develop a text that reflects SPSSI's broader, more eclectic approach to the discipline.

Most books summarize the principles, methods, and findings of social psychology. The present volume is no exception. Beyond this, however, we have several other goals. Probably our most salient goal is to focus attention on social issues and problems. Naturally, many traditional social psychology texts mention social problems; but, these texts usually do so in a cursory manner more as a form of window dressing. The chapters in the present book typically have such material as a core, focal concern. A common format is to describe a problem in some detail, and then indicate how the social psychological material covered in the chapter could be applied to help solve the problem. Such an approach offers students concepts that they can use in order to better understand issues that arise in their own lives. As one person commented, a SPSSI book should—above all else—demonstrate the value of "humanism—research, as a way of improving the individual's and society's condition."

Another important goal of this text is to meet the needs of students. We tried to select materials and examples that would be interesting to undergraduates. Also, the book itself, along with Barbara Maddex's Student Study Guide, is designed to facilitate learning. For instance, the text per se has chapter outlines, a glossary, and chapter summaries. The Student Workbook has learning objectives, a short synopsis of the material covered in the text, multiple choice questions, and a listing of key terms. A unique, important feature of the Student Workbook is the case problems designed to help students improve their skills in applying knowledge to practical situations.

To ensure that the manuscript was meeting our goals, we classroom tested it. Not once, but three times (twice at the University of Manitoba and once at New Mexico State University). Revisions and final polishing of the manuscript benefited greatly from the detailed feedback our students provided.

This book reflects the joint efforts of many contributors. We believe this is one of the book's greatest assets. All the authors are experts in their own areas, and thus were able to write more competent, up-to-date chapters.

Like most editors of multi-authored texts, we have been concerned with achieving a reasonable degree of consistency throughout the book. On the one hand, we wanted to avoid overlap, omissions, and major differences in style. On the other hand, we believe the diversity of views espoused by the contributors accurately reflects the complexity of the field and adds to the book's richness. Thus, we have tried to strike a balance between the contributors' individuality and their interdependence.

Having said this, we should repeat that our role was akin to that of a play's director. Although we guided, honed, and coordinated, the chapters are the work of the contributors. Collaborating with these colleagues has been a pleasure for us and one of the most exciting aspects of developing this book.

Our final product is a social psychology text that is traditional in its organization. After an introductory section, we proceed from chapters on individual processes (socialization, attitudes, attribution, and social perception) to a focus on interpersonal relations (attraction, intimate communications, sexuality, aggression, helping, social exchange, and interpersonal influence) to chapters on group and broader influences on behavior (group dynamics, intergroup relations, the environment, organizations, and social change). Throughout the various chapters, however, several social issues appear. These social issues pertain to: prejudice (Chapters 2 and 16), social justice and the judicial system (Chapters 3, 13, and 16), environmental concerns (Chapters 4, 5, 13, and 17), sex roles (Chapters 3, 9, and 10), media violence (Chapter 11), mental health (Chapter 15), and wife abuse (Chapter 19). Throughout the book (Chapters 5, 8, 9, 11, 12, 18, and 19), there are discussions relevant to increasing personal and organization effectiveness. Thus, we feel that we have both communicated the basic knowledge of the field and met our goal of providing a unique focus on social problems.

Professors will be pleased to know that Ron Riggio has prepared an extensive Instructor's Manual to accompany the text. In addition to a test bank, it contains: suggestions for lecture material, information on films and audiovisual aids, suggestions for classroom projects/demonstrations and supplementary references.

We would like to close with a message especially for students. We believe social psychological knowledge is at its best when it can be given away to an ever widening circle of people. If this text is to succeed, it should leave you wiser—more insightful about your social world and yourself. The questions considered in social psychology have fascinated us for many years. We hope that this book stimulates your interest in these questions and provides some excellent answers. And beyond the information we have communicated, we hope the book will help you to better formulate and answer social psychological questions of your own.

Daniel Perlman
P. Chris Cozby

ACKNOWLEDGMENTS

As anyone familiar with publishing is well aware, most books are written only when the authors have the help and support of many other individuals. We have been very fortunate in this regard.

The initial idea for this volume was championed by Larry Wrightsman. He read the initial prospectus, chapter outlines, first drafts, and the entire second draft of the manuscript. In a manner he has done with so many other publishing projects in social psychology, Larry astutely and unselfishly helped give birth to this book.

We would like to express a very special thanks to Jeff Rubin. His contributions to the book extend far beyond those called for by his role as co-chair of the SPSSI Publication Committee. For four years, we've had periodic "Thursday evening phone calls." Jeff has provided friendship and sage consul. Being one of psychology's truly outstanding writers, he read and offered suggestions on how each chapter could be polished. When problems arose, Jeff took time (even on foreign holidays with his family) to offer compassion plus his superb problem-solving and negotiating talents. This Advisory Committee consisted of Lois Biener, Gary Alan Fine, Diane Ruble, Dalmas Taylor, June Louin Tapp, and Lawrence S. Wrightsman.

The members of our SPSSI Advisory Committee have helped us solidify a team of contributors, provided guidance on broad policy decisions pertaining to the book, and reviewed various chapters in draft form.

Our institutions and the people involved with them have facilitated the completion of this project. At California State University, Jeannie King compiled the integrated bibliography and the glossary. At the University of Manitoba, Joan Embleton very ably served as secretary, obtained permissions, and repeatedly took care of "little" matters that otherwise would have slowed our progress. Both Manitoba's department head, John McIntyre, and Dean of Arts, Fred Stambrook, have not only been most tolerant of the time devoted to this undertaking but also helped create an atmosphere conducive to getting work done.

At Holt, we have worked with Roz Sackoff and Arlene Katz. They have been tolerant of the additional complications caused by a multi-authored book, and aided us in keeping the project moving forward. Not only have they helped us do our best in preparing the manuscript, their own very considerable skills have also added greatly to the design and production of the finished volume.

A number of colleagues have commented on first and/or second drafts of the manuscript. These readers have provided very useful feedback for improving both the scientific contents and the expository style of the book. While the number of readers is fairly large, each has had their distinct impact; we are especially grateful for the care and thoughtfulness that went into their advice. Seven scholars read the entire manuscript:

Russell Bennett, Bemidji State University

Marilynn Brewer, University of California at Santa Barbara

Charles Carver, University of Miami

Susan Green, George Washington University

David A. Schroeder, University of Arkansas

Martin Sofer, Catholic University

Rodney Wellens, University of Miami

The following psychologists read portions of the manuscript:

Richard Archer, University of Texas at Austin

Chris Argyris, Harvard University

Paul Bell, Colorado State University

Ellen Berscheid, University of Minnesota

Philip Brickman, University of Michigan

Larry Christensen, Texas A & M

Sheldon Cohen, University of Oregon

Nina Colwill, University of Manitoba

Cynthia Deutsch, New York University

Robin DiMatteo, University of California at Riverside

Nancy Eisenberg, Arizona State University

Lorenz J. Finison, Wellesley College

Ira Firestone, Wayne State University

William A. Fisher, University of Western Ontario

Alan E. Gross, University of Maryland

Ronald D. Hansen, Oakland University

Bob Helm, Oklahoma State University

Herman Hosch, University of Texas at El Paso

Alice M. Isen, University of Maryland

James Jaccard, Purdue University

Rudolf Kalin, Queens University (Canada)

Edward Krupat, Massachusetts College of Pharmacy

Marianne La France, Boston College

Laurie Larwood, Claremont Mens College

Richard Lippa, California State University at Fullerton

Geoff Maruyama, University of Minnesota

F. Stephen Mayer, California State University at Fullerton

Clara Mayo (1931–1981), Past SPSSI President

Charles McClintock, University of California at Santa Barbara

John McConahay, Duke University

Michael Mend, California State University at Fullerton

Fredrick Miller, New York University

Norman Miller, University of Southern California

Stanley Morse, Massachusetts Institute of Technology

Christopher Olson, Ohio State University

Stuart Oskamp, Claremont Graduate School

Marilyn Rands, Wheaton College

Bertram H. Raven, University of California at Los Angeles

Richard Rozelle, University of Houston

Brendan Gail Rule, University of Alberta

Susan Saegert, CUNY Graduate Center

Steven Slane, Cleveland State University

William Smith, Vanderbilt University

Cecelia Solano, Wake Forest University

Michael Storms, University of Kansas

Elizabeth Tanke, University of Santa Clara

James Tedeschi, SUNY at Albany

Harry Triandis, University of Illinois

Ladd Wheeler, University of Rochester

Allen Wicker, Claremont Graduate School

David A. Wilder, Rutgers University

Alvin F. Zander, University of Michigan

If social psychology has one central focus, one simple message to offer, it is the interdependence between people. We rely on, are influenced by, and seek intimacy with others. For us, the most important others in our lives are our families—Elizabeth and Anton, Jeannie and Josh. They have listened to our aspirations; offered advice, support, and encouragement; and engaged in their own activities during the weekends and evenings we worked on this project. In short, they have given us an optimal blend of solitude and sociability. We are very glad that it is with these individuals that we share our greatest interdependence.

Daniel Perlman
P. Chris Cozby

FOREWORD

Traditionally, the current president of SPSSI writes the foreword for text-books published during his or her presidential year. Clara Mayo should have had this honor. However, her untimely death during her first months of office has led me, as past president of SPSSI, to contribute this piece in her stead.

SPSSI (The Society for the Psychological Study of Social Issues) is a non-profit organization that has been in existence for nearly fifty years. Its mission has been, and continues to be, the application of social scientific knowledge to the broader understanding of various social issues. Throughout its existence, the Society has consistently been interested in, and concerned about, education. The publication of textbooks has been viewed as a way not only of providing technical knowledge to students but also of providing a perspective on research values.

There are many introductory social psychology textbooks currently available, most of which provide a technically competent treatment of research findings in social psychology. This book, I am confident you will agree, is very different. Indeed, it is unique. Although the SPSSI social psychology text is as diverse and extensive in its coverage of traditional topics as its competitors, this book has been guided by the assumption that social values, social issues, and social problems are of central importance—and are therefore worthy of attention in their own right. The distinguished contributing authors, in addition to presenting material in their own fields of expertise, have picked particular social issues or problems for special attention. In this way the book's focus is continually directed to the tight and inextricable ties between knowledge in the abstract and its application to real and pressing social concerns.

In keeping with SPSSI's values, the authors of this exciting new book have produced a volume that presents traditional academic social psychology in the appropriate context of its social relevance. As a result, the readers of this book will be given a unique social problem orientation that may enable them to understand better their social environment, and possibly to behave in ways that improve the quality of their own lives and the lives of others.

Leonard Bickman

BRIEF CONTENTS

CONTENTS

PART

4

Introduction

PART 1

SOCIAL PSYCHOLOGY: DEFINITION, HISTORY, AND PERSPECTIVES

1

- Social Psychology: What Is It?
- What Topics Do Social Psychologists Study?
- Historical Roots of Social Psychology
- Challenges and Perspectives
- Summary

No man is an island entire of itself. . . . Every man is a piece of the continent, a part of the main.

John Donne

A man wholly solitary would be either a god or a brute.

Aristotle

Humans are social animals. Society has been exalted and society has been damned, but without a doubt, others play a major part in our lives. In essence, studying people as social animals is what social psychology is all about.

The field is usually described as a new one, which is correct in the sense that contemporary social psychology, as we presently know it, is less than one hundred years old. The issues that concern social psychologists today, however, are much the same as those that have concerned people throughout the history of civilization. Many of the basic phenomena that social psychologists examine—attraction for others, aggression, helping and kindness, justice, persuasion, and so on—are almost universal aspects of social behavior. Coming to understand such behaviors is a fascinating and important pursuit. Helping you to learn about and better understand these phenomena is the primary goal of this book.

In this chapter the field of social psychology will be introduced, defined, and distinguished from related disciplines. We will identify the topics social psychologists study and trace the history of the field. Finally, some perspectives on the future of social psychology will be offered.

SOCIAL PSYCHOLOGY: WHAT IS IT?

"Social psychology," wrote Gordon Allport (1968, p. 3) in what has become a classic definition, is "an attempt to understand and explain how the thought, feeling, and behavior of individuals are influenced by the actual, imagined, or implied presence of others." In other words, **social psychology** is about how people affect and are affected by one another. Often, as Allport's definition makes clear, other people can influence us without being physically present.

Beside defining what falls within the boundaries of the discipline, you also need to know what to exclude. For you, as a student just becoming acquainted with the field, making this discrimination can sometimes be difficult. You may also be vague on how various disciplines differ.

For instance, after reading Allport's definition, you may wonder how social psychology is different from general psychology, child development, or sociology. General psychology is a broader field, not restricted to *social* influences on behavior. In many ways, the process of early socialization (the transmission of cultural values to the young), a concern of child psychologists, fits nicely within Allport's definition of social psychology. Indeed, as we will see in Chapter 3, developmental and social psychologists do share an interest in this topic. They also share interests in such phemonena as children's peer relations or moral development. These two subareas in psychology are not synonymous, however: while developmental psychologists are uniquely interested in growth and change over the life cycle, this emphasis is considerably less important in social psychology. Also, the interests of developmental psychologists extend beyond social influences to a host of other factors that can shape an individual's maturation. Sociology is concerned with the nature and structure of society. Whereas psychologically trained social psychologists focus primarily on interpersonal relations, sociologists focus more on large aggre-

---

This chapter is written by Daniel Perlman and P. Chris Cozby.

SOCIAL FOCUS 1.1
Sociological Social Psychology

Historically there have been, and there are now, two social psychologies. . . . One is a social psychology written by psychologists, the other a social psychology written by sociologists. Neither is totally remote from the influence of the other . . . but the two tend to differ in definition and in execution. (Stryker, 1977, p. 145).

Differences between sociological (SSP) and psychological social psychology (PSP) can be identified in terms of the leading contributors to the field, the topics investigated, the research methods most commonly used, and the predominant theoretical orientations. Among those scholars whose work has had important impact on sociological social psychology (Perlman, 1979) are such individuals as Howard S. Becker, Herbert Blumer, Charles Horton Cooley, Harold Garfinkel, Erving Goffman, and George Herbert Mead. Methodologically, sociological social psychologists do more survey studies than they do laboratory experiments. The reverse is true for psychological social psychologists (Wilson & Schafer, 1978). Sociological social psychologists have done several widely cited participant observer studies; psychological social psychologists rarely use this technique.

House (1977) has identified two major, distinctive focuses of sociological social psychology: symbolic interactionism and "psychological sociology." Symbolic interactionism has its roots in the work of Cooley, Mead, and others. Cooley introduced the famous notion of the "looking-glass self." He suggested that we first imagine how our acts will be seen by others, then we imagine how others will judge us, we experience feelings such as mortification or pride, and finally, we adjust our behavior accordingly. In more recent times, Herbert Blumer has been a principal champion of symbolic interactionism. He believes that "human beings act toward things on the basis of the meanings that the things have for them" and that "the meaning of such things is derived from, or arises out of, the social interaction that one has with one's fellows" (Blumer, 1969, p. 2).

The major emphases of symbolic interaction have been summarized by House as follows: first, meaning is not inherent in external objects—rather, it is given by the perceiver—and second, the interpretation of situations occurs via human interaction. Thus symbolic interactionists do not see human behavior as an automatic response to fixed stimulus conditions. For symbolic interactionists, "to understand social life is to understand the processes through which individuals interpret situations and construct their actions with respect to each other" (House, 1977, p. 167).

Psychological sociology, the second focus of SSP, had its roots in the writings of Emile Durkheim, Max Weber, and even Karl Marx. This body of theory and research has concentrated on the effect of macrosocial structures (for example, social class, religion, type of community) and macro processes (such as social mobility, urbanization, industrialization) on people's personalities and their behavior.

gates of people. Thus sociologists, more so than psychologists, deal with the influence of social class and social institutions.

Social psychology has been described as lying between psychology and sociology. Actually, there are both psychologists and sociologists who consider themselves social psychologists. This text primarily reflects the psychological perspective. Some of the unique concerns of sociologically oriented social psychologists are reviewed in Social Focus 1.1.

WHAT TOPICS DO SOCIAL PSYCHOLOGISTS STUDY?

To convey more concretely what social psychology is about and to provide a preview of the rest of the text, we want to briefly introduce the major topics social psychologists study. The text can be divided roughly into four parts, a general introduction followed by three substantive sections. The substantive sections are arranged in a sequence that focuses first on basic individual processes, then on interpersonal relations, and finally on the broader influences on behavior—the influences of groups, organizations, and the environment.

This flow from the individual to the larger social context will not be a completely linear progression. Some topics actually involve both individual and group processes, so that one could make a case for placing them at more than one point along the continuum. Nonetheless, this continuum is of value as an organizing principle and is worth keeping in mind as you progress through the course.

The first substantive area of social psychology is called basic individual processes. Four major topics at this level are socialization (Chapter 3), attitudes (Chapters 4 & 5), attribution (Chapter 6), and social perception (Chapter 7). Socialization is the process by which people develop personality attributes as well as learn the norms and values of their so-

ciety. We commonly think of socialization as occurring during childhood, but as Chapter 3 will show, it can take place throughout life. An attitude is an evaluative reaction to some object. For instance, in a conversation between two students, one might say "I like running" and the other might say "Cigarette smoke really irritates me." Both have expressed attitudes. Social psychologists have been interested in measuring attitudes, as well as in studying how people's attitudes develop and are changed.

Attribution processes are the ways we explain the actions of ourselves and others; social perception is how we see others. These topics could be considered interpersonal phenomena, since they involve perceiving and explaining the behavior of others. We prefer to classify them as basic processes, however, since they occur within the individual.

The second substantive area of social psychology is interpersonal relations. The major topics in this area include communication (including self-disclosure), interpersonal attraction (whom we like), sexuality, the ways we relate to others (that is, aggressively versus altruistically), and social influence processes (conformity and obedience). Social influence and attitude change are similar. Yet attitudes can change for reasons beyond the influence of others, and not all social-influence attempts are directed toward changing attitudes; often social influence is directed toward changing behavior. Interpersonal processes are a major part of social psychology.

The third substantive area of social psychology includes the broader influences on our behavior such as groups, organizations, and the environment. The study of groups focuses attention on additional aspects of our social world: roles, status hierarchies, communication patterns, norms, and division of labor. Not only will we explore the dynamics operating within groups, but will also examine the relationships between groups. We will answer such questions as, why does prejudice de-

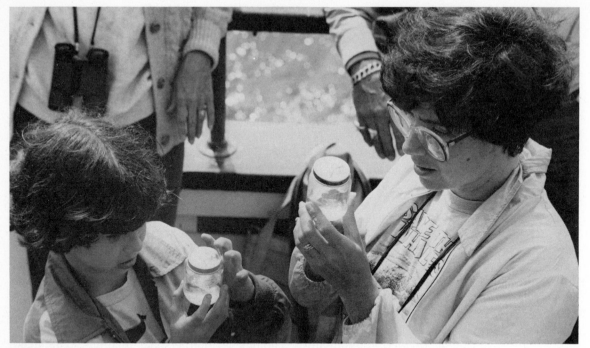

Over 2,000 years ago Aristotle implied that common interests promote friendships. Many contemporary social psychologists hold this same view.

velop? and, what are its consequences? Beyond face-to-face groups, there are larger social organizations such as churches, political parties, communes, and multinational businesses. Social psychologists have been interested in what attracts and holds people to organizations, as well as what effect organizations have on the productivity and attitudes of their members. With regard to environmental factors, psychologists have done research on how we interpret, evaluate, react to, and act on our natural and man-made surroundings.

Consideration of these broader influences on behavior brings us to the role of social psychologists in policy formation and social change. Social psychologists can analyze social problems, offer information to policy makers, assist in setting up social programs, and assess the impact of social changes. We will conclude the text with a chapter on this important topic.

HISTORICAL ROOTS OF SOCIAL PSYCHOLOGY

Aristotle and Plato

It is not difficult to trace social psychological thought back through a long period of history. Consider the following passages that deal with the topics of persuasion and friendship:

We believe good men more fully and more readily than others. . . . It is not true, as some writers assume . . . that the personal goodness revealed by the speaker contributes nothing to his power of persuasion; on the contrary, his character may almost be called the most effective means of persuasion he possesses.

They are friends, then, for whom the same things are good and evil, and who are friends and enemies of the same people. . . . Men like, too, those who have done good to themselves, or those for whom they care. . . .

We like also those who, we think, wish to do us good. We like our friends' friends, and those who like the persons whom we like; and those that are liked by those that are liked by ourselves; and those who are the enemies of our enemies—who hate the persons whom we hate.

These passages were actually written by Aristotle, but contain many insights that are still worthy of our consideration today. For the ancient Greeks, explanations of social behavior were often tied to theories of how to govern. Thus, Allport (1968) claims that social psychology essentially started as a branch of political philosophy.

Besides Aristotle, one of the other outstanding Greek philosophers was Plato (427–347 B.C.). Basically, Plato believed that people band together for the aid group members provide one another in achieving their needs and goals. Plato asked, "What is the best form of government?" He reasoned that since people band together for efficiency in satisfying their needs, specialization of tasks would help. He saw three roles: one for rulers, one for soldiers, and one for artisans or workers.

Plato claimed that some people were blessed at birth with leadership potential. Their leadership abilities, however, would need to be honed via a long training program, and at each step of the way, the trainees would need to be tested. By the end of their training, all rulers should have developed certain characteristics, which included being altruistic, being able to face danger, being indifferent to materialism, and the like. Plato's view of society has been called an elitist one. He saw the three groups as forming a social hierarchy, and saw no reason for workers to question their lot in life. He

believed they were made from different materials than rulers, and therefore, their lower position was just.

In contemporary terms, Plato attributed great importance to genetic determinism. He was one of the earliest social philosophers, however, to discuss what we today would call socialization or education. He had what social psychologists would now call a trait theory of leadership.

Besides his views of society, Plato claimed that the human spirit consisted of three components: affect, conation, and cognition. Plato thought these were located in the abdomen, the breast, and the head, respectively. Affect refers to our feelings and emotion, conation to striving or action, and cognition to thoughts and intellectual analysis. Although Plato's anatomical ideas have been discarded, many social psychologists still find his trichotomy of phenomena useful. Indeed, these concepts were used in Allport's definition of the field. Later in this text, you will see that various theoretical approaches to social psychology differ in the attention they devote to these three aspects of human functioning.

Simplified Explanations of Social Behavior

In the eighteenth and nineteenth centuries, a series of social philosophers kept searching for one simple mechanism to explain all social behavior (see Allport, 1968). The three most popular explanations were hedonism (pleasure seeking), egoism (power seeking), and **sympathy** (imitation).

Jeremy Bentham (1748–1832) articulated the principle of **hedonism** (or utility, as he called it), maintaining that people act solely to enhance their pleasure. The experience of pleasure varies along several dimensions such as duration, intensity, and certainty of occurring. In Bentham's view of man, we are constantly engaging in mental calculations to achieve the maximum amount of gratification. Herbert Spencer extended this doctrine by connecting it to Darwin's ideas, claiming that pleasurable actions generally promote survival and therefore have evolutionary value.

Thomas Hobbes (1588–1679) was a champion of **egoism.** He did not deny the importance of pleasure seeking, but he maintained that to obtain pleasure, one must first have power. Therefore, he claimed that power was the most basic of all motives. The constant, insatiable striving for power leaves the human species in a continual "war of all against all." Hobbes believed that people form governments and agree to social constraints to protect themselves from other power-seeking individuals.

The notion of imitation was contained in Adam Smith's 1776 book, *The Wealth of Nations.* This doctrine was more systematically elaborated over a century later by a Frenchman, Gabriel Tarde (1843–1904). He asserted that "society is imitation." In short, Tarde believed that behaviors are acquired by copying others. He offered several other more refined laws of imitation, claiming, for instance, that people imitate members of their own culture in preference to foreigners and that members of the lower classes imitate members of the upper classes, rather than vice versa.

Criticisms and questions can be raised with regard to each one of these simple, unitary explanations of behavior. Does all behavior result in pleasure? If our actions are acquired via imitation, how do novel behaviors and innovations arise? Beyond these criticisms of specific explanations, there are criticisms of this general approach. With several suggestions as to the key for explaining social behavior, how do we decide which factor is really most important? Perhaps even more telling is the question, Is anything that simple? Is it realistic to explain all behavior with only one or even just a few ideas? Thus these simple explanations of social behavior have faded in their importance, yet they made an important contribution to the understanding of human behavior. These same basic ideas, in only slightly modified form, can clearly be found in contemporary social psychology.

The Beginnings of Contemporary Social Psychology

Another writer at about the time of Bentham was Auguste Comte (1798–1857), who classified the various sciences into different groups. He coined the term "sociology," and is often credited with being the father of social psychology. This is not so much because he did social psychological work, but rather because he saw the need for social psychology and identified the phenomena the field should investigate. For him, a discipline was needed to understand the individual's behavior in its social and cultural context.

Although a number of studies of relevance to social psychology were done in the 1880s and early 1890s (see Haines & Vaughan, 1979), what is typically identified as the first experiment in social psychology was published by Norman Triplett in 1898. At that time bicycle racing was a major activity. For the sports fans of the day, this posed an interesting question: do bicyclists ride faster alone against a clock or in competitions against other riders? Factors such as better pacing could be advanced for why cyclists do best alone against a clock, yet Triplett found that cyclists rode faster in competition. To verify this finding, Triplett had children, ages 10 to 12, crank a fishing reel. Each did this three times alone and three times in competition with others. Triplett found that the children generally cranked faster when competing than when alone.

To keep this, and most subsequent social psychological findings, in proper perspective, one should note that superior performance in competition was only a group tendency. Actually, half the subjects did better in competition, a quarter did less well, and for the others, competition had no effect on performance.

Most social psychological findings are statistical generalizations; there are almost always individual exceptions.

Nonetheless, Triplett's study was an auspicious beginning. The basic question addressed by Triplett still fascinates social psychologists. Do people perform better alone or with others? In 1924, Floyd Allport distinguished between **social facilitation** ("the influence of the group upon the individual's movements") and rivalry ("the desire to win"). In 1965, Robert Zajonc wrote a classic article suggesting that the mere presence of other people enhances the performance of dominant (that is, well-learned) responses, but interferes with the performance of nondominant (that is, new) responses. Research on social facilitation persists.

A next milestone in the history of social psychology was the publication of the field's first textbooks in 1908 by Ross and by McDougall. Ross, a sociologist, focused his book on interpersonal processes; McDougall, a psychologist, relied heavily on the notion of instincts in trying to explain social behavior. Both authors based their books primarily on conceptual insights and speculations rather than on empirical evidence. It was not until Allport's 1924 text and the Murphys' 1931 book (and also Murphy, Murphy, & Newcomb, 1937) that there was a sufficient body of knowledge to write an empirically based introduction to the field.

By the late 1920s, and the early 1930s, the ideal of transforming social psychology into an empirical discipline had been accepted. Research techniques were being developed and the amount of work being done was expanding. Some of the milestones between the 1920s and the late 1960s are shown in Social Focus 1.2.

In the 1940s social psychologists contributed to the war effort, turning their attention to such topics as propaganda, building civilian morale, integration of the armed forces, and military leadership (Cartwright, 1948; 1979). Only in the 1950s, however, was the ideal of social psychology as an experimental discipline

really achieved. In 1949 the proportion of articles in the *Journal of Abnormal and Social Psychology* reporting experimental manipulation was a low 30 percent. By 1959 this figure had risen to over 80 percent (Adair, 1980).

CHALLENGES AND PERSPECTIVES

The Challenges of the 1960s and 1970s

Despite its historical roots and established theory, social psychology is still a young field. It is moving steadily ahead, but this progress is not achieved without intellectual confrontation and controversy. In the late 1950s, just as social psychology was achieving status as an experimental science, a number of critical challenges to the field surfaced. These occurred along at least four fronts, having to do with methodology, social relevance, "history", and value biases.

The first challenge to social psychology was a critical examination of the laboratory experiment as the ultimate method in the field. In 1957 Donald Campbell published an article focusing attention on several factors that could undermine the validity of experiments. An implication of this article was that it is harder than was previously realized to conduct an experiment properly. This was followed by an outpouring of work on the social psychology of the psychological experiment. Rosenthal (1966), Orne (1962), and others demonstrated that cues in the experimental situation, the experimenter's behavior, and other similar factors influence the outcome of research. (Campbell's ideas, as well as work on the social psychology of the psychological experiment, will be covered in more detail in the next chapter.)

A second doubt that surfaced during the 1960s concerned the practical relevance of social psychological research (Ring, 1967). Analyses of social psychologists' research habits had demonstrated their heavy reliance on college students and volunteers as subjects. Could the

SOCIAL FOCUS 1.2
Milestones in Social Psychology (1920–1969)

1921 **The Journal of Abnormal Psychology** becomes the **Journal of Abnormal and Social Psychology**, the first journal explicitly devoted to publishing social psychology articles.

1925 Bogardus develops his social-distance scale to measure people's attitudes toward various ethnic groups. Thurstone's (1928) and Likert's (1932) methods of assessing attitudes followed shortly thereafter (see Chapter 4). Gallup founded the Gallup Poll in 1935.

1933 Katz and Braly report on Princeton students' racial stereotypes.

1933 Mayo along with Roethlisberger and Dickson (1939) studied productivity at the Hawthorne plant of the Western Electric Corporation. Productivity increased, whether the amount of lighting in the work area was increased or decreased. This focused attention on importance of supervisory practices and human relations in determining employees' productivity.

1936 The Society for the Psychological Study of Social Issues is founded.

1936 Sherif studies norm formation, using the autokinetic effect (that is, the illusion of movement given by a stationary pinpoint of light in a totally black room). Subjects' judgments of how far the light moves is influenced by the judgments of other observers.

1939 Dollard et al. claim that aggression is a consequence of frustration.

1939 Lewin, Lippitt, and White show that "we feelings" (that is, morale) are higher in democratic than in autocratic or laissez-faire groups. The highest productivity occurs in autocratic groups, but democratic groups are better able to sustain productivity in the leader's absence.

1945 Lewin founds the Research Center for Group Dynamics, located first at MIT and eventually at the University of Michigan.

1949 Hovland and his Yale collaborators publish **Experiments on Mass Communication**, the first of five influential volumes on attitude change and persuasion.

results from these samples be generalized to a broader cross-section of society? Ring noted the tendency of social psychologists to do flamboyant, and sometimes ethically questionable, studies. This, he claimed, resulted in many fads and new frontiers, but little settling in of research.

In an article entitled "Social Psychology as History," Kenneth Gergen (1973) posed a third challenge to the field. A basic assumption of science is that there are stable, general laws of behavior. Gergen contested this assumption. He claimed that social psychology "deals with facts that are largely nonrepeatable and which fluctuate markedly over time. . . . Knowledge cannot accumulate in the usual scientific sense because such knowledge does not generally transcend its historical boundaries" (Gergen, 1973, p. 310). One reason for the changing nature of social phenomena, according to Gergen, is what he calls "enlightenment effects." He believes that social psychological knowledge is being disseminated to the public and that this knowledge, often covertly prescriptive in character, is changing behavior.

The fourth and most recent challenge to social psychology was articulated by Edward Sampson (1978), who maintains that social psy-

1950 Research on **The Authoritarian Personality** is completed by Adorno and his associates. This type of person manifests submission to authority, prejudice toward ethnic minorities, and the like.

1951 Asch demonstrates conformity to erroneous peer judgments in a line-judging task.

1957 Festinger publishes **A Theory of Cognitive Dissonance.** He argues that people avoid dissonance, a state in which they hold conflicting beliefs or cognitions.

1958 Heider publishes **The Psychology of Interpersonal Relations,** containing his seminal statement of attribution theory (see Chapter 6).

1959 Thibaut and Kelley publish **The Social Psychology of Groups,** describing the theory of social exchange.

1962 Schachter and Singer offer a theory that emotions are a function of both physiological arousal and social cues concerning how this arousal should be labeled.

1963 Milgram publishes on obedience, showing that subjects will obey an experimenter's command to administer intense electric shock to another human being.

1965 Jones and Davis publish a paper that stimulates research on attribution and social cognition.

1965 A paper on equity theory by Adams defines an important rule of social exchange.

1968 Latane and Darley explain why bystanders often fail to help people in emergencies.

1969 Campbell, in a paper entitled "Reforms as Experiments" shows the relationship between social science methods and political action.

(We will wait a few years before speculating on the "milestones" that may have occurred since 1970.)

chology grew out of, and serves, the needs of a "male-dominant Protestant-ethic-oriented, middle-class, liberal and capitalistic society" (p. 1335). In short, he believes the discipline is biased and constrained by a particular set of social values.

Perspectives for the 1980s

The challenges of the 1960s and 1970s will undoubtedly strengthen, rather than diminish, social psychology during the next decade. These challenges do, however, imply certain corrective trends for the future. One of our goals is to manifest these trends as themes in this text. Let us consider each of the challenges, treating the issue of practical relevance last, rather than second.

The first challenge was directed toward laboratory experiments. Critical examination of laboratory methods has led to new safeguards and sophistication in conducting experiments. It has also led to our Perspective 1: a greater appreciation of the need to have converging evidence from different sources collected in different ways. Besides simply diversity in methods, social psychologists must strive for diver-

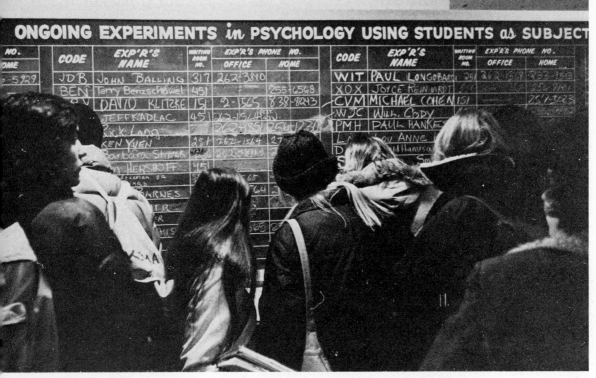

ONGOING EXPERIMENTS in PSYCHOLOGY USING STUDENTS as SUBJECT

Many critics claim that too many social psychology experiments use college students as subjects. As will be manifest in this text, we believe the advancement of social psychological knowledge is best served by studying people of diverse ages and backgrounds.

sity in the ages and backgrounds of the people they study.

Gergen's view of the transient nature of social science findings has stimulated a great deal of debate (see Manis, 1976). In our opinion, Gergen has exaggerated the importance of enlightenment effects. We would be very happy if large segments of the world's population were familiar with the current wealth of social psychological knowledge, but we seriously doubt that this is the case. Further, just because social facts change, that does not mean that the underlying processes of social behavior are unstable. Instead, it implies that social psychologists should more systematically incorporate historical and cultural factors into their theories. This brings us to a second perspective

of the present text: the need to search not only for simple relationships between variables but also for the limiting conditions under which these relationships hold.

Sampson's challenge to social psychology was that the field is dominated by the values of middle-class, American values. It would be unrealistic to deny the influence of these values on social psychology as we know it today, yet within the United States and around the world, other groups are being attracted to the profession. Clearly, others besides middle-class American males are contributing to the field and will continue to do so. Although not directly a resolution of Sampson's challenge, a third perspective of the text is sensitivity to cultural variation. Gender differences, as well as as ethnic or racial differences in behavior, will be identified throughout.

The final challenge was to the practical relevance of social psychology. Even in the 1960s, lack of relevance was a valid criticism for only a segment of the profession. Since the 1930s there has continuously been a group of social psychologists committed to the application of scientific knowledge. Indeed, this commitment was one of the main reasons why the Society for the Psychological Study of Social Issues (SPSSI), the organization sponsoring this volume, was founded (see Social Focus 1.3). Kurt Lewin (1951), one of the most influential early members of SPSSI, eloquently championed this view in his statement that "there is nothing as practical as a good theory." Lewin's philosophy will be a final perspective manifested in this text.

As one way of demonstrating the utility of social psychology, most of the chapters in this book will include a focal social problem. The problem will be described, relevant research cited, and ways of alleviating the problem discussed.

Of all the current trends in social psychology, the shift toward a more applied emphasis is, perhaps, the most important. Much of the exciting new work in the field is currently being conducted in applied settings dealing with topics such as the legal system, health care, problems of energy conservation and en-

Social psychology is shifting toward a more applied emphasis dealing with such topics as health care and problems of the elderly.

SOCIAL FOCUS 1.3
The Society for the Psychological Study of Social Issues: Profile of an Organization

SPSSI, The Society for the Psychological Study of Social Issues, was a product of the depression. Basically, SPSSI got its start as a response to the high unemployment rate among psychologists. During the early 1930s, the dominant ideology of older, leading members of the psychological community was Social Darwinism (see Finison, 1976, 1979). This elite believed in the survival of the fittest. They thought the way to reduce unemployment problems was to increase the entry standards for prospective members of the profession, enhance psychology's image with the public, and lower the supply of psychologists to be consistent with the demand for their services.

SPSSI was formed by a younger group of psychologists reacting against this restrictivist position. The founding members of SPSSI had an expansionist orientation toward unemployment. They believed the social order could be changed, and that psychologists collectively should attempt to improve their employment opportunities. They noted many places in society where the services of psychologists were needed.

The initial founders of SPSSI were sympathetic to socialistic views, but very shortly the leadership of SPSSI came from "the mainstream of American liberalism" (Finison, 1979, p. 35). Almost immediately a significant proportion of psychologists became SPSSI members, and one of SPSSI's founders, E. C. Tolman, became president of the American Psychological Association, the major national organization of psychologists.

Besides employment issues, the founders of SPSSI had other goals. In circulating a petition to create their group, they said SPSSI would be an official body for

1. the promotion and protection of research on "controversial" topics,
2. the administration of timely referenda,
3. the authoritative interpretation of the attitudes of the socially-minded psychologists respecting important group conflicts, and
4. the support of all progressive action that promises to aid in the preservation or creation of human values (cited in Finison, 1979, p. 30).

Although SPSSI's course has changed slightly over the years, it still retains many of its original goals. The organization's purpose is currently stated as follows:

vironmental stressors, and reduction of group conflict in integrated schools. Not only is this work applied; it also demonstrates the validity of Lewin's views, since it is generally grounded in the theories and basic research findings of social psychology. It should be further noted that there are now many more opportunities for advanced training in applied social psychology.

As social psychology progresses through the 1980s, the emphasis on applied work is likely to continue. If the spirit of Kurt Lewin's approach to social psychology is followed, however, a renewed interest in theoretical de-

The Society for the Psychological Study of Social Issues is a group of over 3,000 psychologists and allied social scientists who share a concern with research on psychological aspects of the important social issues. . . . In various ways, the society seeks to bring theory and practice into focus on human problems of the group, the community and the nation as well as the increasingly important ones that have no national boundaries. (Inside cover, *Journal of Social Issues*).

In 1945, SPSSI started a scientific publication called the *Journal of Social Issues*. While this publication is only one of the organization's undertakings, an examination of its pages helps to chronicle the Association's focal concerns. In analyzing the *Journal of Social Issues* over its first 34 years, McGrath (1980) identified three major concerns addressed by SPSSI members. He calls them the three Ps: prejudice, poverty, and peace. As used by McGrath, each concept actually encompasses a broad set of phenomena.

Prejudice refers to discrimination against a wide variety of groups (racial, ethnic, and religious groups; women, homosexuals, the aged, and so forth). This concern has extended beyond questions of prejudice per se to more general social analysis. For instance, SPSSI members have been involved in the race and intelligence debates. They have also been concerned about civil liberties—protection of freedom of speech, the rights of minorities, legal due process, and the like, which are somewhat related to the matter of prejudice (see Chapter 3).

McGrath (1980) uses poverty "to encompass the whole range of issues involving socio-economic class, economic/industrial systems, and organizations, technology, as well as the problems of the poor."

The third main focus of SPSSI, according to McGrath, has been peace. Here, the concern has been with conflict and violence, war and peace, and justice. The concern has been at the domestic level (violence toward youth in families) as well as at the national level.

Times change, and specific issues change; but the values of SPSSI as an organization have persisted. Today, as when it was founded, SPSSI stands for a concern with social issues, a belief in the usefulness of scientific knowledge, justice and equality among people, and the promotion of human welfare.

velopment will occur as well. As more applied work is done, it is likely that current theories will need to be revised or new theories developed in order to account for the new knowledge gained in the real world.

Despite this continued trend toward an applied social psychology, it is important to note that it may be unwise to forget the value of basic theory and research that indeed appears to have no practical value. Such research may eventually have great practical utility. This has been true in psychology and it is certainly true in sciences such as chemistry, physics, and biology. A possible trend that may occur has been advocated by Hilgard (1980). Using an analogy drawn from the sciences, Hilgard notes that each science has a basic and an applied "wing." For example, theoretical physics is intertwined with applied engineering. Hilgard advocates that psychology follow a similar path in which two fields of basic and applied psychology coexist, with separate academic departments and training programs. This may indeed be feasible. For this arrangement to flourish, however, the basic researchers must still maintain the perspective that their work is ultimately to be transferred to the applied area.

Social Psychology as an Evolving Spiral

How much has social psychology changed since the time of Plato and Aristotle? Crutchfield and Krech (1962) describe the field by saying, "We seem to detect a tendency for thinking on a problem to go full cycle . . . there is a kind of spiral, a recurrence of older conceptions but a more advanced level of complexity and sophistication" (p. 10). Thus, they believe that many of the major ideas about social behavior have recurred several times in history.

Many parallels between early social analyses and contemporary social psychological views can be drawn. Three examples will suffice to illustrate this point. First, revised formulations of Tarde's notion of imitation are a pervasive aspect of modern social psychology. For instance, they can be found in Bandura's (1977) work on modeling (see Chapter 3). Second, reinforcement is a concept clearly akin to hedonism. Third, Aristotle's belief ("they are

friends, then, for whom the same things are good and evil, and who are friends and enemies of the same people") was echoed in Newcomb's 1956 presidential address to the American Psychological Association. Newcomb phrased this proposition as follows: "Interpersonal attraction always and necessarily varies with perceived similarity regarding important and relevant objects (including persons themselves)" (p. 579).

But the reappearance of ideas is only one aspect of the point being made by Crutchfield and Krech. The other aspect that needs emphasizing is their view that these ideas are continually becoming more complex and sophisticated. In other words, the field can be seen as an evolving spiral in which our concepts continually advance. They become more useful, precise, and better understood as time passes.

Besides the continuous growth of ideas, another more abrupt shift has taken place. From the time of the ancient Greeks to the beginning of this century, social analysis was conceptual in nature. In this century, the discipline has rapidly become an empirical enterprise. Contemporary social psychologists, as you will see in the next chapter, are experts in designing experiments, collecting data, and doing statistical analysis. The latter has provided a whole new way of testing and validating our understandings of social processes. It gives an objective basis for deciding which ideas are correct and which are not. Thus, the empirical approach provides an important foundation for the continued development of the field in the years ahead.

SUMMARY   Social psychology is "an attempt to understand and explain how the thought, feeling and behavior of individuals are influenced by the actual, imagined or implied presence of others" (Allport, 1968, p. 3). The topics social psychologists study can be organized along a continuum going from individual processes, to interpersonal relations, to the broader influences on behavior.

Social analysis is almost as old as written records. The Greek philosophers, such as Aristotle and Plato, addressed many issues (for example, friendship, attitude change) still of interest to social psychologists. In the eighteenth and nineteenth centuries hedonism, egoism, and imitation were offered as simple, sovereign theories for explaining all social behavior. Comte is often credited with being the father of social psychology. What is conventionally called the first social psychological experiment was reported by Norman Triplett in 1898. Between the 1920s and the 1950s, social psychology became established as a predominantly experimental field.

Since the profession of social psychology is still relatively young, it is not surprising that the field has witnessed several lively debates in the past two decades. Challenges occurred along four fronts having to do with methodology, social relevance, "history", and value biases. Partially in response to these challenges, the present text offers four perspectives for the 1980s: (1) an appreciation of the need to have converging evidence from different sources, (2) a commitment to identifying and articulating the practical relevance of social science findings, (3) the need to identify the historical and other factors on which simple relationships between variables are contingent, and (4) sensitivity to gender as well as ethnic or racial differences in behavior.

Social psychology is currently moving toward more research on applied problems in real-world settings. Consistent with Lewin's dictum, "There is nothing as practical as a good theory", the future of social psychology appears to promise greater integration of theory and application.

In terms of intellectual growth, Crutchfield and Krech view social psychology as an evolving spiral. Certain key ideas have occurred more than once, but these conceptualizations have become more complex and sophisticated over time. In terms of determining the validity of various concepts, an abrupt shift has taken place during the twentieth century, as social psychologists now rely heavily on empirical techniques.

SUGGESTED READINGS

Allport, G. W. The historical background of modern social psychology. In G. Lindzey & E. Aronson (Eds.), *Handbook of social psychology* (Vol. 1, 2d ed.). Reading, Mass.: Addison-Wesley, 1968.

Marrow, A. J. *The practical theorist.* New York: Basic Books, 1969.

West, S. G., & Wicklund, R. A. *A primer of social psychological theories.* Monterey, Ca.: Brooks/Cole, 1980.

RESEARCH METHODS IN SOCIAL PSYCHOLOGY

2

INTRODUCTION

One difference between social psychological and commonsense explanations of human social behavior is that social psychologists use scientific procedures to evaluate hypotheses about social behavior. Conducting social psychological research is like solving a puzzle or a mystery. Typically, what we do is observe social behavior, form hunches about the causes or reasons for that behavior, and then procede to gather evidence to support or refute our hunches. To understand social psychology, one needs to understand the scientific procedures used in gathering such evidence. Only through an understanding of the methods of social psychological research can the reader critically examine the research that is reported.

This chapter is more than just a tool to be used in reading subsequent chapters, however. The procedures used to scientifically evaluate hypotheses about human behavior are intriguing in and of themselves. How do we gather evidence in support of our hypotheses? What kinds of evidence are good for what kinds of purposes? How do we measure and determine the causes of social behavior? Answering these questions is a difficult but rewarding task. We hope both to convey a knowledge of the procedures of social psychological research and to communicate its excitement.

The chapter is organized into five sections. In the first we describe the nature and assumptions behind a scientific and empirical approach to social behavior. Here we also introduce a social problem to illustrate research methods in social psychology. The second section sets forth three criteria, which we call research validities, that can be used to evaluate social research, to differentiate research whose conclusions are sound from research whose conclusions should be more tentative. With

this as background, in the third section we outline various ways in which social research is conducted, discussing the relative advantages and disadvantages of these methods from the point of view of the research validities. In the fourth section of this chapter, which discusses the important issue of ethics in the conduct of social research, we identify potential ethical dilemmas facing the social researcher, as well as typical solutions to them. Finally, in the fifth section we look at social psychological research itself as a social activity, influencing social norms and being influenced by them in turn.

A SCIENTIFIC APPROACH TO SOCIAL BEHAVIOR

What Is Involved in a Scientific Approach?

In any scientific endeavor there is a curious relationship between observation and theorizing. We usually start off by observing a phenomenon. From our observations we construct hypotheses, both about the processes that cause what we have observed and about the effects of what we have observed upon other phenomena. These hypotheses may then lead us back to further observation, through which we attempt to demonstrate or, more strongly, to verify our hypotheses. Thus a scientific approach to any phenomenon usually goes from observation that yields hypotheses or that results in a theory, back to observation in the hopes of confirming the theory. In principle, this back and forth between theory and observation is a never-ending process: further observation leads to modification of theories, which leads to still more observation, and so forth.

A variety of examples of theoretical hypotheses are listed below, differing in the types of social behavior they address, the confidence with which they are made, and the extent to

---

This chapter is written by Charles M. Judd.

which they refer to very abstract versus very specific social behaviors. Nevertheless, all of these hypotheses have some elements in common. First, and perhaps most trivially, they have all been bases for actual social psychological research. Second, they all argue that the behaviors they focus upon are caused by some prior social process or force. That is, they all discuss the relationships between some theoretical cause or causes and some theoretical effect or social behavior to be explained. In the first example, the theoretical cause is attitude similarity, and the theoretical effect on which the hypothesis focuses is interpersonal attraction. In the second example, the cause is dominance behavior in groups, and the effect is eventual conflict.

1. People with similar attitudes will be attracted to each other (Byrne, 1969).
2. The two most dominant members in small groups will usually conflict at some point during the life of the group (Bales & Cohen, 1979).
3. Racially integrated housing projects reduce prejudice among the occupants (Deutsch & Collins, 1951).
4. If confronted by the need to make a decision that involves risk, groups will make riskier decisions than will individuals (Kogan & Wallach, 1964).
5. Believing that a specific member of the opposite sex is attractive may cause that person to behave differently, even when the belief is not explicitly communicated (Snyder, Tanke, & Berscheid, 1977).
6. The greater the number of people who see a victim in distress, the less likely to offer help is any one witness (Latane & Darley, 1970).

From the fact that these hypotheses take the form of assertions about the causes of social behavior, we can infer that one of the assumptions of a scientific approach to social behavior is that such behavior is determined. That is, this approach assumes that social behavior is not a random process, that we can identify factors that cause behavior. While this assumption may seem trivial to some, to others it is likely to seem that we are denying the individual's freedom to act in accordance with personal wishes in spite of social pressures. Such is cer-

tainly not our intention; while a scientific approach argues that social forces exert causal effects upon behavior, we do not presume to predict perfectly social behavior.

A second assumption of a scientific approach is that the theoretical phenomena we discuss in our hypotheses have some parallel or equivalent form in reality. In other words, we assume that there exists a class of actual behaviors that indicate or represent the theoretical phenomena of interest in our hypotheses. In the first hypothesis we assume that "attitudes" and "attraction" are only abstract representations of observables; that there exist certain behaviors that indicate attraction and certain measurable phenomena that indicate attitudes.

In a slightly more formal sense, our theories deal with what have been called *constructs* (Cronbach & Meehl, 1955), relatively abstract classes of phenomena. When we engage in observation, we gather information on *indicators* or things that we believe represent or measure the constructs. The links between the theoretical constructs and the indicators of the constructs we observe are called the *operational definitions*. Deciding what are the best measures or indicators of the constructs of interest is a very difficult task that we will discuss in more detail later.

What Does Observation Do for Theories?

Scientific research involves a curious relationship between theory and observation, in part because the process of observation is informative for our theories in a number of different ways. In other words, research goes back and forth between hypotheses and observation because observation serves different functions at different times in the research enterprise. What are the various ways in which observation aids the development of theory? There are at least four.

First, we initially observe in order to for-

Observation frequently provides the initial basis of social psychological theory and research. What might the man on the left learn by observing the interactions of this couple?

mulate theory. We observe children playing together to form some initial ideas about friendship choice. We observe people interacting in groups to form hunches about what makes a good leader. We watch members of different racial groups interacting to put together hypotheses about factors that maintain stereotypes. In all of these cases we observe while we are putting together a theory or hypothesis. Observation guides us in that process.

Once we have a theory or hypothesis, we use observation in order to assess its validity. For instance, we could attempt to demonstrate that each of the six hypotheses listed earlier holds in some specific setting. We could show

that interpersonal attraction goes up as attitude similarity increases; we could demonstrate that measures of overt prejudice are lower in integrated than in nonintegrated housing developments; or we could show that there is a relationship between the probability of aiding a victim and the number of observers of the victim requesting help. In all of these examples we would be attempting to demonstrate that observed behavior is consistent with our hypothesis.

Beyond demonstration, can observation be used to "prove" a hypothesis? Unfortunately, both scientific experience and philosophical analysis (Popper, 1959) have shown us that observation cannot, in fact, prove a theory. In other words, try as we may to prove a hypothesis through a critical experiment, there will always remain the possibility of other explanations for the observations we record, explanations that compete with our hypothesis and that account for our experimental data equally well.

While science does not proceed by proving hypotheses, we can attempt to test competing or rival hypotheses. If our theories survive such tests, then we may have gained evidence that our original hypothesis is correct. Strictly speaking, we can never in a final sense show a theory to be right. We can, however, conduct research to demonstrate that it is wrong. If the theory can withstand this attack, then we may place increased trust in it.

The third use of empirical observation is to define the limits of the generality of the theory; that is, once a hypothesis has been demonstrated, we may want to see whether it holds true in a new situation or with a different population. In essence, this use of scientific observation amounts to a further development of the hypothesis beyond the circumstances of the original demonstration.

Finally, the fourth use of observation is replication. By this we mean that we may conduct an experiment or a study a second, third, or even fourth time, attempting to recreate the conditions of the first time as closely as possible, in order to develop confidence in the findings of the study.

Illustrating the Uses of Observation

To make this discussion of the uses of scientific observation more concrete, we illustrate it with a research example that will be used repeatedly in this chapter.

One of the most recurrent social problems that social psychologists have addressed is racial prejudice, which may be defined as a negative attitude toward some racial or ethnic group. Usually this prejudice is accompanied by a set of stereotypic beliefs about the way in which members of the racial or ethnic group think and behave. (An elaboration on the nature of prejudice and stereotypes is contained in Chapter 16.) Racial prejudice almost inevitably leads to discriminatory behavior: not letting members of the racial or ethnic group act in ways that are open to others. Such discrimination inhibits the ability of members of the racial or ethnic group to realize their potential and to contribute to society at their ability levels.

In response to this social problem, many social psychologists have conducted research on factors that lead to a reduction in prejudice. We can illustrate the course of social research and

Social psychologists have used several measurement techniques to study prejudice. How can we measure or attempt to reduce the extreme prejudice shown by these young men wearing the Nazi swastika.

the purposes of observation by examining a hypothetical social psychologist looking at racial prejudice. Probably the first step that must be faced is the precise definition of the theoretical construct that is of interest here—prejudice. Assuming that the researcher agrees with us that racial prejudice can be defined as a negative attitude toward a specified racial or ethnic group, the next step is to identify indicators of this construct, or specific ways in which prejudice can be assessed. We have already said that this step, deriving the operational definition for theoretical constructs, is a crucial one. There are a variety of different indicators or measures of prejudice that might actually be used. Social Focus 2.1 summarizes ways in which data can be collected. Problems of data collection are discussed as well. The crucial issue in collecting data concerns whether the indicators adequately represent the constructs of interest. This issue, known as the construct validity of measures, is discussed in the next section.

Once having decided how to measure prejudice, the researcher may use observation to formulate hypotheses about factors that reduce prejudice (the first way in which observation informs theory). A survey might be conducted to examine how various social and economic characteristics of individuals are related to their degree of prejudice.

Let us suppose that one result of this initial survey is the discovery that people who live in integrated residential areas exhibit less racial prejudice than people who reside in segregated areas. This observed relationship may lead the researcher to construct a theoretical hypothesis about the *causal* relationship between integration in residential areas and racial prejudice. For instance, the researcher may conclude from this initial observation that living in an integrated neighborhood reduces prejudice because it gives individuals the opportunity to get to know each other as individuals, rather than as members of a racial or ethnic group.

Once this theoretical hypothesis has been formulated, the researcher may collect empirical data to test the hypothesis. To do this, the researcher may design a study similar to one conducted by Deutsch and Collins (1951), in which women who lived in one of two different sorts of low-income housing projects—racially segregated and racially integrated—were interviewed. In other ways the two sorts of projects were quite similar. Deutsch and Collins showed that women who lived in the integrated housing projects exhibited less prejudice than the women in the segregated projects.

Following this initial demonstration, research might be conducted to assess alternative explanations for the Deutsch and Collins (1951) result in order to falsify the hypothesis. As we will see later in this chapter, since this study used a correlational design, it is difficult to assess cause and effect among the variables. For instance, it might be that the difference in prejudice between the integrated and segregated projects in the original study was due to something other than integration per se. Perhaps those who chose to live in the integrated projects had different attitudes from the start than those who lived in the segregated projects. The difference in the original study might be due to initial prejudice levels rather than to integration, and thus not be supportive of the hypothesis that integration causes a reduction in prejudice.

If, indeed, initial prejudice levels did differ, then for the original hypothesis to hold, research would have to be conducted to demonstrate that integration produces racial tolerance *over and above* any initial differences in prejudice. To do this, one might want to watch people as they move into either segregated or integrated projects, and make sure that they are as nearly equivalent as possible. If we could show that there were no initial differences in prejudice and yet, later, that prejudice levels were reduced in the integrated projects, the original hypothesis would have survived the attempted falsification.

Beyond demonstrating that the hypothesis

SOCIAL FOCUS 2.1
Measuring Social Psychological Variables

PROCEDURES FOR GATHERING DATA

In social psychological research we must measure the variables that are relevant to our research hypotheses. This nearly always means that we wish to order individuals on some scale or scales so that those who are closer together on the scales are more similar on the constructs they represent than individuals who are further apart. There are four major ways of gathering data to measure social psychological variables.

Questionnaire Data. Social researchers give questionnaires to the individuals they study, and the responses to the questions posed are used to order the individuals on scales. The questions may use either a *closed-end* or an *open-end response format.* In the former the individuals respond by selecting one response from a set of alternatives. In the latter individuals respond in their own words and the responses are then coded by the researcher to order the individual on a scale. This coding is called *content analysis.*

Interview Data. Questionnaires are useful for gathering information that individuals have at their fingertips, so to speak. To gather information on relatively deeper motives or values, it may be necessary to probe an individual's responses to questions through an interview.

Observational Data. By observing people's behavior we are often able to gather quite informative social psychological data. The advantage of observation over questionnaires or interviews is that the observation can be *unobtrusive;* that is, individuals may be unaware that they are being assessed (Webb, Campbell, Schwartz, & Sechrest, 1966; Webb, et al, 1981). This alleviates the problems of social desirability and demand characteristics discussed below.

Archival Data. Sometimes information on social behavior may already have been collected by recording agencies of various sorts (libraries, income rec-

seems to hold, empirical observation can be used to assess the generality of the hypothesis to settings and populations other than those included in the original research. For instance, the researcher may want to extend the generality of the hypothesized effects of residential integration beyond low-income housing projects. The effects of residential integration upon racial attitudes among residents of suburban housing developments might therefore be examined. If effects different from those demon-

strated in the low-income housing projects are found, the hypothesis may be modified in order to specify how characteristics of the residents of a community influence whether integration leads to reduced prejudice.

The final use of observation is replication. The original demonstration study, or one of the subsequent studies conducted in response to falsification attempts, may be redone, replicating as closely as possible the conditions of the original research. The purpose of this replica-

ords, educational records, and so forth), whose purposes were not social research. The social psychologist can occasionally make use of these archives.

PROBLEMS IN MEASURING SOCIAL PSYCHOLOGICAL VARIABLES

Beyond the issue of construct validity, which refers to whether a variable measures the construct that the researcher intends to measure, there are three measurement problems encountered by the researcher.

Measurement Reliability

Social psychological variables differ in the amount of error they contain. Those that contain relatively little error are called reliable measures, which researchers naturally attempt to use. There is extensive literature on how to assess the **reliability** of measures (for example, Nunnally, 1978).

Social Desirability. Individuals usually want to "put their best foot forward." They may be reluctant to inform researchers of their fears, prejudices, and what they see to be negative qualities. Responses to questionnaire items may reflect this social-desirability effect as much as the construct they are designed to tap. Unobtrusive measures reduce this problem.

Demand Characteristics. Individuals who are studied form hypotheses about what the researcher is looking at and what sorts of responses are expected. Accordingly they may attempt to provide the desired responses. Responses given with the goal of satisfying the researcher's apparent desires are responses to the demand characteristics of the research setting. Orne (1969) has written at some length about the pervasiveness of demand characteristics in social research.

tion study would be to increase confidence in the hypothesis as originally demonstrated.

CRITERIA FOR EVALUATING SOCIAL RESEARCH

Observation or empirical research in social psychology interacts with theories or hypotheses, and is used to formulate, demonstrate, elaborate, and modify a hypothesis. The quality of research depends upon the degree to which it is informative for formulating or supporting the hypothesis. One piece of research may be much more useful in building or examining a theory than another. In this section of the chapter we examine three criteria of research quality or validity that determine the extent to which a piece of research is theoretically useful.

As we have seen, research hypotheses fol-

suggest

low a certain form: they posit a causal relationship between two constructs, one being the cause and the other the effect. They also refer to a particular population and a particular setting or settings. In the example discussed in the previous section, the causal construct is integration in housing projects and the construct that is presumed to be affected is racial prejudice.

The first issue in evaluating social research is whether the variables or indicators actually measured in the research do a good job of representing the constructs of theoretical interest. This issue is referred to as the **construct validity** of the research (Cronbach & Meehl, 1955; Cook & Campbell, 1979). In research on residential integration, we would want to know whether, in fact, our measures of prejudice did a good job of measuring prejudice. We would also want to determine that we had adequately assessed the degree of residential integration where the research was conducted.

The second issue in evaluating social research is whether we can reach causal conclusions about the relationships we observe in our research. Suppose we find that integrated living arrangements are in fact associated with lower prejudice. Since the hypothesis that motivated the research argues that integration *causes* reduce prejudice, we would want to ask whether any factors other than integrated housing may be responsible for the lowered levels of prejudice that are observed. The question of whether the relationships in our research are causal ones is the issue of **internal validity** (Campbell & Stanley, 1963).

The final issue in evaluating social research concerns the question of whether its results or conclusions can be generalized to various populations or settings of interest. For instance, in the Deutsch and Collins (1951) study of integrated housing, we would want to know whether the obtained results could be generalized to other housing projects in other areas of the country. The question of generalization from a piece of research is the issue of **external validity** (Campbell & Stanley, 1963; for a slightly different definition see Judd & Kenny, 1981).

While the above paragraphs define the three validity issues, in order to understand how research can be conducted to be most informative for a theory, we need to discuss factors that can threaten the construct validity, internal validity, or external validity of social research. Only by pointing out what the problems are in conducting informative research will we be in a position to conduct more adequate studies. Below we discuss each of the three validities in more detail.

Construct Validity

✳ Construct validity, the extent to which the variables or indicators used in research adequately represent the constructs of theoretical interest, concerns the adequacy of the operational definitions of the constructs.✳ If the variables that we measure do a poor job of representing or capturing what is of theoretical interest, the research may be theoretically uninformative.

As we have seen, a theoretical hypothesis posits a causal connection between two constructs, one of which is the presumed cause, the other that which is affected. Both must be represented or given operational definitions in a research study. The variable that represents the causal construct is frequently called the **independent variable** or the *treatment*. The variable that represents the affected construct is called the **dependent variable** or the *outcome*. To discuss the construct validity of research we must question whether each type of variable adequately represents the theoretical construct of interest.

To illustrate the intricacies of this criterion, we will examine the construct validity of a dependent measure designed to assess prejudice, such as might be used in a study examining the effects of integrated housing. Earlier it was pointed out that there are many different ways of measuring prejudice. We can ask people directly; we can develop indirect questions; we can ask them to record their behavior with minority group members; or we can observe their behavior. Suppose that we operationally define prejudice for purposes of study in two of the above ways: we ask them how much they like members of other racial groups and we observe the frequency of their interaction with minority group members.

Undoubtedly both of these variables are indicators of prejudice; that is, to at least some extent they do in fact capture what we mean by the term prejudice. They both, however, capture or represent other things as well. The first measure, a questionnaire asking for feelings toward various racial groups, undoubtedly measures what has been called **social desirability** as well as prejudice. By social desirability we mean that generally people want to portray themselves as open-minded and unprejudiced. Differences on the prejudice measure probably reflect both differences in actual prejudice and differences in how positively individuals wish to portray themselves.

The second measure of prejudice also measures other constructs as well as prejudice. Using frequency of interaction with minority group members as the dependent variable, we would undoubtedly find that individuals who live in integrated housing projects speak more frequently to minority group members than individuals who live in segregated projects. Whether that means that the residents of the integrated projects have less negative attitudes toward the minority group is not necessarily indicated by the data. They may speak with minority group members more frequently because their living arrangements force them to do so, rather than out of choice. In other words, we may infer something about the effects of integration on prejudice when, in fact, we are really not looking at prejudice at all.

How do we assess the construct validity of the indicators used in research? How do we determine whether our measures sufficiently assess what we want them to assess? There are two answers to these questions, both necessary to assure validity. First of all, <u>construct validity</u> can be <u>achieved</u> only <u>if</u> we are sufficiently

precise in defining the theoretical constructs. For instance, what precisely do we mean by prejudice? More specific theoretical definitions usually lead to more valid operational definitions.

Second, whenever we can, we should measure constructs in multiple ways. If we measure prejudice in five different ways and if all of them yield results that are quite consistent with each other, then we may have more confidence that, in fact, we did assess prejudice than if we measured it in only one way. The same need for multiple indicators holds true for independent as well as dependent variables. If we measure integration in two different ways and if both ways show equal relationships to prejudice, then we can have increased confidence that the construct has been successfully represented in the research.

Internal Validity

Suppose we replicate the Deutsch and Collins (1951) study of the effects of housing integration on prejudice. We have two groups of individuals: those who live in integrated housing and those who live in segregated housing. Suppose we find, as did Deutsch and Collins (1951), that the former group shows less prejudice than the latter. We would like to argue that the different housing arrangement *caused* the difference in prejudice. In fact, however, there may be a variety of other factors that are responsible for the difference in prejudice between the two groups. The issue of internal validity concerns the extent to which we are able to rule out those other competing or rival causes. Only by eliminating these competing causes can we have confidence that the different housing arrangements were the causal factor.

Campbell and Stanley (1963), Cook and Campbell (1979), and Judd and Kenny (1981) have made lists of rival or competing causes that threaten the internal validity of research, some of which are given below.

Selection. Those who choose to live in integrated housing may already be less prejudiced than those who live in segregated housing. A difference in prejudice is then not caused by the housing arrangements, but rather reflects only the fact that different sorts of people live in the different types of housing.

History. If we first study individuals who live in segregated housing and only later look at those who live in integrated housing, differences in levels of prejudice may be due to events occurring during the time interval between the observations of the two groups. Historical events may have lessened prejudice in all individuals, while housing arrangements may have had no effect at all.

Experimenter expectations. In some quite creative research, Robert Rosenthal (1964, 1966, 1969) has shown that researchers can subtly and unintentionally influence the individuals they study. For instance, in our example, researchers when they interview those who live in the integrated housing may unintentionally communicate to them the expectation that they should be relatively free of prejudice. This expectation may act as a self-fulfilling prophecy, so that these individuals portray themselves as less prejudiced than they might in the absence of the researcher's expectation. Because the researcher's expectations of those who live in segregated housing and those who live in integrated housing are likely to differ, those expectations constitute a threat to internal validity. As we will see subsequently in Chapters 6 and 7, expectancies of this sort not only operate in experiments but also have a profound effect on our everyday lives.

External Validity

To change our example slightly, suppose we conduct research on the effects of integration on the racial prejudice of children in elementary schools. We may be interested in generalizing our findings to many other elementary schools and many other school children, throughout a city, throughout a region, or even all across the country? The external validity of research refers to the extent to which desired generalizations from the research can be made to populations of interest. To what extent do we have confidence in reaching conclusions about some large group or *population* of individuals from the small group or *sample* of individuals actually observed?

Generalizing from samples to populations can be done only when the sample is representative of the population. Quite a bit of statistical work has been conducted on the question of how a representative sample can be taken from a population. Only if the sample is randomly drawn from the population can we approximate representativeness. In its simplest form, random sampling from a population of interest means that each individual in the population has an equal chance of being included in the sample of individuals actually observed in the research. For instance, suppose we wish to generalize our research on prejudice in elementary schools to all schools in Massachusetts, the state in which the hypothetical research is to be carried out. We decide that we can interview students in no more than 50 elementary schools across the state. There are approximately 1000 elementary schools in the state. In order to form a simple random sample of 50 of these 1000 schools, the probability that children in any one school will be interviewed should be exactly 50/1000 or .05. All schools in the state should have exactly this probability of inclusion in the sample. To draw the sample we would like to have the equivalent of a die with twenty faces. We would roll that die for every school. A school would be included in the sample if a given one of the twenty faces came up. For all of the other nineteen faces the school would be excluded from the sample.

It should be apparent from this example that in order to have confidence in generalization we need to define precisely the population to which we want to generalize. Drawing a random sample is possible only if we have access to all potential individuals or units in the population. If we wish to generalize a study's conclusions to some other population, we must engage in theoretical speculation: why should the conclusions be the same or different in the population of interest? Such speculation needs to be supported by further empirical research.

External validity is then maximized by the following techniques. First, we must define the theoretical population of interest prior to conducting the research. Second, through a table of random numbers or some other tool, we must assure ourselves that indeed a random sample has been drawn from the population. Third, if we are unable to draw a random sample for some reason, then we can generalize the conclusions of our research through theoretical speculation that is backed up by further research.

Priorities and Relations among the Three Validities

Both construct and external validities assess the relationships between the theoretical phenomena in a hypothesis and the phenomena examined in actual research. Construct validity refers to the relationships between constructs and variables. External validity refers to the relationships between populations and samples. In essence, both validities assess the adequacy with which the theory is examined in the research.

Internal validity is concerned with something quite different. It concerns the possibility of reaching causal conclusions. It is sometimes the case that designing a study to increase its internal validity lowers its construct and/or its external validity. Thus, these three validities may conflict and it may be necessary to establish priorities among them.

To eliminate most of the competing causes

(such as selection) that constitute threats to internal validity, we need to "control" them. In other words, we need to conduct our research in a setting in which we can make sure that competing causes are not present.

Imagine a researcher concerned about demonstrating the causal effects upon prejudice of racial integration in classrooms. This researcher decides that as many as possible threats to internal validity should be eliminated, and therefore sets up two classrooms that are as identical as possible, using the same teacher, the same curriculum, and so forth. The only difference in the two classrooms is whether or not the students are racially integrated. By making sure that this is the only difference, the researcher has effectively eliminated many competing causes and thus enhanced internal validity. At the same time, however, it may be quite difficult to generalize from the school children who participate in this research to a broad population of interest. Because a special school has in essence been set up to control for competing causes, the researcher has most probably observed a selected sample of school children, a sample that probably is not representative of the population of interest. It is frequently true that the demands of internal validity mean that special settings and samples must be used, and hence construct and external validity may be reduced.

In a complementary way, a researcher interested in the same phenomenon, the effects of racial integration in schools, who decides that external validity is supremely important, will be certain to randomly sample from the elementary school rooms in the population. Within this sample the researcher will then study the relationship between integration and prejudice. While such researchers may have confidence in their powers of generalization, there are likely to be many uncontrolled competing causes in the research that inhibit conclusions of causality. For instance, integrated classrooms are more likely to be found in urban than in rural areas. Hence, differences in attitudes may be due to the urban-rural difference rather than to the integration variable.

Because the control necessary for eliminating competing causes frequently conflicts with the dictates of external and construct validity, researchers inevitably make priority decisions among the validities. Traditionally, in much of the research reported in the social psychological journals, internal validity is given the highest priority. This is, however, a priority decision that researchers usually make only implicitly. Tradition encourages them to emphasize internal validity. Hence, much social psychological research is conducted in highly controlled settings without worrying about the consequences for construct and external validities.

Rather than accept this tradition-given priority system, we suggest that the relative importance of each of the three validities may depend upon the purpose of the research. In the beginning of this chapter we presented four ways in which research is used in theory development. Perhaps only for the second way, demonstrating causal relationships, should internal validity be pursued at the expense of the other validities. In research that is concerned primarily with exploration, generalization, or replication, one could argue that a different set of priorities is called for. At any rate, we believe that research can clearly be informative even if the dictates of internal validity are not all met. (See Judd & Kenny, 1981, for an elaboration on priorities among research validities.)

DESIGNS FOR SOCIAL RESEARCH

Let us again suppose we are interested in the effects of residential integration on racial prejudice. There are a number of different research designs that might be employed to examine these effects. Most simply, we might find an integrated residential area and measure prejudice levels among the residents. We might find low levels of prejudice and be tempted to conclude that integration reduces prejudice. What might be wrong with this conclusion?

The most glaring problem with this conclusion is that it is based upon a single group of individuals, all of whom reside in an integrated area. Because we do not have other individuals with whom to compare those we have observed, we do not know whether in fact prejudice is *relatively* lower in integrated residential areas than in segregated ones. Only by comparing a group of individuals who do not reside in an integrated setting to a group of individuals who do can we conclude anything about the relationship between integration and prejudice.

In a more general form, to have any confidence in the effects of a particular treatment, such as integration, we must observe at least two groups of individuals: those who get the treatment (that is, live in an integrated area) and those who do not (that is, live in a segregated area). The former group of individuals is referred to as the **treatment group,** the latter as the **control group.** The treatment and control groups differ on the independent variable. If that independent variable is degree of residential integration, the treatment group has a high value on it, while the control group has a very low or even zero value on it.

Nearly all social psychological research designs have at least these two groups of individuals: those who receive the treatment and those who do not. A fundamental issue in research design concerns the procedure by which individuals wind up in one group or the other. This procedure, called the *assignment rule,* has a major impact upon a study's internal validity. Different types of assignment rules, or different ways of deciding who is in the treatment group and who is in the control group, have quite different implications for our ability to reach causal conclusions from the research. Because the assignment rule is so important, it makes sense to distinguish among research designs according to the assignment rule that is used.

Each of the three types of social research designs—experiments, quasi-experiments, and correlational designs—is discussed and illustrated in the following sections. Each has its own strengths and weaknesses, which we will try to make clear.

Randomized Experimental Designs

A research design that has perfect internal validity is one in which the treatment and control groups show no differences on the dependent variable when the treatment makes no difference or has no effect. In other words, if residential integration has no effect at all on prejudice, we would hope to find no difference in prejudice between the treatment and control groups. Any differences that we do find when we know the treatment had no effect would be due to other causes that compete with the treatment. Therefore, in a research design that has perfect internal validity, those differences would be eliminated.

How can we design a study that would show no differences on the dependent variable between the treatment and control groups if the treatment produces no effects?

The only way we can be sure that the treatment and control groups will not differ in the absence of a treatment effect is to use a **random assignment rule.** We would want to do something like flipping a coin to determine whether an individual should live in the integrated or segregated housing project. In its most usual form, a random assignment rule is one in which every individual has the same probability as every other individual of being in either the treatment or the control group. Randomization here, in randomized experiments, is used for quite a different purpose than when it is used to select a random sample from a population. In the latter case, we select a random sample in order to be able to generalize to the population (to increase external validity). In the case of randomized experiments, individuals are randomly assigned to levels of the independent variable to eliminate threats to internal validity.

To use a random assignment rule it is necessary to have control over who receives the treatment and who does not. For many sorts of constructs such control is not feasible. Although the preceding discussion presupposes that we could assign individuals to housing projects, it is unlikely that a researcher could really exert experimental control over such a treatment variable.

Because treatment variables such as degree of residential integration are not particularly amenable to experimental control, researchers may modify or "scale down" a treatment variable in order to gain the benefits of experimental control. For instance, instead of looking at residential integration, a much more modest independent variable may be used—for example, degree of integration in a short-lived social group. While it is unlikely that individuals could be randomly assigned to different housing projects, such an assignment procedure is possible if the treatment is a small group meeting in the research laboratory. The use of such a scaled-down treatment variable has substantial benefits from the point of view of internal validity, but it almost inevitably raises questions about the construct validity of the treatment variable. Does integration in a short-lived social group represent the theoretical construct of interest? Does it represent integration in living arrangements?

Multigroup experiments. In the examples used so far, randomized experiments have included only two groups: a treatment and a control group. In fact, however, experiments frequently use many groups and many treatments to which individuals are randomly assigned. Suppose, for instance, that we are interested in the effects upon racial prejudice of face-to-face contact with members of other races. We could simply set up two groups, a treatment group in which individuals perform tasks of some duration with members of a different racial group, and a control group whose members interact with members of the same racial group. We would gather more information, however, if there were multiple treatment groups in which the duration of face-to-face contact with members of another racial group was varied. For instance, we might define two different treatment groups. In the first there might be a single contact of an hour's duration; in the second, contact might happen for an hour every day for a week. We might conceivably even want to set up a more complex experiment with ten treatment groups, differing in the amount of interaction involved.✻Using multiple treatment groups permits us to calculate how much treatment is necessary before effects are observable. The graph in Figure 2.1 illustrates a hypothetical case in which multiple treatment groups would be useful. Suppose the actual causal relationship between the amount of interracial contact and prejudice level was as depicted in this graph. If we chose only two experimental groups, a control group (0 hours of interracial contact) and a single treatment group (5 hours of interracial contact), we would conclude that the treatment produced no effect upon prejudice. If, instead, our single treatment group interacted for 20 hours, we would conclude that interracial contact made a difference, but we wouldn't know anything about the form of the relationship between the treatment variable and the outcome. Only by forming numerous treatment groups can relationships like that in Figure 2.1 be demonstrated.

Experiments may also employ ✻multiple treatment groups that differ not on one independent variable only but simultaneously on many. For instance, we may suspect that greater amounts of interracial contact lead to a decrease in prejudice levels only when the contact is in a cooperative context. If the interracial contact is over a competitive issue, more of it

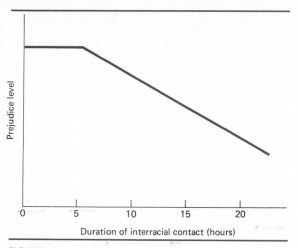

FIGURE 2.1
Hypothesized relationship between prejudice level and duration of interracial contact

may conceivably lead to higher levels of prejudice (Weigel, Wiser, & Cook, 1975). If we wanted to test this hypothesis we would randomly assign individuals to multiple treatment groups that differed both in the duration of interracial contact and in its context—cooperative or competitive. We could then have six treatment groups, representing the combinations of three levels of contact duration and two levels of the cooperativeness/competitiveness of the contact. These six treatment groups are defined by the cells of Table 2.1, each one representing a specific combination of levels of the two independent variables.✻Experimental designs like this, in which two or more independent variables are combined or crossed to yield multiple treatment groups are called _factorial experimental designs_.

✻The advantage of factorial designs is that they permit us to test what are called _interactions_ between treatment variables. In the hypothesis about the combined effects of duration of interracial contact and the cooperativeness/competitiveness of that contact, we suggested that greater amounts of contact may affect prejudice differently, depending upon the cooper-

TABLE 2.1
A Factorial Design Created by Crossing Two Independent Variables: Duration of Interracial Contact and Cooperative/Competitive Context

	COOPERATIVE CONTEXT	COMPETITIVE CONTEXT
One Hour Duration	Treatment Group #1	Treatment Group #2
Ten Hours Duration	Treatment Group #3	Treatment Group #4
Twenty Hours Duration	Treatment Group #5	Treatment Group #6

ativeness/competitiveness of the task. A possible form of this prediction is graphed in Figure 2.2. Independent variables are said to interact whenever the effect of one of them upon the dependent variable depends upon the level of the other independent variable. In the example in Figure 2.2, the effect upon prejudice of duration of contact depends upon whether the contact is competitive or cooperative. If cooperative, more contact reduces prejudice. If competitive, more contact increases it. Interactions such as this between two independent variables can be examined only in a factorial design where independent variables are crossed or combined to yield the treatment groups.

FIGURE 2.2
Predicted effect of duration of interracial contact on prejudice for different task types

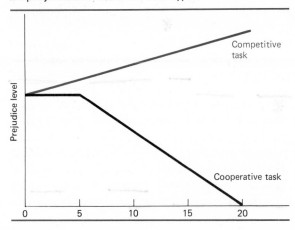

Quasi-Experimental Designs

It is frequently impractical to assign individuals randomly to treatment conditions, even though we may still believe it important to conduct research to estimate the treatment effect. In such cases, quasi-experimental designs are typically used. A quasi-experiment is a research design in which assignment to treatment groups (that is, to levels of the independent variable) is not random, but in which the researcher has been able to collect data from the individuals before the treatment commences, as well as at the conclusion of the research.

To illustrate a **quasi-experimental research design,** suppose that in the Deutsch and Collins (1951) study on residential integration, levels of prejudice had been assessed before the residents moved into either the integrated housing projects (the treatment group) or the segregated ones (the control group). Assuming the researchers were not able to assign individuals randomly to groups, they would have then been using a quasi-experimental research design.

In another example of a quasi-experimental design, Ball and Bogatz (1970) conducted research to evaluate whether the television program *Sesame Street* affected young children's cognitive abilities. While they found it difficult to randomly assign children to a treatment group, where the program was watched, or to a control group, where it was not, they were able to measure all the children's ability levels before any child had watched the program.

Both of these examples illustrate a quasi-experimental design known as the *nonequivalent control-group design*. In this design, there are both a treatment group and a control group, but individuals have *not* been randomly assigned to them. In fact, we usually can only make guesses about the variable or variables that constitute the assignment rule. While the assignment rule is usually unknown, the research has been able to measure the dependent or outcome variable both before any individuals have received the treatment as well as at the conclusion of the treatment.

In the absence of a random assignment rule, the internal validity of the research may be quite low. Because individuals in the treatment group are likely to differ from those in the control group, we would expect to find differences on the outcome variable even if the treatment exerted no effect at all. In other words, if we find differences on the outcome variable at the conclusion of the research, there exist plausible rival explanations for these differences, other than a treatment effect.

While quasi-experiments can never achieve the internal validity of well-conducted randomized experiments, the pretreatment data can be used to reduce the threats to internal validity. In the nonequivalent control-group design, the dependent or outcome variable is measured at the start of the research, before any treatment has been received by the individuals, as well as at the conclusion. This pretreatment measure allows the researcher to estimate how individuals in the treatment and control groups would differ on the outcome variable at the end of the research if the treatment were totally ineffective. The researcher can then look for treatment effects above and beyond the difference that we would expect to find on the outcome variable between the treatment and the control groups.

Conclusions about the causal effects of in-

dependent variables in quasi-experimental research designs must necessarily remain more tentative than causal conclusions from randomized experiments. The difficult task facing the researcher who uses a quasi-experimental design is to estimate how the treatment and control groups would differ at the conclusion of the research if in fact the treatment were ineffective. Meaningful conclusions about the causal effect of the treatment depend upon the accuracy of this estimate. A great deal of attention has been recently devoted to the study of procedures for analyzing quasi-experimental data to increase internal validity (Cook & Campbell, 1979; Judd & Kenny, 1981).

One of the reasons quasi-experimental research designs are receiving increased attention is that through them we can conduct research on independent variables that are not readily amenable to experimental control. Randomly assigning individuals to treatment groups may not be possible when the treatment is a school curriculum, a type of housing, a treatment for mental illness, or a drug rehabilitation program. And yet it is important to evaluate these treatments. While quasi-experiments must reach only tentative causal conclusions, they are valuable tools, as social researchers move beyond the research laboratory to examine treatments designed to alleviate social problems.

Correlational Designs

Social researchers very frequently collect information on a set of individuals at only one point in time. They interview them, they observe them and record their behavior, or they distribute survey questionnaires. The massive public-opinion polls conducted by political pollsters and large survey organizations fall under this general rubric. With this type of information, we are usually interested in examining associations among variables. For instance, we may want to know if prejudice varies with education or with residential area, if political opinions vary with region of the country, or if the incidence of certain diseases varies with diet.

With information or data collected in this way, it may seem slightly inappropriate to speak of a treatment variable and an outcome variable. And yet, in the case of each of the examples in the above paragraph, it remains possible to identify a variable that can be labeled a treatment because we see it as causal, even if we do not control its delivery. For instance, we assume that if education and prejudice are related, education causes a decrease in prejudice and not the other way around. Thus, ✳ even in surveys where we are discovering relationships between variables, we usually have theoretical assumptions about which variable is the cause and which the effect, about which variable is the treatment and which the outcome.✳

Correlational designs are designs in which we do not know the assignment rule by which individuals receive different levels of the treatment variable and in which we interview or observe individuals on only one occasion. To use our prejudice example, suppose we interviewed individuals and ascertained both the integration of their residential area and their level of prejudice. In such a case, the residential integration variable is the treatment and we do not know for certain the process or rule by which individuals wound up in different residential areas. In contrast to the procedure in quasi-experimental designs, in correlational designs we interview the individuals only after the treatment has been received.

Because we do not gather pretreatment information in correlational designs, it is nearly impossible to eliminate threats to internal validity. In our example, it is next to impossible to establish that differences in prejudice between people who live in different residential areas are *caused* by the treatment variable. They

may just as probably reflect differences in prejudice that existed before the individuals moved into the particular residential areas.

Another example will further clarify the nature of correlational designs. Suppose we conduct a political survey and find that sentiment toward the president varies with region of the country, with residents of the southern states showing greater approval of presidential performance than residents of the northern states. Such a survey uses a correlational design: we do not know the assignment rule that has determined who lives in which sections of the country. We are also unable to interview all these residents prior to their being located in different sections. In this example, it would be quite difficult to argue that the treatment variable, region of the country, per se *causes* differences in approval of presidential performance. It is likely that different sorts of people, with different values and general political beliefs, live in the different regions of the country. These differences between people probably cause differences in approval of presidential performance from one region to another. Region of the country itself is not the most likely cause.

Because in correlational designs it is almost impossible to eliminate threats to internal validity, some might wonder whether such designs can ever be useful in informing social theory. There are, in fact, crucial stages in the development of theory when such designs are quite useful and informative. For instance, when we are beginning to formulate hypotheses concerning the causes of a particular social behavior, information about the behavior's relationship to other variables can be quite valuable. Further, there are cases in which our goal is to predict social behavior rather than to explain the causes of the behavior. Political pollsters are content to predict votes; they need not worry about what causes someone to vote one way or another. If our job is one of prediction, then correlational designs are sufficient. If we find that sentiment toward the president varies with region of the country, we can predict differences in voting across the country, even if we do not know what causes the different attitude levels.

Since information from correlational designs is relatively easy to gather, compared to experimental and quasi-experimental designs, and since the information is useful for theory construction and prediction, such designs are extensively employed in social research. Almost everyone has been surveyed, questioned, or interviewed by political pollsters and marketing researchers. Although the correlational design employed in this sort of empirical social research may not have very high internal validity, the ease with which information can be collected means that frequently quite high external validity can be achieved. Thus, research conducted with a correlational design may sacrifice internal validity for the sake of external validity. In conducting a survey, we can engage in random sampling and thus may be able to generalize from our sample to the population of interest. Random sampling is a lot harder to accomplish when conducting a true experiment. Most of us are willing to answer a few questions from a pollster; fewer of us may be willing to participate in an experiment that requires a commitment of time and energy.

ETHICS IN SOCIAL RESEARCH

No discussion of research procedures is complete without consideration of the potential ethical problems that social research may pose. Social research is conducted upon human beings. The impact of the research upon the participants must inevitably concern us.

Potential ethical problems in social research fall into three rough categories. First, occasionally researchers may cause harm to the participants in the research. Harm, if it occurs in so-

All of us have been asked to fill out some sort of survey.

cial psychological research, is usually of a psychological rather than of a physical nature. Second, in some social research, to avoid the threat of demand characteristics and social desirability, we deceive the participants about the purposes and procedures involved in the research. Such deception raises ethical issues. Finally, we inevitably collect information on individuals in social research. In doing so we may violate their privacy by gathering information that they would rather not disclose. These three potential problems are briefly discussed below.

Clearly psychological and physical harm to participants in research is something that should be avoided. While this conclusion seems straightforward, it is unfortunately difficult to predict when research will cause harm. Psychological harm that results from participation in research can take many forms: guilt, embarrassment, the discovery that one has the potential for cruel behavior (for example, Milgram, 1974), and so forth. An experimental treatment may quite unexpectedly induce feelings of inferiority or guilt in an individual. The same treatment in one context may devastate a participant, while in another context or for another participant no harm results. So, while it is relatively easy to say that harm to participants in social research should be avoided, it is more difficult to predict when psychological harm may be induced. Fortunately, experience has demonstrated that very few of the studies conducted by social psychologists do much actual harm.

Earlier in the chapter the threats of social desirability and demand characteristics were discussed. These threats are eliminated primarily through two procedures: unobtrusive information collection and deception concerning the phenomena of interest. Deception in social research raises ethical problems because it violates an implicit contract that can be said to exist between the researcher and the research participants. Whenever social research is conducted we essentially negotiate a contract with the participants to secure their participation in the research. Deception in social research violates the contract under which the participant freely entered into the research.

The final ethical problem in the conduct of social research concerns the use of information that is generated about the participants. Part of the implicit contract negotiated between a researcher and the participants concerns the participants' willingness to provide personal information on their beliefs, values, and behavior for the purposes of research. Nearly always it is assumed that this information will be used only for research purposes and that personal anonymity will be maintained in all research reports. Ethical problems are raised when these two assumptions are not met. For instance, if information on research participants' behavior is used to make slanderous remarks about the population from which the sample was chosen, the information is no longer being used for research purposes. Likewise, if information on individual participants is released or presented in a context where the participants can be identified, then the contract established for the use of the information has normally been violated.

Researchers employ a number of procedures to overcome or obviate these potential ethical problems. In general, the ethical issues posed in social research are not black and white. Rather, there are many fine shades of gray where some benefits may accrue to the researcher as a result of some practice that has a small potential of causing ethical problems. Deception in experimental research best illustrates this. Mild deception may be very useful in eliminating threats to the conclusion of the research. At what point, however, does deception become more than innocuous? At what point does it become unethical? There is no simple answer to this question, and yet it is a question that the social researcher must attempt to answer responsibly.

Most typically, where deception has been used, participants are _debriefed_ at the conclusion of the research. The debriefing is conducted with the purposes of eliminating all deception and of ensuring that the research participants show no evidence of psychological harm as a result of the research experience. Debriefing is without question an important and necessary procedure in social research. And yet, for at least two reasons, it does not constitute a sufficient way of overcoming ethical dilemmas. First, it has been demonstrated that even when participants are thoroughly debriefed they may continue to show effects of the deception (Ross, Lepper, & Hubbard, 1975). Second, as a way of spotting and alleviating psychological distress, debriefing comes too late. Potential distress to participants in research should be eliminated before it happens, rather than alleviating its effects afterwards.

Problems of data confidentiality are usually handled by ensuring that information remains strictly anonymous. This is best achieved by destroying any information that links questionnaire responses, observation, or any other information with individual participants. In other words, all information that can be used to identify individual participants is destroyed. Sometimes this procedure cannot be adopted if the research is to be successfully concluded. For instance, if we are conducting what is called a *panel survey*, where the same participants are repeatedly interviewed, it is essential to be able to link later responses to earlier responses from the same individuals. In cases like this, where it is not feasible to destroy identifying information in the short run, the researcher is under an obligation to make sure that the data remain strictly confidential. At the conclusion of the panel survey, it then becomes important to destroy identifying information.

A final way of dealing with ethical issues in social research involves the use of research review panels, composed of the researcher's colleagues. Fortunately, most institutions where social research is conducted have such panels, through which research proposals routinely pass. As stated previously, experience has shown that such panels seldom see danger in most social psychological studies. Nevertheless, it is helpful to have others to whom the researcher can turn for advice about potential ethical problems. Because it is sometimes difficult to see potential ethical problems that may arise, nearly all research proposals should be routinely reviewed.

THE SOCIAL CONTEXT OF SOCIAL RESEARCH

One of the implicit goals of this chapter has been to convey the idea that a scientific approach to human social behavior does not dictate one and only one method of research. There is not a single research method that is "science." Rather, there are many techniques for gathering empirical data to inform theories.

Because the techniques of science are not dictated and because the theories we formulate and examine change, the conduct of social research is inevitably affected by the context in which it is conducted. In other words, social research is not conducted in a vacuum. Both the choice of theoretical problems to be worked

on and the procedures for working on them are influenced by values in the society as a whole and by the values and expectations of the researcher's professional colleagues.

The most direct way in which social research is influenced is through funding agencies. Social research increasingly relies upon governmental agencies and foundations for research funds. These agencies and foundations have agendas, either explicit or not, for the type of social issues on which they believe research to be important. Thus, researchers are not entirely free to choose the theoretical problems on which they will work. To the extent that the researcher needs to secure outside funding, the choice of the subject to be studied depends upon what the funding agencies decide to fund.

More broadly, the content of social research is influenced by the value consensus in society as a whole. As certain social problems receive more attention in the press, as the public at large becomes interested in social issues, researchers tend to focus their research on related theoretical issues. During the height of the cold war, it is no coincidence that a great deal of social psychological research was conducted on bargaining, negotiation, and conflict resolution (for example, Deutsch & Krauss, 1960). Likewise it is no coincidence that during the 1970s we began to see for the first time research on women's employment and educational aspirations (see Smith-Lovin & Tickamyer, 1978).

The final source of profound influence upon social research, both content and procedures, is the profession in which the researcher has been trained. Graduate education, in part, serves to socialize the scientist, to provide exposure to problems that the discipline finds interesting and to procedures that the discipline finds useful. Earlier in the chapter we stated that social psychologists have traditionally emphasized internal validity more than either external or construct validities. This is an emphasis that is learned by social psychologists during their professional training. Training in other disciplines within the social sciences (for example, sociology or economics) would lead to a slightly different priority list among the three validities.

While social research is conducted in a social context and is influenced by the values of both the society and the discipline, research may also exert effects upon that context. In other words, research is both a social product and a social agent, causing changes in the social context from which it emerges.*There are three ways in which social research can have an impact upon the larger social context of which it is a part. First, research may modify behavior by making clear to individuals and social groups their prejudices and biases. In this sense research may ultimately transform that which it studies (see Gergen, 1973). Suppose we find, for instance, that some sorts of groups are not very efficient at brainstorming (Janis, 1972). We might, as a result of this research, restructure our groups so that they are more efficient.

Closely related to the above situation, where research may transform that which it studies, is the impact that research may have on informing social policy. A great deal of research is currently devoted to the evaluation of policy decisions. This research has the goal of informing policy choices and thereby influencing the society of which it is a part.

The final way in which social research affects the social context from which it emerges is by leading to changes in the values and ideologies commonly accepted within the society. Research may help alter the value assumptions of large parts of the society by pointing to inaccuracies or inadequacies in those assumptions. As an example, social research has been instrumental in changing the notion that separate educational facilities of minority children can be equal (Clark & Clark, 1947). In at least a mild way, social research has played a role in forcing our society to acknowledge that racial discrimination inevitably has social and personal costs.

SUMMARY

This chapter has been long and fairly complex. A lot of difficult and yet important material has been covered. We started by focusing on the ways in which empirical research interacts with theory, how theory guides our research, and how in turn research can inform theory. One of the crucial points in this part of the chapter was that research informs theory in a variety of different ways, that research serves more than a single function in formulating theories, and hence that there is likely to be a diversity of research methods that are useful. We then considered three research validities: construct, internal, and external validities. Construct validity refers to the relationships between variables in the research and the constructs of the theory. Internal validity refers to the causal relationship between the treatment and outcome variables in research. And external validity concerns the generalization from samples to populations of interest. Some discussion of trade-offs among these validities was included.

In the next section of the chapter, we presented the basics of research design, focusing on the rule by which individuals are assigned to treatment groups as an important factor for differentiating among these designs. True experiments are maximally efficient in internal validity since they employ a random assignment rule. Quasi-experiments use a nonrandom assignment rule, but attempt to equate groups on the basis of a pretreatment measure. In correlational designs, the assignment rule is unknown and all data are collected at the conclusion of the treatment.

Ethical issues in social research were next examined. The ethical problems of harm to participants, deception, and invasion of privacy were discussed, as were procedures that are normally used to circumvent ethical problems: debriefing, anonymity of data, and ethical review panels.

Finally, the chapter concluded with a discussion of social research as itself a social product. Like every other human activity, social research is influenced by the social context in which it is conducted. In turn, it may also influence that context by informing policy decisions and causing changes in the values adopted by our society.

SUGGESTED READINGS

Campbell, D. T., & Stanley, J. C. *Experimental and quasi-experimental designs for research.* Chicago: Rand McNally, 1963.

Cozby, P. C. *Methods in behavioral research.* Palo Alto, Cal: Mayfield, 1981.

Crano, W. D., & Brewer, M. B. *Principles of research in social psychology.* New York: McGraw-Hill, 1973.

Judd, C. M., & Kenny, D. A. *Estimating the effects of social interventions.* New York: Cambridge University Press, 1981.

Kidder, L. H. *Selltiz, Wrightsman & Cook's Research methods in social relations* (4th ed.) New York: Holt, Rinehart and Winston, 1981.

Individual Processes

3

SOCIALIZATION: THREE AGES, THREE RULE SYSTEMS

From February through May, 1973, members of the American Indian Movement occupied the village of Wounded Knee on the Pine Ridge Oglala Sioux Reservation in South Dakota. By staging their protest at Wounded Knee, the site of the 1890 massacre of Indian women and children by U.S. government troops, AIM leaders sought to draw public attention to treaty obligations ignored by the federal government and the relationship of these broken treaties to the problems of American Indians. After seventy-one days, the government forces, equipped with armored antipersonnel carriers and M–16 rifles, and the Indians, equipped with limited small arms and meager food supplies, negotiated an end to the occupation.

Government indictments arising out of the occupation resulted in the scheduling of over one hundred trials to be held in Sioux Falls, South Dakota. The defense established that a fair trial for the leadership cases could not be held there and won a change of venue for the trials of Russell Means and Dennis Banks, who were indicted on charges of conspiracy and aiding and abetting. The trial of these AIM leaders convened on January 8, 1974 at the federal courthouse in St. Paul.

The members of the jury were instructed to listen to the case brought against these two men by the state and judge, to the best of their ability, whether these two men were guilty or not of violating society's written codes or laws. These judgments are not always easy to make. One of the key factors influencing the verdict in this case was the history of **legal socialization** that each member brought to the jury's deliberations.

Socialization is the process by which people come to adopt the codes of conduct of their society and gain respect for its rules. Whether called socialization, internalization, or conscience development, the process describes how members of a society acquire its norms and act within them without loss of individuality. Socialization shapes our views about which behaviors violate society's codes of conduct.

In this chapter we will discuss socialization as it occurs throughout the life cycle. As our subsequent examination of the Wounded Knee trial will illustrate, socialization is not a process that ends with the end of childhood. Rather, it is a lifelong developmental process whereby the individual becomes a member of society, adding onto or learning new codes of conduct, as the society or the individual's place in society changes over time. We will discuss three phases of socialization and three contexts in which socialization can occur. We will consider childhood as a time when many of the codes of conduct are acquired in the context of the home; adolescence as a time when the individual questions the fairness of the codes, attempting to legitimize them, often in the context of the school; and adulthood as a time when long-held beliefs can be challenged and new understanding achieved. We have chosen the courtroom as a context in which to discuss adult socialization.

THEORIES OF SOCIALIZATION

Psychologists have devised a number of theories to explain how human beings are socialized. These theories vary in (1) whether human nature is seen as antisocial, prosocial or neutral, (2) whether individuals are viewed as playing active roles in their own socialization, (3) the importance assigned to biological fac-

---

This chapter is written by June Louin Tapp, Megan Gunnar and Daniel Keating.

tors, and (4) whether socialization is viewed as a developmental phenomenon involving predictable, age-related changes. Alone, none of the theories described below can explain human socialization. As social animals whose survival depends on the ability to live together in social groups, the processes that govern our socialization are probably complex and over-determined. Thus we need a combination of theoretical approaches to understand how socialization works. In this section we describe four theoretical approaches that have had a significant impact on the study of socialization.

Psychoanalytic Theory

Sigmund Freud developed psychoanalytic theory in the early part of the twentieth century. After working with mentally disturbed patients, he came to view the development of personality as a dynamic process involving powerful conflicts between an individual's instinctual desires and the demands of society. According to Freudian psychoanalytic theory, these conflicts shape the development of three personality structures: the id, the ego, and the superego.

The **id** is believed to be a primitive structure, housing the instinctual desires of the individual. It is the only aspect of personality at birth and is oriented toward immediate gratification of needs and wants. Society would not function well if all its members were to demand that their needs, wants, and desires be satisfied immediately. At first, parents provide the controls the child does not yet possess. Later, with the emergence of the **ego**, the child develops means of self-control. Initially, the ego deals with conflicts between the id's demands and the demands of parents or authority figures. It is the ego's job to find ways of satisfying the id without violating parental sanctions. To do so, the ego develops *defense mechanisms,* which serve to hold the id in check

until its desires can be satisfied in socially appropriate ways.

The **superego** corresponds roughly to the conscience. It includes moral values and prohibitions. Once the superego has developed, many of the control functions of parents and society are transferred to the self. Conformity to society's rules becomes less a matter of fear of external punishment, and more a matter of wanting to avoid the feelings of guilt that arise when we do not live up to our own internal standards.

Freud believed that the development of these three components of personality was regulated by an internal, developmental timetable; that the timetable, in turn, was regulated by biological changes in the parts of the body that served as the primary sources of sexual gratification. His theory has thus been labeled a theory of *psychosexual* development. The emphasis on the sexuality of the young child has been one of the most controversial parts of his theory. Many modern psychoanalytic theorists deemphasize the role of sexuality, focusing instead on the role of *psychosocial* conflicts in socialization and personality development. Social Focus 3.1 compares Freud's psychosexual theory to a psychosocial theory proposed by another psychologist, Erik Erikson (1968).

If we look at Social Focus 3.1, we find that according to Freudian theory, the superego is supposed to emerge at the end of the phallic stage, when the child is about six years old. We know now that children of this age tend to view rules as absolutes; often they are harsher in their interpretations of rules than are adults. This may explain why the superego is frequently stricter and more demanding than one's parents. As the child matures, the demands of the superego should become more tempered and humane. This will happen, however, only if the values represented in the superego remain conscious and changeable. It is when they are repressed that they remain immature, producing unrealistic guilt feelings and a harsh moral stance in the adult (Baldwin,

SOCIAL FOCUS 3.1

A Comparison of Freud's Psychosexual and Erikson's Psychosocial Stages of Social and Personality Development

| Approximate Chronological Age | PSYCHOSEXUAL STAGE | | PSYCHOSOCIAL STAGE | |
	Body Region or Label	Description	Crisis	Significant Person and Events
0–1 year	Oral	Needs center around and people are valued according to their capacity to provide oral gratification.	Trust vs. Mistrust	Mother; her love and responsiveness.
1–3 years	Anal	Voluntary control of anal sphincters becomes source of both pleasure and frustration as toilet training begins.	Autonomy vs. Shame and Doubt	Parents; the way they react to the child's assertive behaviors, and continuing dependency needs.
3–6 years	Phallic	The Oedipus Conflict: Love of opposite-sex parent and anger towards same-sex parent. Anxiety leading to identification with parental values and the development of the superego.	Initiative vs. Guilt	Family; conflicts between self and others threatens child's sense of initiative and produces feelings of guilt.
6–12 years	Latency	Child's sexual urges are relatively quiet. Energy is expended in school work and vigorous play.	Industry vs. Inferiority	School and peers; intense social comparison among peers.
12–17 years	Genital	Movement toward mature sexual relationships; a reawakening of many earlier conflicts.	Identity vs. Confusion	Peer groups and "heroes;" hormonal, social, and cognitive changes force the adolescent to search for a new, more adult-like identity.
Young Adulthood			Intimacy vs. Isolation	Friends and lovers; the search for meaningful relationships.
Adulthood			Generativity vs. Stagnation	Spouse, children, others; needs of self and family vs. needs of society in general.
Old Age			Ego Identity vs. Despair	Self in relation to others and the past; summing up—satisfaction vs. dissatisfaction.

1968). Freud spent little time discussing the development of the superego in older children and adults. The development of moral reasoning after early childhood is dealt with more extensively in the next theory to be described.

Cognitive-Developmental Theory

Cognitive-developmental theory grew out of the work of Jean Piaget (1932), who was primarily interested in the kinds of reasoning children use in solving logical problems. His work on logical reasoning led him to believe that children's thought processes undergo predictable, qualitative changes with development. Older children do not just solve problems better than younger children; they take in, organize, and act on information differently. Piaget and other cognitive-developmental theorists believe that there is an invariant sequence in the kind of cognitive changes occurring with development. People progress through the sequence at different rates, but no step in the sequence is ever skipped, and once a higher level of reasoning is attained, it is never lost. Thus development proceeds in a forward direction (Maccoby, 1980). In addition, cognitive-developmentalists believe that children play a very active role in their own socialization. They argue that the effect of any socialization experience will depend on how the child perceives or interprets the experience. The same experience may be perceived differently by children who are at different cognitive levels.

Cognitive-developmentalists have been especially concerned with developmental changes in moral reasoning. Piaget was one of the first psychologists to examine how children think about moral issues at different ages. He tried to understand what children know about rules, where they think social rules come from, and how they decide whether a rule is just or right. He came to believe that a major change in moral reasoning occurs during middle childhood (ages 7 to 9). He argued that younger children operate according to a *morality of constraint*. They use an egocentric (self-centered) mode of moral reasoning. They see rules as heteronomous, that is, as emanating from authority figures and thus external to themselves. To the younger child, rules are unalterable realities, in the sense that they have always been and will always remain the same. Reasons for compliance are based on a unilateral respect for the authority figures associated with the rules. Children at this stage of thought equate punishment with wrongdoing (wrong acts are the

ones you are punished for) and judge the deviance of an act by how much damage is done, while paying less attention to the intentions of the person performing the act. Older children, Piaget argued, operate on a *morality of cooperation*. They use a more autonomous, sociocentric mode of moral reasoning. Rules are viewed as social contracts, agreed upon by members of a social group. Through participating with others in making rules, older children come to understand that rules can be made and changed through discussion and by new agreements between individuals. Children operating according to a morality of cooperation view compliance as necessary for the maintenance of social order. They attempt to take the other's perspective (**role taking**) and judge the seriousness of a misdeed more in terms of intentions than actions.

Kohlberg (1969) has taken Piaget's basic framework, refined it, and extended it to cover changes in moral reasoning during adolescence and adulthood (see Social Focus 3.2). Kohlberg's third level goes beyond Piaget's morality of cooperation in that more mature individuals can distinguish between social rules and moral principles. In stage 5, the first stage in the postconventional or "principled" level of Kohlberg's system, an individual feels a moral obligation to attempt to change a rule through acceptable procedures, if the rule is not morally just. In stage 6, a person's sense of personal commitment to what he or she believes to be universal ethical principles is so great that neither external pressure nor even a previous agreement (social contract) is sufficient to permit the individual to comply with rules that violate personal beliefs. In Social Focus 3.2 we also describe Tapp's (1974, 1977) legal-levels model, which reveals similar developmental changes in the realm of legal reasoning. Tapp's views, which will be presented in more detail later in this chapter, are based in part on the work of Piaget and Kohlberg.

A number of studies now indicate that peo-

SOCIAL FOCUS 3.2
Description of Level of Moral and Legal Reasoning

PIAGET'S STAGES	KOHLBERG'S LEVELS	TAPP'S LEVELS
Stage of Heteronomous Morality. The individual operates on a morality of constraint. Rules are viewed as moral absolutes. The consequences of the act are attended to more than are the intentions of the actor. The individual believes that people who violate rules will invariably be punished by some authority—god or natural force.	**Preconventional Level.** **Stage 1: Punishment and obedience.** The rightness and wrongness of actions are defined by their consequences. An act is wrong only if one is caught and punished. **Stage 2: Naive Hedonism.** Rules are conformed to in order to obtain desired rewards. The intentions of the actor now partially define the seriousness of a violation.	**Preconventional Level: Law-deferring.** Individuals exhibit a mode of legal reasoning based on fear of punishment or deference to power. The focus is on external consequences and authority. Instrumental hedonism tempers legal valuations. Egocentric notions of retaliatory justice and literal exchange are pervasive. The generality of law is absent in reasoning about legal actions and attitudes.
Stages of Autonomous Morality. The child now operates on a morality of cooperation, a moral relativism. She realizes that social rules are arbitrary agreements that can be changed and challenged by the consent of people.	**Conventional Level.** **Stage 3: "Good-Boy" or "Good-Girl."** Morality is defined in terms of what helps or pleases. Intentions are now very important in determining wrong-doing. **Stage 4: Law-and-Order Orientation.** Laws are accepted without questioning. Orientation is towards maintaining social order.	**Conventional Level: Law-maintaining.** People are concerned with fulfilling role expectations. Commitment to the community is tied to performing as a good-girl (woman) or good-boy (man). Justice is synonymous with majority vote; individual rights are lost to group norms; equality means only the impartial application of rules. Rights are easily confused with privileges conferred by one's social role. Social norms must be maintained for orderly living.
	Post Conventional Level. **Stage 5: Social-Contract Orientation.** Social welfare and the will of the majority define the legitimacy of social rules. Laws may be viewed as unjust, but must be obeyed until they can be changed by social consensus. **Stage 6: Universal-ethical-principles Orientation.** Right and wrong are determined by one's conscience, based on ethical principles. Violation of one's principles produces feelings of guilt and self condemnation.	**Post Conventional Level: Law-creating.** Individuals have a legislative perspective. These principled-thinking individuals see the need for social systems, yet differentiate between the values of a given social order and universal ethics. In a postconventional frame of reference, legal directives are human constructs reflecting the consensual participation of equals moving toward shared expectations. While valuing social systems, individuals at this level appreciate the need to make independent ethical choices and can distinguish principles of justice from concrete laws and societal conventions.

ple do progress through these levels of moral reasoning. Progression from one level or stage to the next, however, does not appear to be as abrupt as was once believed (Flavell, 1977). Persons may use different levels of moral reasoning in their judgments in different situations. Thus, individual reasoning styles may reflect a mixture—the operations of somewhat more and somewhat less mature levels. One level, however, is usually dominant or modal (Rest, 1973; Tapp & Kohlberg, 1977; Tapp & Levine, 1974). This has led a number of researchers to question whether cognitive development really involves complete, qualitative changes in the way people think. A second question about this approach is whether moral reasoning is related to moral behavior. Predicting moral behavior has been a central issue in the next theory to be discussed.

Children learn sex roles through observation and usually imitate what they learn.

Social-Learning Theory

Social-learning theorists believe that the vast majority of human behavior is learned. People develop in accordance with the opportunities and experiences afforded them in their environment. Following the lead of Albert Bandura (1977), social-learning theorists believe that many behaviors are acquired through observational learning. What the observer acquires are symbolic representations of a model's actions. What is learned is then encoded into memory to serve as a guide for later behavior. We do not need to imitate a behavior in order to learn it. For example, a little boy may learn how to put on makeup by watching his mother, although he may never put on makeup himself.

Four interrelated processes are involved in observational learning (Bandura, 1977). Before an observer can learn much from a model, he or she must actively attend to the model's behavior. Attention is affected by characteristics of both the model and the observer. Memory and motoric processes are also involved. We may learn how to perform a behavior, but then forget what we have learned (memory component). Or we may need to practice one or more of the motor actions required in order to perform the behavior (motoric component). Remember learning to whistle or ride a bike? These behaviors were learned by watching others, but needed to be perfected through practice. Finally, there is a motivational aspect to observational learning. Whether or not we perform a behavior depends on whether we expect to be reinforced or punished for doing so. The little boy in the above example may never use what he knows about putting on makeup because he has learned that imitating such feminine behavior is not approved of in his social group. As with social behavior, we learn a great deal about social rules and sanctions for behavior through observation, by attending to what others tell us, and by observing the consequences of others' actions. The little boy may have been told that boys do not do girls' things, or he may have observed another boy being admonished for putting on his mother's makeup. Bandura calls these instances of *vicarious* reinforcement and punishment.

Ethological Theory

While social-learning theorists argue that most behaviors are learned, ethologists argue that we are biologically predisposed to learn certain patterns of behavior because of their adaptive value. Like other animals, we have a long evolutionary history. Thus, they argue, we cannot ignore the role that adaptive pressures during evolution have played a part in shaping our social behavior (Cairns, 1979). Furthermore, ethologists believe that we cannot understand the adaptive significance of behavior by observing how people act in the kind of contrived laboratory settings used so frequently by developmental or social psychologists. Instead, they believe that behavior must be studied in naturalistic settings. In attempting to understand the behavior of any species, an ethologist first maps or describes the behavior as it occurs in that species' natural habitat. These descriptions are called *ethograms.* From these ethograms the ethologist then attempts to identify *homologies* or similarities in behavior patterns, motivation, and developmental processes among members of the species (Tinbergen, 1972). Once these have been identified, the ethologist attempts to understand what function the behavior may serve in the survival of that species.

Although all ethologists are concerned with the role of evolution in determining adaptive behavior, they differ in the extent to which they believe that explanations of behavior in evolutionary terms are sufficient. Some ethologists like Eibl-Eibesfeldt (1975) and E. O. Wilson (1975) propose that evolutionary influences are the primary causes of behavior. Others, like Hinde (1970) and Tinbergen (1972), believe that in order to adequately explain behavior, both proximal (immediate) causes and ultimate (evolutionary) causes must be taken into account.

Both the methods and concepts employed by ethologists are beginning to have an impact on the study of human social development. Of special importance have been the attempts of John Bowlby (1969, 1973) to combine concepts from ethology with those from psychoanalytic theory to explain the nature, function, and consequences of the child's social relations during infancy. Bowlby proposed that, throughout evolution, survival of the human infant has depended upon the maintenance of proximity to a primary caretaker who is capable of satisfying the infant's biological needs for food, warmth, and protection from predators. As the result of these survival pressures, human infants have a strong biological predisposition to become emotionally attached to one or a few primary caretakers. Furthermore, Bowlby argued that the origins of psychopathology can be traced to disruptions in the infant's "love" or attachment relationship(s). Many of Bowlby's ideas have been strongly criticized (see Rutter, 1972). Modern ethological concepts, however, have served to reorient studies of early social development in the direction of identifying cross-cultural and cross-species similarities in the establishment and regulation of early social relationships. The results of some of this work are discussed later when we consider processes of socialization in the context of the family.

Two Persistent Issues in Describing the Processes of Socialization

The nature of human nature. Any theory of socialization, whether it is an explicit theory like those just described, or an implicit theory like those held by the man or woman on the street, must at some point deal with the following questions: What is the nature of human nature? Are we basically self-serving individuals whose impulses must be checked and controlled in order for society to function? Are we basically social beings adapted to live in social groups and develop social relationships? Are we neither social nor antisocial by nature, but a product of our experiences, which may lead us in either direction? Or, should we view human nature as a dynamic entity—an entity that changes with age as natural capacities develop and alter the individual's understanding of the social world?

If we look back at our four theories of socialization, we can see that they all describe human nature differently. Freudian theory presents us as creatures imbued with dangerous impulses that must be controlled in order for society to function. Social-learning theory describes people as rational beings who act to optimize the chances of receiving the good things from life (reinforcement) and minimize unwanted consequences (punishment). Ethologists, on the other hand, view human nature as having worked to help ensure the survival of the species. This does not mean that we always act in accordance with the needs of our immediate social group. Rather, in the long run our behaviors should result in sufficient reproductive success to ensure that our genes are represented in the gene pools of future generations. Finally, the cognitive-developmental perspective presents a view of human nature that changes with development.

The problem of interaction. Almost all of us would now agree that socialization is not a one-way street. The question of just who is being socialized and who is doing the socialization depends on one's perspective. When we assimilate a new member into a group, we may alter the behavior of that individual to conform to group norms, but the presence of that individual also alters the nature and functioning of the group. Think of two people having a child. The parents take on the task of socializing the child, but the presence of a baby in the family dramatically alters the lives of the two adults. The baby socializes the parents into their new role as parents, just as the parents attempt to socialize the child into the culture. Socialization is an _interactive process_, with each individual, at one and the same time, being both the agent and the object of the process. This is true

throughout one's life-span and in the many contexts in which socialization occurs.

None of the theories of socialization, to date, have captured the totally interactive nature of these processes. Freudian theory views society as pressuring the individual to conform against the individual's own will. Social-learning theory explains how the behavior of individuals is shaped or molded by their own experiences. Cognitive-developmental theory describes individuals as active (perhaps the most active) agents of their socialization. Historically, however, many cognitive-developmental theorists have focused on proving that individuals pass through predetermined stages of development, rather than emphasizing the interactive nature of the processes promoting cognitive and social growth. Finally, ethologists have been some of the most vocal proponents of an interactive approach. In attempting to describe social actions, they have realized the need to devise codes or behavior categories that capture the interactional flavor of social behavior. Nonetheless, ethological theory—emphasizing as it does the evolutionary, biological bases of social behavior—still tends to present an image of the individual as being directed by forces beyond his or her own control.

SOCIALIZATION IN THE FAMILY

During early childhood, one's family is probably the most important agent of socialization. In attempting to socialize the child, parents establish rules and attempt to enforce them through reinforcement, punishment, and example. Parents differ in how clearly they state the rules, how consistently they demand compliance, how they deal with deviant behavior, and so on. In this section, we will consider how variations in patterns of child rearing are related to two aspects of behavior: moral development and the development of sex roles and sex differences.

Moral Development

✳ All morality consists of a system of rules, and the essence of morality lies in the respect the individual acquires for those rules (Piaget, 1932). Most adults do not act as though moral norms (such as honesty, justice, and fair play) are externally imposed constraints. Instead, they act as though those moral norms are *internally* valued codes of conduct. In this section we examine how different experiences in the family affect internalization of normative standards that then serve as guidelines of appropriate or permissible behavior between individuals.

Warmth and affection. The emotional relationship between parent and child forms the context in which socialization occurs within the family. Generally speaking,✳ parental love and affection facilitate socialization, while parental rejection and hostility are frequently related to the development of antisocial behaviors (Hoffman, 1970; Patterson, 1976). Why is parental love so important?

Attachment theorists like Bowlby and neo-psychoanalytic theorists like Erikson point to the role of parental love in the establishment of basic trust. They argue that✳ children who experience a warm, loving parent-child relationship will develop trust in people and a positive, cooperative social orientation. Conversely, children who experience a cold, rejecting parent-child relationship will be suspicious of others and will develop a negative, hostile social orientation. Current research supports this view. Children who experience a loving, secure attachment relationship during infancy and early childhood do appear to be more open, cooperative, and friendly towards others (Arend, Gove, & Sroufe, 1979; Main, 1973). As we will see, trust and a positive orientation toward others forms the basis for many aspects of moral socialization. Accordingly✳ parental love and affection early in childhood lay the groundwork for moral development.

Parent-child relations are important in the individual's development. Individuals who have warm, loving relationships during their early childhood tend to be more open, cooperative, and friendly toward others.

While we usually view parents as the ones who determine the emotional quality of the parent-child relationship, characteristics of the child also play an important role. No doubt it is easier to love and accept some children than others. For instance, recent studies indicate that babies whose physical appearance and behavior deviate significantly from the norm elicit less positive emotional responses from adults (Lamb, in press; Park, 1977).

Discipline. In attempting to develop a moral sense in the child, parents have many techniques available to them. Because discipline encounters occur often during the early years—approximately 5 to 6 times per hour (Wright, 1967, as cited in Hoffman, 1979)—parents have frequent opportunity to exercise different discipline strategies. It seems reasonable that the type of discipline parents use will influence the child's moral development. Developmental social psychologists have examined three classes of parental discipline: *power-assertion, love-with-drawal,* and *induction* (Hoffman, 1970).

According to Freudian theory, children internalize parental values because they are afraid of being punished by the all-powerful parent. (Freud called this defensive identification. He believed that this was the major process underlying the development of a superego or conscience.) Use of power-assertive discipline—including physical punishment, deprivation of privileges, or threats of both—should enhance moral internalization, according to Freudian theory (Hoffman, 1970; Sears, Maccoby, & Levin, 1957). Developmental psychologists, however, have found consistently that use of power-assertive techniques impedes moral development. Contrary to Freudian theory, children who experience frequent power-assertive discipline tend to feel less guilty when they break a rule, fail to comply with adult requests when it is clear their behavior is *not* being monitored, and have an external moral orientation. Basically they believe that rules should be obeyed in order to avoid punishment, rather than because the rules are right or just. In attribution-theory terms (see Chapter 6), these children appear to attribute their behavior to external sources of control. This may impede the internalization of moral values and movement to more mature levels of moral reasoning. In addition, parents who frequently use power assertion also tend to be more hostile and rejecting (Patterson, 1976). A combination of power assertion (which may lead children to see their behaviors as externally controlled) and hostility (which may lead to lack of trust in others) seems to be a good formula for poor moral development in children. This does not mean, however, that occasional use of power assertion when the child is particularly disobedient will have these effects. In fact, there is some evidence that moderate use of power assertion by an otherwise warm and loving parent does inhibit unwanted behavior in the child (Parke, 1974; Sears, Maccoby, & Levin, 1957).

Freud also argued that children are motivated to obey their parents out of fear of losing the parent's love. (He called this <u>anaclitic</u> identification.) Although Freud believed that anaclitic identification played a lesser role in moral internalization, neopsychoanalytic theorists like Erikson (1968) have argued that threats to the security of the parent-child bond serve as powerful motivating forces in socialization. Accordingly, frequent use of love-withdrawal discipline should promote moral internalization. On the whole, this hypothesis has fared much better. Children who are deprived of nurturance by an adult do appear to become motivated to gain that adult's approval (Hartup, 1958). Frequent use of love-withdrawal discipline is also associated with the inhibition of anger on the child's part (Hoffman & Salzstein, 1967). And there is some evidence that children who experience frequent withdrawal-of-love discipline develop rather harsh, punitive consciences (Hoffman, 1970). These children, however, seem to value the letter rather than the spirit of the moral rule. They develop moral systems that are rigid and rather inflexible. They have not really developed a principled moral orientation; rather, in Kohlberg's scheme, they remain at the good-boy, good-girl level of moral reasoning.

The pattern of parental discipline most conducive to moral internalization appears to be a combination of induction plus a warm, loving parent-child relationship outside of discipline encounters (Hoffman, 1979). Induction is defined as reasoning with the child and placing special emphasis on the effects that the child's actions have on other people. Statements like "You hurt Mary's feelings by what you said," "Mr. Jones has worked very hard on his garden, and he will be very disappointed when he sees how you trampled down his flowers," and "You don't like it when others do that to you, so how do you think they feel when you do it to them?'' are instances of inductive discipline. Parents using induction also frequently encourage children to repair or make amends for the damage they have caused (apologizing to Mary, offering to help Mr. Jones fix up his garden). In social-learning-theory terms, parents who use induction are serving as verbal models of the principles underlying moral rules. In cognitive-developmental terms, they may be fostering moral development by encouraging the child to take a role or view the situation from another's perspective. Both processes, combined with a sense of basic trust growing out of a loving parent-child relationship, may explain why induction is such a powerful technique in moral internalization.

Morality as a trait.   So far we have been talking as if morality were some kind of unitary attribute. That is, we have been talking as if some children are more moral than others. According to this perspective, morality is a trait that predisposes people to behave in certain, consistent ways. As with other traits (such as aggression, dependency, sociability), there is heated debate among psychologists over whether individuals are consistent enough in their behavior across situations to make it reasonable to say that one person is more ''moral'' than another. If we look closely at moral behavior, we find that people vary a good deal from one situation to the next. The child who steals cookies from the cookie jar on one occasion may or may not be the one who cheats on a test, or lies about where he or she has been. Even various aspects of moral behavior (moral feelings, thoughts, and behavior) do not always go together. Children who tend to feel guilty if they violate a rule may not necessarily resist the temptation to do so. Children who tend to conform to rules may do so because they fear being caught *or* believe that ''good people'' will be rewarded (external orientation), rather than because they believe the rules are right and just (internal orienta-

Play and team experiences can influence the adoption of sex-role behaviors.

tion). Given these possibilities, how can we talk about the development of morality? First, there is evidence that as children mature and as their moral reasoning becomes more principled (see Kohlberg's stages 5 and 6), moral thought, feelings, and emotions become more consistent (Grim, Kohlberg, & White, 1968; Schwartz, Feldman, Brown, & Heingartner, 1969). Second, we now have evidence that even though behavior does vary over situations, if we average a person's behavior across several situations, a more cohesive picture of personality begins to develop (Epstein, 1979). This is similar to statements we might make about our own morality: ''Well, at times I do lie, but on the whole I'm a fairly honest person.'' The child's experiences in the family may not predict the child's "morality" in every situation, but they may predict the child's average moral disposition.

The Family and Sex-Role Socialization

✳ Sex-role typing is the process whereby children acquire the behaviors that their culture deems appropriate for their sex. There are three aspects of sex-role typing. First, there is one's sex-role *orientation* or perception of one's own masculinity or femininity (or androgyny). Second, there is sex-role *preference* or the extent to which we want to behave in ways deemed appropriate for our sex. The little girl who refuses to wear dresses and thinks dolls are boring has made a clear statement about her sex-role preferences. Finally, there is sex-role *adoption*. This refers to others' perceptions of the femininity or masculinity of our behavior.

Across a number of cultures there is consistency in sex-role standards. While exceptions do exist, obedient and responsible behaviors are generally valued in women, while assertive, achievement-oriented, and self-reliant behaviors are generally valued in men (Barry, Bacon, & Child, 1957). Our own U.S. society is in a period of transition. We recognize that "male" characteristics (like self-reliance and assertiveness) are valuable in some situations, while "female" characteristics (like nurturance and emotional expressiveness) are valuable in other situations. Concepts such as androgyny are being introduced to describe individuals who can be nurturant (feminine) in situations where nurturant behavior is called for and dominant and assertive (masculine) in other situations (Bem, 1974).

In this section, we examine the development of sex typing in the family. Because we will be concerned with familial influences, we will not examine the role of biological and other factors. This does not mean, however, that these factors are unimportant in the development of sex differences. Obviously, too, there are preliminary stages in sex typing. First, children must learn that there are two sexes and be able to distinguish between them, so as to identify their own gender. Only then do children begin to consciously learn about the sex-role standards and stereotypes of society.

Parents, as well as other social agents, attempt to get children to adopt certain sex-role attitudes and beliefs. In many cultures, including our own, male roles are assigned greater value and importance (D'Andrade, 1966). Perhaps because of this, boys experience greater pressure to behave in sex-appropriate ways than do girls (Fling & Manosevitz, 1972; Lansky, 1967). It is all right for a young girl to be a tomboy, but it is not all right for a young boy to be a sissy. This training begins early. In one study, fathers with their 12-month-old sons or daughters were seen in a waiting-room situation. There was a shelf with toys for the children to play with (two trucks, two dolls, a shovel, and a carpet sweeper). The shelf was constructed so that the children could not reach the top; instead, the fathers had to make the toys available. ✳Fathers did not restrict the range of toys they made available to daughters; that is, girls were given both trucks and dolls. They did, however, avoid giving their 12-month-old sons dolls to play with, although they readily gave their sons the trucks (Gunnar, 1975).

✳Fathers appear to be more active than mothers in children's early sex-role training (Hetherington & Parke, 1979).✳They also show a strong preference for having a son rather than a daughter before the child is born, especially if the child is the firstborn. Fathers are more extreme than mothers in perceiving physical differences between sons (large, coordinated, active) and daughters (small, fragile, and pretty) at birth (Rubin, Provenzano, & Luria, 1974). And they spend more time talking to and playing with sons than with daughters during childhood. It is as if fathers believe they must supply something extra if a son is to develop into a "man," while the development of a daughter can be more safely entrusted to a wife's hands.

As children develop, they often imitate the behavior of their parents. A number of theories emphasize the importance of observing and imitating the same-sex parent in the development of sex typing. Characteristics of the parents influence sex-role learning for both boys and girls. Once again, it is the father who seems to play the more influential role. *Fathers who have warm, loving relationships with their sons and who take an active, dominant role in discipline have sons who are more traditionally masculine in their sex-role orientation, preference, and adoption (Hetherington, 1965). Fathers also influence their daughters' femininity. Masculine men who enjoy their wives' femininity and reinforce their daughters' attempts to be feminine have daughters who adopt more traditional sex-role orientations and preferences (Hetherington, 1967).

At first glance, these findings seem to fit with the psychoanalytic notion of identification. But children are not really identifying with their parents in the sense of becoming carbon copies of their mothers' femininity or fathers' masculinity. Instead, *children seek out information about appropriate sex-role behavior from a wide variety of sources (parents, peers, teachers, media, and so forth). Relationships within the family function to encourage or discourage children from embarking on this task. *Disruptions in the family interfere with sex-role development in both boys and girls, but the effects seem to be greater for boys. Masculine orientation, preference, and adoption are impaired in homes where the mother is dominant and the father plays a peripheral role (Hetherington & Parke, 1979). Father absence (physical or psychological) also disrupts sex-role development, but once again, sons are affected more than daughters. This is especially true if father absence occurs before the age of

5 years. So far, the effects on daughters seem to be limited to the girls' ability to form relationships with members of the opposite sex and do not really become apparent until adolescence (Hetherington, 1972).

Within the family, not only parents but also siblings influence a child's sex-role development. A central tenet of social-learning theory is that children learn sex-role concepts from a wide variety of models. Thus siblings, peers, teachers, and television, as well as parents, should influence sex-role development (Shaffer, 1979). In fact, the number of children in the family, their ages and distribution do influence a child's masculinity or femininity (Sutton-Smith & Rosenberg, 1970). Children who have siblings of only the same sex display less cross-sex behavior. *Boys raised only with brothers and girls raised only with sisters are more masculine and feminine, respectively. In father-absent homes, children with older brothers are more aggressive and less dependent than children with older sisters or no older siblings. As these findings suggest, even within the family a child's sex-role development is not based solely on parental behavior, but is influenced by siblings of both sexes and by the total family environment (Shaffer, 1979).

Thus, the family has a great impact on socialization during childhood. Emotional relations between parent and child form the context in which socialization occurs. While parents may use reinforcements and punishments to modify their children's behavior, children, too, play an active role in their own socialization. Even during childhood, agents of socialization other than the parents influence social development. Children and adults develop their rule-guided systems for human interaction from encounters across a number of social systems—family, school, work, and political and legal systems. With age, the child moves out of the family context, and experiences in the context of the school become increasingly more important in the socialization process.

THE ADOLESCENT IN SCHOOL: RULE LEGITIMATION AND PERSONAL IDENTITY

In most postindustrial Western societies adolescence has been traditionally viewed as a time of transition between the dependency of childhood, centered on the home and family, and the independence of adult life. Since the early part of this century, this interim period of semidependency and semiautonomy has become more clearly identified as a formally defined part of each individual's development (Elder, 1980; Kett, 1977). During the same historical period, more and more adolescents have remained in the schools for all or most of the teen-age years. In 1970, for example, over 90 percent of 14- to 17-year-olds were in high school, and nearly 60 percent of 18- to 21-year-olds were enrolled in college (Elder, 1980).

This implies that schools become a highly significant, perhaps even primary, agent of socialization for the society at large. Key social lessons, which in an earlier historical period might have been learned in any of a wide variety of work or community contexts, are more frequently taken into the school setting—and often transformed in the process. Kett (1977) cites as an example of this the frequent practice in the early nineteenth century of placing children as helpers (or formal apprentices) with other families at an early age, sometimes as young as ten. The work and life of children and adolescents were far more community based than school based; this trend has been largely reversed in contemporary U.S. society.

Such changes make an analysis of *what* the schools are socializing adolescents toward, and *how* they are doing so, a crucial social issue. We examine the implications for adolescent socialization in the sections below.

Adolescent Development

Before turning to specific examples of school socialization influences on adolescents, we consider some preliminary issues that provide necessary background. First, there is the broad question: What is going on in the development of the typical adolescent that the school may influence? We recognize there are no satisfactory *brief* answers to this question—and that the "typical adolescent" is a convenient fiction. Nevertheless, we note some salient aspects of adolescent development, especially those that are relevant to socialization.

Cognitively, adolescents are in the process of becoming more effective abstract thinkers. They are far more likely to think about things logically than when they were younger, and they are more likely to take seriously and to try to think more clearly about a wider variety of issues—including deeply troublesome ones like social justice and personal identity (Erikson, 1968; Keating, 1980; Marcia, 1980). Moreover, adolescents are likely to extend the rule acquisition process that was important during childhood to rule legitimation. While continuing to learn the rules of the society and to refine their application in practice, many adolescents begin to wonder *why* these particular rules and expectations exist and *whether* they are necessarily the best rules we could have as a society.

The ability to think logically and to deal with hypothetical situations clearly contributes to this kind of thinking and questioning of social issues among adolescents (Keating, 1980). But so does a more psychodynamic variable, the search for identity (Erikson, 1968; Marcia, 1980). In his psychosocial theory of development, Erikson attempted to combine a basically psychoanalytic perspective with a recognition of the importance of the social environment in which the psychoanalytically defined issues are worked out. His theory has had a profound influence on current research and thinking about adolescent development. From this perspective, one of the compelling reasons for adolescents to learn how to understand and analyze social rules and expectations, as well as to follow them, is that they are trying to understand their *own* identity and their own place in that society.

We can see then that not only are adolescents becoming increasingly *able* cognitively to think seriously about social issues in a more fundamental way, but also that they are increasingly *motivated* to do so by virtue of concerns about their own identity status. One outcome of this is that, in fact, older adolescents are better able to understand and articulate the social rules (and the reasons for their existence) than are younger adolescents.

Although this general developmental progression is quite consistent, we must be careful not to make too much of it. The political and social "consciousness" even of older adolescents and college students is, by any objective criterion, still quite primitive (Gallatin, 1980). Late adolescents typically use political ideas and concepts, but frequently with little understanding. Zellman and Sears (1971) reported, for example, that adolescents support more strongly than children the abstract ideal of civic liberties (for example, free speech), but still have difficulty with specific instances (such as the idea that Communists should be able to teach in the schools). It is important to understand the level at which adolescents (or adults) deal with complex social issues.

Let us now look at the school's contribution to the socialization of adolescents in two specific areas: sex-role stereotyping and social conformity. In doing so, it is important to understand what we mean by school as a socializing agent. Obviously, school does not designate a person or group as specifically as, say, family. What we mean here by the term "school" is everything involved in the social structure of formal schooling in this society, including not only teachers, counselors, administrators, and students, but also the societal attitudes about schools, societal expectations about the outcomes of schooling, and so on.

Sex-Role Stereotyping

As we have already seen, sex-role orientation, preference, and adoption are important social acquisitions of the childhood years. But the development of ideas, attitudes, and behavior connected to one's gender assignment clearly continues throughout the adolescent years. Most of the peer activity in the preadolescent years is organized in same-sex grouping; that is, boys tend to affiliate with boys and girls with girls. Beginning at the age when students normally begin junior high school (about 12 or 13), however, interactions between the sexes rise in frequency and importance within the peer group (Coleman, 1980; Dunphy, 1963). One by-product of this is that the socially approved *roles* for each gender take on added importance. In order to be successful and accepted within the group, adolescents must acquire an impressive array of sex-typed attitudes and behaviors.

This also is a period of heightened conformity pressures in general. Pressure to conform to the norms of the peer group probably peak between 13 and 15 years of age (Conger, 1977). Recall as well that this is an important period for the development of personal identity and the construction of many important values that individuals carry into adulthood and throughout the life cycle. The combination of all these factors—initial attempts at adultlike heterosexual interaction, heightened conformity pressures, and the prominence of questions about personal identity and values—makes the adolescent vulnerable to a variety of external influences in the shaping of socially approved sex roles. Acquiring and practicing these roles obviously has a tremendous influence on the individual's subsequent self-image and self-definition.

What specific effect does the school have in this process? *There are two related areas in which schools play a major part: the accepted *style* of achievement and the accepted *content* of achievement in the academic setting. Let us look at these in more detail.

During the primary school years, there already exists an expectation that girls will be more cooperative than boys, and boys will be more competitive than girls. In fact, during these years girls typically have an easier time in the school setting, because their style is more in line with the preferred style of most elementary schools. But during these years there is still considerable overlap between the sexes, so that competitive girls and cooperative boys are not unusual. Although cooperation is the generally preferred style, competition in boys is still expected and rewarded.

In these respects, the shift to high school is a dramatic one. Competitive activities and attitudes in girls regarding *academic* matters are discouraged, but in boys are highly rewarded. Girls may compete socially, but highly visible academic competence has usually been a social handicap, especially if that competence is at the expense of boys in a competitive setting.

Psychologists have often made a distinction between "agency," which involves acting toward a defined, visible goal, and "communion," which involves getting people together and maintaining social relationships. This difference is very much a part of the general sociocultural pattern (Feather, 1980). Boys are expected to (and do) have more interest in agency, which is concerned with the organism as an individual and manifests itself in self-protection, self-assertion, and self-expansion, whereas girls are expected to have more interest in communion, which is descriptive of the individual organism existing as a part of some larger organism and manifesting itself "in the

sense of being at one with other organisms" (Block, 1973, p. 515).

The effectiveness of this sex-differentiated set of expectations and rewards is dramatically illustrated in a recent study by Ahlgren and Johnson (1979). They surveyed over 2400 students from the second to the twelfth grades on their attitudes about academic cooperation and competition, deriving a "cooperative preference" score for each student. Boys and girls are different throughout the age range studied, with girls being more cooperative than competitive and the boys showing the opposite pattern. In addition, there was a highly significant and interesting interaction of age and sex differences, with the distance between the boys' and girls' attitudes showing a dramatic increase during the eighth through tenth grades. This is partly a result of the boys becoming even more competitive during this time, but even more, it is a function of the girls becoming much *less* competitive.

The impressive consistency with which girls tend toward cooperation and communion and boys strive toward agency and competition is perhaps easier to understand when we examine the socialization pressures pushing them in those directions. Not only are there pressures inducing individuals to adopt the socially approved sex-stereotyped roles, there are also considerable obstacles to those who would go against the expectations. A well-documented recent example of this process was reported in the context of an ongoing study of adolescents who are high achievers in mathematics (Keating, 1976). The low number of high-achieving girls was a major concern in this study, particularly since far fewer girls than boys continue to take mathematical instruction through the high school years. This may greatly diminish career and further education options.

Fox (1976) reported a study in which she selected some of the highest-achieving girls in the seventh and eighth grades to teach them advanced mathematics and to encourage them in a variety of ways to develop their abilities. They were quite successful in the special program. They encountered some problems, however, when they returned to their regular school, identified high achievers in mathematics—a traditionally male dominion. Concerning the girls' return to their home school, Fox reported the following:

One interesting difference is found between the eight girls who were successful and the seven girls who had difficulty. Only one of the eight successful girls reported having problems with her teacher and guidance counselor. All of the seven girls who were less successful reported problems with the school. Many of the problems began before school started. Parents as well as girls called to say that they were having problems with the schools. . . . It is difficult to believe that teachers would deliberately try to fail some of the girls. More than one parent or student reported, however, that the teacher had told the student that the girls could [not] possibly know algebra well enough . . . to do well (pp. 202–209).

These experiences are contrasted with the generally positive reception of male advanced-mathematics students and with schools' expectations that such advancement was appropriate (Keating, 1976). ✳Not all of the socialization pressures are exerted on girls, although they seem stronger for them during adolescence. This is an intriguing contrast to the pattern in childhood discussed earlier.✳But it is clear that adolescent boys who do not measure up in the "spirit of competition" suffer considerably, although the site of these pressures is more often the athletic field than the classroom during these years (Coleman, 1961). Ludwig and Maehr (1967) showed, for example, that for boys with a below-average self-image, criticisms of athletic skill from a physical education teacher were devastating not only to their perceptions of their athletic ability but also to their overall self-image.

These examples illustrate in several ways the socializing influence that schools have on developing adolescents. The content of the socialization is by and large in accord with the expectations of the larger U.S. society. A growing number of researchers have begun to question the value of rigid stereotyping (Bem, 1974; Spence & Helmreich, 1978). It is obviously a highly important topic, impinging as it does on the development of personal identity and basic values.

Political Socialization

In addition to adolescents' expanding interests in questions of personal identity, there is also an expansion of interests beyond the immediate here and now. Among the topics usually included in this wider horizon are questions about social justice and the broader political background of contemporary society. As noted by Adelson (1975), Gallatin (1980), and Tapp and Levine (1974), the increased sophistication of the late adolescent to cope with such issues, when compared to the early adolescent, is evident in moral, legal, and political thinking. Despite this increased interest and ability, most individuals develop through adolescence with basically superficial and unexamined ideologies. They spend little time examining serious moral, legal, and political questions. Often they even have little recognition of how profoundly their implicit, unanalyzed, and unarticulated ideologies affect their personal identity and values (Adelson, 1975; Marcia, 1980). A related observation made by Piaget is that "idealism" is common during the adolescent years. He noted that adolescents' cognitive capacity for logical analysis leads to unsubstantiated and simplistic social solutions, since their knowledge of the complexity of reality lags (Inhelder & Piaget, 1958).

What effect do schools have on this process? Although we would like to believe otherwise, schools most probably contribute little help to the adolescent in developing complex

SOCIAL FOCUS 3.3
Labor Versus Business: Textbook History Versus Reality

A crucial aspect of society's influence in the development of one's own personal identity is the information about the past experiences of the society, whether that is communicated formally or informally. A major route for the communication of this information in contemporary U.S. society is through the schools, especially through formal courses in the history of the U.S. Within the past several years, a number of historians have begun to examine the accuracy of information in high school history textbooks. Sparked by concern over honesty of "official" information arising from the Vietnam and Watergate experiences, these historians have discovered troubling inconsistencies in the textbook treatments of several highly controversial topics.

One of the more interesting and rigorous analyses was done by Jean Anyon of Rutgers University. Anyon (1979) examined the contents of a variety of high-school level U.S. history textbooks. She focused on the economic and labor history from the Civil War to World War I. This time period is a crucial one in the development of the economic structures that continue today:

By the beginning of World War I, industrialization and incorporation had produced considerable wealth for some, an affluent middle class, and economic and social problems that have endured: urban poor, persistent unemployment and marginally employed workers; labor-management conflict; low wages and poor working conditions for many of the non-unionized; and the control of a major portion of the United States economic resources by a relatively small number of corporations. (p. 364)

Anyon examined a variety of specific issues reflecting the divergence between textbook history and the reality of those times. She noted that a view of history which emphasizes the benefits of these economic developments and discredits serious consideration of the alternatives is to the advantage of major corporations. (Note that these corporations benefit the most from existing economic arrangements and publish the most widely-used textbooks).

Perhaps the most interesting example is the treatment of the radical movements of that historical period. If one's goal is to insure social conformity, a useful tool is to convince others that alternative solutions are either nonexistent or "evil." Anyon's analysis of 17 current textbooks suggests how this might be achieved:

thinking about political and social issues. Instead, schools appear to support conformity to existing social norms, and are unlikely to create conditions or contain experiences that encourage or challenge moral, political, and legal reasoning. Adolescents are both implicitly and explicitly socialized by schools *not* to challenge the status quo (Silberman, 1970). In what specific ways is this accomplished? Let us look at some examples.

One obvious way lies in the concealment of critical information about this society which would likely lead to deeper questioning. Fitzgerald (1979) analyzed the content of a wide variety of history textbooks in the United States from the last fifty years. Her most significant

Although socialism has been a popular response to industrialization in virtually every capitalist country in the world, and although the American Socialist Party at the turn of the century was regarded as significant by dominant political and economic groups, twelve of the books do not describe the American Socialist Party or its platform, nor do they mention radical sympathies among various groups in the population. Of the five books that discuss the Socialist party, all but one contain disparaging comments about the intentions of socialists, and four of the five make statements that minimize their influence. They argue, as do the ten books which do not describe the party, that only a few people were attracted to radical ideas; one implies that honest men were not.

The emphasis on the insignificance of the socialist movement in the United States can be contrasted to accounts of the period more sympathetic to the goal of redistribution of economic power and ownership. These discuss socialism at the turn of the century as an important indication of social protest and dissent, citing as proof the popularity of socialist leaders such as Eugene Debs, Bill Haywood, and Elizabeth Gurly Flynn. James Weinstein presents evidence of the electoral success of the Socialist Party between 1910 and 1920, when 150 Socialists were elected to state legislatures. In 1912, at the height of their popularity, 1,200 Socialists were elected to office in U.S. cities, among them 79 mayors in 24 states. In 1912 Socialist Eugene Debs received nearly a million votes for president (Woodrow Wilson was elected that year with six million votes). These figures lead one to challenge the textbook trivialization of socialism in the United States and to question the claim, made by one text, that socialism was the "nightmare . . . of the American people in general." (pp. 369-370)

On other issues which Anyon examined (treatment of economic groups, labor unions, industrialists and labor conflict), similar distortions are evident. If social knowledge is an important aspect of socialization, and socialization plays an important role in identity development, then perhaps we need to think more deeply and critically about how that knowledge is communicated to developing adolescents. Analyses like Anyon's provide a useful example of the directions for this critical re-examination.

finding is that the texts systematically excluded or played down negative features of U.S. history. This was especially obvious in their treatment of oppressed people—blacks, women, and Indians in particular. Without a balanced factual account, adolescents clearly learn myths about U.S. history that are nicer than reality. Whether such learning is conducive to critical, informed analysis is a serious question (see Social Focus 3.3).

A second and more implicit example is the school's practice of expecting conformity and reacting negatively to deviance. This may be observed in the teaching of democracy in the high school classroom, contrasted with the distinctly authoritarian organization of the vast majority of schools (Silberman, 1970, Tapp & Levine, 1974). Moreover, high-achieving students also find the pursuit of an appropriate education difficult because they are not "average" (Keating, 1979). The message to students is quite clear: conforming and average students are desired. The atmosphere for criticism, for deep thinking, and for a desire for significant changes has not been evident in schools, nor has this been a great source of concern in the training of teachers in schools of education.

The preceding analysis and illustrations have indicated that schools do play a major role in the socialization of adolescents. At the moment, this is largely accomplished through a complex system that encourages them to conform to existing social norms. Even though many adolescents come to question these norms as young adults, most accept the legitimation of the rules with little additional analysis, and the legitimation of these rules becomes an integral part of their personal identities and value systems. As we will see, however, experiences in adulthood may lead individuals to question the rule systems they unwittingly accepted as legitimate in adolescence.

THE LEGAL WORLD OF THE ADULT: RULE APPLICATION AND THE EXERCISE OF AUTONOMY

We have seen how the home and school are important institutional contexts for teaching values, rules, and norms to children and adolescents. With adulthood, other contexts become important places for learning the codes of conduct in one's cultural or national group.

We also know that socialization is an ongoing, interactive process with evolving definitions and expectations. For example, parents and teachers (and police, too) respond differently to a four-year-old and a fourteen-year-old, who say, "That's not a good rule," or "That's not fair!" Thoughts and experiences

about law and justice change over the life-span *and* develop in situations other than the home and school. A kiss provides a useful analogue. A kiss at four means something different to the sender and receiver than it does at 8, 10, 40, and 80 years of age. Kisses, like legal beliefs and behaviors, are identifiable evolving phenomena, characteristically different over time, place, and person. As in the case of kissing, an understanding of the legal socialization process requires describing how children, young people, and adults see their legal worlds.

In the past decade or so, researchers have increasingly acknowledged the educational function of the law, and therefore its importance as a socializing institution. Since the laws of a land provide guidelines for appropriate social behavior, the law controls as well as facilitates human interaction. Optimally, internalization of and respect for society's rules involves participation in making and maintaining laws. One place where adults—the public—in the U.S. society can make and maintain law and justice is the jury box.

In this section of the chapter we examine an aspect of the socializing role of the law—specifically, jury service—on adult figures. Using a famous U.S. trial as a case in point, we describe the effect of a nine-month jury experience on the legal reasoning or jurisprudence of the jurors. Before making that analysis, we present a cognitive model of legality, summarize cross-cultural and developmental data on legal beliefs, and discuss socialization strategies. Finally, we briefly consider the jury's role, and the implications for public participation, in the administration of justice.

A Cognitive Theory of Legality

Legal socialization basically involves the development of a sense of law consciousness and a sense of justice. Through this process, people learn standards for making social judgments and for using the legal system to conduct hu-

Contact with the law serves to socialize members of society and to influence their levels of legal reasoning.

man affairs. Naturally, the legal system also influences these affairs. Every day encounters with laws regulating home and family life, schools and child-care facilities, and office and work conditions mean that few individuals escape direct engagement with the legal system ("the long arm of the law"). In contemporary U.S. society, many legal figures—like the judge in court or the cop on the beat—educate about the law and thus act as socializing agents. Their actions illustrate the role of the law as socializer. Further, from the 1950s on, the law has been used by many groups—women, children, ethnics—to express grievances and gain rights. Thus, in addition to serving as a socializer, the law has also served as a mobility belt in American society.

Different psychological approaches (each with a different view of humankind) have been used to study how persons learn their culture's codes of conduct. The advantage of a cognitive developmental approach, broadly conceived, is that it can incorporate other theoretical systems. In this chapter, recognizing that probably

"both (cognitive-development and social-learning) formulations are right to a degree" (Maccoby, 1968, p. 253), we describe the cognitive theory of legality used in legal socialization studies since the late 1960s by Tapp and associates (Tapp & Kohlberg, 1977; Tapp & Levine, 1974).

The utility of a cognitive-developmental model is its identification of underlying reasoning structures with definable characteristics, basic to psycholegal judgments. The Tapp-Levine model of legal reasoning applies Piaget's (1932) and Kohlberg's (1969) moral stage typology to the realm of law. It also draws upon social psychological and legal/philosophical (jurisprudential) thought.

Social psychology provided additional support for this legal levels model (e.g., Bandura & McDonald, 1963; Hoffman & Saltzstein, 1967). Social psychology has long employed an interactive levels approach to interpret individual, social, or cultural phenomena. For example, as is discussed in Chapter 15, Kelman (1958) characterized the phenomenon of social influence into three progressively deep levels (compliance, identification, and internalization).

The Tapp-Levine cognitive model of legality also draws upon the work of lawyer Lon L. Fuller (1969) and moral philosopher John Rawls (1971). Evidently, philosophers and psychologists describe a similar advance from a dependent (heteronomous), hedonistic, and uncritical state to an independent (autonomous), altruistic, and rational stance in matters of legality.

Patterns of Legal Reasoning and Development

Tapp and Levine's model of legal reasoning has three legal levels: I—**Preconventional;** II—**Conventional;** III—**Postconventional.** Level I is a law-deferring, punishment-oriented stance; II is a law-maintaining conformity posture; III is a law-creating, principled perspective. Each level represents a distinctive way to characterize rights, roles, and responsibilities in relation to the legal system. Together, the three comprise a developmental (but not always invariant) sequence where higher levels (III > II > I) reflect more accommodative, integrative, and complex structures of reasoning. "Higher" here simply means better at conflict resolution or problem solving and integrating differences, both logical and psychological. Each level of legal reasoning is best viewed as a successive transformation of thought (restructuring of ideas) about legal matters. The three major progressions display increasing cognitive complexity, intellectual sophistication, and ethical awareness. (A description of the three legal levels is contained in Social Focus 3.2.)

As can be seen in Social Focus 3.2, legal levels are characterized by certain legal reasoning styles. A level I (preconventional) view of law and of legal obligation focuses on external consequences and authority; an instrumental hedonism tempers these legal valuations. At level II, the conventional law-maintenance level, people worry about fulfilling role expectations; they obey or disobey for personal and social conformity reasons. At postconventional level III, developmentally advanced (cognitively complex) persons see the need for social systems, but differentiate between the values of a given social order and universal principles. Martin Luther King may have been a twentieth-century example with such a postconventional reasoning capacity; Thomas Jefferson, an eighteenth-century one.

Each of the three characterizations is based on the answers of children and adults in six countries to classic jurisprudential problems, such as the meaning of rule, law, rights, fairness, and compliance. To assess legal reasoning, an open-ended questionnaire, known as the Tapp-Levine Rule-Law Interview (TLRLI), has been developed. The interview focuses on five substantive areas: the value and function of rules and laws, the conditions of legal compliance, the changeability and breakability of rules or laws, the dynamics of justice/fairness, and the nature of rights consciousness. It permits classification of legal reasoning according to three cognitive-developmental levels. The basic 15-item version appears in Social Focus 3.4, and a classification of responses into the three levels in Social Focus 3.5.

Basic Evidence on the Psychological Limits of Legality

The Tapp-Levine Rule-Law Interview has been used cross-culturally and developmentally across age and occupational groups in classroom, courtroom, and cellroom contexts on samples totaling nearly 6000 individuals. Responses from four types of populations in and outside the United States were analyzed: (1) primary-age school children from kindergarten to grade 3 (5 to 8 years); (2) middle-school preadolescents from grades 4, 6, and 8 (10 to 14 years); (3) college men and women in diverse university settings (17 to 21 years); (4) adult groups of graduating law students, school teachers, federal penitentiary inmates, day-care parents, and jurors (20 to 60 years).

Data from these studies have revealed, for example, that *across cultures there are detectable regularities in legal thought; that is, the same stages of development are present in all cultures.* For example, two questions dealing with how individuals ideally and really define obligations to legal systems (Why should people follow rules? Why do you follow rules?) were posed to school children in six countries (Denmark, Greece, India, Italy, Japan, and the United States). In all six countries middle-school children typically gave conventional (II) answers. On both questions, younger children consistently gave more preconventional (I) responses. The few children with postconventional (III) answers were 8th-graders. These age trends in this cross-national sample suggest a universal pattern of development in young

SOCIAL FOCUS 3.4
Tapp-Levine Rule Law Interview (TLRLI: 1980 version)

1. What is a rule? Why is that a rule?
2. What is a law? Why is that a law?
3. Why do we have laws? Why should we have laws?
4. Can some things be fair and right to do even when there are no laws about them? How can this be?
5. What is a fair law? Why is it fair?
6. What is a right?
7. What kinds of rights should people have? Why?
8. What kinds of rights do people have? Why?
9. What would happen if there were no laws anywhere at all? Why?
10. Why should people follow laws?
11. Why do you follow laws?
12. How and why can laws be changed?
13. Are there times when it might be right to break a law? When, if ever?
14. What does it mean to be right?
15. Can a person be right and break a law? How can this be?

people's understanding of the dynamics of legal compliance.

These studies also showed that *the incidence of higher legal level is greater in older groups; that is, the movement from I to II to III is related to age and development.* For example, on the question: "What would happen if there were no rules?", a marked progression was evident in U.S. youth from kindergarten through college. Primary children worried about violence and crime in a world without rules (I). Adolescents shifted from egocentric concerns about physical punishment to a conventional social concern about organizations governing human relations (II). Principled legal reasoning (III) emerged only at college, but only a few then believed people could regulate behavior by using universal principles. Adult groups also primarily considered rules in law-maintenance terms (II), reasoning that anarchy and chaos would engulf a society without rules. Social Focus 3.6

contains examples of child and adult answers to selected questions, categorized by legal level.

Overall, these findings from varying age, cultural, and occupational groups support several recurrent themes on the origins of jurisprudence and the psychological limits of legality. First, there is a pattern of legal reasoning that progresses from a preconventional law-deferring to a conventional law-maintaining to a postconventional law-creating orientation (I to II to III). Second, this progression is marked by more developmental (age) than situational or cultural effects, but the variation among occupational groups reveals the interactive nature of legal development. Third, over all groups, the conventional perspective was found to be modal. Nevertheless, by the late adolescence, and particularly by college age, sizable minorities exhibited postconventional principles. This form of legal reasoning, however, did not dom-

SOCIAL FOCUS 3.5
Classification of Interview Categories by Legal Levels*

SUBJECT/QUESTION	LEVEL I: LAW-DEFERRING PRECONVENTIONAL CATEGORIES	LEVEL II: LAW-MAINTAINING CONVENTIONAL CATEGORIES	LEVEL III: LAW-MAKING POSTCONVENTIONAL CATEGORIES
1. **Value and Function of Rules and Laws:** What would happen if there were no rules? (What would happen if there were no laws anywhere at all?)	**Violence-crime:** Laws prevent concrete physical harm like specific bad acts or crimes. They secure physical necessities.	**Personal desires not principles:** Laws restrain bad, guide weak, and insure personal control over greed. **Anarchy-disorder-chaos:** Laws maintain social order. **Impossible to imagine:** Society cannot exist without rules. Abstract regulation is requisite for society.	**Human beings as self-regulatory:** Guide behavior via principles and distinguish law from moral principles.
Function of Rules and Laws: What is a rule? What is a law?	**Prohibitive:** Functions as proscription or flat command restraining actions that serve no positive social good.	**Prescriptive:** Functions as shared guide. Generalizes whole system rules as facilitating, "maintaining society," or "preventing anti-social behavior." **Enforcement:** Distinguishes between badness of act and consequent punishment.	**Beneficial-rational:** Functions to achieve rational purpose behind law, usually for maximizing personal and social welfare consequences. Cognizant of the utility of agreed-upon standards.

inate in any age group.*Fourth, while no person's answers are 100 percent at any one level, college and adult groups were more postconventional than preconventional. In contrast, preadolescents typically gave conventional answers and primary-school children reasoned at this level with significant frequency.*Finally, from an empirical perspective, the legal-levels data derived from cross-cultural, developmental, and cross-occupational responses to the TLRLI's open-ended, classic jurisprudential questions are reliable. There is also some evidence, theoretically, of congruence (overlap) between philosophical and psychological models of legal thought, suggesting that ethical codes of conduct evolve interactively—that is, in response to natural and social inputs.

Beyond demonstrating the developmental progression of legal reasoning, this cognitive approach has also been used to study the relationship of legal reasoning to moral judgment *and* to determine the impact of socializing strategies on development of an ethical legality. Taken together, these works offer support for a legal-reasoning construct and for an age-related sequence in the growth of ideas on law and justice.

Socialization Strategies

To date,*the conventional or system-maintenance level (II) has been modal in most societies, but recent studies show that individuals

SUBJECT/QUESTION	LEVEL I: LAW-DEFERRING PRECONVENTIONAL CATEGORIES	LEVEL II: LAW-MAINTAINING CONVENTIONAL CATEGORIES	LEVEL III: LAW-MAKING POSTCONVENTIONAL CATEGORIES
2. **Conditions of Legal Compliance:** Why should people follow rules? Why do you follow rules? (Why should people follow laws?) (Why do you follow laws?)	**Avoid negative consequences:** Punishment reason for conformity. Simple compliance, not respect for rules. **Authority:** Obedience to power figures as ultimate guides. Rules derived from them. "Badness" of proscribed activity confused with badness of disobeying authority's rule.	**Personal conformity:** Confuses obedience with socially desirable behavior in order to be good and maintain what law-makers think is "good" behavior. **Social conformity:** Requires compliance to be fair to other obeyers and to avoid chaos.	**Rational-beneficial-utilitarian:** Obedience to maintain individual and social welfare based on rational, mutual decision-making, and utilitarian considerations. Obedience from weighing consequences. **Principled:** Obedience guided by principles like sense of justice, independent of society. Conform only with principled rules.
3. **Changeability of Rules and Laws:** Can rules be changed? (How and why can laws be changed?) **Breakability of Rules and Laws:** Are there times when it might be right to break a rule? (Are there times when it might be right, to break a law?)	**No:** Laws are fixed, permanent, or quasiphysical things. **No:** No differentiation between legal and moral. Badness of law- or rule-breaking equated with badness as such. **Yes:** Simple "yes" but no differentiating moral norm from prudential directives.	**Yes:** Laws not for "good of all" because they permit unkindness or are made by uncharitable persons. **Morality of circumstance:** Extreme circumstances justify breaking. Recognizes socio-moral function of rules to which law obedience is instrumental.	**Yes:** For reasons of social utility, rational purposes, and to change unprincipled laws. **Morality of rule:** Justify breaking when law immoral or unjust, when law violates moral principles.

Note: Questions in parentheses are the 1980 version of the Tapp-Levine Rule Law Interview (TLRLI).
*The classification schema is part of the more extensive conceptualization of legal development in Tapp and Levine (1971, 1974). Box 3.5 is adapted from Tapp, J.L., & Kohlberg, L. Developing senses of law and legal justice. In J.L. Tapp & F.J. Levine (eds.), **Law, justice, and the individual in society,** 1977.

have the potential to reach the third or highest level of legal reasoning (Rest, 1973, 1979; Tapp & Keniston, 1976; Tapp et al., 1981) The dominance of conventional legality in children, youths, and adults suggests that social experiences in particular environments can limit or extend an individual's natural capacity. As psychologists, we want to know the socializing conditions that move persons to make autonomous choices and to use law in a just manner.

As developed by Tapp and Levine (1974, 1977), four socializing strategies seem basic to stimulating movement to a higher level of legal reasoning and thus socializing for an ethical legality.

1. **Legal knowledge.** This strategy involves transmitting information. Effective socialization includes "schooling" about rights, rules, and remedies. Such education allows individuals to become creators as well as consumers of law. Without substan-

SOCIAL FOCUS 3.6
Examples of Child and Adult Responses to Selected Questions TLRLI

AREA/QUESTION	LEVEL	CATEGORIES	AGE/OCCUPATION	STATEMENT/ANSWER
Value and Function of Rules and Law	I	Violence/crime	Grade 2	People would go around killing other people, stealing things, and kidnapping people.
What would happen if there were no rules?	II	Anarchy/disorder/chaos	Grade 4	It would be a lot of disorganizing in the world.
	II	Anarchy/disorder/chaos	College	There would be utter chaos and confusion.
	III	Human as self-regulatory	College	If people were capable of acting responsibly and morally, nothing would happen.
			Wounded Knee juror	People can regulate themselves.
Conditions of Legal Compliance	I	Avoid negative consequences	Grade 2	People would be doing anything. The police would try to catch them. It would be bad.
Why should people follow rules?			Law student	To avoid costs of not following them.
Why do you follow rules?	I	Authority	Grade 6	Because my parents, school, and the city want me to.
	II	Personal conformity	Grade 2	Not to be bad. Not to do things they are not supposed to do.
	II	Social conformity	Grade 8	Sometimes it's for their own good. They should follow rules because you go back to confusion again, if you didn't have any rules.
			High-school	To maintain order and achieve objectives of society.

tive knowledge of law and the legal process, individuals cannot as effectively use a service, invoke a right, redress a grievance, question a police officer, or hire a lawyer. Knowledge alone, however, is not a sufficient condition to stimulate integrative, independent, and critical thought.

2. **Mismatch and conflict.** Mismatch in value orientations or value conflicts stimulates the construction of more complex forms of thought. Some argue that increases in disequilibrium afford excellent conditions for development. In both cognitive-developmental and social-learning theories, conflict has been identified as a strategy in value education. As Haan, Smith, and Block said, "Conflictless experiences are probably incompatible with both moral and cognitive growth" (1968, p. 200).

3. **Participation.** Through participation, an individual can gain an appreciation of someone else's framework. The centrality of such perspective taking to mature moral thought and action is emphasized by cognitive-developmental psychologists (Flavell, Botkin, & Fry, 1968). In addition to role-taking opportunities, participation emphasizes reciprocity and cooperation. To the extent that

AREA/QUESTION	LEVEL	CATEGORIES	AGE/OCCUPATION	STATEMENT/ANSWER
	III	Rational/beneficial/utilitarian	Grade 8	For the benefit of everyone. It makes everything easier actually and easier to live with.
			High-school	To accomplish greatest good for all concerned.
	II	Principled	College	People should only follow those they think are fair and just.
			Wounded Knee juror	Every rule is set up so everyone can be treated fairly.
Breakability of Rules and Laws	II	Morality of circumstance	Grade 8	It depends on what's going on. If it's a matter of life and death—you know something pretty important—then it's all right.
Are there times when it might be right to break a rule?			Prisoner	Prevailing circumstances of unusual condition merit breaking them.
	III	Morality of rule	College	When the rule is immoral or unjust because I believe that people are morally accountable for their actions.
			Prisoner	Not all rules are fair, good, or ethically desirable.
			Wounded Knee juror	If they aren't good and you care enough about the fact that they're not good, then you have to break them.

participatory experiences stimulate empathy, enhance tolerance for dissent, and foster critical abilities and internal controls, they embody a postconventional legality.

4. **Legal continuity.** Rule-creating and fair-play op-
✳   portunities (and thus experience of justice and injustice, obedience and disobedience, and so on) occur in many daily contexts: home, school, church, union. All these rule-guided systems are experientially "legal." This broader view of the law emphasizes the rule-making power and connection of various legal systems from family to school to government. Recognition of the continuity among various rule or justice systems should help persons define the interdependent nature of legal activity.

THE CASE OF WOUNDED KNEE

While we have seen that age is a crucial variable in the socialization process, we also know that situational variables vitally affect the rate and direction of development. Since socialization and resocialization continue through the life cycle (Brim & Wheeler, 1966), actual participation by adults in the institution of law can aid individual legal development. A basic question, then, is the extent to which institutional settings, particularly legal ones use—or can use—the socialization strategies that stimulate change.

In contemporary U.S. society, jury participation is a major mechanism for citizen involvement in decision making. In the course of a trial, jury service provides information about the legal system to the jurors whose previous contacts with law were limited, an opportunity for participation and role taking, exposure to new—often conflicting—ways of thinking about rule systems, and an occasion to connect jurisprudential ideas (meanings of law, justice, and rights) from one "legal" setting to another. If these four conditions (legal information, participation, conflict, continuity) operate optimally, jurors should progress to a higher level of legal reasoning.

The chance to work on the jury selection for the Wounded Knee trial provided an excellent opportunity to explore in a real-life setting the socializing effect of jury service on legal development. The trial, a result of incidents between the U.S. government and American Indians in South Dakota, was held in Minnesota. It took nine months, and the federal government lost. To gain a perspective on this socializing context, we examine the impact of a jury experience on the legal reasoning of adults and identify the relevant socializing strategies. We draw heavily on the in- and out-of-courtroom exploratory studies of Tapp and her associates.

Selection of the Jury

The Wounded Knee trial began with selection of the jurors. Of the 93 prospective people originally called, 55 were excused (7 for cause, 48 for hardship). After 14 days of the *voir dire* (detailed courtroom) questioning, 38 persons were candidates for the 12 person jury. A jury selection team for the defense consisted of the defendants, attorneys, and social scientists. The questions in the voir dire ranged from basic demographic items (age, religion, marital

status) to attitudes toward Indians and beliefs about the law. During this questioning, Tapp and her associates rated each potential juror's level of legal reasoning and authoritarianism. The prospective jurors challenged by the government's lawyers were predominantly young, single, female, urban residents, with some college education. They tended to affiliate with the Democratic party, had some contact with Native American people, tended to support Indian self-determination, and defined law as process rather than fixed rule. The defense lawyers tried to remove the middle-aged or over, those residing in rural areas, white-collar workers, Republicans, those with noncommittal attitudes toward Indians, and those with a law-and-order mentality. The 26 challenged jurors included 12 females and 14 males, ranging in age from 19 to 81 (mean = 49.9).

The 12 impanelled jurors (individuals left after the defense and prosecution challenges) included 7 females and 5 males, aged from 20 to 53 (averaging 29.3). The impanelled jury was predominantly urban, college-educated, and youthful: 9 jurors were 32 or younger; 7 had some college education; the others were blue-collar workers. On Native American self-determination, 7 jurors supported it. Of the twelve, 6 had sympathy for Indian people; 5 were noncommittal. Of the 12 jurors, 7 saw as legitimate the right to protest (Zimbrolt, 1974).

The Research Study

To examine the effects of a public trial on adults, Tapp and her associates (Aliotta & Tapp, 1981; Tapp & Smolka, 1975; Tapp & Keniston, 1976) studied three groups. First, there were 9 people (2 males and 7 females, mean age = 31) who served as jurors in the Wounded Knee trial. Second, there were 14 challenged jurors, 9 males and 5 females (average age = 46). Finally, 23 randomly selected, potential jurors were used. They included 11 males and 12 females with a mean age of 44 years.

After the trial, interviews and questionnaires were given to all three groups. The Tapp-Levine Rule-Law Interview was administered along with measures of self-esteem and authoritarianism. A set of open-ended questions was designed to get jurors to describe socializing experiences related to the trial.

According to a cognitive theory of legality, the impanelled jurors—those asked to serve on the Wounded Knee jury—should have had more opportunities for legal development than the challenged jurors or the random jurors. The impanelled jurors would have been actively exposed to the four socialization conditions. Accordingly, they should have moved to higher legal levels in nine months than the other two groups and beyond their own earlier level. Theoretically, jury service on a trial, especially a controversial one, should promote socialization to more principled levels of legal thought.

Also there are implications for personality development related to legal socialization. For example, in terms of a cognitive theory of legality, individuals at lower reasoning levels should be more authoritarian and less tolerant. On the other hand, legal level maturity should be associated with personal growth toward autonomy and tolerance.

The Effects of Participating in the Wounded Knee Trial

Level classification and movement. Let us examine some of the evidence that indicates the positive socializing effects of a public trial on a group of adult citizens. Of the 38 prospective (petit) jurors, the percentages in levels I, II, and III, based on in-courtroom assessments, were respectively 19, 67, and 12 percent for the challenged jurors; for impanelled jurors, they were 8, 50, and 42 percent. This distribution of legal levels at the beginning of the trial suggests the

effect of the peremptory challenges in the jury selection process, but not jury socialization. About one-half (20) of the prospective (petit) group were also identified as being mixtures of levels. The prevalence of a conventional level replicated the finding of widespread level mixture within individuals.

Responses to the Tapp-Levine Rule-Law Interview in the after-trial study revealed that none of the people in either group were at the preconventional level (I). Among the random jurors, 40 percent were at II; 60 percent at III. In the challenged group, 50 percent were conventional (II) and 50 percent postconventional or principled (III). But, among the impanelled jurors, everyone (100%) scored at the postconventional level by the end of the Wounded Knee trial. Incidentally, the correlation between courtroom ratings and questionnaire scores of legal level was also significant, thus giving confidence in the validity of the courtroom ratings.

The fact that all the impanelled jurors exhibited principled thinking after the trial as opposed to 42 percent before the trial illustrates an important change in the legal reasoning of that group. While initially there were more III types among impanelled jurors, the dramatic shift of the entire group to a postconventional position suggests important influences, both social and interactive, that acted upon them during the trial. What were some of the social variables in the experience that might explain this movement to a higher level of legal reasoning? What socializing effect did the Wounded Knee trial have on the legal reasoning of jurors with varying degrees of involvement—that is, the impanelled, challenged, and random jurors?

The impact of socialization. The socialization questions in Tapp's study were keyed to the issues (strategies) of legal information, conflict, participation, and continuity. Two socialization questions discriminated well among the juror groups: the one anticipating trial outcome; the other, knowledge of the jury selection process.

The effects of information and participation can be seen in the 75 percent acquittal-vote forecast of the impanelled jurors (who felt the government had no case or evidence) compared to the 23 percent vote of the challenged jurors and 17 percent of the random jurors. The impanelled jurors became sufficiently knowledgeable about the jury process so that nine months later 100 percent of them had some notion why they were selected to the jury. Only 54 percent of the challenged and 48 percent of the random jurors could give reasons for their selection.

The effect of the jury experience is further illuminated by answers to the legal information question: Do good motives justify breaking the law? Almost 88 percent of the impanelled jurors, compared to 8 percent of the challenged and 25 percent of the random jurors, gave principled-level answers. Impanelled jurors, typically worried about the person and the system, reasoned that "It depends on the motives" or "It can be beneficial to the legal system" or "If it is a bad law." The greater percentage of principled responses from the impanelled jurors suggests they had a distinctly different experience over the nine months, began at a higher level of legality, or both. The difference between 88 percent and 8 percent, however, further suggests that jury service is an important "social" experience, capable of stimulating movement to "natural" higher levels of legal reasoning.

To get at the issue of change and further probe the socializing dimensions, the following questions were asked of the impanelled jurors:

1. How did this jury experience affect you? Your ideas?
2. Do you think you experienced any lasting or permanent change as a result of jury duty?

Overall, they described their experience with some passion and fervor. They saw the trial and jury duty as more important than did the challenged or random groups. Many impanelled jurors saw jury service as a socializing and educative experience. Over two-thirds felt that the jury experience changed them, their lives, and their ideas about compliance, rights, fair rules, and laws. In addition to the adamant affirmative answers to these questions, two-thirds of the impanelled jurors felt that the jury situation provided information, produced conflict, demanded participation, and allowed role taking (perspective shifting). All felt more able to link their newfound values to rule-guided settings (government, home, community) beyond the courtroom. Most reported changes in their attitudes toward minorities, government, and the meaning of law and justice.

Legal reasoning patterns. The after-trial assessment of legal levels showed that on many issues the juror groups were similar. Differences, however, emerged on issues of authority, law function, compliance (obedience), rule breakability, and the meaning of rights. For example, on the question, What would you do when told to do something wrong by someone in charge?, 67 percent of the impanelled jurors appealed to universal moral principles as a basis for disobedience, while only 21 percent of the challenged group did so. On the question, What would happen if there were no rules?, all the challenged and random jurors answered at the conventional level. Only the impanelled jurors gave postconventional answers, opting for the possibility that humankind is capable of self-regulation. In answering the question, What kinds of rights should people have?, the impanelled jurors expressed a "rights-conscious perspective" (III) in greater numbers than either the challenged or the random jurors (45 percent versus 29 percent versus 14 percent). In general, challenged and random jurors felt that people's rights should be system related; that is, for maintenance of the legal system. In contrast, impanelled jurors viewed rights as a basic component of human dignity. One impanelled juror summed it up this way: "When I think of rights in this country, I think of life, liberty, and the pursuit of happiness. No one can take that away. If you didn't have these rights, you wouldn't be a person. You'd be an animal."

Personality and legality.   In considering the personality correlates of legality, Tapp and her associates found a negative relationship between legal maturity and authoritarianism: higher legal-level jurors were less authoritarian. Analyses of other personality dimensions revealed, for example, that impanelled jurors, after the trial, scored higher on self-esteem. And, high self-esteem went hand in hand with being at a higher level of legal reasoning. Apparently, those with high legal reasoning and high self-esteem scores have a greater sense of justice.

The Jury as Socializer and Symbol

The noticeable shift and difference on matters of law and justice between the impanelled jurors and the challenged or random jurors suggest that jury service can be an important socializing (and educative) experience. While the Wounded Knee jury study showed that adults answered classical jurisprudential questions at one of three legal-reasoning levels, this research also indicated that more advanced, complex levels may result from experiences in an ecologically valid, socializing setting like a jury. If this is the case, it is important to maintain the jury process—not merely for the sake of justice and symbolism, but for the sake of having a vehicle to socialize more principled legal reasoning. Jury duty then becomes an activity not only for the idle and anonymous, but also for all persons who wish to become more autonomous, competent, and ethical in their judgments about personal and societal codes of conduct.

One juror's answer to the question, What do you think of the jury process?, captured the jury's importance to and for adults: "I guess I always felt that this was a system of justice. If it wasn't for the jury, what would it all be about, what would we all be up to?" This last refuge of public participation in the judicial decision-making process is important to maintain in the United States, as de Tocqueville (1835/1961, p. 337) observed over 100 years ago:

> The jury contributes powerfully to form the judgement and to increase the natural intelligence of a people and this, in my opinion, is its greatest advantage. It may be regarded as a gratuitous public school ever open in which every juror learns his rights, enters into daily communications with the most learned and enlightened members of the upper classes and becomes particularly acquainted with laws, which are brought within the reach of his capacity by efforts of the bar, the advice of the judge, and even by the passions of the party. I think that practical intelligence and political good sense of the Americans are mainly attributable to the long use which they have made of the jury in civil cause.

Finally, psychologists' involvement in the jury-selection process may have moved both the professional and the public to review the meaning of a fair jury in terms of its socializing and symbolic significance.

SUMMARY   As we have discussed, socialization involves the processes whereby individuals come to internalize the social conventions, normative guidelines (rules), and moral codes of their society. They are bidirectional, interactive processes, in which the individual can take an active, as well as a passive role. While social rules and concepts of morality appear to be externally imposed (heteronomous) during childhood, with maturity the individual plays an active role in internalizing social norms, differentiating social conventions from moral rules, *and* abstracting and organizing a personal set of ethical principles. The results are codes of conduct that guide relationships and define roles as well as responsibilities between persons in social systems.

Socialization spans the life cycle. It involves the development of emotion and cognition as well as belief and behavior. Different theories of socialization emphasize different personality and social-development domains. We outlined four theories (psychoanalytic, social-learning, cognitive-developmental, and ethological) that have had an impact on the study of socialization. While pointing out the strengths and weaknesses of each theoretical approach, we noted that a combination of approaches will probably be necessary in order to understand the processes governing socialization.

Just as socialization is not a phenomenon peculiar to any age period, it is also not a phenomenon that occurs in only one context. We chose to discuss socialization in three rule systems (home, school, and jury). Throughout the life-span, however, socialization experiences are encountered in a variety of settings. Indeed, both the reiteration of social themes across contexts, as well as the clashes between beliefs and norms (rules) encountered as one moves across contexts, play a role in promoting more mature, integrated value systems.

For early and middle childhood, we focused on socialization as it occurs within the family. We noted that children's emotional relationships with their parents, the parents' attempts to get their children to view the social world from another's perspective (role taking), and children's own active attempts to understand the nature of social rules (as well as processes such as observational learning, reinforcement, and punishment) play important roles in socialization.

With adolescence, we considered socialization in school settings. While adolescents are developing cognitive capacities that should lead to a critical assessment of social rules and conventions, too often schools seem to be structured to discourage or actively repress this process.

Third, we described how the experience of serving on the jury (for the Wounded Knee trial) seemed to promote the development of more mature, complex, and ethical modes of legal reasoning in adults. While we know that most persons acquire their beliefs (ideas) about law and justice over the life cycle, the legal-socialization experience of jury service underscored the interactive aspect of the process. After all, each juror brought a history of socializations in U.S. culture to the courtroom context. That history, including experiences in the home, the school, and the law, shaped jurors' reaction to the trial, and, participation in the trial, in turn helped the jurors reformulate and internalize new codes to guide subsequent psycholegal reasoning and conduct.

SUGGESTED READINGS

Baldwin, A. L. *Theories of child development.* (2nd ed.) New York: Wiley, 1980.

Tapp, J. L. & Levine, F. J. (Eds.), *Law, justice, and the individual in society: Psychological and legal issues.* New York: Holt, Rinehart and Winston, 1977.

4

ATTITUDES AND BELIEFS

- Introduction: Three Mile Island
- Definition of Attitudes
- Measurement of Attitudes
- Attitude Formation
- Summary

INTRODUCTION: THREE MILE ISLAND

On December 30, 1978 the Three Mile Island nuclear power plant began generating electricity. Located about ten miles south of Harrisburg, the capital of Pennsylvania, the plant had cost almost one billion dollars and taken ten years to design and build. It was an inspiring example of advanced technology, heating water by nuclear fission and using this water, in turn, to heat "clean" water in separate pipes. The water in this secondary system of pipes was thereby turned into steam and rushed through a series of turbine blades, producing electricity. Working at full capacity, the plant could generate about $400,000 worth of electricity each day.

Dominating the landscape around the plant were four hourglass-shaped towers, forty stories high, which were designed to cool the water in the secondary system of pipes. Nearly a million gallons of water per minute could be cooled by these structures. The plant had other equally impressive features. The structure housing the nuclear reactor was built with steel and concrete walls strong enough to withstand the direct impact of a jetliner. Other safety features also seemed faultless. Each essential system had at least two backups, and most were programmed to begin automatically when needed. In fact, almost half of the money spent in the design and construction of the plant was for safety systems.

But shortly before 4:00 A.M. Harrisburg time, Wednesday, March 28, 1979, something went wrong. An air valve was opened to flush out some sludge from a filter in the water system. Unfortunately, the valve either stuck or was inadvertently left open. As a result, water that was needed to cool the nuclear reactor leaked out of the open valve. This accident would not necessarily have been serious if the backup systems had operated as planned. Three pumps automatically came on to supply cooling water to the reactor. What the operators in the control room did not know, however, was that the pipes from these pumps to the reactor had been closed two days earlier for maintenance. And the warning light on the control panel that would have told the operators that the pipes were closed was obscured by a red caution tag indicating that a switch on the panel needed repair.

As a result of this series of problems, the fuel rods in the nuclear reactor overheated and were damaged. Radioactive water leaked onto the floor of the structure housing the nuclear reactor and was automatically siphoned into an adjoining pump house that had no shielding. Radioactive gas then escaped from a vent in this pump house.

For several days it was unclear what might happen, as complications continued to mount. Metropolitan Edison, the company in charge of the plant, and General Public Utilities, the owner of the plant and parent of Metropolitan Edison, argued that things were under control. Other sources argued that a "meltdown" of the plant's radioactive fuel was possible—an event that might have disastrous consequences. A meltdown can occur if the fuel rods get so hot that they melt their container, thereby releasing the radioactive material. Public concern became so great that President Carter visited the plant.

Eventually the operators were able to stabilize the reactor, cool the nuclear core, and shut down the plant. The crisis was over, but its ramifications were just beginning. The cleanup costs will be from $500 million to $1 billion, and even then the plant may never be usable.

Charges that Metropolitan Edison had withheld and distorted information were denied by

---

This chapter is written by James M. Olson and Mark P. Zanna.

The controversy surrounding the Three-Mile Island Nuclear Power Plant incident and the protests against such plants illustrates the importance of attitude and social behavior.

the company. Plant operators who were blamed for the incident claimed that the systems that caused the problems had malfunctioned before, but nothing had been done. Investigators hired by the U.S. Nuclear Regulatory Commission reported that the plant came within 30 to 60 minutes of a meltdown and warned that similar accidents could happen at other plants. Consumer advocate Ralph Nader called for the dismantling of all U.S. nuclear power plants as soon as possible. Surveys of the people living near the Three Mile Island plant showed that attitudes toward nuclear power were quite negative, with almost 50 percent voicing opposition and only 34 percent expressing support.

One of the most startling aspects of the Three Mile Island accident was that it occurred only shortly after the release of "The China Syndrome," a movie that dealt with just such a possibility. The parallel between real life and the movie was frightening and almost certainly served to heighten people's reactions to the accident. For example, the film portrayed the management of the fictitious plant as being unconcerned about public safety; the public's suspicions about the honesty of Metropolitan Edison may have reflected their exposure to the movie.

It seems likely that nuclear power will become one of the most hotly debated issues of the 1980s. Already, "anti-nukes" are organizing pressure groups to fight what they perceive as "greedy" utility companies. On the other side of the fence, many "pro-nuke" industry officials argue that nuclear power constitutes an essential source of energy in our world of declining resources. Energy versus safety: which is the more important?

This is a complex issue with many arguments for each side. It is clear, however, that people's **attitudes** toward nuclear power will play an important role in the final outcome. Just as public opinion turned against American participation in Vietnam and eventually led the government to end its involvement, so the tide of public opinion on this issue may be crucial.

Of course, nuclear power is not the only environmental issue facing our society. For example, the possibility of gasoline and oil shortages is frightening to many North Americans, yet it seems difficult to get people to conserve energy. Why do people fail to conserve when they appear to have favorable attitudes toward conservation? How can we induce such behavior? These are questions of social engineering and again relate in important ways to the concept of attitudes.

There are also some environmental issues that have not even entered public awareness. Acid rain is one such issue. Many of our students in 1979 had never heard of the acid rain problem, yet it poses a potentially deadly threat to many of our lakes. The fumes released from some industrial plants combine with moisture in the atmosphere to form a weak sulphuric acid. This acid then falls as rain and, if allowed to continue over a period of time, builds up in lakes until the water is so acidic that plant and fish life is impossible. Many of our lakes have already "died"; many others are in danger of doing so. In this case, strong attitudes about the issue have not yet formed, but may develop in the near future.

Thus, there are many important environmental issues confronting our society. Some are potentially divisive (for example, nuclear power), some appear to have consensus but little concerted action (for example, energy conservation), and some have yet to arouse wide public concern (for example, acid rain). For all of these issues, however, people's attitudes will be very important. One's attitude toward an issue—favorable or unfavorable—probably influences one's behavior. Consequently, if anything is to be done about these environmental problems, the public will have to become concerned (that is, develop appropriate attitudes) and press for change.

This chapter and the one to follow will discuss how attitudes are formed and changed, and how attitudes influence behavior. Attitude research and theory will be presented with environmental issues used to illustrate the basic principles.

DEFINITION OF ATTITUDES

What, exactly, is an attitude? Because the term is a popular one in daily life, almost everyone has an idea of its meaning. Social psychologists, however, must define the concept carefully if they want to use it to explain people's behavior. Although many different definitions have been proposed by various theorists, certain elements are common to most of them.

One of the simplest definitions was suggested by Bem (1970, p. 14): "Attitudes are likes and dislikes. They are our affinities for and our aversions to situations, objects, persons, groups, or any other identifiable aspects of our environment, including abstract ideas and social policies." Thus, attitudes are our evaluative (good/bad) *feelings* toward particular targets; they are affective, or emotional. This evaluative or affective quality is probably the most important characteristic of the concept of attitudes. Attitudes refer primarily to the favorability of our feelings toward particular targets.

Note that attitudes always have a *referent*—that is, they always refer to feelings about or toward some object (attitudes *toward* police, attitudes *toward* nuclear energy, and so on). People often think of attitudes in more general terms, such as "The baseball player has a bad attitude." When social psychologists speak of attitudes, however, they always have particular referents in mind.

Note also that this concept has wide generality. We can have favorable or unfavorable feelings (attitudes) toward virtually anything: people, objects, issues, events, situations, policies, groups, abstract ideas, and so on. This generality might seem to make the concept less interesting; is it sensible, for example, to talk about someone's attitude toward green cars?

There are a number of answers to this possible criticism. First, if people happen to have strong feelings about green cars, then it *does* make sense to talk about their attitude, because their feelings may influence their behavior. Second, even though the concept of attitude has wide generality, social psychologists have typically been interested only in attitudes that are important to people. For example, the kinds of attitudes that have stimulated the most research have been attitudes toward groups of people (blacks, Jews, women), social issues (abortion, capital punishment), and ideologies (communism, the existence of God). Clearly, people's feelings toward these targets are often very strong. Third, the generality of the concept of attitude may prove to be useful. If social psychologists can come to understand how people's important attitudes develop, change, and influence behavior, then they may be able to extend the principles to feelings (attitudes) that are not so involving or important. Thus, making the attitude concept a general one (evaluative feelings toward an object) seems worthwhile.

Beliefs, Behavioral Intentions, and Behavior

It is important to distinguish the concept of attitude from some related concepts. For example, how do attitudes differ from **beliefs?** Fishbein and Ajzen (1975, p. 12) explain the distinction in the following way: "Whereas attitude refers to a person's favorable or unfavorable evaluation of an object, beliefs represent the information he has about the object. Specifically, a belief links an object to some attribute."

Thus, a belief associates some attribute or characteristic with an object. For example, the belief "apples are red" links the object "apple" to the attribute "red." The belief "nuclear power plants are a health hazard" links the object "nuclear power plants" to the characteristic "health hazard." Note that, like attitudes, we can have beliefs about virtually anything (people, groups, objects, issues, and so forth) and the attributes or characteristics that can be linked to the object are almost unlimited (traits, qualities, other objects, and so on).

People may differ in the strength of their beliefs. For example, one person may be absolutely certain that nuclear power plants are a health hazard, whereas someone else may believe that nuclear plants are only a possible health hazard. This point reveals another aspect of beliefs: they are what people see *subjectively as probabilities* that objects have certain attributes. In other words, a belief links an object to an attribute *at some level of probability* between 0 and 1. For example, although most people associate the attribute "red" with the object "apples," they also know that apples can be green, yellow, and so on. Thus, they may have the specific belief that "apples are red 80 percent of the time" (belief strength = .8). Similarly, someone may believe that "nuclear power plants are 100 percent certain to be a health hazard" (belief strength = 1.0), whereas a different person may have the belief that "nuclear power plants are only 20 percent likely to be a health hazard" (belief strength = .2). These two beliefs are linking the same object (nuclear power plants) to the same attribute (health hazard), but at different levels of probability. Finally, these beliefs form the basis for one's attitude. Whether one has a positive or negative attitude toward something depends on whether the relevant beliefs are evaluated positively or negatively and the strength with which the beliefs are held. The way beliefs combine to form attitudes will be discussed in more detail later in this chapter.

Another important concept is **behavioral intentions.** Whereas attitudes are feelings toward an object, and beliefs are cognitive links between the object and various attributes, behavioral intentions are a person's intentions to perform specific behaviors. For example, one may intend to oppose nuclear power plants whenever possible; that is, one may intend to behave in ways that are unfavorable toward nuclear power plants (for example, sign a petition, attend a protest rally, write letters to politicians, and so on).

Behavioral intentions, like beliefs, are subjective probabilities; that is, they are people's personal estimates of how likely it is that they will perform particular behaviors. When we intend to behave in certain ways, it means that we are likely to do so. If asked, we could provide an estimate of how likely it is that we will carry through our intentions. Thus, although intentions influence how we behave, they do not make it absolutely certain that we will perform particular actions.

This brings us to the final concept that we need to consider here—behavior. Behavior refers to an individual's overt, observable acts. Whereas attitudes, beliefs, and behavioral intentions are internal and not directly observable (and therefore must be inferred from subjects' answers to questions), behavior can be observed directly. Of course, behavior is ultimately what most social psychologists are primarily interested in; the goal of research and theory is usually to understand and explain people's actions.

In later sections, we will discuss the relations among attitudes, beliefs, behavioral intentions, and behavior. We will use a model developed by Fishbein and Ajzen (1975) to suggest that a person's beliefs about an object influence the attitude that is developed toward

the object, that attitudes influence how a person intends to behave toward an object, and that behavioral intentions influence (but do not completely determine) how a person actually behaves toward an object. Thus, although these concepts are separate, they are related to one another in important ways.

In this context we should mention that one common view of attitudes in the past was that they had three components: a cognitive component, consisting of the person's beliefs about the object; an affective component, consisting of the person's feelings toward the object; and a behavioral component, consisting of the person's tendencies (or intentions) to act in particular ways toward the object. In other words, this three-component view of attitudes combined beliefs, feelings, and behavioral intentions into the concept of attitude. This view is now less widely accepted, at least in part because it confuses some important distinctions among these concepts. Our position will be that attitudes are a person's feelings toward an object; beliefs, behavioral intentions, and behavior are separate (though related) concepts.

Why Are Attitudes Important?

Now that the concept of attitude has been defined and distinguished from some related concepts, the question can be asked, Why are attitudes important? That is, why have social psychologists given a great deal of research attention to people's evaluative feelings toward various objects, groups, and issues?

There are a number of reasons why evaluative feelings may be important. First, it is generally assumed that attitudes are relatively enduring; that is, people's feelings toward objects and issues are probably quite stable over time. Although attitudes can and do change, such occurrences are not random: something happens to cause the change. Thus, for example, individuals do not typically fluctuate from being in favor of nuclear power plants one day to being opposed the next day. If attitudes fluctuated substantially over short periods of time, then they would have little value as predictors of future behavior. Because they are relatively enduring, they can be studied, measured, and used to predict actions.

Second, attitudes are learned. We are not born liking or disliking nuclear power plants; we *learn* to like or dislike them. Consequently, the processes of attitude formation and change can be studied, and it may be possible to develop programs that encourage socially desirable attitudes (such as, favorable attitudes toward energy conservation).

Third, and most important, attitudes are assumed to influence behavior; that is, people's actions are believed to reflect their feelings toward relevant objects and issues. Indeed, interest in the attitude concept has always been based on the assumption that attitudes influence behavior. In 1935, Allport defined an attitude as a predisposition to respond in a consistent manner toward all objects and situations with which the attitude is related. Thus, if we are to understand, predict, and influence human behavior, then we must investigate and understand attitudes.

MEASUREMENT OF ATTITUDES

If attitudes are to be studied scientifically, then ways of measuring them accurately must be developed. We mentioned earlier that attitudes are internal and unobservable; no one has ever seen an attitude. As a result, researchers must infer individuals attitudes toward objects from their overt behavior, such as responses on a questionnaire or actions in a structured situation. Thus, attitude measures are always indirect—they are assumed to reflect people's evaluative feelings.

What does it mean to say that a measure of attitudes should be "accurate"? Accuracy involves at least two components: reliability and validity. **Reliability** refers to a constancy in subjects' scores (that is, to a lack of random fluctuation in subjects' scores). A person who completes the measure on two different occasions should receive approximately the same attitude score on both (called *test-retest reliability*), and two different judges should assign approximately the same attitude score to one person's performance on the test (called *inter-rater reliability*). *Validity*, on the other hand, refers to whether the test actually measures what it is supposed to measure, rather than whether subjects' scores are "constant." For example, does the measure *really* assess subjects' attitudes toward nuclear energy? Attitude researchers have gone to considerable lengths to develop measurement techniques that accurately reflect respondents' evaluative feelings. Several of these techniques are described below.

Self-Report Paper-and-Pencil Measures of Attitude

The most common approach to measuring attitudes uses self-report paper-and-pencil measures, in which respondents are asked to answer one or more items on an attitude questionnaire or scale. Presumably, their attitudes on the issue(s) influence how they answer the questions. Public-opinion polls, for example, measure attitudes in this way. In social psychological research, three types of self-report paper-and-pencil measures are most widely employed.

Self-rating technique. Guilford (1954) and Taylor and Parker (1964) have argued that a single, general question can often provide a good measure of respondents' attitudes. For example, if a researcher wants to measure attitudes toward capital punishment, then subjects can be asked, "In general, how favorable or unfavorable are you toward capital punishment?" Answers are indicated by placing an X on a scale ranging from "Very unfavorable" to "Very favorable":

| Very unfavorable ____: ____: ____: ____: ____: ____: ____ Very favorable |

Alternatively, the item can be phrased, "If I were to rate my attitude toward capital punishment, I would say that it is," with answers indicated on the same scale as above.

The advantages of this technique are, of course, that it is very simple and fast, and that it gets directly at what the researcher wants to measure. One disadvantage is that respondents can easily fake their answers if the question relates to an attitude that they would rather not admit. In addition, some people may be unable or unwilling to express an overall, global attitude that oversimplifies the complexity of their position. Thus, a multi-item attitude scale might allow respondents to indicate better the various aspects of their attitudes.

Semantic differential technique. Osgood, Suci, and Tannenbaum (1957) developed a very simple technique for assessing the general meaning of a concept. The concept that is to be rated is written at the top of the page. Below the concept are a number of 7-point scales with opposing adjectives at each end (for example, good-bad, pleasant-unpleasant). Respondents place an X on each scale to indicate how they would rate the concept on that particular dimension.

For example, subjects could be asked to rate capital punishment on the scales "good-bad," "nice-awful," and "fair-unfair" (see page 83). Their answers could then be scored from 1 to 7 on each scale, with favorable answers (good, nice, fair) getting high scores and unfavorable answers (bad, awful, unfair) getting low scores. Subjects' total scores could then be calculated by summing their scores on each item;

high total scores would reflect favorable overall attitudes toward capital punishment and low total scores would reflect unfavorable overall attitudes.

The semantic differential technique can be used to measure things other than attitudes. For example, respondents can be asked to rate a concept on such scales as heavy-light, weak-strong, active-passive, and fast-slow. These dimensions do not reflect evaluative feelings (attitudes), but rather the concept's general meaning to the respondents. Thus, when the technique is used to measure attitudes, only some adjective dimensions are appropriate—namely, those that reflect subjects' evaluations of the object. The most common evaluative dimensions used in semantic differential measures of attitudes are good-bad, nice-awful, pleasant-unpleasant, fair-unfair, and valuable-worthless.

The advantages of this technique are that it is relatively simple, fast, and direct, while not forcing respondents to make a global, overall judgment. Like the self-rating technique, however, it may be open to faking by respondents. Another problem is that sometimes the presented adjective dimensions are upsetting, ambiguous, or completely irrelevant to the concept being rated. For example, asking respondents to rate the attitude object "abortion" on the scales "nice-awful" and "pleasant-unpleasant" may seem distasteful or insulting. Similarly, the meaning of "fair-unfair" in the context of abortion is ambiguous—fair to whom? Such ambiguities can be irritating to respondents.

When researchers exercise good sense, however, and avoid asking respondents to make ambiguous or upsetting ratings, the semantic differential technique can provide an effective measure of attitudes. The flexibility of the technique is appealing, and its simplicity is certainly a virtue.

How would you rate CAPITAL PUNISHMENT on each of these scales? Place an "X" in the appropriate box to indicate your rating.

Good ____: ____: ____: ____: ____: ____: ____ Bad
Awful ____: ____: ____: ____: ____: ____: ____ Nice
Fair ____: ____: ____: ____: ____: ____: ____ Unfair

Likert's method of summated ratings. Likert (1932) developed a technique for measuring attitudes that has remained one of the most popular methods. The researcher begins by collecting or designing a large number of statements (for example, 20 or 30) on the issue of interest, each of which is phrased in a clearly favorable or unfavorable direction. For example, if a researcher wants to measure attitudes toward capital punishment, then two of the statements might be "Capital punishment is a deterrent to murder" (favorable to capital punishment) and "Capital punishment is immoral" (unfavorable). Some readers may have noticed that these two statements actually measure subjects' *beliefs* about capital punishment, rather than their evaluative feelings per se. The assumption underlying the technique is that an individual who holds mainly unfavorable beliefs about an object will have a negative attitude toward the object, whereas an individual who holds mainly favorable beliefs about an object will have a positive attitude toward the object. Thus, the Likert technique indirectly measures attitudes by assessing the extent to which someone holds positive or negative beliefs about an attitude object.

All of the statements collected by the experimenter are presented to subjects, who indicate agreement or disagreement with each item by circling the appropriate answer on the following scale:

Strongly Disagree: Disagree:
Undecided: Agree: Strongly Agree

Answers are scored from 1 to 5, with high scores reflecting agreement with favorable statements *or* disagreement with unfavorable statements. (Thus, favorable and unfavorable items are scored in opposite directions; that is, 1, 2, 3, 4, 5 versus 5, 4, 3, 2, 1.) Total scores can then be calculated by adding up respondents' answers to all of the questions (hence, the name *summated ratings*). High total scores reflect favorable overall attitudes on the issue, and low total scores reflect unfavorable overall attitudes on the issue.

The most important feature of Likert's method is the *item analysis* procedure, which is performed after subjects' total scores have been calculated. In any pool of statements designed by the researcher, some items can be expected to be ambiguous, poorly phrased, or even unrelated to the attitude being measured. That is, some statements may not *discriminate* between respondents with favorable and unfavorable attitudes (in which case, of course, the statements should not be included in the scoring). For example, suppose that a researcher wanting to measure attitudes toward capital punishment includes the following statement in the original set: "Capital punishment is unpleasant" (an apparently unfavorable item). Perhaps, though, everyone would agree with this—even people who believe that capital punishment is necessary (although unpleasant). If this is the case, then the item does not discriminate between favorable and unfavorable subjects and should be excluded from the scoring.

The item analysis procedure identifies such ineffective statements. Across all subjects, scores on each individual statement are correlated with the total scores for the whole set of statements combined. Any statements that do not show a substantial positive correlation with the total scores are discarded, since responses on those items are unrelated to subjects' attitudes (as measured by the total scores). After the ineffective statements have been identified, respondents' attitude scores are *recalculated* by adding up their answers to all of the remaining statements (that is, discarding the ineffective items). These scores are then taken to reflect subjects' overall attitudes on the issue.

Likert's method of summated ratings has

| Very unfavorable ____: ____: ____: ____: ____: ____: ____ | Very favorable |

* the advantage of ensuring (via the item analysis procedure) that all items tap the same underlying dimension. Thus, confidence in the

reliability of the scale is increased. Likert scales are also relatively easy for subjects to answer and do not force global, overall judgments. The disadvantages of the technique are that it is more time consuming than some other methods, and that the researcher must construct a large number of statements on the issue. Nevertheless, the technique is simple enough for its advantages to more than compensate for the increased work. As with all self-report paper-and-pencil measures of attitude, respondents can fake their answers if they would rather not admit their true attitudes. This problem may be less serious with a Likert scale than with the techniques described earlier, however, since a large number of statements are included in the scale.

Measuring Attitudes Toward Nuclear Power Plants

The self-report paper-and-pencil measures of attitudes described above are general techniques that can be modified to measure any particular attitude. That is, they are frame-

works that can be adapted for any specific attitude object.

For example, the techniques could be used to measure respondents' attitudes toward nuclear power plants. The self-rating technique could be employed by asking subjects, in general, how favorable or unfavorable are you toward nuclear power plants?

The semantic differential technique could also be used. Subjects could be asked to make the following ratings:

Nuclear Power Plants

| Good ____: ____: ____: ____: ____: ____: ____ Bad |
| Nice ____: ____: ____: ____: ____: ____: ____ Awful |
| Worthless ____: ____: ____: ____: ____: ____: ____ Valuable |

Finally, Likert's method of summated ratings could be used if the researcher designed a set of statements about nuclear power plants. Three such statements might be:

1. Nuclear power plants pose a grave threat to public safety.

   Strongly Disagree: Disagree:
   Undecided: Agree: Strongly Agree

2. Nuclear power is necessary to solve our future energy needs.

   Strongly Disagree: Disagree:
   Undecided: Agree: Strongly Agree

3. The owners of nuclear power plants cannot be trusted to behave in the best interests of the public.

   Strongly Disagree: Disagree:
   Undecided: Agree: Strongly Agree

Of course, if Likert's method were used, additional statements would be required, and an item analysis would be performed on the statements after respondents had answered all of the items.

A remaining question that we have not addressed is whether one self-report paper-and-pencil measure of attitudes is better than another. We have described three techniques; which one is best? There is no clear answer to this question. Each technique has its advantages and disadvantages, as described above. Moreover, Jaccard, Weber, and Lundmark (1975) compared four self-report paper-and-pencil measures of attitudes (including the three that we have described) and found that all had good reliability and validity. Thus, there were no clear "winners"; all of the measures seem to provide satisfactory methods of attitude assessment. The best recommendation, therefore, might be to use two different measures. All of the techniques are relatively easy, and having two measures of attitudes allows the researcher to check the consistency of respondents' scores across assessment techniques. Of course, any self-report measure is open to possible faking by respondents. Nevertheless, the techniques that we have described seem to provide reliable and valid measures of attitudes across a wide variety of content domains.

Problems with Self-Report Paper-and-Pencil Measures of Attitude

With any self-report measure of attitudes, there are several problems that can reduce the reliability and validity of the scores. These problems involve respondents failing to answer the questions honestly or carefully.

Social desirability. We all like to present ourselves to others in a favorable way. Consequently, if a question on an attitude scale has a clearly "desirable" answer, then we may be tempted to shift our response toward that answer even if it is not true. For example, imagine that a question asked, "Do you ever get so upset that you feel like hurting someone?", with possible answers ranging from "Never" to "Very often." For this question, "Never" is obviously the most socially desirable or acceptable answer. Thus, even if we occasionally get so upset that we feel like hurting someone, we

may answer "Never" because we want to present ourselves in a favorable way.

Acquiescence. **Acquiescence** refers to a tendency to agree with some or all questionnaire items regardless of their content. There are two kinds of acquiescence response sets (Bentler, Jackson, & Messick, 1971). An *agreement* response set is the tendency to agree with all items regardless of how they are phrased. For example, someone may agree with both "I rarely feel tired" and "I often feel run down." An *acceptance* response set is the tendency to agree with all positively worded statements (for example, "I always tell the truth") and to disagree with all negatively worded statements (for example, "I never lie").

Individuals differ in the extent to which they manifest these response sets. Clearly, though, agreement and acceptance response sets lead to answers that do not accurately describe the respondent.

Carelessness. If respondents are careless in their answers to an attitude scale, then the scale cannot accurately measure their evaluative feelings. Carelessness can arise if respondents are uninterested or unmotivated, or if the scale is so long that it becomes tiresome.

Ways to minimize problems with self-report measures. There are a number of simple procedures that can minimize the problems described above. First, making the attitude scale anonymous reduces the pressure to present oneself in a socially desirable way, as does stressing that there are no "right" or "wrong" answers on the items. Researchers should avoid selecting items for the scale that have a clear, socially desirable answer. Second, stressing the importance of the task and keeping the questionnaire as brief as possible reduce carelessness on the subjects' part. Third, the effects of acquiescence response sets can be eliminated by creating a *balanced scale*—half of the items are scored so that agreement gets a high score, and half are scored so that agreement gets a

SOCIAL FOCUS 4.1
The Bogus Pipeline

Self-report measures of attitudes have an inherent problem in that respondents may not answer questions honestly. For example, subjects may give "socially desirable" answers to questions that pry into things that they would rather not admit. Although certain procedures may reduce pressures for presenting oneself in a favorable way, it is impossible to be certain that respondents' answers are honest.

Jones and Sigall (1971), however, developed a technique that is designed to induce total honesty. They call the technique the *bogus pipeline,* because it is presented to subjects as if it were a "pipeline to their souls" (that is, a kind of lie detector). Subjects are connected to an impressive-looking machine (called an "electromyograph"), which purportedly records tiny muscle movements that reveal "inner feelings." Subjects are led to believe that the machine can accurately indicate their attitudes on a scale from −3 (very unfavorable) to +3 (very favorable).

To convince subjects that the machine really works, they are asked a few preliminary, innocuous questions, and the needle on the meter immediately moves to precisely the correct answer for the subject. In reality, the machine does not measure subjects' reactions at all. The needle is controlled by an experimental assistant, who knows the subject's answers on the preliminary questions because they were obtained earlier in a different experiment. Most subjects are completely convinced, however, that the machine can assess their true attitudes.

Subjects are then asked the critical attitude questions. For these questions, they receive no feedback from the machine, although they believe that the experimenter is recording the needle's movement. Subjects are told that the experimenter wants to see how much they are "in touch with their inner feelings." Thus, they are asked to guess what the machine is revealing about their atti-

---

low score. For example, a Likert scale should include equal numbers of statements that are favorable and unfavorable to the attitude object. Since favorable and unfavorable statements are scored in reverse directions, a tendency to agree with all statements will be cancelled out across the set of items. Finally, alternative techniques may be developed that attempt to circumvent problems such as social desirability. One such technique, called the **bogus pipeline,** is described in Social Focus 4.1. Although the technique holds promise for as-

sessing attitudes on topics that have a strong social desirability bias, it has practical and ethical limitations that make its widespread use unlikely.

ATTITUDE FORMATION

We stated earlier that one of the reasons it is important to study attitudes is that they are learned. People's attitudes toward various ob-

tudes; that is, they are asked to predict where the needle moves to on each question, along the -3 to $+3$ scale. Presumably, if they believe that the machine is revealing their true feelings to the experimenter, then they will be totally honest in their predictions. Their predictions can be used as a measure of their attitudes.

Several studies have shown that the bogus-pipeline technique produces less socially desirable answers than standard self-report paper-and-pencil measures. For example, Sigall and Page (1971) found that the bogus pipeline led subjects to admit more negative views of blacks than did standard self-report measures. Similarly, Quigley-Fernandez and Tedeschi (1978) found that the bogus pipeline increased the rate of confessions from subjects who were provided with illegitimate information about how to perform well on an experimental test.

The bogus-pipeline technique has also been criticized, however (Cherry, Byrne, & Mitchell, 1976; Ostrom, 1973). For one thing, even though subjects are thoroughly debriefed (that is, the nature of the deception is explained completely), the deception may be upsetting. Thus, there are ethical questions about the legitimacy of its widespread use. Second, the procedure is very involved and time-consuming. Consequently, unless the attitude topic is clearly open to social desirability distortions, the practical advantages of paper-and-pencil measures probably offset concerns about respondents' honesty. Finally, it is not yet certain that the bogus-pipeline technique is more accurate than paper-and-pencil measures on all attitude topics. For example, it may be that a bias to give socially *undesirable* answers is introduced by the procedure.

Thus, the bogus-pipeline technique has certain limitations that make its widespread use unlikely. Nevertheless, it may be a useful tool for assessing subjects' attitudes on some topics.

jects, groups, and issues develop over the years. As a result, researchers have been very interested in the processes of attitude formation: how and why do attitudes develop?

It seems clear that the way we feel about objects or people depends upon what we know about them; that is, attitudes (feelings) depend somehow on beliefs (knowledge). We explained earlier that attitudes and beliefs are related, though conceptually distinct, constructs. We are now suggesting that to understand attitude formation, we must examine people's beliefs. How, exactly, are attitudes and beliefs interrelated?

Fishbein and Ajzen (1975; Ajzen & Fishbein, 1980) have presented a comprehensive model of the relations among attitudes, beliefs, behavioral intentions, and behavior. Basically, these authors suggest that a person's beliefs about an object determine how that person feels toward the object (that is, the individual's attitude). In turn, the attitude determines the person's behavioral intentions with respect to the object. Finally, these behavior intentions

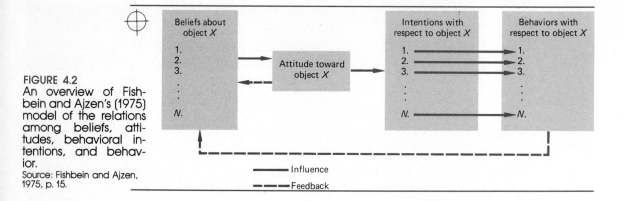

FIGURE 4.2
An overview of Fishbein and Ajzen's (1975) model of the relations among beliefs, attitudes, behavioral intentions, and behavior.
Source: Fishbein and Ajzen, 1975, p. 15.

determine how the person actually behaves toward the object.

Fishbein and Ajzen assume that humans are usually quite rational and make systematic use of the information available to them. They propose that "people consider the implications of their actions before they decide to engage or not engage in a given behavior" (Ajzen & Fishbein, 1980, p. 5). Hence, they call their approach a *theory of reasoned action*. Figure 4.2 presents an overview of their model.

We will return to consider this overall model in the following chapter. For now, let us consider only the hypothesized relation between attitudes and beliefs. It makes sense to propose that our feelings are dependent upon our knowledge, but precisely how does this dependency operate?

Recall that beliefs are cognitive links between an object and an attribute, and that the links are made at some level of probability (from 0 to 1). For example, imagine that you have three primary, salient beliefs about someone you know. You are confident that this person is friendly (belief strength = .8), quite sure that the person is intelligent (belief strength = .7), and suspect that the person is conceited (belief strength = .5). Note that your beliefs link the attributes friendly, intelligent, and conceited to the person. Also note that you *value* these attributes differently. For example, you

may evaluate friendliness and intelligence positively and conceit negatively.

Fishbein and Ajzen hypothesize that attitudes toward an object, issue, or person can be predicted by calculating the sum of the salient beliefs about the target, weighted by the belief strengths and the evaluations of the attribute in each belief; that is, for each belief, multiply the belief strength by the evaluation of the attribute. Next, add up these products for each belief. This sum will reflect the overall attitude.

Continuing the example above, suppose that on a scale from -3 (bad) to $+3$ (good), you evaluate friendliness as $+3$, intelligence as $+2$, and conceit as -2. To calculate your overall attitude toward this person, Fishbein and Ajzen would multiply $+3 \times .8$ (friendliness), $+2 \times .7$ (intelligence), and $-2 \times .5$ (conceit), and add up the products ($2.4 + 1.4 - 1.0 = +2.8$). Thus, your overall attitude toward this person would be favorable, which makes sense because there are more positive than negative attributes.

Thus, Fishbein and Ajzen propose that a person's attitude toward some object is determined by a complex combination of the salient beliefs about the object. Studies have shown that, indeed, it is possible to predict subjects' attitudes, as measured by the semantic differential technique, from their salient beliefs, as explained above. These studies have success-

SOCIAL FOCUS 4.2
Attitudes toward Nuclear Power Plants as a Function of Salient Beliefs

Imagine that two individuals, George and Robert, have similar salient beliefs about nuclear power plants, but hold these beliefs at different strengths (levels of probability). According to Fishbein and Ajzen's (1975) theory of reasoned action, George and Robert will form different attitudes toward nuclear power plants.

Attributes Linked with Nuclear Power Plants

	HIGH ENERGY SOURCE	HEALTH HAZARD	NECESSARY FOR FUTURE ENERGY NEEDS	TOO EXPENSIVE
(a) George's belief strength (0 to 1)	1.0	.3	.8	.2
(b) George's evaluation of attribute (−3 to +3)	+3	−3	+3	−2
(a) × (b)	+3.0	−0.9	+2.4	−0.4
(c) Robert's belief strength (0 to 1)	.9	1.0	.3	.5
(d) Robert's evaluation of attribute (−3 to +3)	+3	−3	+3	−2
(c) × (d)	+2.7	−3.0	+0.9	−1.0

Using Fishbein and Ajzen's formula, George would be expected to have a strongly favorable overall attitude toward nuclear power plants (3.0 − 0.9 + 2.4 − 0.4 = +4.1), whereas Robert would be expected to have a slightly unfavorable overall attitude toward nuclear power plants (2.7 − 3.0 + 0.9 − 1.0 = −0.4). Thus, the differing strengths with which these two persons hold particular beliefs would lead to very different overall attitudes.

Note that this example is relatively simiplified. Not only can people differ in the strengths of their beliefs, but they may, in fact, hold entirely different beliefs (that is, may associate different attributes with the object). Moreover, people may differ in their evaluations of the same attribute. For example, one person might evaluate the attribute "high energy source" very positively (+3), whereas someone else might not value this characteristic so highly (+1). Thus, there are many ways that people can develop different attitudes toward some object or issue (which explains the wide variety of attitudes on most issues in real life).

fully predicted subjects' attitudes toward blacks (Fishbein, 1963), political candidates (Fishbein & Coombs, 1974), and birth control pills (Jaccard & Davidson, 1972), among others. Social Focus 4.2 illustrates how two people might develop different attitudes toward nuclear power plants on the basis of their respective beliefs.

In summary, then, it seems that our attitudes toward an object depend on the beliefs we have about that object. Consequently, if we are to understand attitude formation, we must consider where beliefs come from. The next section addresses this issue.

Sources of Beliefs

Where do we obtain knowledge about various objects, persons, groups, and issues? There are two basic sources: direct personal experience and other people. Of course, these general categories can be broken down into many more specific sources.

Direct personal experience. Much, perhaps most, of our knowledge comes from our personal experiences. We learn firsthand that our mothers feed us, comfort us, and care for us. We learn that apple juice tastes good, that we dislike (or like) liver, and that peanut butter sandwiches are heaven on earth. We also learn about people—Carole is funny, Stuart is aggressive, Robert is shy, and so on.

Fazio and Zanna (in press) have discussed the importance of direct personal experience in the formation of attitudes. They have shown that the attitudes (feelings) toward an object of someone who has had actual behavioral experience with the object will be more clear and more confidently held. Presumably, knowledge gathered from personal experience can be trusted more than information obtained from other people.

Other people and institutions. In addition to direct personal experience, we get a lot of information from other people and institutions. Indeed, for many social issues (for example, capital punishment, abortion, nuclear power plants), we have had no personal experience with the relevant objects. Thus, we depend on others for our information and beliefs.

Parents. Our parents have a profound influence on our beliefs. We generally respect, trust, and love them; thus it is not surprising that we adopt many of their beliefs (and resulting attitudes).

For example, high school seniors tend to support the same political party and express the same denominational preference for churches as their parents (Jennings & Niemi, 1968). In addition, children's levels of racial prejudice are related to the level of prejudice their parents express (Epstein & Komorita, 1966b), and the impact of school desegregation on reducing prejudice in children depends, in part, on their parents' attitudes toward integration (Stephan & Rosenfeld, 1978).

Peer groups. We also depend on our friends and peers for information. From the time children begin school, and especially in the high school years, peers serve as an important *reference group*—a group whose beliefs, attitudes, and behaviors provide a standard against which individuals compare themselves. Because we all want to be popular and accepted, we often adopt the beliefs, behaviors, and dress of our peers.

A famous study of reference groups was conducted by Theodore Newcomb (1943) at Bennington College, a small liberal arts college for women in New England. Many of Bennington's students came from conservative, upper-class families. Most of the faculty and senior students, however, were quite liberal. Newcomb traced a class of incoming students through their four years at the college and found a clear shift toward more liberal attitudes and beliefs during the four years. Thus, the women's peer group had an important influence on their views. In addition, a follow-up study twenty years later (Newcomb, 1963) showed that the women's liberal attitudes and beliefs had generally persisted, and that the women had married relatively liberal men. Thus, it seems that the women did not become more liberal merely to achieve prestige at the college; their Bennington peer group had an enduring impact on their attitudes.

Institutions. We have extensive contact with institutions from a very early age. The most important institution for shaping our beliefs is almost certainly the school system. Schools teach us to value democracy, to respect our elders, to obey authority figures, and so on. In short, the school system socializes children into the beliefs and value systems of the society (see Chapter 3). We do not want to imply that this is necessarily undesirable; the point is that schools have a pervasive impact on our beliefs and attitudes (see, for example, Tolley, 1973).

A second important institution is the church. Obviously, churches influence our religious beliefs—was Jesus the Son of God?, does Hell exist?, and so on. In addition, however, churches inculcate more general value systems. For example, Christianity probably leads to different attitudes toward targets such as work and women than does, say, Islam. Thus, our exposure to a particular religion (and to a particular denomination within that religion) has a major impact on our beliefs.

Mass media. The final source of beliefs that we will consider is the mass media. Television, radio, movies, newspapers, and magazines are so central to our daily lives that it is difficult to imagine what it would be like without them. It has been estimated that by the time the average American youth finishes high school, as many hours have been spent watching television as in school (Oskamp, 1977).

The mass media are influential in many ways. First, they transmit a great deal of information that we would not otherwise be able to obtain. For example, news coverage of the Three Mile Island accident kept the public abreast of developments. Most of our information (and hence, beliefs) about far-off events comes from the media. Second, the media select events to emphasize in their communications, and usually interpret or comment upon ongoing incidents. As a result, readers/listeners may form different beliefs or attitudes than they would have formed if they had personally witnessed the occurrence (Lang & Lang, 1959). That is, the media define "reality" for the viewers, which can influence what they "learn." Finally, the media can have entirely unintended effects on the beliefs, attitudes, and behaviors of the viewers. For example, some researchers have argued that violence on television increases viewers' aggressiveness and their fear of being victims of violence (see Chapter 11). Thus, there is increasing evidence that the mass media have pervasive effects on our beliefs and attitudes. We rely heavily on the media for our information about the events and issues that occur outside our daily lives.

Note that our discussion of the sources of beliefs has not mentioned the interdependence of the various sources. For example, our parents select the church that we attend as children, our friends and peers influence the television programs we watch, the mass media influence our teachers, and so on. That is, all of these sources operate within a *system*, which means that, inevitably, each source is influenced by each of the other sources. The combined impact of the total system on our beliefs is profound.

A Different Perspective On Attitude Formation

To this point, we have considered the belief sources of our likes and dislikes. Are all of our evaluative feelings (attitudes) determined by, or dependent upon, our beliefs? Some theorists have said no, that attitudes can be influenced by factors that do not involve our knowledge about an object. That is, affect can become associated with an object or issue independently of our beliefs about that target. Below we describe two factors that may play a role in attitude formation, but that may not be mediated by cognitive beliefs.

Mere exposure. The **mere-exposure** hypothesis (Zajonc, 1968a) asserts that merely the repeated exposure of an individual to a particular stimulus enhances the individual's attitude toward the stimulus. That is, repeated exposure to an object leads us to like the object more—familiarity leads to positive attitudes. The advertising industry seems to follow this principle—new products are announced in a flurry of repetitious, attention-grabbing commercials. Presumably, if consumers are familiar with a product's name, then they may feel positively toward it and be more likely to buy it.

Note that Zajonc's hypothesis does not require the development of beliefs, except in the existence of the object. We develop favorable attitudes through *mere* exposure or *mere* contact, without interaction or other psychologically significant processes. Mere perceptual exposure to an object is enough to produce liking.

Is there any empirical evidence to support this hypothesis? Zajonc (1968a) reports several experiments that show an effect of exposure on liking. In one study subjects were shown ten Chinese characters for two seconds at a time. Each subject saw two of the characters only once, two others twice, two others 5 times, two others 10 times, and a final two 25 times. In addition, the experimenter had two characters that the subjects never saw at all. Subjects were told that the experiment dealt with the learning of a foreign language and were instructed to pay close attention to the characters as they were presented.

Following the exposure trials, subjects were told that the characters were in fact Chinese adjectives, and that their task would be to guess what the characters meant. The experimenter said that he realized how nearly impossible this task was, and that he therefore did not require guesses about the precise word meanings. Instead, it would suffice if subjects indicated on 7-point, good-bad scales whether each character meant something good or something bad, because these Chinese characters all meant one or the other. Subjects then estimated the favorability of each character's meaning, including the two characters that they had not been shown during the exposure trials. There was a strong, direct effect of exposure frequencies on subjects' estimates of the characters' meanings. The more often subjects had seen a character, the more favorable they estimated its meaning to be. That is, mere exposure led subjects to predict that a Chinese character had a favorable meaning. These results clearly support Zajonc's mere-exposure hypothesis.

In a second experiment, Zajonc (1968a) used the same experimental design as with the Chinese characters, but the stimuli were faces of men (photographs of graduating Michigan State University seniors taken from the MSU yearbook). Again, subjects saw the stimuli different numbers of times, from 0 to 25, for two seconds each time. Following the exposure trials, subjects were asked to rate on a 7-point scale how much they might like the man in each photograph. The more often subjects had seen a face, the more they said that they would like the man. Thus mere exposure increased estimates of liking.

These studies do not constitute the only support for the mere-exposure hypothesis. Social Focus 4.3, for example, describes a clever, more recent demonstration of the principle. Nevertheless, some researchers have criticized Zajonc's position (for example, Jakobovitz, 1968; Maddi, 1968). For example, the mere-exposure hypothesis seems inconsistent with the common observation that repeated exposure to a stimulus can lead to satiation and boredom. In addition, people often seek novelty and ex-

---

SOCIAL FOCUS 4.3
"Mirror, Mirror, on the Wall": Facial Images and the Mere-Exposure Hypothesis

Mita, Dermer, and Knight (1977) reasoned that individuals are more likely to be exposed repeatedly to their mirror facial images than to their true facial images. Thus, if the *mere-exposure hypothesis* is true (see text), one should prefer a facial photograph that corresponds to one's mirror image rather than to one's true image. Conversely, close friends are almost certainly exposed more often to the true than to the mirror image and therefore should prefer a photograph that corresponds to the true image.

To test this reasoning, Mita, Dermer, and Knight recruited a total of 61 female subjects, who posed for two frontal facial photographs. Only one of the negatives was developed, however, and two copies were printed to be mirror (that is, reversed) images of each other. The print corresponding to how the target appears to the subject herself when looking in the mirror was designated the *mirror print;* the remaining print, corresponding to how the subject appears to others, was designated the true print.

Subjects returned for a second session and brought with them either a close female friend (Study 1) or a boyfriend (Study 2). Subjects and their friends were asked individually to indicate which of the two prints they "liked better." Forty-one of the 61 subjects in the two studies indicated a preference for the mirror print rather than the true print. On the other hand, 37 of the 61 friends preferred the true print. Thus, expressed preferences for mirror versus true prints corresponded to the frequency with which subjects were probably exposed to each image, although admittedly the effect was not overwhelming (approximately one-third of the subjects did not select the predicted print).

These findings are particularly interesting because the mirror and true facial photograph were almost indistinguishable, and participants had no suspicions about the actual purposes of the study. Yet, different patterns of preferences were obtained from the subjects than from their friends. Familiarity with an image seemed to increase liking for it, as Zajonc's (1968a) hypothesis would suggest.

---

citement, a behavior that appears to contradict a preference for familiarity.

How can these apparent inconsistencies be reconciled? Perhaps the most plausible view is that all are true to some extent. That is, familiarity (mere exposure) generally increases liking, but *over*exposure can produce boredom. Further, although familiarity is generally positive, we sometimes want novelty and excitement. Thus, people seek a sort of equilibrium—a balance between familiarity and novelty. Certainly, the general validity of Zajonc's mere-exposure hypothesis cannot be denied; repeated exposures to a previously neutral stimulus have been shown to enhance an individual's attitude toward the stimulus. From our perspective, the most important aspect of this effect is that it does not appear to be mediated by the individual's beliefs about the stimulus object. Thus, affect can become associated with an object independently of our knowledge about it.

The two photos above represent the kinds of photos shown to subjects in the Mita, et al. experiments. The photo on the left is a true image; the photo on the right is its mirror image.

One important qualification to Zajonc's hypothesis should be mentioned, however. It seems that repeated exposure to an initially *disliked* stimulus can sometimes make our attitudes even more negative (Brickman, Redfield, Harrison, & Crandall, 1972; Perlman & Oskamp, 1971). For example, repeated contact with (or exposure to) someone we dislike may simply provide us with a series of unpleasant experiences, which may intensify our negative feelings for that person. Thus, the mere-exposure hypothesis may not generalize to initially disliked stimuli; results have been more consistently supportive, however, for exposure to initially neutral and initially liked stimuli.

In a recent paper, Zajonc (1980) has gone beyond the mere-exposure hypothesis and argued that we can like or dislike an object before we have any meaningful beliefs about it. That is, our affective reactions to objects may be fairly independent of cognitive processing. In his paper Zajonc discusses a number of experimental results that support the hypothesis that "feeling" and "thinking" are under the control of separate systems, which combine to determine how we process information. Again, then, this hypothesis is consistent with our suggestion that attitude formation is probably not wholly determined by beliefs and knowledge.

Classical conditioning. A second process that can play a role in attitude formation without involving beliefs is **classical conditioning.** Classical conditioning occurs when a stimulus comes to evoke a response that it did not previously evoke, simply by being paired with some other stimulus that "naturally" evokes the response. For example, if an animal is given an electric shock immediately following the presentation of a particular sound, then after a number of such pairings, the sound alone will produce signs of fear, muscle tenseness, and so on. To take a personal example, one of the authors was, as a child, very fond of oatmeal cookies. Unfortunately, overindulgence one evening, when he was not feeling well to begin with, led to a night of distressful illness.

To this day, oatmeal cookies evoke a very unpleasant reaction, even though he knows that the oatmeal cookes were not, in themselves, the cause of the illness. That is, the negative feelings toward oatmeal cookies are not mediated by **beliefs;** somehow, affect has become linked directly with oatmeal cookies, independently of beliefs about them.

Many of our attitudes probably include some classically conditioned affect. A pleasant evening around a fireplace increases liking for those present, problems during a visit to a city (for example, losing your wallet) lead to unfavorable feelings toward the city, and so on. An interesting study by Griffitt and Veitch (1971) illustrates this process. Subjects in this experiment worked on a number of tasks in a small chamber. Two independent variables were manipulated to produce different kinds of affect in the subjects. For half of them the effective temperature in the chamber (considering both temperature and humidity) was uncomfortably hot (about 94°F), whereas for the other half, the effective temperature was comfortable (about 73°F). In addition, half of the subjects participated under "crowded" conditions, with 12 to 15 persons jammed into the chamber, while the others participated in groups of 3 to 5. After working on the tasks, subjects rated how much they liked a stranger (actually, an experimental assistant). Extreme heat produced less liking for the stranger than did a comfortable temperature, and a crowded chamber produced less liking than did an uncrowded chamber. Thus, negative feelings aroused by environmental conditions generalized (were conditioned) to an innocent bystander.

Classical conditioning, then, is a second process that can influence attitude formation independently of beliefs. Although Fishbein and Ajzen's (1975) theory of reasoned action explains how many of our attitudes are formed, it probably does not tell the complete story. Under some circumstances, affect can become linked with an object or person *directly*.

Formation of Attitudes Toward Nuclear Power Plants

What are the sources of the public's attitudes toward nuclear power plants? It seems unlikely that many of us have had direct personal experience with nuclear energy. Unless we live near a nuclear plant, we probably depend on others for our information and beliefs.

Certainly, the mass media have had an important influence. Reports on the Three Mile Island incident, interviews with experts on nuclear power, commentaries on the pros and cons of nuclear energy, and so on, have received increasingly wide exposure in the last few years. In addition, movies like "The China Syndrome" have influenced many people's beliefs and attitudes.

For today's adults, therefore, the mass media have probably been the most important source of beliefs. For today's children, on the other hand, sources other than the mass media may play a role in the formation of beliefs and attitudes about nuclear power plants. Today's children are learning about nuclear energy from their parents, friends, and teachers, as well as from the mass media.

It is interesting to speculate on the role of mere exposure. Because today's children will grow up with nuclear energy, they can be expected to be more familiar and comfortable with it. Thus, attitudes may slowly become more favorable toward nuclear energy, as the public has more exposure to it and as children mature to adulthood. Of course, if frightening incidents such as the Three Mile Island accident continue to occur, then attitudes can be expected to become more negative toward nuclear energy, despite increased familiarity. (In fact, as mentioned earlier, repeated exposure to initially disliked stimuli can make attitudes even more negative.) Environmental disasters can certainly have a dramatic impact on public attitudes. In 1969, for example, an oil spill near Santa Barbara, California, covered 25 miles of beaches with crude oil. This crisis prompted an overwhelming protest from the community and "radicalized" many citizens on environmental issues (Molotch, 1971).

SUMMARY

Attitudes are evaluative (good-bad) feelings toward objects, issues, persons, or any other identifiable aspects of our environment. They are assumed to be learned, relatively enduring, and important determinants of behavior. They can be distinguished from beliefs, which are cognitive links between an object and some attribute or characteristic, and from behavioral intentions, which are an individual's intentions to perform specific behavior with respect to some object, issue, or person.

Numerous techniques for measuring attitudes have been developed. The most common techniques are self-report paper-and-pencil measures, such as the self-rating technique, the semantic differential technique, and Likert's method of summated ratings. With any self-report measure of attitudes, however, there is the problem that respondents may not answer the questions honestly or carefully. Social desirability, acquiescence, and carelessness produce response biases that can potentially affect the scores. A relatively new measurement technique is the bogus pipeline, which is designed to induce total honesty. This technique raises ethical questions, however, and seems unsuitable for widespread use.

Our attitudes are based on our beliefs. That is, the way we feel about something or someone depends on what we know about it or them. Fishbein and Ajzen (1975) have proposed a theory of reasoned action, which specifies how beliefs are combined to produce our attitudes. This model has been shown to predict people's attitudes very well.

Thus, to understand attitude formation, we must consider where beliefs come from. The most important sources of our beliefs are probably direct personal experience, our parents, our peer groups, institutions such as the school system and the church, and the mass media.

Our attitudes may also be influenced, however, by factors that are not mediated by beliefs. Specifically, through such processes as mere exposure and classical conditioning, affect can become linked directly to an object or person.

SUGGESTED READINGS

Ajzen, I., & Fishbein, M. *Understanding attitudes and predicting social behavior*. Englewood Cliffs, N.J.: Prentice-Hall, 1980.

Oskamp, S. *Attitudes and opinions*. Englewood Cliffs, N.J.: Prentice-Hall, 1977.

5

ATTITUDE CHANGE AND BEHAVIOR PREDICTION

INTRODUCTION

The distinction between attitude formation and attitude change is rather arbitrary. As described in Chapter 4, attitudes toward an object, a person, or an issue form when we obtain information (and form beliefs) about the target, and/or when affect becomes linked directly to the target through such processes as mere exposure and classical conditioning. In similar fashion, attitude change occurs when we form new beliefs and change old ones about the target, and/or when new affect becomes conditioned to the target. Thus, attitude change involves the same basic processes as attitude formation. There is one important difference, however: the individual already has some feelings toward the object. These preexisting feelings may produce resistance to the new information.

Almost inevitably, belief change is an important component of attitude change. If you want to modify someone's feelings toward an object, then you will probably attempt to change that person's beliefs about it. This strategy is precisely the one employed by most mass-media campaigns. For example, campaigns to change people's attitudes toward smoking typically present information about the deleterious consequences of this habit.

Attitude change theorists have taken various perspectives on belief change, its relation to attitude change, and the conditions that facilitate both kinds of change. We will examine, in the first section of this chapter, five of the most influential attitude change theories in social psychology. These theories differ most clearly in their assumptions about the motives that precipitate attitude change.

Fishbein and Ajzen's (1975) theory of reasoned action, which specifies the relations among beliefs, attitudes, behavioral intentions, and behavior, qualifies as a sixth important theory. Their model might well prove to be the most influential of all. While the theories described below focus specifically on attitude change, Fishbein and Ajzen's model is a more general formulation, encompassing attitude formation, attitude change, and the relations between attitudes and other concepts. It is especially helpful in understanding the relationship between attitudes and behavior. This topic will be the focus of the last part of the chapter.

BALANCE THEORY

A number of attitude change theories can be classified as **consistency theories.** Consistency theories postulate that humans try to maintain psychological consistency among their beliefs, attitudes, and behaviors; that is, people are motivated to maintain a sense of order and compatibility among their cognitions, feelings, and actions. When individuals become aware of inconsistencies in their beliefs and attitudes, they are motivated to restore consistency. Thus, belief and/or attitude change should occur if individuals obtain new information that is inconsistent with their previous opinions, or if inconsistencies in their existing beliefs and attitudes are made salient.

Heider's (1944, 1958) **balance theory** is an early consistency theory, remarkable in both its simplicity and its intuitive plausibility. The model is concerned primarily with situations involving two persons and an attitude object. Balance theory postulates that when two persons have a strong, positive, affective relationship, they will feel either "balance," if they share important attitudes, or "imbalance," if

---

This chapter is written by James M. Olson and Mark P. Zanna.

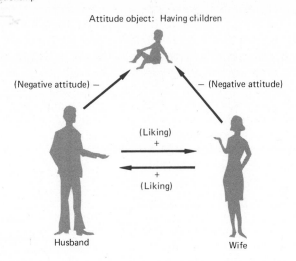

(a) Balanced relationship

Attitude object: Having children

(Negative attitude) −

− (Negative attitude)

(Liking)
+

+
(Liking)

Husband

Wife

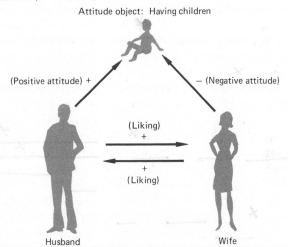

(b) Unbalanced relationship

Attitude object: Having children

(Positive attitude) +

− (Negative attitude)

(Liking)
+

+
(Liking)

Husband

Wife

FIGURE 5.1
Examples of balanced and 204 unbalanced relationships

they differ in their most valued attitudes. *Balanced* relationships are postulated to be psychologically comfortable, stable, and resistant to change. *Unbalanced* relationships are postulated to arouse discomfort or stress, to be unstable and open to change. For example, if a husband and wife hold the same attitude toward having children, then the relationship will be stable and comfortable, at least with respect to children. If one spouse wants children and the other does not, however, then there will be stress, instability, and pressure for change of some kind. Figure 5.1 depicts these contrasting possibilities.

Balance theory predicts exactly the reverse of the above when two persons dislike one another. In such circumstances, the negative affective relationship is balanced if the persons differ in their important attitudes, whereas it is unbalanced if they hold similar attitudes. For example, if you discover that someone you strongly dislike shares your religious beliefs, then balance theory predicts that you will experience stress and be motivated to restore balance to the relationship. If, on the other hand, you learn that a disliked other holds different religious beliefs from your own, then balance theory predicts that there will be no pressure for change.

The fundamental assumption in balance theory, then, is that we like (or should like) people who share our important opinions, and we dislike (or should dislike) people who hold different views on issues that are important to us. Phrasing this assumption differently, people we like should share our important opinions and people we dislike should hold different views from our own.

Balance theory postulates that when this fundamental assumption is violated, we are motivated to restore balance to the relationship. How can balance be restored? First, we can change our attitude toward the object or issue. For example, if a husband wants children and a wife does not, then she could convince herself that children would be rewarding, after all. Alternatively, we can change our attitude toward the other person. That is, we can come to dislike others who disagree with our viewpoints and come to like others who share our important attitudes. Of course, this alternative may not be viable in some circumstances, such as the husband-wife example above. Finally, we can try to convince the other person to change his or her attitude and thereby restore balance to the relationship. For example, the wife could try to convince her spouse that children would be a burdensome responsibility.

Heider suggests that we will make whatever change is least costly to restore balance to a relationship. Thus, in positive affective relationships, we are likely either to change our attitude toward the object or to attempt to change the other's attitude. In negative affective relationships, we are likely to change either our attitude toward the other or our attitude toward the object.

Problems with Balance Theory

Although balance theory has had an important influence on later consistency models and has stimulated some interesting applications (for example, Feather, 1967; Fischoff, 1979; and see Mower-White, 1979, for a recent review), its lack of specificity has limited its usefulness. Frankly, the theory is just too simplistic. For example, it does not consider *degrees* of liking for the other and for the attitude object; clearly, the amount of distress we feel in an unbalanced relationship will depend on how important the attitude object is to us, as well as how much we like or dislike the other person. In addition, Heider does not provide clear guidelines for predicting how balance will be restored in a particular relationship. Finally, the theory probably overemphasizes the need for balance—we often disagree with people we like, or recognize that we share attitudes with disliked others, without experiencing distress. Our relationships with others are based on similarity across a range of important topics; we know that people cannot agree (or disagree) about everything. Moreover, there is evidence that we prefer positive rather than negative affective relationships with others (whether the other person agrees with us or not) and agreement of opinions rather than disagreement (whether we like the other person or not), which can override the preference for balanced versus unbalanced relationships (Zajonc, 1968b).

DISSONANCE THEORY

Festinger's (1957, 1964) **dissonance theory** is also a consistency model, but is more elaborate than balance theory. Dissonance theory postulates that we are motivated to maintain consistency among our *cognitive elements*. Cognitive elements are simply beliefs or bits of knowledge. Thus, "It is raining today," "I like chocolate cake," "New York is an exciting place," and "George is intelligent" are all cognitive elements.

Festinger hypothesizes that cognitive elements are either *irrelevant*, *consonant*, or *dissonant* with one another. Irrelevant cognitions are beliefs that are completely independent. For example, the four beliefs listed above may exist simultaneously in someone's head, without having any implications for one another. Irrelevance probably describes the majority of the relations among our beliefs.

Consonant cognitions are consistent with one another. They are compatible, or support each other. For example, the beliefs "I exercise regularly" and "Exercise is good for my health" are consonant. Festinger postulates that people prefer consonant relations among their cognitions.

Dissonant cognitions are inconsistent or incompatible; they psychologically contradict one another. For example, the cognitions "I smoke" and "Smoking causes cancer" are dissonant with one another, as are the cognitions "I hurt Bob's feelings" and "I like Bob." Awareness of dissonant cognitions produces *psychological dissonance*, which Festinger describes as an unpleasant state of tension or discomfort. Because dissonance is unpleasant or aversive, people are motivated to reduce it. Festinger's theory is primarily concerned with the effects of dissonance on people's beliefs, attitudes, and behaviors.

For example, imagine that you want to purchase a car. You have narrowed your alternatives down to two possibilities. One is a large, comfortable, almost luxurious Chevrolet; the other is a small, economical, and much cheaper import model. Each alternative has its pros and cons, but eventually you choose the cheaper model. There will be both consonant and dissonant relations among your postdecisional cognitions. "Car B is economical" and "I bought car B" will be consonant, as will "Car A is expensive" and "I rejected car A." On the other hand, "Car A is luxurious" and "I rejected car A" may arouse psychological dissonance. Festinger postulates that we experience postdecisional dissonance after most of our important decisions and choices.

What are the effects of such dissonance motivation? That is, how do we reduce our discomfort? There are three ways that dissonance can be reduced. First, we can change one or more of the dissonant cognitions to make it (them) consonant with our other cognitions. For example, we can decide that car A was not luxurious; in fact, it was no more comfortable than car B. Second, we can add new, consonant cognitions. For example, we can decide that car A would have been an inconvenience in the city; its size would have made parking difficult. Third, we can change the importance of one or more cognitions. We can either increase the importance of consonant cognitions or reduce the importance of dissonant cognitions. For example, we can decide that good gasoline mileage is really important because gas prices are going up, or we can decide that luxury is not important because a car is simply a means of transportation—comfort is irrelevant.

Younger, Walker, and Arrowood (1977) obtained some interesting evidence for the effects of making a decision on people's cognitions. These authors interviewed people who were playing games of chance at the midway of the Canadian National Exhibition in Toronto. They asked bettors how confident they were of winning and how lucky they felt that day. Some bettors were on their way to place bets when they were interviewed; others had already placed their bets, but did not yet know the outcome. Younger et al. reasoned that people who have committed themselves to a choice should feel more dissonance when they think about the possibility of losing than should people who have not yet made an irrevocable choice. Thus, committed bettors should express more confidence and feel luckier than uncommitted bettors. The findings supported these predictions.

What factors influence how much postdecisional dissonance is experienced? First, important decisions arouse more dissonance than unimportant decisions. Second, as the attractiveness of the alternatives becomes more equal (that is, as the decision becomes more difficult), the amount of postdecisional dissonance increases (Brehm, 1956). Finally, the similarity between the alternatives affects dissonance (Brehm & Cohen, 1959). If the alternatives have a lot of features in common (that is, are similar), less dissonance will be aroused than if the alternatives are very different. This is because with similar alternatives, no matter which alternative is chosen, many of the features of the rejected alternative will be obtained. For example, a choice between two cars will arouse less dissonance than will a choice between a car and trip to Europe. In the former case, you get a car no matter which alternative is chosen, whereas in the latter case, your decision involves giving up something that is very different from what you will get.

Applications of Dissonance Theory

One important application of dissonance theory is to decision making, as discussed above. The theory can also be applied, however, to other phenomena. A controversial aspect of dissonance theory is its explanation for the effects on an individual's beliefs and attitudes of counterattitudinal behavior. This phe-

nomenon is called **induced compliance:** a person is induced to behave in some way that goes against his or her attitudes.

One of the most famous dissonance experiments examined induced compliance. Festinger and Carlsmith (1959) had subjects work for one hour at an extremely boring task. At the end of the hour, subjects were told that the experiment was actually looking at the effects of expectancies about a repetitive task on performance of the task, and that they were in a "no expectancy" condition. Subjects were told that other participants, in an "enjoyable expectancies" condition, were led to believe that the task would be enjoyable. Having explained the study in this way, the experimenter went on to tell subjects that a research assistant who usually provided the "enjoyable expectancies" to subjects was sick. In addition, subjects were told that someone was waiting to take part in the study and that this participant was supposed to be in the enjoyable expectancies condition. This ruse enabled the experimenter to ask the subjects if they would be willing to tell this next subject (actually, a confederate) that the task was enjoyable and lots of fun. Half of the subjects were paid $1 for telling this lie, and half were paid $20.

Festinger and Carlsmith reasoned that this induced compliance would arouse dissonance between the cognitions "The task is boring" and "I told another person that it is enjoyable." Subjects who were paid $20, however, would have the additional cognition that "I was paid a lot of money to tell another person that the task is enjoyable," which would be consonant with their behavior. Thus, these subjects should experience less dissonance than subjects who were paid only $1. Providing good, external reasons for behaving counterattitudinally should automatically reduce the amount of dissonance that is experienced, because the external reasons are consonant with (that is, explain) the counterattitudinal behavior.

Subjects were asked, after they told the lie, how much they had actually enjoyed the repetitive task. Those who were paid only $1 for saying that the task was fun reported enjoying the task more than did subjects who were paid $20 for the lie. Presumably, $1 subjects reduced their dissonance by changing one of the dissonant cognitions—they convinced themselves that the task was not so boring after all. Thus, these results are consistent with what dissonance theory would predict, although they may seem counterintuitive.

The explanation that dissonance theory proposes for the effects of induced compliance, however, has been challenged by some researchers. Social Focus 5.1 discusses the induced compliance controversy; essentially, the debate concerns whether it is necessary to postulate dissonance motivation to explain the results.

Another application of dissonance theory

has been to the phenomenon of **selective exposure.** Festinger postulated that because of the motivating effects of dissonance, people will actively seek (selectively expose themselves to) information that is consonant with their beliefs, attitudes, and past behaviors, whereas they will actively avoid information that is dissonant or inconsistent with their beliefs, attitudes, and past behaviors. This idea is intuitively plausible and has stimulated a great deal of research. Some findings have supported Festinger's predictions (for example, Brock & Balloun, 1967; Frey & Wicklund, 1978; Mills, 1965), but other findings have seemed inconsistent with the hypothesis (Rosen, 1961; Sears, 1965).

Wicklund and Brehm (1976) point out that many factors besides the dissonance-arousing or dissonance-reducing potential of a piece of

People who feel dissonance because they smoke, yet know the dangers of smoking, might reduce their dissonance by deciding to quit their smoking habit.

SOCIAL FOCUS 5.1
The Induced Compliance Controversy

Festinger and Carlsmith's classic study of *induced compliance* (see text) stimulated much debate about dissonance motivation. Numerous follow-up studies also showed that when individuals are induced to perform a behavior that is discrepant with their attitudes, they later change their attitudes to make them more consistent with their behavior (for example, Linder, Cooper, & Jones, 1967). As long as subjects feel that they are free to refuse to perform the behavior, their actions will modify their attitudes.

A common paradigm for studying induced compliance involves asking subjects to write an essay that goes counter to their opinions. Antiabortion subjects, for example, might be asked to write an essay that argued in favor of making abortions more easily available. If they willingly write the essay, then dissonance is presumably aroused between their cognitions "I am against abortion" and "I willingly wrote a proabortion essay." Since the second cognition cannot be changed, these subjects may reduce their dissonance by changing the first cognition to make it more consonant with their actions—that is, they may change their attitudes to become more proabortion. In fact, several studies have demonstrated this very effect. Compared to subjects who are *required* to write a counterattitudinal essay (that is, who are not given an opportunity to decline performance of the behavior, and who therefore should not experience any dissonance), subjects who willingly write the essay manifest significantly more attitude change in the direction of their advocated position.

Dissonance theory explains this effect in terms of a motivation to reduce the unpleasant tension resulting from the inconsistent (dissonant) cognitions. There are, however, other possible explanations. Bem's (1967, 1972) **self-perception theory** of attitude change provides one alternative interpretation. According to self-perception theory, "Individuals come to 'know' their own attitudes, emotions, and other internal states partially by inferring them from observations of their own overt behavior and/or the circumstances in which this behavior occurs" (Bem, 1972, p. 2). That is, when we are asked for our attitude on a particular issue, we think back over our past voluntary actions that related to that issue and infer our attitude from those behaviors. Thus, subjects who have willingly written a counterattitudinal essay will include this behavior in their analysis of past actions, will express opinions consistent with these actions, and will therefore appear to change their attitudes. On the other hand, subjects who were required to write the essay will not include this behavior in their analysis (since it was not voluntary) and will manifest no apparent attitude change.

Note that Bem's theory does not involve any kind of internal motivation or discomfort. Instead, subjects' attitudes are presumed to change only because

information will influence whether we seek it out or avoid it. If information is useful to us, for example, then we may seek it out, even if it is also potentially dissonant with our beliefs. Similarly, curiosity can motivate us to approach

dissonant material. Thus, we do not "stick our heads in the sand" and avoid all possibly upsetting (dissonant) information. On the other hand, Wicklund and Brehm conclude that when these factors (usefulness, curiosity, and

subjects have performed a new behavior that enters into their dispassionate analysis of their relevant actions. In the same way that we normally infer other people's attitudes from their overt actions (what they say and do), Bem argues that we infer our own attitudes from what we have said and done in the past.

Several studies have been conducted to test these competing explanations of the effects of induced compliance. Results have been equivocal, however, with some experiments supporting dissonance theory (for example, Green, 1974; Ross & Shulman, 1973) and others supporting self-perception theory (for example, Snyder & Ebbesen, 1972). One finding that clearly supports dissonance theory over self-perception theory is that induced compliance appears to arouse aversive, unpleasant tension or discomfort (Zanna & Cooper, 1976). Thus, negative affect seems to play a role in the effects of counterattitudinal behavior on attitudes.

There is a third possible explanation, however. Tedeschi, Schlenker, and Bonoma (1971) have proposed an **impression management theory** of attitude change. These authors argue that we are socialized to want to appear consistent to others. As a result, subjects experience evaluation apprehension when they are induced to behave counterattitudinally. That is, they are apprehensive about what the high-status experimenter will think of them after they have behaved in a way that is inconsistent with their attitudes. To avoid possible negative evaluations by the experimenter, subjects make themselves appear consistent by reporting attitudes that are in accordance with their behavior. Thus, these authors suggest that induced compliance does not produce real attitude change at all. Instead, subjects are merely trying to manage the experimenter's impression of them by making themselves appear consistent. In support of this reasoning, Gaes, Kalle, and Tedeschi (1978) found that when the bogus pipeline was used to measure subjects' attitudes (see Social Focus 4.1), induced compliance did not produce attitude change.

How can these various explanations of the effects of induced compliance be reconciled? It seems likely that all are true in some situations. Dissonance theory, self-perception theory, and impression management theory all have intuitive plausibility and some empirical support. One proposed integration comes from Fazio, Zanna, and Cooper (1977), who suggested and found evidence that behavior that is only slightly discrepant from one's attitudes produces attitude change that is mediated by self-perception, whereas behavior that is highly discrepant from one's attitudes produces dissonance-mediated change. Thus, no single theory is likely to "triumph" over the others; the task that faces researchers is determining each theory's proper domain of application.

so forth) are controlled or taken into account, the available evidence strongly supports the idea that we actively seek out consonant information. These authors do not believe that active avoidance of dissonant information has been conclusively demonstrated, although some evidence does exist for this half of the selective-exposure hypothesis (for example Mills, 1965). Finally, there is evidence that personality variables may influence the extent to which people manifest selective exposure (Olson & Zanna, 1979). Taking personality into account may help to resolve some of the inconsistent findings.

Problems With Dissonance Theory

Dissonance theory has stimulated a tremendous amount of research and has led to a variety of interesting applications. Nevertheless, several problems have been encountered in testing the theory. First, it is difficult to obtain a precise measure of dissonance motivation. The theory postulates that certain conditions will produce uncomfortable tension, but quantifying the tension has proved difficult. Part of this problem relates to the fact that it is impossible to know all of the cognitive elements that may be relevant (either consonant or dissonant) to a particular element in a person's mind.

Second, dissonance theory does not allow precise predictions of how dissonance will be reduced—whether an individual will change a dissonant cognition, add consonant cognitions, or change the importance of cognitions. This has made the theory rather elusive with regard to disconfirmations.

Finally, the theory does not take into account individual differences in sensitivity to dissonance, tolerance for dissonance, or preferred modes of reducing dissonance (Shaffer, 1975); yet people probably differ on all of these dimensions. For example, many of us can tolerate quite comfortably minor inconsistencies in our beliefs and attitudes; thus, it is not clear that everyone (or even anyone all of the time) is as concerned about consistency among cognitions as dissonance theory would suggest.

FUNCTIONS OF ATTITUDES

Balance theory and dissonance theory seem to suggest that it is relatively easy to change people's attitudes: make them aware of inconsistencies among their beliefs, or induce them to behave counterattitudinally, and their beliefs and attitudes will change to restore consistency. Yet our intuitions and experience tell us that attitude change is not so easy to produce—in fact, it is often very difficult to change people's opinions. Two other theories are more consistent with our intuitions and help explain why people's attitudes are not always malleable.

Katz's (1960) **functional approach** to attitudes is one of these theories. Katz argues that an individual's beliefs and attitudes meet important needs—that is, attitudes perform certain functions for the individual. Consequently, attitudes will often be resistant to change.

Katz identifies four functions of attitudes. Many of our attitudes form as a result of the rewards and punishments we have received for past actions. Such attitudes perform an *instrumental* function: they help us to maximize future rewards and minimize future punishments. For example, you may develop a favorable attitude toward someone who is kind to you; your positive attitude will induce you to continue interacting with this person, which will in turn increase your rewards.

Attitudes can also perform a *knowledge* function, by helping us to understand and interpret events that would otherwise be difficult to explain. For example, one nation's hostile actions against another may be rendered more understandable by the attitude that the people are bad.

A third function is to protect individuals from admitting to themselves basic, uncomplimentary truths. These *ego-defensive* attitudes protect the person's self-esteem or self-concept. For example, racial prejudice may give insecure people a sense of superiority.

Finally, attitudes can perform a *value-expressive* function. Value-expressive attitudes allow individuals to express their uniqueness, identity, and values. Roman Catholics, for example, may adopt attitudes expressed by the Pope to indicate their devotion to the church.

An important aspect of Katz's analysis is that the same attitude can perform different functions for different people. For example, imagine that three students have negative attitudes toward the same course. One student's negative attitude may form because the course seems boring (punishing)—thus performing an instrumental function. In the second case a negative attitude may form because the student cannot understand receiving a low grade. To make sense of this unusually poor performance, the student decides that the course is a bad one; thus this attitude performs a knowledge function. The third student, who also did poorly, may form a negative attitude because of a suspicion (perhaps subconscious) that he or she is a poor student. To avoid admitting this uncomplimentary truth, the student decides that the course is boring and unfair; this attitude performs an ego-defensive function.

A functional approach to attitudes helps to explain why attitude change is often difficult. According to the theory, to change someone's attitudes, you must address the needs that the attitudes satisfy. For example, instrumental attitudes can be changed only by providing new rewards or punishments, while removing the old contingencies. Attitudes that fulfill a knowledge function can be changed only by providing alternative ways of understanding the confusing events. Ego-defensive attitudes are probably the most difficult type to change. It can be done only if the underlying threat or insecurity is removed. And finally, value-expressive attitudes can be changed only by changing the underlying values or by making the person aware that the attitudes do not really fit with the values.

Thus, Katz's model suggests that simply providing new information (beliefs) will rarely be enough to change people's attitudes. His approach also implies that balance theory and dissonance theory overestimate the impact of minor inconsistencies on attitude change. A functional perspective on attitudes therefore provides a useful contrast to the theories discussed earlier.

In this context, we should mention an interesting technique known as **value confrontation** (Rokeach, 1968, 1973), which contains elements of both the consistency models and the functional approach to attitudes. This technique is designed to induce people to change the importance they place on certain values and thereby to affect their behavior. It is relevant to the functional approach because it is directed at basic, underlying values (similar to value-expressive attitudes); it utilizes a strategy, however, that is more compatible with the consistency models.

In essence, value confrontation involves convincing subjects that the priorities they assign to certain values reflect uncomplimentary truths about themselves. For example, Rokeach (1973) asked university students to rank-order 18 values, including freedom and equality, from most to least important. Most subjects ranked freedom higher than equality. Rokeach then suggested to the students that their rankings showed that they were more concerned about their own freedom than about the freedom of others. Notice that this interpretation was designed to make salient an inconsistency within the participants' value systems. Postexperimental follow-ups showed that this confrontation resulted in a restructuring of the values (with equality being ranked higher than it had been before) and, more interestingly, in a greater response rate to a letter soliciting help for a civil rights organization. This latter, behavioral measure was taken three to five months after the value confrontation, which makes the findings even more impressive.

Thus, basic values (and relevant behaviors) can be affected by carefully designed strategies. Rokeach's value-confrontation technique provides a nice example of how different theoretical perspectives can be integrated productively.

When people are highly ego-involved in an issue, such as abortion, it is very difficult to change attitudes.

Problems with the Functional Approach

Although Katz's theory has many interesting implications (see Kiesler, Collins, & Miller, 1969, and Oskamp, 1977, for good discussions of the functional approach), it has not generated much research. There is one primary reason for the paucity of experimental investigations of attitude functions: no effective techniques for measuring the functions have been developed. At the present time, there are no clear guidelines for determining which function an attitude performs for an individual. Moreover, an attitude could potentially perform more than one function for the same person, making the measurement problem even

more complex. Obviously, a theory cannot be tested if its central concepts cannot be accurately measured. Thus, the functional approach, while intuitively appealing, must await the development of satisfactory measurement techniques before it can be expected to have much impact on attitude change research.

SOCIAL-JUDGMENT THEORY

Another theory that helps to explain why it is often difficult to change people's attitudes is Sherif and Hovland's (1961) **social-judgment theory.** This theory (as well as the approach described in the next section) is primarily concerned with the effects of persuasive *messages* on attitudes, rather than with the *self-persuasion* processes that were emphasized in the earlier theories. That is, whereas balance theory and dissonance theory emphasize the effects of individuals' awareness of inconsistencies in their beliefs and attitudes, social-judgment theory is primarily concerned with the impact of a persuasive message from some external source on an individual's opinions.

Social-judgment theory provides a unique perspective on attitudes and attitude change. Sherif and Hovland distinguish three separate regions that can be located along any attitude dimension—called **latitudes**—that differ in their acceptability to the individual. The *latitude of acceptance* is the range of positions on the attitude issue or scale that the person finds acceptable or agreeable. The *latitude of rejection* is the range of positions that the person finds unacceptable or objectionable. The *latitude of noncommitment* constitutes those positions that the person finds neither acceptable nor objectionable.

Thus, social-judgment theory recognizes that our responses to statements about an issue depend on our own attitudes. If a statement is reasonably congruent with our own view, then we will probably find it acceptable; if it and our attitude are somewhat discrepant, then we may find it neither acceptable nor objectionable; and if it and our belief are highly discrepant, then we will probably reject it.

Sherif and Hovland also propose that when we hear a statement that falls within our latitude of acceptance, we interpret it as being even closer to our own view than it really is. This phenomenon is labeled **assimilation**—we "assimilate" acceptable statements toward our own position. On the other hand, when we hear a statement that falls within our latitude of rejection, we interpret it as being even further from our own view than it really is. This phenomenon is labeled *contrast*—unacceptable statements are seen as being even

more different from our own position than they really are.

How can this theory help to explain why it is often difficult to change people's attitudes? Here, we need to consider the final important aspect of Sherif and Hovland's formulation: The effects of *ego-involvement.* Ego-involvement refers to the importance of an attitude or issue to the individual. Thus, high ego-involvement means that the person is very committed to or involved with the issue. Note that the meaning of ego-involvement is different from that of ego-defensive attitudes, described in the last section. Ego-defensive attitudes protect the person from admitting some uncomplimentary personal truth. Ego-involvement does not refer to the function that an attitude performs, but to how important the attitude is to the person.

Social-judgment theory postulates that highly ego-involved persons have larger latitudes of rejection (that is, find more positions unacceptable) than do people who are less ego-involved. Since the latitude of acceptance remains about the same size irrespective of ego-involvement (Sherif, Sherif, & Nebergall, 1965), this means that the latitude of noncommitment becomes smaller as ego-involvement increases. In addition, highly ego-involved persons are hypothesized to assimilate and to contrast more strongly than less ego-involved persons. That is, ego-involvement increases the tendency to interpret acceptable statements as being closer to one's own position than they really are and to see unacceptable statements as being further from one's own position than they really are.

Figure 5.2 illustrates these postulated effects of ego-involvement, showing why it is difficult to change the attitudes of highly involved persons. A message that advocates a position within the target person's latitude of rejection will be rejected and therefore produce no attitude change. Since highly ego-involved persons have large latitudes of rejection (see the "High involvement" box in Figure 5.2, they will reject most messages. Further, since highly

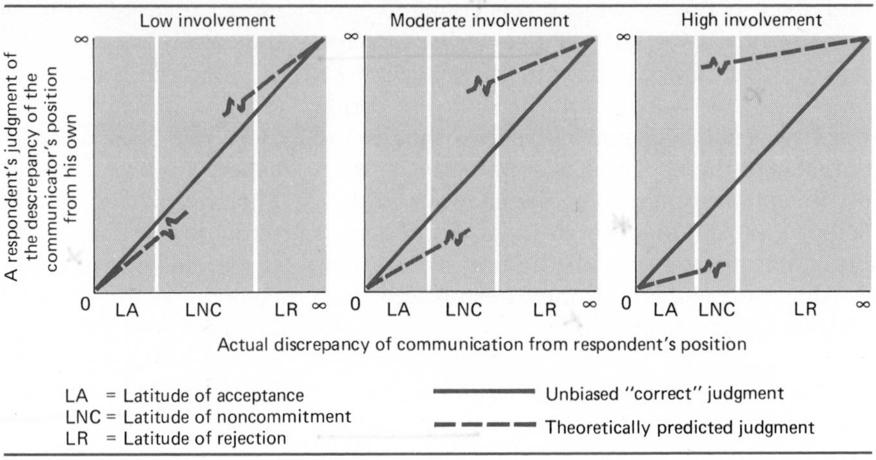

FIGURE 5.2
Postulated effects of ego-involvement on latitude widths and perception of messages (assimilation/contrast).
Source: Kiesler, Collins, and Miller, 1969, p. 247.

ego-involved persons assimilate strongly (note that the dotted lines differ more markedly from the solid line in the "High involvement" box), they will tend to see messages within their latitude of acceptance as advocating basically their own views and will feel no pressure to change their attitudes. When a message advocates a position within the target's latitude of acceptance, it will produce attitude change only if it is seen as advocating a position that is at least somewhat different from the attitude the person presently holds, an unlikely possibility for highly ego-involved people.

Thus, the only way to produce much change in the attitudes of highly ego-involved persons, according to social-judgment theory, is to present a message that advocates a position within their latitude of noncommitment. Presumably, such messages will be neither rejected nor assimilated to the person's own position and will therefore motivate attitude change. But highly ego-involved persons have very small latitudes of noncommitment; consequently, even this strategy may fail, since it will be difficult to tailor a message to fall precisely in the correct location.

As this analysis shows, social-judgment theory provides a good explanation of why attitude change in the real world is often difficult. Whereas laboratory experiments typically

focus on attitudes that are not particularly important to the individual, attempts to change people's attitudes in the real world are usually directed at involving issues. That is, we usually want to change the opinions of people who are highly ego-involved (for example, individuals who are prejudiced or who disagree with us on important issues such as abortion and capital punishment). In such circumstances, our targets have a large latitude of rejection, a small latitude of noncommitment, and assimilate strongly within their latitude of acceptance. As a result, our persuasive messages are unlikely to produce attitude change.

Experiments conducted to test predictions from social-judgment theory have yielded rather inconsistent findings. Although the majority of studies have supported the theory (for example, Freedman, 1964; Miller, 1965; Rhine & Severance, 1970), nonsupportive results have also been reported (Petty & Cacioppo, 1979; Rule & Renner, 1968). From our perspective, the most important aspect of social-judgment theory is that it provides a plausible explanation for the effects of ego-involvement, a factor that makes attitude change in the real world more difficult. Thus, the theory fits nicely with our intuitions about real-world attitude change, in contrast with some of the earlier theories.

One interesting application of social-judgment theory is reported by Varela (1971), who has designed systematic strategies for changing people's attitudes outside the laboratory. Varela argues that it is important to "feel out" your target person's latitudes of acceptance, noncommitment, and rejection, so that you can tailor your persuasive appeals to fall within appropriate boundaries. We recommend Varela's book; it is an intriguing application of social psychological principles to real-world persuasion situations.

Problems with Social-Judgment Theory

Social-judgment theory provides a unique perspective on the structure of attitudes (involving the three latitudes) and on how persuasive messages are perceived (assimilation versus contrast). Nevertheless, it has been sharply criticized. First, the theory lacks precision. It is difficult to make specific predictions about attitude change because many variables that might be important (for example, the relationship between the source of the message and the target person) are not considered in the theory. This lack of precision results partly from the fact that the theory is quite narrow in its scope.

Second, some of the findings that have apparently supported the theory can be interpreted in other ways. Thus, there is debate about whether social-judgment theory's explanations for the findings are valid. For example, the classification of subjects into high- and low-ego-involvement groups often confound attitude extremity with ego-involvement—highly involved subjects have more extreme attitudes. This confounding is problematic for interpreting the results clearly (see Kiesler et al., 1969).

As a result of these problems, social-judgment theory has had less impact on researchers than other approaches, including the consistency models described earlier. Nevertheless, Sherif and Hovland's formulation is intuitively appealing and, with some modifications, may yet provide a more precise framework.

THE YALE COMMUNICATION RESEARCH PROGRAM

The final approach to attitude change that we will consider is not really a theory at all. Rather, it consists of a comprehensive program of research conducted at Yale University in the 1940s and 1950s, led by such prominent psychologists as Carl Hovland, Irving Janis, Harold Kelley, and Muzafer Sherif. These researchers, interested in specifying the factors that affect the success of a persuasive message, conducted a large number of studies that carefully manipulated specific aspects of the persuasion situation and looked at the effects of the manipulations on attitude change. Their work was not designed to develop a systematic theory of attitude change. Instead, the program can be viewed as a collection of experiments that addressed different questions about persuasion and provides, overall, a wide-ranging analysis of this phenomenon.

The theme of the Yale Communication Research Program can be summarized by a single question: Who says what to whom with what effect? The "who" in this question is the *source* of the message; "says what" refers to the *message itself*; "to whom" is the *audience* or target of the message; and "with what effect" refers to the *impact* of the message on the audience. The Yale researchers investigated the characteristics of each of these factors that influence persuasion. We summarize below some of the general trends in these studies (see McGuire, 1969, for a more complete review).

Source Characteristics

What kinds of communicators are most likely to be successful? Perhaps not surprisingly, research has shown that attractive, likable, similar, and familiar sources are generally

SOCIAL FOCUS 5.2
The Sleeper Effect: Source Credibility and Attitude Change Over Time

Several experiments in the Yale Communication Research Program (for example, Hovland & Weiss, 1951; Kelman & Hovland, 1953) found evidence of a fascinating interaction between source credibility and the passage of time in attitude change. Specifically, these studies showed that although messages from high-credibility sources produce more *immediate* attitude change than do messages from low-credibility sources, *over time* the effects of source credibility on attitude change disappear. That is, the amount of attitude change produced by high-credibility sources decreases over time (as would be expected due to forgetting of the material), whereas (and here lies the controversy) the amount of attitude change produced by low-credibility sources actually increases over time. This latter effect for low credibility sources has been termed the **sleeper effect:** attitude change increases as subjects "sleep" on the message.

The explanation proposed for the sleeper effect involves two processes: *discounting* and *dissociation.* Initially, subjects discount the message because it comes from a low-credibility source and thereby suppress any attitude change that might have resulted from the message itself (that would have occurred if subjects had known nothing about the source's credibility). Over time, however, subjects forget who provided the information. That is, the source and the message become dissociated in memory. As a result, the message produces delayed attitude change because the discounting cue (low source credibility) is no longer paired with the message content.

This hypothesis is interesting because it predicts an unexpected increase in persuasion over time. At the same time, the explanation has intuitive appeal—it is often very difficult to remember where or from whom we heard something.

Unfortunately, some researchers have been unable to find evidence of a statistically significant increase over time in attitude change following a message from a low-credibility source. Gillig and Greenwald (1974), for example, report seven experiments that failed to show significant sleeper effects.

We would be forced to conclude that the sleeper-effect hypothesis is invalid, therefore, except for a recent paper by Gruder, Cook, Hennigan, Flay, Alessis, and Halamaj (1978). These authors point out that several conditions are necessary for the sleeper effect to occur, that statistical tests of the effect must have adequate power, and that forces that can counteract sleeper effects must be minimized. The details of their analysis are beyond the scope of the present chapter. An illustrative point, however, is that researchers should obtain evidence to show that over time subjects have, in fact, forgotten the credibility of the source. Otherwise, the sleeper effect cannot be expected to occur.

In two experiments, Gruder et al. show that when the necessary conditions are met, when adequate statistical tests are used, and when counteracting forces are minimized, statistically significant sleeper effects can be demonstrated. Thus, although sleeper effects are limited in the sense that particular (and rather stringent) conditions must be met, it seems that the original arguments of the Yale researchers concerning this interesting finding were valid, after all.

more successful at producing attitude change than are unattractive, disliked, dissimilar, and unfamiliar sources. The source characteristic that has received the most attention, however, is *credibility*. Credibility consists of two components: expertise (amount of knowledge) and trustworthiness (lack of intention to manipulate or to deceive the audience—that is, lack of ulterior motives). Although credible sources generally produce more attitude change than noncredible sources, there is some debate about the roles of expertise and trustworthiness in these effects. Findings indicate clearly that expertise is important; trustworthiness, however, seems to be important in some circumstances, but not in others.

Eagly, Wood, and Chaiken (1978) have proposed an attribution analysis of source credibility. Essentially, they suggest that listeners form expectancies about the likely position that a communicator will espouse, based on their perceptions of the communicator's values and the situational pressures. If the anticipated position is subsequently espoused then the communicator will be seen as biased (noncredible), and little attitude change will occur. If, on the other hand, listeners' expectancies are disconfirmed (that is, the communicator argues for an unexpected position), then he or she will be seen as credible, and greater attitude change will result. This research demonstrates nicely that source credibility is not a static quality; perceived credibility involves an interplay between the source's characteristics and the audience's expectancies.

The most controversial effect of source credibility on attitude change concerns its effects over time. Social Focus 5.2 addresses this controversy.

Message characteristics

How should a message be organized and presented to have the most impact? For example, should a speaker present both sides of the issue or only his or her own side? If both sides are presented, which should go first? Is it a good idea to state the conclusions explicitly, or is it better to let audience members draw their own conclusions? Should the message be repetitive? And so on.

There are no absolute answers to these questions. For example, one-sided versus two-sided messages are differentially effective with people who are initially favorable versus initially unfavorable toward the speaker's position. One-sided communications do more to strengthen the opinions of initially favorable listeners than do two-sided messages. On the other hand, two-sided messages are more effective than one-sided messages at changing the attitudes of initially unfavorable listeners (Hovland, Lumsdaine, & Sheffield, 1949). In addition, two-sided messages are less likely to be seen as biased or manipulative (Jones & Brehm, 1970).

One of the most interesting issues concerning message characteristics is whether or not "scare tactics" are effective. Will a message have more impact if it arouses fear in the listeners?

Studies exploring this question have yielded conflicting results (see Higbee, 1969, for a review). Some researchers have found that a highly fear-provoking message produces less attitude or behavior change than a low-fear message (for example, Janis & Feshbach, 1953), whereas other researchers have found that a high-fear message is more effective (for example, Leventhal & Singer, 1966). Faced with these contradictory results, theorists have tried to identify the psychological processes that mediate the effects of fear on attitude and behavior change.

McGuire (1969) has argued that a fear-provoking message reduces the audience's desire to pay attention (since it is aversive), but simultaneously increases their willingness to accept the speaker's recommendations (since they do not want to suffer the consequences that are described in the message). These po-

We are continually bombarded by attempts to influence our attitudes, beliefs and behaviors. Many of the American oil companies have directed much of their advertising toward influencing us on environmental issues.

tentially competing effects of fear arousal may explain the inconsistent results in past studies. McGuire further suggests that a curvilinear relation exists between fear arousal and persuasion: moderate levels of fear will produce more attitude change than low levels, but extremely fear-provoking messages are so aversive that people will avoid them and will not change their attitudes.

Rogers and Mewborn (1976) have taken a different approach. They suggest that there are at least three ways in which high fear may produce more compliance with a speaker's recommendations than low fear: (1) listeners may perceive that the depicted event (for example, lung cancer) is more serious, (2) listeners may believe that their susceptibility to the event is greater, and (3) listeners may be more convinced that the recommendations (for example, quitting smoking) will be effective in avoiding the event. In a careful set of experiments, Rogers and Mewborn found that fear increased subjects' intentions to comply with the speaker's recommendations by leading subjects to perceive the event as more serious. The effects of fear on intentions to follow the recommendations were not mediated by subjects' perceived susceptibility to the event or by their belief that the recommendations would be effective in avoiding the event. Interestingly, the more subjects believed that the recommendations would be effective in avoiding the event (whether subjects were fearful or not), the more they intended to follow those recommendations. This suggests that it is important to include specific directions in the message about how to comply with the recommendations—if people do not know exactly what they should do and why it will be effective, they are unlikely to change their behavior (see also Leventhal, Singer, & Jones, 1965).

Audience Characteristics

Are some people more easy to persuade in general than others? That is, ignoring differences that are specific to a particular attitude (for example, ego-involvement), are there stable differences between individuals in their persuasibility across all attitude domains?

Although many studies have explored this question, there is little evidence to support the hypothesis that people differ substantially in their persuasibility. For example, intelligence might seem to be a characteristic that should affect people's reactions to persuasive messages. Yet there is no consistent evidence that higher intelligence either increases or decreases persuasibility. McGuire (1968) suggests that intelligence may have two competing effects on persuasion that "cancel one another out." On the one hand, intelligent persons will be better able to understand the message and therefore appreciate its content. On the other hand, intelligent persons may be more critical and/or more confident of their own opinions, which will decrease their susceptibility. Thus, a straightforward relation between intelligence

and persuasibility should not be expected.

Some researchers (for example, Janis & Field, 1959) have found that females are more persuasible than males. The suggestion has been made that the socialization of females leads them to be more conforming and therefore more easily influenced (Hovland & Janis, 1959). In a recent comprehensive review of the literature, however, Eagly (1978) concludes that this generalization is inaccurate. Although some evidence (to be further discussed in Chapter 14) suggests that females are more responsive to group pressure than are males, there do not seem to be reliable sex differences in attitude change following a persuasive message. Thus, attempts to change the attitudes of females are probably no more likely to be successful than attempts to change the attitudes of males.

In summary, then, there is little evidence to suggest that some people are more persuasible in general than others. At least, researchers have been unable to identify any relevant characteristics, if they exist. Scales developed to measure persuasibility itself have generally evidenced only weak correlations with attitude change following subsequent influence attempts (for example, Linton & Graham, 1959). It seems likely that the effects of personality variables on persuasibility depend on other factors, such as the style of the message, the prestige of the speaker, and the complexity of the arguments in the message. Thus, large individual differences in persuasibility across attitude topics probably do not exist. Nevertheless, many audience characteristics that are specific to the particular attitude topic, such as familiarity with the issue, ego-involvement, and favorability to the speaker's position, do seem important (as mentioned earlier).

Effects of the Message

Hovland, Janis, and Kelley (1953) argued that to understand the impact of a persuasive message it is important to distinguish among five steps that must occur in the process of persuasion. These steps are *attention, comprehension, yielding, retention,* and *action* (see also McGuire, 1969). In order for a message to have the impact that the speaker intends, the audience must pay attention to the message, understand it, accept (that is, yield to) its arguments, remember or retain the content, and act on the new attitude. Failure to achieve one of these steps will mean that subsequent steps also will not occur.

The value of these distinctions is that they can provide a novel perspective on the effects of various factors on persuasion. For example, perhaps attractive sources are more effective in producing attitude change than unattractive sources because people pay more attention to attractive speakers. To take another example, source credibility may be important, at least in part because listeners will be more willing to yield to credible speakers. In similar fashion, it may be possible to analyze other factors that have been shown to affect the success of a persuasive message (for example, fear appeals, audience characteristics such as ego-involvement, and so forth) and locate the stages where they exert their impact. This perspective could potentially improve our understanding of the persuasion process by suggesting some of the mechanisms that may mediate the factors' effects on attitude change. In addition, awareness of the five steps can sensitize communicators to the importance of the audience's attention, comprehension, and so on, and thereby provide helpful clues about how best to maximize attitude and behavior change.

Problems with the Yale Communication Research Program

The major problem with the Yale Communication Research Program was stated early in this section: the experiments do not provide a systematic theory of persuasion. Although the studies are methodologically sound, they are directed toward specific persuasion questions rather than theoretical issues. As Brown (1965) puts it, "The work has been well done . . . but it lacks something of intellectual interest because the results do not fall into any compelling pattern" (p. 549).

Despite this limitation, the Yale program has had an important influence on subsequent attitude-change research. Perhaps its most important contribution has been that it demonstrated the value of an experimental approach to persuasion (Kiesler et al., 1969). At a time when controlled experimental work was not common in this area, the Yale researchers employed careful manipulations to examine the factors that might influence the success of a persuasive message.

CHANGING ATTITUDES ABOUT OUR ENVIRONMENT

What do these five theories of attitude change tell us about the possibility of changing people's attitudes toward environmental issues? A few examples will serve to illustrate the value of the theories. Before we begin, however, a few comments on how the theories relate to one another will probably be helpful.

The theories we have described provide quite different perspectives on attitude change. The consistency theories (balance and dissonance) postulate a motivation to maintain consistency among beliefs, attitudes, and behaviors, and explain attitude change in terms of the negative arousal that results from awareness of inconsistencies. The functional view postulates that attitudes satisfy important needs for the individual and that to change attitudes, one must provide alternative ways of satisfying these needs. Social-judgment theory distinguishes the latitudes of acceptance, noncommitment, and rejection, and postulates that messages that advocate positions within these latitudes will be differentially successful.

Finally, the Yale Communication Research Program, which is not really a theory, explains attitude change in terms of source, message, and audience characteristics.

Which of these perspectives is most valid? How can the conflicting approaches be reconciled? The answer to the first question depends on whom you talk to. Consistency researchers would vote for their approach, social-judgment researchers would vote for their perspective, and so on. It seems most likely that all of the theories are true to some extent or in some situations. Certainly, people are often bothered by inconsistencies and sometimes change their attitudes to restore consistency; certainly, attitudes sometimes protect our egos or express our values; certainly, assimilation and contrast occur, and ego-involvement affects attitude change. Although it may seem dissatisfying to conclude that all of the theories have value, this is probably the most reasonable conclusion, at least at the present time. Each theory provides a plausible explanation for some instances of attitude change. Taken together, we get a more complete view. Perhaps someday someone will develop an inclusive, comprehensive theory of attitude formation and change that integrates all of the perspectives. Fishbein and Ajzen's (1975) model is a step in this direction. Nevertheless, at the present time, each of the more limited theories that we have described has some unique value for explaining instances of persuasion. Humans are complex beings with many motivations and needs; it should not be surprising that the attitude-change literature includes an array of plausible perspectives.

An interesting distinction in the domain of attitude change has recently been suggested by Petty and Cacioppo (in press). These researchers have identified two separate categories of persuasion processes: persuasion via the central route, which occurs when a person is motivated to consider thoughtfully the relevant information, and persuasion via the peripheral route, which occurs when a person is not par-

ticularly concerned about the issue and when persuasion results from factors other than a careful consideration of the relevant information (for instance, because the person likes the source). When an individual is highly ego-involved with an issue, then persuasion will most likely occur via the central route; when involvement is low, then persuasion may occur via the peripheral route. Further, persuasion via the central route is likely to produce more enduring changes in attitudes than is persuasion via the peripheral route.

This distinction has received some empirical support (see, for example, Chaiken, 1980; Cialdini, Petty, & Cacioppo, in press) and seems to provide a valuable perspective on persuasion. It may be possible to examine the various theories of attitude change and determine whether they relate to persuasion via the central or the peripheral route; in turn, it may be possible to integrate the theories along a continuum of attitude-change phenomena. For example, Fishbein and Ajzen's (1975) theory of reasoned action seems to deal primarily with persuasion via the central route; on the other hand, much of the research conducted in the Yale program has examined persuasion via the peripheral route. It will be interesting to see whether or not this recent conceptualization is adopted widely by researchers in the next few years and fulfills its potential of providing an integrative framework within the persuasion literature.

Turning now to environmental attitudes, what are some of the implications of the theories that we have described? Let us provide two examples. Attitudes toward nuclear power plants are becoming polarized, as we discussed earlier. Taking a social-judgment perspective, it becomes apparent that changing people's attitudes toward nuclear energy is going to become more and more difficult. Simply put, people are becoming highly ego-involved with this issue. Conservationists are very concerned about the health risks of nuclear plants. On the other hand, industry officials have a lot to lose if nuclear power is abandoned. Government officials, who must satisfy the public's competing demands for energy and safety, are caught in the middle. Thus, this issue has all of the elements necessary for high ego-involvement.

Because people are becoming highly ego-involved, social-judgment theory predicts that their latitudes of rejection will grow and their latitudes of noncommitment will shrink. In addition, assimilation and contrast can be expected to occur more strongly within the appropriate latitudes. Thus, attitude change will become increasingly difficult. What this means is that we can probably expect some intense conflict and public debate about nuclear energy in the years to come, as the opposing "camps" become more and more committed. Social-judgment theory provides a convincing account of the course of divisive, involving issues such as nuclear energy.

What about environmental issues that are not as ego-involving? How can attitudes toward such issues be changed? Energy conservation provides one example. Although most people support the idea of conserving energy, many of us do not seem to have strong feelings (at least, not with respect to our own conservation behavior). How can we make people more concerned and thereby increase their energy conservation? Dissonance theory provides some ideas. For example, increasing people's public commitment to conservation (for example, via a petition) should change attitudes and behaviors to be more consistent with the advocated position. Similarly, if one could induce even minimal increases in conservation and subsequently emphasize the social value of such behavior, then attitudes and future behaviors should again shift toward the induced behavior. As we will see in the next section, programs derived from dissonance theory have, in fact, been successfully applied to the domain of energy conservation.

Thus, the theories described in this section seem applicable to environmental issues. Perhaps the reader can think of some possible applications of balance theory, the functional perspective, and the Yale Communication Research Program for changing attitudes in the environmental domain.

ATTITUDES AND BEHAVIOR

Throughout this chapter we have talked about the basic assumption that attitudes influence behavior; people's actions are assumed to reflect their feelings toward objects and issues. Much of the scientific interest in the attitude concept is based on this assumption. In this section we will examine the assumption directly by reviewing research that has studied attitude-behavior consistency.

In 1934, LaPiere published a paper that many attitude researchers found troubling. LaPiere had traveled throughout the United States with a young, well-dressed, Chinese couple, visiting more than 250 establishments, including restaurants, hotels, and "auto camps." They were refused service because of the couple's race at only one establishment. Six months later, LaPiere sent each establishment a questionnaire that included the question, Will you accept members of the Chinese race as guests in your establishment? Of the 128 establishments that returned the questionnaire (almost exactly 50 percent of those that were visited), only one answered yes, whereas 118 (92 percent) answered no. (Nine establishments said that it would depend on the circumstances.) Thus, the vast majority said that they would not serve Chinese customers, whereas LaPiere had already shown that they would.

What are we to make of this apparent inconsistency between reported attitudes and actual behavior? In fact, the findings are easily explained. Dillehay (1973) points out that the people who answered the questionnaires were very possibly not the same ones who served LaPiere and his Chinese companions at the establishments. Clearly, this circumstance could have led to the apparent inconsistency. Proba-

A classic study in social psychology showed that most restaurant owners would serve a Chinese couple even though their verbally expressed attitudes predicted that they would not. When do attitudes predict behavior accurately?

bly more important, however, is the fact that it is much easier to state in a questionnaire that one will not serve Chinese guests than it is to refuse to serve a well-dressed Chinese couple standing before you, accompanied by a white male. That is, the measure of attitude did not correspond to the behavioral measure in terms of the pressures of the situation, termed **situational thresholds** (Campbell, 1963). As Oskamp (1977) puts it, "Discrimination against members of another race is much harder in the face-to-face personal situation than in the abstract written-letter situation" (p. 228).

Thus, investigations of attitude-behavior consistency must equate the measures of atti-

tudes and behaviors in terms of situational thresholds. Many early studies did not satisfy this requirement. Wicker (1969) reviewed more than thirty studies that examined attitude-behavior consistency and found that the typical correlation between measures of attitudes and measures of behaviors was approximately .30, a fairly weak relation. Wicker concluded that there was "little evidence to support the postulated existence of stable, underlying attitudes within the individual which influence both his verbal expressions and his actions" (p. 75)—a discouraging conclusion, to be sure.

As we implied above, however, many of the studies reviewed by Wicker failed to equate their attitudinal and behavioral measures in terms of situational thresholds. Thus, these studies often did not provide a fair test of the ability of attitudes to predict behavior; they probably underestimated the actual correlation between feelings and actions. Further, there was yet another problem with many of the early studies on attitude-behavior consistency. To understand this problem, we must return to Fishbein and Ajzen's (1975) theory of reasoned action.

Fishbein and Ajzen's Model

Fishbein and Ajzen (1974, 1975; Ajzen & Fishbein, 1973, 1980) have argued that there has been a basic misconception inherent in most studies of attitude-behavior consistency. Fishbein and Ajzen's theory of reasoned action was presented in Chapter 4 (see Figure 4.2). These authors argue that the favorability of a person's attitude toward some object determines the overall favorability of the person's behavioral intentions with respect to the object. In turn, behavioral intentions predict actual behaviors.

The important aspect of this model for attitude-behavior consistency is that attitudes predict only the *overall* favorability of the *class* of behaviors toward the object. For example, your attitude toward another person will predict, according to Fishbein and Ajzen, how favorably you will act in general toward the person, but your attitude will not predict (at least, not nearly as well) *specific* behaviors toward the person (for example, whether you will offer to treat them to a cup of coffee). This argument reflects the fact that favorable (or unfavorable) attitudes can be manifested in many different ways. Thus, different people may act somewhat differently even when they hold similar attitudes. Presumably, however, such idiosyncratic differences should even out across the whole set of behaviors that are relevant to the object, and therefore attitudes will predict the

favorability of the class of actions more effectively.

To take an example from the environmental domain, people's attitudes toward conserving energy may not strongly predict specific conservation behaviors, but should predict the overall class of such behaviors. Thus, favorability toward energy conservation will be only weakly related to whether or not an individual rides the bus to work, turns down the thermostat at night, or buys a fuel-efficient car. When all of these behaviors (and others) are taken into account at the same time, however, attitudes toward conservation will be strongly related to the overall "conservationness" of the class of actions. These predictions were in fact supported in a study by Hope and Cozby (1981).

Fishbein and Ajzen correctly point out that most of the studies on attitude-behavior consistency reviewed by Wicker (1969) used measures of general attitudes toward an object to predict specific behaviors. That is, these studies assumed that general attitudes should predict specific actions, whereas the more appropriate view is that general attitudes predict the favorability of the class of behaviors toward the object.

Fishbein and Ajzen argue, therefore, that to provide a fair test of the attitude-behavior relation, **multiple-act behavioral criteria** must be used. Multiple-act behavioral criteria are simply measures of behavior that include a large number of actions toward the object. Such measures assess the overall class of actions relevant to an object, which is what attitudes should be expected to predict.

Many studies (for example, Fishbein & Ajzen, 1974; Weigel & Newman, 1976) have shown that measures of attitudes correlate highly (typically, .50 to .90) with multiple-act behavioral criteria, whereas the typical correlation between measures of attitudes and specific behaviors is much lower (around the .30 level noted by Wicker, 1969). For example, Zanna, Olson, and Fazio (1980) measured subjects' attitudes toward religion. These attitudes correlated weakly (.09 to .38) with subjects' reports of specific religious behaviors, such as attending religious services and praying in private. A multiple-act behavioral criterion, however, consisting of a questionnaire that assessed ninety actions relevant to religion, correlated more highly (.54) with subjects' attitudes.

Thus, attitudes do, in fact, predict behaviors. Our feelings about an object determine the general favorability of our class of actions toward it. The expectation that general attitudes should predict specific behaviors is unreasonable. When a more appropriate perspective on consistency is adopted, the existing evidence shows that people act in ways that are generally congruent with their attitudes.

Predicting Specific Behaviors

Two questions are raised by Fishbein and Ajzen's analysis of attitude-behavior consistency. First, if general attitudes toward an object do not predict specific behaviors toward that object, then how can specific behaviors be predicted (if at all)? Second, *why* are general attitudes only weakly related to specific behaviors? That is, what other factors besides attitudes determine our specific actions?

Fishbein and Ajzen (1974) present evidence that specific behaviors can be predicted by measuring people's attitudes toward the *behavior* itself. For example, whether or not individuals ride the bus to work may be predictable from their attitudes toward riding the bus to work, whereas their more general attitude toward energy conservation will not predict this specific behavior as strongly (as noted above). Thus, attitudinal and behavioral measures should be at the same *level of specificity:* attitudes toward specific behaviors will predict specific behaviors, whereas general attitudes toward objects will predict the overall favorability of the class of behaviors toward the ob-

jects (multiple-act behavioral criteria). Thus, even specific behaviors can be predicted. The problem with many past studies has been that they have failed to equate attitudinal and behavioral measures for level of specificity.

But why do general attitudes not predict specific behaviors? For example, why do attitudes toward religion not predict whether or not an individual will attend church on a particular Sunday? What factors other than attitudes are relevant?

Many researchers have identified nonattitudinal factors that can lead to apparent attitude-behavior inconsistency. (For discussions of some of these factors, see Calder & Ross, 1973; Fishbein & Ajzen, 1975; Oskamp, 1977; and Schuman & Johnson, 1976.) Five such factors are listed below.

1. **Competing attitudes and values.** Behaviors are often relevant to more than one attitude or value. For example, a student with a favorable attitude toward a course may also have a favorable attitude toward skiing, and so not attend class on some beautiful winter day.

2. **Lack of volitional control over the behavior.** Attitudes cannot predict behavior if the behavior is beyond the control of the individual. A drug addict may desperately want to conquer the habit, but be completely unable to do so.

3. **Lack of available alternative behaviors.** Attitudes cannot predict behavior if the individual has no alternatives. A student may hate statistics, but enroll in such a course (and attend regularly) because the student's program requires that course.

4. **Norms.** Often our behavior is guided by normative constraints rather than by our feelings. For example, we usually try to be polite to people, even those we dislike.

5. **Unforeseen extraneous events.** Obviously, unexpected occurrences can affect our performance of specific behaviors. We will not attend a party that we were looking forward to if we are sick or if our car breaks down that evening.

These nonattitudinal factors illustrate that behavior is not completely predictable from attitudes. This should not be surprising; behavior is not completely predictable from *anything*. The important point that we have tried to make in this section is that attitudes do affect behavior, and this can be observed when appropriate measures are used. Thus, the assumption that underlies social psychologists' interest in the attitude concept seems justified. By coming to understand attitudes, we will learn a great deal about why people behave as they do.

Individual Differences in Attitude-Behavior Consistency

There is evidence that some people act in accordance with their attitudes more than do other people, and that each of us acts more in accordance with some of our attitudes than with others. That is, there are variations in attitude-behavior consistency.

Let us first consider one individual difference that is specific to particular attitude domains. Several experiments (for example, Fazio & Zanna, 1978; Regan & Fazio, 1977) have shown that personal behavioral experience with an object increases attitude-behavior consistency. For example, Fazio and Zanna (1978) measured subjects' attitudes toward participating in psychological experiments. Some subjects had taken part in experiments before, others had not. Subsequently, subjects were given the opportunity to volunteer for future studies. Individuals who had participated in experiments before acted in accordance with their expressed attitudes (that is, volunteered for future studies if they had favorable attitudes, but did not volunteer for future studies if they had unfavorable attitudes), whereas those who had little or no previous experience as subjects manifested less attitude-behavior consistency. Thus this finding suggests that we act more in accordance with attitudes that are based on direct behavioral experience than we do with attitudes that are formed without the benefit of personal experience.

There is also evidence that some people behave more in accordance with all of their attitudes than do other people. That is, some people manifest more attitude-behavior con-

sistency across all attitude domains than do others. The personality construct of **self-monitoring** (Snyder, 1974, 1979) is relevant to this issue. Low self-monitors generally act in ways that are consistent with their internal states (attitudes, values, moods), whereas high self-monitors are more responsive to situational cues in making their behavioral choices. For example, low self-monitors typically "say what they think," whereas high self-monitors are more flexible (or, if you like, manipulative) in that their statements and behaviors will depend on the circumstances. As would be expected from these descriptions, low self-monitors manifest greater attitude-behavior consistency than do high self-monitors (Snyder & Swann, 1976; Snyder & Tanke, 1976; Zanna, Olson, & Fazio, 1980).

Thus, although attitudes influence everyone's behaviors to some extent, there are variations both between domains (for the same person) and between persons (across all domains) in attitude-behavior consistency. By taking these variations into account, a better understanding of the attitude-behavior relation should be possible.

Attitude-Behavior Consistency in the Environmental Domain

Do people's attitudes toward environmental issues predict their actions? That is, do people behave in accordance with their environmental attitudes? One relevant finding is provided by Bowman and Fishbein (1978). These authors attempted to predict voting behavior on a referendum about nuclear power plants in Oregon in 1976. The referendum asked citizens whether limits should be placed on the construction of nuclear power plants. Bowman and Fishbein sent questionnaires to 500 voters living in Portland, Oregon. The questionnaires assessed respondents' general attitudes toward nuclear power, their attitudes toward the specific act of voting yes on the referendum, their beliefs about the issues, and their intentions to vote yes on the referendum. Following the election, subjects were contacted and asked how they had actually voted.

The results strongly confirmed Fishbein and Ajzen's (1975) theory of reasoned action. For our present purposes, the most important finding was that attitudes toward voting yes predicted actual voting behavior very well (the correlation was .84). It is also interesting to note that general attitudes toward nuclear power predicted the specific act of voting less effectively, although the correlation was still substantial (.66).

Thus, attitudes in the domain of nuclear power do seem to predict relevant behaviors. But we have mentioned before that nuclear energy is a heated issue (no pun intended). What about energy conservation, where people often seem to express favorable attitudes without doing much to conserve energy themselves? Do attitudes predict actions in this domain?

Olsen (1981) has reviewed numerous studies that examined the ability of beliefs and attitudes to predict energy conservation. Surveys show that about half of all Americans believe that the energy problem is real and serious, and less than one-fourth are completely unconvinced of the problem. Further, consistent with Fishbein and Ajzen's (1975) theory of reasoned action, general attitudes toward the energy problem are not strongly associated with reported conservation behaviors, but beliefs about specific, personal consequences of using less energy predict behavioral intentions and behavior quite well. That is, individuals' attitudes toward specific behaviors (based on their beliefs about the personal consequences of those behaviors) are better predictors of intentions and actions than are more general attitudes. For example, people who anticipate experiencing negative, personal consequences from the energy crisis are more likely to report that they intend to conserve than are people who do not anticipate negative, personal consequences (Hass, Bagley, & Rogers, 1975). In a study that measured actual energy consumption (rather than intentions to conserve), Seligman, Kriss, Darley, Fazio, Becker, and Pryor (1979) found that individuals' beliefs about whether using less energy would affect their personal comfort constituted the best predictor of conservation, whereas more general beliefs and attitudes (for example, beliefs about the energy crisis) did not predict subjects' actions nearly as well. Thus, perceived personal consequences were again shown to be important.

These studies show that people's specific beliefs about, and attitudes toward, energy conservation do predict their behaviors. But is there any way to increase conservation directly? That is, can we affect behavior, rather than simply using beliefs and attitudes as predictors? This is a question of social engineering (that is, creating a desirable social environment), which has been addressed by a few researchers.

Pallak and Cummings (1976) contacted homeowners and asked them to participate in a study of energy conservation. Some subjects were told that the names of all participants in the study would be published in the local newspaper. Other subjects were told that their participation would be completely anonymous. A third group of homeowners served as a control group and were never actually contacted by the experimenter (their meters were simply read at the same times as those of the other, informed participants).

Results showed that the public commitment group used less energy than did the other two groups, who did not differ from one another. Thus, as would be predicted from dissonance theory, inducing subjects to commit themselves publicly to a position changed their behavior to be consistent with their commitment.

Seligman and Darley (1978) showed that simply providing feedback to homeowners about their energy use increased conservation. Two groups of homeowners participated in this experiment. One group was provided with meters, mounted outside their kitchen windows, which displayed the amount of electrical energy that was consumed that day. The second group was not provided with such meters.

Results showed that the homeowners who were provided with feedback consumed an average of 10.5 percent less electricity than did the no-feedback group. Thus, a constant reminder of energy use increased conservation.

The studies described in this section are encouraging because they show that attitudes influence behaviors in the environmental domain, and that socially desirable behaviors can be increased via relatively simple techniques that are derivable from existing theories. Thus, the findings from social psychological research can be applied to the important area of environmental attitudes and behaviors. We will return to the topic of environmental concerns in Chapter 17.

SUMMARY

Although the distinction between attitude formation and attitude change is rather arbitrary, researchers have proposed a variety of theories to explain how existing attitudes can be altered. Balance theory and dissonance theory are consistency models and focus on the effects of being aware of inconsistencies among one's beliefs, attitudes, and behaviors. The functional approach to attitudes postulates that attitudes satisfy important needs for the individual and that to change attitudes, one must provide alternative ways of satisfying these needs. Social-judgment theory focuses on whether an individual judges the position advocated in a persuasive message to be acceptable, unacceptable, or neither; the persuasive impact of the message is postulated to depend on how the message is perceived. Finally, the Yale Communication Research Program analyzes persuasion in terms of source, message, and audience characteristics.

Each of these theories has problems or limitations, as well as some unique value for explaining instances of attitude change. Taken together, they illustrate the complexity of the persuasion process and show that a variety of perspectives can usefully be applied to attitude change.

In order for the attitude concept to have much practical value, it must be shown to predict behavior. Although some studies have found apparent inconsistencies between people's expressed attitudes and their subsequent actions, many of these studies did not equate the attitudinal and behavioral measures in terms of situational thresholds and/or level of specificity. As Fishbein and Ajzen (1974, 1975) have pointed out, attitudes toward an object predict the overall favorability of the class of behaviors toward the object. When general attitudes are used to predict specific behaviors, many factors can lead to apparent inconsistency. Examples of such factors are competing attitudes and values, lack of volitional control over the behavior, lack of available alternative behaviors, norms, and unforeseen extraneous events. Thus, multiple act behavioral criteria should be used. Numerous studies have shown that attitudes predict such criteria very well.

SUGGESTED READINGS

Calder, B. J., & Ross, M. *Attitudes and behavior.* Morristown, N.J.: General Learning Press, 1973.

Varela, J. A. *Psychological solutions to social problems: An introduction to social technology.* New York: Academic Press, 1971.

Zanna, M. P., & Cooper, J. Dissonance and the attribution process. In J. H. Harvey, W. J. Ickes, & R. F. Kidd (Eds.), *New directions in attribution research* (Vol. 1). Hillsdale, N.J.: Lawrence Erlbaum Associates, 1976.

Zimbardo, P. G., Ebbesen, E. B., & Maslach, C. *Influencing attitudes and changing behavior* (2d ed.). Reading, Mass.: Addison-Wesley, 1977.

ATTRIBUTION THEORY

6

- Why Do We Make Attributions?
- Classifying Causal Attributions
- Information Used in Making Causal Attributions
- Effects of Causal Attributions
- Biases and Information Processing in Making Causal Attributions
- Summary

The desire to know why things happen and why people do the things they do seems to be an essential part of being human. We often ask ourselves why we did well or poorly on an exam or why someone did or did not ask us to a party. We also wonder about why other people do things. Why was Jerry so friendly to Mary? Or why was the teacher so mean to JoAnn yesterday? Children ask these types of questions, too. Many of us have seen young children asking why until their mothers reach the end of their knowledge or patience.

Attribution theory is the scientific study of these why questions. Attribution theorists generally assume that people act like scientists, constantly trying to make sense of their worlds and forming theories about why things happen in the ways they do. **Causal attributions** are the answers to these why questions. They serve as mediators between all the stimuli we encounter in our world—the things we see, hear, and touch—and the responses we make to these stimuli. These responses include our thoughts and feelings as well as our actions. Thus, we do not respond directly to the events around us. Instead, we respond to the meanings or interpretations we give these events, which are supplied, in part, by the attributions we make about the events.

Research on attributional phenomena became the most active area of social psychology in the 1970s. As a result of studying the attributions that people make in order to understand and organize their worlds, attribution theorists have come to understand the types of causes people refer to in different situations, some of the information used to formulate these attributions, and the consequences of making one type of attribution or another. Attribution theorists have also begun to understand the ways in which people's minds work as they consider causal questions. Other questions about how we can best measure attributions and when people make causal attributions (or whether they do) emerged from this research and stimulated further research. Rather than attempting a broad and detailed review, we will look at some of the basic findings of attribution theorists, especially as they relate to the question of how attributions affect what happens in the classroom. By necessity, this review will be selective. For further information about some of the specific developments in this area, we suggest additional readings at the end of the chapter.

Let us look at an example of how some attributional phenomena might operate in a hypothetical sixth-grade classroom (see Social Focus 6.1). The class has just taken a mathematics exam. As everyone expected, Ann and David did quite well, both getting 100 percent on the exam. When we ask why Ann and David did so well, everyone tells us that they are smart and always do well. David confirms this when we ask him. Ann, however, tells us that she studied very hard for the exam and that's why she did so well. Whom do we believe? Given that both Ann and David had studied for the exam, perhaps the most realistic attribution for both of them might have been that they did well because of effort *and* their high abilities. As attribution researchers, however, we would not be overly concerned with who is right. Instead, we assume that the causal attribution made by any particular individual reflects his or her view of the world, and has important consequences for behavior or reactions toward others. Thus, the fact that David focused more on his ability as a cause of his high grade probably reinforced his confidence in himself, while Ann would be less confident about the future and would feel that the only way she can continue to do well is to keep studying as hard as she did for this test.

This chapter is written by John S. Carroll and Irene Hanson Frieze.

SOCIAL FOCUS 6.1
Meet Your New Class

In order to demonstrate how some of the principles of attributions can be applied to real-life events, this chapter will take the classroom situation as an example. To make this example more concrete, we will consider a hypothetical sixth-grade classroom in a large urban school. The cast of characters in this classroom is deliberately assembled across performance, ability, race, and sex categories to illustrate attributional issues and empirical results. Some of these ideas help to explain the bases of stereotypic differences among types of people.

The main teacher in this classroom is Ms. King who has been teaching for a number of years. She is quite concerned with students doing their best in class and works hard to encourage the students she feels are interested in studying and learning. She has little patience with students who are not interested in school and who are disruptive in class. Mr. Jackson is a student teacher in the classroom. Like Ms. King, he is white, but their similarities end there. He cares most about making sure students develop a positive self-concept. Although he does not discourage academic performance, he certainly does not stress it. On the other hand, he is enthusiastic about athletics and urges his students to develop their skills in sports.

We will also be considering six of the students in this sixth-grade class. First, there is Ann. She is intelligent and helpful in class. She always does her homework and volunteers for extra projects. Debbie, by contrast, is not especially intelligent and rarely does her schoolwork. She is active in several clubs and enjoys her social life more than anything. Both Ann and Debbie are white. Michael is also white. Like Debbie, he rarely does his schoolwork. He also tends to "act up" in class and is only really happy when he is playing baseball or football. Several of his teachers, however, have suspected that Michael is really very intelligent, even though he does poorly in school. David is Jewish. He tries very hard in school. Good grades are important to him, since he wants to become a lawyer and he wants to go to a good undergraduate college. He and Ann often compete for the highest grades in the class. David, however, typically speaks up more in class than Ann. Barbara and William are both black. Barbara is quite intelligent and is good at basketball. She divides her time outside the classroom doing schoolwork and practicing for the girls' basketball team. William is an average student in the class, although he lacks self-confidence and tends to think of himself as less intelligent than he really is.

Attributions could lead to other consequences as well. On this particular exam, William and Debbie both failed, getting only 50 percent correct answers. When asked privately about why he did so poorly, William tells us that he really isn't very good in math and that this grade reflects his low ability. Debbie, on the other hand, admits that she really doesn't care about school at all and that she got a low grade because she was busy with planning a dance for her church group all week and had no time to study. As a consequence of his attribution of the grade to his low ability, William feels even more discouraged about ever doing

What explanations will these students give for their success or failure on the exam? In this chapter we will discuss attributions of this sort and explore their importance.

well and feels little if any motivation to study more for the next test. Debbie secretly believes that she could do well if she wanted to, but she just doesn't care about school. She suffers no loss of self-confidence after the exam. She may or may not study for the next one, depending on her social schedule at the time.

This example illustrates three key issues in the attributional approach. First, given any particular event, such as getting a high grade on an exam, people seem naturally to interpret the event in reference to plausible causes. The specific attribution that is made, however, depends not only on the event itself but also on what is known about the context of the event, knowledge about relevant past events, and personality or motivational factors that affect attribution. Both David and Ann got 100 percent scores on the exam, yet they attribute their performance to different factors, because David is confident of his high ability in mathematics, while Ann lacks this confidence and believes her efforts in studying were crucial. Other students, aware of Ann's consistently high performance, believe she is smart. Ann's sister, aware of Ann's study habits, might be more inclined to agree with Ann rather than Ann's classmates.

Second, attributions have a commonsense explanatory logic. As we have just seen, Ann, David, Debbie, and William all answered our questions about why they did well or poorly by telling us about one or two events or characteristics that could plausibly account for their results. They did not tell us about the hours they had spent watching Sesame Street at the age of two, nor did they mention their genetic heritage from their parents, even though scientific research has suggested that both of these factors may be important determinants of mathematics performance.

It appears that each culture has its own ideas about the basic reasons why things happen. Malinowski (1948) considers science, religion, and magic as alternative systems of belief that are directed at answering questions such as Where did we come from?, What happens when we die?, and Where does the sun go at night? These belief systems also provide categories of reasonable explanations for the why questions of concern to attribution theorists, questions such as Why does it rain? or Why did Mary's baby die? In some societies, a heavy rain is attributed to the rain god's being angry. In our society, we perceive the rain as being caused by movements of air masses.

Third, events will have different effects depending on the attributions made about the events. David attributed his success to his high

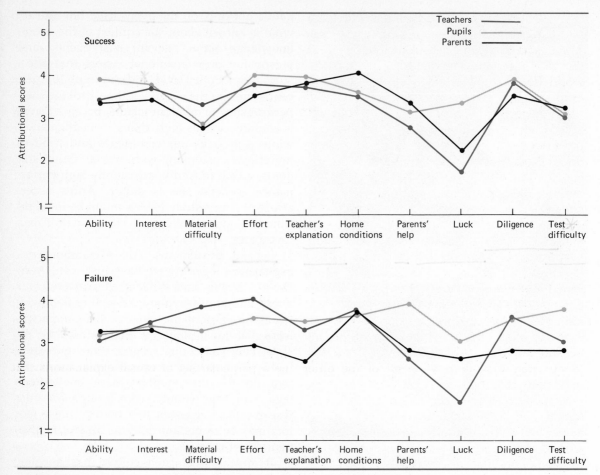

FIGURE 6.1
As demonstrated here in graphic form, teachers, pupils, and parents may make attributions for the same event—a pupil's grade in a mathematics course.

ability in math, so he feels very confident on the next test, and probably will be attracted to mathematical puzzles and further math classes. Ann attributes her success to hard work, and therefore is less confident than David about her future performance and may not seek out mathematical tasks. In both cases, the attributions for what is nominally the same event affect the self-concepts and future choices of these students.

WHY DO WE MAKE ATTRIBUTIONS?

In the situation we have just looked at, we asked people why they felt they had gotten a good or a poor grade. Obviously, one of the reasons for making an attribution is to answer a specific question. Some researchers believe that this is a major reason people make attributions and that without the instigating question, no attribution would be made (for example, Langer, 1979). Others believe that people are constantly making causal attributions in order to understand, predict and control their world (for example, Heider, 1958). According to this second point of view, students make attributions about their exam grades in order to predict what types of grades they can expect in the future and to know how to act in order to do well on future tests. Social Focus 6.2 discusses some of the issues in investigating attributions when the researcher does not ask the questions.

Recent research has suggested that people are more likely to make attributions about events that are unexpected or about failures (for example, Wong & Weiner, 1981). Thus, David may not consciously ask himself why he got another high grade on the math test. Since high grades are common for him, he may accept one more high grade as a fact of life, not questioning it. If Michael, however, got a high grade after doing poorly on all of the other math tests this semester, he and others might well question this unusual grade. In such a situation, an attribution to Michael's ability would be unlikely. Instead, Ms. King might suspect cheating or exceptionally good luck as the cause of Michael's grade. Michael, however, might say to himself that all of the studying he was able to do because of the bad weather and his having to stay home every afternoon was paying off. Similarly, if Barbara got a C instead of her usual A on the exam, she would be highly motivated to try to explain this poor grade, perhaps making an attribution to unfair grading of her exam, or her bad luck in not studying the right things. In short, the challenge to our ability to predict or control events may stimulate attributions.

In addition to the rational goals of prediction and control, people may also make attributions in order to enhance their self-image and feel better about themselves. Attributions are also made to justify our actions. Many peo-

ple may feel that Debbie's attribution for her low grade to her lack of interest may be a defensive attribution, which allows her to avoid thinking that she does not have much ability in mathematics. In general, there is a tendency to take credit for our successes and to avoid responsibility for our failures. We also tend to perceive the causes of events that benefit or harm people in ways that make the world less threatening to us. These types of "biases" in attributions will be discussed in more detail later in the chapter.

CLASSIFYING CAUSAL ATTRIBUTIONS

One of the first issues that must be resolved in studying causal attributions is how we conceive of the attributions themselves. As discussed earlier in the chapter, there appears to be a particular set of causal explanations that are relevant for any particular situation. This is true even if people disagree on the relative importance of various causal factors (see Figure 6.1). Thus, poor scores on classroom exams might be attributed to lack of ability, lack of effort, not being interested in the subject, not caring whether one does well, having a poor teacher, or unfair grading practices (Frieze & Snyder, 1980). Losing a football game might be attributed to some of the same factors: not having much ability to play football, not trying hard enough, not being interested in playing, or being refereed unfairly. In a sports situation, however, there are a number of other commonly used attributions, such as the other team being better, not being up for the game, or having the home-field advantage (Frieze, McHugh, & Duquin, 1976). Other lists can be developed for any situation. For example, crimes are committed because of drugs, alcohol, need for money, victim precipitation, influence of friends, mental problems, and so

SOCIAL FOCUS 6.2
Listening in on Causal Attributions

Attribution researchers typically measure attributions by asking subjects to produce ratings of causes, such as, How much was the event due to something about the actor? or ratings of dispositions, such as, How helpful is the actor?

A major problem with this approach is that asking for attributions may influence subjects' thought processes: subjects may make attributions only when asked to by the researcher (Enzle & Shopflocher, 1978), or they may use only certain attributional categories when these are provided within the question itself (Miller, Smith, & Uleman, 1981). It would certainly be helpful to observe attributions without heavy-handedly asking about them.

A possible strategy for observing attributions without biasing them uses a technique called _verbal protocols._ This technique was developed for the observation of mental processes in studies of problem solving and decision making (Ericsson & Simon, 1980; Payne, Braunstein, & Carroll, 1978). In these studies, subjects are given a task, such as solving a math problem, making a chess move, shopping in a store, or selecting an apartment. While they consider the information they have and make their judgments, they "think aloud" into a tape recorder about everything they see, read, or think about. The resulting verbal protocols are transcribed, coded, and used as indicators of the thought processes involved in doing the task.

The verbal protocol technique has been used to "listen in" on causal attributions without asking subjects to make attributions. Carroll and Payne (1977) wanted to know whether expert parole decision makers, whose job is to decide whether a prisoner should be released on parole or kept in prison, would try to determine _why_ the prisoner had committed criminal acts. They asked five experts from the Pennsylvania system to "think aloud" while they investigated actual case material from parole applicants.

The following excerpts are from a parole case that was being decided as the expert talked about his thoughts:

All right, well, the first thing I usually do is see what he's here on. Since it is a, you know, this guy's been convicted of burglary. Pled guilty to it.

Now this is not too bad. He broke a window and entered a food market. He left . . . with . . . a cardboard box containing 37 cartons of assorted cigarettes totaling so much money. So he stole a bunch of cigarettes, and, he did this with, uh, one other person. So, that is really not too bad . . . .

So, well, I wanna look at prior records to see if the present offense is along with other types of behavior . . . . But, both reports indicate that he hasn't been in trouble since '64 'til '75.

He indicated he was intoxicated at the time of the crime . . . . He also indicated to the counselor that when he found himself out of work that he started hitting the bottle. Which is . . . why there would be some alcohol abuse.

The difficulties that the guy had in the past, the records would show that it was due to alcoholism, you know. Uh, and since he's been here, uh, he has been participating in AA [Alcoholics Anonymous].

I think the area that we're gonna be concerned with, or the parole agent should be concerned with this man, is that of his alcohol problems.

The guy has the ability to be stable out there.

OK, you know, what he did was so, was done so impulsively, man. He was out, he had been drinking with this cat, and uh, they were drunk, and they needed cigarettes, and he went into this place and he got the cigarettes.

The alcohol is probably an escape to dealing with, uh, depressions or whatever. . . . You know, with superior intelligence—and he's not usin' it. . . . So— I would seek, I would seek therapy also in the areas of trying to get him to realize, you know, his capabilities.

We see in these excerpts several interesting features relevant to attribution theory. First, the expert attributes this crime to drunkenness, and further attributes past "difficulties" to alcoholism. Second, information about past events (prior record) is obtained, suggesting that criminal behavior is unusual for this man and therefore the crime is "impulsive" and the prisoner can be "stable" (crime-free) in society. Third, the alcohol use is itself attributed to his emotional reaction ("depressions or whatever") to losing his job. Finally, the response of the expert was to direct therapeutic efforts toward the attributed cause.

In subsequent research, Carroll (1978) asked Pennsylvania Parole Board members to fill out a questionnaire immediately following actual parole hearings. The questionnaire included an item requesting "opinions on underlying cause for offense committed." The most frequent causes given were alcohol-abuse problem, drug problem, long-term greed for money, sudden desire to get money, victim precipitation, drunk at time of crime, influence of associates, lack of control, mental problems, and domestic problems (these account for 75 percent of all causes). Consistent with the above example of a crime attributed to "drunk at time of crime," when the parole experts attributed a crime to an unstable, temporary cause, they considered the prisoner a better risk and were more likely to grant parole. When crime was attributed to a stable, enduring cause, the prisoner was seen as a poor risk and more likely to be denied parole.

This analysis of actual parole-board decisions indicates how important attributions can be. Without some idea about why the parole applicant had committed the crime, the board member would have much more difficulty making a decision and preparing a treatment plan.

forth (see Social Focus 6.2). Since these lists can become endless, most attribution theorists have, instead, looked for abstract underlying categories or dimensions that can be used to classify the specific causal attributions made by people in any situation. The three primary dimensions along which attributions have been classified are internality, stability, and controllability.

Heider (1958) first differentiated between

	STABLE	UNSTABLE
TABLE 6.1		
A Three-Dimensional Model for Classifying Commonly Made Causal Attributions for Doing Well or Poorly in School		

	STABLE	UNSTABLE
Internal—Factors in the Student Controllable	Diligence or laziness Long-term interests Intrinsic motivation	Trying hard or not trying Short-term interests
Uncontrollable	Ability Knowledge or background Personality	Fatigue Mood
External—Factors Outside the Student Uncontrollable	Difficulty of the subject Quality of teaching	Luck Outside interference

Source: Modified from Frieze, in press.

internal and **external** forces as causes of events. According to Heider, one of the earliest questions we ask about an event is whether it was caused by the person or not. As Heider saw it, when Michael, or anyone else, takes a test, his performance is a function of his *personal force* pitted against the *environmental force;* the greater his personal force, the higher his grade.

This distinction between personal causes internal to the actor and environmental causes external to the actor constitutes the fundamental causal dichotomy that has been investigated by attribution researchers. For example, Jones and Nisbett (1971) proposed that actors tend to attribute their own behavior to situational (external) causes while observers tend to attribute the actor's behavior to personal (internal) causes. According to this actor-observer hypothesis, if Debbie flunks an exam, Ms. King will tend to attribute her failure to her personality (she's lazy), while Debbie may attribute her low grade to an unfair test or other external factors, such as writing the test in a noisy room. Support for this hypothesis has been found in studies dealing specifically with classroom situations (for example, Miller, 1976).

Weiner and his coworkers (1971) recognized a second dimension, stability, underlying most attributions. This refers to how changeable or permanent causes are. For instance, a student's ability or the difficulty of a test are relatively **stable,** enduring causes. How hard students try (effort) and how successfully they guess on specific multiple-choice items (luck) are relatively **unstable,** or fluctuating causes of test performance.

A third dimension along which attributions can be classified is **controllability.** The causes of an event can be called controllable if the behaviors (or causes) leading up to the event are within the actor's capacity to manipulate. Thus, effort illustrates a controllable cause. Inasmuch as actors cannot dictate the environmental antecedents of events, external causal factors are usually noncontrollable.

Table 6.1 indicates how some of the commonly cited causes of academic performance can be classified along these three dimensions. All of these classifications, however, depend upon the context of the situation and the interpretation given to them by the perceiver. So, individual causes may sometimes appear in different cells than shown in the table.

INFORMATION USED IN MAKING CAUSAL ATTRIBUTIONS

A good deal of attribution research has been concerned with what information people use in making causal attributions. For example, in trying to decide why she got a poor grade, Barbara might think about how hard the test seemed, how well others had done on the test, how well she had done on other tests in the class, how much she had studied, and how she was feeling the day of the exam. People appear to use such information in rather consistent ways in deciding what causes performance. This section will review how some of these and other sources of information are used in forming causal attributions. We will also look at some of the differences among people in their use of various sources of information.

Information about This Event

The event we are attributing itself contains considerable information about plausible causes. Simple physical events are typically believed to happen because of some immediately preceding event that has been observed (Michotte, 1963; Siegler & Liebert, 1974). For example, lightning strikes a house and the lights in the house go off. We assume the lightning caused the lights to go off because of the temporal connection. If the lights went off one hour after the lightning we would not make such an attribution.

Observing students taking a math test provides some direct evidence about plausible causes. If David works rapidly, rarely erases anything, shows no overt signs of anxiety, and hands in the test early, we infer high ability. If William bites his pencil, continually erases and crosses out his work, frowns a lot, and hands in the test late, we infer low ability. It is obvious that the manner or style of behavior influences our interpretation of events. Sometimes we try to manipulate the impressions others have of us by pretending low effort or low anxiety or otherwise managing our overt behavior.

The event itself may suggest causes. For example, doing very well on an exam implies high ability, much more than doing very poorly implies low ability (Reeder & Brewer, 1979). Particularly brutal crimes imply mental illness in the criminal (Hendrick & Shaffer, 1975). Kruglanski and his colleagues (1978) and Carroll and Weiner (1981) have suggested that events evoke causal hypotheses that are checked for confirming information. In short, we know a lot about the likely causes of events simply from the nature of the event itself.

Jones and Davis (1965) proposed that attributions about the personal dispositions underlying intentional (chosen) actions would depend on an analysis of the effects or consequences of the chosen act compared to the effects of plausible alternative (nonchosen) acts. They define a **correspondent inference** as attributing an act to an underlying intention and disposition that is consistent with the act. For example, if Ann helps Mr. Jackson, a correspondent inference would attribute her helpful behavior to her intention to help, produced by her being a helpful person.

We tend to make a correspondent inference when there are fewer **noncommon effects** of the chosen act, effects that are unique to that act. For example, let us assume that in a few years Ann applies to several colleges and is accepted by three of them—Smith, Harvard, and the University of Chicago. According to Jones and Davis, in order to understand her final decision we would have to compare the effects of each decision. Table 6.2 summarizes some of the common and noncommon effects of each choice (adapted from Schneider, Hastorf, & Ellsworth, 1979, p. 50).

If we assume that the factors listed in Table 6.2 are Ann's most important criteria for decid-

	TABLE 6.2	
	Common and Noncommon Effects of a Decision to Attend a Particular College	

	SCHOOLS	
Smith	Harvard	University of Chicago
High academic reputation Scholarship available	High academic reputation Scholarship available	High academic reputation Scholarship available
Small town All female	Big city Coeducational	Big city Coeducational
Far from home	Far from home	Close to home
Father did not attend	Father attended	Father did not attend

Common effects combined in boxes; noncommon effects outside boxes.

ing which college to attend, then her choice tells us informative things about her. If Ann chooses Smith over the others, we attribute this action to those effects that are not shared with Harvard or the University of Chicago, such as location and composition of student body. But because there are two noncommon effects, we are not sure which is more important. If Ann chooses Harvard, we can be fairly certain that the noncommon effect of going to the same school her father went to is a determining factor, since it is the only effect not shared by the other schools. She may, however, have also wanted to go far from home but not to a women's college.

In a study supporting these ideas, Newtson (1974) presented scenarios in which students chose to "babysit for a professor" with either one or two effects of this choice, and either two or four effects "foregone" in nonchosen alternatives. The one noncommon effect always present was ingratiation with the professor. The student was judged more ingratiating when there was one noncommon effect of babysitting, rather than two, and when more effects were foregone in order to babysit. In ef-fect, we learn most about people when they choose an action for one reason and are uninfluenced by many other reasons.

Information about What Other People Did

Jones and Davis (1965) also proposed that noncommon effects that are socially desirable, or expected of everyone, are relatively uninformative and do not produce correspondent inferences. When the noncommon effects are unusual, however, or even socially undesirable, we learn something new and unique about a person. For example, choosing a school with a good academic reputation over schools with poor reputations gives us little insight into Ann, since nearly everyone would do that. If the noncommon effect were unusual, such as wanting an all-female school when most students desire coed schools, we make a stronger correspondent inference. As a second example, if a politician delivers a speech strongly favoring conservation and government regulation to a group of executives from major oil companies, we would make a correspondent infer-

When people act consistently with our stereotypes (or category-based expectancies), we often have attributions which spring instantly to mind without much thought or analysis of their behavior.

ence that these views represent personal convictions.

Kelley (1967) included a similar idea in his theory of the attribution process. He defined **consensus** as the degree to which behavior is similar across people. If others behave similarly, the act has high consensus; if others behave differently, the act has low consensus. High consensus suggests a stimulus attribution: if everyone gets an A on a test, the test must have been easy. Low consensus is a more vague cue that could imply a person attribution (David is the only one who got an A, because he is smart) or a circumstance attribution (David was lucky) or a more complex attribution (David studied the right material).

According to the Weiner et al. (1971) analysis of achievement events, consensus is of particular importance for assessing task difficulty. The distribution of test scores indicates how hard the test was and, more specifically, how

hard it would be to get any particular score. Research on achievement situations has confirmed that if everyone does well or poorly on a test, attributions are made to a situational factor such as the test or the teacher (Frieze & Weiner, 1971). This means that William would not change his low assessment of himself if we gave him an easy exam on which he could do well. As soon as he found out that everyone else did well too, he would simply make the realistic attribution that the task was easy. This same process may occur for the mentally retarded or for those with learning disabilities. If they realize that they are being given easy tasks to do, they will not attribute their successes to themselves and therefore will not take responsibility for them or even feel particularly good about doing well (Gold & Ryan, 1979).

A particularly important type of consensus information is what Jones and McGillis (1976) call category-based expectancies. These are essentially stereotypic ideas of how categories of people behave. We have expectations for males, females, whites, blacks, youths, aged people, students, jocks, Catholics, Jews, computer-science majors, business majors, librarians, blondes, and so forth. When an individual behaves consistently with the stereotype, we may make a "snap attribution," relating this behavior to the stereotype. Only if our expectancies are violated do we do more thoughtful attributional analyses to gain unique information (correspondent inferences) about the person. Thus, a black student at the top of his class or a female math whiz should prompt more attributional analysis than more stereotypic events (when the observer holds these stereotypes, of course).

Information about the Actor's Past Behavior

Kelley (1967) posited that attributors find information about an actor's past behavior highly informative for interpreting present behavior. He labels past instances of the same behavior toward the same stimulus object **consistency**. Behavior toward different stimulus objects he labels **distinctiveness** information. Jones and McGillis (1976) have also discussed this information, which they consider produces target-based expectancies.

For example, suppose that Mr. Jackson praises Barbara for her coursework after she does well on an English test. If Mr. Jackson has praised Barbara often in the past, his behavior is high in consistency. But if he has rarely praised Barbara, it is low in consistency. If he has praised only Barbara, his behavior is high in distinctiveness, because it is specific to Barbara. If he praises other students, however, his behavior is low in distinctiveness.

Research on achievement situations has indicated that performances that are consistent with our expectations result in attributions to stable factors such as ability and task difficulty.

(These, of course, mean there will be no change in expectations for the future.) Performances that deviate markedly from expectancies lead to unstable attribution, particularly luck, and therefore to little change in expectation. Events are often explained away if they do not fit our expectations. Only performances moderately different from expectancies will bring into question our estimates of ability and our expectancies for the future (Valle & Frieze, 1976).

Kelley also proposed that if we wish to determine why a particular event occurred, and if we have information about past behavior (Kelley, 1971), then we will systematically analyze three sources of information: consistency, distinctiveness, and consensus. His **Covariation Principle** (Kelley, 1967) assumes that the event is attributed to the factor with which it covaries, and that the possible causal factors are the person, the stimulus object, and the circumstances.

To see how the covariation principle operates in a particular example, let us again consider the situation in which Mr. Jackson praises Barbara. As shown in Figure 6.2A, when there is high distinctiveness (Mr. Jackson does not typically praise all the students), high consistency (Mr. Jackson has praised Barbara before), and high consensus (others praise Barbara too), the typical attribution that would be made by anyone having this information is that the cause of the praise is Barbara (for example, "Barbara is a good student"). In a situation like that in Figure 6.2B, where Mr. Jackson commonly praises lots of students as well as Barbara and others do not praise Barbara, we tend to assume that Mr. Jackson is praising Barbara because he is a supportive person, or for some other factor in Mr. Jackson. Figure 6.2C demonstrates a situation where all the teachers are being particularly supportive of all the students, a situation that has not typically happened in the past. Such a case is attributed to the unique circumstances of the situation (for example, it is graduation day). These patterns

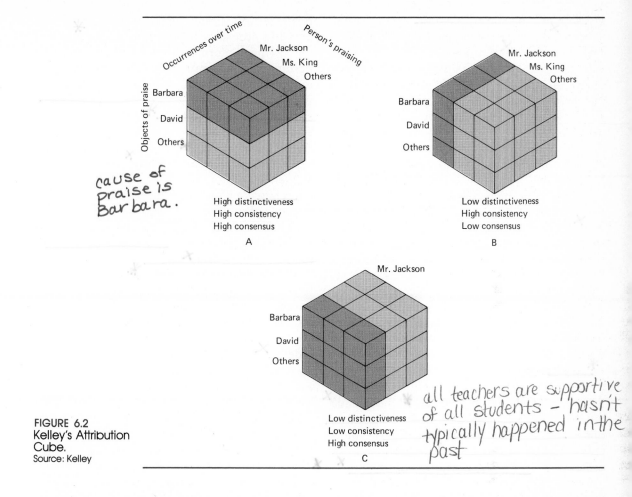

FIGURE 6.2
Kelley's Attribution
Cube.
Source: Kelley

[handwritten: cause of praise is Barbara.]

[handwritten: all teachers are supportive of all students — hasn't typically happened in the past]

of attributions were substantially supported in a study by McArthur (1972).

Orvis, Cunningham, and Kelley (1975) demonstrated that people can make causal inferences even if they do not have all three sources of information. For example, Orvis et al. (1975) found that the same person attributions were made to a cue of low distinctiveness (Mr. Jackson praises everyone) as to the full three-cue pattern of low distinctiveness, high consistency, and low consensus. Similarly, the same stimulus attributions were made to a cue of high consensus (everyone praises Barbara) as to the full three-cue pattern. Kelley (1972) assumes that we make assumptions about how

the world operates and we use these assumptions and our knowledge about events and their likely causes to make attributions rapidly and efficiently on the basis of incomplete information.

Information about One's Own Feelings

As noted by Jones and Nisbett (1971), a person has access to information that is typically unavailable to an observer of that person's behavior. We are aware not only of our complete history of experiences (consistency and distinctiveness), but also of our inner feelings and goals. When people want to do well or spend a lot of time on a task, they are more likely to make an effort attribution (Frieze, 1976). Consider poor William, who flunked his exam a little while ago. To an outside observer who sat in on class today, William's failing grade is all the observer knows about William, and the grade is probably unusual in the class, since most students pass any given test. It is quite natural for the observer to assume that this low-consensus event is due to William, and to further assume high consistency ("I bet he has done poorly all year long"). Thus the observer assumes that his limited observation of William represents William's ability level, and the observer compares William to the other students. In contrast, William has the opportunity to compare his grade to his past record of performance. He also knows how much he studied the night before, how important this test was to him, how he felt during the test, and how hard he tried. He may agree with the observer, but his superior information may lead him to attribute his failure to lack of effort, lack of interest, an unfair test, or bad luck. Monson and Snyder (1977) suggest that attributions about one's own behavior would in general be more accurate than an observer's attributions because of the enhanced access to information.

Social psychologists have discovered, however, that people often lack direct access to their inner states and end up in a role comparable to that of an observer in inferring what their inner states must be. In the first analysis of this type, Schachter (1964) argued that our experiences of particular emotions are not biologically fixed, but instead consist of a general level of arousal and situational cues that produce an inference about which emotion is being "felt."

In a classic experiment demonstrating this effect, Schachter and Singer (1962) gave subjects an injection of adrenalin, which produces increased heart rate and other symptoms of physiological arousal. Subjects were told that the injection was a vitamin supplement under-

going testing. Some subjects were told to expect the arousal symptoms as a side effect of the vitamin (informed group), others were told nothing about symptoms or side effects (ignorant group). Half the subjects in each group were exposed to a "euphoric" confederate, a student who behaved in a merry, happy way. The remaining subjects were exposed to an "angry" confederate. Subjects who could not explain their arousal in terms of the vitamin side effects (the ignorant group) reported feeling relatively happier in the presence of the euphoric rather than the angry confederate. In contrast, subjects whose arousal could be referred to the vitamin (the informed group) did not show this effect.

Schachter's reasoning has produced a way to reduce negative emotions people feel toward various objects or situations. In "misattribution therapy," anxiety, fear, or pain can be considered as arousal plus cues. New cues are provided to direct attributions in a safer direction and reduce these negative emotions. For example, Nisbett and Schachter (1966) gave misattribution subjects a placebo pill which, they were told, would produce physiological arousal. While supposedly under the effects of this pill, subjects were given electric shocks. These subjects tolerated more shock than control subjects who had been told that the placebo pill would produce unrelated side effects. Presumably, the misattribution subjects attributed their arousal to the pill rather than to the shocks, and thus believed they feared the shocks less. Similarly, Storms and Nisbett (1970) gave insomniacs a placebo pill that supposedly either aroused or relaxed them. Insomniacs given the arousal pill reported getting to sleep faster than before the pill, whereas relaxation-pill subjects said it now took longer to achieve sleep. Presumably, insomniacs actually have presleep arousal that they worry about. Misattributing this arousal to the pill—although it may lead to "pill dependency"—allows them to feel comfortable about their arousal and get to sleep more quickly. Those

SOCIAL FOCUS 6.3
Attributional Conflict in Couples

As we all know, members of a couple do not always agree on everything. In order to study attributional disagreements, Orvis, Kelley, and Butler (1976) asked each member of young heterosexual couples to describe a time when the couple disagreed about why that person did something. Each also described a situation in which they disagreed about something the other member of the couple had done. In describing incidents involving criticism, teasing, or fighting, people were more likely to recall their *own* behavior as caused by factors in the situation, other people, their own psychological or physical state at the time, their beliefs, their concerns for other people, and the fact that the activity was a generally desirable one. These data suggest that these people were most likely to see the causes of their own behaviors as due to external factors or unstable factors.

When asked about the partner's perception for these same behaviors, they more often felt that the partner was making an attribution to their general characteristics, to the fact that they had a negative attitude toward the partner, or to an attempt to attain desirable consequences. The tone of these explanations was largely negative, with attributions being made to causes such as the lack of ability of the person, his or her selfishness, or ulterior purposes behind the actions.

Imagine, for example, that you have been dating someone for a while. When you and your partner disagree about your behavior, such as criticizing your partner for leaving a mess, your partner tends to see your criticism as part of a more general pattern of behavior, representing your pettiness or dominating nature. You, however, view your own behavior as a single incident. This type of disagreement, which parallels the actor-observer bias, is very hard to resolve, because both people believe their behaviors are justified and that they understand themselves.

This same study also found that the behaviors of women were attributed by both members of the couple more to factors in the environment, other people, her lack of ability to deal with the situation, and her insecurity about the relationship. Male actors were more often seen as doing something because it would ultimately lead to good things. Such attributions appear to support the stereotype that women feel they have less control over their lives than men and that others also see them this way.

The areas of disagreement were also analyzed. Disagreements about male behavior generally arise from insensitive behavior toward the partner or some type of sports activity. Disagreements about female behavior more often centered around avoidance of some activity, behaving emotionally, or doing something with their partners. The stereotype of active, aggressive males and passive, emotional females seems to emerge once again.

who feel aroused even after taking a relaxation pill may worry even more about their problem and find it harder to sleep. (For a more recent discussion of the application and limitations of misattribution therapy for treating insomnia, see Storms, Denney, McCaul and Lowery, 1979.)

Bem (1967, 1972) expanded Schachter's analysis by proposing that when internal cues about attitudes or emotions are "weak, ambiguous, or uninterpretable" (1972, p. 2), people infer these inner states from "observations of their own behavior and/or the circumstances in which this behavior occurs" (p. 2). As discussed in Chapter 5, this **self-perception theory** offers a reinterpretation of attitude-change phenomena uncovered in research on dissonance. Bem posited that subjects do not have a clear idea about their own attitudes toward unpleasant dissonance tasks, and therefore infer that they are motivated to lie when paid enough money, but infer that they are telling the truth when paid a small sum.

Self-perception theory also suggests that our beliefs about why we do enjoyable things, our interests or intrinsic motivation, can be altered by external cues. Lepper, Greene, and Nisbett (1973) introduced attractive drawing materials into preschool classrooms and observed children's free play for two weeks through a one-way mirror, after which time the materials were removed from the classroom. Children who played a lot with the materials were selected to participate in an individual experimental session in a separate room. In this session, each child was asked to play with the same drawing materials under one of three conditions: (1) in the expected-award condition, children were shown a "good player" certificate and asked if they wished to draw in order to win the award; (2) in the unexpected-award condition, children were asked to draw and unexpectedly received the same award after they finished; and (3) a no-award condition. Two weeks later, the drawing materials were reintroduced into class for several days, and children's free-play interest was again unobtru-

sively observed. The results clearly demonstrated that the expected-award children were no longer as interested in the activity as the remaining children. Thus, once the children label their activity as a means to an end (a way to get the award) rather than an end in itself (a fun thing to do), their intrinsic interest decreases.

Research suggests that external constraints other than rewards may also produce decrements in interest. Lepper and Greene (1975) showed that a child's interest in an activity initially performed with an adult watching is subsequently reduced when the adult is absent. Amabile, DeJong, and Lepper (1976) showed that a deadline can make adults less interested in an activity at a later time when no deadline is present. In short, it is the attribution, "I am doing this for some extrinsic goal—to get an award, please someone, get attention, beat the deadline" that produces a decrement in subsequent interest in the task for its own sake.

The above research has been frequently used to question the general wisdom of using rewards to motivate behavior. Many educators advocate the use of operant conditioning procedures such as a "token economy." To address this issue, Greene, Sternberg, and Lepper (1976) set up a token economy in an actual classroom. Children were rewarded each day for twelve days for doing certain math problems. When rewards were withdrawn, the children worked less at such problems than they had before the rewards were begun.

We should recognize, however, that operant procedures often work very well. Rewards can *increase* interest in a variety of ways, particularly if the activity is of low interest to begin with. If Debbie hates studying, rewards may increase her studying even when the rewards are stopped. Also, if rewards are presented so that they are not salient as the reason for behavior, so that the rewards are there but behavior is attributed to oneself, then interest does not suffer. Rewards can be presented as a "fringe benefit" (Johnson, Greene, & Carroll, 1978), or unspecified (Ross, 1975), or less tangible rewards such as approval can be used (Anderson, Manoogian, & Reznick, 1976), or subjects can be told they are interested in the activity itself rather than the reward (Pittman, Cooper, & Smith, 1977).

EFFECTS OF CAUSAL ATTRIBUTIONS

Our discussion of the information used to make attributions has already gone beyond the point when a person makes an attribution. We have shown that attributions affect students' and teachers' behavior and have explored important topics such as intrinsic motivation and misattribution therapy. In this section we will systematically discuss how attributions affect our beliefs about the future, our attitudes toward ourselves and others, and our behavior in a wide range of situations.

Expectations for the Future

Stability of attributions. Weiner et al. (1971) proposed that expectations for future performance are a function of past performance and the stability of attributions for past performance. David's success on an exam is thought to be more strongly indicative of future success if it was due to a stable cause, such as ability, than to an unstable cause such as effort. After all, a smart student is still smart next year, but the fact that Ann studied hard does not necessarily mean she will study hard next time.

Research has been remarkably consistent in supporting this theory. Weiner, Nierenberg, and Goldstein (1976) gave subjects from zero to five success experiences and then asked them why they succeeded and whether they would succeed on the task in the future. The results clearly showed that for both internal and external causes, expectancy for success varied with the stability of attributions for success. Subjects who felt they succeeded because of their ability or the ease of the task felt they would do better in the future than those who attributed success to effort or luck.

Valle and Frieze (1976) found similar effects for expectations regarding others' performance. Business school students were asked to imagine they were employers evaluating an employee who had performed above average in sales. Predictions for future sales and willingness to promote were higher when the employee's performance was attributed to stable factors (see Figure 6.3). Carroll (1978) found that stability mediated the expectancies for risk of recidivism (committing another crime) of parole applicants made by actual parole-board members on actual cases. Those cases whose crimes were attributed to stable causes were considered worse risks and were more likely to be denied parole then those whose crimes were attributed to unstable causes.

Sex and race differences. As we noted earlier, even though Ann and David do equally well in school, Ann tends to attribute her successes more to effort, while David is more likely to say he does well because he is smart. David also seems more generally confident about his abilities than does Ann. Research supports the general conclusion that women are less confident about their abilities, especially in doing tasks with which they are unfamiliar. Women and girls tend to underestimate how well they will do on intellectual tasks, on tasks involving physical skills, and on artistic tasks. Men and boys tend to overestimate how well they will do (Crandall, 1978). Other studies have found that females are less likely to make ability attributions for success but make more lack-of-ability attributions for failure, or that they tend to attribute both their successes and failures more to luck (Frieze, Parson, Johnson, Ruble, & Zellman, 1978). These effects, however, do not always appear, especially in

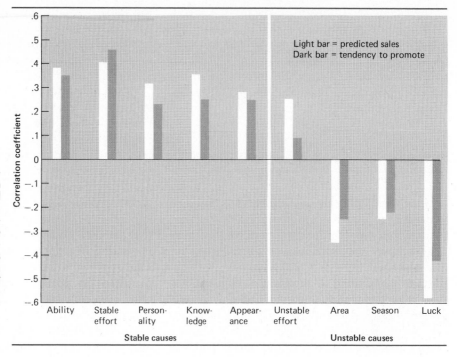

FIGURE 6.3
Relationship of Attributions for Success with Predicted Sales and Tendency to Promote. Attributions affect predictions for the future and promotion decisions as shown in this figure, adapted from a study of employer decisions about life insurance sales personnel.
Source: Valle & Frieze, 1976, p. 584.

recent studies (Frieze, Whitley, Hanusa, & McHugh, in press).

Sex differences in expectancies and attributions are reinforced by the attributions that others make about the performances of girls and women. Other people expect males to do better than females on nearly every task that has been studied (O'Leary & Hansen, 1979). There is also a tendency to attribute female successes, more than male successes, to high effort or to luck (Feldman-Summers & Kiesler, 1974; Frieze et al., 1978). Presumably, the consequences of these sex differences would leave women at a disadvantage because they would avoid tasks requiring high ability and less often receive credit (or credit themselves with self-esteem) for their accomplishments.

Just as our stereotypes lead us to feel that females are less competent than males, racial stereotypes include the idea that blacks are less intelligent and less motivated to do well in

school than whites (Feldman, 1972; Karlins, Coffman, & Walters, 1969). It would be reasonable to assume that blacks would incorporate these stereotypes into their self-images and would lack confidence in their abilities, as William does. This does not always appear to be the case, however, and in fact, some studies have found that black children have higher expectancies than do white children (Entwisle, 1979). It does appear, nontheless, that blacks are generally less likely to see their successes as due to factors in themselves and instead attribute them more to external factors such as luck (Murray & Mednick, 1975). Blacks are also more likely to attribute their failures to external factors. Overall, they see themselves as having less control over the events in their lives than do whites. In many ways, Barbara is typical of black students. When she did poorly on the exam, she attributed it to bad luck, which is an external cause. Of course, luck attributions are

Research suggests that race and gender are related to the reasons people give for their successes and failures. Males and whites are generally more apt to attribute their successes to internal factors.

also more common for women, so that she may have been following the typical pattern for women instead.

Interpersonal self-fulfilling prophecies. Expectations we hold about others' performance can lead us to behave in ways that subtly encourage our expectations to come true. Thus, as shall be noted in subsequent chapters as well, our expectations or prophecies create their own truth. For example, Rosenthal and Jacobson (1968) told teachers that a new intelligence test had indicated that some of their students would be "late bloomers," expected to show a late growth spurt of I.Q. These designated students had actually been selected by chance and did not differ in this respect from their classmates. By the end of the year, however, the

late bloomers actually showed greater I.Q. gains than their classmates. Apparently, teachers came to expect these late bloomers to excel and changed their behavior toward them in such a way as to make excellence more likely. Attributions play an important role in this process.

Teachers' reactions to high-expectation students include attributing their success to high ability and effort, while attributing their failures to lack of effort or external factors. Thus, teachers give high-expectation students more attention and contact, and reward or punish them differently because of the attributions that are made. For example, Cooper (1979) found that elementary school teachers believe that high-expectation students are more personally responsible for success than other students. Brophy and Good (1974) found that high-expectation students were praised more and blamed less than low-expectation students in classes that were homogeneous in ability (so that performance differences were probably attributed to effort). Cooper (1977) has also shown that students who were criticized by the teacher, after initiating discussion, attribute their outcomes less to effort. Thus, teacher behaviors influence students' achievements through a variety of channels, including access to opportunities, rewards and punishments, and self-perceptions. All of these channels are, however, linked to the teachers' attributions.

Evaluations

Another implication of causal attributions is the evaluations or rewards and punishments given others' performances. We also make evaluations of our own performances. Weiner et al. (1971) suggested that the ways we reward and punish performances are based partially upon the internality of the underlying causal attribution for the performance. For example, if Ann does well on a test, Ms. King will think more highly of her—and she will think better of herself—if her success is attributed to herself rather than to the situation or some other external factor. In contrast, should Debbie do poorly, evaluations will be more negative if the failure is attributed to Debbie. In short, evaluations are more extreme for internal causes, more moderate for external causes.

Research has generally supported the above reasoning for attributions to effort. Weiner and Kukla (1970) had subjects pretend they were teachers evaluating students who had just taken a test. The "teachers" were told how each student did, the student's level of ability, and how hard the student tried. As might be expected, students who did better received higher rewards. Among students with the same performance, however, those who tried harder were rewarded more. In addition, stu-

dents with lower ability were rewarded more than students with higher ability for similar performance, perhaps because it was inferred that the students low in ability had to put forth extra effort to do as well.

More recent research has suggested that one's emotional reactions to a particular performance are mediated by the attributions made. Weiner, Russell, and Lerman (1978) had subjects tell how they had felt during a "critical incident" in their lives when they had succeeded or failed at an academic exam because of ability, effort, personality, other people's actions, or luck. Although people generally feel good when they succeed and bad when they fail, self-esteem feelings of competence, pride, and shame do seem to be mediated by self-attributions. Success due to internal causes produces the most enhanced self-esteem, and failure due to internal causes lowers self-esteem the most.

The fact that evaluations of others are not easily related to ability has led Weiner (1980b) to modify his original position. He now distinguishes internal causes that are under one's *control*, such as trying hard, from those that are not under one's control, such as ability. Research indicates that students are rewarded and punished according to internal-controllable factors (effort). Similarly, students report being less willing to lend class notes to another student if the notes are needed because the student did not try to take notes (internal and controllable), compared to other reasons why the student lacked the notes (Weiner, 1980a). Thus, evaluations of others seem to reflect internal-external and controllability attributions.

Achievement Motivation

Educational psychologists have been quite interested in the applications of attribution theory to classroom situations and, as noted earlier in this chapter, there has been a great deal of attributional work done in educational settings. One of the earliest of these applications was the attributional analysis of **achievement motivation** proposed by Weiner et al. (1971). Educators are interested in this, since students with high-achievement motivation have many of the characteristics teachers want. Those with high-achievement motivation work harder, especially if they feel that they are not doing as well as they should be doing. They also like to do challenging tasks and tend to resist doing things they feel are too easy or too hard. They get high grades and are active in school organizations (Weiner, 1972). Both David and Ann appear to have high-achievement motivation.

Weiner et al. (1971) proposed that achievement motivation might be reinterpreted as a pattern of attributions in achievement situations. Students high in achievement motivation attribute success more to high ability and high effort, and attribute failure more to lack of effort. If David gets an A, he attributes his performance to himself, feels a great deal of pride, and therefore is interested in other achievement tasks. He works hard because he perceives an effort-outcome relationship: the harder he tries, the better he will do. If he fails, he is confident that trying harder will bring success.

In contrast, students like William, who are low in achievement motivation, attribute success to external factors and attribute failure to lack of ability. When William gets an A, he feels the test was easy or he was lucky. He therefore feels little pride and has little interest in other achievement tasks, nor does he try very hard. If he fails, he blames his low ability and gives up. He does not perceive the effort-outcome linkage. He chooses very easy or very hard tasks because they will not embarrass him by confirming his low self-estimates of his ability.

Research has generally supported the attributional analysis in the attributional patterns of high- and low-achievement-motivated subjects. Fyans and Maehr (1979) found that students who attribute their achievement to ability prefer tasks in which competence is necessary to do well. In contrast, students who attribute success to luck avoid ability tasks and choose games of chance. Such preferences should reinforce self-attributions and serve to make ability-oriented students more skillful (they get to practice their skills) and luck-oriented students less skillful.

Even more interesting, however, have been the education programs based upon the attributional analysis. Dweck (1975) identified a group of children who endorsed lack of ability as the cause of failure. All showed severely impaired performance, following failure occurrences on math problems. These children were randomly assigned to one of two conditions: (1) success-only experiences, in which they received a constant dose of easily solvable problems intended to bolster confidence, and (2) success-and-failure experiences, which allowed for attribution retraining. When the students failed, the attribution was made by the experimenter to lack of effort. After the training period the success-only group showed no improvement when they again encountered failure, and some were even more incapacitated by failure. The attribution-retraining group showed marked improvement, with none of the children exhibiting reduced performance following failure and most showing *better* performance after failure. They also showed increased tendency to attribute failure to lack of effort. Andrews and Debus (1978) found supporting evidence in training sixth-grade boys to attribute failure to lack of effort. Compared to control subjects who were not trained, these subjects attributed success and failure more to effort, and showed increased persistence in the face of failure even on a four-month follow-up.

These results strongly support the idea that the achievement syndrome of choosing achievement tasks, working hard, and persisting in the face of failure depends upon perceiving the effort-outcome relationship. If success is attributed "away" to luck or the task, and failure is attributed to unchangeable low ability, then no sequence of outcomes can change the attribution pattern. Only if the person can be taught to connect effort and outcome can success experience begin to raise self-esteem, estimates of ability, and achievement behaviors (see Weiner, 1980b).

BIASES AND INFORMATION PROCESSING IN MAKING CAUSAL ATTRIBUTIONS

As we have already discussed, the attribution theories of Jones and Davis (1965) and Kelley (1967) proposed a rational, logical, scientific process of combining information into an attribution. Kelley best exemplifies this approach by calling the attributor a "naive scientist" and describing the attribution process as a "naive analysis of variance" similar to the formal statistical analyses conducted by scientists.

These same theorists recognized that people do not always follow these rational rules. Kelley calls the shortcomings of the attributor "biases, errors, and illusions" (1967, p. 219). Extensive research and theoretical discussion has centered on identifying these biases and determining whether they arise from motivations of the perceiver to feel good and look good to others, or cognitive limitations of the perceiver in attention, recall, and processing of information.

More recent work has challenged the interpretation of attribution theorists that there are rational models and biases that are deviations or distortions in the models. We can instead recognize that biases are existent only when a rational model is proposed for what is an "unbiased" attribution. If attributions are based on different processes that do not derive from the rational models, then the biases may reflect aspects of the actual attribution process rather than a problem or error. In this section we will describe the major biases, and then explore some new ideas about the attribution process.

Protecting self-esteem. Heider (1958) first recognized that perceivers protect their self-esteem by making excuses for events they wish to ignore. He quotes Cocteau's reply to a question of whether he believed in luck: "Certainly. How else can you explain the success of those you detest?" (p. 98). People tend to enhance self-esteem by taking more responsibility for good events or successes than for bad events or failures (for example, Miller & Ross, 1975), and also tend to attribute successes to more stable causes than failures, making success seem more likely in the future (Frieze & Weiner, 1971; Miller & Ross, 1975). Thus, we are more likely to say that we did well on a test because we are good in that subject or because we are smart than we are to say we failed a test because we are dumb. As Snyder, Stephan, and Rosenfield (1979) and others have pointed out, these strategies for maintaining our self-esteem are most useful when the internal attributions for success and the external attributions for failure are plausible. Thus, if Ann should do poorly on a test, after doing well consistently on past tests, it would be quite plausible for her to make an external attribution of bad luck. Attributing her successes to effort or to her ability would be plausible. If William suddenly did very well on an exam, however, it might not be a plausible explanation for him to say that he is now smart, although he might be able to say that he had studied unusually hard for the test.

These general success-failure effects also appear when we are making attributions about other people. Thus, Ms. King and Mr. Jackson are also more likely to see the good grades on the test as resulting from the high abilities of their students than they are to blame the students' low abilities for failure. Ms. King might see failure more as lack of effort, while Mr. Jackson would cite temporary personal difficulties. Thus, there have to be other reasons for the "bias" than self-esteem maintenance. One possibility is that we tend to expect successes more and expected things are attributed more to internal and stable factors (Miller & Ross, 1975).

Protecting self-esteem can be a complicated issue. Berglas and Jones (1978) found that males who had experienced noncontingent success—that is, there was no relationship between their effort and their performance—used a self-handicapping strategy. This strategy was to set up an obvious external cause for failure by choosing to take a drug that would retard their future performance. These subjects actually arranged to fail, but to fail in a way that preserved self-esteem. They preferred this situation to the possibility that they might fail after taking a performance-enhancing drug, even though success should be more likely in this latter case.

Hedonic relevance. Motivational biases can intrude upon attributions in other ways. Jones and Davis (1965) proposed that correspondent inferences are made more strongly if others' behavior provides rewards or punishments for the attributor. They call this **hedonic relevance.** Correspondence is even greater if others are thought to have directed these consequences deliberately toward the attributor. This latter case is called **personalism.** For example, if Ann helped Michael with some classwork, Mr. Jackson might be more inclined to make a correspondent inference (Ann is helpful) than another teacher, because Ann indirectly aided Mr. Jackson as well. If Mr. Jackson believed that Ann helped Michael in order to please Mr. Jackson, correspondence should be even higher.

Overattributing to persons. Heider (1958) also noticed that attributors have a strong tendency to attribute causality to people. When we observe a person's behavior, we tend to believe the person was free to choose and in-

tended the behavior. Heider pointed this out in his comment that "behavior engulfs the field," referring to a perceptual process of focusing on the person and the behavior, while environmental forces fade into the background. Ross (1977) calls this the "fundamental attribution error." Research demonstrates that even when students are assigned to defend or attack an issue (for example, legalization of marijuana or the Soviet invasion of Afghanistan), attributors who *know* students have been assigned their positions still believe the defending students are more in favor of the issue than the attacking students (for example, Jones & Harris, 1967). Similarly, subjects assigned to make up questions for other subjects are thought by all observers to have superior general knowledge, even though they chose to present questions that they could answer and thus had to look good (Ross, Amabile, & Steinmetz, 1977).

Problems with consensus. Attributors seem to have some difficulty dealing with consensus information. Finding out that most subjects in an experiment deliver painful shocks to another subject does not affect judgments about what one subject would do or why a subject would do it (Nisbett & Borgida, 1975). In general, consensus information provided by the experimenter is underutilized. The only domain in which consensus of this type is used is the achievement domain. People readily interpret test scores or grades in relationship to class averages, the "curve," and other forms of consensus. This appears to be a well-practiced skill that is rarely applied to other settings.

Subjects are quite willing, however, to generate their own consensus information and use it. Several studies (for example, Hansen & Donoghue, 1977) have shown that subjects make more extreme attributions about people who act in unreasonable ways or differently from how the subject thinks he or she would perform. Ross, Greene, and House (1977) asked subjects to walk around campus wearing a large signboard. Those who agreed to do this thought 62 percent of students would wear the sign. Those who refused thought only 33 percent of their peers would wear the sign.

*Ross (1977) has emphasized that subjects use their own feelings and behavior as an index of how others will feel and behave. This **false consensus** effect means that people consider themselves normal and typical and whoever differs is thought of as unusual and different. Because different behavior is therefore low (false) consensus, the behavior is attributed to the person. For example, Michael rarely studies and therefore believes most other children rarely study, and that those who study a lot are bookworms. In contrast, Ann studies a lot and believes most others do also, and thinks children who do not study are lazy know-nothings.

Perseverance. Attributions are easy to make, but hard to undo. We have already noted that attributions are often made quickly on the basis of stereotypic expectancies. The tendency to attribute acts to people, especially if they behave differently from ourselves, is another instance of a snap attribution. Once an attribution is made, however, it seems to take on a life of its own and to persevere even in the face of conflicting evidence. Ross, Lepper, and Hubbard (1975) randomly told subjects they had succeeded or failed on an experimental task. Later, subjects were correctly informed that their earlier success or failure had been randomly determined by the experimenter. Yet, "success" subjects continued to feel they had higher ability than "failure" subjects. Similarly, once subjects explain why a person might commit suicide or contribute to the Peace Corps, they come to believe the event they explained is more likely than do those who did not explain this event, even when they understand that these events are hypothetical. Thus, asking Ms. King why William might fail mathematics could lead her to think about low ability and thus create more pessimistic expectations. So, think positively!

Models From Cognitive Psychology

The investigation of cognitive biases has resulted in challenges to the basic theoretical statements of attribution theory. Do people attempt to make the logical analyses proposed by Kelley (1967) and Jones and Davis (1965) but make errors, or do they do something different and simpler altogether? At this time, it is clear that people are capable of making involved logical analyses of causation when told to do so and provided with some assistance (for example, neat summaries of consistency, distinctiveness, and consensus). As social psychologists became more aware of research in cognitive psychology, however, they recognized that built-in limitations in human information processing would preclude the general use of these sophisticated logical rules (for example, Carroll & Payne, 1976; Fischhoff, 1976; Nisbett & Ross, 1980). Instead, simpler processes were proposed that are consistent with studies of other cognitive processes and often draw their models directly from work in cognitive psychology.

Salience. One explanation for the fundamental attribution error is that people are perceptually prominent or salient to observers. Jones and Nisbett (1971) argued that actors and observers differ in their attributions because they differ in their physical viewpoints. The situation is salient to the actor, but the actor is salient to the observer. Storms (1973) created a situation in which two actor subjects conversed, while observers watched one of the two actors. Actors perceived themselves as more influenced by situational factors than did observers who watched them. When actors saw videotapes of themselves taken during the conversation, however, so that they now received the visual information from the physical viewpoint of an observer, their attributions became similar to those of the observer. Regan and Totten (1975) found that instructions to empathize with one of two actors led observers to subjectively shift their point of view and affected attributions about the actor with whom they empathized.

Taylor and Fiske (1978) summarize a large number of studies indicating that whatever attracts attention or is more memorable tends to be thought of as causally potent. For example, one woman in a group of men or one black in a group of whites is highly salient. Such a "solo" individual is reacted to more strongly than if the same person acts the same way in a more mixed group and is often perceived as a typical member of the ethnic or gender group. (More will be said about solo individuals, or "tokens," in Chapter 18).

Categories. Complex real-world knowledge tends to be organized around categories, plausible scenarios or scripts about common situations (Abelson, 1976), or prototypical instances that represent a fuzzy category (Cantor & Mischel, 1979). A **script** is a story or play that organizes situations, roles, characters, and behaviors. For example, the "restaurant" script includes information about the physical setting (tables, chairs), the roles (waitress, cashier, customer), and the action (getting seated, ordering, serving, eating, paying). **Prototypes** are specific examples that represent a category. Other instances can be good or bad fits to the category, depending on how similar they are to the prototype. If the prototypical bird for you is a robin, you have little difficulty classifying a sparrow or a horse. But what about an eagle, an ostrich, or a chicken?

We understand people by utilizing knowledge organized in scripts and prototypes. Ethnic and gender stereotypes are simply one obvious instance of such categories. Other categories are readily apparent. For example, if you know that Michael is a lineman on the school football team, this evokes an image for us of a "big jock with a low I.Q." If you found out that Michael flunked a math test, you might use your "dumb jock" stereotype to suggest an attribution to low ability. If Michael did

very well on a test, you might think of some plausible scenarios or scripts (Abelson, 1976), such as cheating, a roommate who tutors Michael in exchange for telephone numbers, or extra help from the teacher, prompted by a call from the coach. If Michael consistently does well, we may eventually accept a smart jock, but somehow it is faster and easier to "understand" behavior that is consistent with easily evoked categories or prototypes.

This suggests that specific attributions may emerge from a rapid process of category activation. Which category is activated is a function of context and salience. When we hear someone got an A, certain categories are very accessible, such as a brilliant student, a hardworking student, and an easy course. These categories include information organized like little stories about various participants, their behavior and motivations, and plausible subplots. The prototypical stories are somewhat different for a math test than for an English test. When you see visual cues, like Michael's appearance, some cues become highly salient. If Michael is big, has a mashed nose, speaks slowly, and seems to always be clenching and unclenching his hands (as if around a football or quarterback's neck), one salient category is strongly evoked.

Hypothesis testing. Kruglanski et al. (1978) and Carroll and Weiner (1981) have proposed that attribution processes involve the rapid generation of one or more plausible attributions, and another stage when information is considered to validate these attributional hypotheses. The generation of hypotheses is based on salience and prototypes, or general knowledge and context. When we test a hypothesis such as, "Michael flunked because he is a dumb jock," we do not proceed as scientists, logically and inductively assembling all relevant information. Instead, we search for confirming (consistent) evidence. If Mr. Jackson finds out that Michael is indeed on the football team, he may feel confident in his con-

SOCIAL FOCUS 6.4
Attributions of Responsibility

Attribution theorists are not the only people interested in causality. For centuries legal scholars have analyzed issues of causality, culpability, and responsibility. More recently there has been the recognition that legal distinctions cannot be separated from commonsense ideas of causality. Roscoe Pound pointed out over fifty years ago that for determinations of what the reasonable man would do or think in any situation, "we must rely on the common sense of the common man as to common things" (1923, pp. 951–952). At the same time that Heider was laying the foundations of attribution theory in his 1958 book, Hart and Honore were writing *Causality in the Law* (1959), must reading for the serious student of causal reasoning.

Heider's discussion of responsibility presents almost a legal analysis. He posits five levels of responsibility that move from very primitive to progressively more sophisticated consideration of events:

(1) Association—people are held responsible for anything connected with them; for example, being congratulated when your home team wins the Superbowl.

(2) Causality—people are held responsible for anything they caused, even accidentally. Suppose you are arguing with a friend who gets so excited he hits his hand against a table and breaks a bone in his finger. How would you feel? Would he blame you?

(3) Foreseeability—people are held responsible for anything that could have been foreseen or predicted, even if it was unintentional. For example, you try out a small restaurant in a tough neighborhood. To save money you park on the street. After dinner you discover your car has been stolen. What would you or your friends think?

(4) Intentionality—people are held responsible only for what they intended to happen. Accidents, mistakes, oversights, and side effects are not your fault.

(5) Justifiability—people are held responsible only for what they intended and chose freely. If people are forced to intend the act, and if anyone else would have felt and acted this way, then they are not held responsible.

clusion regarding Michael's test performance, although this is certainly not scientific proof. If Mr. Jackson discovers Michael is not on the football team, the hypothesis is not necessarily dropped. Maybe Michael is on the wrestling team. The hypothesis is really only discarded when a better hypothesis is available and checked out. Snyder and Cantor (1979) and Hansen (1980) find strong evidence for such confirmatory strategies. Lest you think these strategies are peculiar or naive, there is good evidence that scientists are also confirmation-biased (Kuhn, 1962).

Heuristics. One of the most important generalizations arising from recent work in cognitive psychology is that people are flexible and adaptive, although within limits. We use a variety of strategies or heuristics for making judgments and switch from one to another in dif-

These five levels reproduce many legal distinctions in criminal responsibility. In the case of a death, accident is an acceptable reduction in responsibility. If the event is foreseeable, however, as in playing with a loaded gun, there is potential responsibility for a charge of manslaughter. If the death is intended, a charge of murder is brought. If the death is intended but justifiable, as in self-defense, responsibility is removed. It is interesting to note that causality is sufficient to produce legal responsibility for certain crimes such as parking tickets or trespassing. In these instances, the courts need not establish any criminal mental state (mens rea) before meting out punishment.

Attribution theorists have frequently equated responsibility judgments with causal attributions. They assumed that responsibility is another term for an attribution to the person. Recent work, however, has established that questions of responsibility and questions of causality are quite different and, in fact, responsibility may be the more basic judgment.

According to Hamilton (1980), causality is assigned by using a "but for" rule: the event would not happen but for cause X. Another way to think of this is that the cause was necessary and could have been absent. When Ann gets an A on an exam, we immediately think of studying hard as a cause "but for" which she would have done less well. In contrast, responsibility is assigned by using a "could have done otherwise" rule: the person who had a reasonable choice is held responsible. If Michael goes out on a date instead of studying for the exam, we hold him responsible for his poor performance, because he could have done otherwise.

Hamilton proposes that in most situations attributors act not as "intuitive scientists" looking for causes, but as "intuitive lawyers" assigning responsibility. This viewpoint helps to explain the fundamental attribution error, where we overattribute behavior to persons. Because we believe people nearly always could have done otherwise, we tend to hold them responsible for their actions. The fundamental attribution error thus rests on our society's belief in free will.

ferent situations. Some attribution theorists have begun to catalogue the heuristics found in studies of human judgment and use them to account for attributional biases (Nisbett & Ross, 1980). However, a more complex view harks back to Kelley's (1972) description of attribution processes as a "repertoire" of thought models. Subjects are quite capable of making attributions in different ways, and for different reasons. They can use a rational model like the

Covariation Principle, and they can draw their attributions from everyday stereotypes.

Researchers are beginning to understand the basic attributional processes and when they occur. They are successfully avoiding the problem of concluding that everyone always makes attributions in the same way unless they make a mistake or have a bias, the dominant view of a decade ago. They are also avoiding the pitfall of saying everyone is different and every situation is different. Models from cognitive psychology have proved very useful. Social Focus 6.4 discusses a model derived from yet another discipline—the law. An impressive and coherent body of research is accumulating and attribution theory is continuing to expand and develop.

SUMMARY   Attribution theory is the study of people's beliefs about why things happen. Although much of the early research was done with college students in laboratory settings, there has been an increasing number of applications of attribution theory to a variety of social problems. This chapter has discussed attribution theory from the perspective of how attributional concepts help us to understand student and teacher behaviors in the classroom.

Attributions are made in order to predict and control events. People are most likely to make attributions about things that are unusual or unpleasant. Thus, students who typically succeed might not wonder why they got yet another A on a test. But the same students might well ask a series of attributional questions about a low grade.

There are many different kinds of attributions, and different situations produce different attributions. In classroom settings, the most typical attributions for student success are ability, effort, motivation, help from others, and an easy test. Luck is also occasionally mentioned. Opposite attributions are made for failure.

These and other attributions can be classified along several dimensions. Attribution researchers have most frequently considered whether the cause is internal to the person or in the external environment. Causes can also be classified according to how changeable or stable they are and whether they are under the control of the person.

In making causal attributions, the event itself provides information to the person trying to understand the event. Jones and Davis theorize that we examine the effects of an action and the effects of alternative actions to make attributions. Along with the event itself, we also use information about how other people have reacted in similar situations. If everyone behaves the same way, their actions tell us little about their unique characteristics. Jones and Davis propose that we make correspondent inferences about people when their actions have few noncommon effects and low social desirability (or consensus, in Kelley's terms).

Another source of information is the behavior of the person in the past. Kelley labels previous behaviors toward the same and different objects as consistency and distinctiveness. Kelley proposes that people use the Covariation Principle to examine consistency, distinctiveness, and consensus, and attribute an event to the cause with which it covaries.

Another major source of information is the knowledge we have about our own feelings. Schachter and Bem have argued, however, that people may not always know exactly how they are feeling and may use external cues about the environment to help them label their feelings. Training people to mislabel their feelings (or in some cases to more properly label their feelings) has been used in the treatment of insomnia as well as other disorders.

Our intrinsic motives can also be altered by mislabeling our own behavior. Giving people a reward for doing something they already enjoy may actually decrease their intrinsic motivation to do the activity. Once they perceive their behavior as a means for getting a reward, they may not do the activity unless the reward is continued. Rewards can be used, however, to increase interest in tasks we are not particularly motivated to do on our own.

Causal attributions have a number of consequences for the person making the attribution. The stability of the underlying cause has an effect upon our expectancies for the future. Performance attributed to ability or other stable factors lead to the expectancy for similar performance in the future. Successes or failures attributed to unstable causes lead one to expect changes in performance levels in the future. These stability effects appear to mediate sex and race differences. Women and blacks expect to perform at lower levels than men and whites. Expectancies may also lead to self-fulfilling prophecies, where the initial expectations influence the ways we react to others, which in turn affect their performances.

Attributions also influence the evaluations we make of others and of ourselves. We reward and punish performances more if they are attributed to internal causes than to external causes. Achievement motivation seems to require a belief that our own efforts produce success. Low achievers who give up when they do poorly can be trained to make different attributions and persist so as to achieve.

Several models for how people make causal attributions were also reviewed in the chapter. Kelley as well as Jones and Davis proposed very rational, logical models. Compared to these rational models, there seem to be a number of "biases" in the ways that people make attributions. Successes are attributed more to internal factors than are failures. This serves to maintain self-esteem. Our attributions are also influenced by their hedonic relevance and we tend to attribute events to people rather than environmental effects, whenever possible. People may not take proper account of consensus information in making their judgments about causality. Finally, once we make an attribution we tend to stick with it, even in the light of disconfirming evidence.

New models adopted from cognitive psychology suggest that attributions may be made in simpler ways. These models highlight the importance of salience, categories or prototypes, hypothesis testing, and heuristics or strategies.

SUGGESTED READINGS

Frieze, I. H., Bar-Tal, D., & Carroll, J. S. *New approaches to social problems: Applications of attribution theory.* San Francisco: Jossey-Bass, 1979.

Harvey, J. H., Ickes, W. J., & Kidd, R. F. *New directions in attribution research* (Vols. 1 & 2). Hillsdale, N.J.: Lawrence Erlbaum Associates, 1976, 1978.

Harvey, J. H., & Weary, G. *Perspectives on attributional processes*. Dubuque, Iowa: William C. Brown Company, 1981.

Schneider, D. J., Hastorf, A. H., & Ellsworth, P. C. *Person perception*, (2d ed.). Reading, Mass.: Addison-Wesley, 1979.

Weiner, B. A theory of motivation for some classroom experiences. *Journal of Educational Psychology*, 1979, *71*, 3–25.

7

SOCIAL PERCEPTION AND FACE-TO-FACE INTERACTION

- Introduction
- Impression Formation
- Perception of Emotions
- Impression Management
- Face-to-Face Interaction
- Summary

The cancer wing was Ward No. 13. Pavel Nikolayevich Rusanov had never been superstitious, had never thought he could be, but something inside him sank when they wrote "Ward 13" on his registration card. They should have had the tact to call it something like "prosthetic" or "intestinal," not "13."

The double doors to the ward were kept wide open, yet as he crossed the threshold Pavel was assailed by a damp, fusty mixture of smells, partly medicinal. With his sensitivity to odors, it was hard to bear. . . .

In the aisle stood a stocky, broad-shouldered patient in rose-striped pajamas. His whole neck was bandaged tightly and thickly almost up to the lobes of his ears. The pressure of the white wrappings prevented him from freely moving his heavy, squat head, with its thick mop of brown hair.

This patient was talking hoarsely to another who listened from a bed. When Rusanov entered, the patient in the aisle turned to him with his entire torso, on which his head seemed tightly fixed and immobile, looked at Rusanov indifferently, and said:

"Here comes another cancer."

Pavel did not consider it necessary to reply to this familiarity. He felt that the whole room was looking at him, but he did not want to respond by glancing around at these strange faces or even saying hello.

—Aleksandr Solzhenitsyn
The Cancer Ward

INTRODUCTION

Imagine that you are about to visit a hospitalized friend in a cancer ward like the one the Russian author Solzhenitsyn is writing about. You will be talking to some patients and gaining some understanding of them. You will also be looking at them and listening carefully to their voices. Perhaps you will sympathize with their feelings, perhaps not. But you are not the only observer; the patients will also form an impression of you. You know this and so may be careful about how you act.

Even before you arrive at the hospital, you have some ideas about how the social interaction will proceed. The fact that the setting is a hospital and the fact that the patients have cancer will probably influence how you feel about and behave toward the people you meet. Nevertheless, the interaction will take form as a result of how you and others behave. Your visit may be pleasant or unpleasant. Although this situation is a special one, the basic processes involving how we get to know and interact with other people are a key aspect in the understanding of all social relations. In this chapter, we explore this field of inquiry, called *social perception,* by focusing on the topic of serious illness, a concern in the important and emerging area of "health psychology."

It is estimated that over three million Americans have a history of cancer, and that almost a million new cases will be diagnosed this year. The social problems created by such illness traditionally have not been directly studied by social psychologists, although many basic concepts of social psychology can be readily applied to an analysis of social interaction under these circumstances. Disease may appreciably affect our perceptions of, our reactions to, and our interactions with others. Understanding such interactions can help us achieve fulfilling and meaningful relationships with friends and family members who become ill.

Before we consider research on social perception, it will be useful to consider briefly the difference between perceiving objects and perceiving people. First, in contrast to perceiving an inanimate object, <u>social perception involves</u>

This chapter is written by Howard S. Friedman.

understanding another active, independent life. It involves another's (action.)

Second, our actions produce reactions in others. Our understanding of and approach to other people affects how they behave. In short, social perception involves another's (reaction.)

Third and finally, your actions are received by the other and return in some way to affect you. In short, social perception involves (interaction.)

The ways we know and deal with other people are necessarily quite different from the ways we approach objects. Knowing others is a communication process. This recognition of the give and take of social interaction is what differentiates social psychology and social perception from experimental psychology and object perception.

IMPRESSION FORMATION

The Effect of Context on Meaning

Suppose that a male friend of yours has been dating an attractive woman named Sue. Sue seems to be a very friendly, sincere, and mature individual, and you think that she is a good match for your friend. Your friend complains to you, however, that Sue sometimes seems very cold and aloof, especially where sexual matters are concerned. Sue does not like to have her body touched. You notice that this information seems to fit with other knowledge you have about Sue: she refuses to go to the beach, she wears attractive but formal clothing, and she doesn't like to talk about having children. You may conclude that Sue is a very inhibited or hung-up woman. Suppose you find out that Sue had breast cancer two years ago and had a breast surgically removed. If you realize that mastectomy is very threatening psychologically and often quite damaging to the self-concept of women, at least in the short

term, this one new bit of information may dramatically change your impression of Sue.

This example illustrates the extreme importance of context of social perception. A piece of information can have one meaning in one context but a very different meaning or impact in another context. The process of drawing inferences about the personality and mood of another is called *impression formation.* To a large extent the study of impression formation involves the study of context effects.

The importance of context in inferring the personal characteristics or traits of others was studied extensively by the psychologist Solomon Asch (1946). The basic paradigm of the Asch experiments was as follows. He gave subjects lists of traits that supposedly described a person. He then asked their impressions of this hypothetical person, using several written measures. For example, one group was given the following list: intelligent, skillful, industrious, warm, determined, practical, cautious. Another group's list consisted of intelligent, skillful, industrious, cold, determined, practical, cautious. Although the two lists differed in only one word—warm versus cold—very different overall impressions resulted. Subjects judged the first person to be much more generous and wise than the second person. The traits "warm" and "cold" were very important influences on impression formation. When polite-blunt was used instead of warm-cold, overall impressions were not affected very much as a function of the differing lists. Warm and cold were very important traits in impression formation; they were a key part of the whole impression. Asch therefore called warm and cold **central traits.** In our example of Sue, it is likely that the characteristic of having had a mastectomy would have a very influential or central impact on our overall impression of her in the circumstances described.

Impression formation is an important aspect of social perception. Our impressions of others' traits and emotions is the subject of the first half of this chapter. (The relevant cognitive attribution and inference processes were described in more detail in Chapter 6.) The second half of the chapter deals with the other key aspects of social perception, namely, the processes of communication and interaction.

Physical Attractiveness and Initial Impressions

When college students are asked to describe the characteristics of an ideal spouse, they often list characteristics such as "warm," "interesting personality," and "a desire to have fun." Students also list physical attractiveness as important, but not extremely so. When the actual dating preferences of college students have been studied, however, it has been found repeatedly that most college students desire to go out with the most physically attractive person (Berscheid & Walster, 1974). These findings indicate that physical attractiveness is important in forming our *first impressions* of other people. Perhaps it is true that later on in the development of a relationship, a warm personality assumes most importance, but at the beginning, beauty is very salient and influential.

Physical attractiveness is important not only in dating relationships but in the initial stages of impression formation in other circumstances as well. It has been shown that with little other information to go on, people assume that physically attractive people have many other positive traits. For example, attractive people are seen as nicer, kinder, and even as more intelligent. In one study, elementary school teachers seemed willing to judge the ability of students on the basis of their physical attractiveness (Clifford & Walster, 1973).

Physicians have reported that the physical attractiveness of a patient may affect the reactions of the doctor (Lasagna, 1970). For example, an unattractive patient who cannot be kept clean may receive less care than an attractive one. Since physical attractiveness can affect the reactions of both medical personnel and a patient's visitors, it has been suggested that cancer patients should be willing to make extensive efforts to keep themselves looking as attractive as possible (Donovan & Pierce, 1976).

Primacy and Recency Effects

When initial information such as first impressions of attractiveness has a greater impact on overall impression than does later information, a **primacy effect** has occurred. When later or more recent information has more influence on social perception than does initial information, then there is a **recency effect.** Which one will occur is important, since it affects such matters as whether one should go first or second in a debate or advertising campaign, whether one should put all one's efforts into making a good first impression on a date or save the best for later, and whether controversial or traditional information should be gathered first in trying to make an important decision.

Both primacy and recency effects have been shown to occur, but it is enlightening to consider some of the factors that may make one more likely than the other in a given situation. They reveal some of the different ways we go about perceiving other people. Often the first piece of information we obtain about another person or situation is extremely important. It anchors our thoughts, and subsequent information is *assimilated* into this first impression, thus producing a primacy effect. For example, if you learn that you are about to visit a cancer ward, then you have information that is relevant to the situation at hand, and you may tend to understand subsequent information in terms of this one overriding fact. Nurses are often urged to make a very positive first impression on their patients, so that the nurses' subsequent actions will be seen by the patients as being done for their benefit. Furthermore, if you pay more *attention* to the first pieces of information you receive about another person, then you are more likely to be influenced by first impressions. Our limited memory may, however, sometimes produce recency effects. You may hear something about another person in advance, but forget some of this information by the time you actually meet and interact with that person. For example, the impressions of a child who has been told what it is like in a hospital may be influenced by an actual visit, both because of greater salience of the immediate stimuli and because some previous conceptions have been forgotten. Thus, information will have differential importance as a function of the circumstances surrounding the impression formation.

Cue Combination

Although meaning always depends on context, it is also true that we associate a particular meaning with an isolated stimulus. For example, if you see someone with a very broad smile, you will usually infer that this person is happy. But what happens if you also receive another cue? For example, what if you hear the person also making somewhat positive statements while smiling? If you now think that the person is happier than you did at first, then a *summation model* of person perception is operating. You are adding or summing the two positive cues in coming to a conclusion. What if instead, however, you now think the person is less happy than you did before, because although the smile is very broad, the words are positive but not extremely positive. In this case, you are *averaging* the two cues. Averaging is thus a second model for combining cues. Finally, consider the case in which you see someone with a smiling face making very negative statements. You may add or average the two cues and decide that the message is a neutral one, but this is not likely. Instead of trying to integrate the two pieces of information, you might ignore or *discount* the sentences and rely only on the happy face in forming your impression. Or, you might bring in other aspects of the context and conclude that the person is happy and that the negative sentences are an aspect of teasing or kidding (Bugental, Kaswan, & Love, 1970; Friedman, 1979a). Research has shown different models of impression formation to be valid in different circumstances. The important point to remember is that we can often gain a better understanding of how impressions are formed by an analysis in which we examine the individual stimulus elements and the ways in which they are combined.

Stereotypes

In order to help make sense of our world, we often classify people according to our expectations of how they will behave; for example, you may think that nurses are nurturant, practical, and caring. The expectations we have about a category of people are known as a **stereotype.** Many people erroneously think of cancer patients as being dirty, depressed, near death, in pain, full of repressed feelings, crippled and weak, and so forth, when in fact this description fits relatively few of them; it is an overgeneralization. We sometimes make this cognitive error in person perception because we try to fit people into categories formed by abstract images called *prototypes* (Cantor & Mischel, 1979). In fact, very few people fit perfectly into the cognitive categories we use to help us understand the social world.

In addition to overgeneralizing, many stereotypes are very inaccurate. For thousands of years people have tried to infer character traits from facial appearance, a field known as *physiognomy* (see Figure 7.1). For example, Aristotle wrote that men with small foreheads are fickle. Today, some people believe that large foreheads or ''eggheads'' are a sign of high intelligence. Despite the extensive interest in this field, there is no validity to the simple physiognomic approach. Then why have people con-

FIGURE 7.1
The field of physiognomy suggests that we can know a person's personality characteristics on the basis of facial appearance (such as a large forehead). Interest in this field continues, although there is no evidence to substantiate its claims.

tinued to use physiognomy for so many years? The answer is that people have a very strong need to infer consistencies in other people's personalities. In the absence of personal experience, we may turn to invalid cues to form impressions and try to predict another's behavior. Social Focus 7.1 illustrates a fanciful case of impression formation based on very limited cues.

It is important to note that even if a relationship, is found between a physical characteristic and a behavioral tendency, it is not necessarily true that the behavioral tendency is innate or that all people of that "type" will nec-

essarily behave in that manner. Rather, it may be that the relationship is caused by social processes. For example, if it is found that most fat people are jolly, it may be that fat people often act jolly because they are expected to do so by other people. As expectations change, so may behaviors. This phenomenon is an important part of social relations and will be considered in detail later in this chapter.

When one person judges another, there are certain systematic biases or errors in perception that come into play. One of the most important of these is the **halo effect,** which refers to the tendency most people have to form an overall impression of another person as either good or bad on the basis of partial information, and then allow this global impression to influence subsequent judgments of that person. Our perceptions of physicians are often produced by halo effects. Many people believe that doctors are more wise, more kind, and more dedicated than most other people, even though these traits do not necessarily have anything to do with medicine. Doctors who have good personalities and good rapport with their patients appear to be seen by their patients as very skillful (in a technical sense), although there is no necessity for the two sets of attributes to be related (cf. Ware, Davies-Avery & Steward, 1978). Such overgeneralization is a good example of a halo effect.

Halo effects can also be negative. In the extreme, we sometimes think of someone who tells bad news as a bad person. Consider the following example:

The role of the bearer of bad news has never been a comfortable one. In ancient times, the messenger returning from the battlefront with news of defeat was frequently made responsible for the defeat itself and executed on the spot. Such an attitude still exists; the physician in announcing to the patient that he has cancer is held responsible for the disease. He looks upon himself, and may be looked upon, as being the creator of the event rather than merely its reporter (Krant, 1976, p. 270).

Physical attractiveness affects our initial impressions of others.

to be called 'person perception' " (1961, p. 494).

Some of our perceptions based on expressive style are merely stereotypic. For example, people often think they can infer personality from voice qualities (for instance, that people with breathy voices are sexy), but such judgments are largely inaccurate (Kramer, 1963). Recent research using videotapes has been more fruitful. For example, information about a person's degree of masculinity or femininity and extraversion or introversion can accurately be inferred from observing expressive style (Lippa, 1978a, 1978b). Other studies (Buck, 1975; Friedman, DiMatteo, & Taranta, 1980) have successfully related emotional aspects of expressive style to personality traits. People who are very emotionally expressive tend to be dominant, impulsive, and like to be the center of attention. The great importance of emotions in social perception is discussed in the next section.

Expressive Style

If asked about the personality of the cartoon character Donald Duck, you would have little trouble describing him. In fact, many producers feel that a character like Donald becomes successful only when a "personality" emerges. We can draw inferences about Donald Duck because of what he does. Partly it is what he says, although he usually isn't saying much of anything. Most of what we know about Donald Duck comes from the way he talks, the way he walks, and the way he laughs, cries, squawks, and quacks. Such actions make up the distinctive, expressive style of an individual, one of the earliest objects of attention in the study of impression formation (Allport & Vernon, 1933). In fact, Allport claims that "the expressive manner and style of the other is an important (perhaps the most important) factor in our understanding of personality—in what has come

PERCEPTION OF EMOTIONS

When patients are told that they have cancer, medical personnel, friends, and family often pay close attention to the patients' emotional reactions. Are they angry, or distressed, or depressed? We perceive emotion. Cancer patients, in turn, receive information about the emotional reactions of those around them. Furthermore, people with cancer receive important information about how others are reacting to their emotions. Are friends sympathetic, does the doctor understand feelings, and so on? The patient then experiences new emotions in response to the emotions of others. Here we see the processes of perception, communication, and reaction that are central to social perception. How do we gather information about the emotions of others and what kinds of information can we obtain?

SOCIAL FOCUS 7.1
How Do You Feel about R2D2?

One of the highlights of the hit movie "Star Wars" was the robot named R2D2. If you've seen the movie then think how you would answer the question, "How do you feel toward this robot?" When asked this question, many people reply that they feel very positively toward R2D2. People think that R2D2 is cute, R2D2 is likable, R2D2 is the kind of robot they would like to have in their homes. Why is this? Why do people like this robot?

When asked this question about *why* they like R2D2, that is, why they formed this positive impression about this robot, people give a variety of answers. Some people say they like R2D2 because he says such cute things. Actually, in the movie, R2D2 never does say anything. He only emits robot sounds—various kinds of squeaks. So it's not something that R2D2 says that makes people like him. Other people say they like R2D2 because of the things he does. They think that R2D2 is a hero. But the fact remains that R2D2 is a robot whose functions are programmed. He is not a person who can do heroic things through free will; and he is liked before he saves anybody. So this is probably not the real reason people like R2D2. Other people say that they like R2D2 because of the way he squeaks, that is, because of the sounds he emits. There may be some validity to this idea, since we saw earlier that paralinguistic cues—vocal tones that accompany speech—influence our perceptions. And R2D2 does seem to have pleasurable kinds of sounds, rather than harsh, grating sounds; but overall, these paralinguistic cues that come from R2D2 are probably not sufficient to explain the overwhelming degree of popularity that the robot has among the viewers of "Star Wars." Finally, R2D2 is certainly not very attractive physically. If asked to describe a goodlooking date, most college students would not list the physical characteristics of R2D2, but they still come to like R2D2 very quickly. Why then is R2D2 so attractive?

A hint as to the likely reason for R2D2's popularity comes from the mistake many people make in incorrectly remembering that R2D2 actually talks. People

Expression of Emotion

The study of the expression and identification of emotions goes back over one hundred years to Charles Darwin. He collected judges' ratings of photographs of facial expressions of emotion to see whether judges would agree and whether they could identify the emotion. He also observed infants' expressions and attempted to study expressions cross-culturally. Darwin concluded that much emotional expression is biologically based, a conclusion supported by recent research (Ekman, 1973). Importantly, research demonstrates that we can obtain precise information about the emotions of others from <u>facial expressions</u>, from <u>tone of voice,</u> and from <u>body movements.</u>

Most researchers agree that there are <u>at least six basic facial expressions of emotion</u> (in addition to neutrality): happiness, anger, sadness, surprise, disgust, and fear (see Figure 7.2). Other basic facial expressions sometimes included are <u>contempt</u>, <u>interest</u>, and <u>pain</u>. Facial expressions of emotion can be controlled or

think that R2D2 talks, even though he really does not, because his squeaks are *responded to* by the human actors in the film. These human reactions to the performances of R2D2 give us (the audience) a lot of the information we have about R2D2. R2D2's human friends always react very positively toward the actions and squeaks of R2D2; it is very clear that they are really quite fond of R2D2. We observers in the movie audience in turn form our impressions of R2D2 on the basis of the reactions of these human film actors, not on the basis of any direct reaction to R2D2 that we might have ourselves. We like R2D2 because the good guys in "Star Wars" also like R2D2.

The case of R2D2 illustrates how we form impressions of many people with whom we do not have extensive, direct contact. We may have very strong impressions about various political figures, various show-business personalities, and other people in the news, even though we do not have any direct personal contact with these people and may not even know very much about these people. We form our impressions on the basis of the reactions of other people to these politicians, show-business personalities, and other public figures. Similarly, if many of your friends have taken a certain college course before you, you may have a very vivid impression of what the professor in charge of that course is like, even though you have never met the professor yourself. You form your impression on the basis of the reactions of others. Sometimes the impressions we form in this way can be very unfortunate in that they do not give us a chance to form our own impressions through direct interaction with the person. For example, you may have a certain idea about a fellow college student. You may have heard that someone in your class is not a very friendly person. If, however, you have not endeavored to find out for yourself if this is the case, you may be making a serious error. If we don't want to risk treating people as robots, then we should be very wary about forming impressions of other people solely on the basis of the reactions of others.

exaggerated, or may sometimes be blends of two or more expressions (Ekman & Friesen, 1975). Much of the time, however, they are quite natural and allow us to communicate quite a bit of information very rapidly to people of various backgrounds.

Specific information about emotions is also expressed through one's tone of voice, which is comprised of those sounds, primarily variations in pitch, that accompany the spoken word. The tone of voice may be independent of the words that are being said. An ill person,

for example, may say "I'm all right," but you may detect from the tone of voice that the person is not all right and actually feels quite sad. In interactions between patients and medical personnel, patients may be quite attentive to the voice tone of the practitioner. Other *paralinguistic* cues such as pauses, stutters, and tempo also communicate important information.

A final important source of information about specific emotional states is found in a person's body movements. It is often quite

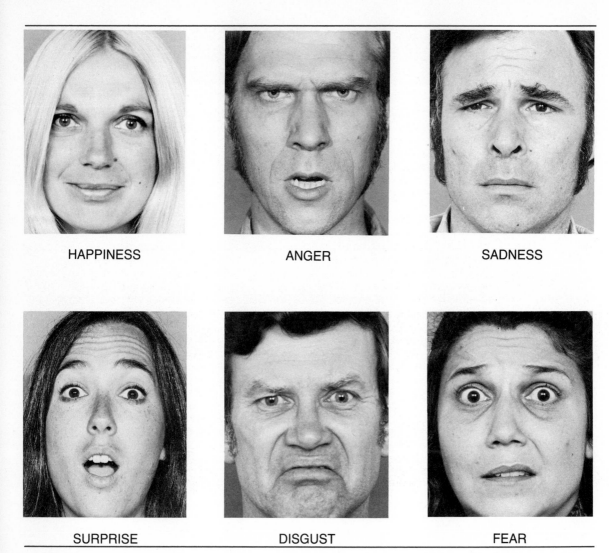

HAPPINESS ANGER SADNESS

SURPRISE DISGUST FEAR

FIGURE 7.2
The six basic facial expressions of emotion

easy to tell a happy gait or bounce from a depressed or painful march. In addition, such body cues as fist clenching, foot tapping, finger drumming, lip biting, and rigid posture may be signs of distress or anxiety. Nurses can sometimes detect pain from a patient's squirming. Just as we infer traits from the way a person moves (expressive style), we can also infer hour-to-hour changes in emotion from body movements.

The combinations of emotional cues are also quite important. If a person with a very tense body and a very nervous voice has a smile, it may be that the smile is "forced" and is not indicative of real happiness. The consistency of the cues matters (DePaulo & Rosenthal, 1979).

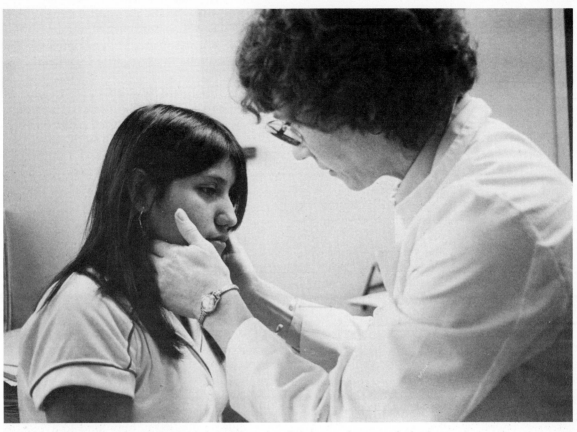

Touching frequently communicates information about status and power. A doctor may touch a patient but the opposite rarely occurs.

Nonverbal Intensifiers

In a romantic film, the viewer can always tell who is about to fall in love: the prospective lovers' eyes meet and you can almost hear the wedding bells ringing. Looking into another's eyes is known as **eye contact.** Social psychological research has indeed found that people strongly in love are likely to spend more time gazing into each other's eyes than people not in love (Rubin, 1973).

Recognition of the importance of eye contact in social perception dates back many years to the sociologist Georg Simmel, who noted the importance of the eyes to social intimacy and reciprocity. The gaze may be one-sided, however; people may be stared at and not reciprocate. People generally realize when they are being looked at and see this nonverbal cue as an attempt to open an interaction (Ellsworth, 1975). However, in many circumstances, being *stared* at is quite negative. An incapacitated patient does not, of course, like to be stared at. Research demonstrates that the meaning of eye contact depends on the context in which it occurs. If the situation is a positive one, then a glance may open communication channels and increase positive feeling. If negative contextual cues are present, however, such as, for example, a disgusted facial expression, then negative feelings will probably increase (cf. Ellsworth & Langer, 1976). For this reason eye behavior can be considered a *nonverbal intensifier.*

Medical personnel have long recognized the importance of *touching* in healing. For example, the faith-healing technique called laying on of hands has long been popular, although of course it is not used in modern scientific medicine. Nevertheless, nurses of cancer patients are constantly urged to pay close attention to touch. Physical contact seems to reassure patients and may even reduce pain. On the other hand, we can all imagine situations in which it is quite unpleasant or threatening to be touched by another person; being grabbed, pushed, or molested is negative. Hence touch is also a nonverbal intensifier.

Status and Touching

Touching also communicates information about status and power (Henley, 1977). Imagine two people standing together, with one touching the other, perhaps with a hand on the shoulder. Knowing nothing else about these people except that one is touching the other, decide which person in the dyad should get which label in the following pairs of status positions: boss/secretary; captain/private; teacher/student; doctor/patient. It should be clear that touching is associated with status. Higher-status people often touch lower-status people but the reverse is quite rare. In the medical setting there are many practical reasons for the doctor to touch the patient, but few reasons for the patient to touch the doctor. Nevertheless, pragmatic reasons aside, the doctor's ability to touch the patient gives the doctor added power over the patient. In fact, one of the defining characteristics of the doctor's role is that the doctor can invade the patient's body. Cancer

patients can easily come to feel controlled and helpless when they are touched in many different ways by various medical personnel who do not take the time to establish interpersonal rapport.

If you doubt the importance of this aspect of touching, then try to put your arm around your professor or your physician or your own town's mayor or most prominent businessman. The right to touch another person often indicates higher status.

Interpersonal Rapport and the Perception of Emotions

Although many cancer patients encounter serious medical problems, these problems are often not their greatest source of difficulty; cancer patients often have significant problems in their interpersonal relationships. People who are told they have cancer are likely to have a high degree of fear and uncertainty and so may look to others to help define their condition (see Chapter 13 on social comparison). Family and friends may be quite confused, however, and while sympathetic, may tend to avoid the patient. Patients, in turn detect this ambivalence and have a difficult time coping with their disease. Social support groups, including groups of other cancer patients such as Make Today Count, may prove beneficial (Wortman & Dunkel-Schetter, 1979). The communication of feelings is also very important to the establishment of the proper rapport between physicians and their patients. When the physician-patient relationship is a good one, patients are more likely to cooperate with their treatment (DiMatteo, 1979). How can we scientifically study a vague notion like "rapport"? We can pay close attention to nonverbal communication.

A key process in understanding emotions is termed *empathy.* Empathy is the experiencing of another's feelings to the point that one reacts similarly? For example, if you see a friend crying at the funeral of her husband and you begin crying also, then you may be having an empathic response. Although empathy seems very important to the development of intimate relations, to friendship, and to compassionate behavior, and has been studied in various ways (Hoffman, 1977), we do not yet know much about this social process (Clark, 1980). A number of basic questions remain puzzling. Is empathy a susceptibility to unconsciously "catch" the mood of others? Is empathy primarily a cognitive ability in which we come to understand the situation of another person and then experience the emotional reaction? Is empathy related to or a result of an ability to detect correctly the emotions of others? We do not yet know the answers to these questions, but an interesting approach involves one's ability to "decode" or understand others' emotions.

There have been many studies of **nonverbal sensitivity**—the ability to detect accurately the emotions of others. We saw above that emotions are communicated through facial expressions, voice tones, and body movements. The most extensive research relating emotional detection to characteristics of social interaction used an instrument called the Profile of Nonverbal Sensitivity or PONS (Rosenthal, Hall, DiMatteo, Rogers, & Archer, 1979). The PONS is a film test in which people are shown a series of very brief nonverbal messages of emotion and are asked to interpret them. The research has shown that children become more nonverbally sensitive as they grow older; that the degree of cultural similarity affects one's ability to detect nonverbal cues; that nonverbal sensitivity is not related to general intelligence; and, most importantly, that nonverbally sensitive people tend to be better adjusted and more interpersonally skilled. Thus, the quality of our social interactions may be affected by our success at "reading" the nonverbal messages of emotion expressed by others.

Individual Differences in Perceiving Emotions

The question often arises as to which categories of people are most successful in emotion detection. What makes someone able to "read" the emotions of others? This question is a difficult one, but there are some clear findings that have to do with individual differences. Perhaps the most interesting difference is a sex difference.

Over the past fifty years, accumulated evidence has indicated that women are more nonverbally sensitive than men. When asked to interpret facial, body, and vocal cues of emotion, which have been expressed through photos, films, videotapes, and tape recordings, women tend to perform better than men (Hall, 1978, 1979). This female superiority may help to explain the idea of "women's intuition"; many women may be especially attuned to the emotional nuances of the social situation.

Because of its many implications, it is important to understand what social psychologists mean when they assert that women are more nonverbally sensitive. First of all, such a conclusion does not in itself explain why women are more sensitive. Some people may conclude that the difference comes from genetic makeup and is therefore a basic law of human nature. This is naive, because psychologists know that genes themselves cannot cause such complex social differences; at the very least, any such genetic makeup must develop in a certain environment to have its effect. Furthermore, there is no evidence that the differences are genetic. Since most of our social skills come from experience, it is much more likely that the sex difference is a result of socialization. For example, it has been suggested that it is tied to sex roles. Since social sensitivity, empathy, nurturance, and a "socioemotional" orientation are characteristic of the female role, girls may be more likely than boys to learn the appropriate nonverbal skills. It has also been suggested that women's nonverbal superiority may result from the female's common position of social powerlessness and passivity. Since men have traditionally held the power in many social situations, women may be forced to carefully monitor the cues of those in power and to observe the activities of the male leaders (for example, Henley, 1977). Such practice may produce greater nonverbal sensitivity. Sex differences thus raise a number of interesting questions concerning the development of nonverbal skills.

A second important point concerning the meaning of sex differences in nonverbal sensitivity is that the findings do not in any way suggest that women *should* be more sensitive. This point may seem obvious to you, but social psychology has shown that existing differences and existing roles often become expectations. What is, is often seen as what *should be*. For example, you may have heard such statements as "If God had wanted women to be surgeons, He wouldn't have made them so squeamish"; or "It's crude and unnatural for men to be nurses." Such statements are rationalizations of the way things are, and often form the basis for unfair discrimination, as when men are denied admission to nursing schools.

A third and final important point concerning the interpretation of sex differences in nonverbal sensitivity is that average group differences do not tell us much in themselves about the characteristics of individuals. You may or may not be more sensitive than your boyfriend or girlfriend. Although women may be more sensitive on the average, it is also true that there are innumerable men who are more nonverbally sensitive than most women. In statistical terminology, the distributions of male sensitivity and female sensitivity have considerable overlap.

A final important but understudied issue in the perception of emotions involves the expresser or "sender." It is clear that some people accurately communicate their feelings to others, while others appear relatively inscrutable. For example, it is very easy to tell when some cancer patients are fearful, but very difficult to discern the emotions of others. These differences seem to be related to basic aspects of personality. It may also be that women are slightly more expressive than men (Buck, 1975, 1979; Hall, 1979). Some of the difficulty in studying how people express feelings results from the fact that they sometimes control their feelings in order to create certain impressions. As we saw earlier, people, unlike objects, are active entities that respond to the demands of the social situation. This important phenomenon is the topic of the next section.

IMPRESSION MANAGEMENT

The Presentation of Self

When people get married or become parents, they tell all their friends and acquaintances. They send out announcements, show people pictures, and enjoy talking about the happy event. When people get cancer they do not usually tell all their friends and acquaintances, even though they may need help; they are likely to be very careful about the information they reveal about their condition. Controlling or managing the information that we reveal about ourselves is common to most of our social interaction. This social psychological phenomenon is known as the **presentation of self.**

The ways we present ourselves to others has been extensively analyzed by the sociologist Erving Goffman (1959). Shakespeare said that "all the world's a stage," and Goffman takes a similar viewpoint, viewing people as actors and social interaction as drama. For this reason, his analysis is sometimes called the "dramaturgical approach." People are concerned with the impressions they give, even though these impressions may not actually correspond to their true selves. Like stage actors, people sometimes mouth certain speeches in order to have an effect on their audiences, but save discussion of personal matters for the times when they are offstage.

The fact that we often try to present ourselves in a favorable light has important implications for our sense of identity. Part of our sense of self comes from other people. Children whom most adults consider very smart and cute will probably incorporate some of these adult reactions in their own sense of self. When this notion is coupled with the idea of impression management, however—that is, of presentation of self—a problem arises. On the one hand, we are presenting certain acted images of ourselves to other people, which may be quite different from our true selves. On the other hand, we are constantly receiving feedback from other people in response to our acted or presented selves, and this feedback affects our true sense of self. To some extent, we become the actor whom we portray!

This conflict between our inner thoughts and the impression we give to others may be especially important for cancer patients. People may give their friends the impression that everything is fine at the same time that they are struggling with some very serious problems of illness. Their friends will then treat them as fine. The patient may thus not be able to get the support needed from friends.

Stigma

If it is maladaptive to hide the fact that one has cancer, why do people do so? Why are people willing to admit that they have been in a car accident or have had a heart attack, but are often unwilling to admit that they have cancer? The answer is that there is a tremendous **stigma** associated with cancer. Solzhenitsyn's fictional character Pavel was immediately labeled a cancer.

The term "stigma" refers to some characteristic of a person that is discrediting and usually suggests something bad about the moral status

of the individual (Goffman, 1963). Stigma is actually a property of interpersonal relations, since it is the group that defines what conditions are stigmatizing and reacts accordingly toward the stigmatized individual. For example, some people view blindness or homosexuality as stigmatizing, while others do not.

The stigma associated with cancer has a long history. In the Middle Ages people believed that nothing could be done to help cancer patients; in the seventeenth and eighteenth centuries many physicians believed that cancer was contagious; cancer patients were isolated and a sense of shame was associated with the disease (Cassileth, 1979). In recent times cancer has remained a stigmatizing disease, viewed by many people as almost as "bad" as venereal disease. It is often viewed as a disease of the unclean, as ugly and painful, and sometimes as punishment for bad deeds (Donovan & Pierce, 1976). Unfortunately, this view of cancer is also held by many health-care practitioners who try to avoid cancer patients. The stigma associated with cancer is tremendously destructive. Many forms of cancer actually have a very good cure rate; others, while ultimately fatal, allow patients many years to live.

Self-Monitoring of Behavior

People with a stigma may try to hide this characteristic from other people and "pass" as normals. Like stage actors, they try to perform a certain role. People differ, however, in the extent to which they control their own behavior. Some are very concerned with acting in an appropriate way in various social situations; they try to see what behaviors are appropriate and then try to manage the impression they create. Such people are called "high self-monitors" (Snyder, 1974, 1979). Others are not so concerned with the situational appropriateness of their behaviors and are low on self-monitoring. These individual differences can be measured by the self-monitoring scale (Snyder,

Deceiving others involves controlling facial, body, and voice cues. Thus, it is easier to successfully deceive someone when speaking over the telephone or when the body is hidden by a desk.

1974). For example, high self-monitors agree with items like "I'm not always the person I appear to be," whereas low self-monitors agree with items like "My behavior is usually an expression of my true inner feelings, attitudes, and beliefs." Because of their impression-management skill and orientation, high self-monitors tend to change their interpersonal behavior in accordance with the demands of the social situation, and so affect the impression others form about their personalities (Lippa, 1978a, 1978b).

It has been suggested that many older people who are ill are very good at understanding both the verbal and nonverbal cues of those around them that indicate that the subject of death should not be discussed. They may suppress their feelings and expressions and thus be cut off from needed communication with their families and medical personnel (Peak, 1977), which is unfortunate, since it may increase the fear, loneliness, and pain sometimes associated with dying. In this case, usual self-monitoring—a necessary aspect of most smoothly flowing social interaction—becomes destructive. When carried to an extreme, impression management may turn into deception.

Deception

Sometimes people lie. They say something they know to be untrue in order to convey misinformation to another person. For example, parents may tell a child that he has a minor case of "weak blood," when in fact the child has leukemia. Or a patient may tell the doctor that she feels perfectly fine to avoid the embarrassment or fear of discussing a painful lump in her breast or a suspicious bleeding. The reasons for lying are varied, but it is something that most people learn at a very early age.

To avoid being deceived, we must be able to tell when someone is lying to us. Even young children hospitalized with cancer can usually tell that something is definitely very wrong. They may notice changes in voice tone and the other nonverbal cues of the people they interact with. Sometimes children with leukemia react negatively to attempted deception on the part of their parents, and may be depressed and uncooperative. The problem may be that the children develop a lack of trust and may even feel abandoned—they know that they are sick but their parents deny it (Cantor, 1978).

To be successful at deception one must know how to control the information one transmits to others. One key concept in hiding or detecting deception seems to be anxiety. For example, relatives of cancer patients who have not been told that they have cancer often feel tremendous stress and anxiety in carrying on the deception. The anxiety of lying is the basis for most of the lie detector tests used sometimes by the police. Such instruments measure physiological changes in the body that are associated with increased anxiety, and thus can sometimes tell when a person is lying (Lykken, 1974). Anxiety also appears in communication. There is some evidence that the anxiety of lying produces a higher pitch in the liar's tone of voice. Furthermore, people use this cue of a high-pitched voice to infer that the speaker is lying. Liars may also change their patterns and fluency of speech (Mehrabian, 1971; Apple, Streeter, & Krauss, 1979).

Successful liars must hide clues that they are lying and may also have to conceal their true feelings. As with self-monitoring, people vary in the extent to which they are aware of the subtle cues they are emitting. There are also differences as a function of the channel and the situation. For example, people do not have to control body cues when they are talking on the telephone; to deceive over the phone involves only the successful control of one's voice. In face-to-face interaction, people may be more careful to monitor other cues (Krauss, Geller, & Olson, 1976). There is also some evidence that liars try very hard to control their facial expressions, but pay less attention to their body movements. Thus, cues of deception may "leak" from body movement (Ekman & Friesen, 1974). In the medical setting there is evidence that physicians who are especially sensitive to body cues may be better able to satisfy the interpersonal needs of their patients, presumably because they are more likely to detect when their patients are uneasy or are not telling the full truth (DiMatteo, Friedman, & Taranta, 1979).

Charisma and Emotional Expression

In many medical settings there are certain physicians who are very popular with patients. In many other occupations, too, such as politics, teaching, and sales, there are certain people who possess a characteristic commonly known as "charisma." Research indicates that charisma may be related to nonverbal expressiveness (Friedman, Prince, Riggio, & DiMatteo, 1980). People who have the desire and the ability to express their emotions and so inspire others are charismatic, and with this dramatic flair tend to be able to influence others in face-to-face interaction.

You may wonder how laboratory research on social perception can actually study seemingly vague constructs like charisma, self-monitoring, and nonverbal sensitivity. The answer often involves the use of film, videotape, and audiotape. For example, in one study of charisma (Friedman et al., 1980), we asked a number of undergraduates to be individually video-taped while attempting to express emotions, while greeting others, and while engaging in various forms of natural social interaction. These various videotapes were edited and shown to raters who judged the success of the students at the various tasks. At other sessions, the students provided detailed written information about their personalities and how they described themselves. They also judged film clips of other people expressing emotions, were rated by their friends on various dimensions, and engaged in other laboratory studies. In this way, we gathered a variety of information about each person and then examined the relationships among the various measures. It was found that people who described themselves on a questionnaire in a way termed "charismatic" were people who were rated as expressive by their friends, were more likely to work in jobs involving social influence, had dominant personalities that excited and stirred others, and were above average in ability to express emotions. Such precise laboratory findings can be further tested in real-life situations involving social interactions such as those between doctors and patients. In this way, the various aspects of self-presentation can be systematically isolated.

Who Do You Trust?

Excessive concern with the topic of impression management may lead us to the pessimistic conclusion that people are constantly deceiving and manipulating others. In fact, there has been a good deal of research on what is called Machiavellianism. A Machiavellian tries to manipulate others in social interaction; exploitation is common (Christie & Geis, 1970). For example, Machiavellians may take advantage of others in situations where cooperation is expected. Many people, however, are very trusting—they expect that the word of another individual can be relied on. People who trust others lie less often and respect the rights of

others. Importantly, people high in trust often tend to be happier and better adjusted than less trusting people (Rotter, 1980); they are not less intelligent or more gullible than others, and their positive social orientation seems quite beneficial for society.

FACE-TO-FACE INTERACTION

When we examined how people form impressions of the traits and emotions of others, the focus was directly on the perceiver. For example, the perceiver can be presented with a series of traits listed on a piece of paper, or can be shown a picture of a facial expression and asked for a judgment. When we looked at impression management, however, it became evident that people "perform" in front of other people. Actually, most of our social perception occurs during face-to-face interaction. In such situations, the perceiver may transmit expectations to the other and in turn may receive feedback.

Perceptions and Actions

We saw earlier that Asch found warm and cold to be central traits in impression formation. Do these traits have implications for face-to-face interaction as well? A study by Kelley (1950) applied the traits warm and cold to real people in a real interaction. Students in a class were given notes that supposedly described a guest lecturer who would appear in class that day. To half the students the lecturer was described as industrious, critical, practical, determined, and cold. For the rest of the students, he was described as industrious, critical, practical, determined, and warm. The teacher who was described then actually led the class in a discussion. After he left, the students filled out impression ratings of him. As Asch had found, the central traits had an important effect on students' overall perceptions of the instructor. Especially important is the effect that the trait impressions had on social interaction. The students who believed the instructor to be warm tended to ask more questions and begin more interactions with the instructor than did those who thought him cold. This finding points to an extremely important aspect of social perception, namely, the effect of interpersonal expectations on face-to-face interaction.

Expectations and the Self-Fulfilling Prophecy

At the turn of the century there was quite a bit of interest in talking animals. There were talking dogs, pigs, and Clever Rosa, the mare of Berlin. Most of these animals were performers and their owners made their living in this way. Although scientists were interested in the possibility of intelligent animals, they had to dismiss most of these cases as circus acts involving tricks or deception. The animals were trained by people.

An exception was the horse named Clever Hans. Hans was owned by Mr. von Osten, who allowed scientists to study his horse carefully. Clever Hans seemed to be very smart. He could add, subtract, multiply, and divide and tap the correct answer out with his right forefoot (see Pfungst, 1965). For example, when asked "What are the factors of 28?", Hans tapped out consecutively the correct answers: 2, 4, 7, 14, 28. He also seemed to be able to read German and analyze musical tones. The case of Clever Hans is extremely important to the understanding of social perception.

Most investigators looked at the mind of Hans for the answer to his secret powers, but one psychologist, Pfungst, (1965), tried something different. He found that Hans could not answer a question correctly if the questioner did not know the right answer or if the questioner was not visible to Hans. Pfungst thus suspected that people were somehow sending cues to the horse about when to start and stop tapping. After systematic investigation, Pfungst found this indeed to be the case. When observers leaned forward to watch his hoof, Hans would start tapping. When Hans approached the correct answer, the experimenters would change posture, and when they lifted their heads, Hans knew to stop tapping. Hans would even respond to such very subtle cues as the observers' raising of their eyebrows. Thus, the key to Hans's success lay not in the mind of the horse but rather in the expectations and communications of the investigators.

The observers expected Hans to give the correct answer and their expectations in turn caused Hans to give the right answer. As discussed in Chapter 6, this phenomenon is called the self-fulfilling prophecy. To demonstrate that this applies to humans and not just to horses, Pfungst himself played the part of Hans. By closely observing his questioners, Pfungst was able to tap out the correct answer to various questions to which he did not have the answer.

We saw in Chapter 2 that the expectations of the experimenter may be an important source of error in scientific experiments; the experimental subjects may be heavily influenced, just as Clever Hans was influenced. Such effects in experiments are sometimes called artifacts, because they are made by the experimenter rather than being a more natural form of behavior. The self-fulfilling prophecy is an important phenomenon, however, not only in the conduct of scientific experiments and in our interaction with animals, but also in our normal social interaction.

In the medical setting, medical personnel generally have very definite expectations about patients who have been diagnosed as terminally ill. These expectations may sometimes come to hasten the death of their patients (Kubler-Ross, 1971). For example, in one study, the time it took nurses to answer patients' calls was measured, and it was found that terminally ill patients had to wait longer than other patients.

It is sometimes hard to appreciate the power of expectations and the self-fulfilling prophecy, which can even operate on a mass scale. One interesting example occurred when Johnny Carson joked on television that there was a toilet-tissue shortage. It was not true, but so many people believed him and ran out to stock up that a shortage did, indeed, result. But we are especially interested in the direct effects of expectations on people. A striking example of the power of such expectations comes from a study of mental institutions.

Can Expectations Produce Mental Illness?

We have seen that the doctor's role and the patient's role are composed of expectations about what doctors and patients can and should do. Such expectations are very strong in mental institutions, where the role of a mentally disturbed person (often termed "psychotic") is very well defined. These expectations were dramatically revealed in a field study by Rosenhan (1973). Rosenhan and seven other "normal" people appeared at various mental institutions around the country and said they were hearing voices. They did so in order to be admitted to the mental institutions (which they all were), but they then immediately stopped showing any abnormal signs; they acted normally and observed what went on. These pseudopatients were never detected by the hospital staff; even worse, their normal behavior was ignored or misunderstood. For example, if they got bored (something very common in mental institutions), they might stand in the lunch line or pace the hallway. Such behavior was seen by the staff as psychopathological. Even their note taking was seen as further evidence that they were mentally ill. Overall, their experience was a very unpleasant one. Many mental patients are indeed seriously troubled people who need help from others; but many others are re-

sponding in large part to the demands of the institution in which they find themselves. Some patients are in a "catch 22" situation: if they try to protest that they are perfectly normal, this protestation may be taken as further evidence of their mental illness. The popular book and movie, "One Flew over the Cuckoo's Nest," deals with just this problem. The hero, who is sent to a mental institution for psychiatric evaluation, is a very likable and in many ways quite normal individual. Yet the expectations and the rules of the mental institution act perversely to make the hero more and more psychotic.

Placebos and Expectations

Wise physicians use new drugs and therapies to fight cancer while they are still effective. This is an application of the famous medical dictum, "Treat as many patients as possible with the new remedies while they still have the power to heal" (Shapiro, 1971). It is often true that medical treatments that work quite well when they are first introduced on the medical scene become less and less effective as time goes on. As treatments are studied in more detail and as negative results become more apparent, medical personnel become less confident in the new treatment and their patients do less well. This phenomenon illustrates the importance of expectations in medical settings. If medical personnel expect a therapy to work, they are more likely to engage in helpful behaviors and to communicate positive expectations to their patients, who in turn do better; a self-fulfilling prophecy is at work.

Some people find it difficult to believe that social perception is a key factor in reactions to illness. Their doubts arise from the incorrect assumption that illness is a biological process with no psychological elements. In fact, the mind is very important to physical well-being. A good example concerns pain. You may have thought of pain as a direct function of physical trauma—the more physical damage to your body, the greater the pain. Actually, the feeling of pain depends in part upon what you think about your pain. For example, you may cut your toe but not feel much pain until you look down and see all the blood. Soldiers on the battlefield who are wounded often do not feel their pain until they arrive at the hospital. Similarly, you may have noticed that young children who fall down when running may be somewhat confused; they look to others to label their feelings. If the parents are pitying and comforting, the child may begin to cry, but if the parents make light of it, then the child may begin to laugh. Even with cancer, there are tremendous individual differences in reactions, depending upon what people think about their cancer. Indeed, one increasingly popular method of treating cancer involves visualization (Simonton, Matthews-Simonton, & Creighton, 1978). By imagining that they are overcoming and fighting their cancer, many patients are better able to cope with the stresses and pain.

Sometimes knowingly and sometimes unknowingly, medicine has long employed the **placebo** effect in treatment. The *placebo effect* is the psychological or psychophysiological effect of a therapy that does not have specific activity for the condition being treated (Shapiro, 1971). Sometimes the placebo is a pill—such as a sugar pill—which is inert. In other cases the placebo may be a certain treatment, such as an exercise regimen, that does not have any direct physiological effect on the disease being treated. Placebos seem to be effective because many patients respond to the belief that they are being helped. Placebos can even produce physiological changes in the body and may sometimes interfere with other established treatments (Jones, 1977). As with other expectations, placebo phenomena are often communicated nonverbally (Friedman, 1979b); it is not hard to imagine that patients catch the enthusiasm or discouragement of their physicians.

When the medical community fails to offer patients the positive expectations they need to help deal with disease, they may turn to faith healers. We saw above that one method of faith healing involves the laying on of hands. Another type of faith healing involves treatment with exotic drugs. An example of this phenomenon is provided in Social Focus 7.2. Other faith healers employ special prayer rituals. In some cases special diets are suggested. Unfortunately, such healers are often dismissed as quacks. Actually, their healing is often a prime example of social perception processes at work, and so can and should be scientifically studied by social psychologists.

The whole area of expectations and disease is becoming increasingly important. It is now evident that the views people and medical personnel have about disease and health can have a significant impact on actual health. The ways people perceive and cope with the stresses of life, the quality of their interpersonal relationships, and the expectations and atmosphere of medical-care facilities all have a significant influence on health (Antonovsky, 1979; Taylor, 1979; Totman, 1979).

Accommodating Other's Expectations

Building upon what we know about perception, communication, and the self-fulfilling prophecy, we can achieve a sophisticated understanding of the importance to social perception of face-to-face interaction. An important study of the process of social interaction by Snyder, Tanke, and Berscheid (1977) examined the self-fulfilling nature of the physical-attractiveness stereotype. In this study, pairs of male and female students became acquainted with each other by using microphones and headphones. Before the conversations, the perceptions of the males were experimentally manipulated. Each male was given a picture that was supposedly of his female partner. Actually the experimenters gave the males preselected pictures that varied in the physical attractiveness of the pictured female. The conversation between the males and females was recorded, and judges later rated the female's half of the

SOCIAL FOCUS 7.2
Krebiozen, Laetrile, and Crocodile Dung

Throughout the history of medicine, almost every conceivable substance has been used to treat disease, including hooves of asses, eunuch fat, human perspiration, and crocodile dung (Shapiro, 1971). Interestingly, these treatments often helped patients, although the drugs had no specific effects for the disease being treated. They worked because of the placebo effect: physicians and patients believed that they would help and so they did help somewhat, at least temporarily.

It seems that the more serious the disease, the more dramatic and sweeping are false claims of a new cure. As a serious and often life-threatening disease, cancer has been subject to many claimed, astounding, miracle cures. Two "miracle" drugs—Krebiozen and Laetrile—are of special interest.

In 1951 a medical panic was created when Dr. Andrew Ivy, a leading physiologist, announced the discovery of a drug, Krebiozen, that could destroy malignancies. Thousands of cancer patients tried to obtain the new drug, but its production was tightly controlled. Many patients who did obtain Krebiozen showed dramatic improvement. Case-by-case testimonials were given for this dramatic cure. It was many years before it became clear that Krebiozen had no specific action in fighting cancer; it was a placebo. Typical of patient reactions was the case in which a man, confined to his bed with tumors, was administered this new miracle drug, and was soon out of bed with shrinking tumors. When it became clear, however, that Krebiozen was not effective in fighting cancer, this same patient collapsed and soon died.

In recent years an almost identical scenario has been played out with the drug Laetrile. Supposedly an anticancer drug, Laetrile is an extract of apricot

conversation on such dimensions as, How intimate or personal is this person's conversation? The judges' ratings showed that females who were believed (unknown to them) to be physically attractive actually behaved in a more sociable manner. (The women who were talking to men who thought that they were physically attractive acted attractively.) In other words, the objects of a stereotype confirmed the expectations of the (male) stereotype holders. These women actually "became" different people according to the expectations of their partners. (The males who interacted with women whom they believed to be physically attractive behaved in a more confident, attractive, and out-going manner and so influenced their partners to respond in kind.)

We have seen that women are somewhat better than men at reading nonverbal cues of emotion. According to traditional sex roles, women are not expected to be dominant, controlling, assertive, and manipulative. Yet greater nonverbal sensitivity would seem to give women an advantage, in relationships where power is involved. A resolution to this apparent contradiction has been offered by Rosenthal and DePaulo (1979). They suggest that women are more accommodating than men. That is, although women on the average tend to be good at detecting what it is that others

pits. Although Laetrile has been banned by the federal government as ineffective, thousands of Americans cross into Mexico seeking the drug and many claim miracle cures.

Krebiozen and Laetrile are only two of the many drugs and procedures proclaimed as miracle cures at regular intervals in history. Regardless of whether such drugs are ever shown to have any true physiological value, they illustrate a fascinating aspect of the process of social perception. In most of these cases, the cure somehow acquires a mystical or even religious significance—witness pilgrimages to religious shrines. Further, the cures are usually promoted by a small group of proponents who are not supported by most of the scientific community. Very often individual testimonials, rather than scientific experiments, are cited as proof of the cure's effectiveness. Finally, the cures generally seem most attractive to people who are desperate, who see them as a last hope, and who are very emotionally aroused in some way.

It is important to remember that most of these miracle cures do have some positive effect, at least in the short term. When people expect to improve and are expected to improve by those around them, they often do improve. Unfortunately, scientists often view such procedures as quackery, while the proponents of the cure view the scientists as closed-minded and authoritarian. This polarization could probably be minimized if the scientific and medical communities achieved a better understanding of social psychology. The medical community should be willing to take into account the very real effects of interpersonal relations on a person's physical health.

want them to do, women may be relatively poor at detecting or interpreting subtle, hidden cues. In other words, sex roles may socialize women to see those cues that it is polite to see and to respond accordingly. Along these lines, it has been found that women may adjust their nonverbal style to fit the personality of the men with whom they are interacting (Weitz, 1976). For example, when getting to know dominant men, women tended to react more submissively in terms of their nonverbal communication. Such accommodation did not occur in interactions in same-sex dyads. Again, such accommodation occurs very quickly, and is very subtle.

Interpersonal accommodation is extremely important in medical settings. Doctors, nurses, family, and friends all have definite expectations about what illness means and about how patients should react to illness. Patients will often perceive these expectations and adjust their behavior to fit them. The patient's new behaviors will then be taken as proof that the expectations were correct and so the cycle will continue. For example, a doctor or nurse may expect a cancer patient to get weak. The patient will detect this expectation and may react accordingly. The medical personnel will then see that the patient is indeed looking weaker, and so they first of all reinforce or approve this change in behavior, and second, come to expect further deterioration. Thus, a smooth interaction is established between the patient and other people involved, but the relationships are very destructive. It is important to remember that this process of interpersonal accommodation is common to most, if not all, of our usual social interaction. It helps our relationships proceed smoothly. What is adaptive in normal situations, however, can be quite maladaptive in special situations such as the medical setting.

SUMMARY   Social perception is the process by which we form an impression of and establish a relationship with another person. This process involves inferring the traits and emotions of the other and defining mutual expectations. Taken together with the attributional processes described in the Chapter 6, social perception underlies most social relations.

We have examined social perception in terms of an important social issue—cancer. More precisely, we have explored impressions of, reactions to, and interactions with *people* who have cancer. We do not study people under microscopes. Rather, people are active entities who respond to our behaviors and who in turn affect our actions.

One important aspect of social perception concerns the ways we form impressions of the personalities of other people, impressions that are heavily influenced by contexts. We interpret the actions of others in terms of the background or contextual information we have available. Central traits such as warm and cold form a key part of the whole impression.

First impressions are often an important aspect of social relations. Physical attractiveness is a key factor in the initial stages of impression formation. Physically attractive people are often seen as having many other positive traits as well, a special problem for many cancer patients who are trying to deal with attacks on their bodies. Primacy effects, in which initial information has a greater impact than later information, may occur, as people attempt to integrate later information into the picture they have formed on the basis of first impressions. In understanding impression formation, it is often instructive to try to understand how final impressions result from a combination of the individual elements or pieces of information.

People's stereotypes often interfere with forming an accurate impression of another. Biases of overgeneralization in perception, such as the halo effect, occur as people try to organize or make sense of the various pieces of information about others that become available. In addition, many stereotypes have little if any basis in fact.

A second major aspect of social perception involves the communication of emotions. Much of our information about the feelings of others comes from their facial expressions, their vocal cues, and their body movements. These cues combine with each other and with words to provide a fantastic yet subtle array of information. We generally do not consciously think about this information, but make good use of it. The universality of many of these cues of emotion permit impression formation and interaction with people of very different backgrounds.

The feelings we perceive in others can be intensified through gaze and through touching. Mutual gaze (called eye contact) and mutual touching are an essential aspect in the creation of intimacy in interpersonal relations. The intimacy, however, may be positive or negative, depending upon the context in which the interaction occurs. Nonverbal cues, especially touching, may also give us important information about status and power in a relationship.

Empathy is an important but understudied component of impression formation. Research indicates that nonverbal sensitivity may be an important construct in understanding the success or failure of various social interactions. It has been found that women are more nonverbally sensitive than men, but the precise causes and implications of this difference are not yet clearly understood.

Certain conditions, such as cancer, may stigmatize the individual in the eyes of certain groups of perceivers. To present a favorable or expected impression in various situations, people engage in impression management. Like stage actors, people play certain roles, revealing certain attributes and hiding others. People differ, however, in the extent to which they self-monitor their behavior.

The presentation of self that is common to most social interaction sometimes develops into distinctive attempts at deception. Most people, however, watch for cues that the person they are dealing with may be lying. Often, deception is revealed as anxiety. In different situations, different cues of deception become important. In face-to-face interaction, it may be that cues of deception are often leaked through body movements.

Some people are very good at communicating their emotions to others and may achieve a good deal of social influence. Other people attempt to subtly manipulate others. Ultimately, smooth and positive social relations depend upon mutual trust.

The final basic aspect of social perception involves the process of face-to-face interaction. The perceiver's expectations will generally affect the perceived, thus altering the nature of the social interaction. A self-fulfilling prophecy occurs when expectations result in the realization of these expectations. Such processes are especially likely in hospitals and mental institutions, but are also common in ordinary face-to-face interaction. Since our impressions of others' behaviors influence and change those behaviors, social interaction must be an integral part of the study of social perception.

In many medical interactions placebos are a crucial, though possibly unrecognized, aspect of treatment. Medical personnel form impressions of the personalities and feelings of patients, and patients form impressions about the practitioners. These mutual impressions then combine to form the nature of the social interaction and the treatment. The nature of the social interaction will affect the patient's pain, the patient's success in coping with disease, and sometimes even the patient's course of recovery. When positive expectations are absent in the medical setting, some patients will seek help in nontraditional settings such as faith healing.

Social psychologists have at times achieved a sophisticated understanding of the subtleties involved in the process of social perception. The nuances of interpersonal accommodation are not obvious to the naive observer, but become very clear when examined from a social psychological perspective. Given the importance of social perception to such settings as the medical one, we should strive to bring this knowledge to where it will be useful.

SUGGESTED READINGS

Cantor, R. C. *And a time to live: Toward emotional well-being during the crisis of cancer.* New York: Harper & Row, 1978.

DiMatteo, M. R., & Friedman, H. S. (Eds.) Interpersonal relations in health care. *Journal of Social Issues,* 1979, *35*(1), whole issue.

Goffman, E. *Stigma: Notes on the management of spoiled identity.* Englewood Cliffs, N.J.: Prentice-Hall, 1963.

Henley, N. M. *Body politics: Power, sex and nonverbal communication.* Englewood Cliffs, N.J.: Prentice-Hall, 1977.

Jones, R. A. *Self-fulfilling prophecies: Social psychological and physiological effects of expectancies.* Hillsdale, N.J.: Lawrence Erlbaum Associates, 1977.

LaFrance, M., & Mayo, C. *Moving bodies: Nonverbal communication in social relationships.* Monterey, Cal.: Brooks/Cole, 1978.

Schneider, D. J., Hastorf, A. H., & Ellsworth, P. C. *Person perception.* Reading, Mass.: Addison-Wesley, 1979.

Totman, R. *Social causes of illness.* London: Souvenir Press, 1979.

Interpersonal Relations

PART **3**

8

INTERPERSONAL ATTRACTION

- Introduction
- The Importance of Reinforcement
- The Development of Relationships
- The Nature of Love
- Passionate Love
- Dissolution of Relationships
- Summary

INTRODUCTION

The newspaper television listings on February 15, 1981 contained the following story:

Fred Rogers, better known to TV viewers as Mister Rogers, is bringing divorce into his neighborhood. The personable creator and producer of . . . Mr. Rogers' Neighborhood . . . has a one-hour special about divorce. . . . "We started the show out by saying that in 1990, 40 percent of America's children will be living with one parent, mostly because of divorce," said Rogers. (Haise, 1981 p. 4)

Social psychologists who study **interpersonal attraction** are interested in why we are liked by others, how relationships develop into friendship and love, and also how and why relationships dissolve. Questions of liking and loving are deeply personal for most of us, but they are also important for society as a whole. Further, as vividly illustrated by the Mr. Rogers television show, marital dissolution is a fact of life facing increasing numbers of persons in our society, and is having an impact not only on individual families but numerous social institutions as well. In fact, statistics on divorce frequency indicate that about 40 percent of today's marriages in the United States will end in divorce, the highest rate ever (Norton & Glick, 1976). Statistics such as this underscore the importance of studying how and why interpersonal relationships develop and dissolve. In addition to the fact that many relationships end in divorce, it is also true that many individuals have problems in initiating relationships. In this chapter and the one that follows, we will explore social psychological research on the determinants of attraction, the causes and consequences of divorce, and the dynamics of loneliness and intimacy. As the research of social psychologists reveals more information about interpersonal attraction, it should be possible to be better able to help people with problems in initiating or maintaining relationships.

THE IMPORTANCE OF REINFORCEMENT

Most of what is known about interpersonal attraction can be explained in terms of reinforcement theory. Both Byrne and Clore (1970) and Lott and Lott (1974) have postulated that we like people who reward us and dislike people who punish us. According to Byrne and Clore, when another person has done something to reward you, positive feelings are generated. These positive feelings lead you to evaluate the other person positively and say such things as "I like that person." Lott and Lott state that besides liking someone who provides direct reward, we also like someone who is simply *associated* with rewarding experiences. For example, if there is a class that you particularly enjoy, you may come to like the other students in the class. The principle of generalization is also used to explain the fact that once you have come to like (or dislike) someone with particular characteristics, this feeling will generalize to others who have similar characteristics. For example, a person whose first love as a young teenager had red hair may develop a generalized preference for dating others with red hair.

In the remainder of the chapter, we will trace the development of interpersonal relationships from attraction to love, and then consider the dissolution of relationships. A model provided by Levinger and Snoek (1972) is a useful format for organizing this information.

This chapter is written by P. Chris Cozby and Daniel Perlman.

THE DEVELOPMENT OF RELATIONSHIPS

Levinger and Snoek hypothesize that people go through a series of stages or levels as relationships develop. These levels are termed zero contact, awareness, surface contact, and mutuality. Figure 8.1 illustrates the four levels with two circles, each representing a person in the relationship, overlapping more and more as the relationship progresses. At each level, different factors are important as determinants of attraction. A relationship may stop at any level or may progress to the next level. As the levels are described, imagine that you are one of the circles and that someone you know is the other circle.

Zero Contact

In Figure 8.1, **zero contact** is depicted as two circles with no point of contact. Obviously, considering all the people who are around us in relation to the number of people actually known, most people coexist at this level. Even though the two people have no relationship, it is important to know what factors will lead to their becoming aware of one another and thus beginning a relationship.

The most important determinant of such awareness is called **propinquity,** meaning physical closeness. Of the many people you could potentially become acquainted with, you come to know only a few. Usually this occurs because, just by chance, you happen to find yourself physically in proximity to the other person. You may have sat next to each other in class, worked in the same place, or lived in adjacent apartments or houses. Considerable evidence demonstrates that propinquity is, in fact, a determinant of liking. For example, Festinger, Schachter, and Back (1950) showed that apartment-house residents who live next to one another and on the same floor are much

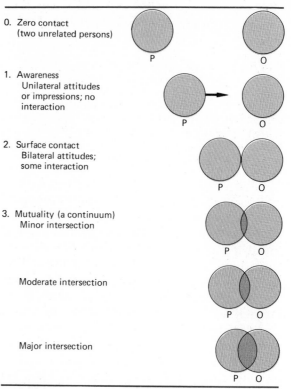

FIGURE 8.1
Levinger's stages of relationships.
Source: Levinger and Snoek, 1972.

more likely to know and be friends with one another than residents who live on different floors or in different buildings. Similarly, students who sit next to one another in class, even when assigned to their seats alphabetically, are more likely to report that they are friends than are students who sit farther away (Byrne, 1961; Segal, 1974). One intriguing implication of propinquity is that such an important part of one's life—those with whom we come to have deep interpersonal relationships—is to a great extent determined by chance. Many married couples will tell you that if both of them hadn't gone to a particular party, hadn't taken the car to a particular garage on a particular day, or in general hadn't done something at a particular time, they would undoubtedly never have met and would now be married to someone else.

Thus, the influence of propinquity is due in part simply to the fact that physical closeness increases the probability of meeting. Also, if the physical proximity occurs when people meet in a setting such as a church or a job, the chances of liking increase because they may share similar attitudes and interests. In addition, the phenomenon of mere exposure is probably operating. Recall from Chapter 4 that repeated exposure to a stimulus increases liking for that stimulus. Research indicates that when people are repeatedly exposed to others who are originally neutral or somewhat favorable, they come to like them more and more (Saegert, Swap, & Zajonc, 1973; Zajonc, 1968). Finally, the fact that simply anticipating that we must interact with someone increases liking may be part of the propinquity phenomenon (Darley & Berscheid, 1967; Tyler & Sears, 1977).

Awareness

The level of **awareness** is depicted in Figure 8.1 as an arrow extending from one circle to the other. This is unilateral awareness, in which only one person is aware of the other. Bilateral awareness, with both persons aware of each other (and aware that the other is aware!), is likely. There is no actual interaction—your impression of the other is based on observable, external characteristics such as clothing, physical features, or the way the person seems to act around others.

Much of the research on social perception and attribution discussed in Chapters 6 and 7 describes relationships at the awareness level. We form impressions, making many judgments about what the other person is like. Most important, a decision of whether to pursue the relationship further is made at this stage. The ability to progress from awareness to the next level, surface contact, or from surface contact to mutuality, is a problem for many people who are shy or experience dating anxiety (cf. Zimbardo, 1977). Social Focus 8.1 describes some aspects of social-skills training, a technique for helping people learn to interact with others and thus develop relationships (Curran, 1977; Lindquist, Kramer, Rhyne, MacDonald, & McGrath, 1975).

Physical attractiveness. As we briefly noted in Chapter 7, an external characteristic of the other that has been studied extensively by social psychologists is **physical attractiveness.** One has only to look at advertisements on television and in magazines to know how important physical attractiveness is in our society. Early studies of physical attractiveness confirmed that people hold a stereotype that "what is beautiful is good" (see Dion, Berscheid, & Walster, 1972). That is, people assume that physically attractive persons possess more highly desirable characteristics than those who are less attractive. Dion et al. report that attractive individuals are assumed to be more sensitive, kind, sociable, interesting, outgoing, strong, poised, and exciting than less attractive persons. They are also assumed to have some negative characteristics, however, such as vanity, egotism, and sexual promiscuity (Dermer & Thiel, 1975).

Later research has indicated that our beliefs about physical attractiveness are quite pervasive and have considerable impact on individuals (Dion, 1980). In fact, the influence of physical attractiveness can be observed among children as young as three years old. Dion (1977) reports that these children prefer looking at pictures of other children who are more attractive. Also, adults treat physically attractive and unattractive children differently. In another study by Dion (1972), college students preparing to become teachers read a description of a child's behavior, presumably written

SOCIAL FOCUS 8.1
Learning Social Skills

Social-skills training allows people to learn new behaviors for interacting more effectively with others. Depending on the individual, skill training may help people to overcome their anxieties about being in social situations; or it may assist people in more accurately assessing their social performance. (Many people are overly negative in evaluating themselves.) Finally, skill-training sessions may simply provide participants with new, more effective ways of behaving. An excerpt from the leader's manual for one such training group is shown below. Here we have a recounting of what takes place in developing the skills necessary to initiate a conversation.

1. Group members offered a variety of possible conversation-starting remarks, included examples of those they had used in the past, and discussed the pros and cons of each.
2. Several important points were made during the discussion by the members and the leaders:
   a. Different settings require different kinds of opening lines: For example, opening lines to use in a classroom situation might include:
   "Can I see your notes for a minute?"
   "What do you think of this lecturer?"
   "Have you found time to get to the special reading assignments?"
   b. It is more important to be natural than to try to be extra suave or dramatic.
   c. You do not have to come on strong at the beginning.
   d. Use a question to open a conversation rather than a snide comment or critical statement, as it can be very difficult to respond to the latter. Not only are they difficult to respond to but it is easy to alienate the person before you get to know her.
   e. Once the conversation has started, be sure to listen closely to what she says so you can ask further questions.
3. Some of the ways of opening or starting a conversation are listed below:
   a. Where are you from?
   b. Is anyone sitting here?
   c. Do you come here often?
   d. Hi. I've seen you here before and wanted to talk to you.
   e. How long have you been at this school?
   f. Have you always lived around this part of the country?
   g. Are you taking any courses you are particularly interested in this semester?
   h. Where do you live on campus? How do you like living there?
   i. Have you decided what you are doing this summer yet?
   j. Did you read about _____ in the paper?
4. The group discussed that while many of these were cliché beginnings, it was most important to start somewhere and to be genuinely interested in the conversation. Hopefully the two of you would soon discover topics of mutual interest.
5. Group members were encouraged to ask personal questions about the other person's feelings and interests like:
   a. What do you like to do with your spare time?
   b. Are you happy here in school?

Source: Lindquist, Kramer, Rhyne, MacDonald, and McGrath, 1975.

by the child's teacher. In one condition, the behavior was *very* bad: the child had thrown a snowball packed with a sharp piece of ice at the head of another child. In the other condition, the behavior was only *mildly* bad: the child had thrown a snowball at another child's leg. Attached to each description was a photo of the child, who was shown to be either attractive or unattractive. The subjects then made judgments about the child. The attractive and unattractive children were treated differently, but only in the very bad behavior condition. When the child was attractive, the behavior was excused as a temporary transgression. The unattractive child, however, was blamed, and the behavior was assumed to be typical for that child.

It is not surprising, then, to find that physically attractive people grow up to actually have higher self-esteem, be less shy, date more frequently, and have greater social skills than less attractive individuals (Curran & Lippold, 1975; Goldman & Lewis, 1977; Jackson & Huston, 1975). Interestingly, hospitalized mental patients *are* less attractive than nonhospitalized individuals (Farina, Fischer, Sherman, Smith, Groh, & Mermin, 1977). It is not clear whether low attractiveness is a contributing cause of mental illness or whether such individuals are more likely to be hospitalized because clinicians perceive them to be more poorly adjusted (Cash, Kehr, Polyson, & Freeman, 1977).

Physical attractiveness also influences very important decisions that we make about others. For example, physically attractive job candidates are more likely to be hired following a job interview than less attractive applicants (Dipboye, Arvey, & Terpstra, 1977; Dipboye, Fromkin, & Wiback, 1975). Also, the physical attractiveness of a defendant affects jurors' perceptions. In mock jury trials, attractive defendants are usually less likely to be judged guilty and receive more lenient sentences than unattractive defendants (Efran, 1974; Sigall & Ostrove, 1975).

Finally, attractiveness is a factor in decisions about whom we desire to date and marry. Early research indicated that when people express their desires for *potential* dating or marriage partners, they choose the most attractive persons possible (Walster, Aronson, Abrahams, & Rottman, 1966). *Actual* choices, however, seem to follow a **matching principle.** That is, people choose partners who are about equal to themselves in physical attractiveness. Evidence that people choose similar partners has been obtained in several investigations (Murstein, 1972; Price & Vandenberg, 1979; Berscheid, Dion, Walster, & Walster, 1971), and the effect occurs for both opposite-sex pairs and same-sex friendships (Cash & Derlega, 1978).

The matching principle is explained in part by the fact that the decision to ask someone for a date is determined both by the attractiveness of the other person *and* by the probability of being rejected (Shanteau & Nagy, 1979). The highest likelihood of actually making a decision to date occurs when the other is similar in attractiveness. In casually dating couples, the more attractive partners have more opposite-sex friends, and the less attractive partners worry more about their partner's interest in other relationships (White, 1980). Over time, couples who are dissimilar in attractiveness have less stable relationships, so that the relationships of highly similar couples are more likely to last over a long period of time (Hill, Rubin, & Peplau, 1976).

What makes a person physically attractive? It is generally true that within a given culture the standards of what constitutes attractiveness are learned by those in the culture. The nature of the standards, however, differs from culture to culture. In general, people who conform to the current standards tend to be perceived as attractive.

In today's U.S. and Canadian culture, a few generalizations about attractiveness standards are possible. First, people who are not overweight are seen as more attractive than those who are (Lerner & Gellert, 1969). Males who

At the awareness stage of a relationship, external characteristics such as physical attractiveness are the most important determinants of attraction.

are tall (at least up to about six feet) are seen as more attractive than shorter men (Graziano, Brothen, & Berscheid, 1978). Such things as smiling, eye contact, and posture also contribute to perceptions of attractiveness (McGinley, McGinley, & Nicholas, 1978; Kleinke, Staneski, & Berger, 1975). In terms of body features, most males prefer women with medium-size legs, medium breasts, and medium to small buttocks (Wiggins, Wiggins, & Conger, 1968), while females prefer a "V-shaped" male with broad shoulders and a torso that tapers to small buttocks (Lavrakas, 1975). It should be noted that there are personality and social-class

differences in what body type is preferred. To a large extent, whether two people find one another attractive is dependent on whether they somehow fit each other's individual preferences.

In today's society, physical attractiveness is more important in judgments about females than about males (Krebs & Adinolfi, 1975; Morse, Gruzen, & Reis, 1976). It remains to be seen whether changes in sex-role standards will lead to less emphasis on female attractiveness or more emphasis on male attractiveness.

It is worthwhile to point out that the research on physical attractiveness does have extensive practical implications. For example, therapists helping an unattractive person may now consider such treatments as a different hairstyle, choice of clothing, or cosmetics. Also, a very unattractive person who has had problems obtaining employment may be likely to engage in criminal activities such as robbery. In these cases, plastic surgery may be a better (and probably less expensive) means of rehabilitation than imprisonment.

Surface Contact

At the **surface-contact** level, the two individuals begin to interact, shown in Figure 8.1 as contact between the two circles. The nature of the interaction is quite superficial and predictable. Think of what you say to someone during your first casual conversations. You probably ask each other a number of questions regarding such things as college major, desired occupation, hobbies and interests, and attitudes. The kinds of activities engaged in are quite predictable as well—for example, a movie, a dance, or dinner at a pizza parlor. Despite the superficiality of the interaction, surface contact is very important. You are learning about the other person and making judgments concerning your desire for future interaction. This learning and decision process may occur not only in face-to-face interaction but also through such mechanisms as newspaper ads (see Social Focus 8.2).

At the surface contact level, people interact and discover whether they are similar to one another. Finding that interacting is rewarding is important at this stage.

The importance of reinforcement in attraction can be easily seen at the surface-contact level. That is, liking occurs when two people find that interacting with one another is reinforcing. Interpersonal-attraction researchers have generally neglected the fact that liking for another is based on *specific behaviors* that comprise the interaction. For example, suppose you know someone who always gives you helpful information when you have a question about your car. This leads you to say, "I like this person." It is very likely that you will want to interact with that person on occasions when your car is having problems. Just because you

like that person, however, interaction on other occasions does not necessarily follow. You may not interact with the person when there is a basketball game, because the person doesn't reinforce basketball-watching behavior. Thus, many relationships are maintained at a surface-contact level in which the two individuals interact only in very specific situations. Relationships that develop further (for example, into what might be called friendships) require that a number of different types of behavior be reinforced. In other words, you interact with another person in a *variety* of situations.

It must be noted that reinforcement in a re-

ple for dating relationships. The crucial feature of this method of finding a dating partner is that it attempts to increase the likelihood that a suitable match will occur. In effect, this short-circuits the information-gathering process that takes place during awareness and surface-contact stages. An individual who secures a date can be assured that they will like many of the same things (if you hate cats and sailing, don't contact the Aquarian woman) and that the other will possess, or not possess, certain characteristics (such as being a nonsmoker).

Research on the advertisements placed in singles' newspapers reveals that people try to find someone whose overall level of desirability on various characteristics matches their own (Cameron, Oskamp, & Sparks, 1977; Harrison & Saeed, 1977). For example, people who describe themselves as attractive (using terms such as cute, good figure, good-looking) desire attractive partners. Interestingly, *females* who describe themselves as attractive are likely to stipulate that their partners should be financially well-off. Also, females tend to be more concerned with the partner's occupation, education, and financial status, while males are more concerned with the appearance of the partner. If you like what you see in an ad, you can write a letter to the person: the newspaper serves as intermediary to preserve anonymity. The letters are usually similar to the ads in that the writers state their interests, physical characteristics, and personality traits, and they then usually give a phone number to arrange a date (Cozby & Jebousek, 1977). The writers do not reveal a great deal of intimate information, but instead try to emphasize that because of their characteristics, they are desirable or rewarding people.

In general, the process of date selection via newspaper ads follows the same rules that we see in regular date selection. What we don't know is whether the relationships that begin with a newspaper ad, a computer match, or a "foto-date" are more likely to be satisfying and to progress toward deeper levels.

lationship cannot be one-sided. Social-exchange theory (see Chapter 13) emphasizes that for the relationship to continue, each person in an interaction must reinforce the other. Thus, your relationship with the car expert may be maintained because you thank the person profusely and tell everyone how smart he or she is. In this case, you are exchanging the status you confer on the other for the information you receive. Of course, the other's information-giving behavior is reinforced by your status-giving behavior.

Foa and Foa (1976) have provided an interesting classification of the various rewards that people exchange. As shown in Figure 8.2, these are called love, status, information, money, goods, and services. These general classes of rewards are seen as varying on two dimensions: *concreteness* and *particularism*. Something concrete tends to be tangible rather than symbolic. Thus, goods and services are more concrete, while status and information are more symbolic. Particularism implies that the nature and value of the reward depend upon the particular person and the nature of the relationship. Thus, money is low on particularism, while love is high on this dimension. Foa and Foa propose that people normally pre-

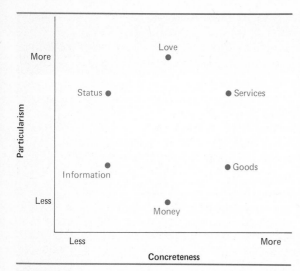

FIGURE 8.2
Rewards People Exchange
Source: Foa and Foa, 1976.

subject in the study. After reading this questionnaire, the subject indicated how much he or she liked the other person. The results from studies such as these show a strong positive relationship between similarity and liking. Byrne has reported that this effect occurs with such regularity that a mathematical equation is able to relate the proportion of similar attitudes to liking (Byrne & Nelson, 1965; Schonemann, Byrne, & Bell, 1977). Note that it is the *proportion* of similar attitudes that is important, not just the number of attitudes. You are equally attracted to a person when you share 7 of 10 similar attitudes as when 70 of 100 attitudes are similar.

Later research showed that the effect of similarity is not limited to laboratory situations. In a study by Byrne, Ervin, and Lamberth (1970), male and female students were paired on the basis of their responses to an attitude questionnaire. Half of the pairs were highly similar, while the other half were dissimilar. Each couple was then brought together and sent for a short "coke date" at the student union. When the couple returned, each person rated the other. It was found that the similar couples indicated greater attraction for one another than did the dissimilar couples. Further, the similar couples actually stood closer to one another when they returned.

fer exchanging rewards of the same type (for example, love for love) or rewards that are close to one another in the classification system shown in Figure 8.2. For example, the exchange of status and information seems appropriate, as does that of money and goods. The exchange of more distant rewards, however, such as love and money or status and goods, seems less likely.

✳Two important factors that lead to liking at the surface-contact level are attitude similarity and social approval.✕These have been studied extensively by social psychologists.

Attitude similarity. Attitude similarity leads to liking. This conclusion is justified on the basis of many studies conducted by Byrne and his colleagues (Byrne, 1971). In Byrne's early studies, which were quite artificial, subjects filled out attitude questionnaires. For each subject the experimenter then filled out a blank questionnaire with answers that had varying degrees of similarity to the subject's stated attitudes. The subject was given this questionnaire and told that it was completed by another

Social approval. When someone gives you social approval, your behavior is being reinforced. Positive evaluations, such as a compliment or the words, "I like you," lead to liking. The effect of social approval on liking has been demonstrated in a number of studies (for example, Byrne & Rhamey, 1965).

Both with attitude similarity and with social approval, a liking response is likely to occur because most people have learned that interacting with others who agree with them or evaluate them positively is, in fact, rewarding. For example, at least two sources of reinforcement are occurring in the case of attitude similarity (cf. Davis, 1981). First, if you know that you and someone else are similar, you can anticipate that you will like many of the same things and therefore minimize the chances of conflict. You have learned that it is easier to interact with others who share similar attitudes and interests. Also, since attitudes are in some ways "summaries" of many behaviors (cf. Fishbein & Ajzen, 1975), the person who agrees with your attitudes is essentially expressing approval of those behaviors.

The positive effect of praise or agreement will not occur when the praise is interpreted as *ingratiation* (Jones, 1964). Ingratiation is an attempt by a person to give praise and engage in other behaviors that will produce liking in someone else. The praise is not genuine, but rather a tactic that may lead the other to like and bestow favors upon the ingratiator. Most of us learn that there are specific situations in which praise is likely to be ingratiation. In most cases, these are situations in which one controls potent reinforcers that the other desires. For example, a professor may be suspicious of a compliment from a student when it is given right after the final exam. The same compliment, however, given after grades have been posted (when the professor no longer controls the grade reinforcer), may be accepted as genuine.

Mutuality

Levinger and Snoek (1972) describe **mutuality** as a continuum in which the two circles or people begin to overlap. Three degrees of overlap are shown in Figure 8.1. At the beginning level of mutuality, you and the other begin to spend more time together and disclose deeper and more intimate information about yourselves (see Chapter 9 on intimate communication). You express your feelings about things and your feelings for each other. Both verbal and nonverbal expressions of attraction will be exchanged. You begin to do things you find mutually enjoyable.

In evolving friendship we see the development of a unique relationship between two individuals. As the two circles overlap more and more, we can begin to think about the relationship moving from liking to love.

Being "hard to get". In the next section we will turn to a more detailed consideration of the nature of love. First, however, let us look at the common belief that being "hard to get" makes a person more attractive to others. Does, in fact, the appearance of being unwilling to develop a relationship make a person more desirable? This is a problem that faces many people who write letters to "Dear Abby." Typically, the writer is a female who has sex with a male she likes and is then rejected by him. The general response from Abby is that if we withhold our feelings of attraction from the other, we will be perceived as more valuable and hence more desirable. Is this truly a way to develop a love relationship? A series of experiments was carried out by Walster and her colleagues to find out (Walster, Walster, Piliavin, & Schmidt, 1973).

In one experiment, a female acted either hard to get or easy to get for a potential date arranged by a computer match. Contrary to the hard-to-get notion, there was no difference in the males' liking for the two females. Perhaps the hard-to-get phenomenon is limited to explicitly sexual interactions. To explore this, Walster et al. had a prostitute act hard or easy to get for clients. Again, being hard to get did not enhance liking for the female.

Undaunted by these results, they conducted yet another study. This time they found a crucial ingredient for when being hard to get enhances liking. The results showed that males are most attracted to a female who is hard to get for others but *easy to get* for themselves. A uniformly easy-to-get or hard-to-get female is not highly attractive. It is possible to explain this by assuming that most males have not been reinforced by interacting with such females in the past. More specifically, the hard-to-get-for-others/easy-to-get-for-self female is the one most likely to actually deliver unique and potent reinforcements to the male.

THE NATURE OF LOVE

You may be wondering what can be said about love that hasn't been said somewhere before. Novelists, poets, songwriters, and philosophers have written about love. We all talk about love, and somehow we just know that love is important in marriage and deep interpersonal relationships. Only recently have researchers begun to attempt scientifically to study the nature of love. This, of course, is not an easy task and some people may think that researchers should not even approach the topic. It is important, however, to study love, because the results of the research will lead to a greater understanding of ourselves and our relationships with others.

Conceptions of Love

When we speak of love, we are usually describing a relationship in which there is intense affection between two persons whose lives are intertwined (Berscheid & Walster, 1978). There is a true mutuality between two persons that grows through the type of developmental process described earlier. Ultimately there may be a total unity, with a complete overlap of our two circles.

Of course, such an ultimate bond may be difficult to achieve or will occur at only rare moments. Love and relationships with those we love are often less intense than "total unity."

Nevertheless, most people in our culture believe that love is a prerequisite for the commitment to another that is made in marriage, and that two persons should be in love before engaging in sexual intercourse (Hunt, 1974). This is, of course, our ideal—sex can occur at the surface-contact level, as in prostitution or in brief sexual encounters with another. It is also worth noting that love, in which very personal sources of reinforcement are important in mate selection, is only one basis for marriage. Although love is important in our culture, other cultures may stress nonlove factors—for example, political alliances or economic considerations—as the basis for marriage (cf. Rosenblatt, 1974). In fact, even in our culture males and females differ in the extent to which love is important in choosing a spouse (see Social Focus 8.3).

Given that love is important in deep interpersonal relationships, how can scientific research help us understand the nature of love? Let us begin by looking at an attempt to measure the amount of love between two people.

Rubin's Love Scale

Psychologist Zick Rubin (1970) has endeavored to define and measure love, using traditional techniques of test construction. He generated a large number of self-descriptive statements that reflected various aspects of love relationships as discussed by numerous philosophers, psychologists, and other writers. He then gave these statements to undergraduates at the University of Michigan. Using a technique of "item analysis," he chose a final thirteen items that best reflected feelings of love for another. In later research, nine items were used (Rubin, 1973). Three of the items are illustrated in the following paragraph. On each, the person answers with a particular other in mind, and indicates the degree to which the item does, in fact, describe the relationship.

The items on the love scale reflect three components of love. The first is *attachment-dependency:* "If I were lonely, my first thought would be to seek _____ out." The second component is *caring:* "If _____ were feeling badly, my first duty would be to

SOCIAL FOCUS 8.3
Females Are More Romantic—or Are They?

Our common stereotype tells us that females are more romantic than males. Love movies and romantic novels are devoured by females, while the stoic male scoffs at such "mush." Research is beginning to show, however, that our stereotypes may be all wrong. This should really come as no surprise. In traditional American society, the male is the breadwinner, while the female is totally dependent on him for her economic support, status, and financial security. Sociologist Willard Waller describes the situation in rather blunt terms: "There is this difference between the man and the woman in the pattern of bourgeois family life: a man, when he marries, chooses a companion and perhaps a helpmate, but a woman chooses a companion and at the same time a standard of living. It is necessary for a woman to be mercenary" (quoted in Rubin, 1973, p. 205). Thus, males can afford to use their romantic feelings as the basis for marriage, but women must be concerned with their own economic well-being. Rubin (1973) notes that this is why parents are more concerned with whom a daughter marries than a son.

Support for the conclusion that males are more romantic comes from a study by Rubin (1973). On a scale designed to measure belief in a romantic ideal, males were more likely than females to agree with statements such as the following: "A person should marry whomever he loves regardless of social position," and "As long as they love one another, two people should have no difficulty getting along together in marriage." Males also *disagreed* with statements such as "Economic security should be carefully considered before selecting a marriage partner."

In another interesting study, it was found that women are more likely than men to initiate the breakup of a dating relationship (Hill, Rubin, & Peplau, 1976). A conclusion drawn by Hill et al. is that men fall in love more readily than women and women fall out of love more readily than men.

What does the future hold? Cross-cultural research shows that romantic love is more important in societies in which only one member of the couple has primary responsibility for the economic well-being of the family (Rosenblatt, 1974). On the basis of this evidence, we might speculate that as more and more American families come to depend on the income of both spouses, there could be a decrease in the importance of love as a basis for marriage.

cheer him (her) up." The final component is *intimacy:* "I feel that I can confide in _____ about virtually everything." These three components would seem to reflect our conception of love as mutuality in a relationship.

Rubin gave his love scale to 182 dating couples. The couples had been dating for as long as six or seven years or as briefly as just a few weeks (the average was about one year). Each member of the couple filled out the scale separately and answered the questions in two ways. First, they responded as to their feelings about their boyfriend or girlfriend. Second, they answered with their best same-sex friend in mind. Several interesting results emerged from this research.

An initial finding was that scores on the love scale correlate highly with couples' saying they are "in love." Another finding was that men and women differ in their love for their best same-sex friends. Females love their friends more than males. There was no difference in how much males and females said they loved their dating partners. This result supports the view that female same-sex friendships are closer and more intimate than male friendships. Males usually express love feelings only in the context of opposite-sex relationships.

There was also a strong relationship between scores on the love scale and estimates of the likelihood of eventual marriage to the partner. As noted before, love and marriage remain closely intertwined in our society.

Another interesting finding concerned the amount of eye contact or mutual gaze between the dating partners. Since eye contact is part of intimate communication, Rubin predicted that couples scoring high on the love scale would spend more time in mutual eye contact during a conversation than low scorers. This prediction was supported in a laboratory investigation (Rubin, 1970).

Finally, Rubin followed up on the couples six months after they filled out the initial questionnaire (Rubin, 1973). He asked the couples to indicate whether their relationships had become more intense, less intense, or had remained the same. He found that, in general, persons who originally had scored high on the love scale reported that their relationship had become more intense. More interesting was a finding that believing in a "romantic ideal" is an important factor in whether love propels the couple toward a more intense relationship.

Recall that love may be only one basis for a relationship and that other factors such as economic security may also serve as a basis for marriage. As it turns out, there are individual differences among people in our society in how strongly they adhere to the romantic ideal. Rubin found that when both partners were romantic, their love scores were highly related to the intensity of their relationship six months later. When both partners were nonromantic, however, there was no correlation: that is, being in love did not necessarily mean that their relationship would become more intense. The major conclusion is that feelings of love may occur irrespective of a belief in the romantic ideal, but only a romantic person who believes in that romantic ideal will use these feelings as a basis for marriage.

Reinforcement and Equity in Love Relationships

A high score on the love scale may be interpreted in reinforcement terms to mean that the partner in the relationship is *uniquely* providing a *wide variety of classes of strong positive* reinforcers (Dermer & Pyszczynski, 1978). According to these authors, saying that you are in love or agreeing with the items on Rubin's love scale is a verbal indication that the other person has provided strong reinforcers that are not readily available from anyone else.

The fact that both attachment-dependency (receiving reinforcements) and caring (giving reinforcements) are components of the love scale underscores the importance of mutual reinforcement in the maintenance of relationships. Research also indicates that *equity* contributes to the development and maintenance of strong interpersonal relationships.

Equity is a rule of fairness in social exchange. It exists when one's rewards from a relationship are proportional to one's investments—that is, each person in a relationship gets about what he or she deserves. The equity rule was seen earlier in this chapter when the principle of matching levels of physical attractiveness was discussed. If both partners are not similar in attractiveness, the relationship may be perceived as inequitable. Note, however, that an equitable relationship can exist when the partners are dissimilar in attractiveness, if

For most people in our society, love is thought to be the basis for marriage. The marriage of this famous couple captured the imagination of people in countries throughout the world.

personal contributions such as good looks and intelligence, emotional contributions such as being a loving person, and day-to-day contributions such as being an agreeable person. They were then asked to rate their overall outcome from the relationship—how much they got out of it—by considering benefits such as love, security, and excitement. They were also asked to indicate their partner's contributions and outcomes. Data were collected for two points in time.

The results were clear. People in equitable relationships had stable relationships that lasted over time and they expected their relationships to continue. Inequitable relationships were more likely to break up, and members of such couples were pessimistic about the future of the relationship. This was true irrespective of whether the partner was getting more or less than he or she deserved. Finally, the fact that equity is necessary for the progress of a relationship is shown by a finding that equitable couples had engaged in more intimate sexual behaviors than inequitable couples. (We will discuss this study more extensively in Chapter 13.)

Need Compatibility and Complementarity

It is often assumed that mutually reinforcing relationships are more likely to occur when the two persons have needs that are either compatible or complementary. Need compatibility occurs when the two people are similar in such needs as affiliation (desire to be with others). Need **complementarity** occurs when the two have needs that are opposite and complementary. Most work on need complementarity has focused on dominance-submissiveness and nurturance-succorance. For example, the person who is high on nurturance (need to give love) will have a complementary need with another who is high on succorance (need to receive love), and someone who is highly dominant will have a complementary need with

other factors compensate. For example, Berscheid and Walster (1978) report that when one member of a couple is less attractive than the other, that person is likely to possess compensatory qualities, such as being rich, loving, and self-sacrificing.

On a more general level, the importance of equity in interpersonal attraction is shown in a study by Walster, Walster, and Traupmann (1978). These researchers asked members of dating couples to rate their overall contributions to a relationship—the amount they felt they deserved. They were asked to consider

someone who is very submissive. Although either need compatibility or complementarity could be applied to either same-sex or opposite-sex friendships, research has focused on their role in romantic relationships and marital choice.

Evidence for need compatibility was obtained in a study by Meyer and Pepper (1977). Married couples classified as having well-adjusted or poorly adjusted marriages were given tests to measure a number of different needs. Members of the better-adjusted couples were more similar than members of the poorly adjusted couples on the needs for affiliation, aggression, autonomy, impulsivity, and nurturance. These results imply that when couples are very different on these needs, there is a greater chance of conflict and also less chance that the two individuals will enjoy doing the same things. For example, in a couple dissimilar on affiliation needs, one person greatly enjoys being with others, while the other person does not; in couples who differ on impulsivity, one person likes to do things on the spur of the moment, while the other is more cautious and methodical. In such cases it is easy to imagine how each person might find the other's behavior annoying or objectionable.

There was no evidence for need complementarity in the Meyer and Pepper study. Although a theory of complementarity needs was proposed many years ago (Winch, 1958), most of the research does not find support for complementarity (cf. Levinger, 1964; Levinger, Senn, & Jorgensen, 1970; Murstein, 1972). The one exception is a study by Kerckhoff and Davis (1962).

Parental Interference

In Shakespeare's *Romeo and Juliet*, attempts by the loving couple's parents to keep Romeo and Juliet apart served only to intensify their feelings for one another. Is it possible that parental interference increases love? There is reason to believe it should, since attempts to keep us away from something usually increases our desire for it (Brehm, 1966). In a study to test this idea, Driscoll, Davis, and Lipetz (1972) gave several love scales to couples, along with a measure of parental interference. They found that love and parental interference were related in the expected way: the greater the interference, the greater the love. Further, when they tested these same couples six to ten months later, they found that increases in parental interference during that time were accompanied by increases in love. The lesson to parents should be clear!

So far we have been discussing a type of love characterized by deep attachment, caring, and mutuality. In the parental-interference study, the researchers found that interference was more strongly related to a passionate type of love than to the more companionate type we have been concerned with. In other words, the interference increased feelings of intense passion for the other person, but not the feelings of caring, intimacy, sharing, and so on. This raises the possibility that there are two kinds of love, one an emotional passion and the other a deep level of mutuality. Let us now examine the nature of this more passionate love.

PASSIONATE LOVE

Walster and Berscheid have suggested that people experience both companionate love and another type of love—an intense emotional experience—that can be called passionate love (Berscheid & Walster, 1978; Walster & Berscheid, 1974). This is the love we feel in our bodies, the heart-throbbing type of love (as one popular song put it, "can't you hear my heartbeat, it's a love-beat"). Walster and Berscheid reasoned that since this type of love is an emotion, much like fear or anger, we can understand it by considering it as a type of emotional state. Consequently, they analyzed love using a theory of emotion developed by Stanley Schachter (1964).

Schachter's Theory of Emotional States

As was discussed in Chapter 6, Schachter posits that our experience of any emotional state (for example, anger, fear, or elation) is the result of two factors operating together. First, there must be some physiological arousal. Second, the exact emotional state is determined by the cognitive attribution we make to explain and label the physiological arousal. The theory states that we must have physiological arousal and that we simultaneously cognitively interpret and identify the arousal on the basis of the immediate situation and past learning experiences.

Berscheid and Walster, in applying Schachter's theory to passionate love, suggest that we come to feel that we are "in love" in much the same way. We experience passionate love whenever (1) we are in a situation in which "our hazy, jumbled, inconsistent ideas as to what love is combine to tell us that 'this may be love,' and (2) we are intensely physiologically aroused—for whatever reason" (Berscheid & Walster, 1978, p. 160). It doesn't matter much where the arousal comes from, as long as we come up with an attribution that "I must be in love." Thus, the arousal may come from uncertainty or concern over rejection, sexual stimulation, or even some unrelated event such as being in a dangerous situation.

Two very interesting studies illustrate the usefulness of this analysis of passionate love. In an experiment to test Schachter's theory, Valins (1966) showed male students slides of nude females. As the slides were displayed, the students were given feedback about changes in their heart rates, through earphones that were hooked up to a machine that was supposedly monitoring their heart rates. In actuality, the feedback was bogus. For some of the slides, students heard no change in heart rate; for other slides, there was either a rapid increase in heart rate or a sudden decrease in rate ("my heart stood still"). Valins reasoned that students would interpret their heart-rate change in terms of their attraction for the female who apparently was responsible for the change. In fact, this is what occurred. The males rated the females associated with a heart-rate change as much more attractive than the no-change females. Although this study was not directly concerned with love, but rather with attraction, the results are consistent with the theory of love we have been discussing.

In a more direct test of the theory, Dutton and Aron (1974) tested males while they were standing on a shaky suspension bridge over a deep gorge. People certainly feel arousal in such a situation and most of the time we would expect them to label the arousal as "fear." What if, however, a male talks to an attractive female while on the bridge? Is it possible that he will attribute some of the arousal to his love or sexual feelings for the female? Results indicated that he will. Males on the suspension bridge, approached by a female experimenter, included a great deal of sexual imagery in short stories they were asked to write about an ambiguous picture; most of them also called her later (she had given them her name and phone number in case they wanted more information on the research). This did not happen when the same female approached males on a safe concrete bridge nearby—here there would be no arousal and hence no love. It also did not happen when a male experimenter was on the suspension bridge—here there would be arousal but being in love with the male is not a very likely attribution.

Kenrick and Cialdini (1977) have criticized the research supporting an attributional analysis of attraction. They begin by noting that according to Schachter's work, the source of arousal must be unclear if it is to be misattributed to another person and be interpreted as passion. They then argue that the men in Dutton and Aron's study should have attributed their arousal to the obvious source—the bridge. Kenrick and Cialdini, consequently, do not consider such studies evidence for the two-component theory. More recently, they have presented evidence that the misattribution of arousal does not readily occur in many situations in which the source of actual arousal is relatively clear (Kenrick, Cialdini, & Linder, 1979).

Kenrick and Cialdini prefer to interpret the findings in terms of reinforcement principles. They suggest that since the men on the bridge were probably experiencing fear, the female experimenter who appeared so calm may have had the effect of reducing the fear. Thus, by reducing fear, the female served as a reinforcer. Kenrick and Cialdini do indicate, however, that the two-component attributional theory does appear to be appropriate, "given a situation involving a highly ambiguous and diffuse state of arousal, for which there is no clear and salient cause, and given the presence of an individual of the opposite sex who meets all the standards for a romantic label" (1977, p. 389).

DISSOLUTION OF RELATIONSHIPS

It is rarely easy to end a relationship, whether it be a marriage or a dating relationship, yet we do end them. What factors cause a relationship to dissolve? What are the consequences of divorce? Although current research cannot provide definitive answers to questions such as these, there is a growing literature and interest in the topic (cf. Levitin, 1979; Moles & Levinger, 1976). Three types of causes of dissolution will be examined: relationship factors, individual factors, and alternative attractions.

Relationship Factors

Relationship factors refer to problems within the relationship itself (in contrast to factors within the individual or factors external to the relationship). It is important to recognize that both members of a couple may be good, desirable people and they may be attracted to one another, although for some reason they have not been able to sustain a *relationship* between them. In some cases, their interaction

may be characterized by conflict and discord. In other cases, it may be characterized as "empty": the relationship lacks the intimacy, caring, and attachment of the mutuality level discussed previously. The members of the couple do not communicate with one another and cease to be dependent on one another for mutual reinforcements (Levinger, 1976).

Research indicates that couples who remain together or report being satisfied with their relationships have more positive exchange of reinforcement and are similar on a number of characteristics. For example, a good index of marital happiness is the frequency of sexual intercourse minus the number of arguments (Howard & Dawes, 1976).

In a large-scale study that followed dating couples over a two-year period, Hill et al. (1976) were able to compare 117 couples who had stayed together with 103 couples who had broken up. They found that the couples who broke up were more likely to be different in age, educational aspirations, intelligence, and physical attractiveness than couples who stayed together. In addition, the relationships of the couples who broke up were characterized by unequal involvement of the two partners—typically one member of the couple was less involved than the other. Of course, this was a study of relationship dissolution *before* marriage (as the researchers note, "the best divorce is the one you get before you get married"). Still, it is true that many people marry despite the potential for future conflict arising from dissimilarity, or when the dissimilarities have not yet surfaced. This is likely, for example, when people marry at an early age or because of premarital pregnancy. Such marriages have high incidences of divorce (Furstenberg, 1976).

We all know of relationships that remain intact despite all apparent problems. For example, some couples stay together because it is the "right" thing to do. Individual factors and alternative attractions are important in determining whether relationships will actually dissolve.

Individual Factors

Individual factors are characteristics of one of the individuals that cause that person to prefer to dissolve a relationship. One important such characteristic is being raised in a family affected by divorce. Statistics show that children of divorced parents are more likely to become divorced themselves (Pope & Mueller, 1976). Although one might speculate that such children would be motivated to avoid divorce, apparently a subtle learning takes place during childhood that makes dissolving their relationships more likely.

Another individual factor that has been studied is the need for power. Stewart and Rubin (1976) reported that men high on the need for power were more likely to break up their relationships than were men low on this need. Women's need for power was not a factor in relationship stability. One possible explanation is that men with a high need for power establish a Don Juan syndrome, in which power is sought by engaging in many short-term "conquests" of women.

Alternative Attractions

Levinger (1976) proposes that people consider the reinforcements received in their present relationship as well as the reinforcements available as alternatives to the present reinforcement. They also consider the various costs or punishments that they presently receive, along with the costs of dissolving the relationship. Anything that makes breaking off the relationship more costly will be a force for maintaining the relationship. Anything that makes breaking off the relationship more rewarding will lead the person toward dissolving the relationship.

The types of rewards and costs considered would include children, the availability of an alternative relationship, the monetary situation, or the value of independence. A man may decide to stay in a marriage because he would

miss the children or feel guilty about leaving them without a father, because he has no alternative relationship, or because he feels that giving up whatever love and security he now has would not make it worthwhile to leave. He may also stay because he feels a divorce would result in an undesirable reduction in his standard of living.

Such factors could, of course, be considered by the woman as well, and many other specific examples could be given. The main point here is that changes in these factors will change the likelihood that the relationship will be maintained. Although such changes may often arise from individual circumstances, they can also result from societal changes such as no-fault divorce laws that make it easier to obtain a legal divorce (Stetson & Wright, 1975).

An interesting finding related to this discussion concerns the timing in breakups of dating relationships. In the Hill et al. (1976) study of college students, relationships were most likely to dissolve at the end of the school year in May or June, at the beginning of the school year in September, or during the semester break. It is probably easiest to break off an undesirable relationship at times when unpleasant confrontations and trauma can be avoided. Also, a separation during the summer may raise a person's estimates of the attractiveness of alternative relationships. There may be similar timing patterns in marriage, although these are probably not as regular as among college students. For example, it may be easiest to actually initiate the divorce when the husband or wife gets a new job in another town or when the children have left home.

Consequences of Divorce

Ending a relationship is a traumatic experience for most people, although the person who initiates the breakup is generally happier and less depressed (but more guilty) than the other member of the couple (Hill et al. 1976). There are feelings of fear and panic at the thought of being alone, and extreme anger directed at the spouse. At the same time there are feelings of ambivalence, as the person realizes that he or she also has strong feelings for the spouse (Weiss, 1976). Such feelings are vividly illustrated in the following quotes of recently separated individuals who particpated in seminars conducted by Weiss:

When the idea occurred to me that I could live without Dave and be happier, my immediate next feeling was just gut fear. It's really hard to explain. It was just terror.

I don't like him. As a man I find him boring. If I met him at a party I'd talk with him for about two minutes and then I'd say, "I'll see you." But the emotional tug is still there. He is still attractive to me.

Divorce is also likely to be traumatic for the children as well. In fact, many people decide to not get divorced "for the sake of the children." This may not be a wise decision, however, since children from a divorced family may suffer less psychological stress than children from intact but unhappy families (Bane, 1976). Research on the impact of divorce on children indicates that children from divorced families do, in fact, show increases in problem behaviors at home and at school during the year following the divorce; however, the problems appear to become much less pronounced after two years following the divorce (Hetherington, Cox, & Cox, 1979). Also comparisons of adults who either did or did not come from divorced family backgrounds indicate that the long-term effects of divorce, in terms of overall adjustment, appear to be minimal (Kulka & Weingarten, 1979).

Many people now believe that divorce can, in fact, be a positive experience—"the chance of a new lifetime" (Brown, Feldberg, Fox, & Kohen, 1976). This may be especially true for women who feel their lives are empty in the role of wife and mother and whose husbands are hostile when they attempt to develop careers, seek further education, and so on. Perhaps that view is correct, but even so, divorce is likely to be painful and may create many new problems. Some argue that the government should fund divorce centers to provide the kind of help—child care, legal assistance, counseling, and so on—that is needed to face these problems (Brown et al., 1976). This is likely to be a source of much public debate in the future.

A final consequence of divorce seems to be a new marriage. In the United States, 80 percent of the people who get divorced eventually remarry. This is not surprising, since most of us have strong needs for the kinds of satisfactions a marriage relationship can provide.

SUMMARY

Interpersonal attraction research focuses on factors involved in the initiation, maintenance, and dissolution of interpersonal relationships. Much of this research is grounded in reinforcement theory: people are attracted to those who reward their behaviors. A model of relationship development proposes that relationships develop through four levels: zero contact, awareness, surface contact, and mutuality.

Propinquity or physical closeness is an important determinant of whether people will progress from zero contact to a level of awareness. Propinquity generally results in increased liking for others.

At the level of awareness, attraction toward another is based on external characteristics of the other. One important characteristic is physical attractiveness. Research shows that people generally have positive perceptions of physically attractive others, and also that more physically attractive people possess such qualities as high levels of self-esteem and social skills. People generally prefer to have relationships with highly physically attractive others. Research supporting the *matching hypothesis* indicates, however, that close friends and spouses are usually similar in attractiveness.

At the surface-contact level, individuals' attraction for one another is based on the reward value of their interaction with each other. Foa and Foa have identified six classes of reinforcers that people exchange with one another: love, status, information, money, goods, and services. These rewards vary in terms of concreteness and particularism. Two important factors leading to liking at the surface-contact level are attitude similarity and social approval. Attitude agreement or praise do not, however, lead to liking when they are interpreted as ingratiation attempts.

Mutuality is characterized by increasing levels of intimacy and interdependence. Relationships develop into what are called friendship and love. Research on whether the appearance of being hard to get makes one more desirable to others indicates that the most liked other is one who is hard to get for others but easy to get for oneself.

Rubin developed a love scale that reflects three components of love: attachment-dependency, caring, and intimacy. Scores on the love scale are related to saying one is in love, degree of mutual eye contact, and likelihood of a relationship progressing. Reinforcement and equity are important in love relationships. The expression of love is viewed in reinforcement terms as an indication that the other has provided a variety of positive reinforcers that are not readily available from anyone else. Research also indicates that equitable relationships are more stable and intimate than inequitable ones.

Need compatibility, or similarity in needs such as affiliation, has been found to be related to marital adjustment. There is little evidence that need complementarity, or opposite and complementary needs, is an important factor in the development of relationships.

Berscheid and Walster suggest that passionate love is an emotional state and use Schachter's two-factor theory of emotion to explain this type of love. According to this theory, love is experienced when there is physiological arousal and a situation in which this arousal is labeled as love. There is some controversy regarding whether research supporting this analysis of love should be interpreted in reinforcement terms.

Three types of causes of relationship dissolution were identified. Relationship factors include problems stemming from conflict within the relationship itself. Individual factors include being raised in a family affected by divorce, and the need for power. Alternative attractions are the reinforcements available from alternative relationships, along with consideration of the costs of dissolution of a relationship.

SUGGESTED READINGS

Berscheid, E., & Walster, E. *Interpersonal attraction* (2d ed.). Reading, Mass.: Addison-Wesley, 1978.

Dion, K. K. Physical attractiveness, sex roles, and heterosexual attraction. In M. Cook (Ed.), *The bases of human sexual attraction.* London: Academic Press, 1980.

Levinger, G., & Moles, O. C. *Divorce and separation: Context, causes, and consequences.* New York: Basic Books, 1979.

Murstein, B. *Love, sex, and marriage.* New York: Springer, 1974.

Walster, E., & Walster, E. *Love.* Reading, Mass.: Addison-Wesley, 1978.

Zimbardo, P. G. *Shyness.* Reading, Mass.: Addison-Wesley, 1977.

LONELINESS AND INTIMATE COMMUNICATION

9

Chapters 7 and 8 described general issues of interacting and developing relationships with others. We develop friendships, fall in love, and dissolve relationships. More generally, we *communicate* with others through both verbal and nonverbal means. The act of communicating and others' reactions to our communications have implications for the development of self-esteem, of a self-image, and perhaps even of the ability to grow as a person (cf. Jourard, 1971). This chapter will focus in detail on the role of intimacy in our relationships. We will explore feelings of loneliness, the functions and processes of disclosing information about ourselves to others, and the influence of sex roles on our abilities to be intimate. Finally, we will explore questions of whether there can be too much intimacy in a relationship.

LONELINESS: THE NEED FOR INTIMACY

The sad feeling of loneliness, of being cut off from meaningful relationships with other people, is something that disturbs many of us. Consider the following statements by three lonely people.

Anne: I'm basically a loner. I don't really associate with a lot of people. In high school, I didn't stick with any particular group. I didn't become close to anyone.

Helen: This is my first semester at _____ University. I transferred from a community college in my home town to come here to school. It's been awfully lonely for me; being away from home, my family, my friends, and my boyfriend has been rough. I miss my boyfriend a great deal. I miss being with him. Sometimes I just sit in my room dreaming about him, wishing he was with me, and I feel sorry for myself. I feel lonely and lost. I think to myself, here I am on my own for a while. I feel like such a baby at times, missing home and the people. What am I going to do with my life? I enjoy being home much more, but I can't stay there. I must be independent. I must support myself and live alone. All these things scare me and I often think about them.

Pearl: I guess my life can be described as a lonely one. I'm all alone now that my son has moved to Arizona. I don't see him much anymore. Most of my friends have died and it's hard to get around to see the people I do know now that I can't drive any longer. I look forward to my son's telephone calls on Sundays.

All of these people are lonely, although the conditions leading to their loneliness are different. Anne is chronically lonely—a "loner" who doesn't develop relationships with other people. Helen has decided to go away to school and finds herself lonely because she is away from others she cares about and hasn't yet developed new relationships at her school. Pearl finds that being elderly has imposed upon her certain circumstances that have isolated her from others.

People usually do not want to be isolated. Survey studies indicate, however, that the experience of loneliness is widespread in North America (Peplau & Perlman, 1982). One nationwide survey asked, "During the past few weeks, did you feel very lonely or remote from other people?" (Bradburn, 1969). Twenty-six percent of those surveyed answered yes. Those who described themselves as very lonely or remote from other people also tended to report being depressed or very unhappy. More than half of a sample of widowed men in a telephone survey reported severe feelings of loneliness in the preceding week. A smaller, though still substantial, proportion of widowed

---

This chapter is written by Valerian J. Derlega and Stephen T. Margulis.

Loneliness affects many people in our society. For the elderly, loneliness is frequently caused by isolation and separation from loved ones.

women, 29 percent, also reported that they felt lonely and remote from other people during the same time period (Maisel, 1969). The social isolation caused by the death of a spouse seems to place a special burden on the elderly widower. Such men are less likely than widows to have (or find) meaningful, alternative relationships to help them after the spouse's death. It seems that widowers' susceptibility to social isolation and loneliness contributes to their high suicide rate (Bock & Webber, 1972).

The experience of being alone is a central fact of human existence. Very few of us want to be alone most of the time, but we put up with it as a fact of our lives. This loneliness is part of living. But loneliness has been aggravated by a number of contemporary developments. The great mobility of many Americans has had the effect of cutting friendship and family bonds. City life also has radically changed friendship patterns. Many city people tend to form limited relationships with others.

The experience of loneliness seems to derive in part from the absence of intimate relationships—that is, not having a confidant or companion with whom we can communicate intimately (Derlega & Margulis, in press; Haas-Hawkings, 1978; Lowenthal & Haven, 1968). A confidant can assist an individual to achieve important socially mediated goals, such as companionship, knowing that someone cares, and social feedback. When one does not have or loses an intimate partner (for example, through divorce, death of a friend, moving to a new community) loneliness may be the result, since these and other important social needs cannot be satisfied. In such circumstances, **self-disclosure** becomes an important vehicle to reduce loneliness. We establish social contact by divulging information about ourselves to others, and by being receptive to their self-disclosures.

WHAT IS SELF-DISCLOSURE?

It is important to note that self-disclosure can vary on many dimensions. For example, one may give information to another about many areas of one's life and yet reveal only shallow, superficial material. You may tell another person that you are a college student majoring in psychology, that you enjoy tennis, that pizza is your favorite food, that you were born in Kansas, and that you have two older brothers. Such a recital indicates many facets of your life, but the bearer really knows very little about what you feel strongly about, what your hopes, fears, and aspirations are, or in essence, what makes you unique as a person. Such disclosure is characterized by breadth but not depth. On the other hand, disclosure may be deeply personal and intimate, but focus on only one or two content areas of one's life, such as sexual feelings or emotions.

Self-disclosure can be classified on the basis of two types of intimacy, descriptive and evaluative (Morton, 1978). **Descriptive intimacy** refers to the disclosure of otherwise unavailable factual information about yourself (for example, a detailed account of your sex life or a car accident). **Evaluative intimacy** refers to the disclosure of personal feelings or judgments (for

example, an intense expression of love, anger, or shame).

Self-disclosure can also be transmitted by means other than language. Nonverbal behavior (duration of eye contact, distance maintained from the listener, hand gestures, facial expressions, and so forth) and paralanguage (such as voice inflection, pitch, stress) can convey much information to an observer, especially about such things as the discloser's status, emotional state, and liking for the listener. Such nonverbal behavior may reveal more than does verbal communication (Mehrabian, 1972). One difference between verbal and nonverbal channels is that the discloser often has much less control over and awareness of the information that is being transmitted nonverbally (Ekman & Friesen, 1969).

SELF-DISCLOSURE AND PRIVACY

To self-disclose or not to self-disclose? When considering this question we must examine the issue of **privacy** regulation. If we can choose how much or how little to divulge about ourselves to another voluntarily, privacy is maintained. Social psychologist Irwin Altman (1975) defines privacy in the following manner:

Privacy is conceived of as an *interpersonal boundary process* by which a person or group regulates interaction with others. By altering the degree of openness of the self to others, a hypothetical personal boundary is more or less receptive to social interaction with others. Privacy is, therefore, a dynamic process involving selective control over a self-boundary, either by an individual or by a group (p. 6).

It is important to note that privacy (or the desired state of contact with others) may vary for an individual from time to time. Depending on circumstances, we may either seek out or avoid others. Privacy does not mean avoiding all contact with others. It represents the barrier or boundary we wish to maintain around ourselves at any point in time (Altman, 1975, 1977).

Self-disclosure is a major mechanism people use to regulate privacy. Briefly stated, adjustment in self-disclosure outputs and inputs is an example of boundary regulation, and the extent of control we maintain over this exchange of information contributes to the amount of privacy we have in a social relationship. We can view self-disclosure in a relationship in terms of an opening and closing of boundaries (Derlega & Chaikin, 1977; Margulis, 1979). The *self* (or *personal*) *boundary* separates the sender and his/her information from a recipient. A closed self boundary means that key information is concealed or withheld. An open (or lowered) self boundary means that key information is shared. A second boundary, the *dyadic boundary,* is based on the communicator's perception that what passes between the two will be separated from everyone else. It is—as viewed by the discloser—the boundary within which it is safe to disclose to the invited recipient and across which the self-disclosure will not pass. That is, the disclosure is safe with the recipient, as perceived by the discloser. Figure 9.1 illustrates how the self and dyadic boundaries operate in practice.

FUNCTIONS OF SELF-DISCLOSURE

What happens when we disclose? We run the risk, of course, that the disclosure recipient may somehow use the information against us. The "plunger" or "quick self-discloser" may be regarded as "anathema, to be avoided at all costs" (Luft, 1969, p. 130). On the other hand, if self-disclosure is appropriate (that is, part of an ongoing relationship, occurring reciprocally, in small steps, and with the feelings and reactions of the recipient taken into consideration)

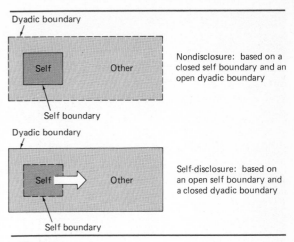

FIGURE 9.1
Self-disclosure as a function of self and dyadic boundary adjustments

a number of benefits may occur, including self-expression, self-clarification, social validation, relationship development, and social control (Derlega & Grzelak, 1979).

Expression

Self-disclosure enables individuals to express their feelings. Those who have suffered grief after the death of a close friend or relative may talk about their feelings of loss. Players on a basketball team may laugh and joke jubilantly after winning an important game. Self-disclosure seems to provide a release for pent-up feelings in such situations. Social institutions sometimes legitimize the expressive function of self-disclosure. After a death, a period of bereavement may be observed during which it is acceptable to express grief.

Self-Clarification

Self-disclosure may be useful in increasing personal clarification; it may help individuals who disclose information, or who anticipate

We frequently self-disclose to express our feelings. This fan is clearly happy as evidenced by his nonverbal behavior.

disclosing information, to clarify their own opinions on issues. According to objective self-awareness theory (Duval & Wicklund, 1972), individuals' anticipation of speaking about themselves causes them to focus attention on themselves instead of on the environment. The anticipation of talking in front of other persons increases speakers' attention to the consistency and integration of their ideas.

Objective self-analysis seems to operate through a process of critical self-evaluation. Anticipation of giving a talk (and perhaps being evaluated by others) will make salient these evaluative processes within a person.

Speakers attempt to reduce ambiguity and inconsistency in their own thinking to avoid self-criticism and possible criticisms from others.

Personal clarification may occur in many settings, not just when a person is expecting to talk to an audience. Writing a letter, keeping a diary, or perhaps even talking to oneself aloud, can increase objective self-awareness and, in turn, consistency in thought. Duval and Wicklund (1972) suggest that objective self-awareness occurs only when a person is not actively addressing an audience, such as when preparing to talk, during speech pauses, or after delivering a speech. The act of speaking or delivering a talk is seen as reducing the person's focus on the self and increasing attention on the outside environment.

Social Validation

According to Festinger's (1954) theory of social comparison, people look to "social reality" to obtain feedback and ultimately to validate their self-concepts. Other persons may help individuals to define the appropriateness and correctness of their attitudes, beliefs, feelings, and values. Consulting with and confronting others, or seeking the advice of friends and associates, may help a person to decide on a course of action in dealing with a situation. This function of self-disclosure is called social validation.

Relationship Development

As discussed in Chapter 8, self-disclosure frequently occurs when people develop close intimate relationships (cf. Rubin, 1970). In disclosure reciprocity, for instance, one person's disclosure tends to elicit self-disclosure from another. Self-disclosure may also contribute to relationship maintenance. One partner may listen to and help meet the other partner's emotional needs, and this process provides positive outcomes in the relationship.

Social Control

Self-disclosure may sometimes operate as a tool for controlling, and even exploiting, others. Persons may use information about themselves (including their intentions, beliefs, values) to increase their control over their own and others' outcomes. Self-disclosure may be used as an ingratiation technique to gain others' social approval or to make them feel good about themselves (for example, "I feel—as you do—that the energy crisis is a serious problem"). People may even provide misleading in-formation about themselves or provoke other persons to disclose in order to learn about their intentions and expected behavior. In other words, self-disclosure *can* be a tool for social manipulation. Social Focus 9.1 describes the possibility that modern electronic technology can invade our privacy.

GETTING TO KNOW YOU

How do people decide what information to reveal about themselves? Do people differ in the kinds of information they reveal? What are the pluses and minuses that affect people's decisions to self-disclose?

Consider the following description by a college student, Joan, about her experiences when she first enrolled at college. She was away from home for the first time, and she was sharing a dormitory room with another woman. She explained how she got to know her roommate and friend, Janet:

When I came on campus, I really didn't know anybody. I was pretty busy the first couple of weeks. Going to classes, buying books, learning the campus, and getting my fall schedule straight—all these things took a lot of time. My roommate had already been here for a semester, and she helped me find my way around. She pointed out the buildings to me and showed me where my classes were.

In the first few days we talked about general stuff: where we came from, what we were interested in. I really didn't know her very well then. One night, though, she and I were both studying in our room, and we got to talking about our personal lives. We had done the same things when we were younger, we had gotten into the same kinds of trouble. It was funny because our lives were kind of parallel to each other. We came from the same types of backgrounds.

We talked about some pretty serious things. We were talking about our boyfriends, how they were having serious drug problems and how we didn't want to date them any more because of it. I think she knows me pretty well now. I can start to say

SOCIAL FOCUS 9.1
Two-Way Cable TV and Electronic Snooping

Consider the following situation:

A priest and a former nun are being interviewed on a cable-TV talk show in Columbus, Ohio, on the issue "What is it like to be a homosexual in Columbus?" The interviewer notes that an estimated 80,000 homosexuals live in the Columbus metropolitan area, which has an overall population of more than one million people. The interviewer then asks television viewers the following question: How many viewers have a friend, relative, or acquaintance who is homosexual? "If you do know a homosexual," the interviewer says, "press button No. 1 on your home console for yes; if you do not, press button No. 2 for no." Viewers at home use the console next to the channel selector button on their televisions to answer the question. Within seconds, a computer supplies the results, which are presented on viewers' television screens: yes—65 percent; no—35 percent.

The marriage of information technology and television has created two-way interactive cable TV. One-way cable TV carries signals, such as first-run movies, directly into the subscriber's home. Two-way interactive TV allows the viewer to transmit messages back to the sender through the cable system. Experts predict that two-way TV will offer home-based entertainment, classroomlike instruction, bill paying, shopping, home security, medical and disaster emergency preparedness, and political and community participation, and will attract 50 percent of American households to cable TV during the 1980s. What will be done with all the information subscribers send over their cable systems? Will cable operators treat information provided by their customers as privileged, or will the information be sold or passed along to confidential clients such as mail-order houses, credit-rating companies, the Internal Revenue Service, and so on?

Currently, only a few communities in North America have two-way TV. The best-known system operates in Columbus, Ohio. The heart of the system is called QUBE (a trade name that doesn't stand for anything). It is a computer that scans subscribers' households every six seconds to find out if the TV is switched on, to what channel, and what was the last message transmitted by the viewer to the computer. Messages from the viewer to the computer are punched on a five-button console. The first two buttons are used to indicate yes and no. The five buttons can be used to answer multiple-choice questions or to punch up number codes, to select, for instance, a product displayed on the television screen.

Two-way cable TV holds great promise. The QUBE system has, for instance, significantly increased public participation in town meetings and public hearings. Two public meetings on an urban redevelopment plan in the Columbus area drew about 125 people each. When the meetings were held on two-way cable TV, the computer reported that 2000 residents participated in the two-and-a-half-hour town meetings. The question remains, however: what happens to the information that is collected? Can the computer collate a subscriber's responses, merge them with other information on file about the subscriber (including information such as address, income, social background, and so forth) and create a file or dossier on the viewer's household?

At present neither the U.S. Congress or state legislatures have enacted restrictive laws, nor has the industry developed policies to protect personal disclosures derived from cable TV. Experts feel that controls are coming. Until then, protection will be a matter of the cable TV operators' own policies (QUBE's operators restrict access to the computer and its records). Some local communities have restrictions to protect subscribers; other communities do not.

Psychologically, subscribers regard two-way TV as "fun." As one subscriber put it, "It gives you a sense of power, a sense of directing something far away." For instance, an audience participation program similar to the *Gong Show* is presented by QUBE. Viewers direct the show by pressing yes or no to say whether an amateur act should continue. If a majority of the viewing audience presses no, the act is ended in midperformance. On the other hand, viewers seem only vaguely aware that personal information may be tabulated and passed along to others. As one young woman said about the QUBE system, "I don't feel that I have any reason to be afraid—I may be naive, but I don't care if my opinions are recorded."

Cable-TV operators could, however, profit from the sale of information about their subscribers. For instance, the following uses (none of which are illegal) could be made of information you might provide on two-way cable TV:

1. After your recent vote during a televised town meeting about busing children to integrate public schools, you begin to receive mail and phone calls from fund-raising groups, charities, and political groups that ask for your support.
2. After watching an X-rated film, a publisher of a "skin" magazine is notified of your selection. The publisher sends you a sales brochure in a plain manila envelope.
3. A subpoena has been prepared for you. To make sure you are home to receive it, the cable operator has been paid to monitor when you turn on the TV and to report this immediately.
4. You use your two-way TV to order on credit a product advertised on TV. The store's credit manager reports that your credit payments are in arrears. You cancel the order until you are able to transfer sufficient funds from your bank account to the store's account. However, a national credit-rating company, a confidential client of the cable operator, learns that your order has been rejected. This information is put into your dossier for the next customer who purchases your credit information.

The ultimate abuse of individual privacy by two-way TV was portrayed in George Orwell's novel *1984*. Households were under constant TV surveillance. Less chilling, but still potentially dangerous, are the abuses of files that could be obtained from two-way cable-TV subscribers. So long as businesses and government rely on personal information about individuals, there is a possibility of such abuses. It is to be hoped that the restraint of cable operators and active consumer and community monitoring will be sufficient to protect subscribers' disclosures. Industrywide regulation by cable operators, legislative action, and local ordinances can also address this potential social problem.

something and she can just pick it right up and say what I was going to say.

She tells me just about everything about herself. She wants me to go to her house to meet her family and friends. We do a lot of things together now. We go to parties together, to Zero's [a local campus hangout], and to the basketball games.

How did Joan and Janet decide what information to reveal about themselves? Do Joan and Janet differ from other people in the types of information they reveal? What benefits did they expect to derive from their disclosures? Social-penetration theory, developed by social psychologists Irwin Altman and Dalmas Taylor (1973) provides a useful framework for examining patterns of self-disclosure in a relationship.

Self-disclosure, according to Altman and Taylor, is one part of the *social-penetration* processes that accompany the development of close friendships. Social penetration refers to the overt and internal, subjective events that occur between two individuals as their relationship develops. It includes verbal (such as self-disclosure), nonverbal (such as smiling, eye gaze, hand gestures, head nods), and environmentally oriented behaviors (such as use of spatial distancing). It also involves the development of a subjective picture of the other person, including a forecast of what an interrelationship would be like.

According to social-penetration theory, individuals generally disclose more information as a relationship progresses to more intimate levels. They will talk more intimately, disclose information about an increasing number of areas, and within each area they will disclose more pieces of information and dwell on them for a longer time.

These stages may be represented as a series of "wedges" being driven into one's personality, as shown in Figure 9.2. At each stage of the relationship more information is disclosed

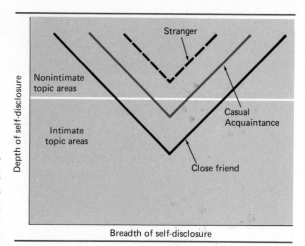

FIGURE 9.2
Breadth and depth of self-disclosure at three stages of a relationship
Altman and Haythorn, 1965, p. 422.

at superficial than at intimate levels. As the relationship between individuals advances—as they change from strangers to casual acquaintances to close friends—disclosure expands on both the breadth and depth dimensions: the wedge therefore widens and deepens as the individuals exchange more information and at greater levels of intimacy.

Two important aspects of Figure 9.2 should be noted. First, disclosure in some areas may remain at the same level of intimacy as the relationship develops. If individuals enjoy talking at certain levels of intimacy about sports, hobbies, or other common interests, disclosure will continue at these levels in the future, even though it may become deeper in other topics. Second, disclosure proceeds gradually into more intimate areas, primarily because of the greater potential for embarrassment in these areas. Persons who move too quickly into intimate levels of disclosure may suffer crises if unexpected costs arise. For instance, new roommates may be very open with each other and subsequently find out that the information disclosed has been used to ridicule them. Our prospects of being hurt are reduced when we carefully gauge the effects of disclosure at each level of intimacy.

An example of the developmental changes in self-disclosure was reported by Dalmas Taylor (1968) in a longitudinal study. Fifteen pairs of college roommates, who were not acquainted initially, were studied for one semester in dormitories at the University of Delaware. During the first, third, sixth, ninth, and thirteenth weeks of the semester, two types of self-disclosure measures were administered. One questionnaire inquired about the sorts of activities roommates had shared during the preceding three weeks. The second questionnaire asked subjects to indicate whether they had revealed information about themselves to their roommates in each of forty content areas (such as religion and family). Supporting the concept of disclosure as wedgelike, breadth of self-disclosure tended to be greater for superficial material than for intimate material. In both superficial and intimate areas of exchange, self-disclosure increased in depth as a function of the number of weeks the roommates had known each other. There was also a tendency for breadth of disclosure to increase at a faster rate for superficial areas of disclosure.

Besides the wedge shape, there are other possible patterns of disclosure in an intimate relationship. In a summer romance, persons may disclose highly intimate information about themselves in very limited areas. Breadth of disclosure is approximately the same at every level of intimacy. These relationships are likely to be very fragile and short-lived. There are areas in which the individuals have not built up a working relationship with each other. Subsequent disclosure of intimate information that is unacceptable to the other person may precipitate a quick end to the relationship.

Usually, self-disclosure increases gradually over the various stages of a relationship (see Social Focus 9.2), but there are exceptions. Disclosure may vary at different rates, depending upon the nature of the material being talked about. For instance, certain topics may be considered taboo, even among close friends. A Protestant and a Catholic who are otherwise very close may be unable to talk with each other about abortion. The topic is highly emotional, and discussion tends to lead to controversy and bitterness. For similar reasons, husbands and wives may tacitly agree not to discuss their premarital sexual experiences.

BREAKING UP

Just as relationships can progress into more intimate areas, a reversal of this process can occur. In the latter case, the relationship produces fewer rewards for the individuals and a possible increase in the costs incurred by continued interaction. Two persons may discover that their personality styles conflict. For instance, they may both want to dominate the relationship. In other cases, an individual may like another person very much, but find out that the other doesn't want to become intimate.

For individuals who have been intimate, the deterioration process of their relationship may be compared to a film being shown in reverse (Altman & Taylor, 1973). A gradual decrease in breadth and depth of exchange of information occurs. Disclosure returns to more superficial areas, where the costs connected with further interaction are slight. The person who experiences an unfavorable reward/cost ratio may think, "Why should I take a chance and trust him any more with my feelings? I am only going to get hurt." The reversal in self-disclosure processes will continue until the individuals have found a mutually acceptable level of exchange. Former lovers may find it suitable to be "just good friends." In other cases, where the rewards have become so meager and the costs so great, the individuals may want to have nothing to do with each other.

SOCIAL FOCUS 9.2

SOCIAL FOCUS 9.2
Friendship and Acquaintance as Demonstrated by a Self-Disclosure Questionnaire

Think of a casual acquaintance and one of your closest friends. First circle the statements below that you discuss with your friend in private conversation. Next, list the statements you would discuss with a casual acquaintance. Finally, list the statements you have not shared with anyone.

1. Whether or not I have ever gone to a church other than my own. (2.85)
2. The number of children I want to have after I am married. (5.91)
3. How frequently I like to engage in sexual activity. (10.02)
4. Whether I would rather live in an apartment or a house after getting married. (3.09)
5. What birth control methods I would use in marriage. (9.31)
6. What I do to attract a member of the opposite sex whom I like. (8.56)
7. How often I usually go on dates. (5.28)
8. Times that I have lied to my girlfriend or boyfriend. (8.56)
9. My feelings about discussing sex with my friends. (7.00)
10. How I might feel (or actually felt) if I saw my father hit my mother. (9.50)
11. The degree of independence and freedom from family rules that I have (had) while living at home. (5.39)
12. How often my family gets together. (2.89)
13. Who my favorite relatives (aunts, uncles, and so on) are and why. (5.83)
14. How I feel about getting old. (6.36)
15. The parts of my body I am most ashamed for anyone to see. (6.88)

DISCLOSURE RECIPROCITY

In general, disclosure by one individual is met by reciprocal disclosure from the other. According to major theories of friendship formation (for example, Altman & Taylor, 1973; Levinger & Snoek, 1972), if there is no **disclosure reciprocity** in the early stages of a relationship, further development will not occur. Friendships seem to begin when one person risks possible ridicule or rejection by disclosing some personal information. The second person reciprocates by sharing something equally intimate. The first person then responds, either at that time or at a later meeting, by revealing something more intimate. In turn this elicits a comparable disclosure from the other person. Little by little, in a spiraling fashion, this reciprocal exchange builds and strengthens bonds of intimacy, understanding, and trust between the two persons. There are two factors that can abort this developing relationship. First, neither party may be willing to initiate an intimate exchange. Second, the recipient of an intimate disclosure may clam up and not reciprocate.

Why does disclosure reciprocity occur? If I tell you something personal about myself, why should that lead you to respond with an intimate disclosure of your own? One popular ex-

16. My feelings about lending money. (4.75)
17. My most pressing need for money right now (outstanding debts, some major purchases that are needed or desired). (6.88)
18. How much I spend for my clothes. (7.17)
19. Laws that I would like to see put in effect. (3.08)
20. Whether or not I have ever cried as an adult when I was sad. (8.94)
21. How angry I get when people hurt me. (5.33)
22. What animals make me nervous. (3.44)
23. What it takes to hurt my feelings deeply. (9.37)
24. What I am most afraid of. (8.25)
25. How I really feel about the people I work for or with. (7.29)
26. The kinds of things I do that I don't want people to watch. (8.85)

Scoring: The amount of communication is shown by the number of statements circled for each person. Intimacy of communication is found by adding up the number in parentheses for the circled statements, divided by the total number of statements circled. For instance, if you have circled statements 1, 4, 12, 19, and 22 for an acquaintance, 5 indicates the amount you would communicate, and 3.07 (2.85 + 3.09 + 2.89 + 3.08 + 3.44 = 15.35 ÷ 5) would be the intimacy-of-disclosure figure, which is not very much in this example.

Source: From Taylor and Altman, 1966.

planation, which might be labeled the *social-attraction* position, postulates that being entrusted with another's disclosure is considered to be a social reward by the listener (Worthy, Gary, & Kahn, 1969). Since intimate disclosures are usually shared only by close friends, the initial disclosure may be viewed by the recipient as a sign of liking and trust: "Imagine—she told me such personal things about herself. With all these people in the office that she could have talked to, she felt that she could trust me the most." The recipient may reciprocate with disclosure as a sign of liking and to provide a reward to the initial discloser. The following sequence of events summarizes the social-attraction explanation of disclosure reciprocity:

1. A reveals intimate information to B.
2. B infers that A's disclosure was based on his liking for her.
3. B likes A.
4. B reveals intimate information to A.

The social-attraction position makes sense intuitively, but research suggests that steps 2 and 3 may not be necessary for disclosure reciprocity to occur. B may reciprocate A's disclosure even in the absence of liking. The skeptical reader may be thinking, "But do you mean that I am going to match intimacies even if I don't like the person?" Derlega, Harris, and Chaikin (1973) conducted a study to answer this question. They created a situation in which liking for the discloser was manipulated independently of level-of-disclosure input. For example, if liking for the discloser is reduced in some situations under high disclosure input, the social-attraction explanation would predict that self-disclosure should correspondingly decrease.

A situation was arranged in which two college women met for the first time in what was described as an experiment on impression formation. Each participant was told that she would be asked to talk about herself to the other. Actually, one woman was a research assistant who always delivered the same standard disclosure. The other woman was the actual subject. Although the subject believed that the choice of first speaker was due to chance, it was arranged for the assistant to speak first every time.

As part of the manipulation of disclosure input, the female research assistant revealed high intimacy information of either a conventional or deviant nature. For some subjects the high discloser indicated that she was lesbian (deviant high discloser); for another group the high discloser indicated that she was heterosexual (conventional high discloser); for a third group a low discloser revealed very conventional information (conventional low discloser).

It was felt that subjects would like the confederate more when she revealed details of a heterosexual relationship than when the relationship was homosexual. As expected, confessing to a lesbian relationship did not endear our assistant to the subjects. The deviant high discloser was liked less than either the conventional high discloser or the assistant who revealed superficial information. The critical question was whether the subjects would reciprocate and reveal intimate material to a person who was not liked. Subjects agreed to reveal more information and more intimate information to both the conventional and the deviant high disclosers than to the superficial discloser. Furthermore, the two high-disclosure conditions did not differ in reciprocated disclosure.

These results show that liking cannot always account for disclosure reciprocity, for the effect occurred even when the first discloser was not liked. Other studies (for example, Cozby, 1972; Lynn, 1978) have found similar results, giving additional confidence in this conclusion.

Since reciprocity occurs even in the absence of liking for the initial discloser, how else can we account for it? A distinguished sociologist, Alvin Gouldner (1960), proposed that a **norm of reciprocity** governs much of our social behavior. Operating in a quid pro quo manner, people often feel obligated to return the services they have received from others—whether money, favors, or disclosures.

The notion of a reciprocity norm can be traced back to the assumption that people wish to preserve equity, or equality, in their social relationships (see Chapter 13). A person who feels always on the giving end of a relationship will become resentful and angry. Although the feeling may not be as strong, the individual on the receiving end of an inequitable relationship will also be uncomfortable. Few people like to feel that they are in debt to another or that they are exploiting someone. Thus, a move toward equity may originate with the party who is reaping the rewards from the inequity. Without reciprocity, the recipient of high disclosure and the discloser are placed in an inequitable situation. The discloser has invested more in the relationship in the form of high self-disclosure than has the listener.

A study conducted by Chaikin and Derlega (1974a) demonstrated with observer subjects that people may dislike those who violate the reciprocity norm. Subjects watched a video tape of two persons conversing. One woman revealed something about herself, then the other replied. When the second woman's disclosure was equal in intimacy to the first, she was liked. This result occurred as long as the second woman's disclosure matched that of the first, regardless of whether the first woman had been very superficial or somewhat intimate; when the second woman's intimacy level differed from the first's, however, either by being much more or much less intimate, she was disliked. If the second woman was more intimate than the first, subjects thought that she was maladjusted and unusual. When she was less intimate than the initial discloser, she was perceived as cold and unfriendly.

The Chaikin and Derlega (1974a) results imply that only by matching the original revealer intimacy for intimacy can the recipient satsify the norm of disclosure reciprocity. Are social norms that specific, however? In a follow-up study, Berg and Archer (in press) found that a show of sympathy or concern after hearing another's disclosure of an unpleasant experience was preferred over the reciprocating of personal information and was considered more appropriate by observers. The disclosure recipient who indicated a willingness to listen to the communicator's problems was seen as warm, adjusted, and trustworthy. The display of responsiveness seemed to enhance the concerned recipient's attraction for the observer subjects.

Thus, disclosure reciprocity does not *have* to occur every time an initial discloser reveals personal information. There are situations in which reciprocal disclosure is inappropriate and unlikely, or where an intimate revelation elicits withdrawal rather than reciprocal intimacy. For example, certain role relationships, such as priest-confessor or doctor-patient, discourage mutual disclosure. Meetings between peers may also fail to show reciprocity for various reasons. People who believe that their disclosures will lead to rejection or ridicule by the listener, or will be made public, or will be used later to hurt them, may not reveal intimate information, regardless of the level of intimacy of the other person's prior disclosure (cf. Kleinke, 1979).

There is considerable evidence indicating that reciprocity of disclosure during a single encounter is more likely to occur between passing strangers or acquaintances than between two persons who are close friends (Derlega, Wilson, & Chaikin, 1976; Morton, 1978; Won-Doornink, 1979). For instance, Derlega et al. (1976) found that reciprocity of self-disclosure was greater between pairs of strangers than close friends. Immediate reciprocity between strangers or acquaintances may be necessary to prove one's trustworthiness and to propel the relationship into more intimate stages. Between close friends, however, mutual respect and trust have been established over a long time period. The friends hopefully have moved beyond stereotyped rules governing how acquaintances should behave. An individual can respond to a friend's high disclosure in several ways, depending on what is appropriate at the moment. A relationship between friends rests on a foundation of previously established trust; the relationship should not be adversely affected by one partner's failure to reciprocate immediately (Altman, 1973).

Other exceptions to the rule of disclosure reciprocity may occur when recipients perceive that open communication will lock them into unwanted relationships, or that the senders' messages are part of a larger "confidence game" designed to elicit information from or to control the recipients. According to Brehm's (1966, 1976) theory of psychological reactance, perceived threats to important freedoms may produce a negative psychological state. Another person's self-disclosure input, by creating an obligation to reciprocate, may threaten one's freedom of choice to regulate interactions with others. The recipient of an intimate disclosure may experience the following type of conflict. On the one hand, the listener is obliged to reciprocate after listening to another's intimate disclosure. But if the listener returns a disclosure, privacy is given up. A recent study by

Archer and Berg (1978) found that persons who were faced with this dilemma sought to restore their threatened freedom by reducing their self-disclosure. When, however, the intimate stranger told subjects that whatever they wrote was all right, the threat seemed to be eliminated, producing the usual reciprocity effect.

BARRIERS TO SELF-DISCLOSURE AMONG MEN AND WOMEN

The Inexpressive Male

Sociologist Mirra Komarovsky (1976) wrote that "on the one hand, the desire to escape loneliness, to find support, reassurance, appreciation, perhaps absolution—all generate the need to share feelings and thoughts with others. Pitted against these advantages are the risks of sharing, e.g., possible criticism, ridicule, loss of power, and the like" (p. 163). This dilemma is felt acutely by men in North American society who often feel the need to maintain the pose of masculine strength, making it difficult for them to disclose to other men or women.

Consider the following example of a college senior who hid from his girlfriend that he was in psychotherapy (Komarovsky, 1976, p. 164). After he met the woman, she told him that she was in therapy. The student said, "I could not tell her that I too was in therapy. That would show her how unsure and confused I was. A girl wants a strong man. I would be lowering my image in her eyes." This concealment, however, worried him. He kept his secret for the first three months of their relationship, but felt that eventually she would find out the truth. Moreover, he advocated the values of openness, authenticity, and reciprocity in male-female relationships, all of which he compromised by his secrecy.

Sometimes men may fear that when they disclose intimate information they will regress

into a childlike role with others. Consider the following example provided by a male college student at an Ivy League school:

I shall never forget the mistake of telling one of my past girl friends about some of my problems. She became concerned and started offering all kinds of advice. From then on, she always treated me like a little boy, waiting for me to admit some problem and to seek her advice. Our whole relationship changed and I felt terrible that I had forced her into the role of an advice giver. (Komarovsky, 1976, p. 164)

Men find it more difficult than women to disclose personal information about themselves in relationships (Cozby, 1973; Derlega, Durham, Sholis, & Gockel, in press; Jourard, 1971; Komarovsky, 1976). As Kate Millet (1975) wrote, "Men repress, women express" (p. 27). Why? Through a combination of rewards, punishments, and modeling processes a little boy is taught how to be a "man" and a little girl is taught how to be a "woman." Sex-appropriate behaviors are reinforced and thus strengthened, whereas sex-inappropriate behaviors are punished or ignored and thus are reduced in strength and eventually disappear. As part of the social learning of sex roles, boys are usually praised and rewarded for mastery at games and sports, whereas girls are rewarded for their success in relationships with people. Boys are expected to hide their feelings because "big boys don't cry." In contrast, little girls are allowed and even encouraged to show their feelings and emotions. Such childhood conditioning is difficult to overcome.

Besides the role of early child experiences in the development of self-disclosure patterns, cultural norms operate in adulthood to maintain sex-linked differences in self-disclosure (Chelune, 1976; Derlega & Chaikin, 1976; Lewis, 1978). After self-disclosure behaviors are acquired, their maintenance depends on continued reinforcement, which is achieved by expectations of rewards or punishment. Thus, even those men who have the capacity to express their feelings may fear doing so. Men who identify with the masculine role may fear being rejected or ridiculed if they violate expectancies of appropriate sex-typed behavior. Similarly, expressive behavior of women occurs because they continue to expect reinforcement and approval for such behavior. These values are held today by many college students. For example, Derlega and Chaikin (1976) found that male and female subjects rated a male stimulus person as better adjusted when he failed to disclose information about a personal problem than when he did disclose such information. In contrast, a female stimulus person was rated as better adjusted when she disclosed than when she did not. In addition, high disclosers—regardless of whether they were male or female—were considered to be more "feminine" than low disclosers.

Though men have difficulty being intimate, an "ethic of openness" seems to be developing, at least for close relationships (Rubin, Hill, Peplau, & Dunkel-Schetter, 1980). Influenced, perhaps, by the counterculture of the 1960s and the encounter-group movement, self-disclosure is valued in opposite-sex relationships. The modern version of the male role encourages emotional intimacy, at least when it is confined to a close heterosexual relationship (Pleck, 1976). The male's romantic partner is supposed to serve as a source of emotional support and as a confidante. Confirming this view, Komarovsky (1974, 1976) found that males at an Ivy League college disclosed more to their girlfriends than to anyone else. In contrast, men's emotional relationships with other men were weak or absent. The modern male role, while it legitimizes disclosure in opposite-sex relationships, still denies men the opportunity to channel some of their expressive needs into relationships with other men. Men are frequently unable to communicate with other men, especially about feelings that might carry connotations of weakness (Lewis, 1978).

The "male role" inhibits self-disclosure and intimate relationships, especially among male friends.

When Women Don't Disclose

The sex role of the "strong and silent" man promotes low disclosure in males, but women's self-disclosure in certain areas is also inhibited by the roles society expects of them. In a study conducted in the 1940s, sociologist Mirra Komarovsky (1974) found that approximately 40 percent of a group of female college students reported that they had occasionally "played dumb" on dates (for example, by not revealing academic achievements or pretending to know nothing about some subject). Similar surveys conducted in the 1970s (Komarovsky, 1974) indicate a substantial drop in the percentage of those who would deliberately downgrade their intellectual ability in favor of a man.

CAN THERE BE TOO MUCH OPENNESS?

We have noted how self-disclosure plays a crucial role in building close relationships. Negative consequences, however, may result from too much disclosure. Disclosing intimate details about one's life to casual acquaintances may invite negative reactions, ranging from incredulity and amazement to ridicule and avoidance. Self-disclosure may be inappropriate and self-defeating if it is not done at the correct time, in the correct context, and to the correct people. For instance, one study (Chaikin & Derlega, 1974b) found that observers rated disclosure of intimate information to a stranger negatively, leading them to rate the discloser's behavior as inappropriate and maladjusted. Not surprisingly, observers also disliked such a person.

There are norms that prescribe when people should disclose and when they should not. One norm, for instance, concerns status. Sociologist Erving Goffman (1967) noted that disclosure by a low-status individual (for example, an elevator operator) to a high-status individual (such as a business executive) is more appropriate than disclosure in the reverse direction (recall the discussion of touching and status in Chapter 7). In fact, subjects rate self-disclosure to someone of higher status (for example, an older person) as more appropriate and less unusual than self-disclosure to a person lower in status (for example, a younger person). Disclosure to a peer is seen as most appropriate (Chaikin & Derlega, 1974b). Slobin, Miller, and Porter (1968) also found that workers disclose more to their bosses than to immediate subordinates, although not as much as to fellow workers. These results may reflect the notion that the disclosers are placing themselves symbolically on a comparable level with their targets. Since few people desire to reduce their status, self-disclosure to a lower-status in-

dividual is regarded as somewhat inappropriate and unusual.

The timing of a message will also affect how a high discloser is evaluated. Persons who divulge personal information too early in a conversation may be perceived as nondiscriminating and, hence, may be disliked and avoided. In one experiment (Wortman, Adesman, Herman, & Greenberg, 1976), a male confederate confessed that his girlfriend was pregnant. Results indicated that subjects evaluated the discloser who revealed this information at the beginning less favorably than one who did so near the end of the meeting. Why was the later discloser liked more than the early discloser? The value of a person's disclosure seems to rest partially on the listener's perception that the discloser is selective and that the target has been singled out as the recipient. In other words, the listener's reactions depend on whether or not the disclosure input was *personalistic*—intended uniquely for the recipient (Rubin, 1974; Jones & Archer, 1976). If the discloser waits until the end of the meeting to disclose intimate information, the listener may think, "The revealer presumably had time to learn something about me and decide to trust me with this intimate material." Early disclosure leads to the inference that the discloser is "too open" and would have shared the information with anyone.

A final comment about the "appropriateness" of self-disclosure: Many "humanistic" psychologists argue that self-disclosure is necessary for mental health. For instance, Sidney Jourard (1971) wrote that the "healthy personality will . . . display the ability to make himself fully known to at least one other significant human being" (p. 32). Jourard thought that growth as a person, or in psychologist Abraham Maslow's terms, "self-actualization" (the fulfillment of one's unique potential), is stopped when individuals hide information about themselves from others. There may, however, be an important reason for individuals to keep some information hidden. A sense of uniqueness (or individuality) may depend on maintaining some barriers between oneself and others, ultimately by keeping certain secrets (cf. Brock, 1968). Individuals who are completely transparent, who speak openly about deeply personal matters, may have a less clearly defined self-concept than others, just because they do not possess any scarce or unique information about themselves. Individuals need to become aware of the limits to their own "tolerance for intimacy," just as we need to respect and become aware of others' limits (Stein, 1975).

OVERCOMING LONELINESS

This chapter opened with self-descriptions of three lonely people. We have not directly answered the question of what might be done to alleviate their loneliness. It should be obvious by now that we think that a lack of intimacy contributes to loneliness and that developing an intimate relationship is a way to overcome loneliness. But what are some ways that this might be accomplished? Several findings in the research on loneliness suggest strategies that could be employed.

First, programs to help build self-esteem and teach social skills might be introduced in schools. Such programs would be especially useful for chronically lonely persons, such as Anne, who persistently avoid building deep relationships. The promise of this approach is demonstrated in a recent study by Jones (1982), which found that even a few hours of specially designed social-skill training can be highly successful in helping people alleviate their loneliness.

Second, we might encourage new college students to focus on building their network of friendships (cf. Cutrona, 1982). Research is beginning to indicate that people in new settings, such as Helen who left her family and friends to go off to school, should be more concerned with new friendships rather than, for example, finding a new dating partner.

Third, we might suggest that communities need to remove barriers to communication among certain segments of the population. For example, Pearl's loneliness, which stems in part from her inability to drive a car any longer, might be alleviated if she had access to transportation designed to fit her needs. In general, it is important to consider such strategies as research on loneliness increasingly documents the extent to which a lack of intimate relationships is a problem that distresses people in our society.

SUMMARY   This chapter has focused on one class of verbal communications, self-disclosure. Self-disclosure can be defined as what personal information one person gives another. Decisions about self-disclosure will determine the kinds of relationships we have, the number of friends we have, and how well we know others and are known by them. Self-disclosure may even play a major role in overcoming loneliness and social isolation. The experience of loneliness seems to derive in part from the absence of intimate relationships, from not having a confidant or companion with whom we can communicate intimately.

Self-disclosure is a mechanism people use to regulate privacy. Adjustment in self-disclosure outputs and inputs is an example of boundary regulation, and the degree of control we maintain over this exchange of information contributes to the amount of privacy we have in a social relationship. The dyadic boundary establishes the precondition for self-disclosure, ensuring that it is safe to disclose to the invited recipient and that the information will not be leaked to uninvited third parties. The self (or personal) boundary is modified by self-disclosure. We maintain a barrier around ourselves, which is based on nondisclosure. This barrier is opened when we disclose.

A number of benefits may derive from self-disclosure, including self-expression (a catharsis-like effect), self-clarification (talking about one's values and opinions to clarify one's own thinking), social validation (eliciting feedback from others and validating one's self-concept), relationship development (acting as a vehicle for developing close relationships), and social control (operating as a tool for control and perhaps taking advantage of others).

According to social-penetration theory, individuals generally disclose more and more information as a relationship develops. They talk more intimately and disclose information about an increasing number of areas. At each stage of a relationship more information is disclosed at superficial than at intimate levels, reflecting the wedge-shaped pattern of disclosure. Disclosure reciprocity, in which individuals tend to match one another in level of communication intimacy, plays an important role in relationship development.

Men generally find it more difficult than women to disclose personal information about themselves in relationships. Men traditionally have been expected to hide their feelings, while women have been encouraged to show their feelings and emotions. Although an "ethic of openness" seems to be evolving, at least in close relationships, men's emotional relationships with other men are still weak or nonexistent.

Self-disclosure is not a panacea for all human problems. It may not reduce instantaneously people's loneliness, increase their friends, or facilitate self-awareness. Pursued in an appropriate manner, however, it may help in realizing these goals.

SUGGESTED READINGS

Chelune, G. J. (Ed.). *Self-Disclosure: Origins, patterns, and implications of openness in interpersonal relationships.* San Francisco: Jossey-Bass, 1979.

Derlega, V. J., & Chaikin, A. L. *Sharing intimacy: What we reveal to others and why.* Englewood Cliffs, N.J.: Prentice-Hall, 1975.

Goffman, E. *The presentation of self in everyday life.* New York: Doubleday, 1959.

Jourard, S. M. *The transparent self.* New York: Van Nostrand Reinhold, 1971.

Margulis, S. T. (Ed.). Privacy as a behavioral phenomenon. *Journal of Social Issues,* 1977, 33(3).

Peplau, L. A., & Perlman, D. (Eds.). *Loneliness.* New York: Wiley-Interscience, 1982.

10

HUMAN SEXUALITY

- Introduction: Theoretical Emphasis
- Social Issue Focus: Feminism
- Research Findings and the Issues Raised by Feminists
- Sexual Expression
- Summary

INTRODUCTION: THEORETICAL EMPHASIS

Bob is seated in front of a screen on which "X-rated" pornographic slides are projected. His sexual arousal is measured by a small band that he had earlier placed around his penis. Bob is showing little sign of sexual arousal. When the series of slides are over and he is asked to rate how sexually arousing they were, Bob gives them relatively low ratings.

The experimenter then proceeds to mix three drinks using liquids from vodka and tonic bottles and adding some lime juice. He offers the drinks to Bob with instructions to drink them slowly so that they can be absorbed into his system. When Bob finishes drinking, he views a new set of pornographic slides similar in content to the first set. Now, however, the penile band indicates considerable sexual arousal and Bob reports that he found the stimuli highly sexually arousing. When Bob is asked if he felt that the alcohol had anything to do with his higher arousal to the second as compared with the first set of slides, he tells the experimenter that he thinks much of his arousal can be explained by the alcohol.

Bob does not know that the drinks did not contain alcohol. They were only made to look and taste like alcohol. Thus, the effects of drinking were caused by Bob's belief that he drank alcohol and not by any pharmacological effects of the drinks.

The above description is based on the actual findings of a series of studies that compared the cognitive versus the pharmacological effects of alcohol on sexual arousal. The pharmacological view suggests that the effects may be explained by direct chemical effects on inhibitory centers of the brain. The cognitive view (cf Schachter and Singer's work discussed in Chapter 6), in contrast, argues that *believing* that one has ingested alcohol reduces personal responsibility for behavior and provides justification for "taboo" behavior. Such cognitive reasoning may occur at both the subconscious and conscious levels.

Studies of this type (e.g. Lang, Searles, Lauerman, & Adesso, 1980) found that subjects who believed that they had drunk alcohol, regardless of whether they actually had, were more sexually aroused to various kinds of pornographic stimuli, including heterosexual, homosexual, and rape depictions, than those who believed that they had not drunk alcohol. Actually ingesting alcohol had relatively little effect. The impact of believing that one is under the influence of alcohol was found to be particularly dramatic for subjects with high guilt about sex (Lang et al., 1980).

The Cognitive System

We began this chapter with a presentation of research on the cognitive effects of alcohol to draw your attention to a central aspect of social psychological theories of human sexuality. Such theories (for example, Abramson, 1982; Byrne, 1977; Gagnon & Simon, 1973) emphasize the role of the human cognitive system as a mediator of sexual responses. This cognitive system is the result of the unique development of the human brain that enables us to analyze, interpret, and react to events in ways fundamentally different from those of other species.

The theorizing of Abramson (1982) is an excellent example of such an emphasis on the cognitive system. He recognizes the role of such influences as hormones and physiological sensations, but argues that their effects on human sexual expression are a function of the interpretation and meaning they are given in being processed through our cognitive system. Most important in the cognitive system are principles developed as humans grow from infancy into adulthood. Such principles are the result of many different experiences, including

---

This chapter is written by Neil M. Malamuth.

parents' conversations, mass-media exposure, sermons, previous sexual encounters, and so forth. The specific experiences are not typically remembered by the person, but general principles or ideas are developed, such as whether sex is good or bad, what is appropriate or inappropriate sex, and when, where, and with whom sex is sanctioned. These principles determine our attitudes, judgments, and responses to various sexual experiences.

Consider the example of stroking a person's body. Stroking your own body may have the identical physical properties as having someone else stroke your body, but the meaning you attach to that event results in very different sensations. Whether you find the other person's stroking sexually arousing, boring, or disgusting will be determined by your perceptions of the attractiveness of that person and the psychological interpretation you give to the actions.

One of the principles in your cognitive system concerns who is or is not attractive. Commonsense thinking leads us to believe that judgments of attraction are largely biologically determined without any cognitive or learning mediation. As is demonstrated by cross-cultural research (for example, Ford and Beach, 1951) such thinking is clearly wrong. There is little consistency among different cultures in what are considered sexually attractive persons; the very characteristic that in one culture typically increases the person's sexual attractiveness (for example, fatness, skinniness, upright breasts, long pendulous breasts, deformed ears, noses, or lips) may make the person repulsive to members of other cultural groups.

The presentation in this chapter will illustrate how social psychologists have been guided in the study of human sexuality by their emphasis on a cognitive system. In lower animals, sexual acts are primarily determined by hormone levels and other accompanying physiological changes occurring during periods of heat or estrus, a period that maximizes the possibility of conception (Beach, 1965). The human cognitive system has made conception a relatively insignificant motivator of sexual expression. Therefore, explanations of human sexuality based primarily on hormones or similar factors, as well as theories that are simple extrapolations from animals, are inadequate.

Sexual Scripts

According to a particularly interesting social psychology theory advanced by Gagnon and Simon (1973), various principles about sexuality are organized into a program for behavior that can be labeled a script. Scripts, discussed earlier in Chapter 6, specify the whos, whats, whens, wheres, and whys for behavior. They are like theatrical scripts in which the playwright provides directions for behavior. Improviso theatre, in which actors are given general guidelines for behavior but are free to improvise in various ways, may be the most suitable metaphor to apply here.

An illustration of the role of social scripts comes from the present writer's experiences in working with North American students visiting Israel. I once organized a dance between these students and their Israeli counterparts. The scripted behavior for an Israeli female in slow dances is generally not to have direct bodily contact with her dancing partner unless she is intimately involved with him. North American scripts, as you know, frequently prescribe body contact in such dances even when no intimacy is involved or desired. The consequence of the different cultural scripts was that the Israeli males thought that the North American females with whom they danced desired immediate sexual intimacy. The North American males dancing with Israeli partners, on the other hand, seemed very uncomfortable in being kept at a physical distance and later reported that they had been thinking that the Israelis must have found something about them highly offensive.

SOCIAL FOCUS 10.1
Methods Used in Sex Research

As social psychologists, we would like to believe that we can approach the topic of sexuality with the same degree of scientific objectivity and openness as in any other area of human research. Unfortunately, societal attitudes historically have restricted a systematic examination of this area (Byrne, 1977). In recent years scientists have been finding a social climate more conducive to research on human sexual functioning. The following are some examples of the methods sex researchers are currently using:

Surveys

Surveys are frequently used to gather social psychological data about sexuality. While sex surveys appear to have as much validity (that is, they share the same strengths and weaknesses) as surveys in other areas of human behavior (Barber & Perlman, 1975; Perlman, in press), they often pose unique difficulties:

Having developed a rather lengthy questionnaire, I didn't want to take any more of the respondents' time than was absolutely necessary. So, I devised a "branching" technique. I asked all the sexually experienced respondents to answer a long list of questions skipped by sexually inexperienced respondents. As a way of trying out the questionnaire, I administered it to all the students in my social psychology class. I asked them to use alternate seats and assured them their answers would be treated confidentially. After about 15 minutes, many students turned in their questionnaires and left; others continued working. I noticed one boy in the front of the room who was clearly finished but waiting patiently before leaving. Then it dawned on me: time to complete the questionnaire was an unobtrusive measure of sexual experience. After about five minutes, the boy in the front of the room began writing down the names of all the girls he knew who were still answering questions. Needless to say, I have never used these administrative procedures since (Perlman, in press, p.4).

Physiological Assessment of Arousal

For some time, psychologists have been using various physiological measures to study sexual arousal. The penile transducer, a small band that is placed

---

Jemail and Geer (1978) attempted to determine whether people in North American culture actually follow a basic sequence of events in sexual acts that would qualify as a script. According to Gagnon and Simon's theory, such a script would be the most sexually arousing sequence of events to members of our culture because we have learned that this is the appropriate sequence. To test this prediction, Jemail and Geer had male and female subjects rearrange a set of sentences, each of which described an event in a heterosexual interaction,

on the penis, and the vaginal probe, which is inserted into the vagina, have been used for several years. A recent innovation in the physiological assessment of sexual arousal is thermography, the measurement of infrared energy emitted as a function of body temperature (Abramson, Perry, Rothblatt, Seeley, & Seeley, 1981). Using this technique, pictures illustrating hot and cold areas of the body provide means of viewing blood-flow changes that occur during sexual arousal. The identical procedures are used to study the responses of males and females. Since subjects do not insert or attach any devices to their bodies, this technique is less obtrusive than other approaches.

Direct Observation

While investigators have not literally invaded people's bedrooms to observe them, the highly influential work of Masters and Johnson (1966, 1970, 1979) involves direct observations of volunteers engaging in various sex acts, including intercourse. Their research analyzed both heterosexual and homosexual behavior.

Ethical Considerations

Society has often treated sexuality as a taboo topic and many people understandably wish to keep their sexual lives private. It is clear that research in this area needs to be particularly sensitive to ethical safeguards. Below are some examples of the ethical requirements typically required for sex research: (1) Only volunteers who are fully aware of the procedures to be used in the research should serve as subjects. (2) Pressures should not be exerted on people to volunteer. (3) Subjects should not participate in any new activities as part of the research that they have not previously chosen to engage in. (4) Subjects must be free to leave at any time for any reason without any penalty whatsoever. (5) A thorough debriefing must be held to explain any procedures that may involve deception. Subjects in sex studies that follow such ethical safeguards almost uniformly report that they found the experience to be positive and devoid of any negative aftereffects (Abramson, 1977).

under two sets of instructions. Subjects were asked to order the set of sentences on the basis of the most sexually arousing or the most likely sequence. Subjects could choose to discard any sentences they felt did not fit in.

The results indicated a high degree of agreement among subjects in each of these conditions and very high correlations among the sequences with the two sets of instructions. For example, both males and females almost uniformly indicated with both "the most likely to occur" and "the most arousing" instructions,

Social scripts, the scenarios we have about likely sequences of events, influence the meaning we give to social behaviors. Given different patterns of courtship, bodily contact while dancing means different things to American and Israeli students.

a sequence that began with kissing, followed by the male manipulating the female's breasts with his hand and then kissing her breasts. These data suggest that there are culturally shared scripts in sexual interactions and that these sequences define what is most arousing. In future research, it would be desirable to replicate these procedures with cultures that are very different from our own to gain insight into the differences and similarities across cultures in sexual scripts.

SOCIAL ISSUE FOCUS: FEMINISM

Our cognitions are organized in many ways, one of which is the use of scripts, our scenarios about how sequences of behavior should unfold. Another is according to belief systems or ideologies. The feminist movement reflects one such ideology.

In this section, we will focus on the feminist beliefs as they relate to sexual behavior. Among other concerns, feminists have formulated views on the double standard and traditional sex roles, rape, and pornography. These issues have also been investigated by social scientists. In a later section, we will examine research findings as they pertain to these issues.

The term "feminism" has varied associations in people's minds. There are many definitions of feminism, and undoubtedly disagreements exist among people who consider themselves feminists. Yet, in attempting to give a definition for the purpose of this chapter, the one that seems most suitable is that a **feminist** is a person who believes that men and women should have equal opportunities for individual development and for power (Freeman, 1979). In keeping with this definition, the term "egalitarian" (or equalitarian) appears more appropriate than feminist, since the term feminism is often mistakenly associated with femininity. Because of the wide use of the term feminism, however, it will be adopted here, with the understanding that a man can hold feminist views equally as forcefully as a woman. Below is a scale, based on items from Spence and Helmreich (1972), Phelps (1979), and Laws and Schwartz (1977), designed to measure correspondence of attitudes on sexuality with those of feminists.

Instructions. The statements listed below describe attitudes. There are no right or wrong answers, only opinions. You are asked to express your feelings about each statement by indicating whether you (DS) Disagree Strongly, (DM) Disagree Mildly, (AM) Agree Mildly, or (AS) Agree Strongly. Please indicate your opinion by marking, in the space beside each item, the alternative that best describes your personal attitude.

1. If a woman does not find her male sexual partner to be more dominant than she, her sexual adjustment will not be the best.
2. Due to differences in psychological makeup, women usually should engage in sex only in response to loving feelings, while men may often engage in sex for recreation.
3. There should be legal rape in marriage; that is, a wife should be able to deny her husband intercourse.
4. Women have the same sexual drive and needs as men.
5. In terms of sexual relations, women have as much right to be gay, celibate, promiscuous, or experienced as men.
6. The man should always initiate each progressively intimate level of sexual advance.
7. Reaching sexual fulfillment each time a person has intercourse is not as important for a woman as it is for a man.
8. The initiative in dating should come from the man.
9. It is insulting to women to have the "obey" clause remain in the marriage service.
10. A woman should be as free as a man to propose marriage.
11. Women earning as much as their dates should bear equally the expense when they go out together.
12. Women should take the passive role in courtship.

Instructions for scoring. For each item, give a score of 1 if you chose the Disagree Strongly option, a 2 for the Disagree Mildly option, a 3 for the Agree Mildly option, and a 4 for the Agree Strongly option. Then add the scores for items 3, 4, 5, 9, 10, 11, and subtract the scores for items 1, 2, 6, 7, 8, 12. If your final score is 12 or above, your opinions are quite consistent on these matters with those of feminists, whereas if your score is below 12, your opinions do not show a high degree of agreement with those of feminists.

Sexual Scripts, the Double Standard, and Sex Roles

Feminists contend that women and men in Western societies are taught sexual scripts that are based on female powerlessness, dependency, and submission, while requiring men to be aggressive, domineering, and lacking in such areas as tenderness and sensitivity (Phelps, 1979; Laws & Schwartz, 1977). As English (1980) has suggested, the kind of mate people look for is often related to such scripts (for example, women may seek men who are taller, older, smarter, richer, or dominating in other ways). According to the feminist viewpoint, the sexual scripts many people adopt today are to some degree remnants of those popular earlier in history. For example, one Victorian script dichotomized women's roles into that of the good woman (wife) and the bad woman (whore). Part of what was expected of good women was the lack of sexual desires and adherence to a double standard that permitted greater sexual expression for men than for women (Laws & Schwartz, 1977). The double standard of earlier generations taught women that sex, particularly intercourse, was justified only in marriage, or later in history, when a woman was in love or in deeply committed relationships. Men, on the other hand, it is argued, have always been permitted a greater range of reasons for engaging in sexual acts—such as experimentation, developing skills and knowledge, or "just for fun." It is important to stress that this feminist viewpoint does not necessarily prescribe when sex is or is not appropriate, but objects to different standards of permissiveness for males and females.

Where and why, according to the feminist theoretical perspective, did the wife/whore script and the double standard originate? According to this view, it can be traced back to a period in Western society's history in which the system of private property emerged (Clark & Lewis, 1977). This system allowed only men the right to own property, and women were part of a man's property. (Even today, in some languages, such as Hebrew, the word for "husband" is "owner".) Such a system required some means of transferring accumulated property from one male generation to the next. This was done by granting the man's offspring the right to his property, a system that required precise determination of who were his biological offspring. To ensure that a man's children were indeed his offspring, men acquired exclusive rights to use a woman's body by means of marriage; thus the origin of the double standard. A woman was forced to limit her sexual activity to marriage, but in this system a similar requirement did not exist for men— they could engage in sexual activities before marriage or outside it. Women were defined as whores if they engaged in sexual intercourse outside of marriage.

This sexual double standard may partially explain the traditional male/female sexual script and its accompanying sexual roles. The man, permitted by society to engage in sexual activities prior to marriage, attempted to initiate sexual acts. The woman, on the other hand, having severe prohibitions imposed on her for other than marital sex, was not inclined to seek sexual activities. She resisted or at least set limits to sexual activities. Such a double standard created the foundation for divergent goals and possibly antagonistic relationships between men and women. Males were taught to try to "get off" the female as much sex as they could, whereas females were taught to utilize their sexual appeal to get the most material gain (for example, gifts) or long-lasting commitment (marriage) in exchange for sexual "favors." Such a double standard and the resulting scripts, which according to feminists remain to some degree even today, would not appear consistent with the goal of developing relationships of mutual respect and love.

Rape and Pornography

Rape. In fact, double-standard scripts are, according to feminist writers (Clark & Lewis,

1977), one of the major causes of rape. Since women have been socialized not to freely express their sexuality as they desire, but to bargain with it, men have been taught to persuade and coerce women into sex. Such roles of wheedling, bargaining, and coercing may lead to considerable manipulation, mistrust, resentment, and hostility between the sexes. In some instances, such roles, attitudes, and hostile feelings result in the use by males of physical force and violence against women that comes to the attention of the law and results in a rape conviction. According to feminists, however, there are many men in the general population who have attitudes, hostilities, and behavioral inclinations similar to those of convicted rapists. Because of various factors, however, they may not actually commit such a crime or they may not come to the attention of the law even if they do rape. Such factors include the fear of being caught, the use of nonviolent coercive tactics, the failure of women to define certain episodes as rape because they are socialized to expect male sexual aggression and to blame themselves when things get "out of hand," and the failure of victims to report rape to the police because of the ordeal many rape victims have to undergo in the legal process.

Pornography. Another major area of concern for the feminist movement has been pornography (Steinem, 1980). Many feminists argue that much of pornography dehumanizes and degrades women, portraying them as the tools of men. They argue that as an expression of sexist ideology, such materials "promote a climate in which acts of sexual hostility directed against women are not only tolerated but ideologically encouraged" (Brownmiller, 1975, p. 444). In other words, their position is that pornography can contribute, although not necessarily directly, to acts of violence against women by making such acts less reprehensible to people. Feminist writers do not object to sexually explicit materials that portray men and women in humanized and positive relationships (Steinem, 1980). Rather, they object to what they

Does, as many feminists claim, pornography contribute to rape and other forms of sexual hostility toward women?

perceive as portrayals of sexual violence, unequal power relations between men and women, and the degradation of women.

RESEARCH FINDINGS AND THE ISSUES RAISED BY FEMINISTS

In this section we will examine social psychological data that pertain to each of the issues raised by feminists. Are the feminists correct in their views? Whatever the answer, feminism as a social movement deserves considerable credit for making the general public more aware of these issues. And feminists have provided social scientists with new questions that have promoted further research on these topics. Thus social scientists, too, have benefited from the feminist analysis.

The Double Standard and Sex Roles

Research directly relevant to feminist theorizing regarding the origins of the double standard and traditional sex roles are difficult to come by, since these theories concern historical events that cannot be directly tested by psychological methods. We can, however, examine research regarding the current existence of a double standard and of traditional sex roles in

SOCIAL FOCUS 10.2
The Cost of the Traditional Male Script

The script of the traditional male role in Western society has typically emphasized aggressiveness, competitiveness, dominance, and achievement orientation (Cicone & Ruble, 1978). Conforming to such role expectations may have serious costs to the individual. For instance, with regard to health, women have a life expectancy that is about eight years longer than that of men. While evidence suggests that both genetic and sex-role factors may play some part, it is adherence to the traditional male role that accounts for the larger part of men's reduced longevity (Harrison, 1978).

With respect to sexuality, the traditional male role embodies elements that may be in direct conflict with a fulfilling sexual relationship (Gross, 1978). One aspect of the traditional male role in sexual as in other areas of behavior is the heavy emphasis on performance. This performance orientation has been judged as a major block interfering with the expression of one's sexual capacity (Masters & Johnson, 1970). For the male, performance is often simplistically and erroneously equated with a woman's orgasm. Consequently, the male's attention is focused on doing those things he perceives are necessary for the female to reach an orgasm, rather than in fully enjoying the many pleasurable sensations that people can experience in addition to orgasm. The woman, in turn, may feel pressure to experience an orgasm in order to help the male confirm to himself that he is indeed a potent lover. Such pressures stand in direct conflict with the experience of mutual physical exploration, devoid of any set goals or hidden agenda, that leads to the most satisfying sexual experience (Masters & Johnson, 1970).

A recent experiment by Polyson (1978) suggests that it is principally the male who places undue responsibility on himself for sexual "success." This investigator gave both male and female subjects an account of a situation involving sexual dissatisfaction on the part of one of the partners or both of them. When subjects were asked to rate the individuals described, the male (but not the female) received poor scores by male raters only. Interestingly, negative evaluation oc-

sexuality. The data provide some support for the existence of a double standard, although it is clear that such sexism has changed drastically from earlier generations.

The findings in this area may be illustrated with a study of 231 college-age dating couples from the Boston area (Peplau, Rubin, and Hill, 1977). It was found in this study that 82 percent of men and women advocated identical standards for males and females with respect to sex with casual acquaintances or in committed relationships. (Admittedly, the data of this and many other studies are based on samples of educated college students who may be less likely than their relatively less educated counterparts to believe in a double standard.) When students did hold different attitudes for the sexual behavior of men and women, however, they were more permissive toward men.

What the data of this and other studies also show is that to a large degree sexual interactions still follow traditional roles. Such roles, in which the man is the initiator of sexual advances and the woman sets the limits, accord-

curred regardless of whether it was the male or the female who was described as not sexually satisfied in the relationship.

The traditional male sex role requires that the man be a sexual expert. The male who conforms to such an expectation is reluctant to reveal any ignorance or uncertainty. Since there are considerable differences among individuals in what they find most sexually pleasurable, the male who adopts the "expert" role may not encourage his partner to teach him about her idiosyncratic desires and needs. As McCary (1973) has suggested, "For a man to become a good sex partner . . . he must first be willing to admit that he does not know all there is to know. . . . Many men, unfortunately, are unwilling to make this admission because it threatens their ego and masculine self-image" (p. 149). Moreover, honest communication between partners is often barred by such male attitudes because women are reluctant to give honest feedback or make suggestions to a male who is defensive and hypersensitive about succeeding as the "expert."

The traditional male-female sex roles prescribe male initiation and female passivity. The female is consequently deprived of the positive aspects of initiating and directing while the male is denied the experience of relaxing and receiving pleasure. Although many men readily admit to having the fantasy of being actively seduced and made love to by an assertive woman, they are often unable to cope with female assertiveness. Such inability may be caused by the traditional societal emphasis on sexual conquest and dominance as central to male gender identity (Gross, 1978). Not fulfilling the traditional controlling male role in sexual relations may be seen as threatening one's manhood. Interestingly, based on society's traditional attitudes, a man who cannot engage in sexual intercourse is labeled "impotent" or powerless (Goldberg, 1976). It would appear, then, that male power is seen as directly based on sexual performance.

Many men have come to reject the traditional male role in sexual relations. As Julty (1974) indicated, "I don't want to get into bed wearing a tottering crown. That's just too much responsibility and not enough fun" (p. 37).

ing to the research findings, continue as part of the typical script most people follow. The findings of Peplau et al. (1977) indicate that both for couples who did and for those who did not have intercourse, males initiated sex. It was the women's attitudes towards coitus, however, that in most cases determined whether intercourse was engaged in, and if it was, how early in the relationship it first occurred.

These data are consistent with findings that both men and women stereotype descriptions of one person attempting to convince another to "have sex" as male actions, whereas attempts "not to have sex" are stereotyped as female actions (McCormick, 1976). Studies show that women do indirectly communicate their interest or receptiveness to sexuality, or that once certain sexual acts have been engaged in within the relationship, women may initiate the act. In terms of directly initiating sexual acts for the first time, however, it is males who play the traditional role of "making the pass," while the females try to determine where and if limits are set.

Rape

A number of studies were designed to investigate the feminists' contention that "normal" socialization of sex roles often legitimizes sexual aggression and coercion. In support of such a possibility, Kanin and his associates (Kanin, 1967; Kanin & Parcell, 1977) found that over half of the female college students interviewed reported experiencing offensive male sexual aggression during the previous year. Giarusso, Johnson, Goodchilds, and Zellman (1979) similarly found that the attitudes of high school youths to a surprising degree condone the use of force in sexual relationships. Four hundred and thirty-two high school students from representative backgrounds in the Los Angeles area were interviewed concerning whether they thought using force was "okay" in dating relationships. Participants were given descriptions of nine situations and asked to indicate whether they thought it was acceptable "for a guy to hold a girl down and force her to have sexual intercourse" in each of these situations. It was found that in some situations, such as when "she gets him sexually excited" or "she says she's going to have sex with him then changes her mind," a majority of the males and about a third of the females indicated that they thought it was acceptable to use force. About 40 percent of the males similarly believed that force was acceptable when "he spends a lot of money on her," "she's had sexual intercourse with other guys," "she is stoned or drunk," or "they have dated a long time." In fact, only 44 percent of the females and 24 percent of the males rejected the use of force in all nine situations. Clearly, attitudes such as these create a cultural context within which the crime of rape becomes more likely.

In related research, an attempt was made to identify males in the general population who may have relatively higher inclination to rape (but who have not necessarily actually raped) than others. Male college students were asked to indicate how likely they personally would be to rape if they could be assured of not being caught and punished. These students came from varied parts of North America. They were typically asked to indicate their responses on a five-point scale ranging from 1 (not at all likely) to 5 (very likely). This question has been asked under a variety of conditions, including following the viewing of a videotaped interview with an actual rape victim, following the reading of a pornographic description of rape, and without any prior exposure at all. Across these varied studies, about 35 percent of males indicated any likelihood of raping (that is, a 2 or above) (Malamuth, Reisin, & Spinner, 1979; Malamuth, Haber, & Feshbach, 1980; Malamuth & Check, 1980; Tieger, 1981).

To determine whether such a self-report has any validity, comparisons were made, on two types of responses, among men who indicated no likelihood of raping, men who indicated some likelihood of raping, and convicted rapists. These responses were selected because they appear to show reliable differences between rapists and the general population. It has been found that rapists are more likely than males in general to (1) hold callous attitudes about rape and to believe in rape myths (for example, "women ask for it" or "women get pleasure from being raped") (Gager & Schurr, 1976; Wolfe & Baker, 1980), and (2) to show relatively high levels of sexual arousal to sexual depictions of rape that emphasize the victim's suffering (Abel, Barlow, Blanchard, & Guild, 1977). The findings in several experiments clearly were that on both of these responses, men who indicated higher likelihood of raping were more similar to convicted rapists than men who indicated a lower likelihood of raping (Malamuth, 1981a).

Malamuth (1981b) designed an experiment to determine whether self-reported likelihood of raping predicts actual aggressive behavior against a woman. In one phase of the research, male college students were asked to indicate how likely they would be to rape if they could be assured of not being caught. Days later, each of these males participated in what they thought was a completely unrelated experiment. Actually, it was the second phase of the same research. In this second phase, subjects were mildly rejected and insulted by a woman whom they thought to be also a subject. In fact, she was a confederate of the experimenter. She behaved in the exact same way toward each subject. As part of a teacher-learner interaction, the males were given the opportunity of choosing among different levels of aversive noise to punish the woman (the measure of aggression). (Of course, unbeknown to them, she did not actually hear the aversive noise.) The results showed that higher reported likelihood of raping was associated with higher aggression.

Overall, the pattern of the data concerning self-reported possibility of raping indicates some validity for these self-reports as measures of an inclination to rape. Furthermore, these findings lend support to the feminists' contention that in the general population there are many men with the type of attitudes, feelings, and behavioral tendencies that generally characterize convicted rapists.

Pornography

In 1967 the U.S. Congress established the Commission on Obscenity and Pornography to conduct a thorough investigation of this issue. On the basis of several converging lines of evidence, the commission concluded that there was no evidence to support contentions that pornography has antisocial effects. This finding is obviously contrary to the position of the feminist writers cited earlier. In the following sections we will look at some of the research conducted by the commission, as well as criticisms of its work and new data that extend or challenge its conclusions. (While distinctions are often made between the terms pornography and erotica, these are used interchangeably in this chapter to refer to sexually explicit stimuli.)

The commission's surveys of availability of erotica. One line of research in the commission's work dealt with the frequency of sex offenses in Denmark as related to the availability of pornography in that country (Kutchinsky, 1970). Denmark was selected because legal restrictions on the sale of pornography were lifted for erotic books in 1967 and for all other sexual materials in 1969. These surveys reported that sex crimes, which had been relatively stable from 1958 to 1966, dropped in Denmark by about 25 percent in 1967, 12 percent in 1968, and 30 percent in 1969. This led the commission to conclude that, if anything, the legalization of pornography may result in a reduction in sex crimes.

Criticisms of availability surveys and new data. Court (1976) has taken issue with the conclusion that sex crimes in general decline if pornography is made available. He points out that the change in the total number of crimes in Denmark following the introduction of pornography was due to reductions only in certain "minor" crimes such as voyeurism (Peeping Toms), and because certain acts such as homosexual prostitution were no longer considered illegal and were therefore not reported to the police. In fact, according to statistics presented by Court (1976) the crime of rape increased slightly in Denmark following the lifting of restrictions on pornography. Moreover, Court presents data from countries such as England, New Zealand, the United States, Singapore, and Australia, showing that rape generally increased as pornography became more widely available (see Figure 10.1). Court particularly points to the possible adverse effects of violent sexual stimuli (for example, rape, sadomasochism). Such stimuli, as discussed below, have

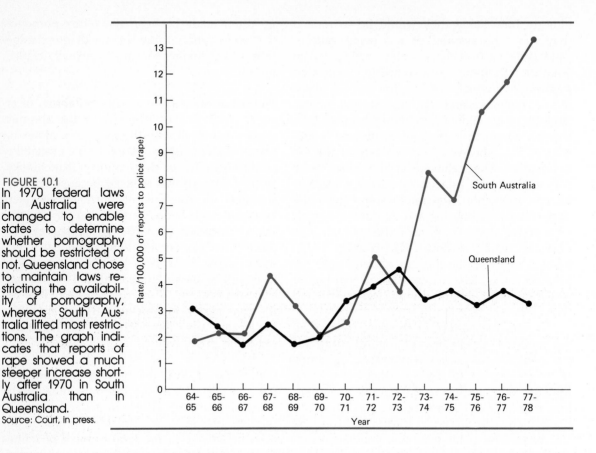

FIGURE 10.1
In 1970 federal laws in Australia were changed to enable states to determine whether pornography should be restricted or not. Queensland chose to maintain laws restricting the availability of pornography, whereas South Australia lifted most restrictions. The graph indicates that reports of rape showed a much steeper increase shortly after 1970 in South Australia than in Queensland.
Source: Court, in press.

become much more frequent in the 1970s than in earlier years. The fact that Court's data are correlational cautions against any simple interpretations or firm conclusions at this time.

The commission's experimental research. In addition to survey research, the commission conducted experiments that enabled random assignment of subjects to various conditions of the experiment (experimental research; see Chapter 2). For instance, Kutchinsky (1971) found that exposure to sexually explicit movies increased the probability of subjects engaging in already established types of sexual behavior in the period shortly thereafter. The experiment by Howard, Reifler, and Liptzin (1970) is another example of the commission's experi-

mental research. It focused on the effects of repeated exposure to erotica on sexual arousal. The results of this experiment showed that repeated exposure of males to erotica for 90 minutes a day, five days a week for five weeks, resulted in lessened sexual arousal to these materials (see Figure 10.2). When new erotic material was introduced, or following two months of nonexposure, there was a full recovery in sexual arousal levels.

Another measure of sexual interest in this experiment—the amount of time subjects chose to spend with the pornographic materials—indicated a rapid decline of interest. The percentage of time spent with the erotic materials decreased from 84 percent on the first day of the three-week exposure period to 26 percent on

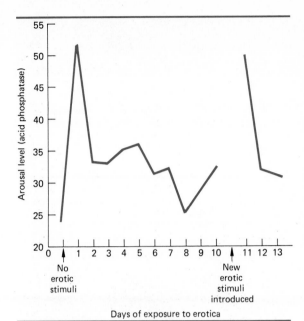

FIGURE 10.2
Measuring acid phosphatase in males' urine can be used as an index of sexual arousal. Males exposed to pornographic materials initially show a large increase in arousal followed by a decline with repeated exposure. When new erotic material was introduced, this pattern repeated itself.
Source: Adapted from Howard, Reifler, and Liptzin, 1971.

the last day of that period. Sex differences in reactions to erotica are discussed in Social Focus 10.3.

There have been several questions raised about the commission's experimental research, especially regarding its generalizability to various groups of people, various settings, different types of pornography, and the like. Generally, however, the conclusions made by the commission with regard to the conditions and stimuli it studied remain intact.

Violent pornography. Clearly, one limitation of the commission's experimental work was that it failed to examine adequately the effects of materials that fuse violence and sex (for example, rape). In fact, most of the stimuli used in the commission's experimental work were of the type that many feminist writers do not object to (for example, films depicting mutually consenting face-to-face intercourse and oral-genital sex). To be fair to the commission's work, it should be pointed out that at the time it conducted its research, explicit violence in erotica was not very common. As revealed in some recent content analyses, however, in the 1970s such materials became more common. For example, Smith (1976) analyzed the content of hard-core paperback books published between 1968 and 1974. He found that in about one-third of the episodes force was used, almost always by a male, to coerce a female to engage in an unwanted act of sex. Furthermore, he found that the average number of acts depicting rape doubled from 1968 to 1974. Similarly, Malamuth and Spinner (1980) analyzed the pictorials and cartoons in *Playboy* and *Penthouse* magazines from 1973 to 1977. While throughout this five-year period about 10 percent of the cartoons were rated as sexually violent, a change occurred in pictorials, with sexual violence increasing from about 1 percent in 1973 to 5 percent in 1977.

The increasing frequency of sexually violent pornography has prompted research designed to directly assess its impact. This research has found that exposure to violent pornography (stories, pictorials, and movies) significantly affects males' responses, but there are no consistent data to show similar effects on females. With regard to males, Malamuth (1981b) found that exposure to two sexually arousing depictions of rape caused some subjects to generate their own violent fantasies. Malamuth and Check (1980) report that exposure of a pornographic portrayal of rape suggesting that the victim may have become sexually aroused as a result of being assaulted (the typical rape scene in pornography) reduced subjects' perceptions of the degree of trauma suffered by rape victims. Similarly (see Figure 10.3), it has been found that male subjects exposed to sexually violent stimuli delivered higher levels of electric shock to a female victim (actually a confed-

SOCIAL FOCUS 10.3
Gender and Erotica

One of the variables that may affect a person's reaction to pornography is gender. In examining the relationship between gender and erotica, two questions arise. Are males and females equally sexually aroused by erotic stimuli? Are both genders equally likely to seek out opportunities to be exposed to erotica?

The data regarding the first question are not very conclusive. Some studies (for example, Griffitt, 1973; Schmidt, 1975) report that males are most sexually aroused by stimuli that are sexually explicit and that depict casual sex or lustful themes, whereas females are more sexually responsive to romantic or love themes. Other studies (for example, Fisher & Byrne, 1978; Heiman, 1975) report that females and males respond similarly to erotic stimuli, with both genders being more aroused by explicit hard-core portrayals involving casual or lustful themes.

The data concerning the second question are much more conclusive. The findings in this area are well illustrated with a recent study by Kenrick, Stringfield, Wagenhals, Dahl, and Ransdell (1980). These investigators reasoned that although females may be as responsive as males to hard-core erotic depictions, they may experience more negative feelings in reaction to such materials. A reinforcement-affect model (Byrne, 1977) would predict that if particular stimuli (for example, sexual materials) elicit positive emotions, then people would be likely to voluntarily expose themselves to such stimuli. If these stimuli elicited negative emotions, on the other hand, people would be more likely to avoid them. Indeed, research studies have consistently found that females evaluate pornographic materials more negatively than males (Fisher & Byrne, 1978; Griffitt, 1973), even if they are equally aroused to them. Thus, a reinforcement-affect model would predict that in a free-choice setting, females would be more inclined to avoid pornography, particularly hard-core materials.

Kenrick et al. (1980) tested this prediction in two experiments. In the first study, college students who had signed up for an experiment (without there being any mention of sexual content) were ostensibly given a choice to view one of two movies. One of these, they were told, was an explicit hard-core film depicting a man and prostitute, whereas the other was a less explicit soft-core film depicting a man and his wife who were very much in love. As predicted on the basis of the reinforcement-affect model, females were more likely than males to choose the soft-core than the hard-core film. In the second experiment, subjects were contacted by phone and asked to volunteer for one of two experiments: a study involving erotica or one involving perception of geometric figures. The re-

erate of the experimenter) than subjects exposed to neutral, sexually nonviolent, or aggressive but nonsexual materials (Donnerstein, 1980; Donnerstein & Berkowitz, 1981; Malamuth, 1978).

Finally, in a recent field experiment, Malamuth and Check (1981) found that males' acceptance of interpersonal violence against women increased as a result of viewing two feature-length movies that contained sexual vi-

sults showed that females were less likely than males to volunteer for the erotica study.

How can these sex differences in desire to view erotica be explained? An obvious explanation raised by feminist writers is the content of such materials, which very frequently portray the degradation and abuse of women (Smith, 1976). This explanation, however, may not be adequate to explain why women avoided the film described as soft-core to a greater degree than males. A second explanation is in terms of sex-role socialization. According to this explanation, some women have been taught that it is not appropriate for them to view and enjoy erotica, that such actions conflict with their femininity.

Fortunately, Kenrick et al. obtained data relevant to the sex-roles explanation. All subjects in their second study had been administered the Bem Sex-Role Inventory (BSRI). This measure is designed to assess whether a person's self-description is in keeping with sex-role stereotypes (a sex-typed individual) or reveals a blend of characteristics stereotypically considered to be masculine and feminine (an androgynous individual). If the choice of viewing erotica is related to sex-role socialization, we would expect differences between males and females classified as sex-typed, but not between men and women classified as androgynous. As the table below reveals, that is exactly what Kenrick et al. found— substantial differences between sex-typed males and females, but no significant differences for androgynous subjects (with the actual percentages being nonsignificantly higher for females).

Percentage of Subjects Volunteering for the Erotica Experiment as a Function of Subjects' Sex and Scores on the Bem Sex-Role Inventory (BSRI)

	SUBJECT'S SEX	
BSRI CLASSIFICATION	MALE	FEMALE
Sex-Typed	85	35
Androgynous	83	100

Source: From Kenrick, Stringfield, Wagenhals, Dahl, & Ransdell, 1980.

olence. (See Figure 10.4). What is particularly revealing about this study is that the sexually violent films ("Swept Away" and "The Getaway") are ones that have been shown on television rather than being X-rated movies. Moreover, the measurement of the effects of the films was done a week following exposure, in a setting that subjects thought was completely unrelated to the film-exposure phase of the experiment. This procedure eliminated the possi-

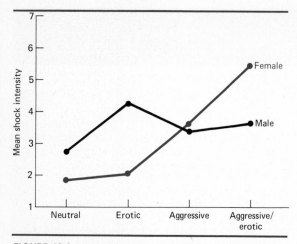

FIGURE 10.3
The Effects of Exposure to Four Types of Stimuli on Subsequent Administration of Shocks to a Female Victim
Source: Donnerstein, 1981.

ble influence of "demand characteristics" and therefore increased confidence in the conclusion that it was the films that caused the differences in attitudes.

Positive effects of pornography. For some time psychologists have used erotic materials as part of therapy designed to help individuals with a variety of sexual difficulties. For example, Wishnoff (1978) exposed women with high levels of anxiety about sex to explicit sexual movies. Compared with control groups, such exposure was found to lower sexual anxiety and increase self-reported willingness to engage in sexual behavior under appropriate circumstances. Gillan (1978) recently reviewed such data, as well as findings from studies on the use of pornography to treat male impotence. She concluded that such "stimulation therapy" may result in considerable improvement for some patients, but that other therapeutic interventions are required as well.

In addition to helping in the treatment of individuals who already have sexual problems, it has been suggested that pornography plays an important social role in helping prevent the development of sexual problems. This suggestion was made by Cody Wilson (1978), director of research for the Commission on Pornography. Wilson points out that there are considerable survey and clinical data to show that

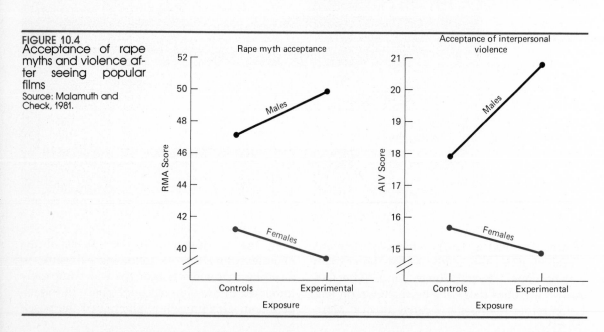

FIGURE 10.4
Acceptance of rape myths and violence after seeing popular films
Source: Malamuth and Check, 1981.

close to half of North American married couples have significant sexual problems, with about 20 percent of survey respondents rating their present sex life as unsatisfactory. Moreover, Wilson points out, the principal sources of such dissatisfaction as well as clinical sexual problems appear to be lack of information, general anxiety about sex, and inability to communicate freely with one's partner about sex. Wilson indicates that some men and women report that exposure to pornography provided them with sex information, reduced their sexual inhibitions, increased their willingness to discuss sex with others, had caused them to try "new things," and generally improved their sexual relationship. Therefore, concludes Wilson, pornography may indeed help prevent the development of clinical sexual problems.

Positive or negative effects? The findings described up to this point seem to justify the conclusion that pornography, like many other types of mass-media stimuli, has some impact on human behavior. For instance, as we have documented, it causes physiological arousal. Being aroused may, in turn, have further effects on our feelings and behaviors. Probably the two major reasons why pornography influences our behavior are because such stimuli communicate information and because they provide models of behavior. Both positive and negative effects have been suggested. In considering the nature and degree of effects, it is useful to focus on the type of sexual script communicated by the erotic stimuli. While distinctions may be made among many different types of scripts, we will focus on the possible differential effects of sexual portrayals of men and women in acts that communicate mutual respect and positive emotions, as contrasted with those that depict exploitation and violence.

INFORMATION. Pornographic stimuli may provide information about what people are like, what kinds of sexual acts people engage in,

and the way different people react to various sexual acts. Thus, stimuli that portray mutually consenting sexual acts that both partners enjoy may be beneficial in providing new information regarding sexual techniques, in suggesting that other people feel good about sex, in educating people about contraception (see discussion later in this chapter), and so on. Concern about sexually violent stimuli may be raised, because the information usually conveyed in these materials is that women are basically masochistic and in need of male domination (Smith, 1976). Such information may contribute to the formation of a sexual script that requires men to be conquerors and suggests that even if a woman seems disinterested or repulsed by a pursuer, she will eventually respond favorably to forceful advances, violence, and overpowering by a male (Johnson & Goodchilds, 1973).

MODELING. While modeling involves several processes (Bandura, 1977), two of these may be particularly relevant to the effects of pornography—imitation and vicarious learning of consequences. By imitation, people acquire new behaviors. Pornography may cause imitation if people learn about sexual behaviors they were previously unaware of. Most people do not, of course, uncritically imitate everything they observe, so such factors as the extent to which they perceive the pornographic portrayal to be realistic or socially acceptable are important determinants of whether modeling will occur. A concern often expressed by feminist writers is that mass-media sexual violence contributes to the perception that certain acts of violence against women are socially acceptable (Brownmiller, 1975).

In vicarious learning of consequences a person does not acquire any new behavior pattern. Rather, by observing the consequences experienced by models, inhibitions over behavior already acquired become strengthened or weakened. Rape and similar acts, as they are portrayed in pornography, nearly always result in the victim becoming sexually aroused and desirous of her assailant; very seldom are there any negative consequences such as arrest (Smith, 1976). People's inhibitions concerning such behavior might therefore become lessened. Similarly, portraying mutually desired sex as resulting in positive consequences may reduce anxiety and inhibitions.

In conclusion, there is evidence that pornography may significantly affect some people's sexual behavior some of the time. This is not to suggest that pornography is necessarily the most or one of the most powerful influences on sexuality. Rather, it is one of the many factors that may affect people's responses. The nature of the effect and the degree of influence exerted may depend, among other things, on the background of the person exposed to the stimuli, the content of the materials, and the sociocultural context in which exposure takes place.

SEXUAL EXPRESSION

Up to this point, we have discussed theoretical approaches and social issues that concern human sexuality. In the final section of this chapter, we will focus on the actual expression of sexuality. First, we will consider some of the reasons people choose to engage in sex. Second, we will look at different ways of answering the question, What is normal and what is abnormal sexual expression? Third, the degree to which sexual attitudes and behavior have been changing over the years will be discussed. Finally, an area of much personal and social importance—contraception—will be highlighted.

Functions of Sex

When we consider the reasons that people engage in sexual acts, it becomes quite obvious that sexuality is closely tied with other diverse social needs that may differ considerably from one person to another. Nelson (1979) recently developed a questionnaire designed to measure the varied functions sex serves for people. The assumptions underlying this scale are that sexual acts can simultaneously serve several different functions and that people vary with respect to what to them are the most important functions (other than conception). The seven functions of sex measured by this scale are given below.

- **Love and affection:** the degree to which a person's sexual behavior is motivated by needs to receive and share affection and intimacy with another person.
- **Hedonism:** the degree to which a person's sexual behavior is motivated by needs for pleasurable stimulation.
- **Recognition:** the degree to which a person's sexual behavior is motivated by a need to be considered competent or skilled.
- **Dominance:** the degree to which the need to control or impose one's will on another motivates sexual behavior.
- **Submission:** the degree to which sexual behavior is motivated by desires to relinquish control or power and by desires for protection.
- **Conformity:** the degree to which a person engages in sexual behavior out of conformity to the expectations of others or in order to gain social acceptance.
- **Novelty:** the degree to which sexual behavior is motivated by the need for excitement and relief from boredom.

Nelson (1979) administered this sexual functions questionnaire to 180 male and 215 female undergraduate students at the University of Florida. Their responses were classified according to which of the seven functions listed above was the most important to them. This investigator found that the most important function for the largest percentage of males was conformity (21 percent), whereas for females it was love and affection (31 percent). The percentages of males for whom the other functions were the most important were as follows: novelty (18 percent), hedonism (17 percent), love and affection (16 percent), recognition (12 percent), dominance (10 percent), and submission (6 percent). For females, these percentages were: submission (18 percent), conformity (15 percent), recognition (10 percent), hedonism (9 percent), novelty (9 percent), and dominance (8 percent). These data clearly show that sex fulfills diverse social needs and that the situation is very much one of "different strokes for different folks."

Models of Normality

What is normal? As you were reading Nelson's (1979) findings, you may have been asking yourself, What are the normal functions of sex? The question of normality is often on the minds of many individuals when they evaluate their own sexuality. This is probably because open communication about sex is often inhibited in our society, making it difficult to engage in social comparison. People consequently may have limited information about the sexual behavior and preferences of others, which they could use to compare with their own experiences. It is easy to conceive of a situation of "pluralistic ignorance" developing under these circumstances. Many individuals may have the same sexual feelings or desires but are unwilling to talk to others about them, because they assume that they alone have these emotions. Each individual fears being labeled "sick" or abnormal, and therefore does not communicate information that may make others realize that they share similar desires and fears.

There are a number of different ways of defining what is or is not normal. Differing models will often lead to opposing conclusions. Zimbardo and Newton (1976) described varied models of defining normality, four of which we will consider in the present discussion of sexuality. We will illustrate the applications of these models to the area of homosexuality.

Defining normality by an **absolute standard model** consists of specifying which behaviors are considered normal and which are abnormal, regardless of the social or cultural context.

Such a standard is similar to a medical judgment of sick versus healthy. A person who has pneumonia, for example, is considered sick, regardless of the context. The term "medical model" is therefore often used interchangeably with an absolute-standard model. Religions often prescribe absolute standards for defining sexual normality. The Bible, for example, speaks in no uncertain terms of which sexual acts are considered permissible and which are strictly forbidden.

Utilizing a **statistical model** relates to the literal meaning of abnormal—deviation from the norm. Such a model is based completely on the cultural or social context. No behavior is considered normal or abnormal in and of itself. Rather, the extent to which it differs from the frequency of that act in a particular culture or group determines whether it is judged normal or abnormal. If a behavior is engaged in by a substantial percentage of the group, it is considered normal. If it is statistically infrequent (or perceived as statistically infrequent), it is considered abnormal.

The *functional approach* considers whether the behavior contributes to the welfare and survival of the species or group. It is often used in evaluations of the behavior of animal species, but it can be applied to humans as well. If a behavior is considered to increase the chances of survival of the species, it is judged normal, whereas a behavior that decreases its survival chances is considered abnormal.

The **tolerance-limit model** primarily concerns whether an act annoys or bothers others. If it disturbs someone in a position to do something about it (for example, report it to the police), it may be labeled abnormal. Of course, the fact that an act offends someone may not be sufficient to result in a label of abnormality. It also has to deviate either from the absolute standard being applied or from the norm of the group.

Normality and homosexuality. The contrasting judgments that may result from adopting each of the above models of normality are well exemplified in considering homosexual behavior. The Bible, as an example of an absolute standard, considers homosexual behavior as an "abomination" (Leviticus 28: 22). People who adopt such a standard are unlikely to change their judgment, even if confronted with information concerning the prevalence of homosexuality throughout history as well as today, or the historical fact that in certain cultures, such as that of the Greeks, homosexuality was not only socially sanctioned, but considered a more refined and worthy mode of sexual expression

than heterosexual behavior (Tannahill, 1980).

Using an absolute standard, many psychoanalysts have generally considered homosexuality to be abnormal (Evans, 1969), a judgment that until recently reflected the position of psychiatry and psychology. Today, psychiatric and psychological organizations no longer consider homosexuality to be a sexual deviancy, but an alternative form of normal sexual expression (Diagnostic and Statistical Manual III). This fact illustrates the possibility that absolute standards of judgment, while stated absolutely at a particular time, may be subject

From the perspective of the statistical model, showing the widespread prevalence of homosexuality leads to the acceptance of its normality.

to modification as new scientific data become available and as cultural and normative changes take place.

From the perspective of a statistical model of normality, the frequency of homosexuality is the critical issue. Both the classical survey of Kinsey and his associates (Kinsey, Pomeroy, & Martin, 1948) and more recent surveys (for example, Hunt, 1974) conclude that about 25 percent of males and a somewhat lower but similar percentage of females in the United States have had some homosexual experience. Additional data, such as Masters and Johnson's (1979) conclusions regarding the many physiological and psychological similarities in same-sex and cross-sex relationships, point to a judgment of normality on the basis of a statistical model.

The functional model would consider the extent to which homosexuality contributes to the survival and development of the group. Clearly, a group that became exclusively homosexual would be judged as engaging in dysfunctional behavior, since it would become extinct. In most societies today, however, overpopulation is a very serious problem. In such a situation, the presence of a significant proportion of exclusively homosexual individuals would be highly functional, in that fewer offspring would be born. Of course, with the availability of effective means of contraception and with opportunities for artificial insemination, the relationship between procreation and same- versus cross-sex partner may become insignificant.

In considering the tolerance-limit model, the question is, How disturbed are heterosexuals by homosexual behavior? Homosexual acts of much intimacy (for example, intercourse) taking place in private may not annoy heterosexuals who might be very bothered by a kiss between homosexuals if exchanged on a street corner or in a park (even though such a kiss between heterosexuals is unlikely to annoy anyone). If sufficiently annoying, such behavior may be called to the attention of authorities and labeled abnormal.

Sexual Attitudes and Behavior

Sexual revolution. In recent decades there has been a great deal of publicity about a "sexual revolution." Has there indeed been such a revolution, a total departure from previous sexual standards? To answer this question, we will examine research findings concerning premarital, extramarital, and homosexual sexuality.

Premarital sexual intercourse. An area that has received particular attention in studies of heterosexual behavior is premarital intercourse. On the basis of surveys conducted with college students (Hopkins, 1977) and the general population (Hunt, 1974; Glenn & Weaver, 1979), the following conclusions can be made with some confidence:

1. There have been very dramatic changes in attitudes toward premarital intercourse and in behavior from the late 1930s through the late 1970s. In each decade greater sexual permissiveness has been found than in previous years, with the 1960s and 1970s revealing the greatest changes (Glenn & Weaver, 1970; Hunt, 1974). Among college students, in the later 1970s about 60–70 percent of males and 50–60 percent of females reported having engaged in premarital intercourse by the end of their teen years (Hopkins, 1977).

2. It appears that while changes in permissiveness are occurring at all age levels and in all segments of the population, the **degree** of change has been considerably greater among college students than other groups. Among the general population, many people still consider premarital intercourse to be wrong. In fact, national probability samples (random polling of the population such as that used by a Gallup Poll) of adult Americans found that in the mid 1970s about 45 percent said that premarital sex was either "always wrong" or "almost always wrong" (Glenn & Weaver, 1979). Age was found to be an important determinant of attitudes in this study, with only about 20 percent of subjects between the ages of 18 and 29 choosing these sexually restrictive alternatives, compared with 42 percent of those between 30 and 49 years, and 64 percent of those more than 50 years old.

3. There have been greater changes in attitudes and coital experiences among females than among males (see Figure 10.5). While in earlier generations males were much more sexually permissive than females, the size of this difference was relatively small by the 1970s (Hunt, 1974).

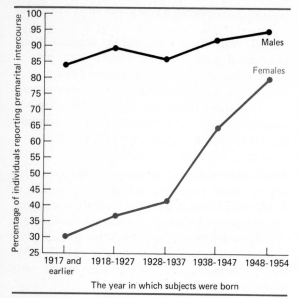

FIGURE 10.5
Percentage of respondents reporting premarital intercourse by date of birth

4. Young people of both genders are engaging in intercourse at a considerably younger age than in previous decades (Hopkins, 1977).

5. The double standard allowing men more sexual freedom than women seems to be gradually disappearing. It remains largely in casual sex or intercourse without strong affection. Both genders, however, are more approving of sexual intercourse for both males and females when emotional ties are involved (Peplau et al., 1977).

The effects of premarital sex on relationships. A number of studies consistently show that at least for individuals involved in long-term relationships, most people do not regret having engaged in premarital intercourse. Moreover, the degree of sexual intimacy reached by couples does not appear to generally affect the stability of their relationships. For example, in the study of couples referred to earlier, Peplau et al. (1977) found three different orientations towards sex: the "traditionals," 18 percent of the sample, abstained from premarital intercourse; the "moderates," about

41 percent of the sample, felt that intercourse should be engaged in only by couples in love; and the "liberals," also about 41 percent of the sample, felt that sex without love is acceptable. There were no significant differences among these three groups with respect to their general satisfaction in the relationships or to what happened to their relationships two years later— they were equally likely to have broken up (46 percent), continued dating each other (34 percent), or married each other (20 percent).

Other areas of sexual behavior. Whereas attitudes concerning premarital intercourse have become increasingly permissive over the years, similar dramatic changes have not occurred with respect to other forms of sexual expression. The findings of the national probability sample referred to earlier in discussing premarital sex (Glenn & Weaver, 1979) indicated that in the late 1970s about 78 percent of Americans considered extramarital relations to be always wrong or almost always wrong. About 70 percent of Americans similarly judged homosexual relations. Moreover, while this survey showed significant increases in the 1970s in the percentage of people holding permissive attitudes toward premarital relations, no similar changes were found for either extramarital or homosexual relations. These data suggest that a "sexual revolution" in general, if defined as a total departure from previously accepted standards, has not occurred in the general population, despite the dramatic changes in attitudes and behavior related to premarital intercourse.

Contraception and Sexuality

The importance of contraception. Contraception during sexual intercourse is not only an important matter for individuals but it is also of critical concern to nations and humanity in general. As early as 1798, Robert Thomas Malthus argued that population was growing in a geometric progression, whereas sources of subsistence were growing in an arithmetic progression. Malthus therefore predicted the future inability of the world to feed itself and suggested that in order to avoid the impending doom people spend their youths, defined as into their thirties, in total sexual abstinence.

Total sexual abstinence does not seem to have gained too many followers, as the data presented earlier about premarital intercourse clearly indicate. The movement toward premarital sexual permissiveness that has taken place in this century has been significantly affected by the development of contraceptive devices (Tannahill, 1980). One would expect, therefore, that modern techniques of contraception would be used very consistently by sexually active individuals. Unfortunately, this does not appear to be so, particularly with teenagers. For example, studies in both the United States and Canada (Alan Guttmacher Institute, 1977; Roberts, 1977) show that only about 20 percent of the millions of teenagers in North America who engage in sexual intercourse use effective contraceptive methods regularly. Consequently, there are about 800,000 unwanted teenage pregnancies in North America each year, a figure that some have described as reaching epidemic proportions. These pregnancies frequently lead to abortions, out-of-wedlock births, and hasty and often short-lived marriages. Presented with such startling evidence about the failure of people to protect themselves from unwanted pregnancies and the human tragedies that often result, one must ask why, and what can be done about it?

Factors accounting for the use of contraceptives.

INFORMATION. Quite obviously, some knowledge is necessary for responsible contraceptive action. Byrne (1979) discussed three areas of knowledge that are of central importance to contraception: the relationship between sexual intercourse and conception, the undersirable consequences of unwanted pregnancy, and the ways in which conception can be avoided.

Accurate knowledge about contraception may be essential for successful contraception, but it is clearly not sufficient. Many individuals who have acquired such knowledge do not consistently use contraceptives (Fisher, Byrne, Edmunds, Miller, Kelley, & White, 1979). It is apparent that other factors must be considered. Attempts to differentiate contraceptive users from nonusers by the use of such general dimensions as maturity, independence, and intelligence have not proven very successful (Sandberg, 1976). Approaches examining sex roles, attitudes, emotions, and imagery specifically linked to sexuality appear to be considerably more promising.

SEX ROLES. The failure to employ contraceptives may be tied to traditional sex roles in which the male is the sexual aggressor and the female the sexual "victim" (Byrne, 1979; Gross & Bellew-Smith, in press). This role relationship mitigates against contraceptive use, as the male does not wish to lose the sexual "conquest" by discussing contraception just prior to an initial sexual encounter and thereby reducing the chances of "scoring." The woman, in turn, does not wish to be seen as "loose" or "easy" by being prepared for sexual intercourse and thus not conforming to the role of a sexual "victim."

ATTITUDES AND BELIEFS. Traditional sex roles may in part be responsible for the common belief that sex should not be planned but should be spontaneous. Roberts (1977), in fact, reports that this was the most common attitude found in the sexually active female teenagers he studied. These teenagers also believed that the use of contraceptives was an indication of a lack of spontaneity.

Barriers to contraception may also result from parental attitudes. Many parents do not discuss or provide information about contraception to their children because they fear that this would legitimize and sanction premarital intercourse in their children's eyes (Abramson, 1980). In addition, some youths may be reluctant to possess contraceptives lest their parents find them (Byrne, 1979).

EMOTIONS. A belief that preplanning about sexual intercourse is unacceptable may result from relatively negative feelings about sex in general (Byrne, 1979). Support for such a hypothesis comes from research showing that consistent users of contraceptives report a more positive emotional orientation to sexuality than inconsistent or nonusers of contraception (Fisher et al., 1979). Presumably, those with more negative emotions may want to avoid admitting that sex is likely to occur or that they have planned for it.

Byrne (1979) argues that feelings about sex are related to contraception in three additional ways:

1. To engage in contraception, a public act is typically necessary in order to obtain the needed paraphernalia (for example, purchasing condoms or discussing contraception with a physician). The degree of aversiveness or embarrassment resulting from such a public act has been shown, as predicted by Byrne, to increase as negative feelings about sex increase (Fisher & Byrne, in press). Thus, people who feel strongly embarrassed about publicly acknowledging that they are planning to engage in sexual intercourse are less likely to take the necessary steps to obtain contraceptives as compared with people who have more positive feelings about sex.

2. Sexual partners need to communicate about their contraceptive plans and practices. Negative sexual emotions would be expected to interfere with such communication. Research indeed suggests that negative feelings about sex are associated with failure to communicate about contraceptives and with incorrect assumptions about the precautions one's partner has taken (Byrne, Miller, Fisher, & White, 1976).

3. For contraceptives to be used, there may need to be a constant reminder on one's sexuality (for example, daily taking of the pill) or direct contact with sexual organs (such as slipping on a condom). Such acts are likely to be distressing to the individual with relatively negative emotions toward sex. Research (Kelley, 1979) shows that general feelings about manipulation of one's sexual organs, as in masturbation, do relate to attitudes regarding the use of contraceptives requiring di-

In North America, there are an estimated 800,000 unwanted teen-age pregnancies each year. Social psychologists are learning about the factors that influence contraceptive use among adolescents.

rect contact with sexual organs. Similarly, attitudes toward other contraceptives are related to general feelings about sexual relations (Kelley, 1979).

SEX GUILT. A concept closely tied to negative emotions about sex is that of sex guilt. It refers to the extent to which a person feels guilty for violating a set of standards for sexual conduct (Mosher, 1979). Since it appears that there is some consistency in how guilty people feel from one sexual situation to another, sex guilt is considered to be a personality variable rather than a transient response to a particular sexual situation. A measure of sex guilt was developed by Mosher (1966) as a subscale of a more general measure of guilt, the Mosher Forced-Choice Guilt Inventory.

In view of the fact that sex guilt has been shown to relate to varied sexual behaviors, we might expect it to relate to contraceptive practices as well. Individuals high in sex guilt may need to create the impression (to themselves and to others) of unintentional sex, thereby reducing the willingness to discuss or use contraceptives (Gross & Bellew-Smith, in press). Indeed, research shows that individuals who score high in sex guilt are less likely to use contraceptive techniques during intercourse than those with low sex guilt (Mosher, 1973). Moreover, Lindemann (1974), from a review of clinical data, concludes that while sex guilt does not prevent sexual activity, it does deter many individuals from obtaining and using contraceptives. This conclusion is consistent with the finding that high-sex-guilt women who were sexually active required more abortions than low-sex-guilt women who were sexually active (Gerrard, 1977).

IMAGERY. Sexual fantasies and images have been shown to relate to sexual behaviors in certain important ways (Heyman, 1979). Byrne (1979) points out that the possibility of conception and its prevention are almost never present in erotic images presented in pornography and other areas of the mass media. These mass-media stimuli therefore fail to provide appropriate role models or imaginative cues. This fact, Byrne argued, decreases the likelihood that people will engage in sexual fantasies that include contraceptives, and consequently also lessens the use of contraceptives.

What can be done. Byrne (1979) makes several specific suggestions designed to increase the use of contraceptives:

1. Accurate contraceptive information should be included in everyone's education prior to and throughout adolescence. This is not necessarily in-

tended to encourage sexual activity, any more than teaching about seat belts is intended to encourage reckless driving. Such information should include considerations of the suffering that usually is caused by an unwanted pregnancy, as well as specific details about obtaining and using different types of contraceptives.

2. Any existing legal barriers to contraception should be eliminated, so that each individual may freely choose whether or not to avoid parenthood.

3. Any child-rearing, educational, or therapeutic practices that reduce guilt and negative emotions about natural sexual functions should be encouraged. Again, no particular sexual life style is being encouraged. Rather, it is simply assumed that people would be healthier and happier if they could choose to experience sex without fear or self-blame.

4. Anything that makes for an equal and honest relationship between males and females should be encouraged. Interpersonal games in which the macho-exploitive male seduces the female are not conducive to the mature use of contraception. An honest relationship is likely to result in more open communication about contraception.

5. Steps should be taken to bring contraception into our sexual fantasies and images. Byrne points out that condom manufacturers have made a start in that direction with magazine advertisements that refer to "sensuous contraceptives" or those that are "shaped for extra pleasure." In other words, contraception can presumably be sold not just for safety's sake, like sensible shoes, but for its erotic qualities. To take a further step, Byrne (1979) suggests that fiction writers be encouraged to include contraception in scenes of romance and/or lust: "Perhaps some research foundation can even be induced to underwrite a hard-core film in which Marilyn Chambers inserts a diaphragm or John Holmes wears a condom. That movie might do more for contraceptive education than dozens of factual presentations" (p. 306). In other words, if contraception is put into the movie's script, it may be more likely to become part of people's sexual scripts.

An additional recommendation for reducing unwanted pregnancies involves changing sexual scripts by broadening a narrow definition for what constitutes desirable sex (Gross & Bellew-Smith, in press). When contraceptives are not available, during particularly vulnerable periods or at any other time, sexual acts other than intercourse (for example, oral sex, mutual masturbation) should be perceived as desirable means of achieving satisfaction.

SUMMARY   Social psychological theories on human sexuality emphasize the role of the human cognitive system as a mediator of sexual responses. In lower animals, influences such as hormones and physiological sensations determine sexual acts, while in humans the effects of these influences on sexual expression are a function of the interpretation and meaning they are given in being processed through our cognitive system. General principles are developed within the cognitive system as a result of life experiences. These principles determine sexual attitudes, judgments, and responses.

According to one social psychology theory, various principles about sexuality are organized into a program for behavior that can be labeled a script. Scripts provide guidelines for behavior. Data suggest that there are culturally shared scripts in sexual interactions and that these sequences define what is most arousing.

The feminist movement has been actively working to bring about fundamental changes in the scripts men and women learn to follow. In the sphere of sexual scripts, issues of concern to feminists include the double standard and traditional sex roles, rape, and pornography. According to the feminist viewpoint (and research data provide some support), current sexual scripts—such as the traditional male/female sexual roles of man as initiator of sex and woman as resisting or setting limits on sex—are remnants of those prevalent earlier in history.

Current sexual scripts are, according to feminist writers, one of the major causes of rape. Women have been socialized not to use their sexuality freely, as they desire, but to bargain with it, and men have often been taught to persuade and coerce women into sex. Such roles of wheedling, bargaining, and coercing can lead to manipulation, mistrust, resentment, and hostility between the sexes, and in some instances to the type of physical force and violence that may result in a rape conviction. According to feminists, however, there are many men in the general population who have attitudes, hostilities, and behavioral inclinations similar to those of convicted rapists, although they may never actually commit the type of act that would get them arrested.

A number of studies have supported the feminists' contention that normal socialization of sex roles often legitimizes sexual aggression and coercion. In related research, it was found that a relatively large percent of college students indicated some likelihood that they personally would rape if they could be assured of not being caught. These findings and related research lend support to feminists' contentions that there are many men with attitudes, feelings, and behavioral tendencies that are similar to those that generally characterize convicted rapists.

Feminist writers also object to what they perceive as portrayals of unequal power relations between men and women and the degradation of women in pornography. They argue that pornography contributes, although not necessarily directly, to acts of violence against women by making such acts less reprehensible to people.

On the basis of several converging lines of evidence, the President's Commission on Pornography in 1970 concluded that there was no evidence to support the contention that pornography has antisocial effects. While more recent research has not generally found undesirable effects of nonviolent sexually explicit materials, exposure to violent pornography has been shown to adversely affect the responses of male subjects.

There is actually some evidence to suggest positive effects of nonviolent erotica. Psychologists have used erotic materials as part of therapy designed to help individuals with a variety of sexual difficulties. It has also been suggested that pornography plays an important social role in helping prevent the development of sexual problems.

Effects of pornography on human behavior may occur because such stimuli can cause physiological changes, communicate information, and provide models of behavior. In considering the nature and degree of effects, it is useful to focus on the type of sexual script communicated by the erotic stimuli, as well as the background of the person exposed to the stimuli and the sociocultural context in which exposure takes place.

When we consider the expression of sexuality, it becomes clear that sexuality is closely tied with other diverse social needs that may differ considerably from one person to another. College students showed varied responses to a recently developed questionnaire designed to measure seven functions of sexual behavior: love and affection, hedonism, recognition, dominance, submission, conformity, and novelty.

There are a number of different ways of defining what are or are not normal sexual behaviors and preferences. The absolute-standard model of defining normality consists of specifying which behaviors are normal and which are abnormal, regardless of social or cultural context. In the statistical model the frequency of the behavior in a particular culture or group determines whether it is judged normal or abnormal. The functional model considers whether the behavior contributes to the welfare and survival of the species or group. Finally, the tolerance-limit model primarily concerns whether an act annoys or bothers others. Contrasting judgments result from adopting each of the above models of normality as exemplified in considering homosexual behavior.

Several conclusions can be made regarding premarital sexual intercourse.

1. In each decade since the late 1930s through the late 1970s greater sexual permissiveness has been found than in previous years with the 1960s and 1970s revealing the greatest changes.
2. While changes in permissiveness are occurring at all age levels and segments of the population, the degree of change has been greater among college students than other groups. In the general population, age has been found to be an important determinant of attitudes.
3. There have been greater changes over these decades in the attitudes and coital experiences of females than of males.
4. Young people of both genders are engaging in intercourse at a considerably younger age than in previous decades.
5. The double standard allowing men more sexual freedom than women seems to be gradually weakening. Both genders are more approving of sexual intercourse for both males and females when emotional ties are involved.

Whereas attitudes concerning premarital intercourse have become increasingly permissive over the years, similar dramatic changes have not occurred with respect to other forms of sexual expression, such as extramarital and homosexual relations. The data suggest that a "sexual revolution" (meaning a total departure from previously accepted standards) has not occurred in the general population.

Although the movement toward premarital sexual permissiveness has been significantly affected by the development of contraceptive devices, modern techniques of contraception are not used consistently by sexually active individuals, particularly teenagers. Factors accounting for the inconsistent use of contraceptives include lack of information about conception and contraceptives; traditional sex roles of male as sexual aggressor and female as sexual "victim"; the belief that sex should be spontaneous; parental attitudes toward discussing contraception; emotions such as negative feelings and guilt about sex; and the absence of information concerning the possibility of conception and its prevention in erotic mass-media stimuli. Several suggestions have been made that are designed to increase the use of contraceptives.

SUGGESTED READINGS

Brownmiller, S. *Against our will*. New York: Bantam, 1975.

Cann, A., Calhoun, L. G., Selby, J. W., & King, H. E. (Eds.). Rape. *Journal of Social Issues*, 1981, 37(4).

Hrdy, S. B. *The woman that never evolved*. Cambridge, Mass.: Harvard University Press, 1981.

Parsons, E. S. (Ed.). Women—Sex and sexuality. *Signs*, 1980, 5(4).

Peplau, L. A., & Hammen, C. L. (Eds.). Sexual behavior: Social psychological issues. *Journal of Social Issues*, 1977, 33(2).

11

VIOLENCE AND AGGRESSION

INTRODUCTION

Have you ever wondered why people intentionally hurt each other? What makes us aggressive, despite the norms and even laws that are opposed to hurtful behavior? Why are some persons' behaviors so dominated by aggressive acts that it is necessary to take the extreme step of permanently separating them from society? On the other hand, why are other persons unable or unwilling to defend themselves even when physically attacked? Have you ever been surprised by the anger that may have caused you to "fly off the handle" at the slightest provocation? Why do individuals in large groups often commit acts of violence they would never consider when acting alone? Why is there so much violence in television progamming? These are some of the questions to which we turn in this chapter.

Aggression: What Is It?

In our everyday language, the word **aggression** is used to refer to a wide range of behaviors, attitudes, and even emotions (Blumenthal, Kahn, Andrews, & Head, 1972; Tedeschi, Smith, & Brown, 1974). For example, a highly competitive salesperson is called aggressive, and aggression is the word sometimes applied to our feelings after we are provoked. In an attempt to achieve clarity and parsimony, researchers have restricted their use of the term to _behaviors that are intended to harm others_. As you can see, then, the examples given earlier in this paragraph do not qualify as aggression in the sense that we will use the term.

One problem faced by researchers attempting to arrive at a working definition of aggression has to do with the _intention_ of the person engaging in the behavior. Ordinarily, inclusion of a notion such as intent, in a definition of a particular type of behavior, is avoided because of the difficulty of clearly establishing what a person wishes to accomplish by a given action. If we consider aggression only in nonhumans, the matter of intention can be avoided, not only because animals cannot fill out questionnaires about their intentions, but more importantly, because the range of behaviors in any nonhuman species that may be called aggressive is sufficiently limited so that such behaviors may be specified and catalogued. In humans, however, the intent of the actor must be included, because some actions that may hurt others (for example, a physician setting a child's broken arm) no one would call aggression, and other actions that do not hurt another person (for example, firing a weapon at an enemy soldier but missing) may safely be considered aggression.

Kinds of Aggression

Numerous classification schemes for aggression have been proposed, and several distinctions have proven useful. First of all, occurrences of aggression may differ in the extent to which they are **provocation motivated** (Zillmann, 1979). That is, in some cases anger predominates, and hurting is aimed at forcing one's tormentor to stop, or at retaliation; this has been termed by Arnold Buss (1971) as angry aggression. Other times aggressive acts may represent a cold-blooded or calculated attempt to gain something—for example, property or money that can be used to purchase anything from food to heroin—by attacking someone, a form referred to as **instrumental**

This chapter is written by Edgar C. O'Neal.
Preparation of this chapter was facilitated by a fellowship from the Margaret Bosshardt Pace and Paul David Pace Fund.

aggression. As a matter of fact, *most aggression involves both anger and extrinsic rewards* (Bandura, 1973). For example, a child who has been teased by a playmate and who hits back in anger also may know that the attack will force the playmate to yield a preferred swing. In general, *"angry" and "instrumental" are terms used to refer to extremes on the provocation-motivated/not provocation-motivated continuum, rather than to mutually exclusive categories of aggressive behavior.

Buss (1971) has made three additional distinctions: direct/indirect, active/passive, and physical/verbal. As can be seen in Table 11.1, which gives examples of the aggression that represents combinations of these, all actions intended to harm others are by no means direct, active, or physical. While aggression that is direct, active, and physical may be the exception rather than the rule, it is the type most often researched, mainly because it is the kind most clearly recognized as a problem for society.

Mark Essex: A Case of Explosive Violence

During the first week of January 1973, a young ex-serviceman, Mark Essex, carried out a series of sniper attacks in New Orleans that left twenty people dead or wounded. The episode ended only after his death on a motel roof. Over six hundred law enforcement officers were mobilized in the final stages of a tragic drama that glued New Orleanians to their television sets in horrified fascination.

There were very few other black families in Emporia, Kansas, while Mark Essex was growing up. Teachers and neighbors remembered him as a happy child and an above-average student with aspirations of becoming a minister. After high school he enlisted in the Navy and trained as a dental technician. While he was stationed at a naval base near San Diego, he was exposed to racial harassment for the first time in his life. He grew embittered, and became friends with a helicopter mechanic at the base who was a member of the Black Muslims. Through the literature of black militancy and through this friend and other similarly dissatisfied acquaintances on the base, he became convinced that he must leave the Navy. After briefly being AWOL, he was granted an early release from the service, and entered a job-training program in New Orleans.

	DIRECT		INDIRECT	
	Active	Passive	Active	Passive
Physical	Stabbing Punching Shooting another person	Physically preventing another person from reaching a goal (for example, a sit-in demonstration)	Setting a booby trap; hiring a hit man	Refusing to perform necessary tasks (for example, refusing to aid a dying enemy)
Verbal	Insulting or derogating another person	Refusing to speak to another person	Spreading malicious rumors or gossip about another person	Failing to verbally support another person (for example, failing to defend a person who has been unfairly criticized)

**TABLE 11.1
Three Distinctions among Types of Aggression**

Source: Adapted from Buss, 1971, p. 8.

In the days preceding his violent rampage, Essex had a few minor skirmishes with police over traffic violations, which left him enraged. He painted slogans such as, "Kill," "Hate white people beast of earth," "Kill pig devil," on the walls of his small apartment. On New Year's Eve, he took the large-caliber carbine he had purchased several months earlier in Emporia and shot a police academy trainee who was entering police headquarters. After several days of hiding out in a church, he commandeered a car at gunpoint and drove to a high-rise motel opposite City Hall. There he shot several hotel guests and firemen sent to fight several small fires he had set in the motel. Finally, police arrived for a siege that lasted forty-eight hours and that required the closing of a major portion of the downtown business district. In this chapter, a psychological "post mortem" of Mark Essex will be used to clarify ways in which research can be helpful in understanding society's problems with violence and aggression.

THE ORIGINS OF AGGRESSION

Was Mark Essex's Violence Biologically Preprogrammed?

Because aggression appears to be such a common—and for many, enjoyable—occurrence, philosophers, and students of behavior

Writings on the walls of the apartment occupied by Mark Essex.

have long speculated that it is somehow "wired into" the biological makeup of human beings. At this point the question may be posed: Was Mark Essex's violent behavior somehow genetically preprogrammed?

Lorenz's "So-Called Evil." The Nobel-prize-winning ethologist Konrad Lorenz based his view of the instinctive nature of human aggression upon his observation of animals in the wild. His very influential viewpoint was presented in a book that appeared originally in German and whose title is translated literally as "The So-Called Evil"; its English edition is published as *On Aggression* (1966).

Lorenz's argument is that aggression is not the evil it is thought to be when you consider its function, or advantages for survival, in animals. First of all, it increases the probability that the more fit, stronger members of a species will survive and reproduce. Second, it serves the function of distributing the members of the species over the available environment, so that each member has a chance of having enough resources—chiefly food and water. In many species individuals mark and defend a specific territory, with the larger animals making the most expansive claims. Aggression also results in a type of dominance order that provides for stable forms of interaction in animal groups (cf. Bernstein & Mason, 1963).

According to Lorenz, aggression is **instinctive,** that is, an unlearned and species-wide behavior, and represents the discharge of an aggressive energy that is constantly building up within the individual. Especially in species that have acquired bodily structures that allow individual members to kill their prey (for example, large teeth in old-world apes and in wolves), aggression is highly ritualized and seldom lethal. Lorenz argues that this is so because of inhibitory cues or signs that an animal receives from the animal with which it is struggling. These cues restrain it from actually killing the other animal. For example, a timber wolf who is losing a territorial contest may bare its neck (making it theoretically possible for the

Does the fighting behavior of animals reveal anything about human aggression? A controversial view is that aggression is instinctive in many animal species including humans.

other animal to kill it). As if there were a genetic tacit agreement between the wolf and its opponent, the vanquished then typically backs slowly out of the disputed territory while the victor stands motionless.

Although Lorenz's observations were entirely of animals, it is clear that his viewpoint is applicable to human aggression as well. For him, all human aggression is spontaneously instinctive; that is, it involves the unthinking discharge of aggressive energy. Because humans in modern societies have fewer opportunities to aggress, discharge of aggressive energy is achieved through competition, achievement, and "militant enthusiasm" for one's country. Even so, Lorenz feels, humans may have an excess of this energy and turn to aggressive spectator sports as an acceptable way of discharging it.

A number of critics have found flaws in Lorenz's interpretation of animal aggression and have suggested that his account may be more applicable to lower animals than to mammals (Zillmann, 1979). For example, there is no evidence that an energy builds up over a long period of time until it is released aggressively (Scott, 1970). The greatest opposition to his position comes from other ethologists who urge extreme caution about directly applying interpretations of animal aggression to an understanding of human behavior (for example, Boice, 1976). The following points also should be kept in mind in regard to the ethological position as applied to humans:

1. The theory does little to help explain the who and the when of human aggression. Why was it Mark Essex, and why did his violent behavior occur on New Year's Eve, 1972, rather than a year earlier or later?

2. There is an overwhelming amount of evidence

that all vertebrates' behavior adapts to a particular environment or a particular situation. Animals can readily be trained to be either aggressive or passive (Kuo, 1967). As we will see later in this chapter, many of the differences in aggresssion among humans can be accounted for by learning, a process not admitted by Lorenz to play a role in aggression.

3. Halloway (1974) rightly observes that human aggression can be internalized, delayed, and controlled. These capacities are hardly implied by Lorenz's "spontaneous instinct."

4. It is highly doubtful that we reduce our tendency to aggress by watching violent sports. As a matter of fact, a number of studies produced results in the opposite direction: increased aggressiveness after seeing an aggressive sports contest. For example, Arms, Russell, and Sandilands (1979) randomly assigned college students to attend a hockey game, a wrestling match, or a swim meet, and administered questionnaire indexes of hostility and anger both before and after viewing the sports events. Increases in hostility followed the wrestling match and the hockey game, but not the swim meet. The related issue of **catharsis** will be taken up later in the chapter.

5. Zillmann (1979) wisely points out that "promoting the belief . . . that aggression is inevitable . . . constitutes a ready-made rationalization for anyone's violent acts. . . ." (p. 59). Ashley Montagu (1978, p. 42) states that "fears that we are predestined by our genes to destroy ourselves . . . [may divert us from focusing] more directly upon the changes to be made in ourselves, our institutions, and our societies."

Chromosomes and Violence

Another direction taken by the search for a biological basis of aggression is to focus on the possibility that a genetic factor could account for variations in aggressiveness. One defect suspected as being associated with extreme aggression is the XYY chromosome anomaly in males. Normal females have two X sex-linked chromosomes and males an X and a Y. In the 1960s, the XYY anomaly was proposed as a possible cause of aggressive behavior because of its apparent high occurrence among prisoners (Jacobs, Brunton, Melville, Brittain, & McClement, 1965) and its possessors were labeled "supermales." The lawyer defending Richard Speck, who murdered seven nurses in Chicago in 1966, was quoted as saying he

would use his client's XYY defect as the basis for his defense. (Just for the record, it was later determined that Speck did not, in fact, possess the anomaly.)

It is now clear that the XYY aberration cannot be a major cause of human aggressiveness. First of all, its frequency is very low (less than 1 in every 1000 births), and most XYY males are never convicted of violent crimes (Witkin, Mednick, Schulsinger, Bakkestrom, Christiansen, Goodenough, Hirschhorn, Lundsteen, Owen, Phillip, Ruben, & Stocking, 1976). In addition, while among criminals there is a higher occurrence of the defect than in the normal population, as many possessors of the anomaly have records of property crimes as of violent crimes.

By far, the majority of persons convicted of violent crimes do not possess the XYY chromosome pattern (Price & Whatmore, 1967). Finally, Bandura (1973) points out that any connection between the XYY anomaly and aggression could well be accounted for by slightly larger than average build and slightly lower than average IQ, a combination associated with higher rates of violent crime in genetically normal individuals.

In a way it was disappointing to learn that the violence of a Mark Essex or a Richard Speck cannot be predicted on the basis of a simple chromosomal analysis. Studies of the XYY anomaly, as well as several studies of aggression in twins (for example, Canter, 1973), generally give a pessimistic reading of the possibility that a simple relationship between genes and aggression in humans will be found.

Violence and the brain. For some years it has been well known that animals will attack other animals when specific locations in the midbrain limbic system are stimulated. Rats and mice launch such attacks against any animal nearby, whereas when monkeys' brains are stimulated, they tend to attack only animals socially subordinate to them or animals with which they have recently had a negative encounter (Delgado, 1969). As you might suspect, by damaging or destroying these limbic structures, animals' aggressive behavior can be drastically reduced.

It occurred to neurosurgeons Mark and Ervin (1970) that research on brain-aggression relationships in animals might offer clues as to surgical procedures that could be used with extremely violent persons. They used several techniques (for example, X-rays, brain-scans, EEG tracings) to locate areas of abnormal electrical activity in the brains of persons with long histories of criminal violence. These sites were then stimulated electrically to corroborate their aggressive "function" and finally, in some cases, the area was surgically destroyed.

Needless to say, the Mark and Ervin project evoked a chorus of criticisms voicing objections to the ethics of psychosurgery used to eliminate a behavior unacceptable to society. Other criticisms of the procedure were made by Elliot Valenstein (1973): (1) In humans, repeated stimulation of the same brain site causes variable results. Certain behavioral effects that are produced by one episode of stimulation of a neural center do not indicate with any certainty that that site is instrumental in always producing that behavior; (2) The side effects of the procedures have often produced devastating physical and intellectual disabilities; (3) In many cases the violent behavior persists even after extensive surgery.

After his death it was discovered that Charles Whitman, the student who shot and killed thirteen persons from a platform at the top of the University of Texas Tower in 1966, had a tumor in a brain area that in lower animals is related to aggression. Such pathologies, however, are not common in extremely violent persons; they exist in people who are not aggressive, and are very difficult to detect (Rubin, 1975). It should be noted that prior to his early release from the Navy, Mark Essex had thorough medical and neurological examinations, which uncovered no evidence of any brain disorders.

It seems clear, then, that brain operations do not offer a solution to our society's prob-

lems with extreme violence and homicide. Such a solution may seem intuitively appealing in view of the dramatic restoration to health possible through surgery in the case of many physical ailments, but it is probably illusory in the case of human aggression.

Does Frustration Cause Aggression?

If you were asked at this point what you think to be the main reason for Mark Essex's violent binge, what would you say? The most frequent answer to this question, in an informal poll of students in this author's social psychology course, was **frustration.** Many examples of frustration can be found in Essex's Navy experiences and in his attempts to gain employment after leaving the service. Did these contribute to his later violence?

The frustration-aggression hypothesis. In 1939 a group of Yale psychologists (Dollard, Doob, Miller, Mowrer, & Sears, 1939) published a theoretical account of aggression, which was based on Freud's early notion of aggression as a product of a "thwarted instinct." The theory made two principal assertions: frustration always leads to aggression and aggression results only from frustration. This appealingly simple formulation gained a considerable degree of acceptance and influence, even though one of the authors of the proposal, Neal Miller, published a "clarification," admitting that frustration frequently produces behaviors other than aggression (Miller, 1941). It is now clear that neither of the original assertions is entirely true. There are situations in which frustration has been shown to result in dependence, withdrawal, resignation, psychosomatic reactions, or drug abuse (Bandura, 1973). Also, we will see later in this chapter that individuals have not always been frustrated when they aggress. For example, Buss (1961) expresses doubt that frustration plays an important role in instrumental aggression. A professional hit man for organized crime carries out his assignment whether he is frustrated or not!

Frustration and aggression: limitations and parameters. All of this is not to say that frustration does not play a role in aggression. Part of the difficulty is in the wide range of experiences that have been labeled frustration. In defining frustration as the "blockage of a goal response," the original formulators of the hypothesis had in mind rather specific operations that could be carried out in experiments with animals. In the many studies with humans, however, frustration has been variously defined, most often involving the withdrawal of an expected reward or task failure, sometimes combined with verbal insult. It is not surprising that these very different treatments do not produce equivalent effects on aggression.

An experiment by Geen (1968) represents a careful attempt to determine the effects on aggression of several of these frustration treatments. College men worked on a jigsaw puzzle under one of four conditions: (1) for a quarter of the men the puzzle was insoluble (task frustration condition); (2) for a second group of men, the puzzle was soluble, but they could not complete it due to interference from the experimenter's assistant (a confederate) who was masquerading as another participant (personal frustration condition); (3) a third group of men were allowed to complete the puzzle but then were verbally abused by the confederate (insult condition); (4) the rest of the men were allowed to complete the task and were not subjected to insult (control condition). All of the men were led to believe they could administer an electrical shock to the confederate on the pretext of correcting his errors in a learning experiment. (The confederate in fact received no shocks.) The lowest shock intensity was used by the men in the control condition, and the highest by those subjected to insult. Intermediate intensities were used by participants subjected to the other two treatments, with those in the personal frustration group giving slightly higher intensity shocks than those in the task frustration group.

What is it about a frustrating experience that makes aggression more likely? For the moment let us exclude verbal insult and concentrate on events that more closely qualify as frustrations under the 1939 definition: task failure and omission of a reward.

UNEXPECTED FRUSTRATION. It was surprising to many journalists that Mark Essex, who committed such extreme acts of violence, did not experience a considerable amount of frustration as a child. It may be particularly significant that he went directly from a happy childhood and adolescence to his unfriendly and frustrating experiences in the Navy. Nothing he had known previously prepared him for his experience in the service and after his discharge.

There is laboratory evidence suggesting that the more unexpected the frustration, the greater the possibility that aggression will result. In an ingenious experiment by Worchel (1974), college men were told by the experimenter that they would be given one of three prizes for their participation, and were asked to rank them in order of preference. In one condition, the participants were informed simply that at the end of the experiment they would be given the prize designated by the assistant experimenter. Other participants were told the prize they would receive would be the one they had ranked highest. A final group was told that at the end of the experiment they would be allowed to choose their prizes. As a matter of fact, at the end of the experimental session, the experimenter's assistant gave men in each of these conditions either their most preferred (no frustration), next most preferred (low frustration), or least preferred (high frustration) prize. Then all the men had an opportunity to aggress against the assistant by confidentially rating him in the knowledge that the rating might affect his continued employment. Higher levels of frustration led to increased aggression (negative ratings) only in the two conditions in which the participants expected to receive their most preferred prize and did not. X

In an experiment by Dengerink and Myers (1977, Experiment I), expectancy of frustration was varied in a way that was very analogous to Mark Essex's rude transition from a world of little frustration to one of high frustration. Some college men were subjected to repeated failures at anagram tasks; others were given anagram problems that guaranteed success. Then they competed for several rounds in a re-action-time contest with an experimental confederate and were allowed to select the intensity of electric shock that the confederate ostensibly would receive on the rounds the confederate lost. The contest was contrived so that on a given number of rounds the participant lost, and received a shock. X Those men who had previously been frustrated by anagram task failure selected lower shock intensities for their opponent when subsequently frustrated in the reaction-time contest than did those whose experience with the anagrams had been successful. X

The fact that X unexpected frustrations produce the greatest aggression X may be an important factor in understanding the causes of riots and mass violence. The tragic urban riots of the 1960s began in the Watts section of Los Angeles, where more funds had been spent for urban renewal and job training than anywhere else. It seems possible that the optimistic political rhetoric of the times (for example, that even the nation's most profound problems can be readily solved by the government programs of a "New Society") made the frustration of continued unemployment and racial inequity particularly unexpected and irksome.

FRUSTRATION THAT DOES NOT REVEAL PREVIOUSLY UNKNOWN DANGEROUSNESS OF THE FRUSTRATOR. In some cases the person responsible for the frustration can be seen as more capricious, dangerous, or powerful because of the way in

which the frustration is brought about. In such cases the frustrator could reduce the aggression that would otherwise result if she or he is seen as a person who might punish or retaliate.

In an interesting experiment investigating the effect of frustration on aggression in young children, Kuhn, Madsen, and Becker (1967) promised four- and five-year-old children candy for watching a film showing an older child in aggressive play. After the movie, half of the children were told they would not get the candy because they had "not paid attention to the movie." X When the children's play was later monitored by the experimenter, those exposed to the frustration were no more aggressive than those not frustrated. X By her frustrating act, however, the experimenter revealed herself as a vengeful and unpredictable person, and moreover, the frustration was linked to the film that was aggressive in content. It is quite possible that fear that the experimenter might disapprove of aggression and even punish children for it prevented the frustrated children from acting out their aggressive impulses. Other similar experiments (for example, Hanratty, O'Neal, & Sulzer, 1972), in which the frustration was caused by the incompetence of an unthreatening frustrator, resulted in a greater amount of aggression from frustrated children than from those not frustrated.

ARBITRARY FRUSTRATION. X If a frustration appears to be particularly capricious and gratuitous, aggression is more likely to result than if it is seen as having been unavoidable. X For example, if you were waiting for a bus and the bus driver did not stop, you would be less angry at the bus driver if you knew the bus needed repair and was heading straight for the garage than if you thought the driver simply did not feel like stopping. Do you think you might experience a similar reaction if you were Mark Essex and learned that your employment opportunities were limited merely because of your race? A number of laboratory experiments have demonstrated that X arbitrary frustration is

SOCIAL FOCUS 11.1
Anger and the Weapons Effect.

Berkowitz (1974) proposed that overt aggression is much more likely when angered persons are in the presence of cues they have come to associate with aggression. Some of the most interesting demonstrations of this tendency occur when firearms are casually displayed to subjects who have been angered in the laboratory. They then deliver more shocks to the provocateur than do angered subjects not exposed to firearms (for example, Berkowitz & LePage, 1967; Ellis, Weiner, & Miller, 1971). For a time, laboratory demonstrations of this **weapons effect** were suspected to be merely a product of "demand," induced by awareness of what the experimenter who leaves firearms lying around might expect of subjects (Page & Scheidt, 1971). It now seems clear, however, that the effect can be obtained in subjects who have little awareness of the experimenter's purpose (Turner & Simons, 1974) and when the weapons are not presented in the context of the same experiment in which aggression is measured (Page & O'Neal, 1977).

This is not to imply that weapons invariably enhance aggression in angered persons. In a field study Turner, Layton, and Simons (1975) determined motorists' aggressive reaction to a pickup truck in front of them, which was deliberately stalled at a green traffic light, by counting the number of times they blew their horns. A rifle displayed on the gun rack of the pickup increased hornhonking only if combined with a bumper sticker reading "Vengeance." The researchers suggested that the violent message may have been required for the motorists to strongly associate the rifle with aggression.

Does past experience using firearms in target shooting or hunting reduce the weapons effect? Jones, Epstein, and O'Neal (1981) reasoned that persons accustomed to using firearms for nonaggressive purposes would not associate them as strongly with aggression. In confirmation of this line of reasoning, these researchers found that angered college men who had a lot of such firearms experience were less responsive to the presence of firearms than were those with less firearms experience. When the weapon was not a firearm, however, but brass knuckles or a switchblade knife, for instance, past weapons experience did not reduce the weapons effect.

It seems clear, then, that the presence of weapons can increase the aggression of angered persons, provided these persons have learned to associate them with aggression. It is interesting to point out, however, that none of the research has included violent criminals or persons such as Mark Essex, whose aggressive resolve had probably been established for some time.

indeed more likely to result in aggression than is nonarbitrary frustration (for example, Pastore, 1952; Burnstein & Worchel, 1962).

The type of frustration that may lead to aggression is therefore rather restrictive: unexpected, arbitrary, and not coming from an agent revealed as capable of punishing aggression. Even when these conditions are met, frustration is perhaps not as important an antecedent to aggression as is verbal insult or physical assault (Baron, 1977; Zillmann, 1979). In one of the principal revisions of the frustration-aggression hypothesis, Berkowitz (1969) theorizes that frustration may result in a tendency to aggress, or an "instigation" to aggression, but does not ordinarily result in overt aggression unless aggressive cues are present. These cues are aspects of the environment, such as firearms, that may have been associated in the past with aggression (see Social Focus 11.1). Indeed, unless frustration (that is, reward omission or task failure) is combined with verbal abuse, cues, or specific guidance in the form of an aggressive model (imitation of aggression will be discussed later), it is a rather weak and unreliable cause of aggressive behavior.

Insult and Physical Attack as Instigators of Aggression

Research strongly suggests that insult and physical **attack** are much more powerful producers of aggression than is frustration (Geen, 1968; Epstein & Taylor, 1967). When we are subjected to a verbal or physical assault from another person, a number of processes are involved that ordinarily combine to make a retaliative attack highly probable.

1. Insults or attacks frequently include a component of frustration, either as an intrinsic aspect of the assault (for example, withdrawal of an expected reward in the form of esteem, or disclosure of a failure in interpersonal relations) or as an accompanying feature of the episode.
2. A counterattack is frequently motivated by concerns of negative reciprocity. If others have hurt us, we feel we have the right to make them feel as bad as we do. The ancient norm of "an eye for an eye" ordinarily leads to retaliation that follows rather closely in magnitude the perceived intensity of the original assault (McDaniel, O'Neal, & Fox, 1971).
3. The tormentor provides an example; the influence of an aggressive model, particularly when we are frustrated (Hanratty, O'Neal, & Sulzer, 1972) can be particularly potent.
4. Frequently the assault involves presentation of aggressive cues (for example, weapons) that can increase the probability of subsequent aggression.
5. Anger is reliably produced by attacks, and in most laboratory settings the magnitude of the anger experienced is highly related to the intensity of subsequent aggression (Geen, Rakosky, & O'Neal, 1968).

Mark Essex did not retaliate when subjected to the cruel and persistent verbal abuse heaped on him from other enlisted men and noncommissioned officers. The images and emotions of these events were to be evoked later, however, and provided fuel for his angry explosion of violence.

LEARNING TO BE AGGRESSIVE

Direct Learning of Aggression

One important way in which aggression is acquired is through learning. In a series of studies with several species, Scott (1970) demonstrated that training an individual animal to be successful in aggression greatly increases its aggressiveness. It seems safe to say that some type of reinforcement or reward ordinarily is a consequence of aggression between humans, especially for the victor. Let us take for example the hypothetical case of two boys fighting in a schoolyard over the use of a swing, and consider the possible sources of reinforcement. First, and most obvious, the winner in the struggle gets the swing, a reinforcement that is *intrinsic*, or a natural consequence of the aggression. Second, the supporters of each fighter may offer encouragement or admiration, such as "Right on, Jeff!", or "Good punch, Jerry," and these *social reinforcers* have been shown to have a potent effect in increasing aggressive behavior (Geen & Pigg, 1970). It is possible that cries of pain from one's victim can also serve as reinforcements, especially for an aggressor who is very angry (Baron, 1977, pp. 262–263). Repeated experience in such situations undoubtedly plays a role in the development of habitually aggressive methods of dealing with interpersonal conflict (Olweus, 1978).

There is another way in which direct learning is involved in aggression, and that is skill training in the techniques of fighting and violence. In some cases persons concerned about their vulnerability to physical assault or rape, obtain training in karate or self-defense techniques. It may have been concerns for his own safety or thoughts of vengeance that led Mark Essex to seek advanced marksmanship training during a period of racial tensions in his Navy experience. Skill training has the effect of increasing one's confidence that an aggressive challenge can be met successfully.

Vicarious Learning and Aggression

The similarity of Mark Essex's actions to those depicted in Walker Percy's novel, *Love in the Ruins* (1971) led to speculation as to whether Essex might have read the novel and have been influenced by the passages in which a sniper occupies a large motel. The novel was not among the materials later found in his apartment, but it was available in New Orleans in paperback edition the weeks preceding. In the case of another violent criminal, however—Arthur H. Bremer—the fact that he read and was impressed by an account of an ambush very similar to his later shooting of George Wallace is documented in his diary (Bremer, 1972, p. 109). More recently, it appears that John Hinkley, the man who attempted to assassinate Ronald Reagan, was influenced by events depicted in the film "Taxi Driver."

There seems to be little doubt that under most circumstances exposure to another person's violent act will increase the chance that we will aggress. A number of processes are apparently involved in producing this result.

Imitation of aggression. During the past two decades research on learning aggression by observation has been largely influenced by the social-learning approach of Albert Bandura (1973). It is his view that children learn aggression much as they learn other behaviors, and that exposure to a violent model yields two types of information: (1) technical how-to information that may make the observer more confident about her or his ability to carry out successfully a violent act; (2) information about the consequences of aggression, about the rewards and penalties of aggressing in a specific way and in a given type of situation. A behavior can be acquired, or made a part of the observer's repertoire of behaviors, if the observer pays attention to it, comprehends and remembers it. But the acquired behaviors will be spontaneously acted out only if the observer is fairly certain that reward—or at least, no punishment—will be forthcoming.

An example of the way in which these propositions of social learning theory have been tested is an experiment by Bandura, Ross and Ross (1963). Young children saw an older child attack a large, inflated "Bobo" doll by sitting on it, kicking it, punching it, and hitting it with a wooden mallet, while saying such things as, "Hit him!" Some of the children saw the model receive punishment for his aggression, some saw him rewarded, and some saw no consequences occurring as a result of his action. Then the children were allowed to play for a while with a number of toys, including a Bobo doll, and their behavior was surreptitiously recorded. Only in the condition in which the model's behavior resulted in punishment did the children not imitate his behavior; nevertheless, these children could later recall the model's actions when asked by the experimenter.

Research on the imitation of aggression in children and adolescents has allowed specification of conditions that may enhance a model's influence on an observer's behavior:

1. The reality of modeled violence increases its ability to elicit aggression in viewers. For example, Thomas and Tell (1974) reported more aggressiveness in children who had viewed a tape of a parking-lot fight when it had been described as an actual fight than when it had been presented

as a dramatized enactment. This general finding was also obtained by Geen (1975).

2. An attractive model and one perceived to be similar to the observer are more likely to be imitated than an unattractive or dissimilar model. Bandura, Ross, and Ross (1963) found that children imitated a model of their own sex more than they did one of the other sex, and numerous studies have demonstrated the efficacy of a model who is similar to the observer in other respects or who is attractive.

3. An observer's spontaneous performance of the model's aggressive behaviors is more likely soon after exposure to the model than later on. In a study in which children were tested both immediately after seeing an aggressive model and on the next day, O'Neal, McDonald, Hori, and McClinton (1977) reported much less imitation on delayed testing. Hicks (1965) found that little spontaneous imitation occurred six months later, although all the children tested could recall the model's behaviors accurately!

Effect of repeated exposure to violence on attitudes toward aggression. In a number of ways attitudes about aggression may be modified by observing aggressive behavior. First of all, observation of aggression may lead to increased permissiveness about violence. A clue to this possibility was offered in early imitation studies in which children who had seen a model aggress not only engaged in more imitative aggression, but also in aggressive behaviors not like those displayed by the model. Investigators speculated that these findings may indicate that one effect of a model's aggressive behavior is to **disinhibit,** or reduce the societal constraints against, aggressive behavior (cf. Wheeler & Caggiula, 1966). In a very interesting study, Drabman and Thomas (1974) showed fourth-graders a violent movie and then gave them responsibility for monitoring the behavior of some younger children. These fourth-graders took longer to report an incident of fighting to the experimenter than did other fourth-graders who had not seen the movie. Evidently, then, exposure to aggressive portrayals can increase tolerance for our own and others' aggressive behavior.

A second and related finding has been that persons who have viewed more violence react

Children frequently learn to be aggressive by observing others who behave aggressively.

with fewer electrodermal responses associated with anxiety (GSRs) than do individuals who have seen little aggression. Cline, Croft, and Courrier (1973) classified young boys on the basis of whether they spent a lot of time (more than 25 hours per week) or little time (less than 4 hours per week) watching TV. Those with heavy television-watching habits had fewer GSRs when exposed to a 14-minute film clip of a bloody boxing match than did the other boys. Similarly, Thomas, Horton, Lippincott, and Drabman (1977) found the time children and adults spent viewing televised violence to be negatively related to GSRs to aggressive films.

The picture emerging, then, is that with repeated exposure to violence, aggression loses some of its "shock" value, and moreover, large amounts of witnessed violence leads to greater acceptance of aggression. An additional question regarding repeated exposure to violence has been investigated: do people who are exposed to more violence have a greater fear of being victims of violence? Results reported by Gerbner and Gross (1976) indicate that heavy TV viewers, as opposed to light TV viewers, were more likely to feel that they might be physically assaulted. But were these findings due to *violence* on television, or a result of television programs in general? Could they have been a result of persons in high-crime areas watching more television?

In a recent study Doob and MacDonald (1979) attempted to answer these questions by interviewing residents of two high-crime police districts in Toronto (one urban and one suburban) and of two low-crime districts (also one urban and one suburban). Questions included time spent watching television during the preceding week, time spent watching violent programs, and a number of items dealing with estimated likelihood of being a violent-crime victim. When the data from all districts were pooled together the results looked very much like those previously reported by Gerbner and Gross (1976). Overall, the amount of time spent watching all types of programming and the amount spent watching violent shows were both reliably related to fear of victimization. Another finding, however, was that people in high-crime areas tend to watch more television and more violent television. So, part of the television-watching/fear-of-victimization relationship found by Gerbner and Gross may have been due to the fact that people who watch more television may be in more actual danger of assault in their own neighborhoods. This does not appear to be the entire story, however, because when Doob and MacDonald analyzed their results district by district, they found that there was a strong positive relationship between television watching and fear of victimization only within the high-crime urban

Aggressive acts take place under many different sets of circumstances. The looting shown above is one way people demonstrate aggressive behavior.

district. The investigators speculated that because this district resembled more closely than did the others the settings commonly encountered on violent television shows, people living in it may have been more inclined to respond with apprehensiveness to violent program content.

In summary, then, it seems clear that watching or reading about other people's aggression can teach the observer a great deal: how to be aggressive, the rewards of aggression, to tolerate aggression calmly, and to become more sharply aware of the dangers of assault from other people. Each of these singly or jointly would seem to make a considerable contribution to the observer's own increased propensity for aggression.

COGNITIVE AND ATTENTIONAL PROCESSES IN AGGRESSION

Under certain conditions a rather deliberate decision-making process precedes an act of aggression. If there is a period of time between provocation and opportunity to aggress, or if the aggression is instrumental, we may contemplate the advantages and disadvantages of a particular aggressive act. The importance of such a cognitive process may be greater if our anger and emotional arousal are not at their most extreme levels (Zillmann, 1979).

Ordinarily, when we are angry or considering aggressive action, we are in an approach-avoidance conflict (Miller, 1948). On the one hand, approach factors may include anticipated rewards for aggressing, hostile wishes for another person, justifications for retaliation or revenge, and anticipated emotional relief (often illusory, as we will see in a later section). Arrayed against these are avoidance factors, such as social prohibitions against aggression, moral reservations about hurting another person, anticipated punishment for aggression, or expected probability of retaliation. These consid-

erations, sometimes termed "aggressive excitatory" or "aggressive inhibitory," respectively, constitute the two horns of the dilemma for a person considering a violent act. The person's ultimate decision may depend upon judgments made about the nature of the provocations that may have occurred, about the moral acceptability of aggression, and about one's own emotional state. It seems likely that Mark Essex underwent a prolonged struggle, with a conflict in regard to violence following his discharge from the Navy; afterward New Orleans friends told reporters that in the weeks before the shootings Essex's long periods of moody silence had been broken by statements such as "I might have to make it happen."

Focus of Attention and Willingness to Engage in Violence

The outcome of the decision-making process we have just described depends in part upon whether the individual is thinking mainly about aggressive inhibitory or aggressive excitatory factors. A number of conditions affect focus of attention during the decision-making process.

A psychological state labeled "deindividuation" by Festinger, Pepitone, and Newcomb (1952) leads to an increase in impulsive, socially prohibited behaviors, including aggression (Zimbardo, 1969; Prentice-Dunn & Rogers, 1980). Deindividuation may be induced by a number of conditions, including anonymity, arousal, loud noise, and drugs, and may prevent individuals from thinking of themselves as individuals, especially in relation to societal and moral behavior standards. Recently Diener (1976) has pointed out that all of the conditions originally theorized to induce deindividuation do not have identical influences on aggression; nevertheless, most of them (for example, anonymity, loud noise, arousal) tend to increase aggression. It is interesting that when we have made the decision to aggress, we may seek to make ourselves deindividuated (Andreoli & Worchel, 1978); Mark Essex did not tell anyone he knew that he was going to the downtown motel where he carried out his assaults, and his identity was not known by the police until after his death. Usually, trained police officers take pains to use the criminal's name when negotiating for the safety of a hostage; the effectiveness of this tactic may be in the "individuation" of the person considering a violent act.

Alcohol consumption serves also to increase aggression, through a mechanism that may be similar to deindividuation. Taylor and Gammon (1975) gave male college student volunteers cocktails containing ginger ale and a low or a high dose of either bourbon or vodka. Peppermint oil was included to disguise the taste of the concoction. Men given the higher dosage chose higher shock settings for their opponents to receive in a reaction-time contest than did those who drank the cocktails lower in alcoholic content; this difference in aggression was observed whether the alcohol was bourbon or vodka. Alcohol may have the effect of reducing inhibitions against aggression, especially in angered persons (Taylor, Gammon, & Capasso, 1976). According to uniform crime statistics issued annually by the FBI (FBI, 1979), alcohol consumption is involved in as much as 67 percent of violent crimes!

A somewhat different approach to the issue of attention during aggressive-behavior conflict is to investigate the factors that cause people to direct their attention inward. Based upon Wicklund's (1975) theory of objective self-awareness, research has determined that stimuli that cause one to think about the relationships between one's behavior and one's standards can have the effect of lowering aggression. Scheier, Fenigstein, and Buss (1974) tested such a notion and tried to make social prohibitions against aggression as strong as possible by not angering the male college student volunteers and by making the target of aggression a woman. To increase self-awareness, half the subjects worked in front of a mirror. Subjects working in front of the mirror

used lower shock intensities to punish a female confederate for preprogrammed errors in a verbal learning task. Carver (1975) used a similar procedure, but prior to the experiment determined by a questionnaire whether his volunteers were in favor or against the use of physical punishment. Among antipunishment males, those who worked in front of a mirror were less aggressive than those who did not; with the propunishment men, however, the effect of the mirror was to increase aggression. These and other studies (for example, Scheier, 1976) indicate that stimuli that direct an individual's attention to self tend to make aggressive behavior more in line with the standards or norms that should apply in the given situation. So, providing stimuli that would cause a member of a group advocating revolutionary violence to focus attention on self might have the effect of increasing the tendency toward aggression. This would be an extremely strong tendency in a situation in which the group's values were particularly applicable.

Perception of Provocation and Threat

During the days preceding his rampage, Essex reacted with extreme rage following encounters with police in regard to two minor traffic violations. Our evaluation of events, particularly those that have negative consequences for us, plays a major role in aggression decision-making processes. A particularly critical aspect of this evaluation is our estimate of the likelihood that our unpleasant experiences were deliberately intended by another person. The process of making conclusions about the causes of events, called *attribution*, was introduced in Chapter 6.

You will recall that the likelihood that frustration will produce aggression is increased when it appears to have been arbitrarily caused—the frustrator appears to have intended the unpleasant experience. It turns out that what we perceive to have been our tormentor's *intent*—rather than the amount of unpleasantness caused us—may be the more important determinant of our tendency to retaliate. Greenwell and Dengerink (1973) had college men oppose a confederate in a reaction-time contest in which on each trial both men set the intensity of a shock to be delivered to the opponent, if the opponent was the slower to react. Actually, on predetermined trials, the subject was led to believe that his reaction time was slower than his opponent's. A light display at the subject's console indicated the intensity of shock presumably chosen by the confederate for the subject to receive. It was contrived to appear to the subject in some cases that his opponent had selected intense shocks, but the shocks actually received by the subject were mild; in other cases the reverse was true. If the light indicated the confederate had selected more intense shocks for the subject to receive, the subject selected more intense shocks for the confederate, regardless of the actual intensity of the shocks the subject received. Data more recently reported by Dyck and Rule (1978) indicate that inferences about the probable intent of the tormentor are more important determinants of retaliation when the precipitating assault is of moderate—rather than very mild or very severe—actual intensity.

Moral Development and Retaliation

The decision to act aggressively often depends upon a judgment that the tormentor "deserves" to suffer. If we are convinced—or can convince ourselves—that we are justified in our action and that it is a matter of punishing a transgressor, then the aggressive inhibitory factors that would ordinarily restrain our aggressiveness would not apply. Reports from those who knew him suggest that Mark Essex had convinced himself that he was entitled to punish white people for the persecution and discrimination he had experienced at their hands (Hernon, 1978).

If we have decided that the person who has caused us pain or frustration deserves to suffer, then the question becomes, How much? It turns out that our judgment about the appropriate level of retaliation may depend partially upon our stage of moral development (Lagerspetz & Westman, 1980). According to Piaget's theory of cognitive development, children prior to the age of seven advocate "expiatory punishment," a principle whereby the greater the punishment for a transgression, the more just that punishment is judged to be. Older children, however, abide by a principle of punishment by reciprocity, in which the magnitude of the punishment should match the seriousness of the transgression. In confirmation of this theory, Zillmann and Bryant (1975) found that seven- and eight-year-old children disliked the prince in a video-taped vignette who overretaliated against his disloyal brother, but that the overretaliation did not reduce four-year-olds' liking for him. Most adequately socialized adults, when moderately angered, very carefully match the intensity of their retaliation to the magnitude of the original provocation (McDaniel, O'Neal, & Fox, 1971) and regard overretaliation as unjustified (Tedeschi, Smith, & Brown, 1974).

The perception and evaluation of the provoking event play important roles in the decision-making process that precedes actual aggression. In actuality, there probably are far more hostile wishes than there are aggressive acts, a fact partly attributable to the interplay of excitation and inhibition that may often hold the provoked person in conflict until the aggressive opportunity is past.

LOSING ONE'S TEMPER: ANGER AND AGGRESSION

With a strong enough annoyance, most of us will fly into a rage, and our behavior is more a product of our emotions than of any rational or semirational decision-making process (Zillmann, Bryant, Cantor, & Day, 1975). Perhaps you have attempted to reason with a friend who is extremely angry and have acquired firsthand knowledge of the futility of such an approach until after the friend has cooled off. Acts of violence committed immediately after extreme provocation are recognized as "acts of passion" and are dealt with more leniently by criminal laws that recognize second degree, or unpremeditated murder.

Anger and Acts of Passion

The physiological arousal produced by extreme provocation has direct influences upon aggression. Bandura (1973) has noted that arousal can increase the probability that "prepotent" aggressive behaviors (those already likely because of disposition, habit, or exposure to a violent model) will actually occur. And, according to Berkowitz's (1969) revision of the frustration-aggression hypothesis, arousal makes it more likely that aggressive cues will result in overt aggression. There seems to be abundant evidence indicating that arousal can increase imitation of an aggressive model (for example, O'Neal, McDonald, Hori, & McClinton, 1977) and aggressive responsiveness to cues associated with aggression (Geen & O'Neal, 1969).

Emotional Labels and the Rhetoric of Violence

A particularly strong relationship between arousal and aggression occurs when we label the arousal as anger. (The notion that emotions include both an arousal and a cognitive—or labeling—component was introduced in Chapter 6.) In the majority of cases we are confident about what to call our provocation-induced arousal: anger. More often than you might think, however, persons are uncertain about the intensity of the emotion they are experiencing. In these cases, individuals' attributions about their arousal—that is, their inferences

about what produced the arousal—can provide the basis of their conclusions as to the proportion of their arousal that represents a given emotion such as anger (Younger & Doob, 1978). For example, individuals who know that they have taken a powerful stimulant drug and then are provoked may conclude that because a part of the arousal is not due to provocation, they are not as angry as would be the case if they had not been aware that the stimulant drug was responsible for part of the arousal.

In a series of creative studies, Zillmann and his associates (Zillmann, 1979) have demonstrated that persons who are unobtrusively aroused and then provoked rate themselves higher in anger and are more aggressive against their provocateurs than persons whose previous arousal was more obtrusive. Zillmann refers to this process of misattribution of arousal as **excitation transfer.** Through misattribution, arousal may be cognitively reassigned to a category such as anger, which, of course, would have a tendency to increase aggression. Recently Bryant and Zillmann (1979) showed that even after hours of delay, excitation transfer can increase the aggression against one's provocateur. Evidently, then, our beliefs about the intensity of our anger can strongly influence aggression, even if those beliefs are inaccurate.

The tendency to use a given emotional label such as anger is partially due to training and socialization. In the days he spent AWOL from the Navy at home in Emporia, Mark Essex read the book, *Black Rage,* written by black psychiatrists William Grier and Price Cobbs (1968). According to later reports by his family, Essex was deeply influenced by the volume, and New Orleans police found a well-worn copy of it in his apartment after his death. Some of the material in *Black Rage* can be understood as instruction for frustrated black people as to appropriate labels for their emotion. For example, Grier and Cobbs (1968, p. 81) write, "Observe that the amount of rage the oppressed turns on his tormentor is a direct function of the depth of his grief, and consider the intensity of a black man's grief. . . ."

The use of labels such as "angry" and "mad" to describe one's emotion undoubtedly makes aggression more likely. In laboratory studies, self-ratings of anger are highly correlated with the magnitude of shock administered to another person (for example, Geen, Rakosky, & O'Neal, 1968). It is quite likely that when we intend to engage in instrumental aggression, we are motivated to search for words to describe our emotional state that will provide justification for our subsequent hurtful actions (Blumenthal et al., 1972). If you wish to use aggression to take something away from someone, it is useful afterward to be able to say that your victim had made you so angry that you were impelled to attack him!

The Catharsis Controversy: Was Mark Essex "Blowing off Steam?"

Popular lore has it that we can "blow off" our anger by attacking the person(s) responsible for our distress. According to the theory of aggression **catharsis,** after we attack our tormentor, we experience (1) a reduction in arousal or anger (emotional catharsis) and (2) a reduced tendency to aggress (behavioral catharsis). In certain of its forms, the theory also assumes that we are relaxed and nonhostile following indirect (attacking a person other than our tormentor), witnessed (watching someone else do the honors), or fantasized aggression. While the term catharsis has been traced to Aristotle, Quanty (1977) points out that Aristotle never applied it to anger or aggression. The authors of the *Frustration-Aggression Hypothesis* (Dollard et al., 1939) strongly argued that "the expression of aggression is a catharsis. . ." (p. 33), and they probably are responsible for introduction of the notion into recent psychological literature. The status of the notion is controversial for psychologists, and most are prepared to draw only preliminary conclusions as to its scientific validity.

Is arousal reduced when angry people retaliate? Under most conditions, it is. An important exception pointed out by Geen and Quanty (1977) is aggression against one's tormentor that might lead to anxiety. For example, when the provocateur is of higher status than you are, aggressing against him or her may give rise to fears about that person's "getting even" in the future (Hokanson & Shetler, 1961). Other examples might include aggression that would lead to public embarrassment or feelings of guilt about behaving aggressively. The anxiety produced by aggression in these cases maintains the high level of arousal that was initially induced by provocation.

But when anxiety is *not* involved, why does aggression frequently lower anger-elevated arousal? Recent research suggests that it is a tension reduction that occurs whenever we engage in a behavior that we have learned is effective in reducing an unpleasant quality of our environment. Often such is the case with aggression—by retaliating, the probability that the tormentor will again attack is lowered.

A very important experiment by Hokanson, Willers and Koropsak (1968) will illustrate this latter point. Angered college students could either shock or reward their tormentors. Male subjects who were able to deliver shocks to their tormentors experienced a reduction in their anger-elevated blood pressure, but when they were able only to reward their tormentors, they experienced no blood-pressure reduction. The pattern for women was reversed: when they could reward their tormentors, their blood pressure returned to normal, but it was unaffected when they were able to retaliate. One explanation for these results is that the men (of 1968, at least) had learned the effectiveness of physical retaliation against their tormentors, while for women the most effective action may have been to placate the attacker. "Take my purse, but don't hurt me," has unfortunately often been the safest reaction for women who are confronted by physical intimidation. A second phase of the study supports this interpretation. Other women were exposed to training, rigged so that if they retaliated against their attackers, future attacks would be of lower magnitude. When these women were subsequently tested, it was found that their blood-pressure response conformed to the male pattern; it returned to normal after they punished their tormentors.

It is important to emphasize, then, that the emotional relaxation experienced by an angered person after engaging in aggressive vengeance, is not, strictly speaking, emotional catharsis. It is, rather, a reduction in tension that could result from performing any act that might be effective in improving the situation. For example, had alternatives—such as joining a black political action group—been available to Mark Essex, these just might have resulted in as satisfying self-expression as did the more violent course followed. There is no physiological imperative that makes aggression the only way angered people can find inner tranquility.

After aggression, is there a reduced tendency to engage in more aggression? When we are angered by another person we no doubt harbor hostile wishes that usually are rather specific about the amount of harm desired. For example, if a schoolboy is kicked in the shin by a playmate, he may wish that the other boy's shin be kicked, but not that his leg be broken! Only if the offense is extreme, or if it has been going on for a very long time, or if the offended person has somehow lost a sense of proportion, does a revenge wish include the permanent injury of the provocateur. (In this respect, we must admit that Mark Essex's aggression represents an unusual extreme.)

There seems to be quite a bit of evidence indicating that when we have personally physically hurt our tormentors, our subsequent attacks are weaker than they would be if we had not previously attacked the tormentor (for example, Konečni & Ebbeson, 1976). Also, if we learn that someone *else* has hurt the person who has angered us, our aggression against

that person will be lessened (Bramel, Taub, & Blum, 1968; Doob & Wood, 1972). Therefore, if we see that harm has been done to our tormentor, under most circumstances we will not retaliate as strongly as we would otherwise.

When, however, we see a person other than our tormentor attacked, the effect upon our subsequent retaliation against our tormentor is very likely to be to *increase* it. Zillmann and Johnson (1973) had angered college men see either a violent film clip, a segment from a travelogue, or no film at all, before having the opportunity to attack their provocateur. Viewing the violent film clip maintained the angered subjects' blood pressure at a high level and produced more aggression than in either of the other two viewing conditions. There is very little evidence suggesting that viewing violence can ever reduce aggression in angered subjects, and, contrary to a catharsis prediction, usually increases it.

In general, then, we must say that there is not much evidence to support the notion of *aggression catharsis*. To summarize:

1. While physiological relaxation is often produced by angry persons' aggression, the relaxation can also be produced by many other types of non-aggressive action.
2. Sometimes seeing one's tormentor suffer can lower an angered person's retaliation against the tormentor, but the reduction in aggression could merely be the result of seeing one's hostile wish fulfilled.
3. Viewing violent scenes usually **increases** aggression from angered individuals.

CONTROL AND PREVENTION OF VIOLENCE

Ideally, it seems that society should be able to identify individuals with a high propensity for violence, and so be able to intervene in the development of a Mark Essex. Much effort and great expense has gone into the attempt to develop ways to predict who will commit violent crimes, but it is generally agreed (for example,

Rubin, 1975) that such prediction is not possible. One reason is that the disposition to aggress comes from many sources. Hans Toch (1969) interviewed a large number of violent offenders and was able to identify a score of personality types, such as "self-image compensators" and "sadists" (similar to the "bullies" in schoolyards, investigated by Olweus, 1978). Furthermore, a large number of the personality types that theorists have offered as descriptive of violent criminals are shared by persons who never commit acts of criminal aggression. Prior to his discharge from the Navy in February 1971, Mark Essex was given a psychiatric examination. In the clinical report, it was noted that he was "impulsive and immature," but there was no statement indicating a propensity toward violence or aggression.

What then can be done to control aggression? A number of strategies have been investigated by social psychologists, some of which would seem to be helpful in reducing the possibility that explosive acts of violence—like those of Mark Essex—will occur, and others would seem to be promising as interventions in milder forms of aggression.

Punishment and Aggression

Intuitively, it would appear that **punishment,** or threat of punishment, would be an effective deterrent to aggression. In fact, however, what would seem to be a simple and straightforward application of aversive conditioning produces highly variable and complex effects in the case of aggression.

Punishment of aggression. When a parent spanks a child after the child has hit a younger sibling, the child will no doubt refrain from attacking the younger brother or sister, for a time (Deur & Park, 1970). In order to work in reducing aggression, it seems clear that the punishment has to be relatively harsh (Shortell, Epstein, & Taylor, 1970). There are a number of

reasons, however, why this effect will be temporary and can, in the long run, actually result in more aggression. (1) A physical punishment reliably produces anger, and aggression aimed at a vulnerable target, such as the younger sibling, may be the result once the parent has left the scene. (2) The parent, by using physical punishment, is presenting the child with a very effective model; and too often the unintended message is: when attempting to gain control of a social situation, hit! (3) The punished child may perceive the younger child as the cause for the punishment, and vow to retaliate when the opportunity arises. These considerations together may account for the positive correlation, reported in a now classic study by Bandura and Walters (1959), between parental use of corporal punishment and adolescent boys' aggression.

More success is typically obtained when the punishment used does not involve hitting and includes removing a child from the sources of the positive reinforcement that often accompanies aggression. Such techniques as **time out,** if employed promptly and calmly by a parent or teacher can break up an aggressive interchange and allow the principals time to cool off. A child who hurts another child is simply seated on a chair away from the action of the play yard or classroom for a prescribed number of minutes. At this point the child can be talked to about alternative, nonaggressive strategies that could be used in situations like the one leading up to the aggression. Time out and other techniques have been found to be more effective in the management of aggression and other impulsive behavior problems in children than is physical punishment or threats of corporal punishment.

Punishment as aggression. If physical punishment is not the most effective means of controlling children's aggression, and has numerous undesirable side effects, why is it used by so many adults? In order to answer the question, it is necessary to consider physical punishment itself as aggression. Parents who use physical punishment almost exclusively in controlling their children's behavior may (1) be unaware of nonpunitive techniques of control; (2) be themselves the targets of physical punishment as children; (3) feel anger about some aspect of their parental role (Fontana, 1973).

Indeed, very often punishment is the justification given by adults for their physical attacks on children. Child abuse is one of the most persistent and perplexing problems faced by society today. It has been estimated that some 500,000 to one million children in the United States are subjected to physical abuse each year. Much of it takes place in the context of the family, which Murray Straus (Straus, Gelles, & Steinmetz, 1979) has characterized as the context for a large proportion of all the violence that occurs in the United States. Undoubtedly, the problem is a complex one, a joint product of individual, familial, and cultural factors (Belsky, 1980).

What can be used to reduce physical abuse of children, often committed in the name of punishment? A number of approaches are being attempted: (1) help professionals who deal with children (social workers, teachers, physicians, child psychologists) to be alert to and recognize symptoms of child abuse; (2) educate prospective parents in appropriate expectations for behavior in children and in effective nonpunitive methods of child guidance; (3) make available centers that receive reports of child abuse and investigate suspected cases. In recognition of the need to evaluate the effectiveness of these and other methods of dealing with the problem of child abuse, the Congress in 1974 established the National Center on Child Abuse and Neglect.

Reducing Television Violence

There seems to be little doubt that television is an extremely important influence on children's behavior. By age 16, the average teenager in the United States has watched television more than he has attended school (Liebert, Neale, & Davidson, 1973)! The amount of aggressive content in TV programming rose consistently from 1954 (17 percent) to 1969 (80 percent), and showed no reduction through 1972 (Gerbner, 1976), although in very recent years the violent content has shown some signs of abatement (Nader & Johnson, 1979). So, young adults have been served since early childhood a very heavy diet of televised violence.

Why do so many persons tolerate and even seek out violent TV programs? It must be admitted that social psychologists have directed much more research at the influence of mass-media violence on behavior than at the reasons why people voluntarily expose themselves to violent TV shows. A number of preliminary answers in regard to the latter question, however, can be offered: (1) themes of physical action, risk, and conflict, which are abundant in violent programs, may be attractive per se, whether or not accompanied by aggression; (2) violent television fare may be more attractive to us when we are angry or after we have engaged in aggression (Fenigstein, 1979); (3) persons high in aggressivity may be those *most* interested in mass-media violence. Criminologist David Agresti conducted a survey of movies selected by violent criminals in state penal institutions and found violent and sexual themes to be highest in popularity (Ruth, 1978).

You will recall from the earlier section on vicarious learning that there are several powerful effects of watching an aggressive model. There is little doubt that early exposure of a young child to TV violence has long-term effects on the child's behavior. In a very important longitudinal study, Eron, Huesmann, Lefkowitz, and Walder, (1972) reported that the amount of time spent viewing TV violence by third-grade boys was reliably related to their aggressiveness—as rated by peers and parents—a decade later. It is important to note that these investigators employed a cross-lagged comparison technique that allowed them to infer that the boys' earlier viewing habits were more closely associated with their aggressiveness a decade later than was their third-grade aggressiveness.

Ordinarily, network censors have been more willing to allow portrayals of provoked violence than of unprovoked aggression "in cold blood." Ironically, much research suggests that justified aggression is not necessarily more desirable than nonjustified aggression in the media. Bandura (1973, p. 133) observes, "Taken as a whole, the data indicate that modeling of defensible violence adds legitimacy and thereby weakens restraints over the use of aggressive solutions for social problems. . . . There is always uncertainty as to whether righteous violence in the moral lesson will legitimize aggressive conduct or depicted punishment will inhibit transgressive behavior." In confirmation of this position, Berkowitz and Powers (1979) reported enhancement of aggression by a violent audiovisual display only when it was preceded by an introduction that made it clear that the aggression to be portrayed was justified.

Fostering the Development of Socially Acceptable Behavior

Inappropriate aggression often achieves objectives for the aggressor that could be gained by socially acceptable means (Brown & Elliot, 1965). For example, a police officer might be able to refer a quarreling couple to a family service agency rather than merely threatening them with a promise to hit them both with his nightstick if he is called again to intervene in their marital disputes. Or, a young boy might be able to suggest taking turns when in conflict with a playmate over the use of a ball in the schoolyard, rather than merely hitting the playmate to take possession of the ball. Usually attempts to reduce a person's inappropriate aggression do not yield satisfactory results un-less they are accompanied by efforts to help the individual develop the socially acceptable skills that could replace the aggression.

Prevention of angry confrontations.   A necessary skill, if inappropriate aggression is to be avoided in favor of socially acceptable alternatives, is the ability to recognize when a situation is becoming so emotion laden that an angry confrontation, and possibly aggression, is likely. Diagnosing another person's emotional state, detecting the often subtle signs of another person's anger, is a first step. Then, the use of distraction or humor to disarm the angry person has been an effective strategy used by human service workers and of demonstrated effectiveness in laboratory tests (for example, Mueller & Donnerstein, 1977). Moderate levels of humor, or even of sexual arousal, can prevent anger from reaching levels that would make aggression likely (Baron, 1977).

Training in verbal resolution of interpersonal conflicts. Verbal skills in coping with conflict situations are crucial in the avoidance of physical aggression. A first step in development of competence in socially acceptable modes of managing conflict with others is *assertiveness*, or the ability and willingness to articulate one's feelings and one's rights. Bandura (1973) has pointed out that often assertiveness and aggressivity in children is negatively related, because children able to inform others about their feelings and rights less often find themselves pushed into situations in which their only recourse is physical force.

Watching another person use verbal methods of coping with a provocative situation has been shown to be effective in reducing the viewer's subsequent aggressive reaction to provocation (for example, Baron & Kepner, 1970; Donnerstein & Donnerstein, 1977). Robert M. Liebert (Liebert & Poulos, 1975) developed a number of brief, video-taped dramatizations that demonstrated both angry or aggressive reactions to a conflict situation and verbal problem-solving approaches toward resolving that situation. The tapes were first successfully tested with young children in the laboratory, and then used as spot prosocial "commercials" on several television stations.

If brief one-shot presentations can have a measurable effect on children's use of aggression, efforts by parents and teachers to demonstrate the use of negotiation techniques and constructive problem-solving reactions to conflict situations would seem to produce even more favorable and long-term effects on children's development.

INDIGNATION AND SPEAKING OUT ABOUT INJUSTICE OR INEQUITY

So far in the chapter, we have focused on violent acts themselves, without much attention to the nature of the provocation. Often an act of violence represents an effort on the part of an individual to express indignation at a perceived injustice or inequity in society. Such a violent result is especially likely to occur when the individual does not have either the skills or power to have an impact upon the social system. Mark Essex is probably a good case in point. When in the Navy, he appealed to his superiors for relief from racial harassment with only mixed results. Therefore, when confronted with racial discrimination in economic opportunity, he may have been extremely pessimistic about the probability that any legal method of seeking redress would be successful. As a matter of fact, when Essex's car was searched by police following his death, on its

front seat were unmailed letters to the Louisiana Department of Employment Security, dealing with his complaints of employers' racial discrimination.

Women have faced a particularly complex set of obstacles in seeking to correct forms of injustice and discrimination based solely on gender. Psychiatrist Teresa Bernardez-Bonesatti (1978) has recently made perceptive observations about the effects upon women of arbitrary sex-role-related prohibitions against the expression of anger. Women who openly express such feelings may face the loss of femininity and sexual attractiveness. Frequently, Bernardez-Bonesatti goes on to say, women therefore direct anger toward self or express it in an ineffectual fashion. Freedom from such arbitrary sex-role restraints in the expression of anger enables women more clearly to see its sources, and even more importantly, to defend assertively their own rights without guilt or recrimination. Both Larwood, O'Neal, and Brennan (1977) and Richardson, Bernstein, and Taylor (1979) found women's expressions of anger directed toward a provocateur to be considerably enhanced by the presence of an audience perceived as supportive of such self-expression.

Anger is an emotion that can as easily fuel positive actions such as exposing the sources of injustice and articulating how equity can be restored as it can violent actions that in the end are harmful and self-defeating. A society committed to equity and justice, one with open and free speech for those who perceive injustice, should expect fewer episodes of explosive and tragic violence as in the case of Mark Essex!

SUMMARY

Aggression is defined as behaviors that are intended to harm others. It may be *provocation motivated* (anger is the predominant motivator) or *instrumental* (primarily a calculated attempt to gain money or property), although in most instances of aggression some of both—instrumentality and anger—is involved. Mark Essex was a young man who in 1973 carried out a series of sniper attacks in New Orleans that left twenty people dead or wounded. He was killed by police, and a psychological post mortem was used as a case-study focus throughout the chapter.

There have been three approaches in investigating the possibility that human aggression is somehow biologically "wired in." (1) Students of animal behavior have focused on the function or survival value of aggression, and conclude that such an analysis is as helpful in understanding human aggression as it is with lower species. (2) A search for a genetic defect—such as the XYY chromosome anomaly—as basis for an understanding of why some persons are aggressive and some are not, has not been successful. (3) While relatively direct relationships exist between the activity of certain brain structures and aggression in lower animals, such relationships are extremely complex in humans, and often depend upon learning and environmental conditions.

Frustration is a relatively weak antecedent of aggression. In order to lead to aggression it must be unexpected, arbitrary, and not reveal the frustrator as a powerful or vengeful person. In contrast to frustration, insult and physical attack are strong instigators of aggression, and reliably evoke attempts to retaliate.

Aggressive skills, and knowledge about the rewards and punishments that may follow aggressing, can be learned either directly or by observing others. Repeated exposure to others' aggression, in addition, increases calm tolerance for aggression in others, but can lead to an increased awareness of the possibility of becoming a victim of assault.

Except when anger is at its most extreme level, focus of attention and interpretation of events can play an important role in aggression. If a person's attention is directed toward self, then behavior conforms more closely to personal values; so if aggression is disapproved, it will be decreased by attention focused on self. By contrast, an attentional state called "deindividuation," which may be induced by such stimuli as being in a large crowd, makes an individual more likely to engage in impulsive socially prohibited acts like aggression. Alcohol intoxication has effects upon aggression similar to those of deindividuation. When attacked, our retaliation is apparently more a function of the perceived intent of our attacker than of the magnitude of the attack. Retaliation also is partially determined by our level of moral development; younger children approve of maximal retaliation, whereas older children disapprove of retaliation that exceeds in intensity the original attack.

The arousal produced by attack or insult can increase aggression, especially if the individual clearly identifies it as anger. An individual's tendency to describe arousal as anger is a product both of learning and of interpretation of the causes of the arousal. In general, the more angry a person feels, the greater the magnitude of the aggression. Angry arousal is often lowered by aggression aimed at one's provocateur, but such relaxation effects can also be produced by nonaggressive behaviors that prove effective in reducing an unpleasant quality of the environment. Angered persons who learn that their tormentor is injured—whether or not they themselves were responsible for the injury—tend to engage in less subsequent retaliation. On the other hand, if angered persons see someone other than their tormentor become the victim of an aggressive assault, their retaliation against their tormentor will be increased.

In general, attempts to predict which persons will be criminally violent have been unsuccessful. The use of physical punishment to discourage aggression may inhibit aggression temporarily, but in the long run may actually encourage aggression. More long-term desirable effects are produced by helping children to learn to discern signs of anger in others, to express freely their own feelings, to develop skills in defusing potentially emotionally explosive situations, and to effectively use negotiation and compromise in conflict situations.

There is no doubt that television is an important influence upon children's behavior and attitudes. The amount of violent programming on television has increased steadily over the past two decades before leveling off somewhat in the past year or so.

Anger in the form of indignation can motivate individuals to speak out about injustices and inequities in society. The use of legal, nonviolent forms of protest depends in part upon freedom to dissent and governmental responsiveness to minority needs.

SUGGESTED READINGS

Baron, R. A. *Human aggression.* New York: Plenum, 1977.

Geen, R. G., & O'Neal, E. C. (Eds.). *Perspectives on aggression.* New York: Academic Press, 1976.

Goldstein, J. H. *Aggression and crimes of violence.* New York: Oxford, 1975.

Straus, M. A., Gelles, R. J., & Steinmetz, S. K. *Behind closed doors: Violence in the American family.* New York: Doubleday, 1979.

Zillmann, D. *Hostility and aggression.* Hillsdale, N.J.: Lawrence Erlbaum Associates, 1979.

12

HELPING

- Learning to Help
- Helping Because of our Emotional Reactions to the Needs of Others
- Processes that Undermine the Motivation to Help
- Situational Constraints on Helping
- Implications for Our Response to Others' Needs
- Summary

"We have met the enemy, and they are us!" The social issue addressed in this chapter is not some problem in California or Connecticut, in Tennessee or Texas; it is a problem with us. It is our failure to respond to the needs of others, whether in California, Connecticut, or right next door.

We are daily confronted with other people in need. They may be far away or close at hand, desperate or only mildly upset. But they are there. You could be faced with the following need situations or with similar ones almost any day.

- You pick up a newspaper. One headline announces that hundreds lost their homes in an earthquake in Turkey; another introduces a story on thousands of refugees who are dying of disease and starvation.
- You turn on the television. A documentary presents the plight of migrant workers in the southern United States; overworked and underpaid, they desperately need help.
- Closer to home, a good friend comes to you in tears, because she has just broken up with her fiance. Another friend is upset over receiving a low grade on a test.
- While jogging down a quiet, country road, you round a corner and come upon a horrible scene. A sports car is on its side, half in and half out of the ditch. On the pavement is the driver, a young woman. She is lying on her back, eyes closed, barely moving. Her face is bloody and bruised; her left leg, clearly broken, is twisted at a grotesque angle.
- Hurrying to a doctor's appointment, you notice a shabbily dressed young man slumped in a doorway in a cold, windy alley. As you go by, he coughs and groans.
- Someone comes to your door asking for contributions to the United Fund.
- Walking to class, you see a poster announcing the annual Red Cross blood drive on campus.
- As a participant in a psychology experiment, you are given the task of observing another student who is performing a learning task under aversive conditions. The aversive conditions used in the experiment are mild electric shocks delivered at random intervals. Because of a traumatic experience with shock as a child, the other student finds the shocks extremely uncomfortable. Clearly, she is in considerable pain.

What do we do when confronted with others in need? Sometimes we help. One can think of dramatic examples in which help has been offered at considerable personal cost and risk to the helper. Consider the case of Alan Brenneka:

Nineteen-year-old Alan Brenneka was surfing about 40 yards off shore at Delray Beach, Florida; there were about 30 other surfers in the area. Suddenly, Brenneka was attacked by a shark. His arm was badly mangled, and he started losing blood rapidly. Two strangers—Mark Schroeder, a 19-year-old surfer, and John McCurdy, a beach walker—responded to Brenneka's cries, swimming out and helping him to shore (Associated Press, November 26, 1976).

Less dramatic but also important is the quiet comfort we give a friend or the contribution we make to the United Fund.

But often, too often, we do not help. Even when helping involves no personal danger and very little cost, we turn away. Why? In this chapter we will attempt to gain some understanding of why we do and do not help. We will find that although there are important and powerful social-psychological processes that encourage us to help those in need, there are also important and powerful processes that discourage us from helping.

Before reading what social psychologists have to say about why we do and do not help, take a few minutes to think about it yourself. Specifically, think whether you would help with each of the needs in the list at the beginning of the chapter. If you are like most people, you would help with some but not with others. On the basis of this reflection, jot down a list of what seem to be reasons why you help and a list of the reasons why you do not help.

This chapter is written by C. Daniel Batson and Mary S. Vanderplas

Once you feel you have reasonably good answers to these questions, read on and see how your answers compare with those proposed by social psychologists.

LEARNING TO HELP

Perhaps the most obvious reason why we help others is that we have been taught to do so. Our parents, teachers, and others use a number of subtle and some not so subtle techniques to get us to share and to care. They provide an example by helping others themselves, and they extol the virtues of helping. They reward us for helping—at times with candy or coins, more often with a warm smile, praise, or a hug. And in various ways these socializing agents try to get us to adopt the welfare of others as an internalized value, so that we will want to help even when they are not around to dole out rewards. They want us to become helpful people.

Systematizing these observations, we can identify five different reasons for helping, all a result of what we learn.

1. We learn that others, who serve as models for us, help.
2. We learn that helping can be rewarding. The rewards may be material (such as money or a prize) or social (for example, thanks or praise). In fact, after being associated with these rewards, helping itself may become a reward.
3. We learn social norms, which tell us that helping, at least under certain circumstances, is expected.
4. We learn that even when there are no material or social rewards we can reward ourselves when we help; we can pat ourselves on the back for being good, caring people.
5. Over time, some of us may internalize the value of helpfulness into a stable personality characteristic, becoming the kind of people who help in a variety of different situations.

Probably your list of reasons for helping included most if not all of these five. But before we assume that these are valid reasons, we need to look at each a bit more closely. For although social-psychological research provides evidence for each, the evidence for some is much clearer than for others.

Learning That Others Help: Modeling

Much of what we learn comes from watching others. So powerful is observational learning that parents of young children often resort to spelling off-color words for fear of what Johnny or Suzie will pick up and use in public. "Not in front of the children" has long been an important maxim of child rearing.

Parents are, of course, the primary models whom children watch to learn how to act. If children see their parents helping others in need, they too are likely to help. Mussen and Eisenberg-Berg (1977) provide much evidence that a relationship exists between parents' modeling of helping and the subsequent helping behavior of their children. For example, identification with parents who were models of social concern and prosocial action was reported to be an important antecedent both to the behavior of Christians who courageously rescued Jews from the Nazis during World War II (London, 1970) and to the efforts of those civil-rights workers who committed themselves wholeheartedly to working for social integration in the southern United States in the late 1950s and 1960s (Rosenhan, 1970).

Modeling is not confined to the parent-child relationship. Bryan and Test (1967) found that simply seeing someone helping a woman change a flat tire made motorists more likely to stop and assist a second woman in a similar predicament.

Other investigators have studied the conditions necessary for modeling to be effective. Hornstein, Fisch, and Holmes (1968) found that similarity between the model and the observer was important. In a series of experiments, pedestrians in New York City came upon a wallet that had been strategically "lost" by a researcher. There was a letter with the wallet, ostensibly written by someone who had found and was returning it. This person, who had supposedly lost the wallet in the act of returning it, was a model of helping behavior for the pedestrians. The letter was written either by an American, a similar model, or by a foreigner, a dissimilar model. Moreover, in some cases the letter revealed that the model was pleased to help, in other cases that the model found returning the wallet an inconvenient nuisance. Results of these experiments suggested that both the similarity and the reaction of the model affected pedestrians' behavior. When the model was similar, pedestrians more often returned the wallet when the model reacted positively to helping than when he reacted negatively. When the model was dissimilar, the model's reactions did not make a difference; helping was relatively low regardless. What seemed to be happening, then, was that the observer looked to the response of a

Children imitate the behaviors of adults; parental nurturance and warmth may enhance this tendency.

similar other to determine whether this helping act had rewarding consequences. When the model responded positively to performing the act, the pedestrian learned not only that helping was appropriate in this situation but that it felt good. And under these circumstances the pedestrian was very likely to help.

Research also suggests that children are more likely to imitate the behavior of more prestigious and more powerful models (Bandura, 1977). Interestingly, however, children have not been found to imitate the helping of an adult who is warm and nurturant toward them any more than they imitate a more distant and aloof adult (Grusec, 1981). This unexpected finding may be the result of the nurturant model seeming more permissive, leading the child to be more self-indulgent. Or it may be because in the studies showing this effect the adult-child relationship has been of only limited duration (typically, no more than an hour or so). More nurturant models may have more positive effects in long-term relationships, such as the parent-child relationship (Hoffman, 1977).

Television and other mass media also provide us with models that we imitate (Rushton, 1979). Think, for example, about our involvement in social causes. A few years ago many people were active in community efforts to recycle paper and metal; their goal was to protect the environment. This concern, at least in part, resulted from environmental protection campaigns being modeled for us through the news media. We learned that many important and respected people were involved in environmental protection; clearly, it was the thing to do. So we got involved, and much good was done to save the country's natural resources and beauty.

Unfortunately, this kind of faddish involvement in social causes stimulated by media models is not likely to last, for the media must always have something new to talk about, not just the same old stuff. They move on to new causes, showing us that many important and respected people are now concerned about, for example, energy conservation and nuclear power. This new information is likely to pressure us to turn our attention to the new cause; after all, we don't want to be passé. As a result, our involvement in any given social cause is likely to be short-lived. It is as if we were being pushed along in a cafeteria line; we focus upon this or that item for a brief period, but then are hurried on to the next. Media modeling may get us uninvolved in helping others as quickly as it gets us involved.

Learning That Helping Can Be Rewarding

Material rewards. If someone offered you $100,000 to help him move across town, you would almost certainly agree. A nickel, on the other hand, would not be enough. It will come as no surprise that money and other direct, material rewards can be very effective in getting us to help. In fact, rewards can not only entice us to help in the present; they can also lead us to help in the future. In one of the numerous demonstrations of the effect of rewards on future helping, Fischer (1963) found that rewarding children with bubblegum for donating marbles to a peer made them more likely to donate again when given another opportunity. This is a simple reinforcement effect; we are more likely to repeat behaviors for which we are rewarded.

Social rewards. Often we help in the absence of any direct material rewards, but we may still anticipate the intangible social rewards of thanks, praise, and esteem in the eyes of our fellows. Gelfand, Hartmann, Cromer, Smith, and Page (1975) found that children who were praised for sharing gave larger donations to other children when subsequently given the opportunity. No doubt you can think of examples from your own experience when you felt rewarded for your helping by someone's thanks, praise, or admiration.

Consistent with such examples, Reis and Gruzen (1976) found that male undergraduates who were asked to allocate a five-dollar reward for successful team performance among themselves and their three partners did so in the way that would gain the most social approval for themselves. Those individuals who thought that the experimenter would know how they allocated the money tended to divide it *equitably*, giving each team member an amount proportional to his input to the team's performance. Presumably, they did this to win the approval of the experimenter, who they had reason to believe would see an equitable division as most fair. In contrast, those individuals who thought that the other team members would know how they allocated the money tended to divide it *equally*, giving each team member the same amount, regardless of his contribution to the team's performance. Presumably, they did this to win the approval of the other participants, who they had reason to believe would see an equal division as most fair. Finally, those individuals who thought that their decision would be known only to themselves tended to give themselves a disproportionally large share of the money. Presumably, with the possibility for social rewards removed, these individuals returned to providing themselves with direct, material rewards. These findings suggest that presenting ourselves in ways that maximize our social rewards is an important determinant of our readiness to give to others.

Social rewards coming from the recipient of help have also been found to affect future helping. Moss and Page (1972) demonstrated that people who had previously helped were more likely to help a second person in need if the earlier help had been received with thanks and gratitude rather than resentment.

Helping as a reward in itself. Not only can direct material rewards and indirect social rewards affect helping, but helping itself can become rewarding. Over time, behaviors that are rewarded can become *secondary rewards.* When this happens, engaging in these behaviors makes us feel good, even when it leads to no other rewards. For most adults in our society, helping is a behavior that has become a secondary reward. To demonstrate this, Weiss, Buchanan, Altstatt, and Lombardo (1971) had participants watch a confederate whom they thought to be receiving electric shocks. When the participants were given an opportunity to help the confederate by terminating the shock, they did so. And their speed of responding increased over time, much as it would if they had been paid for terminating the shocks. Moreover, the increase was greater than could be attributed to practice effects. These results suggested that helping acted as a reward, much as money might.

Building upon the idea that helping can serve as a secondary reward, Cialdini, Darby, and Vincent (1973) proposed that we are more likely to help someone when we feel bad, because we know that helping is rewarding and will make us feel better. Consistent with this "negative state relief" hypothesis, Cialdini et al. found that people who felt bad because they had accidentally harmed someone (or had seen another person harm someone) and were then given a chance to volunteer to make phone calls for a worthy cause were more likely to volunteer than were people who did not feel bad. But when people who felt bad had their negative-mood state relieved by receiving praise or a dollar before being given the chance to volunteer, they did *not* help more. Presumably, they did not help more because they had already had their negative state relieved by the praise or the dollar, and so did not need the secondary reward that comes from helping.

Not only does helping have reward value for a person in a bad mood; it also seems to be rewarding for persons in a good mood. Indeed, the effect seems to be even stronger when people are in a good mood. Weyant (1978) found that undergraduates who were in a good mood because they had just learned that they did

well on an aptitude test helped more than undergraduates in a neutral mood, regardless of the worthiness of the cause or the cost of helping.

What accounts for this pervasive reward value of helping for people in a good mood? Isen, Shalker, Clark, and Karp (1978) have suggested that being in a good mood may bias our memories about the positive and negative aspects of various activities, including helping. They suggest that when we are in a good mood we are more likely to recall and attend to positive rather than negative aspects of our lives. Applied to helping, this makes us more likely to remember and attend to the positive, rewarding features, and less likely to attend to the negative features, such as the costs involved.

Isen and her associates have used a number of ingenious techniques to enhance people's moods—having them succeed at a task, giving them a cookie while they studied in the library, having them find a dime in the coin return slot of a phone booth. She found that each of these experiences increased the likelihood of a person giving help to good causes (Isen, 1970; Isen & Levin, 1972). Presumably, this was because these experiences placed people in a relatively good mood, and this made them more aware of the positive, rewarding aspects of helping and less aware of the negative aspects.

More generally, why do we feel better when we help? That is, what makes helping a secondary reward? In part, it may be because of the prior association of helping with primary rewards, such as gifts or praise. But it seems that there is more involved than simple association. As we grow up, we develop a sense of obligation; we learn that we *should* help.

Learning That We Should Help: Norms

At the same time that we are learning that helping can bring rewards, we are also learning a number of unwritten rules for appropriate behavior in various social situations. These unwritten rules are called **norms,** and compliance with norms is another important reason why we help. It is easy to see the effect of norms on our behavior. For example, we tend to feel comfortable when we dress and act in accord with the unwritten rules of our social group; we tend to feel uncomfortable when we do not. So most of us dress and act in line with the norms of our particular crowd.

There appear to be a number of norms that apply to helping. They tell us that we should help people in need, at least some people under some circumstances. For example, one norm that has been studied extensively is the **norm of reciprocity.** Gouldner (1960) suggested that this norm tells us both that we should help those who help us and that we should not injure them. He believed that this norm was universal, an important part of the moral code of every culture. He also believed that the pressure on us to comply with the norm of reciprocity depends on the circumstances under which the initial help was given, namely, (a) how badly we needed help, (b) our perception of how much the other person gave us relative to his or her total resources (a millionaire who contributes $1000 to the United Fund may be seen as giving less than a struggling student who gives $20), (c) our perception of the other person's motives for helping (for example, was it a bribe?), and (d) whether the other person helped voluntarily or was pressured into it.

There is much evidence that we are motivated to comply with the norm of reciprocity. For example, Wilke and Lanzetta (1970) found a direct relationship between the amount of help received and the amount of help reciprocated. That is, the more help people were given, the more they gave in return. Consistent with one of the qualifications suggested by Gouldner, Pruitt (1968) demonstrated that the amount of help people reciprocated depended not upon the absolute amount they were given but upon their judgment of how much of the other person's total resources had been given

to them. Moreover, this kind of effect has been found in Japan and Sweden as well as the United States, lending some support to Gouldner's contention that the norm of reciprocity is universal (cf. Gergen, Ellsworth, Maslach, & Seipel, 1975).

The norm of reciprocity seems to underlie the principle of equity, discussed in Chapter 13, for equity requires a balance in interpersonal relationships between what individuals receive relative to what they give. Berscheid and Walster (1967) demonstrated the effect on helping of our desire to maintain a fair exchange in our relations with others. They found that people who had accidentally harmed someone else were motivated to help that person in equal measure to the harm done. In their experiment, women who were members of a church auxiliary group were led to act in such a way that they deprived a fellow group member of two books of green stamps. The harmdoers were then given an opportunity to award a bonus of either three stamps, two books, or five books to the woman they had harmed. These awards corresponded to insufficient compensation, sufficient compensation, and excessive compensation for the harm that had been done. It was found that women who could give compensation equal to the amount of harm done—that is, could give two books—were more likely to compensate the victim than were women who could give insufficient or excessive compensation. Thus, it appears that we may be motivated to help in order to restore an equitable relation not only after someone else has helped us but also after we have hurt someone else.

Moreover, it appears that the norm of reciprocity can motivate us to help when we want some reward in the future. And the help that we give need not be to the same person from whom we hope to receive. Instead, at least some of us may help from a sense of *generalized reciprocity,* a feeling that we should get in equal measure to what we give to the world in general. Some people hold a strong belief in a "just world" (Lerner, 1970)—people get what they deserve in life and deserve what they get (see Social Focus 13.1). Perhaps you are such a person. If you are, think what you might do if someone asked you for help shortly before you were to take a big exam in your psychology class. You might reason that if you did something good by helping, you would deserve something good in return, namely, a good grade on the exam. But if you didn't help, you would deserve a poor grade. This logic may sound purely superstitious, but at least some of us seem to think this way. Zuckerman (1975) found that shortly before the midterm exam in a psychology course, students who scored high on a measure of belief in a just world helped others more than did those who scored low. After the exam was over, however, there were no differences. Zuckerman (1975) concluded that those who had a strong belief in a just

world helped more before the exam to make themselves more deserving of a good grade. These results suggest that the norm of reciprocity has a wide range of applicability, for in this study reciprocity was not operating between two individuals. It was operating between an individual and that individual's perception of the world at large.

A second norm that psychologists have suggested motivates helping is the **norm of social responsibility**. This norm tells us that we should help people in need when they are dependent upon us—that is, when others are not available to help and so the person is counting specifically on us. Although such a norm does seem to exist, it has been surprisingly difficult to demonstrate its effect on helping. In fact, after over a decade or research trying to demonstrate an effect, Berkowitz (1972, pp. 68, 77) concluded, "The findings do not provide any

The norm of social responsibility dictates that we should help those in need.

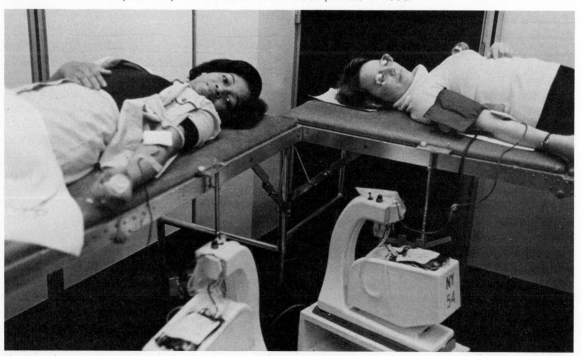

clear-cut support for the normative analysis of help-giving. . . . The potency of the conjectured 'social responsibility norm' was greatly exaggerated."

Why has evidence that the norm of social responsibility leads to helping been so hard to come by? Darley and Latané (1970) have suggested that this norm may be at once too general and too specific to show any clear effect on helping. The norm may be too general in that everyone in our society adheres to it. If this is true, then it cannot account for why one person helps and another does not. On the other hand, the norm may be too specific in that along with it comes a complex pattern of exceptions, situations in which an individual may feel exempt from acting in accordance with the norm. To take an extreme example, if someone is dependent upon you for help with what you believe to be an immoral act, such as performing a robbery, you will probably feel no normative pressure to help. Thus, the norm of social responsibility may be characterized not simply by a rule that says, "If someone is dependent on you for help, then help," but by a more complex rule that says, "If someone is dependent on you for help, then help, *except when* . . . ." And the exceptions may vary for different individuals in the society and for different social situations.

Exceptions to the norm of social responsibility may account for the highly inconsistent effects on helping of such background variables as race and sex. It has sometimes been found that same-race helping is more frequent (Gaertner & Bickman, 1971; Gaertner & Dovidio, 1977; Piliavin, Rodin, & Piliavin, 1969), sometimes that cross-race helping is more frequent (Katz, Cohen, & Glass, 1975), and sometimes that the race of the victim or helper makes no difference (Thayer, 1973; Wispé & Freshley, 1971). Similarly, it has sometimes been found that males help more than females (Schwartz & Clausen, 1970; West, Whitney, & Schnedler, 1975), sometimes that females help more than males (Schopler & Bateson, 1965; Wegner &

Crano, 1975), and sometimes that the sex of the helper makes no difference (Piliavin & Piliavin, 1972; Staub & Baer, 1974), although female *victims* are generally more likely to get help than male victims (Gruder & Cook, 1971). How are we to account for these seemingly contradictory findings? One possibility is that blacks, whites, males, and females may feel exempt from the obligation to help a dependent other in different sets of situations. To provide but one example, black students on a predominantly white campus, acutely aware of their minority status, may feel strong responsibility for helping a fellow black student but very little responsibility for helping a white student (Wegner & Crano, 1975; West, et al., 1975).

Personal norms. Because general social norms like the norm of social responsibility have not been able to predict whether a person will help, Schwartz (1977) has suggested that we should change the focus of our thinking about norms. Rather than thinking about general social norms, Schwartz suggests that we should think of more specific, personal norms. By personal norms he means internalized rules of conduct that are learned from social interaction, rules that vary between individuals within the same society, and that function to direct behavior in particular situations. Applied to helping, a personal norm involves a sense of obligation to perform a *particular* helping act. For example, people may say, either publicly or to themselves, "I ought to give a pint of blood in the blood drive." Such statements appear to be far more predictive of whether a person will give blood than are statements of agreement with more general social norms like the norm of social responsibility. And such specific statements are particularly powerful predictors when one takes account of extenuating circumstances—for example, whether an individual was in town during the blood drive, had no major scheduling conflicts, and was physically fit to give blood (Zuckerman & Reis, 1978). Of course, at this level of specificity, it is not entirely clear whether the statements reflect a sense of personal obligation stemming from internalization of a rule of conduct—a personal norm—or simply an intention to act in a particular way.

Learning to Reward Ourselves for Helping: Self-reward

If we internalize a value that tells us that helping is a good and desirable behavior, we can **self-reward** (Bandura, 1977) for helping. The self-reward takes the form of seeing ourselves as good, kind, helpful people. Quite independent of direct reward, social approval, or even secondary reward, the ability to pat ourselves on the back and feel good about the kind of people we are can be an important source of motivation to help. In fact, it often seems that it is important *not* to have any direct reward, social approval, or secondary reward, if we are to self-reward our helpfulness. For example, the popular practice of making anonymous contributions to charities would seem to reflect, in part, a desire to reassure ourselves that we acted from no ulterior motives, but simply because we really are good, kind, helpful people.

The process of self-rewarding our own helpfulness is rather subtle and complex, so we would expect it to appear relatively late in a child's development. Consistent with this expectation, there is some evidence that self-reward is not an important factor in motivating helping before early adolescence. In one study, Cialdini and Kenrick (1976) found that high school students made larger anonymous contributions when they were in a depressed mood than when they were in a neutral mood, while grade school children made smaller contributions when they were in a depressed mood. Cialdini and Kenrick suggested that this was because the high school students knew that they could self-reward for helping and so improve their mood, but helping was not yet self-rewarding for the grade schoolers.

Learning to Be a Good Person: Personality Differences

Our consideration of the ways we are taught to help has been progressing along a continuum from outside the individual to inside. We began with processes like modeling and direct material rewards, processes that do not assume that the person has an internalized desire to help, only that helping is one way to reach other desired goals. At that end of the continuum, helping is under the control of forces outside the individual. But we have considered increasingly internalized reasons for helping—because helping becomes a secondary reward, because we are responding to the sense of social or personal obligation embodied in norms, and because it is self-rewarding to see ourselves as good, kind, helpful people. We now arrive at the inside end of the continuum. As the desire to be helpful becomes more internalized and more pervasive, one might expect it to be reflected in the personality structure of the individual. Helpfulness, morality, and goodness could become stable personality characteristics. Viewed from this perspective, if some people help while others do not, it is because some have more of these personality characteristics than others.

Explaining why some people help and others do not in terms of stable personality differences is appealing in its simplicity. It implies that there are good, moral, helpful people who help, and there are bad, less moral, less helpful people who do not. All we need to do is measure this personality variable and we will be able to predict how helpful different people will be. Unfortunately, it has not proven this simple. Many researchers have tried to identify some personality variable that might be associated with a stable and general desire to be helpful, but their success has been very limited. To list only a sample of the variables considered, researchers have considered Machiavellianism, authoritarianism, religious orientation, social desirability, alienation, autonomy, deference, submissiveness, trustworthiness, independence, and political liberalism. None of these variables, by itself, has proven to be a consistent predictor of helping behavior. This has led some researchers to turn to composite measures, which seem to be better predictors. For example, Staub (1974) found that individuals' scores on a composite index of prosocial orientation (combining measures of feelings of personal responsibility, social responsibility, moral reasoning, prosocial values, and low Machiavellianism) were positively related to several different types of helping response.

In sum, the empirical evidence is inconsistent. Occasionally, a relationship between personality and helping is found; more often, it is not. Because of this inconsistency, a divergence of opinion exists about whether personality differences are important for an explanation of why we help.

Some researchers emphasize the failures to find personality differences between people who help and people who do not. For example, Rosenhan, Moore, and Underwood (1976) state: "An analysis of the literature with a view to determining whether morality is more strongly influenced by personality (i.e., beliefs, values, attitudes, and dispositions) or situations leads us to conclude that the latter are far more important" (p. 241).

Other researchers emphasize the successes, claiming that an "altruistic" personality type has been identified. In general, these researchers point to composite personality indexes based on a number of personality measures. Rushton (1980), for example, concluded that a classic study of generosity and helpfulness in children, conducted in the 1920s by Hartshorne and May, provided evidence for consistent differences among children in their helpfulness across a range of situations. And Staub (1974) claimed that his general prosocial orientation index related to consistent differences in helpfulness.

Given this divergence of opinion, where do we stand? At this point, we believe that the claim that an altruistic, prosocial personality dimension has been discovered is premature. Although there is some encouraging evidence that a composite index of personality measures may predict individual differences in helping, the evidence is still spotty and inconsistent.

Rather than seeking to uncover a uniquely altruistic personality dimension, some researchers have turned their attention to the way that personality differences that are not explicitly moral in character might affect helping. For example, Wilson (1976) studied the effect on helping of the desire to seek esteem as opposed to seeking personal safety. Esteem-oriented individuals have been found to feel more confident and competent and to rely less on cues from other people when deciding what to do. Safety-oriented individuals, on the other hand, are more anxious and insecure; they frequently look to others for cues when deciding how to act. Wilson reasoned that if highly esteem-oriented individuals witnessed an emergency (hearing an explosion in a room where they knew another person was working), they would be likely to rush to the person's aid regardless of what other witnesses did. But highly safety-oriented individuals were expected to model the behavior of the other witnesses: if the others helped, they would help; if the others did not respond, they would not respond. Wilson found precisely this pattern of results.

In all, we have considered five different forms of learning that lead us to help: modeling, rewards, norms, self-reward, and personality differences. To say that we help because we are taught to is to say, in essence, that we help because it pays to help. Whether the anticipated rewards are obvious, such as money or a hug, or subtle, such as the quiet satisfaction of knowing that we have done something really nice, the assumption is that we help because we perceive the rewards for helping to be greater than the rewards for not helping. As indicated by the empirical evidence reviewed, anticipated reward, whether obvious or subtle, is indeed an important factor in why we help. Some recent research, however, suggests that it is not the only factor; our emotional response when we see someone else suffering is also important.

HELPING BECAUSE OF OUR EMOTIONAL REACTIONS TO THE NEEDS OF OTHERS

Emotional response to the needs of others may not have been on your list of reasons, but there is social-psychological research suggesting that your emotional response may play an important role in determining whether you help. To appreciate the role of emotional response, think about your reaction to one of the need situations described at the beginning of this chapter: you unexpectedly come upon the scene of an auto accident and find a young woman lying unconscious, bleeding, and bruised, with her leg twisted at a grotesque angle. If you are like most people, you will experience strong emotions on witnessing such a scene. Moreover, the emotions you experience will be of two qualitatively distinct types. First, you are likely to experience a substantial degree of *personal distress*, including feeling alarmed, disturbed, upset, and troubled. Perhaps the best way to summarize this cluster of emotions is to say that you feel a sense of horror and, perhaps, "yuk!"

But your emotional response is likely to go

Our emotional response to the plight of others can stimulate helping behavior.

beyond these feelings of personal distress. As you identify with and feel sorry for the young woman, you are likely to experience a second set of emotions, **empathic concern,** including feeling sympathetic, tender, softhearted, warm, and compassionate toward her. Perhaps the best way to summarize this cluster of emotions is to say that you feel sorry for her. While these two sets of emotions often occur together, there is mounting evidence that they are experienced as qualitatively distinct (cf. Batson & Coke, 1981). Moreover, there is also mounting evidence that each can motivate us to help a person in need, but for very different reasons.

Reactions of Personal Distress

Emotions comprising the cluster called personal distress are unpleasant. Typically, when we experience them, we are motivated to act to reduce them. When the situation involves seeing or knowing that someone is suffering—whether it be the young auto-accident victim, starving refugees, or poor migrant workers—there are two ways we can remove our distress. We can help, or we can escape from the situation. Helping can relieve our distress by eliminating the person's suffering, the cause of our distress. Escaping—whether by running from the scene of the accident, by turning the page of the newspaper, or by switching to another TV channel—does not eliminate the person's suffering, but it can eliminate our contact with it. Escaping may not do the person in need any good, but it may be effective in relieving our distress.

Piliavin and Piliavin (1973) have suggested that when we experience distress as a result of seeing someone else in need, our decision whether to eliminate the distress by helping or by escaping will depend on how costly it is to help and how costly it is to escape. Think first about the cost of helping. Helping the young auto-accident victim by calling an ambulance

from a nearby farmhouse would not be very costly. But if the nearest farmhouse were several miles away, the cost of helping would be higher. And think how costly it would be to try to help the starving refugees. To eliminate their suffering effectively would require millions of dollars and thousands of hours.

Now think about the cost of escaping. It would be relatively low when you are reading a newspaper article about the refugees or watching a TV special on migrant workers. All you have to do is turn the page, switch channels, or go do something else. But in the case of the accident victim, the cost of escaping would be high, for you would probably anticipate feeling considerable guilt if you just ran away. And the cost would become even higher if, for example, you recognized the young woman as a teller at your bank, for you would know that seeing her at the bank (or worse, *not* seeing her) would remind you of your failure to help. And what if she opened her eyes, turned, and recognized you? The cost of escaping without helping would escalate immensely; now you could anticipate social censure as well as guilt.

Cost of helping. Consistent with the Piliavins' reasoning, a number of studies have found that people are more likely to help when the cost of helping is low rather than high. For example, Wagner and Wheeler (1969) found that Navy enlisted men were more likely to donate to a worthy cause when the donations were to be deducted from their paychecks at the low rate of $1 a month than when the donations were to be deducted all at once. Midlarsky and Midlarsky (1973) found that male undergraduates who received painful electric shocks when they helped another student with a manual-dexterity task helped less than students who received less intense shocks. Piliavin and her associates found that people were less likely to help a person who collapsed on a subway if that person bled or had a port-wine birthmark on his face (Piliavin, Piliavin, & Rodin, 1975; Piliavin & Piliavin, 1972). These researchers reasoned that it was more costly to help a person who was bleeding or had a stigma.

Cost of escaping. Other studies have found that individuals experiencing a relatively high degree of personal distress are more likely to help when the costs of escaping without helping are relatively high. For example, Batson, Duncan, Ackerman, Buckley, and Birch (1981) reported two experiments based on one of the need situations described at the beginning of the chapter. In each experiment, female undergraduates observed what they thought was another female student, Elaine (actually a confederate of the experimenters), performing a learning task under aversive conditions. The aversive conditions were created by giving Elaine mild electric shocks at random intervals while she was performing the learning task. (In fact, Elaine received no shocks; she only acted as if she did.) Elaine's reactions suggested that she found the shocks extremely uncomfortable. After watching Elaine react to the shocks on the initial trials, the young women participating in the experiments were given an unexpected opportunity to trade places with Elaine, taking the shocks in her stead.

Try to imagine how you would respond if you were faced with this opportunity. The shocks are clearly uncomfortable for Elaine, but she says that if you don't wish to trade places she intends to continue with the remaining trials because she doesn't want to ruin the experiment. At the same time, you probably do not relish the thought of taking shocks yourself. You will likely experience considerable personal distress. What would you do?

If you are like the young women who participated in these experiments, the cost of escaping will have a powerful effect on what you do. In each experiment the young women were far more likely to agree to trade places with Elaine when they thought that if they did not trade, they would have to continue observing her take the shocks (difficult escape) than when they thought that they would not (easy escape).

There seems, then, to be considerable support for the Piliavins' contention that when we feel personal distress as a result of seeing someone suffering, our choice to eliminate the distress by helping or escaping depends on the relative costs associated with these responses. When the costs of helping are low and the costs of escaping are high, we are likely to try to help. But when the costs of helping are high and the costs of escaping are low, we are likely to try to escape.

Reactions of Empathic Concern

While feelings of personal distress lead to motivation either to help or to escape, depending on which response is less costly, feelings of empathic concern seem to produce motivation directed more exclusively toward helping. This is because the emotion of empathic concern is not focused on our own distress; it is focused on the distress of the person in need. And to the degree that we are concerned about that person's distress, only knowing that he or she is no longer suffering will eliminate that concern. Escaping may reduce our personal distress, but it is not an effective means of reducing empathic concern; only helping, or knowing that someone else has helped, will suffice. This suggests that the only cost variable relevant for the empathically concerned individual who is deciding whether to help is the cost of helping. If helping is extremely costly, other considerations may override the motivation to help. But if the cost of helping is not too high, the empathically concerned individual should be motivated to help, regardless of whether it is easy or difficult to escape without helping.

Consistent with this reasoning, several studies show that when bystanders experience a relatively high degree of empathic concern for a person in need, they are motivated to help. Moreover, they are motivated to help regardless of whether the costs of escaping are high or low.

Empathic concern motivates helping. Krebs (1975) created an elaborate experimental situation to determine whether feeling empathy for a person in need can motivate helping. In his experiment male college students served as observers, watching a young man play a roulette game. When the ball landed on an even number the young man won money; when it landed on an odd number, he received an electric shock. After the series of roulette trials was over, the experimenter announced that there would be a final "bonus" trial. On this trial the magnitude of the reward or punishment that the young man would receive was not to be determined by chance as it had been on the previous trials; this time it was to be determined by another person, the observer. The observer could select any one of 21 payoff levels, ranging from one highly beneficial to the young man—a maximum reward of $2 if the ball landed on an even number and an imperceptible shock if it landed on an odd number—to one that was harmful to him—no reward if the ball landed on an even number and a severe shock if it landed on an odd number. But benefiting the young man was not without its cost, for whatever reward the observer selected to be given to the young man would be taken away from money that had previously been given to the observer, and any shock withheld from the young man would be given to the observer. Thus, the observer could help the young man only by incurring costs himself. The observers who were most ready to help under these circumstances were those who displayed the strongest empathic response to watching the young man. They reported identifying more strongly with him and feeling more concern for him. Moreover, they showed the strongest physiological reaction to watching him receive shocks on the earlier trials.

Recent studies (Coke, Batson, & McDavis, 1978) have similarly demonstrated a correlation between empathy and helping. In one study, students listened to a tape of a graduate student in education describing her need for undergraduates to volunteer to participate in her master's thesis research. While the undergraduates listened to the tape, a GSR (galvanic skin response) monitor in front of them registered their supposed degree of emotional arousal as a result of hearing the broadcast. For some, the needle on the monitor rose, indicating that they were highly aroused by the broadcast; for others, the needle remained fairly steady, indicating low arousal. After listening, the undergraduates were asked to report their emotional reactions to the broadcast; then each was given an unexpected opportunity to volunteer to help the graduate student by participating in her research. Those led to believe that they were emotionally aroused by listening to the broadcast reported feeling more empathic concern but not more personal distress as a result of hearing about the graduate student's need, and feeling empathic concern correlated positively with helping.

Empathic concern motivates helping even when the cost of escaping is low. Evidence that feeling empathic concern leads to motivation to help when escape is easy, as well as when it is difficult, comes from the two experiments by Batson et al. (1981), in which female undergraduates were unexpectedly given a chance to trade places with Elaine, taking shocks in her stead. As we reported earlier, those young women who thought that they would have to continue observing Elaine take the shocks were far more likely to agree to take the shocks themselves than were those who thought that they would not have to observe any more. There was, however, another set of conditions in each experiment that we did not report earlier. Some of the undergraduates were led to experience a relatively high degree of empathic concern when observing Elaine. In each experiment these young women were highly likely to agree to take the shocks for Elaine. Moreover, they were as likely to agree when they thought that they would not have to observe her take any more shocks (easy escape) as when they thought that they would (difficult escape).

Overall, the research reviewed in this section provides rather strong evidence for two conclusions. First, feelings of personal distress caused by seeing someone in need motivate helping only when helping is the easiest way to reduce this distress—that is, when it is difficult to escape from exposure to the other's suffering without helping. Second, feelings of empathic concern motivate helping that is not directed toward the goal of reducing the helper's own distress, but toward reducing the distress of the person in need. This different goal is reflected in the fact that empathy leads to helping even when it is easy to escape continued exposure to the other's need without helping.

These two conclusions suggest that only if we are able to get beyond the horror and upset caused by, for example, reading about the starving refugees or watching a TV special on migrant workers, and also begin to feel some

empathic concern for these people, are we likely to be motivated to try to relieve their plight. If all we feel is personal distress, our goal will be to reduce our distress rather than theirs. And by far the easiest way to reduce any personal distress caused by hearing of their suffering is to turn the page or switch channels.

Empathic Motivation for Helping: Could It Be Altruistic?

Because the motivation to help arising from feeling empathic concern seems to be directed toward the goal of reducing another's distress rather than just reducing one's own distress, a number of researchers have suggested that this motivation may be truly altruistic (see, for example, Aronfreed, 1970; Batson & Coke, 1981; Krebs, 1975). Certainly, it seems to fit the dictionary definition of **altruism:** "Unselfish concern for the welfare of others" (Webster's).

If it is altruistic, then the motivation arising from empathy would have important implications for our conception of human nature. Most major psychological theories assume that all human motivation is, at heart, *egoistic,* that everything we do is ultimately directed toward the goal of reducing our own distress or increasing our own welfare. The motivation to help others arising from anticipated rewards or from reactions of personal distress is quite compatible with this egoistic assumption, for even though we are benefiting someone other than ourselves, we are doing it because it ultimately benefits us—we anticipate rewards of money, praise, or a good feeling, or anticipate reduction of an unpleasant and distressing emotional state.

But the motivation to help resulting from feeling empathic concern is not nearly so compatible with the egoistic assumption; it seems to involve seeking to benefit another without regard for the benefit that may ultimately come our way. This motivation suggests that at least

---

TABLE 12.1
Proportion of Subjects Agreeing to Exchange Places with Elaine, A Victim of Shocks

Difficulty of Escaping	SUBJECT'S DOMINANT RESPONSE TO ELAINE'S DISTRESS	
	Personal Distress	Empathetic Concern for Elaine
Easy	.33	.83
Difficult	.75	.58

Note: By trading roles with Elaine, subjects could take shocks in her place and thereby help her. Subjects experiencing concern for Elaine were likely to help Elaine whether or not they could escape from seeing her punished. Subjects experiencing personal distress at seeing Elaine shocked were more likely to help if it was difficult to escape from seeing her shocked. (Table adapted from Batson et al., 1981)

some people, under some circumstances, and to some degree, may transcend egoistic self-concern and show altruistic concern for others. They may do this when and to the degree that seeing the other in need evokes feelings of empathic concern. Even with these qualifiers, this possibility implies a far more optimistic picture of human nature than psychologists have typically painted.

PROCESSES THAT UNDERMINE THE MOTIVATION TO HELP

We have found that there are a number of powerful social-psychological processes that motivate us to help. Still, as we are all too aware, there are many times when we do not help. Why? At least part of the answer lies in the fact that there are also powerful processes that discourage us from helping. It is time to turn our attention to these. Look back at your list of reasons why you do not help, and compare them with the reasons we will discuss.

To organize the social-psychological research let us distinguish between two different types of inhibiting factors. First, there are processes that can undermine or restrict the power of the social-psychological processes motivating us to help. Among these are (1) limitations on the rewards and norms for helping, due to conflicting rewards and norms; (2) limitations on self-reward, due to the presence of other rewards; (3) limitations on our emotional reaction of personal distress, due to our adaptation to media presentations of suffering and our tendency to derogate those in need; and (4) limitations on our empathic concern, due to our perception of the needy as "them," our failure to pay attention to their needs, or our failure to imagine how they feel.

Second, there are situational constraints that may prevent us from acting, even when we are motivated to help. These include (1) deciding that no real need exists, since no one

else is responding; (2) deciding that someone else should help; (3) deciding that there is really nothing we can do; (4) deciding that the needy do not deserve our help; and (5) deciding that receiving help would make those in need feel worse, not better.

Limitations on the Rewards and Norms for Helping

Conflicting rewards. While we are learning that helping is rewarding, we are also learning that it can be costly. You may lightly say, "Sure" to a friend's request to help him move across town. But then you find that it takes the whole weekend. Afterwards, you may feel that it just wasn't worth it. The next time someone asks for such help, you will probably be much more reluctant to say yes. And the lesson is likely to generalize to other situations. You will count the costs of helping more carefully, and the more costly you perceive it to be, the more rewarding *not* helping becomes.

Situations in which the rewards for not helping outweigh the rewards for helping are easy to find. Imagine that you are planning to spend your last $5 on a movie you have been looking forward to seeing. You are walking out the door on the way to the movie, when someone arrives soliciting contributions for the United Fund. Under these circumstances, the rewards of not helping may seem far greater than those of helping. Similarly, if you are given the chance to help Elaine by taking shocks in her stead, the costs associated with helping make not helping look pretty attractive. The shocks may not hurt you as much as they are hurting her, but they will hurt nonetheless.

It seems that if we are to employ learning principles, we cannot simply focus upon the rewards associated with helping. Instead, we must employ a more complex cost-benefit analysis, thinking in terms of *relative reward.* We must ask whether the anticipated benefits of helping are greater than the anticipated costs. A number of social psychologists have emphasized the importance of this kind of cost-benefit analysis for our understanding of helping (for example, Latané & Darley, 1970; Piliavin & Piliavin, 1973). And it will probably come as no surprise to you that the empirical evidence documents the importance of a cost-benefit analysis. For example, Schaps (1972) found that shoe salesmen who were paid on the basis of the number of pairs of shoes they sold were more willing to take the time to help a choosy customer when there were no other prospective customers waiting in the store. Presumably, this was because the potential reward of selling this customer a pair of shoes outweighed the costs only when the costs did not include the loss of other sales.

The costs need not be monetary. Darley and Batson (1973) found that seminary students who were in a hurry to get to an appointment were far less likely to stop and offer aid to a young man slumped in an alley, coughing and groaning, than were seminarians not in a hurry. Some of the seminarians actually stepped over the young man as they hurried on their way! For them, the relative reward of helping was apparently outweighed by the relative reward of being punctual for their appointment.

Another nonmonetary cost of helping is the feeling that we have been pressured into it. This cost can be explained in terms of Brehm's (1966) theory of psychological reactance. According to this theory, reactance is aroused when our freedom to engage in some behavior is threatened. When this happens, we are motivated to reestablish the threatened freedom. Being pressured to help threatens our freedom not to help, causing reactance and reducing the relative reward for helping.

The cost involved in being pressured to help is nicely illustrated in an experiment by Brehm and Cole (1966). Participants were given an opportunity to help a young man, whom they thought to be another research participant, stack some papers. Some of the students felt pressure to help, because the young man had previously given them a coke. Others had not been given a coke. Brehm and Cole found that the students placed in the position of feeling pressure to reciprocate the young man's favor were less willing to help him stack papers. Presumably, this was because they were motivated to reestablish their freedom not to help. Pressure to help can also come from knowing that someone is depending on you for help. And once again, there is evidence that such pressure increases the costs of helping by producing reactance (Jones, 1970).

Conflicting norms. Just as there are rewards for not helping that oppose the rewards for helping, Darley and Latané (1970) suggest that there are norms for not helping that oppose the norms for helping. We may be taught, "Help those in need," but at the same time we are taught, "Mind your own business." Which norm are we to follow? If we follow the former we may help, but if we follow the latter we probably will not.

The power of norms to inhibit helping is clearly demonstrated in an experiment by Staub (1971), in which it was found that seventh-grade children were far less likely to help when helping meant breaking a rule set by an adult. The children were left alone in a room to draw a picture. Some were told that they should not go into the adjoining room where another child was working (prohibition group); others were told that they could go in to get more drawing pencils if they needed them (permission group). Shortly after they were left alone, the children heard a crash and cries of pain; apparently the other child had fallen from a ladder and hurt herself. Those children told that they should not go into the other room were much less likely to go to the other child's aid than those who had been given permission to go in. Especially interesting was the response of one girl in the permission group. Shortly after she heard the crash and the cries of pain, she broke the points on both of her drawing pencils in quick, deliberate movements. Then she ran into the other room.

Undermining Self-Reward with Other Rewards

Earlier, we found that self-reward is an important reason for helping, especially for adults. But if we are to pat ourselves on the back for helping, we must be assured that our helpfulness was motivated by our internal desire to help and not by external pressures such as material or social rewards. If we helped because of external pressure, then we cannot take the credit.

Consistent with this reasoning, it has been found that people who help under external pressure, whether from money, from the norm of reciprocity, or from highly helpful models, are likely to see themselves as less caring, helpful people than are people who help in the absence of these external pressures (Batson, Coke, Jasnoski, & Hanson, 1978; Thomas & Batson, 1981; Thomas, Batson, & Coke, 1981). This undermining of self-perceived helpfulness occurs even though those who help under external pressure would have helped even without that pressure.

These results suggest that we are caught between a rock and a hard place. One important source of motivation to help, the external reward that comes from payment for helping or from doing what we are expected to do, actually undermines a second important source of motivation to help, the self-reward that comes from seeing ourselves as good, kind, helpful people. Consider the long-term consequences of this. As self-reward is undermined, additional external pressure will probably be necessary to get us to help. But this additional external pressure should further erode the chances for self-reward. Over time, the result may be a spiral toward a more and more cynical self-concept, in which personal kindness plays an increasingly minor role.

It is worth noting that studying social psychology may actually contribute to this process, for social psychology teaches us how much our behavior is shaped by external social pressures rather than by our personal characteristics. If who we are and what we do is largely a product of our past and present social environment, how much credit can we take for anything good we may do? It is easy to become very cynical about our own motives.

As we grow more cynical about our motivation, we may actually turn from self-reward to self-punishment for our helping. Instead of patting ourselves on the back for being good and kind, we may begin to kick ourselves for not being able to say no. Think of the way you feel after a child's pleading eyes have gotten you to contribute to a charity about which you know and care very little. Do you feel good and helpful? If you are like us, you feel just the opposite. Rather than displaying your compassion, you feel that you have displayed a very different personality characteristic—compliance. And there is empirical evidence that if you attribute your helping to compliance rather than compassion, you will be less likely to help in the future (Batson, Harris, McCaul, Davis, & Schmidt, 1979).

Limitations on Our Emotional Reaction of Personal Distress

The second basic reason for helping is our emotional reaction to seeing someone else in need. We noted that there are two qualitatively different types of emotional reaction to another person's suffering—feelings of personal distress and feelings of empathic concern. Both seem to motivate helping. Personal distress motivates helping behavior only when the costs of escaping without helping are relatively high. Empathic concern induces helping regardless of whether the costs of escaping are high or low. But each of these reactions can be undermined. Think first of factors that could limit our reaction of personal distress.

Adaptation to others' suffering: A possible consequence of TV news. In the 1960s television newscasting came of age; cameras were taken out of the studios and into the world. The result was that the horror of natural disasters, assassinations, wars, and poverty came into our living rooms. We watched on live television as Jack Ruby shot Lee Harvey Oswald, the assassin of John Kennedy. We saw a South Vietnamese officer put a gun to the head of a Viet Cong prisoner and literally blow out his brains. We were taken to My Lai, where American soldiers massacred defenseless Vietnamese women and children. We were taken into the homes of black sharecroppers in South Carolina, to see the hollow stares and protruding stomachs produced by severe malnutrition and poverty. We were taken to Biafra, to Bangladesh, to Watts, and more.

Reaction to these exposures to others' pain, suffering, and even death was often strong. Many people were horrified; cries were raised that something should be done to overcome injustice and to help those in need. Today, the TV cameras continue to bring others' suffering into our living rooms, but the cries that something must be done are less frequent. Doubtless there are many reasons for this, but we suspect that one reason is that more than a decade of graphic news portrayal of the suffering of others has numbed our feelings of horror and distress. The novelty has worn off; we find ourselves watching news reports and documentaries on human suffering with little more reaction than if we were watching a gripping drama. Real tragedies and fictional ones all blend into "programming," something to provide diversion at the end of the day (cf. Withey & Abeles, 1980). If this suspicion is correct,

then an important source of motivation to help, our reaction of personal distress, has been undermined by the media's presentation of human suffering.

Derogation of those in need. A second process may also undermine our feelings of personal distress; we may derogate the victims of suffering. As we noted earlier, many of us seem to believe in a just world (Lerner, 1970), a world in which people get what they deserve and deserve what they get. This belief implies that if we can convince ourselves that someone else's suffering is deserved, then we should be far less likely to be upset by it. Consistent with this reasoning, Lerner and his associates have found that people tend to derogate an innocent victim of misfortune. Female undergraduates rated another female undergraduate as less attractive and less likable when they saw her receive what they thought were painful electric shocks *and* thought that she would not be compensated for her suffering (Lerner, 1970; Lerner & Simmons, 1966). Presumably, when they thought that she would be compensated, a balance of suffering and reward existed that did not threaten their belief in a just world. But when they thought that she was suffering without compensation, and therefore unjustly, they derogated her. If they could see her as a bad person they could accept that she had something bad happen to her and still maintain their belief that the world is just. (See Social Focus 13.1 for a more detailed discussion of this particular experiment.)

The implication of this research for our reactions to seeing others suffer unjustly is clear. Rather than being distressed by it, we may instead derogate them, concluding that they deserve their pain. This process can lead to what William Ryan (1971) has called **blaming the victim.** He suggests that we are likely to react to the victims of unjust discrimination and oppression in our society by unconsciously blaming them: If they have less, they must deserve less; that is, they must be less deserving people. Ryan notes that the prototypical victim blamer is the middle-class person who is fairly well-off financially. By blaming the victims of poverty and oppression, middle-class persons can reconcile their own relative advantage with a belief that the world is just. And then there is no need for them to be distressed by the victims' plight.

Some research suggests that there are limits on the derogation process. Derogation has been found *not* to occur if one helps the victim (Mills & Egger, 1972) or if one feels no personal responsibility for the victim's suffering (Cialdini, Kenrick, & Hoerig, 1976). Moreover, even if derogation occurs, it may not inhibit subsequent helping (Kenrick, Reich, & Cialdini, 1976).

But these findings provide a basis for only minimal reassurance, for two reasons. First, the helping opportunities in these studies involved no cost to the helper. It is possible that if helping is costly, which it usually is, derogation of the victim of injustice will be preferred to helping. Second, at a societal level, it seems likely that the more advantaged do feel some responsibility for the suffering of the less advantaged. If so, they would not be exempt from the need to derogate. Derogation remains, then, a chilling alternative to being distressed by the suffering of others, an alternative that can lead to smug acceptance of the pain of others as perfectly just and right.

Limitations on Our Emotional Reaction of Empathic Concern

The emotional reaction of empathic concern to another's suffering is, apparently, quite fragile. It can be dramatically affected by our relationship to the person in need and by our frame of mind.

Perception of others as "them." There is a powerful tendency for us to divide people into "them" and "us." "Us" includes ourselves and those to whom we see ourselves as similar; "them" includes those we see as dissimilar. There is evidence that we are far more likely to respond with feelings of empathic concern to the distress of similar others than to the distress of dissimilar others. Stotland (1969) found that people were more likely to become physiologically aroused and to report empathic concern when they were watching a similar other undergo a painful experience than when they were watching a dissimilar other. Krebs (1975) also found effects of similarity on empathy; in addition, he found that people were more willing to help a similar victim.

Hornstein (1976) has noted that shared group membership is an important factor in our experience of concern for others. He suggests that common interests lead to the formation of cooperative ties. These "we-group" ties, in turn, lead us to be concerned about the welfare of others in the group. At their base, these ties may have genetic roots in kinship (cf. Wilson, 1975). But Hornstein (1976) suggests that our uniquely human ability for abstract thought enables us to develop much broader social ties. We can use language to generalize a sense of "we-feeling" based on close kinship relations (for example, parent-child, brother-sister) to others who are not our kin. For example, by thinking of them as "brothers," we can cognitively adopt into our family others who are not genetically related to us, even others whom we have never seen before.

Given the limitation of empathic response to those we see as "us" rather than "them," it is easy to see why the terrible suffering of people in foreign countries, especially hostile countries, arouses very little concern. While it may not be an attractive characteristic of human nature, the restriction of our concern to "us" seems firmly ingrained, perhaps even genetic. Still, this does not mean that it cannot be changed. Presumably, that is the hope of those who preach the "brotherhood of man"; they seek to have us think of everyone as "us."

Not attending to the needs of others. In addition to restrictions on empathy arising from a lack of relationship with the other, there are restrictions that can arise from our frame of mind. In order to experience empathic concern for someone in need, a certain chain of thought is necessary. First, we must attend to the other person's situation; then we must think about how he or she feels about that situation. This chain of thought can be broken at either link, and if it is broken, the empathic response will be undermined. Two factors seem especially likely to break the first link—information load and self-focused attention.

A common stereotype of city dwellers labels them as people who are interested only in getting where they need to go and doing what they need to do, without any concern for the needs of the other people they encounter along the way. Perhaps equally common is the stereotype of small-town dwellers as people who are always concerned, perhaps too concerned, about the welfare of people around them. Consistent with these stereotypes, there is evidence that helpfulness is lower in cities than in towns. For example, Korte and Kerr (1975) found that people living in Boston were less likely than residents of several small towns in eastern Massachusetts to assist wrong-number callers, to return money when they had been paid too much, and to return lost postcards. But why does this city-town difference exist?

Milgram (1970) has suggested that the lower rate of helping in cities may be a product of the higher information load there. Complex and diverse urban environments bombard city dwellers with so much information that they experience an **information overload.** To cope, city dwellers must employ strategies to limit the amount of information they take in. One strategy is to make distinctions between high-priority and low-priority information and to attend only to the former. A second strategy is to spend less time attending to each piece of information and, perhaps, to ignore some pieces

altogether. Along with this strategy may go tactics for dampening the intensity of the incoming information. This tactic may be reflected in limiting involvement with at least some other people to sporadic and superficial interactions. One result of each of these strategies is that attention to the needs of others is likely to be diminished.

Consistent with Milgram's analysis, Weiner (1976) created overload by having some individuals attempt to deal with a number of different types of information simultaneously. They were required to perform two tasks at once, one that involved attending to a series of visual stimuli and another that involved attending to a series of auditory stimuli. Not surprisingly, individuals reported feeling that this experience was "hectic," because there were "so many things to attend to at the same time." Other individuals were in a low-information-load condition. They did the two tasks, but only one at a time. Weiner found that when a young woman unexpectedly came into the participant's room and tripped and fell, individuals in the low-information-load condition were more likely to offer her aid.

Also consistent with Milgram's analysis, Korte, Ypma, and Toppen (1975) conducted a series of studies in Holland in which they compared rates of helping in cities and towns. They found that when all differences due to differences in information load were removed, there were no additional city-town differences.

Many of us can probably recall times when we were so wrapped up in our own concerns that we didn't even notice the needs of somebody else, until it was too late. Or perhaps we noticed but did not become concerned. We may have thought, "I have enough problems of my own without worrying about his." This state of thinking primarily about oneself and one's own needs is called **self-focused attention.**

Wicklund (1979) discusses one aspect of self-focused attention, self-awareness. When one is self-aware, one's attention is directed toward self as an object. Self-awareness can be produced by, for example, observing oneself in a mirror or by listening to a tape recording of one's own voice. If you have ever listened to your own recorded voice or watched yourself on television, you probably experienced some discomfort and embarrassment at the thought of the way you come across to others. Few of us meet our own standards, and being self-aware makes the discrepancy between who we are and who we feel we should be especially salient. What are the implications of being self-aware for helping?

Gibbons, Wicklund, and Rosenfield (1980) found that in the absence of salient external pressure to help, people who were self-aware were less helpful than people who were not self-aware. The self-aware individuals seemed to be too wrapped up in themselves and evaluating their own needs and inadequacies to attend to the needs of others. Similarly, Kary-lowski (1979) found that self-aware individuals were less effective at a task that benefited someone else than at a task that benefited themselves. He concluded that the debilitating effect of self-awareness on helping is due "mostly [to] its interference with empathy" (p. 60).

Finally, Thompson, Cowan, and Rosenhan (1980) found that people who had been asked to imagine their own reactions to a friend dying of cancer were less helpful on a subsequent unrelated task than were those who were asked to imagine the reactions of the friend. These researchers interpreted this difference as being a result of self-focused attention, which created self-concern and inhibited attention to the concerns of others.

Empathic set.   Even if we attend to another in distress, we may not experience empathy, because, if we are to experience empathy, we must also think about how that person feels. This is the second link in the chain of thought necessary for empathic emotion. Our cognitive orientation or "set" seems especially important for this link.

It is possible to view another's suffering through different eyes. Sometimes we seem to look with the cold, clinical gaze of an observer; this has been called an *observe set*. At other times, however, we find ourselves imagining how the person who is suffering must feel. This second way of looking has been called an *empathic set.*

Adopting an empathic rather than an observe set is important if we are to experience empathic emotion. In the classic studies reported by Stotland (1969), some individuals were instructed to imagine how a young man felt as they watched him undergo what they thought was a painful experience (diathermy treatment of a relatively high intensity); others were instructed to watch closely, observing his bodily movements. Although both groups watched closely as the young man displayed signs of distress and pain, only those in the former group, those instructed to adopt an empathic set, showed any substantial increase in physiological arousal or in self-reported feelings of empathic concern. Moreover, a subsequent study by Aderman, Brehm, and Katz (1974) showed that individuals who adopted an empathic set did not derogate an innocent victim; only those who adopted an observe set did.

Adopting the role of detached observer, like all of the reasons for not helping we have discussed so far, undermines our *motivation* to help. But, there are even more reasons for not helping. There are also several situational factors that can further inhibit helping.

SITUATIONAL CONSTRAINTS ON HELPING

Many situations, especially emergencies, are unusual, unexpected, and ambiguous events. Are screams in the night a woman being attacked or two lovers having a quarrel? If the former, something should be done. But what? The appropriate response is frequently not clear, and to respond at all may be dangerous. Further, the action of one bystander is often sufficient. One call to the police is as helpful, if not more helpful, than twenty calls. No doubt others also heard the screams, and someone else has probably helped already.

Latané and Darley (1970) have suggested that once we notice a possible need situation, we must make a number of decisions in sequence before we help. First, we must decide that a need exists; then we must decide that it is our personal responsibility to act; and third, we must decide that there is something we can do to help. Only if we decide that there is need, that we are responsible for helping, and that there is something we can do will we try to help. Latané and Darley further propose that the social context can influence this decision sequence at each step.

What's the Problem? Deciding That No Real Need Exists

Because emergencies involve events that are unusual and ambiguous, we turn to others present, seeking cues to help us decide what is happening. No one wishes to appear foolishly excited over an event that may not be an emergency after all, so we react initially with a calm outward demeanor, while looking at others' reactions. But the others are doing the same. No one appears upset; a state of "pluralistic ignorance" develops, in which everyone decides that since no one else is upset, the event must not be an emergency. And no one helps.

As this analysis would predict, Clark and Word (1972) found that helping was more likely when an emergency was not ambiguous. Further, as this analysis also predicts, in ambiguous need situations people are strongly influenced by the reactions of other bystanders.

Latané and Darley (1968) found that students were more likely to respond to smoke pouring into their testing room when they were alone than when they were with two experimental confederates who did not react to the smoke. More importantly, when three naive students were in the room they were again less likely to respond. Apparently, cues from the others led each to interpret the smoke as benign. Extending this process to a helping situation, Latané and Rodin (1969) found that the presence of one or more strangers reduced the likelihood of individuals responding to a crash and cries of pain from a woman in an adjoining room.

Subsequent research has confirmed that it is not the mere presence of another bystander that affects responses; it is the other's cue value. Ross and Braband (1973) found that if the other bystander (a confederate) was blind, his failure to react to odorless smoke did not affect responses. If, however, the emergency was one that a blind person could notice—a woman's scream—then the confederate's failure to respond did decrease responses. Darley, Teger, and Lewis (1973) found that the presence of another person did not reduce response to an emergency if the two people were seated in a face-to-face position. They were as likely to respond as were alone bystanders. If the two people were sitting back-to-back, however, they were less likely to respond. Darley, Teger, and Lewis reasoned that people able to see one another's initial startle responses were led to define the situation as an emergency, while those not able to see this response were not.

Is It My Responsibility? Deciding That Someone Else Should Help

The presence of other bystanders may also affect whether or not we accept personal responsibility for helping. If there is a crowd, each individual may feel less personal obligation to come forward and help. In Darley and

Latané's (1968) terms, <u>responsibility for helping will *diffuse* among all the bystanders present, making it less likely that any one bystander will help.</u> To test this possibility, Darley and Latané (1968) measured whether people helped another research participant (actually a confederate) who was apparently having an epileptic seizure. At the time of the seizure, some participants believed that only they knew it was happening; others believed that they and one other participant knew, and others, that they and four others knew. As expected, the greater the number of bystanders, the less likely participants were to help.

As the principle of **diffusion of responsibility** would suggest, <u>the knowledge that there are other bystanders does *not* reduce helping, if the others cannot help.</u> If, for example, the others are not in the same building as the person in need, but we are, then we will still shoulder the full responsibility for helping (Bickman, 1972).

What Can I Do? Deciding That You Lack the Skill to Help

A major factor affecting the decision about whether we can help is <u>our sense of competence.</u> In some situations we may feel that we lack the necessary skill to help; we may not have the strength to swim out and save someone caught in a strong undertow, or we may not know what to do if someone has an epileptic seizure. In other situations we may feel only relatively incompetent; we may feel that we could do something, but that others present could do it better. For example, we are likely to defer to the medically trained if someone seems sick (Piliavin, Piliavin, & Rodin, 1975; Schwartz & Clausen, 1970). Finally, at times we may feel a general sense of incompetence, which can affect our readiness to attempt any difficult task, including helping. The most obvious source of a general sense of incompetence is having just failed at some task, and

predictably, people who have just failed are less likely to try to help someone in need (Isen, 1970).

In addition to these three decisions outlined by Latané and Darley (1970)—whether a need exists, whether it is our responsibility to help, and whether we can help—two other decisions seem important when we are trying to make up our minds whether to help. And for each, as for the previous three, the social context can powerfully influence the outcome.

Whose Fault? Deciding the Needy Do Not Deserve Help

We are not likely to try to help people in need if we do not feel that they deserve it. A major factor in deciding whether people deserve help is whether they are innocent victims or have brought their troubles on themselves. Think, for example, how it might affect your reaction if you learned that a friend who was upset over receiving a low grade on a test had, instead of studying, decided to go to a party the night before the test. You would probably not be very sympathetic. And what if he had done this before, and you had reason to believe that he purposely did poorly just so that others would feel sorry for him? If your reactions are anything like those of participants in a study by Schopler and Matthews (1965), who were faced with a request for help from a person who brought his need on himself, you would be very unlikely to help.

Think now about the combined effect of this tendency to help only innocent victims who have not brought their troubles on themselves and the tendency, discussed earlier, to derogate an innocent victim in order to maintain our belief in a just world. The combined effect suggests that a needy person is in a no-win situation. Derogation should lead us to conclude that innocent victims are not innocent after all, that they deserve their fate. And if this is true, they do not deserve our help.

Do They Want It? Deciding That Accepting Help Would Make Those in Need Feel Worse

Even if we overcome the hurdle of deciding that the needy deserve our help, another hurdle looms ahead. Not only may helping be costly to us, it may also be costly to the person we help. We seem to be at least implicitly aware of this possibility when we explain, "I would have helped, but I was afraid he would get mad if I tried."

Why should being given help make a person angry? An answer becomes clear when we consider helping in the context of Homans' (1961) theory of *social exchange*. Homans suggests that, one way or another, social relationships tend to remain balanced in terms of what the various parties give and get. If help recipients cannot give helpers something tangible in return such as payment, or help in some other area, then they must complete the social exchange by giving up status relative to the help giver. Consistent with this reasoning, Greenberg and Shapiro (1971) found that people were not very willing to request or accept a favor when they anticipated not being able to repay it. And Fisher and Nadler (1974) found that receiving help that could not be repaid lowered the recipient's self-esteem. Ironically, self-esteem was especially likely to be lowered for those whom we are more likely to help, similar others. Apparently, this was because recipients are especially likely to compare themselves with similar others, making the loss of status and esteem especially pronounced.

Fortunately, there may be limits on the costs to the help recipient, for it appears that not all of our social relationships are based on the principle of social exchange. Clark and Mills (1979) suggest that our relationships with close friends and family are communal and they provide some evidence that in communal relationships, exchange principles do not apply. Communal relationships seem, instead, to be based on the sense of we-feeling that we found important as a prerequisite for experiencing empathic concern. Helping in these relationships may be motivated by empathy rather than by a careful quid-pro-quo exchange. If so, then in communal relationships there should be less need to refrain from helping out of concern for the costs to the recipient. Of course, we encounter many people in need with whom we do not have a communal relationship.

IMPLICATIONS FOR OUR RESPONSE TO OTHERS' NEEDS

Throughout this chapter our goal has been to try to gain some understanding of why we do and do not respond to the needs of others. The needs are there; each of the social issues considered in this book documents this; so does our daily experience. And although we sometimes try to help those in need, often we do not. If we can understand why we do and do not help, then we may be able to gain better control over our own behavior, bringing it more in line with our beliefs and values.

How have we done in reaching our goal of understanding why we do and do not help? One way to answer this question is to compare the social-psychological understanding we have presented with the reasons you jotted down at the beginning of the chapter. If you are like most students whom we have asked to do this, there will be considerable overlap between the reasons that you listed and the reasons social psychologists have proposed. But there will be some surprises as well. For example, it is common to assume that one reason we help is out of compliance with a social norm that tells us to help, usually called the norm of social responsibility. But, as we found, there is little evidence that this is true. It is also common to assume that helpfulness is a personality dimension, that there are good, kind people who help and bad, insensitive people who do not. Again, we found only limited evidence that this is true.

In addition to these surprises, social-psychological theory and research may have suggested some reasons for helping that you had not considered—for example, self-reward and the emotional responses of personal distress and empathic concern. The theory and research may also have suggested a number of reasons for not helping that you had not considered—the desire to preserve a sense of freedom to choose not to help, derogation of innocent victims of injustice in order to maintain a belief in a just world, the undermining of intrinsic self-rewards with external rewards, limitations on our emotional response to seeing others in need, and situational factors that may lead us to decide either that no need exists (pluralistic ignorance) or that if it does we are not the one responsible for helping (diffusion of responsibility).

But is knowing all of this helpful? That depends on what you do with the information. If it is just something that you retain for the next exam in social psychology, it is not very helpful. If, on the other hand, you begin to look at the need situations you encounter in the light of this information—both the broad social issues discussed in this book and the more individual needs of the people around you—then it may be helpful. It may help you understand why some causes and issues grab you while others do not, why sometimes you can really get involved in and concerned about another person's problems while at other times you cannot, and so on. And understanding some of the psychological factors that affect your responses may enable you to bring your responses more in line with what you feel you should do. There is even some empirical support for this optimistic possibility. Beaman, Barnes, Klentz, and McQuirk (1978) found that learning about some of the situational factors that discourage helping led students to be more responsive to a person in possible need. We hope it will do the same for you.

But at least as important as the prospect of enabling you to be more responsive to the needs of others, we hope that the information we have presented may help you feel better about your helping. If the present analysis suggests anything, it is that the pressures *not* to help are strong and many. When in the face of these pressures we take the time and trouble to reach out and help someone in need, we richly deserve the esteem of our peers, as well as that self-rewarding pat on the back. After all, credit where credit is due.

SUMMARY

In this chapter we asked "Why do and don't people help?" We proposed two broad answers to the question of why we *do* help: because we have been taught to and because our emotional reactions to seeing others in need motivate us to help.

The process of being taught to help takes a variety of forms.

1. Parents, teachers, and others teach us to help by modeling; we learn that helping is appropriate and desirable behavior by seeing them help.
2. We are taught to help by being rewarded when we help. Sometimes these rewards are material; more often they are social—a hug, an approving smile, or praise. In fact, if helping is consistently rewarded, it can become a secondary reward. When this occurs, we feel better when we help, even if no other rewards follow.
3. We are also taught to help as we learn the norms of our society, because certain norms, such as the norm of reciprocity, specify that we **should** help at least some people under some circumstances. Compliance with these norms, especially when the norms are internalized and felt as personal moral obligations, is another important

source of secondary reward. We feel good when we act in accord with normative expectations and bad when we do not.

4. In addition to internalizing specific norms, we may internalize helpfulness as a general value. When this occurs, we cán self-reward for helping. Even when no one else knows what we did, we can pat ourselves on the back for being good, kind, thoughtful people. Self-reward seems to be an extremely important reason for helping among adults.

5. As helpfulness becomes internalized as a personal value, it might be expected that it would find expression as a stable personality dimension. While this certainly remains a possibility, it is yet to be clearly demonstrated.

The second broad answer to why we help is that our emotional reactions to seeing others in need motivates us to help. We considered two qualitatively different emotional reactions, personal distress and empathic concern. The former involves feeling alarmed, disturbed, upset, and troubled. The latter involves feeling sympathetic, tender, softhearted, warm, and compassionate. We found that a reaction of personal distress seems to evoke motivation directed toward reducing our own distress; this motivation leads to helping only when helping is the easiest way to reduce the distress. In contrast, a reaction of empathic concern seems to evoke motivation directed toward reducing the distress of the person in need; this motivation leads to helping even when it would be easy to escape from another's suffering without helping.

In discussing this broad reason for helping, we noted that the motivation to help evoked by feeling empathic concern appears to fit the definition of altruistic motivation. If this motivation *is* altruistic, then a change needs to be made in most psychologists' conception of human nature, for most psychologists assume that the motivation for everything we do is ultimately egoistic.

Turning to the issue of why people *don't* help, we considered both situational constraints and factors that undermine our motivation to help. We started by indicating several ways that our motivation to help can be undermined.

First, at the same time we are learning that it pays to help, both materially and socially, we are also learning that it often pays *not* to help. So when we are confronted with someone in need, we calculate the relative reward of helping, using a cost-benefit analysis. If the costs outweigh the benefits, we are less likely to help.

Second, attempting to increase the benefits of helping relative to the costs by increasing external pressures—whether by offering material rewards (money), by presenting highly helpful models, or by intensifying normative pressure—can undermine another important source of motivation, self-reward. If we helped for extrinsic reasons, we can no longer pat ourselves on the back for being good, kind, helpful people.

Third, our emotional reaction to seeing someone else suffer can also be undermined. Continued exposure through the news media to the suffering of others may dull our feelings of shock and personal distress. And instead of feeling outrage when we see others suffer unjustly, we may derogate them in order to reconcile their suffering with our belief that the world is just.

Finally, our reaction of empathic concern can be undermined. We are far less likely to feel empathy for those we see as dissimilar to ourselves, as "them" rather than "us." In addition, an empathic emotional response may be undermined by our failure to attend to the distress of others—either because we have so many other things to attend to (information load) or because we are so wrapped up in ourselves and our own needs (self-focused attention). And even if we notice their distress, an empathic response may be undermined by our failure to adopt a cognitive set that allows us to recognize and appreciate how the others feel.

With regard to situational factors, we must give affirmative answers to five questions if we are to help, but there are situational pressures encouraging us to answer each negatively.

1. **Is there a need?** Need situations are often unusual, unexpected, and ambiguous. To avoid jumping to conclusions in such a situation, we usually try to remain calm, while observing the reactions of others present. They do the same, observing us. As a result, a state of pluralistic ignorance can easily develop, in which we interpret another's calm demeanor as evidence that no real need exists.

2. **Is it my responsibility to help?** If others can help, we are likely to diffuse responsibility to them. They are as responsible for helping as we are, so why don't **they** help?

3. **Can I help?** Even if we decide that a real need exists and that we are responsible for helping alleviate it, we may decide that we lack the means. If the need is too great or we feel that we do not have the needed skill, we can only say, "Sorry."

4. **Do the needy deserve my help?** Even if we can help, we may decide that the needy do not deserve it. Such a conclusion is especially likely when people have brought their troubles on themselves, or when we can convince ourselves that they have.

5. **Do the needy want my help?** Receiving help can be costly, for the recipient may lose self-esteem. Recognizing this, we may decide not to help out of our concern to protect the needy from losing esteem.

When we look at the overall picture, obviously the question of to help or not to help is a complex one. Hopefully, this chapter has expanded your insights and the sophistication of your answer. But we did not intend this knowledge solely for knowledge's own sake. We hope your increased understanding will make you feel better and be more effective in helping others.

SUGGESTED READINGS

Batson, C. D., & Coke, J. S. Empathy: A source of altruistic motivation for helping? In J. P. Rushton & R. M. Sorrentino (Eds.), *Altruism and helping behavior.* Hillsdale, N.J.: Erlbaum Associates, 1981.

Hornstein, H. H. *Cruelty and kindness: A new look at aggression and altruism.* Englewood Cliffs, N.J.: Prentice-Hall, 1976.

Latané, B., & Darley, J. M. Bystander "apathy." *American Scientist*, 1969, 57, 244–268.

Mussen P., & Eisenberg-Berg, N. *Roots of caring, sharing and helping.* San Francisco: W. H. Freeman, 1977.

Rushton, J. P. Effects of prosocial television and film material on the behavior of viewers. In L. Berkowitz (Ed.), *Advances in experimental social psychology* (Vol. 12). New York: Academic Press, 1979.

13

SOCIAL EXCHANGE

- **Introduction**
- **Equality Versus Equity in Human Affairs**
- **Limitations of Equity Theory**
- **Social Exchange as a Social Issue**
- **Reciprocity, Bargaining, and Conflict Resolution**
- **Societal Implications of Social Exchange**
- **Summary**

INTRODUCTION

In May of 1979 the citizens of California encountered sudden and unexpected shortages of gasoline. Caused in part by a drastic reduction in petroleum exports from Iran, a major oil-producing country that had experienced a revolution earlier that same year, fuel shortages soon spread to other population centers in the United States. Some interesting reactions were produced by this restriction of the gasoline supply to citizens who had become both economically and psychologically dependent on the mobility provided by their automobiles. These reactions can be used to illustrate several aspects of what psychologists call **social exchange**, the central topic of this chapter.

Social exchange implies a reciprocal transfer of goods, services, or sometimes even ideas and feelings among the various parties to a relationship (Foa & Foa, 1974). At a gas station the motorist exchanges money for the fuel possessed by the owner. Usually such transactions are completed without much emotional distress, leaving both parties reasonably satisfied with what they perceive to be a fair deal. Under the pressure of a supply shortage, however, this orderly system broke down. Drivers gathered at stations in the wee hours of the morning, hoping to gain first access when the owners opened for the day. At one station the manager and five attendants were confronted by 75 gas-hungry motorists; when barriers at the entrances were removed, six cars left skid marks on the pavement as they simultaneously charged the pumps (*Newsweek*, 1979 pp. 24–30). Clearly, both owners and drivers were in need of some less chaotic system of distributing gasoline.

If you were the owner of a service station swamped by more motorists than you had sufficient fuel to accommodate, how would you decide whose tanks were to be filled? At least four strategies come to mind:

1. Issue a ticket to each motorist present at the time you opened for business, divide your supplies by the number of tickets, and give everyone a small, equal share. This strategy, however ignores the fact that some cars are nearly empty while others are merely being "topped off." Is it fair to give the latter as much as the former? Furthermore, some drivers may have been waiting all night for you to open, while others arrived around the same time you did. Probably those who have waited longer will protest if they receive no more gas than recent arrivals.

2. Require each driver to indicate on the ticket how much fuel is wanted. The tickets could be placed in a drum and drawn randomly until the supply of gasoline was used up. Here, every driver would have an equal **chance** of getting filled up rather than an equal **share** of available supplies. This strategy has similar drawbacks to the one described above, however.

3. Raise the price per gallon to the point where the quantity people who can afford to buy will fall within the supplies you have on hand. The steady rise in gasoline prices in the United States since the oil embargo by Arab countries in 1973 suggests that this rationing by price may indeed be occurring. Objections have been raised to its fairness on the grounds that the rich will buy all the fuel they want, while the poor will be the ones whose mobility is restricted.

4. Tell the drivers to form a line in order of their time of arrival at the station and fill their tanks on a first come/first served basis. Though it is the most common practice, this too creates problems. During the 1979 shortage in Los Angeles, gasoline lines often stretched for a mile or more, requiring waits of four hours for those at the end. One school teacher waited two hours and arrived at the pumps just as the supplies were exhausted; she burst into tears. Others became aggressive—telephoning bomb threats to station owners—or depressed, telling staff at their local suicide "hot lines" that life without gasoline was not worth living.

Sometimes a blend of the foregoing strategies was implemented, as when owners set a limit of 10 gallons per vehicle, pumped on a first come/first served basis (#1 and #4), or when only cars with odd- or even-numbered

---

This chapter is written by William Samuel.

Long lines of motorists formed at gas stations during the 1979 gasoline shortage. What rule should be used to make sure that the motorists receive their fair share of the available gasoline?

license plates were allowed to line up on odd- or even-numbered days, respectively, (#2 and #4). The points to be made here are that social exchanges occur when people require one another's cooperation so as to gain access to needed resources, and that such exchanges typically proceed according to some formal or informal set of rules.

Social exchange is not, of course, something that occurs only at gasoline stations. Whenever we seek satisfaction of our material or psychological needs from other individuals or groups, and whenever we seek to be treated fairly by them in the process, we are engaged in social exchange. These relationships can include the most intimate and personal, such as dating and marriage, or the most aloof and impersonal, such as receiving an unemployment check or reserving a seat on an airline flight. Some major issues in each of these situations are who decides the rules by which exchanges proceed

and who is responsible for interpretation and enforcement. As we have seen in the fuel shortage example, many different rule systems are possible, and each carries with it certain drawbacks, in the sense that some individuals are likely to have their needs left unsatisfied. The various systems often have different drawbacks, however, which means that each tends to create different groups of dissatisfied people, who can be expected to prefer whichever system provides them with the greatest access to desired resources.

It seems clear at this point that the rule systems we create to facilitate social exchange are closely involved with our concept of justice. As Thibaut and Walker (1975) have noted, justice has both procedural and distributive aspects. Returning to the gasoline shortage example, we have already seen that different procedures for deciding who deserves a fill-up can produce very different distributions of fuel among gas-hungry motorists. Human groups evolve procedures of justice apparently because some rule-regulated system of adjudication is preferable to a chaotic free-for-all among individuals pursuing their own selfish interests. If, however, the procedural system produces grossly uneven distributions of power and material goods, such that large numbers of individuals are left unsatisfied, the system runs the risk of being overthrown and replaced by an alternative model.

Because social exchange is such a widespread and universal phenomenon and because it is sometimes accompanied by strong emotional involvement, psychologists have given it a great deal of attention. We will begin this chapter by examining a formal theory of social exchange called **equity.** We will also consider the competing **equality** rule and the implications that each of these principles has for the conduct of social relationships. One's feelings of fairness or unfairness in such relationships are often the outgrowth of favorable or unfavorable comparisons between one's own lot in life and that of others whom one perceives as similar to oneself. Examination of these *social comparison* processes will be followed by an application of the foregoing psychological principles to understanding the consequences of socioeconomic deprivation and the factors that promote either cooperation or competition in social interaction. The chapter will conclude with a discussion of personality traits that influence one's preferred approach toward social exchange and bargaining.

EQUALITY VERSUS EQUITY IN HUMAN AFFAIRS

There are many methods by which human groups have historically apportioned the good or bad things that result from membership. A few of these are exemplified by such phrases as "winner take all," "share and share alike,"

"privileges of rank," or "to each according to his need." For the most part, however, we will focus on the distinctions between two widely accepted yet somewhat conflicting principles of justice called *equality* and *equity*. Equality implies that no distinctions will be made between individuals in terms of their deservingness of rewards or costs. The first two strategies in our discussion of ways to distribute gasoline during a fuel shortage are examples of the application of the equality rule. Here, everyone was given an equal share of available supplies or was given an equal chance of obtaining the full amount needed. The second two strategies require that distinctions be made among motorists in terms of their ability to pay (#3) or in terms of their ordinal position in a gas line (#4). Both of these strategies imply that some motorists are more deserving of a fill-up than others and so represent an application of the equity rule. The important point is that we develop and use rules for determining the fair and just allocation of resources.

Contemporary Theories of Equity

The contemporary meaning of equity is that the rewards one derives from a social relationship should be directly proportional to one's contributions to that relationship. This idea is expressed in such old sayings as "You get what you pay for" or "You get out of life what you put into it." When all parties to a relationship perceive that they have been rewarded in direct proportion to their contributions, the distribution of rewards will be perceived as fair and equitable, even though persons with unequal contributions will receive unequal rewards (Homans, 1961, 1974).

An attempt at describing this principle in semimathematical terms was made by Adams (1965). He defined **outcomes** as the pleasurable or unpleasurable consequences that result from one's social relationships with others. Outcomes, abbreviated by the letter O, may be thought of as various rewards or costs that are summated to yield a global impression of the overall pleasurableness (or unpleasurableness) of a given relationship. Adams defined **inputs**, abbreviated by the letter *I*, as the personal characteristics a participant contributes to such relationships. If these characteristics are socially valued ones, the participant will be perceived as deserving of rewarding outcomes, but a participant who brings undesirable or antisocial characteristics to an exchange situation will be perceived as deserving costs or perhaps even punishments.

According to Adams, we have a strong desire to maintain equity in our social relationships. This means that two persons, A and B, should be most satisfied when the ratio of their outcomes to inputs is equivalent:

$$\frac{O_A}{I_A} = \frac{O_B}{I_B}$$

The above equation could describe a situation in which A and B are employees working at similar jobs in the same office. Both are about the same age, have worked for the firm for the same period of time, and put in 40 hours per week; in short, they have equal inputs. Consequently, equity requires that each receive the same outcome (say, a salary of $10,000 per year). Now suppose that A is paid $15,000 to B's $10,000. We can diagram this difference by drawing O_A to be $1^{1}/_{2}$ times larger than O_B. If I_A and I_B remain equivalent, there will be an *inequity* in the relationship between A and B:

$$
\begin{array}{cc}
(\$15,000/\text{year}) & (\$10,000/\text{year}) \\
\dfrac{O_A}{I_A} > & \dfrac{O_B}{I_B} \\
(2000 \text{ hours/} & (2000 \text{ hours/} \\
\text{year}) & \text{year})
\end{array}
$$

The symbol between the ratios (>) may be read "is greater than." A's ratio is greater than B's because A is making $7.50 per hour to B's $5.00.

If A and B share this perception of their re-

lationship, each will feel that A is getting more than A deserves and/or that B is getting less than B deserves. For party A, who is on the long end of the inequity, this sense of unfairness produces the unpleasant emotion of guilt; for party B on the short end of the inequity it produces the emotion of anger. To eliminate these unpleasant feelings, both parties will be motivated to restore equity to their relationship. Since there are four variables in the equity equation—O_A, I_A, O_B, and I_B—there are four basic methods of eliminating an inequity. We will consider each in turn.

Increasing the inputs of the advantaged party. To reduce the feeling of being inequitably overpaid, A might begin working overtime and so achieving inputs of 60 hours per week or 3000 hours per year. A's ratio of outcomes to inputs *(O/I)* would then be $5.00 per hour, the same as B's. There is evidence from both laboratory research and studies conducted in real work settings that people who are inequitably overrewarded will often increase their efforts so as to make themselves appear deserving of their higher outcomes (Adams, 1965; Morse, Gruzen, & Reis, 1976; Pritchard, Dunnette, & Jorgenson, 1972). Sometimes the inputs of the overrewarded party may be perceptually inflated rather than actually increased. Lerner (1965) asked subjects to observe two equally productive workers, only one of whom received a reward. Even though it was clear that the reward had been assigned according to an arbitrary, random procedure, subjects nonetheless felt that the rewarded worker had somehow "performed better."

Decreasing the inputs of the disadvantaged party. Returning to our earlier example, if A's inputs do not increase, the disgruntled B may make drastic reductions in work effort. B might end up working about 27 hours per week or 1350 hours per year by means of such tactics as arriving late, leaving early, and taking extra long coffee and lunch breaks; B's *O/I* ratio would then approximate A's $7.50 per hour. As before, research has confirmed the existence of this strategy. One clever pair of investigators examined the performance of 23 major league baseball players who declared themselves "free agents" following the end of baseball's reserve clause in 1975, which had committed a player to remain with one team until traded or retired (Lord & Hohenfeld, 1979). While some "superstar" free agents quickly negotiated new contracts for enormous and widely publicized increases in pay, these 23 played without contracts in 1976 and suffered *decreases* rather than increases in their pay (up to 20 percent lower than 1975 salaries). These players, who can be assumed to have felt underpaid, showed reductions in batting average, home runs, and runs batted in during 1976. Other studies have also demonstrated a tendency for those who feel inequitably underrewarded to

Baseball players who feel their pay is just or equitable perform better than players who are paid less than they feel they deserve.

reduce their work efforts (Evan & Simmons, 1969; Kessler & Wiener, 1972).

Here again, inputs may be perceptually distorted rather than changed in actual fact. B's inputs might be devalued or underrated so that it would seem fair for B to be less highly rewarded than A. This possibility leads us to the intriguing *just-world* hypothesis, which is discussed in Social Focus 13.1.

Decreasing the outcomes of the advantaged party. If neither A's nor B's inputs are increased or decreased, respectively, equity could be restored in our example by A refusing to accept $5000 of his or her salary or by giving $2500 of it to B. While this would seem to be an unlikely solution to the particular equity problem we have been dealing with, it does sometimes occur. Children in a study by Long and Lerner (1974) were paid 70 cents for "market testing" the products of a toy company. Half were told they were being paid more than children their age were qualified to receive, while the others believed they were fully deserving of the 70-cent payment. All children later had an opportunity to donate money to a charity that bought toys for "poor orphans." Those who felt they were overpaid gave about 30 cents, while the equitably paid group gave only 20 cents.

It could be argued that charitable appeals generally strive to create a sense of inequitable overreward and accompanying guilt feelings in the minds of potential donors by inducing them to compare their lot in life with that of victims of undeserved misfortune. Charities rely on the desire of the donor to reduce this inequity through self-sacrifice. Simultaneously, of course, the outcomes of the recipient are being raised. The latter aspect of self-sacrifice is related to the last basic method of equity restoration, to be discussed below.

Increasing the outcomes of the disadvantaged party. The solution to our equity dilemma which should be most satisfying to both A and

SOCIAL FOCUS 13.1
Is the World a Just Place?

Closely related to equity theory is the hypothesis that we have a need to believe in a *just world,* in which good people are rewarded and wicked ones are punished (Lerner, Miller, & Holmes, 1976). This belief begins in early childhood, with one's absolute faith in the justice of rules enforced by one's parents and the magical power of the environment to apply appropriate rewards or punishments for good or bad behavior. According to Lerner, belief in a just world is so firmly established early in life that, as adults, we also come to believe the converse; namely, those who have been rewarded *must* be good, while those who are punished *must* somehow have been wicked. If it were otherwise, if it were generally the case that good people meet with punishment while wicked ones receive rewards, we would find it difficult to support a social system that tolerates such unjust and tyrannical behavior. Belief in a just world, then, is based on a genuine desire for justice, but it carries with it a danger. The danger is that when we are faced with victims of what is really undeserved misfortune, we may distort the victims' personal characteristics so as to convince ourselves that these are "wicked" persons who are getting their just desserts.

An experiment by Lerner and Simmons (1966) provided a classic demonstration of such devaluation of an innocent victim. The subjects were female college students run in groups of four to ten. One member, the future victim, was an accomplice of Lerner's. She was picked in a rigged drawing to work at a learning task while being observed over a closed-circuit television monitor by the other women in the group. In the course of this task, she pretended to be in great pain due to electric shocks that were allegedly being administered as punishments for errors. Because they were supposed to be forming impressions of the victim's personality, the subjects evaluated her on a set of 15 scales, such as intelligent-unintelligent, immature-mature, sociable-unsociable, and so on. Each subject also rated her own personality on these scales.

Subjects in an Endpoint condition believed the experiment was finished after they completed their ratings. Those in a Midpoint condition, however, believed the victim was scheduled to begin another series of painful shocks following the rating period. In a Reward condition, the group could vote to remove the victim from the shock task for the second half of the experiment and to replace this task with one on which she could be expected to earn several dollars (all groups did so).

What were the inequities of the situation? Initially, subjects had no reason to believe that the future victim was different from themselves in any important respect. She was the same sex as they, about the same age, a fellow college student, and therefore roughly equivalent to them in socially valued characteristics, or inputs. After watching the victim suffer on the learning task, subjects should have perceived that her outcomes in life were, at least temporarily, lower than their own. Here is a diagram of the equity comparison:

$$\text{Subject} \quad \text{Victim}$$
$$\frac{O}{I} \quad > \quad \frac{O}{I}$$

This equity comparison should change, however, depending on whether the subject expects the victim to continue to suffer through another series of shocks or succeeds in rescuing the victim from the shocks and providing her with a reward. Shown below are the various equity comparisons, a brief explanation of each, and the subject's evaluation of the victim's attractiveness in the Endpoint, Midpoint, and Reward conditions. On these evaluations, a positive score indicates that the subject perceived the victim as more attractive than herself and a zero score indicates equal attractiveness. A negative score implies devaluation of the victim's inputs, or a perception that she was less attractive than the subject. The maximum possible devaluation would be a score of -120.

Equity Ratio				
CONDITION	SUBJECT	VICTIM	EXPLANATION	VICTIM'S ATTRACTIVENESS
Endpoint	$\frac{O}{I}$	$>$ $\frac{O}{I}$	Victim has lower outcomes than subject due to her suffering punishment on the learning task.	-12.8
Midpoint	$\frac{O}{I}$	$>$ $\frac{O}{I}$	Victim has even lower outcomes than in the Endpoint condition because she is expected to suffer through an additional series of shocks.	-25.8
Reward	$\frac{O}{I}$	$=$ $\frac{O}{I}$	Victim has outcomes equal to those of the subject because, even though she suffered on the learning task, she will receive no shocks during the second half of the experiment and is being given a compensatory cash reward.	-5.1

In the Endpoint condition, the victim's inputs were slightly devalued, thus permitting the subjects to restore a sense of equity to the situation and maintain their belief in a just world. At a subconscious level, subjects were in effect saying to themselves that the victim was the kind of unattractive person who might be expected to create trouble for herself and so deserved to suffer. In the Midpoint condition, where the suffering of the victim was even greater, subjects were required to devalue her inputs somewhat further in order to restore equity and maintain their belief in a just world. In the Reward condition, where subjects were given control over the victim's outcomes and succeeded in rescuing her from an additional shock series, while at the same time providing her with a cash reward that made up for her past suffering, she was perceived as nearly equal in attractiveness to the subjects. Here, it was unnecessary for the subject to devalue the victim, since equity had been restored to their relationship through an increase in the victim's outcomes.

Subsequent research has for the most part replicated these findings, including the observation that a victim who has received a compensatory reward is not (or at least not very strongly) devalued by observers (Kenrick, Reich, & Cialdini, 1976; Lerner, 1971; Mills & Egger, 1972; Simons & Piliavin, 1972). On the other hand, Aderman, Brehm, and Katz (1974) discovered that subjects asked to imagine themselves in the victim's place did *not* devalue her attractiveness and that subjects run alone rather than in groups (as in the original Lerner and Simmons experiment) were significantly less likely to devalue the victim.

Despite the qualifications implied by the results of some studies, it seems reasonable to conclude that, on some occasions at least, we will attempt to restore equity to our relationships with disadvantaged parties by underrating their inputs. In this process, we assure ourselves that the disadvantaged party in some way deserves to be less well-off, and we thereby defend our belief that the world is basically a just place.

B would consist in B successfully appealing to the person in charge of distributing salaries for a $5000 raise. It is the most satisfying solution because, according to Adams (1965), people strive to maximize the overall level of outcomes in social exchange, and this is the only one of the four basic approaches toward equity restoration that would permit both A and B to enjoy outcomes of $15,000 per year. Research has demonstrated that people will initiate appeals for fair treatment when they have been inequitably underpaid and that their satisfaction with the situation improves if their outcomes begin to increase (DeCarufel, 1979; DeCarufel & Schopler, 1979).

You will recall from Chapter 12 that guilty feelings, which may develop either from excessive good fortune or direct involvement in harm doing, are often followed by an effort at helping another person. This can be thought of

as an increase in the outcomes of the disadvantaged party in an equity comparison (Samuel, 1975, pp. 138–146). People in such relationships seem most inclined to restore equity by means of helping and self-sacrifice when they have a clear awareness of their ability to control outcomes. When, instead, they have been made to feel that the other party's disadvantage is an event outside their control, they are likely to restore equity by devaluing the other person's inputs. (Compare, for example, the results for the Reward and Midpoint conditions in Social Focus 13.1.)

LIMITATIONS OF EQUITY THEORY

In an entertaining but nonetheless very scholarly book, it has been persuasively argued that equity theory provides an adequate description of the search for fairness and satisfaction in *all* human relationships, not just those involving economic exchanges (Walster, Walster, & Berscheid, 1978). Not surprisingly, this bold claim has encountered some resistance on both practical and philosophical grounds. Practically speaking, some have questioned the accuracy of the equity formula in predicting what people will perceive as fair—even in economic exchanges, where numerical estimates of inputs and outcomes are readily available. Philosophically speaking, others have been bothered by the implication that human beings can and will be differentiated according to the perceived value of their personal characteristics and that human relationships can be reduced to little more than a bartering of commodities. Both types of criticisms have suggested some limitations on equity theory that will be considered in the paragraphs below.

How Accurate is the Equity Formula?

One of the earliest qualifications of the equity principle to emerge in research on this topic was that people are less disturbed by inequities that go in their favor than by those that go against them. Austin and Walster (1974) led subjects to expect a payment of $1, $2, or $3 for their work at a task and then delivered a pay envelope that contained either the expected amount or one that was greater or less than expected. In general, people who got what they expected were most satisfied that their pay was fair, but underpaid subjects were clearly more upset and dissatisfied than their overpaid counterparts. While people may claim, on paper-and-pencil scales, that they are disturbed by overpayment, they may also, when attached to what they believe is a reliable lie detector, reveal that they are actually fairly happy about the situation (Rivera & Tedeschi, 1976).

On a less selfish-sounding note, it also appears that people will deviate from equity in their allocation of resources if they have an important short-term goal that calls for a different type of distribution strategy. It has been found, for instance, that persons instructed to motivate one who is performing poorly will, for a while at least, give that worker inequitably large rewards (Greenberg, 1978; Greenberg & Leventhal, 1976). Other instances in which people often deviate from the equity principle will be discussed further on in this section.

Conflicts between Equity and Equality

The philosophical objections to the equity concept are based primarily on a contrast between equity and equality as alternative and somewhat incompatible norms by which a society may be organized. According to sociologists, norms are the underlying values by which overt behavior is assumed to be regulated, while **roles** consist in behavior patterns, such as being a good parent, which are defined by norms.

The contrast between equity and equality norms is easy to illustrate. Suppose four individuals—A, B, C, and D—agree to make candles to sell for a profit at a flea market. A and B are equally moderately industrious, and each has 100 candles ready on the appointed day. C works extremely hard and has 200 candles ready, while D parties a lot and produces only 20. All 420 candles are sold for $5 each, raising $2100 to be divided among these persons. The equity solution would be:

$$\underset{\text{(100 candles)}}{\overset{(\$500)}{\frac{O_A}{I_A}}} = \underset{\text{(100 candles)}}{\overset{(\$500)}{\frac{O_B}{I_B}}} = \underset{\text{(200 candles)}}{\overset{(\$1000)}{\frac{O_C}{I_C}}} = \underset{\text{(20 candles)}}{\overset{(\$100)}{\frac{O_D}{I_D}}}$$

The equality norm, expressed in such old sayings as "share and share alike," would specify that each of the partners to this joint venture, regardless of the number of candles contributed, should get an equal portion of the profits—$525, to be exact. In fact, the equality norm can be derived from the equity norm if one assumes either that all persons have equal inputs in all situations or that social justice requires differences in input to be ignored in distributing outcomes. Inputs might then be assigned the arbitrary unit value of 1, producing the following definition of a just world:

$$O_A = O_B = O_C = O_D$$

Adherence to the equity norm is likely to foster a spirit of competition among persons striving to maximize their own share of limited rewards, and those whose outcomes end up smaller are likely to harbor feelings of jealousy and resentment. Equal divisions of resources, on the other hand, generally promote interpersonal harmony and cooperation. Leventhal, Michaels, and Sanford (1972) asked subjects to recommend a division of monetary incentives for good performance among a group whose members differed in their work inputs. When instructed to divide their incentives in a way that would promote cooperativeness, subjects recommended equal shares. Leventhal (1976, p. 218) has reviewed a number of studies that demonstrate that adherence to the equality norm is assumed by most people to promote group solidarity and minimize conflict.

Treating people equally sounds like a "nice" way to behave, while treating them unequally sounds not very nice at all. Consequently, to the extent that each of us wants to be regarded as a nice person, we should find it psychologically difficult to recommend equitable rather than equal distributions of outcomes, when these recommendations must be made in public. Researchers have, in fact, shown that subjects tend to divide rewards equitably among workers making high or low contributions to-

Young children typically use an equality rule rather than equity when allocating resources.

ward the completion of a task only so long as they do not anticipate future interactions with the workers or public disclosure of their role as allocator. Otherwise, they shift towards equality (Reis & Gruzen, 1976; Shapiro, 1975). If rewards are distributed by a committee, however, the equity norm may be adhered to even under well-publicized conditions (Greenberg, 1979). Perhaps being part of a group of allocators makes people less vulnerable to feeling not nice when they recommend adherence to the equity norm.

If the equity and equality norms are truly incompatible, we must experience a great deal of conflict within ourselves whenever we are called upon to recommend a just solution to a distributive problem. Brickman and Bryan (1976) found that children will approve a redistribution of rewards among contributors to a joint task that shifts the existing distribution in the direction of *either* equity or equality (though there was a preference for the latter approach). If children perceive themselves as competitors at a task, they tend to divide the resulting rewards equitably; if they perceive themselves as a team, they shift toward equality, even when the allocator is the more productive and "deserving" member of the pair (Lerner, 1974).

Children appear to undergo a progressive development in their justice principles, much as Piaget (1965) in his classic book, *The Moral Judgment of the Child*, said they do. In a review of more than fifty studies of distributive judgments, Hook and Cook, (1979) found sufficient age-related regularity to conclude that, in general, children under the age of five adhere to the equality norm (though the very youngest may try to keep *all* the reward for themselves), those between six and twelve years of age modify equality in the direction of equity, and only those aged thirteen or older achieve the true proportionality between rewards and contributions specified by equity and distributive justice. Noting that equity is a more complex principle to uphold than equality, Hook and Cook proposed that Piaget's other work on stages of cognitive development suggests that young children may be incapable of fully comprehending and accurately applying proportional concepts.

Walster, Walster, and Berscheid (1978, p. 213) have proposed that the greater simplicity of the equality norm as compared to the equity norm has clear implications for the conditions under which, even as adults, people should prefer equal sharing: (1) when decisions must be made quickly and there is no time for computing relative inputs and outcomes, (2) when the negotiation involved in evaluating inputs is likely to be emotionally unpleasant or in some way particularly costly, (3) when the rewards involved are of small value and hardly worth haggling over, and (4) when the immediate situation in which rewards are being divided is a special occasion that sets no precedent for the future. With regard to the last-mentioned possibility, Walster et al. gave the example of wages paid to teams of professional athletes. For long-term contracts, the amount of pay is proportionate to each athlete's presumed skill, but for the division of prize money following some special event (for example, a Superbowl) the typical strategy is equal shares.

Many critics of equity theory would want to emphasize yet another set of circumstances under which the equity norm would be abandoned: namely, the most intimate of human relationships—friendship, love, marriage, and family life (Deutsch, 1975; Romer, 1977). On the other hand, it has also been argued that there is no necessary reason why equity theory cannot be applied to such relationships, just to see whether or not it increases our understanding of them (Samuel, 1978). Does the equity norm apply to love and marriage? Social Focus 13.2 presents some evidence that bears upon this question (also see Chapters 8 and 9).

In spite—or perhaps because—of such research efforts, some social scientists have expressed dismay at what they see as equity theory's tendency to describe human interaction as always being motivated by a selfish desire for personal pleasure or material gain (Deutsch, 1975; Sampson, 1975, 1977). We will return to these criticisms at the end of the chapter. Assuming for the moment that equity provides a reasonably accurate description of what people mean by fairness in social exchange, another potential source of controversy is the question of who decides what inputs are relevant to a given exchange situation and how they are to be evaluated. Effort and ability are the most legitimate and probably the most common types of contributions considered in decisions regarding the equitable distribution of resources, but people often include superficial and somewhat irrelevant characteristics in their evaluation of inputs—characteristics like age, physical appearance, socioeconomic status, and so forth. In the fuel-shortage example given at the beginning of the chapter, for instance, the typical solution to the distri-

SOCIAL FOCUS 13.2
Is All Fair in Love and Marriage?

Walster, Walster, and Traupmann (1978) asked more than 500 students at the University of Wisconsin who identified themselves as casual or steady daters to describe the quality of their relationships in terms compatible with equity theory. The researchers described a recent study of "marriage contracts" in which young couples had been interviewed as to what they thought each partner was contributing to their relationship and what each was getting out of it. The students were given a few examples of the types of contributions (that is, inputs) that had been mentioned, such as being sociable, physically attractive, loving, and understanding, as well as helping to take care of the home and making decisions. Outcomes were described as material or emotional rewards or costs that the individual had experienced as a consequence of the marriage.

The students were then asked to think about their own relationships and to translate their subjective estimates of their own and their partners' inputs and

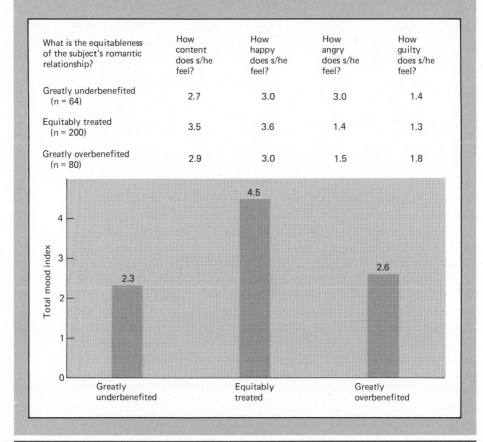

What is the equitableness of the subject's romantic relationship?	How content does s/he feel?	How happy does s/he feel?	How angry does s/he feel?	How guilty does s/he feel?
Greatly underbenefited (n = 64)	2.7	3.0	3.0	1.4
Equitably treated (n = 200)	3.5	3.6	1.4	1.3
Greatly overbenefited (n = 80)	2.9	3.0	1.5	1.8

outcomes onto numerical scales. These numbers were then plugged into the equity equation so that the students could be separated into groups on the basis of the perceived equitableness of their situations. The "greatly underbenefited" and "greatly overbenefited" groups were comprised of students whose ratios were smaller or larger than their partners', respectively, while the "equitably treated" had ratios that closely approximated their partners'. The students also rated how content, happy, angry, or guilty they felt in their relationships, each on a 4-point scale running from "not at all" (1) to "very much" (4). As can be seen below, the perceived equitableness of a relationship had a significant effect on a partner's satisfaction with it.

Clearly, the equitably treated felt more contented and happier and less angry or guilty than either the under- or overbenefited. The angriest partners were the greatly underbenefited, while the guiltiest were the greatly overbenefited. A "total mood index" was calculated as (content + happy) minus (angry + guilty), for a measure of overall satisfaction with the relationship. These results are shown in the diagram and, as anticipated, the equitably treated were the most satisfied.

You probably have already noticed that the largest group of students consisted of those who felt equitably treated. This, too, makes sense, for it is more likely that people will continue a dating relationship in which they feel satisfied rather than dissatisfied. Indeed, these investigators found that the equitably treated were more likely to have a relationship that included sexual intercourse and that remained stable over the three-and-one-half-month duration of the study.

---

bution problem was first come, first served, which treats time spent waiting in line as an effort input that makes a customer deserving of some gasoline. We would probably feel it was an illegitimate use of equity, however, if a male service station owner sold gasoline only to attractive women or drivers of expensive cars, though we are all aware that this sort of thing does sometimes occur.

Even if we restrict our attention to the most legitimate-appearing inputs, effort and ability, we must still face the problem of how these personal attributes are to be measured. In a work situation, a time clock or the quantity and quality of one's products may provide fairly ob-

jective measures of input. In a classroom setting, performance on exams and term papers is often used to evaluate effort and ability. At work, of course, the outcomes to be distributed are dollars, while in the classroom they are grades. How, though, did the students in the love and marriage study by Walster, Walster, and Traupmann (1978) go about assigning a number to their own and their partners' contributions to a dating relationship? It seems absurd to assume that our satisfaction with such relationships is based on a continuous calculation and recalculation of equity ratios. On the other hand, we may all become very adept at such subjective mental arithmetic as we grow up in a social environment. While we generally do not use actual numbers in arriving at these judgments, we all have our own intuitive notions of what does or does not feel fair. When we look at our feelings more carefully, it is in fact often the case that a sense of unfairness accompanies the perception that someone is getting either more or less than legitimately deserved.

It was suggested earlier that outcomes and inputs may be perceptually distorted as well as changed in actual fact, so as to restore a sense of equity to an inequitable relationship. Still more ambiguity is entered into this process of equity restoration by the fact that perceptions of outcomes and inputs are likely to be altered by comparative judgments. Tennis players, for instance, may perceive their inputs of practice and playing ability as large or small depending on whether they compare themselves to other players at the local club, the professionals competing at Wimbledon, or their circle of friends and neighbors. The effect of such comparative judgments on feelings of fairness will be given considerable attention in the section that follows.

SOCIAL EXCHANGE AS A SOCIAL ISSUE

Two individuals may agree that their own relationship is a fair and equitable one but may still remain dissatisfied if they perceive that their outcomes fall short of their expectations or of what others in their social environment are able to obtain. In other words, feelings of fairness and satisfaction reflect not only interpersonal equity but *social comparison* processes as well.

Social Comparison and Social Exchange

According to Festinger (1954), we have a need to evaluate our abilities, beliefs, and gen-

eral circumstances in life. This need is satisfied through comparison with others whom we perceive as similar to ourselves on the relevant evaluative dimension. In general, we may take it for granted that human beings are comparison-oriented animals and that they evaluate not only their abilities and beliefs but also their overall life circumstances—the kinds of jobs they hold, houses they live in, children they raise, and so on—by taking note of where they are relative to the proverbial Joneses. The original focus of social comparison theory has therefore been broadened to include the idea that we seek to compare ourselves with others who are similar to us not only in terms of a particular dimension of ability or belief but also in terms of global characteristics like age, sex, physical appearance, geographical proximity, and so forth (Goethals & Darley, 1977; Samuel, 1973; Suls, Gastorf, & Lawhon, 1978).

A theory of social exchange that incorporated the idea of social comparison was put forward by Thibaut and Kelley (1959), six years before Adams's (1965) formal statement of equity theory. Social-exchange theory was based on the rather simple proposition that people are motivated to maximize rewards and minimize costs in their relationships. A participant whose rewards minus costs do not yield a "profit" is likely to be very dissatisfied with the relationship and to seek ways of modifying or terminating it. An application of this concept to the prediction of marital stability was made by Howard and Dawes (1976). One partner from each of 42 married couples kept track of the frequency of sexual intercourse (a reward) and that of fighting (a cost) over a period of several weeks. Among 30 happily married couples, all but two made love more often than they fought, while the 12 unhappily married couples were unanimous in fighting more than loving. A later replication found a correlation of .81 between the loving minus fighting index and self-ratings of marital happiness among 28 couples (Thornton, 1977).

It is not, however, simply the absolute level

of rewards minus costs that determines whether someone will remain in an exchange relationship, but rather the value of this index of satisfaction relative to the individual's **comparison level (CL).** The CL is set by the individual's past experiences with similar exchanges as well as his or her perception of the rewards minus costs enjoyed by others in the immediate social environment. Thus, couples who perceive that their relationship has deteriorated from one in which loving far exceeded fighting to one in which the two activities occur with about equal frequency may be more dissatisfied than couples in more tempestuous relationships for whom fighting predominated from the very start. Similarly, if one has established a high CL by observing that one's married acquaintances have very loving, harmonious relationships, this could produce considerable dissatisfaction with a marriage in which only a few minor spats occur at long intervals. If instead one has established a low CL by witnessing frequent quarrels among one's married acquaintances, this could produce a great deal of satisfaction with one's own marriage. The phenomenon of CL, though, goes further even than comparative judgments. In a subsequent restatement of their theory, Kelley and Thibaut (1978, p. 9) commented that CL is "the standard that reflects the quality of outcomes that the participant feels he or she deserves." As we have noted before, a person's feeling of deservingness arises in part through comparison with others, but also reflects one's own subjective assessment of one's inputs into a relationship.

Another important concept in social-exchange theory is the *comparison level for alternatives* (CL_{alt}). CL_{alt} refers to the level of rewards minus costs that a person believes could be obtained outside a particular exchange. If CL_{alt} is low, then even a relationship that provides outcomes below each member's CL may nonetheless persist, because neither partner is aware of any more rewarding alternatives. Thus an unhappy marriage may survive if both spouses believe that divorce would bring about a change in their life situation that would be even more unpleasant than their current existence.

Thinking once again about the fuel-shortage example with which this chapter began, we can find evidence of CL and CL_{alt} in people's reactions to the crisis. One reason for the near-panic conditions that developed was that Americans' CL was one of past availability of gasoline in ample supply and (by world standards) low prices. Restrictions on supplies and increases in price were therefore very disturbing and led to such practices as topping off nearly full tanks, which made the shortages seem worse than they actually were. Because Americans had grown to be dependent on their automobiles for the maintenance of even the most basic aspects of their life-styles, they were locked into a dissatisfying social exchange at their local gasoline stations for lack of any better CL_{alt}.

Relative deprivation is a term that has much in common with the notions of CL and CL_{alt}. People feel relatively deprived when, in the process of comparing their own lot in life with that of others with whom they sense a social or psychological affinity, they come off second best (generally leading to feelings of frustration). Blacks in America, for example, may be more prosperous than blacks in any other country, but they sense a national affinity with American whites and in this comparison feel relatively deprived. An escalating sense of relative deprivation among American blacks was emphasized in the *Report of the National Advisory Commission on Civil Disorders* (1968) as a major contributor to the ghetto riots that erupted in many cities during the 1960s and early 1970s. To be sure, other groups besides racial minorities may experience relative deprivation. Manual workers may feel deprived relative to office workers (and conversely), 9-to-5 employees may feel deprived relative to professionals, and anyone can experience pangs of relative deprivation in making comparisons with the Joneses down the block. Reactions to relative deprivation may range from efforts at self-improvement (for example, looking for a better job) through symptoms of psychological stress (ulcers), efforts at making constructive changes in the social system (voting), or, ultimately, violence against the social system in the form of riots or crime (Crosby, 1976). Martin (1980) classifies these reactions as either individually versus system oriented or as hopeful versus frustrated. Thus, a hopeful and individually oriented reaction would be efforts at self-improvement, whereas a system-oriented one would involve activities like voting. A frustrated and individually oriented reaction would be stress symptoms, whereas a system-oriented one would often lead to acts of violence. Underlying feelings of relative deprivation are the perceptions that another, better life is possible and that the deprived individuals deserve better than what they have.

An important question to raise at this point would be how, when a relationship is dissatisfying for one or more parties, it may be restructured so as to provide some relief. Consequently, the next section of this chapter will explore processes of bargaining and conflict resolution.

RECIPROCITY, BARGAINING, AND CONFLICT RESOLUTION

The principle of reciprocity appears to be universal across human cultures and is even observed among higher primates (see Campbell, 1975; Wilson, 1975, p. 120). Reciprocity is expressed in such old sayings as "You scratch my back, and I'll scratch yours" or, on the negative side, "An eye for an eye, a tooth for a tooth." This very elementary notion of fair play underlies all the more sophisticated rules of justice and theories of equity and social exchange that human societies and the social scientists who inhabit them have cared to create.

Despite the modifications in it that are made by moral philosophers and advanced social systems, the reciprocity principle still finds widespread and direct application in human affairs. Often, however, we observe that even simple reciprocity breaks down, and it is with these situations that we will be most concerned below.

The Interaction Matrix

Thibaut and Kelley (1959), who were mentioned above as developers of social-exchange theory, were also pioneers in the use of the **interaction matrix** to describe social relations. To illustrate the operation of a simple matrix we can examine Blau's (1964) analysis of the efforts of employees in business organizations to make a good impression and at the same time enhance their own status relative to others. Suppose two parties to a social interaction, A and B, have just two basic responses they can make toward one another. Each can "express regard" for the other by indicating liking and respect, or each can "withhold regard" from the other. If one party expresses regard while the other withholds regard, the latter has gained in status over the former, since the first party's favorable evaluation of the second is now a publicly known fact, while the second's evaluation of the first remains in doubt. The two responses for each party and the social implications of various combinations of these are shown in Figure 13.1.

In this game of one-upmanship, both parties can benefit if each expresses regard for the other, resulting in an equal-status bond of friendship. Consequently, responses like expressing regard are called the *cooperative choice*. Each party realizes, however, that a cooperative choice carries with it some risk. If A expresses regard but B does not reciprocate, A loses status relative to B, and if B expresses regard while A withholds it, B loses status relative to A. Behaviors such as withholding re-

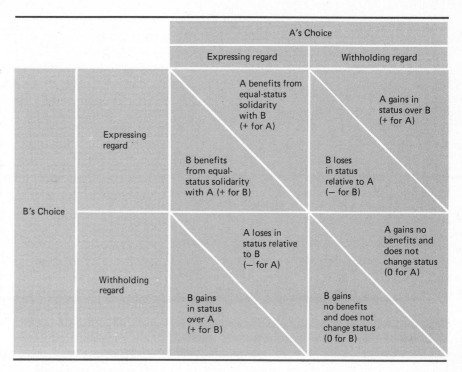

FIGURE 13.1
The social game of one-upmanship displayed in an interaction matrix. For each party, the cooperative choice is to express regard for the other and the competitive one is to withhold regard. If both players express regard, both benefit from gaining a friend. If one expresses regard while the other withholds it, however, the latter party loses in status to the former. Unwilling to risk a loss of status in the event that the other party withholds regard, both players typically opt for the competitive choice.

gard are called the *competitive choice*. What will A and B do? If research on this topic bears any relevance to real life, each of these parties will be sufficiently uncertain of the other's willingness to reciprocate a cooperative choice that both will avoid the risks of such a response and will instead choose to compete. This outcome is shown in the bottom right-hand corner of Figure 13.1. While neither A nor B loses in status by making a mutually competitive choice, it is also true that neither gains the benefit of finding a friend.

Perhaps a parallel to the above situation in the world of international politics can be seen in the relations between the United States and Iran, the country whose revolutionary change of government instigated the fuel shortages discussed at the opening of this chapter. In the course of expressing its grievances against America, the government of Iran held hostage for more than a year 52 officials and employees of the United States embassy in Teheran. In re-

sponse, our government froze Iranian assets in American banks, applied a trade embargo, and assembled an armada of warships off the Iranian coast. A mutually cooperative choice in this confrontation would have involved, on Iran's part, freeing the hostages and resuming normal relations with the United States and, on America's part, lifting economic sanctions and military threats and pledging future noninterference in Iran's domestic politics. A settlement of this sort was eventually arrived at, but only after a year of suspicion on both sides that conciliatory gestures would lead to betrayal and loss of face. As in the interaction matrix, there was a strong temptation for both sides to make mutually competitive choices during a tension-filled period of unlawful incarceration for 52 American citizens that finally ended on January 20, 1981.

Researchers in the area of bargaining and conflict resolution have devised several standardized techniques, called *paradigms*, which they believe provide insights into the psychological processes at work in analogous real-life situations. A few such techniques are described below.

Research Paradigms in Bargaining and Conflict Resolution

All three paradigms to be considered here employ a game-playing format. The settings and rules of these games differ greatly from one paradigm to another, however.

The prisoner's dilemma. Prisoner's Dilemma games utilize an interaction matrix similar to that shown in Figure 13.1. The name for this paradigm was derived from a strategy supposedly employed by district attorneys in order to get one of two suspects to confess to a serious crime for which conclusive proof of guilt is lacking. The two suspects are interrogated separately by the DA, who offers the same deal to each; namely, if one suspect confesses while the other does not, the DA will see to it that the one who turns state's evidence is convicted of a reduced charge carrying a sentence of six months, while the other serves ten years. What the DA does not say, but what the suspects should be able to figure out for themselves, is that if they *both* confess, each will get a five-year sentence. The "cooperative" choice in this case would be for both suspects to remain silent, and both would then be freed for lack of evidence. Keeping silent, however, carries with it the risk of a ten-year sentence if the other suspect confesses. Typically, it is claimed, both suspects end up making the "competitive" choice of confession because each fears betrayal by the other.

The participants in Prisoner's Dilemma (PD) games are, like the suspects in the above example, usually unable to speak to one another. If they could communicate directly, they would probably find it easier to collaborate on a mutually beneficial cooperative strategy, and the results of laboratory research tend to confirm this prediction (see Rubin & Brown, 1975, pp. 93–99). Just the addition to the usual PD situation of an opportunity for eye contact can significantly increase the proportion of cooperative choices made over repeated trials of the game, though hearing the other player's verbal comments appears to be a more crucial factor (Wichman, 1970). Despite the cooperativeness that may be encouraged by communication, however, the typical finding by PD researchers has been that competitive choices predominate, even when cooperation carries no risk of a loss of resources and the only purpose served by competing is to win more than one's opponent. If, on the other hand, a matrix is designed so that a mutually competitive choice is very costly for both players, the majority of choices may become cooperative (Jones, Steele, Gahagan, & Tedeschi, 1968; Komorita, Sheposh, & Braver, 1968; Van Egeren, 1979).

The simplicity of PD games makes it possible for a consistent strategy of play to be programmed into a computer. The four main strategies are (1) *cooperative,* in which cooperative choices are made regardless of whether the other player cooperates or competes; (2) *competitive,* in which competitive choices are made regardless of the other player's behavior; (3) *tit for tat,* in which a cooperative move by the other player is followed by a cooperative move on the machine's part, while a competitive move is answered by a competitive move; and (4) *random,* in which the machine's choices are totally unpredictable from one trial to the next. Some major findings are that *any* of the patterned strategies is superior to the random strategy in inducing cooperative choices, but that the closer a given strategy approaches 100 percent cooperation, the more cooperative choices it is able to elicit from the other player (see Rubin & Brown, 1975, pp. 276–277). On the other hand, when judged by the criterion of how many "points" a given strategy is able to win for its player, tit for tat seems to come out best (Axelrod, 1980a, 1980b). Some studies have suggested that a compromise strategy may be most effective in promoting mutual cooperation, along with maximizing one's own rewards; namely, 100 percent cooperative on the initial trials—to establish a sense of trust—followed by a shift to tit for tat (Komorita & Mechling, 1967; Sermat, 1967).

An attempt at applying findings such as the foregoing to the vitally important real-life issue of nuclear disarmament was Osgood's (1962) proposal for graduated reciprocation in tension reduction, or GRIT. Osgood's proposal has continued to stimulate interest and was summarized and very favorably evaluated by Lindskold (1978).

The GRIT strategy unfolds in several specific steps, beginning with a public announcement by one nation of its desire to reduce tension, accompanied by a schedule of small, self-imposed conciliatory gestures. Each of these concessions must be carried out on schedule regardless of whether the opposing nation responds in kind, and the genuineness of the concessions should be easily verifiable. The underlying idea in all this is that sooner or later the opposing nation's distrust of the conciliatory nation's motives will be reduced, and the norm of reciprocity will be awakened. From that point on, conciliatory gestures will be mutually rather than unilaterally initiated, and tensions should diminish to the point that mutual disarmament becomes a real possibility.

Osgood, of course, was not so idealistic as to advocate unilateral disarmament as a means of inducing cooperation on the part of a heavily armed opponent. He states that the initial, one-sided concessions should be small ones and should never go so far as to jeopardize the security of the conciliatory nation. In the event that the opposing nation responds to conciliation with an act of aggression, the GRIT strategy calls for an appropriately measured counterresponse, a tit for tat. If, on the other hand, the opposing nation does respond with a concession, this behavior, too, should be matched in the precise degree to which it was expressed by the opponent. According to Osgood, retaliatory moves that exceed the opponent's aggressiveness, or conciliatory gestures that fall short of the opponent's concessions, serve to reduce trust and impede progress toward additional cooperation.

The trucking game. Aside from the Prisoner's Dilemma, the single most popular laboratory situation in which to study cooperation, competition, and conflict resolution has been the Acme-Bolt trucking game devised by Deutsch and Krauss (1960). The participants, female employees of a telephone company, were run in pairs but placed in separate booths so they were unable to speak to one another. Each played the role of owner of one of two trucking companies (Acme or Bolt) that were trying to move goods in opposite directions along a highway that contained a stretch of one-lane road, as shown in Figure 13.2. A company was promised a cash payment for successful delivery of its goods to their destination, but "operating expenses" were charged at the rate of one

FIGURE 13.2
The road map used in the trucking game.
Source: Deutsch and Krauss, 1960

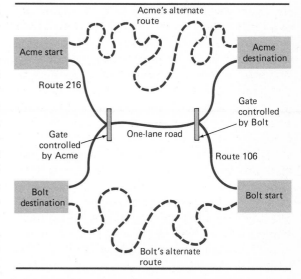

cent per second of transportation time. Past a certain travel time, the company would lose rather than make money on its shipment. Since the one-lane road was shortest, Acme and Bolt were both likely to try to use it but were also likely to lose a lot of time if they became deadlocked in a head-on confrontation. Alternate routes were available for both companies, but these were so long and winding that they were a guaranteed financial loss; only successful use of the one-lane road would return a profit.

On the initial trials, both players generally headed straight for the one-lane road, became deadlocked, and waited to see who would be the first to back down. Eventually one would reluctantly reverse her truck and allow the other to proceed, after which the retreating participant would drive through the one-lane road to her destination. On these early trials, it took so long for the deadlock to be broken that both Acme and Bolt generally lost money. Furthermore, very few participants were willing to be consistently submissive, so after backing down on one trial they would be more determined than ever to wait out their opponent on the next one. Such reactions ultimately led to the emergence of a pattern of cooperation which was the only strategy that guaranteed a mutual profit. Namely, Acme and Bolt took turns at being the first to drive through the one-lane road. In twenty trials of play, they each earned about a dollar.

In a second condition, Acme was given a weapon—a gate that only she could erect to block the one-lane road. Here, the deadlock on the initial trials was typically broken by Acme's reversing her truck behind the gate and then closing it to block the highway. If Bolt then took the alternate route, Acme reopened the gate and drove through the one-lane road to her destination. If Bolt persisted in blocking the main road, Acme would be the first to take the alternate route and so would lose less money than Bolt. Finally, if Bolt backed down in the initial deadlock, Acme simply rushed through to her destination while the hapless Bolt waited to see whether Acme would lift the gate. There

was very little pressure on Acme to cooperate, and the turn-taking strategy seldom emerged. Under these circumstances, both players lost money, but Acme held her losses to about a dollar, while Bolt's losses approached three dollars.

In a third condition, both players had control of gates. Deadlocks were seldom resolved by means of the cooperative strategy, and the time-consuming alternate routes were frequently traveled. Here, Acme and Bolt each lost more than four dollars.

Deutsch and Krauss interpreted their results as indicating that negotiators possessing weapons (as nations do in real life) tend to engage in unproductive confrontations and threats, while unarmed negotiators are more likely to discover mutually beneficial strategies of cooperation. One criticism of this conclusion was that the players of the trucking game, unlike real-life negotiators, could not speak directly to one another. Subsequent replications in which free communication was permitted continued to find, however, that cooperation and joint payoffs were diminished by the availability of weapons (Deutsch & Krauss, 1962; Smith & Anderson, 1975).

Another suggested limitation on the real-world implications of the results was that the participants played for imaginary money (poker chips), while diplomats and negotiators of wage disputes must often bargain for high stakes. Some studies have found that playing for real money increases cooperativeness in the trucking game (Gallo, 1966), but Rubin and Brown (1975, p. 142) expressed doubt as to the reliability of this result on the grounds that, in PD and other types of games, playing for real money has had a very inconsistent effect on overall cooperativeness.

Finally, it has been pointed out that use of the gates in the version of the trucking game in which both players were armed constituted both a threat and an actual punitive gesture. What would happen if, as in real life, the players could threaten their opponents with punishment for noncooperation before they had to commit themselves to an actual punitive gesture? In subsequent replications of the game, the availability of threats that were independent of punishments was sometimes found to increase cooperativeness over what was observed in a no-gates no-threats condition (Shomer, Davis, & Kelley, 1966; Smith & Anderson, 1975). Somewhat analogously, the ability to threaten an opponent with a fine for using a gate increased cooperation over what was obtained in a replication of the original two-gate condition (Pruitt & Gleason, 1978).

Though the results of the trucking game should probably not be generalized too freely to high-stakes negotiations in real life, they do call our attention to the possibility that the threats and weapons possessed by the parties to such disputes may add significantly to the difficulty of achieving compromise and cooperation.

Coalition games. Face to face negotiation is an integral part of the coalition game devised by Vinacke and Arkoff (1957). Participants sit around a Parcheesi board and are told that their goal is to move a marker, by throw of a die, from a common starting square to "home," which is 67 squares away. The first player to reach home wins 100 points, but all players do not have an equal chance of getting there. One may be assigned a "weight" of 4, while others are assigned weights of 3 or 2. If the die came up 5, for example, the 4-weighted player would get to move 20 spaces and a 2-weighted player only 10 spaces. An intriguing feature of the game is that two or more players may enter into a coalition, combining their weights to move one marker farther than either could alone. Thus, if the 3-weighted and 2-weighted players entered into a coalition and rolled a 5, they would move a marker 25 spaces. If they succeeded in reaching home ahead of the other player, they would decide how to divide the 100-point reward between them. Coalitions, once formed, cannot be dissolved for the duration of the game.

Vinacke and Arkoff reported that in nearly two-thirds of the groups who were weighted 4, 3, and 2, the two weaker parties (3 and 2) formed a coalition to defeat the stronger. In these "minimum power" coalitions, the 100-point reward for winning was usually divided equally between the partners. In the cases in which the 4-weighted party joined with one of the weaker members to form a winning coalition, however, the reward tended to be divided equitably, with the more powerful partner getting more. With a few, relatively minor qualifications, these findings have been replicated by other investigators (see Rubin & Brown, 1975, pp. 69–70, 79–80).

In a different version of the coalition game, called Apex, there are four players whose weights are selected so as to place one in a position of clear dominance over the others, but in need of alliance with at least one other in order to win. For example, the weights might be 2, 1, 1, 1, with a minimum weight of 3 being required for a coalition to win. Under these circumstances, minimum power coalitions (that is, 1, 1, 1) were observed only about 20 percent of the time. This happened because the higher-weighted player, the Apex, could easily "subvert" one of the weaker parties by offering half the reward for joining in a coalition. If the three weaker parties banded together to defeat the Apex, on the hand, each could legitimately claim only a third of the reward. When the game was modified, however, so that players could "ding" one another with punitive reductions in points, minimum power coalitions were formed on 62 percent of trials. In other words, the temptation to join the Apex had to be offset by the threat of being dinged by the other weaker parties before minimum power coalitions became viable in this sort of game (Oliver, 1980).

Social Psychological Factors in Bargaining and Conflict Resolution

Some studies of bargaining ask subjects to pretend they are the buyers or sellers of used cars or management or labor negotiators in a wage dispute, while other studies have subjects engage in an actual dollars-and-cents transaction in which they will be allowed to keep what they have bargained for. The general finding has been that an initial demand for large rather than small concessions from one's opponent leads to a deal more favorable to oneself when negotiations are concluded (Chertkoff & Conley, 1967; Hamner & Harnett, 1974). In addition, when one's opponent has indicated a willingness to shift his or her demands in a direction favorable to oneself, this cooperative gesture should be reciprocated with a small shift in one's own position (that is, smaller than the size of the opponent's concession). Bargainers should not make *extreme* initial demands, since the partner may abandon the negotiations altogether, but strong demands combined with small concessions seem to be the best strategy for obtaining a favorable settlement (Komorita & Brenner, 1968; Yukl, 1974).

Bending over backwards to be cooperative in these types of negotiations usually leads to being exploited by one's partner, even if the cooperative party is a "nice guy" who voluntarily renounces use of a powerful weapon (Black & Higbee, 1973; Shure, Meeker, & Hansford, 1965). Only if a powerful but pacifistic party clearly explains why he or she is seeking cooperation will this strategy be likely to be reciprocated by the opponent (Enzle, Hansen, & Lowe, 1975).

Division of rewards. In general, it appears that bargainers who are strong in resources or who have reason to believe they have contributed more toward achieving a negotiated settlement prefer an equitable division of rewards.

Third party mediators are frequently useful in bargaining and negotiation—for example, in international disputes, labor negotiations, and even in marital and family therapy.

Weaker or less productive parties tend to advocate adherence to the equality norm (McClintock & Keil, 1981; Van Avermaet, McClintock, & Moskowitz, 1978). Therefore, a bargainer's choice of a distribution rule appears to be partly determined by a desire to maximize one's own outcomes, since equity increases the benefits of stronger parties, while equality increases those of weaker participants. Alternatively, social norms or outside observers may sometimes dictate that a particular distribution rule must be followed, regardless of the preferences of negotiators.

Role of third parties. Real-life negotiators and even players of bargaining games in a social psychology laboratory are highly motivated to "save face" and to avoid looking foolish or weak (Rubin & Brown, 1975, pp. 44–48). As we saw in our discussion of the trucking game, such attitudes plus the desire to maximize own outcomes can easily lead to an unproductive deadlock. A third-party mediator can be very effective in breaking these deadlocks by providing an outside perspective on what is "fair" and by allowing bargainers to offer concessions to one another via the mediator, rather than directly (Meeker & Shure, 1969; Pruitt & Johnson, 1970). One is reminded at this point of the deadlock reached by Iran and the United States in the long and painful negotiations over releasing the American embassy personnel held hostage in Teheran and of the crucial role played by Algerian diplomats in achieving a negotiated settlement.

A mediator's task is almost never easy, because bargainers usually represent groups who have a lot at stake in the outcome of the negotiations. When groups have their interests represented by a negotiator, they are concerned that the negotiator be competitive and drive a hard bargain. In one study, negotiators whose behavior was kept under surveillance by their constituents made more threats, indicated less understanding of their opponents' position, and arrived at agreements that produced smaller joint rewards than negotiators who were not under surveillance (Carnevale, Pruitt, & Britton, 1979). A mediator, particularly one who is able to reward negotiators for making concessions to one another, can elicit more mutual cooperation and can assist in bringing about final agreements that maximize rewards to both parties (Wall, 1979). The mediator's task is sometimes made easier if all parties feel pressured to conclude a deal prior to an important deadline, but to be most effective in achieving conflict resolution, a mediator must be perceived by both sides as capable and impartial (Brookmire & Sistrunk, 1980).

Personality Factors in Social Exchange and Bargaining

Obviously, a strong ideological commitment to either equity or equality as a method of allocating resources will greatly influence negotiating behavior and willingness to compromise. Aside from such principled commitments, there are other personal characteristics that may also affect bargaining and conflict resolution.

Motivational orientation. Following an idea initiated by Deutsch (1960), researchers have classified bargainers as of three basic types. *Cooperators* strive to achieve the maximum possible rewards for their opponents as well as for themselves. *Competitors* try to maximize their own rewards and at the same time minimize the rewards of their opponents. *Individualists* strive to achieve the maximum possible rewards for themselves and take little interest in whether their opponents are doing well or poorly. In one investigation, a simplified game was used to identify a given participant's motivational orientation, and then subjects of each type were matched against a computerized opponent who played a consistently cooperative, tit-for-tat, or competitive strategy (Kuhlman & Marshello, 1975). Cooperators were nearly 100 percent cooperative in response to a cooperative strategy, and progressively fewer were cooperative in the face of a tit-for-tat or competitive strategy. Individualists were most cooperative (about 60 percent) when matched against a tit-for-tat strategy, and competitors were generally uncooperative regardless of the opponent's strategy. Cooperators, competitors, and individualists also differ in their perceptions of other people, even before having an opportunity to interact with them; each type expects that others are basically cooperative, competitive, or individualistic, respectively (Kelley & Stahelski, 1970; Kuhlman & Wimberley, 1976).

Deutsch's (1960) original emphasis in this area of research was on using instructions to make temporary modifications in subjects' basic personality orientations to see if this would change the likelihood of cooperative, competitive, or individualistic behavior. His cooperation-inducing instructions referred to the subject and other player as "partners" who had a mutual interest in cooperating. The competition-inducing instructions, on the other hand, made it clear that "you're out to beat him and he's out to beat you," while the individualistic instructions stated that "you simply want to win as much money as you can for yourself and you don't care what happens to him." In work by Deutsch and other investigators it has been found that these types of instructions do indeed shift subjects' behavior toward cooperativeness, competitiveness, or individualism, respectively, in each of the three types of bargaining games discussed earlier (Rubin & Brown, 1975, pp. 201–206).

Machiavellianism. Machiavellianism is a personality trait that leads the individual to seek to achieve self-interest goals regardless of the ethicality of the means employed in doing so. A paper-and-pencil scale for measuring this trait was devised by Christie and Geis (1970), who found that high scorers (high Machs) were consistently more successful than low Machs in winning points in coalition games. Low Machs were apparently handicapped by moral feelings that kept them from backing out of unprofitable agreements; also, low Machs were less willing to engage in lengthy haggling over who should get what. One might conclude from these observations that high Machs are simply less cooperative than low Machs, but Christie and Geis found that the former types could be *more* cooperative than the latter when financial incentives made cooperation a more profitable strategy. In short, high Machs, much like the individualists discussed above, adopted whatever approach seemed to offer them the most reward, regardless of the consequences for the other player.

Sex differences. Past reviews of the literature on social exchange and bargaining have noted that women are more cooperatively oriented than men (Terhune, 1970). Women, it was said, avoid conflict and seek accommodative solutions to problems. In addition, men were supposedly more willing to follow the equity norm in dividing a reward among various contributors to a group effort, while women usually preferred equal shares. Leventhal (1976) suggested that women are more affiliation oriented than men and strive toward harmony and loyalty in their relationships. It was observed, for instance, that females expressed greater liking than did males for an allocator who distributed rewards equally and less liking for one who distributed them equitably, the main exception to this rule being a low-input allocator who opted for an equitable distribution and who was liked apparently because he had gone against his own self-interest (Kahn, Lamm, & Nelson, 1977).

Despite the foregoing findings, other reviewers have reported that the literature pertaining to sex differences in cooperativeness and preference for equality versus equity is very inconsistent (Mikula, 1980, pp. 149–150;

Rubin & Brown, 1975, pp. 169–174). Rubin and Brown suggested that females are more attuned to the feelings and motives of other parties to an exchange situation, whereas males are more individualistically oriented. This hypothesized sex difference could account for the inconsistency in the actual behavior of female and male bargainers, since either the interpersonal or the individualistic orientation may sometimes lead to cooperation and sometimes to competition. Mikula apparently feels that the only sex difference to emerge with any consistency is a tendency for males to take a larger share of available rewards. He believes, along with Rubin and Brown, that the nature and direction of any sex differences in social exchange and bargaining will depend on certain yet-to-be-identified features of the particular situations in which men and women engage.

Actually, it would be a good idea to conclude this section on personality factors with the general statement that characteristics of the person practically always *interact* with constraints in the immediate situation to influence social exchange and bargaining. Someone with a personal preference for cooperation may nonetheless become very competitive if betrayed by another player, and a competitive type may engage in a lot of cooperation if it is temporarily advantageous to do so. As was noted earlier in this chapter, people's basic preference for equity or equality as an allocation principle may or may not be expressed depending on short-term payoffs or the degree to which their allocation strategy becomes publicly known.

SOCIETAL IMPLICATIONS OF SOCIAL EXCHANGE

Especially when it is considered separately from psychologists' knowledge of other aspects of human behavior, the literature on equity, social exchange, and bargaining tends to portray human beings as primarily self-interested, calculating, and competitive. Critics of this literature have noted the similarity between equity theory and the competitive values of economic systems based on capitalism. Deutsch (1975) maintained that the theories and research of American social psychologists have been shaped by their culture and that the results they obtained were inadvertently biased so as to paint a picture of human personality that was congruent with cultural values. Sampson (1978) associated the Protestant work ethic, private property, capitalism, selective equality, and scientific methods of searching for objective truth with the historical dominance of masculine values. Masculinity, for Sampson, implies individualistic competition, while femininity implies nurturance, cooperativeness, and desire for equality. Deutsch, Sampson, and other writers on the subject of justice and fairness (for example, Rawls, 1971) have expressed a preference for equality over equity.

Noting the correspondence between the equality norm and the Marxist ideal of "from each according to his ability, to each according to his need," Deutsch (1975) has argued for a normative system that obligates each member of society to contribute as fully as possible so as to maximize the total economic resources available for equal sharing. In exceptional cases, such as a family trying to restore health to a sick member, resources may be distributed neither equally nor equitably, but instead on the basis of *need*. As Mikula (1980) has pointed out, however, a needs rule resembles equity in the sense that it, too, requires some evaluation of deservingness (that is, depth of need). Only the equality rule provides a simple, nonevaluative system for allocating resources. R. L. Cohen (1979) makes the additional observation that *any* allocation rule will run into problems when available resources fall short of what potential recipients both need and deserve.

With all the bad press it has received, one would think that the equity norm would be ashamed to reveal itself nowadays, but such is not the case. More than 2000 years ago, Aristotle wrote in his *Nichomachean Ethics* that "awards should be according to merit," and this idea persists. Furthermore, much as we may want to believe that people do not strive to maximize rewards and minimize costs and that they do not attempt to achieve these ends by driving explicit or implicit "bargains" in their social relationships, to do so is to ignore many of the facts of recorded history as well as the observations of psychologists over the past century.

Rather than pronounce either the equity or the equality norm as more humane or "progressive," we may find it more defensible to say that *both* norms have been important for human groups and that they were in the past, are in the present, and very probably will be in the future applied to socially productive as well as destructive purposes. As has been pointed out several times in this chapter, people may prefer equity and competition in some situations and equality and cooperation in others. When the equity norm is applied, of course, its productive use requires an honest and objective evaluation of legitimate inputs. Given human frailties, it is not surprising that evaluations of equity inputs in real life are often dishonest, subjective, and illegitimate; such socially destructive applications of equity have no doubt tarnished the image of the principle itself.

It may well be that an extreme and inflexible adherence to either the equity or the equality norm would produce a world that was neither very just nor very pleasant. Perhaps sensing this at an intuitive level, we are often in a state of normative conflict within ourselves when attempting to find mutually satisfying resolutions of person-to-person, group-to-group, or nation-to-nation conflicts of interest. Whatever one's preferred approach to social exchange, the feelings of fairness or unfairness that result from these interactions have a profound effect on the quality of human relationships.

SUMMARY

Social exchange implies a reciprocal transfer of goods, services, or sometimes even ideas and feelings among the various parties to a relationship. Rules of fair distribution of resources include equity and equality. The equity rule states that the rewards one derives from an exchange should be directly proportional to one's contributions to that social interaction. Equity theory translates this idea into the mathematical statement that we feel most comfortable in relationships in which the ratio of outcomes to inputs (O/I) is the same for all parties. When an *in*equity exists, there are four basic methods of restoring equity: (1) increasing the inputs of the advantaged party, (2) decreasing the inputs of the disadvantaged party, (3) decreasing the outcomes of the advantaged party, or (4) increasing the outcomes of the disadvantaged party. Outcomes and inputs may be changed in reality or distorted perceptually so as to maintain one's belief that the world is an equitable and "just" place in which all people get what they deserve. Some limitations on the straightforward application of the equity formula to social relationships are that people are more disturbed by inequities that go against them rather than in their favor, and that they may deviate from equity if they have an important short-term goal that calls for a different allocation strategy.

Adherence to the equity norm tends to foster a spirit of competition, while the equality norm encourages cooperation. Equality is the allocation strategy especially preferred by young children and by persons of any age who perceive themselves as a team, who are under pressure to make decisions quickly, who are dealing with rewards of small value, or who feel that the present distribution of resources sets no precedent for the future. Critics have argued that equity considerations do not apply to the most intimate of human relationships—friendship, love, and marriage—but research indicates otherwise.

What Thibaut and Kelley meant by social exchange was the calculation of rewards minus costs and a willingness to remain in a relationship only so long as this difference seems favorable relative to rewards minus costs experienced in the past, rewards minus costs experienced by others with whom one engages in social comparison, or rewards minus costs one might expect from alternative relationships (the CL and CL_{alt}, respectively). Feelings of relative deprivation among American blacks, who compare themselves with American whites rather than with blacks in other countries, may be interpreted in these terms.

An interaction matrix can be used to describe the basic elements of many social exchanges. Each participant may be thought of as having a cooperative and a competitive choice, and most players of these Prisoner's Dilemma games end up making competitive choices because cooperative ones always carry some risk of being exploited. Other types of paradigms used to study bargaining and conflict resolution are the trucking and coalition-formation games.

Social-exchange processes have been examined in laboratory simulations of such real-life phenomena as labor negotiations. Large initial demands followed by small concessions seem to be the most profitable strategy in these situations. Bargainers who are strong in resources generally advocate an equitable division of rewards, while weaker parties prefer an equal split. Mediators can be very effective in breaking the deadlocks that frequently occur in these negotiations.

Some personality factors that have been found to affect social exchange and bargaining are a basically cooperative, competitive, or individualistic approach to social interaction, and the trait of Machiavellianism. In reviews of the literature on social exchange and bargaining, women have been described as preferring cooperation to competition and the equality norm to equity—the opposite of the preferences attributed to men. Subsequent reviews, however, have found that the content and direction of sex differences in social exchange and bargaining was highly inconsistent from one study to another.

Although both the equity and equality norms have their critics and defenders, it seems reasonable to conclude that both norms have been and will continue to be important to human groups. As individuals, we find ourselves adhering to equity norms in some situations and equality norms or a mixture of the two in others.

SUGGESTED READINGS

Homans, G. C. *Social behavior: Its elementary forms*, rev. ed. New York: Harcourt, Brace, Jovanovich, 1974.

Kelley, H. H. & Thibaut, J. W. *Interpersonal relations: A theory of interdependence*. New York: Wiley, 1978.

Mikula, G. (Ed.). *Justice and social interaction*. New York: Springer-Verlag, 1980.

Rubin, J. Z. & Brown B. R. *The social psychology of bargaining and negotiation*. New York: Academic Press, 1975.

Walster, E., Walster, G. W., & Berscheid, E. *Equity: Theory and research*. Boston: Allyn & Bacon, 1978.

14

INTERPERSONAL INFLUENCE

INTRODUCTION

Martin Morganthau had dressed quickly after his examination and was staring out the window of his doctor's office at County General Hospital. Dr. Jordan Fremont strode in briskly and sat down at his desk without raising his eyes from Morganthau's cardiogram. Morganthau stubbed out his cigarette and sat back stiffly in his chair. His mind was racing. He had been feeling less energetic than usual lately. Over the past few months he had noticed that he had trouble catching his breath after walking up stairs or sprinting to catch a taxi. More and more frequently he had been experiencing a painful pressure in his chest. Everyone had been telling him to slow down. Now that he was in his late fifties, president of a thriving import-export business, he could afford to slow down, they said. "Time to rest on your laurels, Martin," they would tell him. That was the last thing Martin wanted to hear. He thrived on the excitement of his business. He wouldn't be the same person if he let others take over the international travel and negotiating that he had been doing for the last twenty-five years. He insisted that he just needed a vacation. He and his wife were planning to spend two weeks in the Bahamas. That would fix him up just fine. He was almost sorry he had agreed to see Dr. Fremont—especially now that Fremont was sitting across from him with his mouth drawn into a grim line.

Dr. Fremont was doing some quick thinking too. Morganthau's cardiogram did not look good. The doctor was thinking about how best to tell his patient that unless he changed his life style—learned to relax more, stop smoking, lose some weight—he was very likely to suffer a major heart attack in the near future.

What approach do you think Dr. Fremont should take? Should he simply state his recommendation, advising his patient of the dangerous consequences of noncompliance? Should he try to educate Mr. Morganthau about the relationships between smoking, obesity, stress, and heart disease? Are there other techniques that might be more effective?

Two floors below Dr. Fremont's office, in one of the hospital's conference rooms, another tension-filled scene was taking place. Ten medical technicians were seated around the table in the middle of a luncheon meeting. From the good-natured joking and informal chatter that had gone on earlier in the meeting, it was evident that the group had developed a strong bond of friendship and colleagueship. The educational programs they had organized for themselves and the social gatherings they had been enjoying over the past few years had resulted in a sense of cohesiveness and group loyalty that they all valued very highly. The joking and chatter had stopped now, however, and the group was quiet as they anticipated the vote that was about to be taken.

At the past two meetings, the question of unionization had been discussed. The technicians had been experiencing considerable dissatisfaction about the lack of response by hospital administrators to their requests for changes in their working conditions. As a consequence, they had been gathering information about the implications of unionization. Today's meeting was the one at which a vote was to be taken on whether or not the group would join a union. It had always been their practice to require unanimity on decisions regarding group activities. No other decision, however, had had as much importance attached to its outcome as this one. Most of the members were strongly in favor of unionizing. They felt that only with the support of a strong union negotiator would they be able to have an impact on hospital policies. But one member had been rather quiet during most of the discussion

---

This chapter is written by Lois Biener.

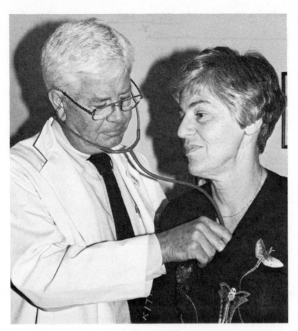

What influence strategies should health professionals use to encourage patients to develop health
promoting life styles and habits?

of unionizing. Although he had never explicitly said that he was opposed to the idea, Paul Drew had always been one of the most conservative people in the group. Several members had expressed concern to each other that Paul might vote no. Roberta Goodman, one of the most vocal advocates of unionizing, was presiding over today's meeting. It was time to take the vote, and Roberta was privately trying to decide whether to make it a secret ballot or to have the members give their votes publicly. She was also debating with herself about the wisdom of waiting for two late members who had already told her they were in favor of unionizing. Perhaps the added power of their presence would help to sway Paul. Do you think the technique of voting would make a difference? Would two more people make it easier to win a unanimous vote for unionization? Why?

Let's look in on one more scene at County

General. This time it takes place at the nurses' station in the pediatrics unit. Marie Russo, a registered nurse, is reviewing the charts of some of the children on the ward. Marie has just resumed her nursing duties half time after having completed her training as an infection-control nurse. During the infection-control course she learned that each year about 5 percent of the 32 million people admitted to the nation's hospitals acquire an infection in the hospital that they did not have when they were admitted. About 15,000 of those people die (Raven & Haley, 1980). Marie found out how to take precautions that would minimize the likelihood of these problems. Now, in addition to her nursing responsibilities, her job as infection-control nurse was to ensure that hospital staff followed the proper procedures as they carried out their daily activities. While Marie was reading through the charts, Dr. Henry Foster approached to instruct another nurse about one of his patients. The child had had a highly contagious staph infection and therefore had been isolated from other children on the unit for some time. The doctor had written a transfer order to have the child moved out of isolation. Dr. Foster, just having seen the child, mentioned that the transfer should occur immediately, because he felt that the child was suffering psychologically from the isolation. Marie was quite surprised and distressed to hear this order. She had given the child some medication a few minutes earlier and knew that the child was still obviously ill with the infection. In fact, she had seen an open sore from which pus was oozing. Moving the child onto the ward at this time would endanger all the other children.

What is Ms. Russo likely to do? Will she try to get Dr. Foster to change the order? How is Dr. Foster likely to respond to such a request?

These situations and the people in them are fictitious, but similar scenes are enacted every day by medical personnel. Comparable situations, in which a person or group attempts to influence the behavior of another person, occur in every workplace and home. Indeed, the influence process is basic to human interaction. It is not surprising, therefore, that a great deal of social-psychological research is devoted to analyzing and understanding how people come to change their behaviors or beliefs as a consequence of interaction with others. In this chapter we will examine some of the social-psychological research on influence by asking what it can tell us about the three scenes at County General Hospital. The following questions will be addressed: What resources or strategies are available to those who seek to influence others? What considerations go into a person's choice of a strategy? What influence techniques are most likely to be effective, and why?

Some Definitions

Throughout this chapter we will use several concepts that have overlapping meanings: influence, power, and status. It is well to pin down what we mean when we use these words.

Power and influence are often used synonymously. To have power over and to have influence with another imply the same phenomenon. In this chapter, however, we will use _influence_ to designate the end state, and _power_ to designate the means to the end. More specifically, the term influence will refer to the outcome of an interaction in which one person changes some aspect of his or her behavior in the direction intended by another. Power will refer to the force that motivates the change. Power can be derived from two sources: from resources the influencer possesses that are relevant for the target of the influence attempt, or from norms that the target has internalized regarding the influencer's right to direct his or her behavior. The particular forms of power available to an influencer will be described in the next section.

It is important to remember that whether or not a particular form of power will be effective

depends on the relationship between the influencer and the target. To give a very simple example, suppose A is a millionaire who wants B to do something. A may offer B lots of money in exchange for compliance. If B needs money, then A can be said to have a great deal of power to influence B, because A has a great deal of what B wants. Suppose B is a hermit, however, and does not want A's money or anything else that A could offer. In that case A would not have power to influence B. While we are accustomed to thinking of millionaires as powerful people, this example illustrates a situation in which a millionaire is quite powerless. In the sections to follow, when we discuss the various forms of power that may be available to influencers, we will be referring to _potential_ power. We cannot know whether it is actual power unless we know whether or not it is effective in an influence attempt.

Status is a third important aspect of group interaction (see Chapter 15) and social life. People have status to the extent that they possess traits that are valued by the society in which they live (Brown, 1965). The more of these traits a person possesses, the higher the status the person is accorded. While some valued traits may originate from an individual's personal characteristics—for example, good looks, skill or intelligence—we will usually be referring to the status that derives from one's social role or position. In general, managers of an organization are accorded more prestige and admiration than their workers; hence managers have higher status than workers. Likewise, in a hospital, doctors have higher status than nurses.

Power and status tend to go hand in hand. Individuals who occupy positions of high status tend to have access to resources that others desire. Individuals in low-status positions tend to be much more limited in the resources they can acquire and utilize.

The three scenes at County General Hospital differ from each other in many ways. We will make use of several of the differences in order to illustrate some of the factors that have important consequences for the influence process. The most obvious difference involves the status of the influencer in relation to the target. In the scene in Dr. Fremont's office we have a high-status influencer seeking to change a lower-status target. Among the medical technicians, the influencer (the majority of the group) and target (Paul Drew) are peers. On the pediatric unit we have a lower-status person (Ms. Russo) attempting to influence a higher-status person (Dr. Foster). Other aspects of the three scenes that will be discussed in this chapter concern the sex of the influencer and target, and the difference between interaction in a group and interaction between two individuals.

THE BASES OF SOCIAL POWER

What resources can an influencer draw upon in an attempt to bring about change in the target? Bertram Raven and his colleagues have devised a useful category scheme for answering this question (French & Raven, 1959; Raven, 1965; Raven & Kruglanski, 1970). They distinguish six potential kinds of social power that an influencer may have available: reward and coercive power, expertise, referent power, legitimate power, and informational power. Each resource has advantages and disadvantages that the influencer will have to weigh in deciding which to use.

Reward Power

Reward power stems from the influencer's ability to provide the target with something the target wants in exchange for compliance with the influencer's request. The reward may be something concrete, such as money or goods or services, or it may be something intangible such as affection, membership in a desirable group, or the like. Suppose, for example, that

Martin Morganthau's insurance company is one of the organizations that offers lower health insurance premiums for nonsmokers. If Dr. Fremont wanted to use reward power, he might promise to write Mr. Morganthau's insurance company when Martin had successfully kicked the habit. A major disadvantage of reward power is that the influencer has to maintain surveillance over the target in order to know whether or not compliance has occurred. Now, if Martin wanted to collect the reward, he would probably make it easy for Dr. Fremont to see that he had stopped smoking, and hence, surveillance would not be difficult. It is possible, however, that he might try to deceive the doctor into believing that he had stopped smoking, when in fact he had not.

Coercive Power

Coercive power derives from the influencer's ability to punish the target for failure to comply with the influencer's request. The punishment may involve the withdrawal of something valued (affection, wages, and so forth), or the infliction of pain or suffering. Like reward power, coercive power requires that the influencer maintain surveillance over the behavior of the target. Unlike the case with reward power, however, the target is likely to conceal the fact of noncompliance. For example, suppose Dr. Fremont threatened to stop seeing Mr. Morganthau unless he stopped smoking. If it were important to Martin to continue as a patient with Dr. Fremont, he might conceal the fact that he was continuing to smoke. Dr. Fremont could easily maintain surveillance over Martin's weight loss by means of periodic physical examinations, so coercive power with regard to weight loss would not be as difficult to implement. In addition to the need for surveillance, another disadvantage of coercive power is that it tends to produce hostility in the target and to make it more difficult to influence the target in the future. Indeed, if

Dr. Fremont carried out his threat and refused to see the patient, there would be no opportunity to influence Mr. Morganthau again.

Expert Power

Expert power derives from the target's belief that the influencer has superior knowledge or abilities in the domain in which the influence is being attempted. To exercise this form of power, Dr. Fremont would simply have to say, "Mr. Morganthau, the results of these tests indicate that you must change your behavior in the following ways in order to maintain your health." If Mr. Morganthau accepts on faith that Dr. Fremont is an expert, which he presumably does, no other explanation should be needed. In fact, expert power is the type that doctors generally rely upon when they interact with their patients. Although there is no problem of surveillance with this form of influence, expert power is likely to be less effective in any situation in which the target believes that the influencer has something to gain by the target's compliance. A television commercial claiming that nine doctors out of ten recommend NUMSYU aspirin for headaches is unlikely to send you off to the drugstore to purchase the brand. Clearly, the NUMSYU Company is paying for the ad in order to increase their sales, so you have good reason to doubt the experts' veracity. Nevertheless, the fact that millions of dollars are spent on TV commercials in which "experts" recommend the sponsor's product indicates that advertisers believe expert power can be effective even when motives are suspect.

Referent Power

Referent power derives from the target's desire to be similar to the influencer. If this desire exists, all the influencer has to do is demonstrate that he or she engages in the desired behavior. Referent power is frequently used by parents, older siblings, and other socializing agents. For example, a mother may point out to her young son that he should help clean the table after dinner because his father does it too. In the case of Dr. Fremont and Mr. Morganthau, the doctor might attempt to enhance Martin's perception of similarity and encourage Martin to increase the similarity. For example, Dr. Fremont might point out that they are both highly respected, successful men in their fifties. They both like working hard and enjoying the monetary benefits of their labors. Perhaps they both enjoy the same sports. If a desire to maintain the similarity could be produced, Dr. Fremont might point out how he had cut down on his office hours, stopped smoking, and lost weight, because he too was suffering from a health problem similar to Martin's.

Legitimate Power

Legitimate power stems from the target's acceptance of the notion that a particular individual, by virtue of his or her role or position, has the right to tell the target what to do. These beliefs usually derive from cultural or organizational norms. For example, children usually believe that their parents have the right to tell them what time to come home. Privates in the army usually believe that drill sergeants have the right to tell them which way to turn during a marching exercise. It is important, however, for influencers to be aware of the limitations of their legitimacy. When children reach a certain age, the norms of their peer group may dictate that it is no longer legitimate for parents to require that they be home at a certain time. Drill sergeants who attempt to tell privates how to vote in a national election will be less effective in gaining compliance in the voting booth than on the marching field. The traditional view of the doctor-patient relationship implies that doctors do have legitimate power.

All of the bases of social power mentioned so far are what Raven calls *socially dependent*. This means that their effectiveness depends on the influencer in some way. With reward and coercive power, the effectiveness depends on the influencer's knowing whether or not compliance has taken place so that rewards can be distributed or punishments meted out. Referent, expert, and legitimate power depend on characteristics of the influencer or the nature of the influencer's relationship with the target. If the characteristics or relationship change (for example, if the user of referent power becomes disliked, if the expert is shown to be a fool, if the legitimate influencer loses legitimacy because of changing social norms), there is no motivation for the target to comply. The last base of social power to be discussed differs from the rest because it is _socially independent_— it does not rely on characteristics of the influencer, but rather on the message content.

Informational Power

Informational power derives from the influencer's ability to provide the target with information that convinces the target that the change being requested is a good one to make. If such information can be provided, then the impetus for change becomes independent of the influencer. For example, Dr. Fremont could provide his patient with information that would demonstrate why it is important to stop smoking. He could explain to Mr. Morganthau that with each puff of his cigarette he is inhaling a substance called carbon monoxide. The problem with carbon monoxide is that it combines with red blood cells and thereby prevents the red blood cells from combining with the oxygen that the body needs. Since less oxygen is getting into the blood, the body has to work harder to get the amount it needs. Therefore the heart has to beat faster, the blood pressure goes up—all in all, a great strain is put on the system.

In order for informational power to be effective, the message must be presented in a convincing manner. A great deal of research in social psychology is devoted to determining what factors increase the effectiveness of persuasive messages. (See Chapter 5.) It also must be relevant to the thoughts and values that support the existing behavior. Certainly Mr. Morganthau values his life. He may, however, consider his life less valuable without the activities he is accustomed to performing.

We have illustrated the six kinds of power by drawing examples from the doctor-patient interaction in which the influencer is a high-status person. Indeed, when high-status people attempt to influence lower-status targets, they often have access to most of these power bases. A recent study by Raven and Haley (1980) demonstrated that when doctors and nurses were asked how likely they were to use each of the six bases of power to influence other hospital staff members, doctors indicated that they were at least "somewhat likely" to use most of them. Nurses, on the other hand, thought it unlikely that they would use more than one or two. (See Social Focus 14.1 for more details about this study.)

This is not to say that influence cannot occur among people of equal status. Peers have access to some very potent sources of power, as we will demonstrate later. It is also possible for low-status individuals to influence higher-status targets, although it may require more effort. Table 14.1 shows how influence could occur in each of the three scenes at County General Hospital, as a consequence of each of the six bases of social power. It illustrates what would have to go on in the head of the target in order for the influence attempt to be effective.

FACTORS THAT INFLUENCE THE CHOICE OF A POWER BASE

It is possible for an influencer to use any of the six bases of social power. As you look over Table 14.1, however, some examples will probably seem more plausible to you than others. How is an influencer likely to choose among

TABLE 14.1
Examples of Motivations for Compliance According to Type of Power Utilized

Base of Social Power	Target's Impetus for Change	STATUS RELATION OF INFLUENCER TO TARGET		
		High to Low (Doctor to Patient)	Equal (Peer Group to Member)	Low to High (Nurse to Doctor)
Reward	Desire to obtain the reward	I'll stop smoking so that I can get lower insurance rates.	I'll vote for the union so the group will like me.	I'll cancel the transfer order so I can get a good evaluation from Ms. Russo.
Coercive	Desire to avoid punishment	I'll stop smoking so that Dr. Fremont won't stop seeing me.	I'll vote for the union so that the group won't reject me.	I'll cancel the transfer order so that Ms. Russo won't damage my reputation.
Expert	Desire to do the right thing and belief that influencer knows what is right	I'll stop smoking because the doctor told me to and he knows how to prevent heart attacks.	I'll vote for the union because, since so many of the others want it, it must be a good idea.	I'll cancel the transfer order because Ms. Russo says it's dangerous and she knows a lot about disease control.
Referent	Desire to be like the influencer	I'll stop smoking because Dr. Fremont did and I admire him.	I'll vote for the union because I want to be like the others in the group.	I'll cancel the transfer order because Ms. Russo says the other doctors follow those procedures.
Legitimate	Desire to conform to social expectations regarding relationship with influencer	I'll stop smoking because I should follow the doctor's orders.	I'll vote for the union because the majority ought to rule.	I'll cancel the order because I ought to heed the infection-control practitioner.
Informational	Desire to behave rationally	I'll stop smoking because I understand how it will ruin my health.	I'll vote for the union because I see how it will benefit the technicians.	I'll cancel the transfer order because I see that the other patients would be in jeopardy.

the various strategies available? Obviously, an influencer must possess the resource necessary for a particular power base in order to choose it. Given this, let's reflect upon the considerations an influencer might take into account when deciding upon a particular course of action.

Costs to the Influencer

There are often significant costs associated with power usage. For instance, with reward and coercive power the influencer will incur the cost of maintaining surveillance. This may require additional time and personnel or other resources such as investment in mechanical surveillance systems. In choosing from among the various power bases that may produce the same level of compliance, an influencer is likely to select the one that involves the least cost.

Negative Emotional States

An influencer who is anxious or feels hostile toward the target will sometimes use coercive power. This was demonstrated in a field

SOCIAL FOCUS 14.1
The SENIC Project: Study on the Efficacy of Nosocomial Infection Control

When the first American hospital was established in Philadelphia in 1751, its sole purpose was to treat and cure the illnesses of the poor. It was felt that by providing them with the care that they otherwise lacked the means to procure, the poor could be restored to social usefulness and be kept out of the alms-houses (Ashley, 1976). By gathering large numbers of diseased people into one place, however, the spread of infection from one to the other was practically ensured. Hence, until a century later, when aseptic techniques were being practiced, those who could be cared for at home had a better chance of surviving their illnesses.

Even now, with the vast technology available to health-care providers, hospital-acquired infections (nosocomial infections) are a serious problem. It is now a condition of accreditation for hospitals that they have an infection surveillance and control program (ISCP). Personnel associated with the ISCP are required to monitor infection risks in the hospital, and formulate and implement policies for reducing risks. They are also responsible for influencing physicians, nurses, and other patient-care personnel to practice techniques that prevent risks.

In 1974 the Center for Disease Control initiated a project designed to evaluate the effectiveness of various programs for reducing hospital-acquired infection (Raven & Haley, 1980). The title of the project is the "Study on the Efficacy of Nosocomial Infection Control," also known as SENIC. The Center recognized that one of the primary factors contributing to effectiveness was the influential power of the infection-control staff in their interactions with other hospital personnel. In order to investigate the influence process, the Center for Disease Control enlisted the collaboration of social scientists at UCLA under the direction of Bertram Raven. In one phase of the study, personnel from 433 hospitals all around the country were interviewed by research staff. Physicians and nurses were asked, for example, what they would do if they saw other staff members using improper procedures. Nurses were asked how they would respond if a doctor asked them to carry out a task that broke with standards of aseptic techniques. Personnel were presented with examples of influence attempts that drew on the various power bases discussed in this chapter. The results of several of the analyses from this comprehensive study are presented throughout this chapter.

study that surveyed supervisors' responses to the poor performance of subordinates. The results showed that white supervisors reported using more coercive strategies with black than with white subordinates and with union than with nonunion subordinates. Presumably, these findings were a consequence of racial prejudice on the part of the supervisors, as well as of their hostility toward union members' ability to resist orders (Kipnis, Silverman, & Copeland, 1973).

These findings have particular relevance to low-status influencers like Ms. Russo and those who lack confidence in their ability to be effective. These individuals are quite likely to experience anxiety at the point when the influence must be attempted. If they don't withdraw entirely from the situation, they may fall into the trap of taking a punitive, coercive stance.

Extent of Change Required—
Long-Term versus Short-Term

When long-term change is desired, as is the case in our doctor-patient example, it is usually more effective and less costly if the target regards the change as a consequence of his or her own choice. If, instead, the target regards the change as externally motivated, then the influencer must see to it that the external forces are continually being exerted in an effective manner. If Mr. Morganthau stops smoking merely to get lower insurance rates, he may well take it up again after his insurance company makes the adjustment on his premiums—especially if he thinks Dr. Fremont will not find out.

A study by Litman-Adizes, Fontaine, and Raven (1978) provides evidence that the various power bases we have been discussing tend to produce differing perceptions of the cause of the change. In that study subjects reacted to scenarios in which a supervisor had successfully influenced a worker with one of the six bases of power. Subjects rated the extent to which the worker's compliance was due to the worker's will (internally caused) and to the supervisor's will (externally caused). Results indicated greater perceived supervisor control for all power bases. Supervisors, however, were perceived to be most responsible and workers least responsible for change, when coercive and legitimate power had been exercised. On the other hand, when referent or informational power had been exercised, workers were seen to be almost as responsible as the supervisor for the change in their behavior.

Sometimes it is possible to use a very subtle reward or punishment and still get the target to make the change. When this happens it is a powerful strategy, because the target may not realize that the change was produced by an external force and instead see the change as being a consequence of his or her own choice. Research on cognitive dissonance has shown that when people make a change that is perceived to be internally motivated, they tend to develop beliefs and attitudes that justify the change and help to maintain it. (See Chapter 5.)

Desire to Perpetuate or Change the
Existing Status Relationship

The form of power used says something to the target about the influencer's perception of their status relationship. An influencer's choice of a strategy can be a way to communicate that perception, and to signal the intention to perpetuate the existing status relationship. Waitzkin and Waterman (1974) point out that a physician's control over the doctor-patient relationship hinges, to a great extent, on his or her ability to control the patient's uncertainty. By using expert power rather than informational power, physicians perpetuate their patients' dependency. The desire to maintain the target's dependency is probably a factor that affects influence strategies in most professional-client relationships (cf. Freidson, 1970).

On the other hand, a desire to equalize the status relationship may be a factor in the choice of informational power as an influence strategy. If Dr. Fremont attempted to provide his patient with the information regarding the need for a behavior change, he would be communicating respect for the patient's ability to review the relevant information and come to his own conclusions.

Influencers who see themselves as of lower status than their targets may avoid particular power bases in order to remain in the target's good graces. Suppose, for example, that Marie Russo emphasized her expertise in infection-control procedures in an attempt to get Dr. Foster to rescind his transfer order for the child with the staph infection. In doing so, she would be implying to the doctor that she knew more than he did on this subject. If Foster were strongly committed to the traditional status hierarchy of the hospital, he might regard Russo's use of this power base as a hostile gesture—an attempt to get "uppity."

In some instances, low-power influencers might choose a power base specifically designed to impress the target with their strength and power. Franz Fanon (1963), in *The Wretched of the Earth,* advocates the use of threats and violence by oppressed groups, even though they may be just as likely to gain concessions from their oppressors with more peaceful methods. When effective, coercive power demonstrates the superiority of the influencer, thereby raising the influencer's self-esteem. In some situations, the status gain may be more important than the change that has been brought about in the target (cf. Raven & Kruglanski, 1970).

Summary

We have seen, so far, that there are a number of different strategies available to influencers and that each strategy has some characteristic advantages and disadvantages. We have also seen that in choosing among potential strategies, an influencer will be affected by many factors: whether or not the necessary resources are at hand; the costs that will be incurred in utilizing a particular strategy; whether a negative emotional state exists; whether the desired change is of a one-shot or long-term nature; and how the strategy will affect the nature of the influencer's relationship with the target.

Let us turn now to research on the influence process to see what is known about the effectiveness of the various strategies. First, we will consider influence situations in which the influencer is a high-status individual and the target is of lower status. Following that, we

will deal with influence among peers, and finally, with situations in which low-status individuals or groups attempt to bring about change.

HIGH-STATUS INFLUENCERS

Following the Doctor's Orders

The problem Dr. Fremont was mulling over when we left him is one that has been of great concern to the medical profession. Studies show that on the average only about 50 percent of patients fully carry out the medical regimen prescribed by their doctors (Sackett, 1976). When it comes to making long-term changes in habitual behaviors—the kind of changes Dr. Fremont is recommending—the level of adherence is likely to be even lower. Patients have disregarded physicians' instructions in a great variety of ways. They frequently fail to take the prescribed dosage of medication. They drop out of treatments designed to control chronic diseases like diabetes and hypertension. It has even been found that mothers, advised to give their children penicillin for ten days in order to cure a painful middle-ear infection, frequently stop giving the medication after five days (Becker, Drachman, & Kirscht, 1972). Nonadherence has been attributed to many things, including disappearance of symptoms, regimens that require complex behaviors, and lack of support in the patient's family (Kirscht & Rosenstock, 1979). Clearly, then, expert power in itself is often ineffective in the doctor-patient interaction. In fact, physicians' desires to maintain their position as experts may be one of the causes of nonadherence. Patients who fail to carry out prescribed treatments frequently do so because they do not really understand what they have been advised to do (Becker, Drachman, & Kirscht, 1972; Hulka, Cassel, & Kupper, 1976). Doctors typically use terminology that patients are apt to misunderstand, as illustrated in the following dialogue. Some physicians use technical jargon even when they expect that it will not be understood by their patients (McKinlay, 1975), an unfortunate example of how an influencer's desire to maintain the dependency of the target leads to the choice of a strategy that undercuts the influencer's effectiveness.

Mother: Do you think he might have developed the murmur, being that my husband and I both have a murmur?
Doctor: No.

Mother: No. Oh, it's not hereditary then?
Doctor: No. (Someone whistling in the room)

Mother: Oh, I see.
Doctor: It is true that certain people have a tendency to rheumatic fever, for instance.

Mother: Mmm.
Doctor: There is a tendency for the abnormal antigen-antibody reactions to be inherited, and therefore they can sometimes be more susceptible.

Mother: Oh, I see. That wouldn't mean anything if uh . . . I would . . . I'm Rh negative and he's positive. It wouldn't mean anything in that line, would it?
Doctor: Unh-unh.

Mother: No? Okay.
Doctor: No. The only thing you have to worry about is other babies.

Mother: Mmm.
Doctor: Watch your Coombs and things.

Mother: Watch my what?
Doctor: Your titres . . . Coombs titres.

Mother: Oh, yeah.

This is a partial transcript of an interaction between a pediatrician and a mother who has just been informed that her baby has a heart murmur. How well do you think she'll watch

her Coombs? (from Korsch & Negrete, 1972).

What kind of influence should physicians be advised to use instead of or in addition to expert power? The value of informational power is not as clear as one might hope. Several writers have pointed out that patients' knowledge about their condition was not related to their tendency to follow the doctor's advice (Kirscht & Rosenstock, 1979; Henderson, Hall, & Lipton, 1979; Sackett, Haynes, Gibson, Hackett, Taylor, Roberts, & Johnson, 1975); but others have shown that some understanding of the reason for the particular treatment does increase adherence (Hulka, Cassel, & Kupper, 1976; Tagliacozzo & Ima, 1970). Evidently information concerning the purposes of a medical regimen and the health consequences of failing to comply does not always provide sufficient motivation to overcome the many resistances people have to changing their habitual behaviors.

It has been shown that surveillance of the patient's behavior increases compliance with medical regimens. Hospitalized patients follow doctors' orders more than day patients, and day patients are more compliant than outpatients. Further, when the frequency of outpatient visits is increased, compliance tends to improve (Haynes, 1976). The fact that surveillance increases the effectiveness of influence suggests that some aspect of coercive power may be operating. It is probably embarrassing to have to face a health-care provider whose advice you haven't taken. On the other hand, since the embarrassment comes from being caught doing something one "ought" not to do—disobeying the doctor—legitimacy might be the power base that is operating. Milgram's studies of obedience, to be discussed in the next section, demonstrate how surveillance affects compliance in a laboratory setting.

It seems that in order for patients to get the most out of their interactions with physicians, many aspects of the provider-patient relationship must be improved. Patients need to become more active participants in their own health care. Lazare, Eisenthal, Frank and Stoekle (1978) recommend that physicians engage in negotiations with their patients. During the process, any conflicts regarding their respective definitions of the problem, its cause, and the appropriate course of treatment can be ironed out. This radical alteration in the concept of the patient's role has been shown to increase patient satisfaction. Proponents expect that it will also increase patient adherence to treatment regimens. Rodin and Janis (1979) emphasize the necessity for getting the patient to internalize the physician's recommendation and feel personally responsible for adhering to prescribed regimens. They recommend a process that first calls for the establishment of trust and cohesiveness between the doctor and patient. This good feeling not only increases the referent power available to the physician, it also makes the physician's positive regard a valued commodity for the patient. Hence, it increases the physician's reward power. Once the rapport exists, patients may be more open to informational influence. Such a procedure reduces the emphasis on expertise, which has often been shown to be an ineffective power base.

Obedience to Authority

The preceding section may have demonstrated that doctors have less power to influence their patients than you thought they had. Next you may discover that they have more power than you thought they had to influence other health-care professionals.

Picture the following scene. A nurse is working the evening shift on Ward C. Things are rather quiet. The telephone rings and she takes the call. It's a Dr. Smith, whom she has heard of but doesn't know personally. He tells her that he has been asked to see Miss Jones, a patient on Ward C, and he wants her to have taken some Astroten before he arrives. He asks the nurse to find the bottle of Astroten which

is on the shelf. When she has found it, he tells her to administer 20 milligrams to Miss Jones immediately. He says he will be there in ten minutes and will sign the prescription order then. He'd like the drug to have started taking effect by the time he arrives. The nurse hangs up the phone and looks at the unfamiliar bottle. Astroten is a drug she has never heard of before. The label on the bottle says the maximum daily dose is 10 milligrams—much less than what has been ordered by the doctor. Nevertheless, she proceeds to prepare the medicine and heads down the hall to the patient's room.

The telephone call that this nurse received, like the calls received by twenty-two other nurses in two hospitals, was part of a study being conducted by Hofling, Brotzman, Dalrymple, Graves, and Pierce (1966). The researchers were concerned about nurses' tendencies to carry out physicians' instructions, even when those instructions were inappropriate. The results of their experiment indicated that indeed there was great cause for concern. Twenty-one of the twenty-two nurses would have administered the overdose. Fortunately, the Astroten bottle contained harmless placebos and nurses were intercepted before they could carry out their missions.

We pointed out earlier that patients seem eminently capable of disregarding doctors' orders. What accounts for the nurses' readiness to obey, even when that obedience might cause grave harm to patients entrusted to their care? Is it the doctors' expert power? Do the nurses assume that the doctors know what they are doing? Maybe. Perhaps you'd argue that the doctors' coercive power accounts for the nurses' obedience. A doctor can probably have a nurse who fails to follow orders fired. More likely, however, it's the power of legitimacy. By virtue of their respective roles in the health-care system, nurses accept the notion that doctors have a right to tell them what to do regarding a patient's medical care. They feel obligated to carry out the orders. Legitimacy as we will see, is an extremely potent base of social power. A series of experiments carried out by Stanley Milgram (1974) demonstrated that fact very clearly.

Milgram's studies of obedience. The studies carried out by Stanley Milgram at Yale University between 1960 and 1963 have become widely known within and outside the field of psychology. The notoriety is probably due both to the intensity of the experience endured by his research subjects and to the fact that his results told us something we didn't want to hear.

Male subjects were recruited for Milgram's studies from the New Haven community by means of an ad in local newspapers. The ad invited men to participate in a study of memory and learning at Yale University. They were told that they would be paid four dollars for one hour of their time. Interested participants were scheduled and when a participant showed up at the appointed time he found two others there. One was another participant and the second was the experimenter. The basic procedure in Milgram's studies was as follows. The experimenter explains that the study is about the effects of punishment on learning. One of the two participants, he says, will be the teacher and the other will be the learner. He asks them to draw lots to determine which participant will play each part. This done, all three people go into an adjacent room where the learner is strapped into a chair ("to prevent excessive movement") and electrodes are taped onto his wrist. The experimenter explains that the learner's task will be to learn a list of word pairs that will be read to him by the teacher. Whenever he makes an error the teacher will administer an electric shock of increasing intensity. Then the second participant is led back to the main experimental room where he is seated in front of a shock generator. The generator contains a horizontal line of 30 switches which are labeled with their voltages. The lowest is 15 volts and the highest is 450. There are also verbal labels on the generator, which go from

"slight shock" to "danger—severe shock" to "xxx." The teacher is instructed to go through a word list with the man in the other room by means of an intercom. Whenever the learner makes a mistake the teacher is to give him a shock. He is to start at the lowest switch, 15 volts, and then proceed to the next higher switch every time the learner makes an error.

As you may have guessed, the learner is not really a naive subject, but rather a confederate of the experimenter who actually receives no shocks. The purpose of the study is to see how far a person will go in inflicting pain on an innocent victim simply because he has been told to do so by an experimenter. The victim had been trained to make numerous mistakes and increasingly strong objections to being shocked. At 300 volts he shouts that he will no longer provide answers to the memory test. The teacher is told to treat the absence of a response as an error. After 330 volts the learner makes no further response to the shocks and no further responses on the memory test.

Should the teacher ask the experimenter's advice about what to do at any point or should he indicate that he wants to stop administering shocks, the experimenter would tell him to continue. If the subject refuses to obey after the fourth prod, the experiment is terminated. If the teacher asks whether the shocks are dangerous, the experimenter tells him that they may be quite painful but will do no permanent damage.

How far do you think the teacher will go in this situation? How far would you go? If you are like other people who have been asked this question after being provided with a description of the experiment, you probably think you would stop somewhere between 120 and 150 volts. In fact, 25 of the 40 subjects (62 percent) who were run in this experiment continued administering shocks until they reached 450 volts, the last switch on the generator. (See the "voice feedback" condition in Table 14.2)

This is an extremely disturbing finding, even though the subjects in the study were by

TABLE 14.2
Maximum Shocks Administered in Various Experimental Conditions

	Remote	Voice-Feedback	CONDITION Proximity	Touch Proximity	Women Subjects	Bridgeport
N	40	40	40	40	40	40
Mean Maximum Voltage	405	367	312	268	370	315
Percentage Obedient Subjects	65.0	62.5	40.0	30.0	65.0	47.5

Source: Adapted from Milgram, 1974

no means unconcerned about the victim's plight. Milgram reports that most of the subjects gave signs of being in great conflict.

Milgram carried out a number of variations on this basic design in order to determine the conditions under which obedience is most likely to occur and the conditions most likely to elicit disobedience. In one series he varied the distance between the victim and the subject. In the "remote" condition, the victim's voice could not be heard. The subject's only knowledge of the victim's reaction was that he pounded the wall at 300 volts and stopped responding to the word association task (which he had done by means of a light signal) at 315 volts. In the "proximity" condition the learner gave the same verbal responses as in the basic "voice-feedback" condition, but was seated in the same room only a few feet from the teacher. In the "touch proximity" condition the learner had to rest his hand on a metal plate in order to receive the shock. When he refused, at 150 volts, to put his hand on the plate, the teacher was ordered to push the victim's hand onto the plate so that the shock could be administered. Another variation included moving the entire operation to a shabby office building in Bridgeport in order to remove the implied approval of Yale University. In still another version of the study, female subjects were

used. As Table 14.2 illustrates, some of these variations succeeded in lowering the percentage of completely obedient subjects; even in the least compelling condition, however, a substantial minority of subjects continued to the highest level of shock possible.

How can we understand this disturbing phenomenon? If the subjects were soldiers and the experimenter were their commanding officer, the torturing of a defenseless civilian would be more comprehensible, although no less horrifying. Why should grown men agree to administer painful, possibly lethal electric shocks to a person whose only crime was making errors on a memory task? Since subjects showed obvious signs of conflict and strain (several had uncontrollable seizures), why did they find it so difficult to say no to a man in a white coat whom they had never seen before and presumably would never see again?

While Elms and Milgram (1966) have found that subjects high in authoritarianism are more likely to obey than subjects who score low on this trait, in general the search for individual personality dispositions that account for obedience in this situation has not been very fruitful (Larsen, Coleman, Forbes, & Johnson, 1972). By varying aspects of the situation, such as the extent of responsibility the subject is given for the victim's well-being and the amount of feedback from the victim, one can raise or lower the amount of obedience much more dramatically than by choosing subjects with particular traits.

The high degree of obedience in Milgram's subjects may be partially due to the fact that they were participating in psychological studies. Orne (1962) and others have argued that subjects become uncharacteristically compliant when they participate in psychological experiments. Assuming that the experimenter must have good reason for what he or she is asking, the subject tends to suspend judgment and fulfill the implicit contract to carry out any request the experimenter makes. Orne demonstrated this tendency to comply in a study that required subjects to complete addition problems. Subjects were left alone in a room and given 2000 sheets of paper, each of which had 224 addition problems. They were told to complete a sheet and then to pick up a card from another stack, which would tell them what to do next. Unfortunately for the subject, every card in the stack read: "Tear up the sheet of paper which you have just completed . . . and go on to the next sheet of paper." Although Orne had expected that subjects would stop performing when they realized that all the cards said the same thing and that all of their finished work was being destroyed. He was amazed to find that subjects persisted at this meaningless task for several hours! When interviewed at the end of the experiment, however, subjects indicated that they did not see the task as meaningless. They had numerous hunches about what they were doing and what might be the significance of their performance.

Orne's research on the peculiar power of psychological experiments has been used by some writers as a criticism of Milgram's study (cf. Wrightsman, 1972). The implication is that if Milgram's subjects had encountered a malevolent authority in more familiar, everyday surroundings, they would have been less willing to obey orders. It seems to us, however, that the point Orne is making is the same that Milgram is making—that when a person is the target of influence in a situation where the influencer is seen as a legitimate authority, regardless of whether that influencer is an experimenter, a parent, a lieutenant, or an employer, the target is very likely to comply.

As Milgram points out, the experimenter is the person in charge and long years have been spent teaching us that we must do what the person in charge says. Initially, we learned through rewards for compliance and punishment for noncompliance. In fact, the first twenty years of a person's life are typically spent in the role of subordinate in hierarchical structures—at schools, in the military, and on the job. As a result, says Milgram, we internalize the rules that help us to know what to do. Once those rules are internalized, the motivation to comply with the authority figure comes not from fear of punishment but from desire to live by the rules. Responsibility for the content of the action is shifted to the authority. The subordinates feel responsible only for how well they carry out the authority's commands. In most instances, this tendency to obey authorities results in the efficient functioning of complex social groups. Imagine, for example, how chaotic life would be in the hospital if doctors had to use informational power to persuade nurses to carry out each of their orders. Occasionally, however, obedience brings about tragedy (Social Focus 14.2).

Milgram carried out two variations in his experiment that did succeed in lowering the level of obedience dramatically. In one variation, the experimenter left the room after giving the initial instructions. He then spoke to the subject over the telephone, giving orders to continue as in the basic design. In this condition only 20 percent of the subjects continued to the highest level of shock. Several of the subjects even "cheated" and gave lower levels of shock than they had been ordered to give. Evidently, the surveillance of the authority was an important component of his power. In the other variation that produced disobedience, the subject found himself to be one of three "teach-

SOCIAL FOCUS 14.2
The Jonestown Massacre—the Ultimate Act of Obedience

In Jonestown, over 900 people complied with Reverend Jim Jones' directive to commit suicide. Why did they do it?

For many Americans the first inkling of the tragedy came with a mysterious one-paragraph newspaper article reporting the ambush of a California congressman in a South American jungle. The next day the newspaper said nothing. Then gradually the story took shape. When all the news was in, we had learned that over 900 people were dead because they had obeyed the directive of their leader, Reverend Jim Jones, to commit "revolutionary suicide." After receiving word that Congressman Leo J. Ryan and members of his party had been killed while trying to help some defectors leave Jonestown, Jones had called his followers together and told them that the time had come for them to carry out the act they had practiced many times in the past. They were to commit mass suicide by drinking a potion laced with cyanide. An hour or so later, practically every member of the People's Temple commune in Guyana was dead.

Why did they do it? What force could compel parents to feed poison to their children, hear them scream in terror, go into convulsions and die? What power could be strong enough to lead hundreds of people to willingly give up their lives? When it was reported that armed guards were circling the group and that many of the bodies showed signs of having been injected with poison, the horrified public embraced the theory that the event was as much mass murder as mass suicide. But from the bulk of the evidence—from the two eyewitnesses who escaped into the jungle, from the grisly tape recording of the event, and from cult members and ex-members who were not in Jonestown at the time—it appears that the majority of the deaths could not be easily attributed to blatant coercion or murder.

On the contrary, reports from all these sources indicate that Jones had every form of power that we have outlined in this chapter. Various forms were effective for various people.

Reward

Some of the members believed that they would be reincarnated. By taking their lives now, they would win peace in the next life and love from Rev. Jones. Jones encouraged this belief during the killings. Clayton, one of the escapees, recalled that Jones was saying, "I love you, I love you. . . . It won't hurt you. It's just like closing your eyes and drifting into a deep sleep . . ." He walked among the followers, embracing them and saying, "I'll see you in the next life." As he accepted the cup of poison, one follower said, "We'll all fall tonight, but he'll raise us tomorrow" (Winfrey, 1979).

Many of the members evidently felt that by committing mass suicide, they would be strengthening their cause. Two guards who were sent to get the visiting attorneys, Charles Garry and Mark Lane, "had this smile on their faces. They said, 'It's a great moment—we all die.'. . . They said . . . that it was a pleasure to die for revolutionary suicide, that this is the way it's got to be done as an expression against racism and fascism" (Winfrey, 1979).

Coercion

It is true that armed guards surrounded the group and some people may have felt that if they didn't drink the poison, they would be killed anyway.

Informational Power

Jones told them that because of the murders of the congressman and some of those with him, the commune would very soon be attacked either by the Guyanese army or the CIA. There was talk of torture and concentration camps. "When they start parachuting out of the air, they'll shoot some of our innocent babies. Can you let them take your child?" ("Hurry, My Children, Hurry," 1979).

Referent Power

Jones was a beloved leader for most of his followers. The group, which was composed of many poor blacks, had given up all their possessions, cut off ties with their families, and followed him to the jungles of South America to start a new society. The fact that he felt it was time to "die with dignity" must have motivated many who wanted to emulate him. "To me death is not a fearful thing," Jones said that day. "It's living that's cursed. It's not worth living like this. . . . I like to choose my own kind of death for a change. I'm tired of being tormented to hell. Tired of it." (Applause) (Ibid.). Jones's referent power for one of the members is evident in this statement heard on the tape: "Like Dad (the cultists called Jones "Dad") said, when they come in, they're going to massacre our children. And the ones that they take captive, they're gonna just let them grow up and be dummies. And not grow up to be a person like the one and only Jim Jones." (Applause) ("Hurry, My Children, Hurry," 1979).

Expert Power

Jones was clearly the expert on what should be done. He controlled everything that happened at Jonestown, and had directed the members' activities for years. Jones's statements to the group emphasize his expertise. "I've tried to keep this thing from happening. But I now see it's the will of the sovereign Being that we lay down our lives in protest against what's been done." As one man said, "I'm ready to go. If you tell us we have to give our lives now, we're ready; all the rest of the sisters and brothers are with me" ("Hurry, My Children, Hurry," 1979).

Legitimate Power

Jones used many techniques to reinforce the feeling that he was the group's legitimate leader and that they were obligated to obey him. By insisting that they call him "Dad" and call his wife Marceline, "Mother," he likened his role to that of a parent. Children must obey their parents. At meetings of the commune, he sat on a chair on an elevated platform almost like a king. He laid the groundwork for his legitimacy during the years preceding the tragedy. He had carried out an extensive program of socialization in which group members were called upon to declare, verbally and in writing, how much they loved him and how important he was to them. There were rewards for acceptable behavior and punishment, often in the form of brutal beatings, for unacceptable behavior (Winfrey, 1979).

In addition to this vast store of personal power available to Jones, there was the equally vast force of peer pressure among the followers themselves. Seeing their friends and relatives killing their children and then taking their own lives undoubtedly convinced many members that suicide was the only alternative for them.

In summary, by analyzing the influence process at Jonestown, an unbelievable, bewildering event becomes an understandable tragedy.

ers'' in a study of the effect of ''collective teaching and punishment on memory and learning.'' Unknown to the subject, the other two teachers were confederates of the experimenter. At two different points each of the confederate teachers refused to continue with the experiment. Only 10 percent of the 40 naive subjects in this condition continued in the experiment until the 450-volt shock was administered.

The Undermining of Authority

It is very significant that the most effective means of undermining the power of the legitimate authority in these studies was to provide the subject with disobedient peers. Seeing the others balk provided the subject with a new perception of the situation. Remember, the basis of legitimate power is the internalized norm that the person in charge, the experimenter, has the right to tell the subject what to do and that the subject is obligated to obey. Norms, however, are effective only so long as they are generally adhered to. By defying the norm, the disobedient teachers allow the subject to redefine the situation as *not* being one in which the rules concerning authority apply. They provide validation for the subject's growing concern about the victim and demonstrate that a natural response to the situation is defiance. The subject also observes that the consequences of disobedience are minimal.

Recall the Hofling et al. study we discussed earlier. In that research the nurses received an inappropriate order from the physician at a time when the ward was virtually deserted. There were no other nurses present with whom the subject could discuss the disturbing phone call. Two other investigators, Rank and Jacobson (1977), felt that the situation for the nurses was unrepresentative of what would usually be found on a hospital ward. Nurses rarely work alone, and if they actually did receive an inappropriate order, they would prob-

ably discuss it with the other nurses before carrying it out. Rank and Jacobson also pointed out that in the Hofling et al. study, the nurses were dealing with a drug they had no experience with and hence had to rely on the physician even more than they usually would. Rank and Jacobson repeated the study with several changes. First, the telephone order from the physician was to administer 30 milligrams of Valium, a well-known drug that is usually administered in 2 to 10 milligram doses. Second, there were other nurses present when the order was given. Rank and Jacobson report that out of the twenty nurses who participated in the study, only two were fully compliant. The other eighteen nurses all tried to verify the order. Twelve tried to recontact the doctor, three tried to contact their supervisors, and one tried to call the pharmacy. The authors attribute the nurses' resistance to their interaction with other nurses. All but one commented to her co-workers about the call. Thus, this and other studies (Redfearn, 1979) demonstrate that a supportive peer group can bolster a subordinate's assertiveness in the face of an inappropriate order from a legitimate authority.

Summary

We have seen so far that although high-status individuals tend to have access to a broad range of power bases, they are not uniformly effective in influencing lower-status targets. Milgram's research has demonstrated that when the target's response to the influence attempt must occur in the presence of a higher-status influencer, legitimate power can be extraordinarily effective. Research on patient adherence to physicians' advice also shows that surveillance by the authority increases adherence. If, however, the target's response is to occur primarily without the influencer's surveillance, the power of a legitimate authority diminishes. Furthermore, since the legitimate power of high-status influencers stems primarily from the target's acceptance of obedience norms, the influencer's power can be severely undermined by information that those norms are not applicable. Peers who challenge the authority of the high-status influencer can provide the target with that information.

PEER INFLUENCERS

Let us consider now the interaction among the group of medical technicians at County General Hospital. Unlike the examples of high-power influence attempts, there is no individual authority figure in this situation. Rather, the influencer is the majority of the group who want to get Paul Drew to vote for unionization. Once again we will ask what resources are available to the influencers and what determines whether their influence attempt will be effective? The answers to these questions are found in the social psychological literature on **conformity.**

The thing that distinguishes conformity from the other examples of **social influence** discussed in this chapter, is that the influencer is a group and the target is a member of the group. Conformity has been defined as "a change in behavior or belief toward a group as a result of real or imagined group pressure" (Kiesler & Kiesler, 1969, p. 2). When conformity occurs, the target's behavior becomes more similar to that of the group; however, tension between the target's initial position and that of the group is an important defining condition.

Most of us wear shoes, for example, and those of us who wear skirts tend to keep them at the length that is currently fashionable. Unless appearing properly shod is the outcome of a conflict between, say, our desire to go barefoot to the symphony and our concern about our reputation, we would consider shoe wearing conventional behavior rather than an example of conformity (cf. Wrightsman, 1972).

A distinction is frequently made between public conformity (sometimes called compliance) and private conformity (internal cognitive change). It is clear that people sometimes say what they think the group wants them to say, but go on believing something different. Likewise, they may refuse to say what the group wants to hear, but privately begin to believe it anyway. Most of the research on conformity relies on observable behavior, however, and while we are aware of the importance of the distinction, in this chapter we will take conformity to mean public compliance with or without private change.

Asch's Studies of Conformity

About thirty years ago Solomon Asch began a program of research that involved a situation not unlike the one encountered by Paul Drew (Asch, 1951, 1952, 1955, 1956). In Asch's experiments individuals found themselves in groups in which they disagreed with the majority. The topic under discussion, however, was not a question of social policy such as whether or not to unionize, where we are not surprised to find disagreement. Rather, the question in Asch's groups concerned a matter of objective fact—whether or not one line was the same length as another. In his research Asch put the power of group pressure to a stringent test. He wanted to discover the conditions under which individuals would forsake the evidence of their own senses in order to go along with the opinion of others. Since Asch's research became the model for hundreds of subsequent studies of conformity, we will discuss his original work in some detail.

When the subjects arrived at the laboratory they were seated at a table with seven other students. These other students were, in fact, confederates of the experimenter. The task seemed quite simple. The experimenter placed two cards on view. The card on the left had a vertical line drawn on it. This was the "standard." The card on the right displayed three vertical lines of varying lengths. These were the "comparison lines." The subject's task was to decide which of the comparison lines was the same length as the standard line. One by one the eight participants were to call out the number designating their choice among the comparison lines. (See Figure 14.1 for an example of the cards.) This procedure was repeated for 18 trials. On 6 trials, the confederates gave what the subject perceived to be the correct answer. On 12 of the trials, however, the confederates unanimously made erroneous judgments.

While there were strong individual differences among subjects, on the average they went along with the erroneous majority 33 percent of the time. That is, on an average of one out of three occasions when the subjects found themselves in conflict with the other group members, they gave the same erroneous response as the rest. This error rate was significantly higher than that of naive subjects who gave their responses in the absence of trained confederates.

Can we use Asch's findings to predict how Paul Drew would respond if he found that everyone else in the group was voting in favor of

FIGURE 14.1
Standard and Comparison Lines used in Asch's
Conformity Experiment
Source: Asch, 1952, p. 252.

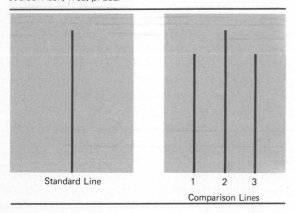

Standard Line	1 2 3
	Comparison Lines

unionization? There are a number of important differences between Paul's situation and the one confronted by Asch's subjects. We already noted that the issue in the Asch studies was a question of objective fact rather than subjective opinion. Another important difference is the fact that the people in Paul's group are acquainted with each other and will be working together in the future, whereas Asch's subjects were brought together only for the sake of the experiment. In order to determine how these and other differences would affect Paul's tendency to conform, we need to understand why people submit to group pressure.

Normative and Informational Social Influence

Why did the subjects in Asch's experiment go along with the group as frequently as they did? What sort of social power were they responding to? Deutsch and Gerard (1955) believe that the power of the unanimous majority derives from two sources. They term the sources *normative influence* and *informational influence*.

Normative social influence occurs when the target is motivated to adhere to what is perceived to be a group norm. As we saw in Chapter 12, a norm is an expectation that is held by group members regarding how they ought to behave. Norms are sometimes explicit; for example, group charters may include attendance norms that specify the number of times a person may be absent before losing membership. More frequently, however, norms are implicit and can be inferred only by observing the behavior of group members. Uniformity in behavior is one cue that a norm is functioning. A teenager who shows up at a party in tie and jacket and observes that all the others are wearing jeans quickly realizes that the group has a norm of informal dress and that he has violated it.

Once one notices that a norm is operating,

what produces the motivation to conform to it? The social power that produces motivation to adhere to group norms may derive from several bases. Referent power may be at work, if the target admires the group and derives pleasure from being similar to the members. Legitimate power may sometimes be operative. One may feel, for example, that if one agrees to be a group member, one is obligated to go along with the will of the majority. Psychologists, however, usually attribute normative influence to the reward and coercive powers of the group. One often goes along with group norms in order to secure the approval of the members and to avoid disapproval or rejection. It is this aspect of group pressure that leads people to regard any conformity as a regrettable form of human behavior. Conformists are seen as individuals who do not think for themselves—who monotonously pattern their behavior after that of others because of their need for acceptance and their inability to stand on their own. This is a rather simplistic conception of conformity, as we shall see.

Informational influence also motivates conformity. When a person regards the group's position as evidence about reality, informational influence is brought into play. Deutsch and Gerard point out that it is to be expected that people will be influenced by the reports of others' perceptions. We have learned from birth that others are usually reliable sources of information. Particularly with regard to perceptions of objective stimuli, like the length of

Studies indicate that when people are highly attracted to a group they are motivated to conform to group norms.

lines, if two people have discrepant impressions, each will attempt to figure out how the disparate views can be reconciled. In the Asch paradigm it seems reasonable for subjects to conclude that the problem is within their own opinions, since several supposedly capable people agree on a different judgment. This type of influence can be seen as a form of expert power; that is, when faced with the fact that everyone else in the group sees things in a particular way, the subject becomes convinced that the other must be right.

Since Asch's original studies, investigators have used an assortment of techniques to uncover the factors responsible for variations in the tendency to conform. Deutsch and Gerard's formulation provides a useful organizing scheme for the research. We will consider first those factors that can be expected to affect the normative pressure of the group and then those factors that affect the informational pressure.

Normative factors. Any variable that increases one's fear of rejection or desire for acceptance by the group should increase the tendency to conform. If the source of the deviant response cannot be identified, one cannot be rejected. Hence, it has been found that when subjects are able to give their responses anonymously, they yield less to group pressure than when their responses are public (Deutsch & Gerard, 1955). Studies have also shown that the more attracted the target is to the group, the greater the conformity (Gerard, 1954; Dittes & Kelley, 1956). Presumably the increased conformity is due to increased concern about acceptance and rejection. It could also be due, however, to the increased referent power of an attractive group. Working on a task that requires cooperative behavior rather than individualistic behavior produces increased conformity (Crosbie, 1975; Deutsch & Gerard, 1955). This may be because cooperative interactions increase the subjects' attraction to the other group members (Deutsch, 1949a); because the

subject may expect harsher treatment for noncompliance; or because cooperative interactions increase the legitimate power groups hold over their members.

One's popularity or status also has an impact on the tendency to conform, but not in the straightforward way that might be expected. If we assumed that higher-status members were more secure about their continued acceptance, we would predict that the higher a person's status, the less that person would feel compelled to go along with the majority. This would account for the ability of group leaders to change norms and to be sources of novel and innovative points of view. The high-status person, however, might also be expected to be the one who serves as a model for the group and hence enacts the norms most consistently. Hollander (1958) devised the notion of **idiosyncracy credits** as a way of explaining these seemingly contradictory expectations. Hollander argues that before leaders can risk deviating from group norms they must first establish "credits" by adhering to norms quite reliably. Only when their loyalty has been clearly established can they afford to deviate and lead the group down unfamiliar pathways.

Predictions about low-status members are equally problematic. To the extent that unpopular members are concerned about their acceptance in the group, we would expect conformity. Knowing that their membership is tenuous, however, they probably do not invest much of themselves in the group. Therefore, having less to lose than members with higher status, they should feel less compelled to conform to norms about which they are conflicted (Homans, 1950). Hence, if we think of status as a mediator of security, we get one set of predictions, but status as a mediator of attraction to the group and commitment to its values yields another set. In fact, most of the research demonstrates that conformity is higher among members of moderate status or popularity than among those who occupy either the highest or lowest status positions (Harvey & Consalvi,

1960; Dittes & Kelley, 1956). This may be because middle-level people are those for whom the sum of the effects of attraction to the group and concern about membership is highest.

Informational factors. Any variable that increases reliance on the group as a source of information or expertise should increase the tendency to conform to the majority judgment. Hence, the more difficult it is to make the judgment and the more ambiguous the correct answer, the more subjects will give up their own responses in favor of those of the majority (Deutsch & Gerard, 1955; Crutchfield, 1955). Likewise, *the more confident people are in their own judgments, either because of a generalized sense of self-esteem (Stang, 1972; Crutchfield, 1955) or because of particular skill in the task at hand (Rosenberg, 1961; Endler, Wiesenthal, & Geller, 1972), the less likely they are to conform.* For the same reason, *conformity is more likely to occur for opinion items than for matters of fact.* With matters of opinion the social validation of others' judgment is an important criterion of correctness (cf. Festinger, 1954). When the issue is one of personal preference, however, such as which of two pictures is more pleasing, the information about others' judgments is less relevant and less conformity results (Crutchfield, 1955).

Any variable that increases the credibility of the influencer should increase the informational value of the influence attempt and hence should increase conformity. It is surprising, therefore, that studies have shown that increasing the size of the group above four does not reliably increase conformity (McGuire, 1968). The absence of a group-size effect may be due to the target's perception that individual group members are not responding independently of each other. If some of the members are seen as simply "following along like sheep," as some of Asch's subjects remarked, then they would not be contributing any new and valid information about the object of judgment. This interpretation is supported by Wilder's (1977) finding that conformity increased as the number of distinct social entities espousing a position increased. He found that four or six people who were said to be members of a single group were not more influential than two- or three-person groups. If, however, the individuals were described as being independent of each other, then the more individuals there were who espoused a particular position, the more the target conformed.

Social Support for Nonconformity

If Paul Drew, the deviant medical technician, wanted to increase his resistance to group pressure, one of the most effective things he could do would be to convert just one of the other members to his point of view. *Asch (1955) discovered that the presence of one deviant from the otherwise unanimous group reduced the amount of conformity to a marked degree.* The reduction in conformity occurred even when the deviant gave a response that was more erroneous than the response of the majority. Furthermore, regardless of the size of the majority, the presence of a single dissenter always reduced conformity to about one quarter of what it had been when the confederates expressed unanimity. This phenomenon has been studied extensively by a number of researchers whose work helps to elucidate the psychological processes underlying the conformity response.

In a review of the studies carried out by himself and his colleagues, Vernon Allen (1975) concludes that both social and cognitive factors account for the liberating effect of the single dissenter. Allen illustrates how three social factors reduce the normative pressure on the subject. He reviews studies that show that if at least one person in the group agrees with the subject, the subject believes that rejection by the majority is less likely. Furthermore, if two people in a group take a position that deviates from the majority, observers are more likely to attribute the deviance to the situation rather than to some flaw in the nonconformer's personality. Hence, if there is a partner in the group, subjects may be less concerned about inviting derogatory remarks about their characters by sticking to their own judgment. Another social factor that may reduce conformity in situations where the target has a partner is the target's opportunity to observe the partner resisting the erroneous judgments of the majority. The partner seems to serve as a model for the subject—demonstrating that it is appropriate and possible to remain independent in the face of group pressure.

In addition to these social factors, Allen's research demonstrates that having just one other person disagree with the majority provides the subject with some important information—that the issue is one on which it is possible to differ. Recall Asch's finding that conformity in naive subjects was greatly reduced even if the partner gave a more erroneous response than the majority. Allen's research has replicated this finding and has shown that as long as the partner appears capable of making a valid response, conformity in the subject is effectively reduced.

Do Some People Conform More Than Others?

Some readers may have been wondering all along whether the tendency to conform isn't more a function of one's personality than of all the situational factors we have been discussing. There are those who are followers, the popular notion goes, and those who are loners. Followers will tend to conform and loners will not. A reasonable amount of research has been carried out in an attempt to discover whether this is true. One of the earliest attempts was made by Crutchfield (1955), who found that conformity in an experimental situation was related to low self-esteem, low intellectual competence, and high scores on the California F scale of author-

itarianism. Reviews of subsequent studies on personality determinants of conformity, however, have generally concluded that the relationships are weak and unreliable (Marlowe & Gergen, 1970). If the tendency to conform were mainly a function of an individual's enduring personality traits, we would expect that the people who conform in one situation would also conform in another. It has been shown, however, that there is little cross-situational consistency in people's tendency to conform (McGuire, 1968). It is more probable that particular personality dispositions interact with features of the situation to determine level of conformity. There are bound to be some areas in which even people with low self-esteem feel relatively competent. They are more likely to resist group pressure when judgments involve those areas. Individuals who score high on need for social approval are likely to conform more if they expect to interact with the group in the future than if they never expect to see the group again. There is one enduring personal trait, however, that has been repeatedly linked to the tendency to conform—femaleness.

The notion that women are more influenceable than men across a wide variety of situations has been subjected to a careful examination in a review by Eagly (1978). Eagly distinguishes among three types of influence studies: (1) persuasion situations in which an influencer presents an argument to a passive audience (the kind of study discussed in the chapter on attitudes and attitude change); (2) conformity situations in which a discrepant position is advanced by a group of people who are not present (typically by having subjects read about the opinions of others before rating their own opinions on a questionnaire); and (3) conformity situations in which the discrepant position is advanced by a group of people with whom the target is interacting. The third type of situation is referred to as a group-pressure situation. It is the only one in which subjects believe that their responses will be seen by the other group members. Eagly searched all social psychological journals and relevant textbook citations for studies that tested the significance of sex differences in subjects of high school age and over. As Table 14.3 shows, the most frequent finding is that there is no difference between men and women in the tendency to adopt the position of the influencer. In the group-pressure category, however, a substantial minority of the studies do show greater conformity among women. Interestingly, studies carried out since 1970 have been significantly less likely to show sex differences than were studies carried out prior to that year.

There are two general ways to explain the moderate tendency toward greater female influenceability. One way is to say it's something about the studies. The other way is to say it's something about men and women. Evidence for the former has been quite compelling. There have been convincing demonstrations that the finding of greater female conformity can be wiped out and even reversed by changing the content of the judgment items. As we have already pointed out, individuals tend to conform more when they are dealing with issues about which they are unfamiliar or uninformed. In studies where items are chosen particularly because they are more familiar to women (for example, items about day care or fashion design), it is found that men conform more (Morelock, 1980; Sistrunk & McDavid, 1971). This explanation contends that most studies use male-type items and that's why we are more likely to find greater influenceability among women. Eagly agrees that the bias in item content may account for some of the sex differences, but points out that it cannot explain why the difference tends to be stronger in group-pressure studies, nor why sex differences were more prevalent in studies carried out before 1970.

The other type of explanation locates the source of phenomena in presumed sex differences that mediate responses in influence situations. Eagly suggests that women have a stronger interpersonal orientation than men, and hence are more concerned about maintaining social harmony. This explanation can account for the fact that sex differences in influenceability were more common before 1970 than after. As sex-role norms liberalize, socialization can be expected to produce fewer and fewer differences between the behavior of men and women. This explanation also handles the other major finding of the Eagly review. It's only when actually confronted with the members of the majority that women's greater motivation to avoid conflict is aroused.

TABLE 14.3
The Effect of Subject Sex on Influenceability

Type of Study	Number of Studies Surveyed	RESULTS		
		Females More Influenceable	No Difference	Males More Influenceable
Persuasion	62	10 (16%)	51 (82%)	1 (2%)
Group pressure	61	21 (34%)	38 (62%)	2 (3%)
Conformity without group pressure	22	2 (9%)	19 (86%)	1 (5%)
	145	33 (23%)	108 (74%)	4 (3%)

Source: Adapted from Eagly (1978).

Summary

We have seen in this section that groups have considerable power to influence their members. The mere existence of uniformity in the behavior or attitudes of a group can potentially endow the group with all of the six bases of power we have described. If membership in the group is important to the target, then the group has reward and coercive power. The tendency to conform because of a desire for acceptance and/or fear of rejection has been termed normative influence. If the target admires the group members and wants to be like them, then the group has referent power. If the target believes in the will of the majority, then the group has legitimate power. If the target believes that the group members are valid perceivers of reality, then the group has expert and/or informational power (termed informational influence).

At effective antidote to group pressure is the presence of at least one other individual who rejects the majority's viewpoint. Research on social support for nonconformity suggests that the existence of another deviant reduces conformity because of the effect the "partner" has on the target's perception of the situation. Specifically, as long as the target is not the only deviant, there is a tendency to believe (1) that there is less danger of rejection, (2) that the majority is more likely to attribute the deviance to something about the situation rather than to negative characteristics in the target, and (3) that there is less reason to question one's competence. It also seems apparent that witnessing the resistance of another person reminds the target of the norm of independence and bolsters the intention to stick to one's guns.

While researchers have looked for evidence of the "conforming personality," the general conclusion is that the relationship between the tendency to conform and any particular personality trait is weak and unreliable. Although many writers suggest that females are more influenceable than males, research has most frequently demonstrated no difference between the sexes. Nevertheless, a substantial minority of group-pressure studies have shown women to be more conforming. It has been suggested that this finding is a consequence of women's strong interpersonal orientation, which leads them to avoid the conflict that would result from resisting the will of the majority.

LOW-STATUS INFLUENCERS

The last situation for us to consider is the one involving Marie Russo, the Infection Control Nurse. If you recall, she was concerned about Dr. Foster's order to move a child out of isolation back onto the ward with other children. Marie knew that the child still had a highly contagious illness and should remain in isolation. Dr. Foster must have felt that the probability of infecting the other patients was low, but hospital policy was clear on this matter and it was Marie's job to see that hospital policy was carried out. What did you predict that she would do? Did you think she would confront Dr. Foster with his violation of hospital policy and ask him to rescind his transfer order? Would she say nothing and permit the child to be moved back to the ward? Or perhaps you predicted that she'd get someone else to intervene and prevent the transfer.

The SENIC Study that was described earlier provides some data that are relevant to this situation. Infection control nurses (ICNs) were asked what they would do if they saw a staff member "breaking technique." The ICNs reported that they would be significantly less likely to speak up to a physician than to a laboratory technician or another nurse whom they saw using improper procedures (Raven & Haley, 1980). Although almost all ICNs believed they would take some action against the violator, they were much more likely to ask another staff member to intervene if the violator was a physician. Furthermore, they believed that even if they did say something to the physician, they would be rather unsuccessful in getting him or her to change procedures.

How can we understand the nurses' reluctance to attempt to influence a doctor and their pessimism about the effectiveness of their efforts? Is it that doctors are particularly invulnerable to influence attempts? Are nurses particularly ineffective influencers? As we will argue below, the answer is yes to both of these questions: doctors *are* relatively invulnerable to influence attempts and nurses *are* relatively ineffective when it comes to influencing them. Furthermore, although we have chosen to examine social influence in a hospital, these characteristics are not unique to health-care settings. Invulnerability of the higher-status party and ineffectiveness of the lower-status party are characteristic of most influence attempts in situations of unequal status.

Social Control and the Invulnerability of Authorities

People in positions of authority or high status usually have a vested interest in maintaining the inequality in their relationships with lower-status individuals (Deutsch, 1973). The more they are able to deflect or resist influence attempts, the greater their freedom of action. This is not to say that the freedom will necessarily be used to the detriment of lower-status individuals. Indeed, the authorities may be striving to carry out their duties and satisfy the needs of their subordinates to the greatest extent of their ability. Nevertheless, it is to their advantage to preserve their superior power. Because of their social position, high-status people often have numerous mechanisms of **social control** at their disposal. These mechanisms function to reduce the likelihood that influence will be attempted in the first place. If influence is attempted, they lessen the likelihood that it will be successful. Ultimately, social control mechanisms serve to maintain the existing power relationships and preserve the existing form of social organization.

Gamson (1968) has described the nature and functioning of a variety of forms of social control. The most straightforward mechanism is the selective use of reward and coercive power. For example, by granting or denying promotions, employers can reinforce behaviors they regard as acceptable and punish behaviors they find unacceptable—that is, behaviors that threaten their authority. More subtle mechanisms than this include regulation of access to power resources and enforcement of norms regarding appropriate influence techniques for lower-status individuals. These two mechanisms will be discussed in more detail.

Regulation of access to power resources. Because they tend to control access to potentially influential positions, high-status individuals can try to ensure that those who obtain the positions will support the status quo. Many university departments have institutionalized this form of control by using the "peel-off principle" in promotion decisions. The peel-off principle is the rule that only those who are of higher status than the candidate can vote on whether or not to grant the promotion. The putative reason for this rule is to prevent junior faculty members from arbitrarily voting against their colleagues as a way of improving their own chances at one of the scarce tenure slots. At the same time, however, the peel-off principle provides the higher-status faculty members with power to eliminate candidates they find threatening.

In addition to regulating the opportunity to launch an influence attempt, authorities can control acquisition of informational and expert power by controlling access to education. The prohibition against teaching black slaves to read is a clear example of this form of social control. The history of the development of nursing education repeatedly demonstrates how limitations were imposed as a way of preventing threats to the authority of physicians and hospital administrators. The following statement in a 1906 issue of the *Journal of the American Medical Association* is one illustration:

> The programs of nursing schools and the manuals employed should be limited strictly to the indispensable matters of instruction for those in their position, without going extensively into purely medical matters which give them a false notion as to their duties and lead them to substitute themselves for the physician. . . . The professional instruction of nurses should be entrusted exclusively to the physician, who only can judge what is necessary for them to know. . . . These maxims should certainly be borne in mind by the physician who has dealings with the nurse, as a matter of simple justice to her that she be not encouraged to take steps that are not in her province. (Cited in Ashley, 1976, p. 78).

Norms regarding appropriate influence techniques. It has been observed repeatedly that when two individuals of unequal status interact, the higher-status party uses behaviors that express dominance and the lower-status party uses behaviors that express deference or submissiveness (Hall, 1959). A boss can call workers by their first names, but workers must use the boss's title and last name (Brown, 1965). The boss can give a worker a pat on the back for a job well done, but a worker who touched the boss in a similar fashion would be considered aggressive and rude. If you think about all the things you learned about "polite behavior" when dealing with superiors, whether the status difference is based on age, expertise, occupational prestige, or the like, you will notice that many of these behaviors function to acknowledge the status difference and indicate to the superior that you have no intention of challenging his position (see Figure 14.2). There are several techniques that low-status influencers *can* use and still comply with the normative requirement of not challenging the target's authority. These techniques include helplessness, ingratiation, and manipulation.

Don't talk back.
Don't speak unless spoken to.
Children should be seen but not heard.
Respect your elders.
. . .

FIGURE 14.2
Social control in the nursery

Helplessness is a form of legitimate power that low-status influencers have available to them. By appealing to the norm of social responsibility (cf. Berkowitz & Daniels, 1963) those who are poor or weak or unable to care for themselves may influence strong, competent targets to help them out.

Ingratiation is a device that can establish reward and coercive power for those who use it. By using tactics such as flattery and agreement (being a "yes man"), low-status people can make themselves more attractive and likable to higher-status people. They can then use their personal esteem and affection as a reward for the high-status person's compliance and the threat of withdrawal of esteem as a punishment for noncompliance (Jones & Gerard, 1967). The potential effectiveness of such tactics are attested to by Kipnis (1974), who describes two experimental studies in which subjects were made managers of a business and given the job of directing groups of workers. The performance of workers varied from poor to above average. The managers had the option of giving pay increases to workers whom they wanted to reward. Results showed that managers rewarded an ingratiating worker who used flattery more than one who was equally competent but did not engage in this form of ingratiation.

In order to conform to status norms, however, ingratiators must be sure to use their reward and coercive power subtly and indirectly. Subtlety is important, because the target must not discover the influencer's real motives. Clumsy attempts at ingratiation are likely to backfire (Kanouse, Gumpert, & Canavan-Gumpert, 1981). Likewise, a direct confrontation that highlighted the high-status person's dependence on the influencer's esteem would constitute a challenge to the target's superiority.

When influencers try to hide their intention to influence, they are engaging in *manipulation*. Hence, ingratiation can be seen as a manipulative form of reward and coercive power. Informational and expert power may also be used by lower-status persons if they, too, are used manipulatively. The doctor-nurse game described in Social Focus 14.3 shows how nurses can influence physicians' medical decisions by making it appear that the physician originated the recommendation.

The techniques available to low-status influencers that are in conformity with status norms can be quite effective in bringing about change in the target. There are, however, two major disadvantages to using these techniques. First, by conforming with the status norms, the influencer reinforces the status discrepancy rather than trying to equalize power and thereby gaining access to the advantages that power brings. Second, the use of helplessness, ingratiation, and manipulation runs counter to our basic social values. They are apt to undermine the influencer's sense of dignity and self-confidence. Since self-confidence is one of the factors that motivates an individual to attempt to influence (Tedeschi, Schlenker, & Linkskold, 1972), relying on these techniques reduces the likelihood that future influence attempts will be made. For these two reasons, norms regarding

As women move into high status occupations they need to use influence strategies not considered traditionally feminine.

appropriate influence techniques for lower-status influencers function to increase the invulnerability of authorities.

Handicaps of Female Influencers

The foregoing has demonstrated how those with high status are protected against successful influence from lower-status parties. Since high-status influencers in our society tend to be male (cf. Johnson, 1978), successful influence becomes even more difficult if the lower-status person happens to be female. Studies have shown that when attempting to influence men, women tend to choose strategies that are normative for those of lower status (Raush, Barry, Hertel, & Swain, 1974; Johnson, 1974). This has been shown to be true even when the woman and man are of equal status. Falbo and Peplau (1980) had college students fill out questionnaires about aspects of their intimate relationships with members of the opposite sex. One part of the questionnaire asked subjects to write essays describing how they got their part-

SOCIAL FOCUS 14.3
The Doctor-Nurse Game

In 1967 Leonard Stein published an article in the *Archives of General Psychiatry* in which he describes certain aspects of the doctor-nurse relationship as a "transactional neurosis."

Stein points out that although physicians have total responsibility for making decisions about the treatment of their hospitalized patients, an important source of information is recommendations made by the nurses. Since they spend much more time with the patient, nurses gain much information that is relevant for their treatment. Instead of engaging in a direct interaction about the patients, however, the staff members play a game in which the object is for the nurse "to be bold, have initiative and be responsible for making significant recommendations, while at the same time (appearing) passive." Stein gives an example of a medical resident being awakened by a 1:00 A.M. call because of a patient's inability to sleep. The resident is covering for other doctors, and is not familiar with the patient in question. The nurse could say, "Dr. Jones, I need a prescription for Pentobarbital mg. 100 for Miss Smith in Ward C. She's having trouble sleeping and has had that drug before." Instead, however, the nurse and doctor engage in a subtle dance in which the nurse describes the patient's behavior, the doctor asks what has been helpful to the patient in the past, then after being told about the medication, says authoritatively, "Pentobarbital·mg. 100 before bedtime as needed for sleep. Got it?" By playing the game successfully, the nurse gains the reputation for being a "damn good nurse" and the doctor gains the respect and admiration of the nursing service. On the other hand, if the nurse is outspoken, she is labeled a "bitch." If a doctor rejects the subtle recommendations made by the nursing staff or fails to recognize them, he is labeled a "clod" and becomes subjected to numerous bureaucratic maneuvers that nurses can use to make a doctor's job difficult.

Stein condemns this "game" as being stifling and anti-intellectual. He encourages members of both professions to take steps to eliminate the game and its inhibitory effect on open dialogue.

Gena Corea describes the consequences of a recent attempt to subvert the game. Under the direction of a progressive male nurse, Thomas Daley, the nurses at St. Agnes Hospital in Philadelphia began to view themselves as colleagues of the physicians rather than their subordinates. "Many nurses Daley hired would call up a physician and politely say, 'Doctor, I think your order to Patient X should be changed for these reasons: A, B, C.' " While some physicians apparently responded well to these breaches of traditional etiquette, others did not. "Open warfare erupted [when] a nurse questioned a doctor's mineral oil order for an elderly burn patient because she feared that the oil, in combination with another drug the doctor had prescribed, could cause oil emboli in the liver and spleen. According to Daley, pharmacology literature upheld the nurse's judgment. 'The physician rescinded the order but still complained to me about it,' Daley told the *American Journal of Nursing.* 'I defended the nurse because it is her obligation to question treatment when she thinks it is detrimental.' . . . . Daley refused to reprimand the nurse. A month later he was fired." The reason? " '. . . inability or unwillingness to cooperate with other department heads' " (Corea, 1977, pp. 74–75).

ner to do something the subjects wanted. Analysis of these responses showed that women were more likely to report using indirect strategies like dropping hints, being especially affectionate, and pouting. Men, on the other hand, were more likely to report direct strategies, like stating one's needs and negotiating.

Johnson (1978) argues that women are socialized to use power indirectly. The ideal of femininity is a woman who is dainty and passive, and women who violate that ideal are responded to negatively. One study demonstrated this by having students respond to descriptions of people exercising authority in four different situations (Jacobson, Antonelli, Winning, & Opeil, 1977). In one case an employer fired a worker for poor-quality work. In another, a police officer threatened to arrest a surly traffic violator. In a third, a professor refused to allow a wayward student to take a makeup exam, and in a fourth, a parent punished a child for failing to carry out a chore. For some students the authority was described as a female and for others the authority was described as a male. Likewise, in some students' booklets the target of the sanction was female, while in others the target was male. Results showed that with the exception of the parent-child situation, students responded most negatively to female authorities being firm with male subordinates. Thus, except for when they are enacting the parental role, females are derogated for exercising direct forms of power over males.

In addition to being criticized for exercising legitimate authority over males, women have been shown to be less influential than men in problem-solving tasks. Studies have shown that both male and female groups are more likely to adopt the suggestion of a male confederate than a female confederate, even though both are equally competent at the task (Wahrman & Pugh, 1972, 1974; Ridgeway & Jacobson, 1977).

It is apparent that norms that govern interactions between women and men are very similar to the norms which govern interactions between low-status and high-status individuals of the same sex. This congruence has not escaped the attention of feminist scholars. It has been pointed out repeatedly that in our society sex is a status characteristic (Radecki & Jennings, 1980; Lockheed & Hall, 1976; Fennell, Barchas, Cohen, McMahon, & Hildebrand, 1978). Being born female automatically places one lower on the hierarchy than males. Thus one can expect that all the advantages that accrue to higher-status individuals, both as influencers and as targets, also accrue to males in their interactions with females. One of the primary objectives of the feminist movement has been to help women undo the consequences of the status inequity. Sex discrimination suits are being used by more and more women to combat denial of access to power resources. More informal means, such as consciousness raising, are being used to demonstrate how sex-role norms function as mechanisms of social control. (See Social Focus 14.4 for a newspaper columnist's view of the right style for women to use to bring about a change in the Constitution.)

Effective Influence by Low-Status Sources

So far we have painted a rather bleak picture for low-status influencers. Must we conclude that they will forever be at the mercy of those above them? That they can do nothing to bring about any significant change in the power distribution, short of discovering oil in their backyard and thereby being elevated to high status? No, we needn't be as pessimistic as all that. There is a growing body of useful literature for individuals who have no special status or expertise, yet wish to bring about a change in the prevailing patterns of behavior. The general message for the individual is "Be deviant!" The message for the group is "Organize!"

The minority influencer. The work of Serge Moscovici and his colleagues has demonstrated

SOCIAL FOCUS 14.4

In Search of Right Rights Style

. . . There is a notion being bandied about that if only, dear lord, those advocates of women's rights would stop being so (1) militant, (2) strident, (3) pushy, they would be (4) successful. If only they could present their cause with The Right Style, why then the doors of equality would open wide to welcome them and all would be right with the world.

This argument has a certain amount of appeal, I grant you. It allows the arguer to profess himself to be a supporter of women's rights, while simultaneously blaming women themselves for any failure. But it is, at heart, absurd, a true comedy of manners. . . .

Last week the ERA came up again in North Carolina, before the same state house which didn't ratify the Women's Suffrage Amendment until 1971.

Many people say that the ERA would have passed years ago except for what one North Carolina legislator described as "the radicals, that's what has hurt this movement from the beginning. If we'd had someone like Bella Abzug or Gloria Steinem come down here, it would set us back 10 years. . . ."

The ERA supporters in North Carolina and elsewhere are conscious of the stylish issue. From all reports they have become studiously moderate, mainstream, homegrown and low-key. So guess what happened in North Carolina last week? The amendment got killed in committee.

Thus we conclude from our search for The Right Style that women have two choices: they can either be so pushy that they are ineffective, or they can be so carefully nonthreatening that they are also ineffective. . . .

Style is an issue, which is only used against women when they are fighting for their own advancement. Ever since suffrage, women have had the choice of being unseemly or unseen.

I am sure that some people are willing to spend their lives searching for the perfect style between high key and low key, seeking the right combination with which to open the safe of equality. But they have better odds at winning the lottery.

Style isn't totally irrelevant, but it belongs in its place, somewhere below that old political standby Power. Style is an issue for those who seek to *influence* the powerholders, not for those who want to *be* the powerholders. (Goodman).

that a single individual without any particular access to resources or status does have the power to influence the behavior of an entire group. The first experiment to demonstrate this "minority effect" was designed as a reverse of the Asch paradigm (Moscovici, Lage, & Naffrechoux, 1969). In this study a group of six individuals were given the task of judging the color of a series of slides. The slides were, in fact, all blue and differed only in their intensity. Four of the six group members were naive subjects who did not know that the other two members were confederates of the experimenter. The two confederates had previously been instructed to call each of the slides green when it was their turn to respond. When the responses of the subjects in the experimental groups were compared with the responses of control groups containing no confederates, results demonstrated that the minority had been influential. Thirty-two percent of the experimental subjects said that a slide was green at least once, while only one of the control subjects ever reported seeing green. This study also demonstrated that the impact of the minority was felt even when subjects made later color judgments on their own.

The minority effect has subsequently been demonstrated for many kinds of group judgments, including the amount of compensation a worker should get for an injury suffered on the job (Moscovici & Nemeth, 1974) and the severity of punishment to be meted out to a fifteen-year-old delinquent (Kiesler & Pallak, 1975). In each of these studies a single group member (who was an experimental confederate) repeatedly and consistently took a position that was quite discrepant from the average judgments of the naive subjects. The studies show that under certain conditions the group moves toward the minority member's position.

There is an important catch in this research, which has to do with the "certain conditions." Rigid and dogmatic repetition of an extreme position is not likely to win the deviant many supporters. In fact, when Asch put one confederate among a group of naive subjects and had him give erroneous responses on the line-judging task, the poor fellow was almost laughed out of the room. The style with which the discrepant view is presented is a crucial determinant of the minority's effectiveness. After reviewing the existing research, Moscovici (1976) argues that the behavioral style of an effective minority influencer must be characterized by investment, autonomy, consistency, and fairness. In other words, the individual must demonstrate a strong commitment to a particular position, an ability to remain independent in the face of group pressure, espousal of a position that is a logical and rational alternative to the one held by the group, and a willingness to

keep an open mind and allow for some concessions to the majority.

Why is the minority influential, you may ask. It seems rather paradoxical to assert that an individual can influence a unanimous majority when we have previously emphasized the power of group pressure. In fact, we are asserting that both positions are true. Unless individuals are strongly motivated to retain their own opinions and to attempt to influence the rest of the group, they are likely to buckle under the pressure of unanimous majority. If the motivation is there, however, then deviant minorities without any particular status have a reasonable chance to have some impact. In fact, because they are minorities, they may even have some advantages. First of all, they stand out and become the focus of attention. This ensures that their position will at least be heard. Furthermore, research on attribution theory (see Chapter 6) suggests that individuals who stand out are seen to have strong dispositional traits (Taylor & Fiske, 1975). While those attributed traits may be detrimental to the influencer's cause (if, for example, the influencer is seen as paranoid or exhibitionistic), the attribution can also be helpful. Minorities who follow Moscovici's four behavioral prescriptions are likely to be seen as sincere, courageous, and competent.

The fact that the minority is presenting a novel point of view can also be an advantage. Normative positions are often boring, and as long as the majority do not feel personally threatened, they may regard the minority view as a refreshing change. A study by Biener (1972) demonstrated that during a color-judgment task, subjects responded quite favorably to a person who presented a discrepant position, if the subjects had first received support for their own perception. If, however, the discrepant person responded *before* the subject received support, the subject rejected the novel point of view and derogated the deviant individual. Since a minority view is, by definition, being presented in a setting where there *is* support for the majority, the majority should be more open to the new position than they would be if it were put forward by a larger discrepant faction.

The problem of the potential threat to the majority introduces another important "catch" or limiting condition for minority influence. Minority influence is more likely to occur when the issue is one in which neither side has a vested interest. For example, minority influence has been demonstrated for judgments of objective stimuli or for solutions to human-relations problems in which subjects have no particular stake in any given outcome. When there is a genuine conflict of interest between the influencer and the target, minority status is apt to be a disadvantage. In these kinds of situations there is power in numbers, and an aspiring low-status influencer would be best advised to round up as many supporters as possible.

Organizing for power. Deutsch (1973) points out that although low-status influencers lack the usual resources of power, they generally do have access to people. The utility of those people is a function of (1) their number; (2) their personal qualities—that is, their competence, dedication, and discipline; (3) their cohesiveness; and (4) their social organization—that is, their ability to coordinate their activities and carry out tasks efficiently. Deutsch argues that the success of guerrilla forces, such as the Vietcong, can be traced to their high social cohesion, their discipline, and their dedication. Oppressed groups also have discontent and a sense of injustice on their side. These are energizers and motivators for potential influencers. When communicated to others, they can win supporters.

Suppose a group has managed to achieve cohesion and good organization. What bases of power are then available to them? With large numbers of dedicated members, low-status groups have, in fact, increased their potential power. They then have the ability to offer high-status targets the reward of their cooperation and also to threaten them with noncooperation. Strategies of civil disobedience and nonviolent resistance have been used extremely effectively by civil-rights and antiwar groups. Some proponents of nonviolent resistance are so convinced of its effectiveness that they recommend that the United States unilaterally disarm and organize its national defense around nonviolent strategies (American Friends Service Committee, 1967).

On the other hand, some groups have used violence successfully. Gamson (1975) studied a random sample of 53 voluntary groups that sought to change some aspect of the status quo in the United States between 1800 and 1945. His sample included political groups of the Left and Right, such as the Young People's Socialist League and the German American Bund. He also investigated professional interest groups such as the Tobacco Night Riders, which sought to break the power of the tobacco trust, and the American Association of University Professors, which attempted to mobilize professors for the achievement of academic freedom. In a fascinating account of the influence attempts of these groups, Gamson analyzes their success and failure according to the strategies they used and the characteristics of their organization. He concludes, to our dismay, that groups that used violence, either as an offensive or defensive tactic, were more likely to succeed than those that did not. He also reports that the nature of the group's goal was related to its success. Those who aimed at changing the policies or organization of the target of influence were more successful than those who attempted to displace the target entirely.

Summary

In this last section on low-status influencers, we have spent more time discussing the *problems* of potential change agents than we have on the strategies they might utilize effectively. We showed how mechanisms of social control in the hands of authorities serve to insulate high-status targets from effective influence from subordinates. By controlling access to power resources, high-status people can prevent challengers from launching influence attempts. The enforcement of norms regarding appropriate behavior for low-status individuals limits potential influencers to strategies based on helplessness, ingratiation, and manipulation. While these forms of influence may be effective in the short run, they tend to perpetuate the status inequity and undermine the self-esteem and self-confidence of low-status individuals. We argued that sex-role norms that prescribe appropriate behavior for women in their interactions with men are actually mechanisms of social control. As a consequence, women are doubly handicapped as influencers when the target is a male of higher status.

Research on minority influence suggests that low-status influencers can have an impact on oppositional groups by presenting their position in a way that demonstrates consistency, investment, autonomy, and fairness. If, however, there is a genuine conflict of interest between the low- and high-status parties, the influencer will do well to mobilize a group of supporters. With a cohesive, competent, well-organized group, low-status influencers gain the ability to exercise reward and coercive powers.

SUMMARY: ADVICE TO THREE ASPIRING INFLUENCERS

Now that we have considered social psychology theory and research on social influence, what advice can we give to the three potential influencers we introduced at the outset?

First, let's consider Dr. Fremont. Being concerned about his patient's risk of a serious heart attack, the doctor wants to influence Mr. Morganthau to stop smoking, lose weight, and cut down on stressful business activities. Dr. Fremont has access to many bases of power, since he is in a relatively high-status position. We would advise him not to rely merely on the traditional power bases used by physicians—expert and legitimate power—because the literature on patient adherence to medical regimens implies that these bases alone are not very effective. While the legitimate power of an authority can be extremely effective, the Milgram studies suggest that it can be easily undermined by lack of constant surveillance of the patient and by the presence of others who don't always follow the doctor's orders.

As consultants to Dr. Fremont we would first acknowledge that habitual self-destructive behaviors are very difficult to change. Consequently, it would be best to apply as many different power bases as possible. Since the changes are long-term ones, it would be well to choose a strategy that encourages the patient himself to take responsibility for the change. Informational power, when effective, makes the influence process independent of the influencer. In itself, however, informational power has not been shown a very effective way of producing adherence. First, Dr. Fremont must establish a viable, supportive relationship with Mr. Morganthau. He must get to know his patient, so that he can provide information that is relevant and convincing. In the process of developing rapport with the patient, Dr. Fremont may also be establishing referent and reward power that can be used to supplement the influence process. It would be useful to involve Mr. Morganthau in a well-organized support group consisting of other individuals who need to make similar changes in their life styles. In that way the social power that derives from group norms would increase the pressure on Morganthau to make the needed changes. This strategy is used in Weight Watchers, Alcoholics Anonymous, and Gamblers Anonymous—just a few of the support groups that use many of the power bases described in this chapter to help members change undesirable behaviors.

Let us now return to the medical technician's meeting, where most of the members are wondering whether Paul Drew will or will not vote in favor of unionization. What could we tell Roberta Goodman, the chairperson? Paul probably realizes that a no vote is apt to earn him considerable disapproval, since he knows that a unanimous vote is necessary for the group to proceed with plans to unionize. In order to assess the normative pressure that group disapproval would exert on Paul, we need to determine how important the group is to him. The fact that Paul is different from the others because of his more conservative views may make him less popular (see Chapter 8). For that reason he may be less invested in continued acceptance.

To assess the informational pressure on Paul, it is necessary to learn something about the assurance with which he holds his antiunion views. The more confident he feels about his grasp of the pros and cons of unionizing, the less influenced he will be by the fact that all the others have come to an affirmative decision. After gathering the information we need about Paul and his feelings about the group, we would not be able to say for sure what his vote would be. The best we could do would be to make a statement about the probability that he would vote yes. Probabilistic information can be quite useful, however, when one has to decide among alternative strategies. Recall that Roberta Goodman, chairperson of the meeting, was trying to decide whether to conduct the vote by secret ballot or to have members report their vote publicly; she was also wondering whether she should delay the vote until two late members arrived. The research we have reviewed allows us to conclude that Paul Drew *is* more likely to go along with the majority if a public vote is taken. The research gives no reason to believe, however, that adding two more yes votes to the situation will make much difference.

What about Marie Russo? What advice can we give her with regard to her interaction with Dr. Foster who, she feels, has given an inappropriate order? First, we would advise her *not* to use the strategies that have been socially prescribed for low-status people and women—ingratiation, helplessness, and manipulation. Rather, we would suggest that she speak quite directly to Dr. Foster. Point out that the child has an infectious disease and that the infection could spread to the other children. She could also point out that it is against hospital policy to move the child out of isolation, and that perhaps another way of reducing the child's loneliness could be found.

Unfortunately, Ms. Russo may find it very difficult to take our advice. As we pointed out earlier, women are socialized to use power indirectly and have probably encountered subtle and not so subtle negative reactions when they have made direct attempts to influence males. This history is likely to raise a woman's anxiety when she attempts to use more direct influence techniques. The same is true of an individual of either sex who attempts to influence a higher-status target. In a sense, such a person is like a minority influencer—a lone individual attempting to stand up against accepted norms that nurses should follow doctor's orders, women should be passive and accommodating, and subordinates should not buck their superiors. To the extent that the analogy applies, the individual is well advised to demonstrate Moscovici's four characteristics: consistency, investment, autonomy, and fairness. These characteristics are ones that are explicitly taught in most assertion-training programs (cf. Smith, 1975). In fact, we would strongly encourage Ms. Russo to organize a support group of nurses with whom she might be able to engage in assertion training. In addition to providing an opportunity for assertion training, the group would serve other useful functions. It would act as a collective partner, similar to the ones we described in the conformity experiments. That is, it would help individual nurses resist the normative pressures to comply with traditional sex-role demands. The group, by its numbers, would also increase the power of individual nurses. With an organized group backing her up, an individual nurse would not be alone in the face of negative reactions that might be evoked by future influence attempts.

We are not suggesting that having read this chapter, you should hire yourself out as a consultant to potential influencers. (You should at least finish this book!) We do hope, however, that you have gotten some idea of how social psychology can be of use to those who want to bring about change.

SUGGESTED READINGS

Gamson, W. A. *The strategy of social protest.* Homewood, Ill.: Dorsey Press, 1975.

Milgram, S. *Obedience to authority.* New York: Harper & Row, 1974.

Smith, J. J. *When I say no, I feel guilty.* New York: Bantam, 1975.

Group and Environmental Influence on Behavior

PART 4

15
GROUP DYNAMICS

- Introduction
- Group Values and Group World
- Group Norms and Standards
- Status within Groups
- Group Leadership and Performance
- Group Decisions and Commitment
- Summary

INTRODUCTION

The significance for individual behavior of groups is that many of the things we value most are best expressed in relationships and group settings. Survival, sex, love, humor, approval, respect, friendship, and many kinds of work require interaction with other people to make them meaningful. Much of the intrinsic satisfaction we get out of life directly involves groups and relationships. Groups have been defined in many ways. After reviewing several of the major approaches, Cartwright and Zander (1968) presented the following definition: "a group is a collection of individuals who have relations to one another that make them interdependent to some significant degree" (p.46). In this chapter, we expand this definition a little to include the two major bases of interdependence (a) shared values and goals, and (b) the joint activities that are needed for members to act on these values and goals: "a group is two or more people who share intrinsic values and who coordinate their behavior in ways that allow them to act on these values."

The coordination of behavior with respect to group goals and activities that represent common values requires the development and maintenance of various structural arrangements for joint regulation, communication, decision making, leadership, interpersonal relations, and group performance. These are some of the topics to be covered in this chapter, but first, let us examine further the significance of groups for individual behavior.

Group and Individual Behavior Potential

Relationships in groups can have important consequences for members. Groups that share value commitments and are coordinated effectively will enhance the **behavior potential** of members. Where members are uncertain about shared values or are organized around issues of little concern, change in individual behavior potential will be minimal. In cases where people are constrained or even forced to act as members of a nonchosen group (prisons, mental hospitals, and so forth), individual behavior potential may be severely restricted. *Behavior potential* is enhanced only when members can *act and interact on values that are central and important to them.* Behavior potential has to do with the choices and options available to group members. It includes a quantitative aspect: that the greater the number of options available, the greater the behavior potential. But, more significant is the *type* of option. Options that allow a member to act on values and needs that are intrinsic and important offer more behavior potential than options that are not so important to the person. For example, if you are involved in running as a sport, the option of entering a race which really challenges you gives you more behavior potential than the option of being only a spectator of the race.

Different groups and relationships bring out different sets of behavior potential. Think about being with your family or going out with your friends. For many people, the kinds of behavior that are possible will be somewhat different when interacting in these two different

---

This chapter is written by John Forward.

The chapter author acknowledges his debt to Peter G. Ossorio (1966, 1978, 1981) whose systematic formulation of Descriptive Psychology has provided the basis for many of the concepts used in the chapter. Descriptive Psychology is a set of logically interrelated concepts that provides a framework for understanding theories and organizing facts in psychology.

situations. Or consider the different sets of behavior potentials brought out when you are with your lover or in a court trial before a judge. Usually, very different values, norms, and social practices are involved in these two situations.

Groups and Behavior Change

The fact that different groups involve different sets of behavior potential accounts for the enormous importance of groups for individual behavior change. *Many of the most significant changes in a person's life are the result of changes in group membership.* Going to school, leaving home, joining the Army, changing jobs, getting married, having children, breaking up, or changing close friends are some examples of these potentially long-lasting changes. That these changes are directly tied to changes in group values and not just changes in circumstances was demonstrated in one of the first longitudinal field studies in social psychology.

Newcomb (1943), as was previously mentioned in Chapter 4, investigated the changes in values and attitudes of female students attending Bennington College during the years 1935–1939. Most students came from wealthy and conservative family backgrounds and had adopted the conservative values and beliefs of their parents. For example, as freshmen, over 60 percent of students endorsed the Republican candidate for president. They also held negative views toward poor people and other ethnic groups and attributed the plight of these people to personal deficiencies or dispositions rather than to societal and situational problems.

At college, the students interacted with faculty who, as a group, held very different values. They were much more committed to social criticism and social justice and supported the liberal policies associated with Roosevelt's New Deal. What was the effect of this change in group values for students? Newcomb found that over the four years at Bennington, a large percentage of students adopted the values and beliefs of the liberal faculty and rejected parental values. Whereas 60 percent had endorsed a Republican candidate in their first year, only 15 percent endorsed the Republican in their senior year.

Moreover, changes in values were associated with participation and involvement in college activities. Students who changed to more liberal values were more popular with other students and more politically active. Compared with those who maintained conservative family values, the new liberals were elected to student offices more frequently, named as friends more often, and even rated as better adjusted according to college medical reports!

Apparently, participation in and acceptance of the values dominant among the college faculty facilitated enhanced behavior potential among the innovative students while in college. But did the changes in values and attitudes persist beyond college, or was it a simple case of conformity to immediate group pressures?

In a follow-up study, 25 years later, Newcomb, Koenig, Flacks, and Warwick (1967) found that the value changes in college had in fact persisted; that is, they were **intrinsic** rather than **instrumental** changes. For example, 60 percent of the Bennington alumnae favored Kennedy (Democrat) over Nixon (Republican) for president in 1960, whereas only 30 percent of a non-Bennington comparison group did so. Bennington graduates read many more liberally slanted newspapers and periodicals and had chosen careers that allowed them to express their liberal values and beliefs (social services, for example). The changed values even influenced their choice of spouse—Bennington women had married men who were significantly more liberal than spouses of the comparison group.

SOCIAL FOCUS 15.1
Values and Generation Gaps

At the time that Newcomb was assessing the long-term stability of liberal value changes in Bennington College alumnae, the children of these women were reaching college age during the "radical" decade of the 1960s. Did the next generation reject parental and family values like their parents before them? From other research done at this time the answer is yes and no.

Block, Haan, and Smith (1969) studied the values of college students in the 1960s and found two different groups on the liberal/radical wing of the political spectrum: the *dissenters* and the *activists.* Both groups were active in protest activities at the time but this was about the only thing they had in common.

The *dissenters* were both rebellious and alienated from society. Although they engaged in protests, they scored low on humanitarian interests. They had also rejected parental values, broken family ties, but had difficulty articulating a set of alternative values. They knew what they did not like but were vague about their ideals for social change. So this group of students had rejected both the conservative and liberal values of parents but did not have a coherent set of alternative values.

The *activists* were an interesting group. Like the liberals, they scored high on measures of humanitarian values. Although they were protesting, they appeared to hold many of the values their parents held. Their criticisms were directed not so much to the liberal values themselves (equality, social justice) but to the hypocritical manner in which these values were held. They saw their parents' generation as saying the right things but not acting on them. The activists apparently were determined at that time to represent the liberal values more honestly, rather than to reject them.

So generational value change may involve giving up parental values for an alternative set of values (Bennington alumnae), giving up family values for no clear set of alternatives (dissenters), or simply trying to represent parental values in better ways (activists).

Groups and Planned Behavior Change

In some cases, group membership change has been incorporated into treatment and therapeutic programs. Therapy groups, Alcoholics Anonymous, group homes for delinquents, and long-term treatment facilities for physical and mental illness represent the intentional use of groups to facilitate behavior change. Unfortunately, these treatment programs do not always work well, particularly where people are committed involuntarily and are, therefore, restricted in behavior potential. In some cases, however, where membership is voluntary, such programs can be tremendously effective in facilitating long-term individual change.

A good example of a group that was formed with the explicit purpose of increasing the behavior potential of members is a field project conducted by Dr. George Fairweather and his colleagues at a large mental hospital in California (Fairweather, Sanders, Maynard, Cressler,

& Bleck, 1969). The project established a halfway house for chronic patients who were ready to be discharged from the mental hospital. The objectives of the halfway house (called The Lodge) were to provide a living-working setting where ex-patients could relearn the skills necessary for survival as self-supporting members of the community. During the course of the project, ex-patients gradually assumed control of domestic tasks (maintenance, purchasing, cooking, and so forth), created a profitable janitorial and gardening business, and developed a completely autonomous decision-making body that made all policy and procedural decisions for the organization.

The contract between the restrictive effects of group process found in a typical large state mental hospital and the liberating effects of life in the halfway house is shown by this excerpt from the journal of a new staff member at the end of his first week at The Lodge:

The difference in atmosphere between this place and the hospital is very striking for someone who steps into it cold and with no preparation as I have done. It really has the feeling of a going business with none of the "marking time" mood of the hospital. . . . The simple fact of sending groups of men out to do productive work in the community for wages has generated a whole series of behaviors which are in contrast to those in the hospital . . . there is a general atmosphere of purposefulness. . . . This activity, plus the general absence of "busy work" or "work as therapy" hospital standards, generates the atmosphere I have described. . . . One characteristic seems common to all of the men and is a direct result of their changed role in this social situation as compared to the hospital—they are all more self-assured and direct in their approach to [the staff director] and me than are people on the ward (Fairweather et al., 1969, pp. 70–71).

These informal observations on the effects of this change in group membership were supported by the results of the overall research project. Compared with a group of ex-patients who had volunteered for The Lodge but had been randomly assigned to the traditional hos-

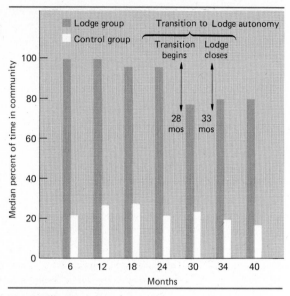

FIGURE 15.1
Comparison of lodge and control groups on time in the community for 40 months of follow-up.
Source: Fairweather et al. (1969), p. 205.

pital after-care program (the control group), Lodge members showed a significant reduction in **recidivism**—the rate at which they reentered the hospital following initial discharge. Forty months after being discharged from the hospital, the median amount of time spent by Lodge members in the community rather than back in the hospital was 80 percent, compared with only 20 percent for the control group (see Figure 15.1). Moreover, for those ex-patients who remained out of the hospital, Lodge members spent significantly more time in full-time jobs (median, 40 percent) than the control group (median, 0 percent).

These dramatic changes have important consequences, not only for the Lodge members who were able to regain significant behavior potential in terms of independence and self-respect, but for society, which regained productive citizens and reduced hospital costs.

To give a complete account of all the factors that made The Lodge such an effective group is beyond the scope of this chapter. The project will be used, however, to illustrate several basic aspects of group structure and function, including group values, group norms and standards, group status and roles, group leadership and performance, and group decisions and member commitment.

GROUP VALUES AND GROUP WORLD

With individual behavior the broad concept of personality captures many of the characteristics of a person that make his or her behavior understandable. Knowing people's dispositions, values, and competencies provides a framework for understanding their behavior in particular circumstances. For example, suppose you overhear someone laughing out loud at a party. If you know the person has a sunny disposition, values a good laugh, and has the ability to create and appreciate humor, you will probably assume that person was enjoying a good joke (and you would be correct most of the time). But if you know the laugh comes from someone who likes to please others or who lacks a sense of humor, you will probably predict that the laughter means "ingratiation" or "playing the fool," rather than enjoying a good joke. Closer observation of the actual interpersonal exchange or knowledge of the circumstances of the act of laughing might confirm or disconfirm your prediction, but by knowing the personality of the person laughing, you will know what is happening most of the time.

The Concept of Group World

With group behavior, the general concept corresponding to personality is **group world.** Group world is the overall orientation of a particular group that includes shared values, norms, attitudes, and practices. By knowing the group world, it is possible to make sense of what the group is doing at any given time. Take the case of a group performing an activity at two different times when an intervening change in group world has taken place. Recall the observation made by the new staff member at The Lodge, presented earlier. He noted that the work activity of ex-patients at The Lodge had a very different significance than similar work at the hospital (both involved cleaning-up types of work). Work at the hospital represented a staff perspective of "keeping the patients busy and out of trouble." Work at The Lodge was an intrinsic part of a developing group world that included values and norms of self-sufficiency, personal competence, cooperation, and survival, as well as organized group practices related to the actual conduct of the janitorial business. The significance of the same kind of cleaning-up work was very different for the men in the hospital and Lodge settings, because of the very different group worlds involved.

For this chapter, we will consider only two of the many aspects of group world: group values (what the group is "really into") and group norms (ways the group expresses shared values).

Group Values

Shared values provide the foundation for any given group world. Values give perspective, meaning, and coherence to the multiple activities in which members participate. There are several features of group values that help explain why values are essential for understanding what a particular group is doing at any given time: (a) values represent the *significance* of group behaviors; (b) values represent the *intrinsic* motivations and involvements of group members; (c) values *organize* all other parts of a group world; and (d) group values restrict or enhance member behavior potential.

a) **Values and significance.** The significance of any specific group activity is the more comprehensive activity or context of which the specific activity is a part. Think of it as a part-whole relationship. For example, a group may be observed making a decision. If we know the group is not just making decisions for the fun of it, we may ask, "What are they doing by making this decision?"; that is, what is the significance of this activity? It may be many things—let's say the decision has to do with ensuring the financial solvency of the group. Again, we can ask the question, "What are they doing by doing that?" The answer might be, "So we can continue to help the needy." At this point the group may respond to a further question by saying there is no further, more comprehensive reason; that is, helping the needy *is* the significance of what they are doing—it is not a part of any larger activity or purpose. It is obvious that for any given activity and any given group, there are a very large number of possible significances. But knowing the central values of the group gives us a good understanding of the significance of any particular group activity.

Of course, what the group members take to be the significance of a group activity may not be shared by outside observers, who may attribute a quite different significance. Take the description of the first job performed by the brand new Lodge janitorial service set up by the ex-mental-patients:

Work started Friday at 9:00 a.m. sharp and everyone put out real good. We worked until noon steadily, although far too . . . slowly. Mr. Rich [worker] needed checks and suggestions on how to solve problems such as how to get clean rags, when and where to move the ladder, and whether the specks were on the inside or outside of the window. . . . Mr. Ward slapped paint on fairly quickly but laid it on unevenly and applied almost equal portions to the walls and the customer's hardwood floors. Mr. Black, in cleaning up, originated a new design in black paint on the customer's rug and unfortunately it was strictly ad lib. . . . still, by 3:30 p.m. all the windows were

in fairly good shape, the painting was done, and some floors had been cleaned (Fairweather et al., 1969, p. 52).

An outside observer who did not know the significance of this group activity for the ex-patients might attribute any number of significances to it. The group could be making a "keystone cops" type of movie, or engaging in very irresponsible behavior, or even getting revenge on the owner of the house. In fact, a few of the early customers reacted to the work in this way. But knowing and appreciating the group and its attempt to develop new group norms and values provides a very different significance for the group's janitorial activity.

b) **Values represent intrinsic motivation.** Values provide not only an understanding of what a group is about but they also represent what members are "really into"—that is, what engages their energy, commitment, and motivation. Rokeach (1973) and others have made a useful distinction between instrumental values (means to ends) and terminal or intrinsic values (ends themselves). In this chapter we are focusing on intrinsic values as those activities expressing values that are engaged in for their own sake. As seen in the last section, the significance of a given activity helps us to locate these intrinsic or terminal values. It is these values that allow for member involvement and satisfaction in the group. They are what make the group worthwhile for members.

c) **Values organize group world.** As mentioned earlier, the shared intrinsic values of a group affect all other aspects of group life—the nature and meaning of group norms, beliefs, attitudes, activities, customs, and practices. In his research Rokeach (1973) has shown that very different sets of attitudes and beliefs are held by people who value *freedom* over *equality*, compared with people who rank equality ahead of freedom in their list of terminal values.

* People and groups who value freedom

TABLE 15.1
Four Value Orientations and the Clusters of Intrinsic Values Associated with Each

		COOPERATION	COMPETITION	RIVALRY	INDIVIDUALISM
Intrinsic Values (Types)	Pragmatic	Common goals Work with others	Win the game Being one-up	Beat the other Domination	Individual goals Independence
	Ethical	Share resources Take others into account	Play by rules Contract ethics	Use any means to obtain ends	"Do your own thing" Make own choices
	Hedonic	"We" feelings Empathy	Satisfaction of winning/being one-up	Anger/hate	Narcissism or satisfaction with being own person
	Aesthetic	Everything working well together	Hard-fought, competent "game"	Nihilistic Imagery	Personal competence

above equality hold much more negative attitudes and beliefs toward the problems of race and poverty and are more prejudiced against homosexuals than people who value equality above freedom. In fact, Rokeach has been able to demonstrate that the different rankings of just these two terminal values is associated not only with contrasting attitudes and beliefs but with very different life styles. It is the same with groups; the shared values make a difference for all other aspects of group life.

Although the research example from Rokeach's work considered only two values, the more typical case with groups is that there are multiple shared values. These values are themselves organized into *value orientations*. Table 15.1 gives an outline of several value orientations that have been extensively researched in social psychology. Note that each value orientation in the table (cooperation, competition, and so forth) is made up of several different types of intrinsic value. This allows for some flexibility in group membership and shared values. For example, some members may join a group with a cooperative value orientation because they value working with others. Others may belong to the same group primarily because they enjoy being with others and still others because of ethical reasons. What they all

share in common, though, is the value orientation of the group.

The power of group value orientations to affect the whole group world has been demonstrated in the famous field studies by Sherif, Harvey, White, Hood, and Sherif (1961), known as the "Robber's Cave" research. The basic research design was to take a group of boys at a summer camp, induce the value orientation of competition and observe the effects, and attempt to induce a change to a cooperative value orientation by means of a variety of procedures. Presumably, since the boys came from middle-class backgrounds, both cooperative and competitive value orientations were "available" for induction in the novel group setting.

The competitive value orientation was induced in three ways. First, the camp was divided into two separate groups and contact was minimized. By the second week, the boys had developed strong loyalties to their groups, as evidenced by the fact that they chose group names for themselves—"Eagles" and "Rattlers." Second, the researchers arranged a series of contests between the two groups, which produced intensified competition. Third (and this really got things going), the researchers allowed one group to show up early for

Continued competition and rivalry has important consequences both within and between groups. In the Robber's Cave Study, competition led to "we're good, they're bad" perceptions and group activities centered around planning (or defending against) attacks.

breakfast and eat all the food before the other group got there. Actually, these inductions triggered more than just healthy competition between the groups. They also induced strong forms of rivalry. A type of warfare ensued, in which the groups raided each other's camp, stole the other group's flags, and engaged in a lot of fighting.

The successful induction of the group value orientations of rivalry/competition changed all aspects of group life, including activities, group perceptions, attitudes, interpersonal relationships, and even leadership. Each group developed group structures conducive to high-conflict situations. Leadership was given to the toughest kids and most of the group activities were centered around planning attacks or defending against attacks. Each group developed strong ingroup/outgroup differentiation, with the ingroup highly valued and the outgroup

strongly devalued. For example, measures taken after one of the contests showed the winners greatly overestimated the margin of victory, while the losers underestimated it. Attitudes and beliefs about other campers became tied almost exclusively to group membership. When asked to rate other camp members on a series of adjective descriptors, 75 percent of the Eagles rated Rattler members as weak, sneaky, and stinkers, while 53 percent of the Rattlers reciprocated the compliment. Any kind of positive interpersonal contacts between the two groups ceased.

In the second stage of the research, various attempts were made to change the value orientations of the two groups from competitive to cooperative. All attempts to appeal to good sense, ethical values, or even outside threats failed to change the rivalry between the Rattlers and the Eagles. Finally, with the time rapidly approaching when the boys would return home—torn, bleeding, and angry—one strategy did work. The researchers arranged a series of incidents that required the whole camp to work interdependently on some common problem or goal. At one time a rag "became stuck" in the camp water line. Both groups cooperated in the search for the problem. On a trip, the camp bus "broke down" and everyone had to push. These activities were successful in eliciting a common, campwide value orientation of cooperation (that is, the pragmatic values pulled in the others). Attitudes, beliefs, activities, and leadership all began to reflect the new system and the boys were sent home at least partly civilized.

Cooperation and competition have also been studied in laboratory-game research (see Chapter 13 on the trucking game and the prisoner's dilemma). Although the laboratory research has been useful for some things (for example, the effects of reward, size, and so forth), it has generally been assumed that it is the distribution of outcomes (rewards, resources) that determines the extent of cooperative or competitive behavior. That is, the scarcer the resources, the more competition is likely.

But this is only the case in cultural/economic groups where competition is a dominant value orientation. Since the boys in the Robber's Cave camp study and the college students in the laboratory-game research had no unique history as *groups*, they naturally resorted to cultural values both available and common to them by virtue of their ethnic or social-class backgrounds.

The middle-class Anglo cultural values of competition and achievement produced the research findings on the relationships between scarcity and competition, rather than the reward structure itself. Research using the same reward structure across children of different cultures shows differing responses to the same experimental situation (Kagan & Madsen, 1972). Children from rural areas of Mexico show cooperative behavior even under competitive instructions. Anglo children in the United States show "typical" high levels of competitive behavior and Mexican-American children show intermediate levels.

It is likely that the different cultural values are adaptive for different sociocultural conditions and that the children have been socialized differently (McClintock, 1974). Perhaps if the Robber's Cave research could be replicated in rural Mexico, the group getting to breakfast first would save some food for the others, since this would be typical of their family situation (that is, necessary for family survival).

d) **Value orientations and behavior potential.** The group value orientations of competition, rivalry, and cooperation offer different sets of behavior possibilities for group members. While *competition* can offer certain satisfactions in winning, being "one-up," and fighting hard (see Table 15.1), there are some very significant restrictions on the behavior potential of members in competition-oriented groups. As seen in the Robber's Cave study, competition involves restrictions on interpersonal openness and warmth, as well as restrictions on the capacity to make realistic assessments of the real world, including the performances of other members or groups. Research on the attributions made to others by people with very competitive laboratory-game strategies shows that such people view the world as a jungle where only the fittest survive. As was noted in Chapter 13, such people are always on guard and expect a lot more competitive behavior from other experimental subjects than the other subjects actually intend (Kelley & Stahelski, 1970).

It is easy to see how the expectations and attributions of highly competitive members can lead to a self-perpetuating cycle. Expecting the other to be competitive can both elicit and produce more competitive behavior in the other, thus reinforcing the initial expectations about people and the world. It is a closed system that does not permit valid feedback from others or accurate assessment of them and can therefore be highly restricting in terms of behavior potential.

The consequences for member behavior in groups that value *rivalry* highly can be even more restrictive and devastating. Not content just to win at another's expense, rivalrous people want to hurt or even eliminate the other. The associated attributions to and expectations for other people or groups cannot be conducive to productive interpersonal relationships. The disposition to work toward increasing the costs to another, even if it means some loss to oneself, was demonstrated clearly in the cross-cultural research of Kagan and Madsen (1972).

Using the experimental game illustrated in Figure 15.2, where the basic choice is either to gain points for both people or hurt the opponent (in relative cost or loss of potential gain), Kagan and Madsen found a significant difference between cultures. North American-Anglo children made significantly more rivalrous choices than Mexican-American children, whereas children from rural Mexico exhibited almost no rivalrous choices at all.

In the United States, using situations that

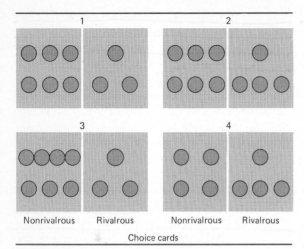

FIGURE 15.2
In the experimental situation, two children sit facing each other; between them is a choice card containing marbles. The chooser may take the nearest set of marbles directly from either the right or left side of the choice card, and other child is allowed to take the remaining marbles from the chosen side. For example, in Card 1, a chooser who selects the right (rivalrous) side takes two marbles and leaves the other child one. A subject who selects the left (nonrivalrous) side takes three marbles and leaves three for the other.
Source: Kagan and Madsen (1972), p. 215.

represent the values of the dominant Anglo culture, several research studies have shown the relative benefits of *cooperative* value orientations. One well-researched setting is the school classroom. In most school systems, resources and academic rewards are typically based on purely competitive or individualistic tasks. Several studies, however, have investigated the effects of structuring learning around cooperative and shared group experiences. In a pioneering study, Deutsch (1949) divided students in an introductory college psychology course into ten groups of five students each. Half the groups were randomly assigned to a *cooperative* situation in which the course grade was based on group effort; the other groups were assigned to the usual *competitive* situation, where the best individual performances re-

ceived the highest grades based on the normal curve.

To obtain ongoing measures of performance, all groups were required to work weekly on logical and visual puzzles and to propose solutions for complex problems in human relations. In addition, students and trained observers recorded various aspects of group and individual behavior.

At the end of the term, the most striking finding was the overall superiority of the cooperative groups. Cooperative group members evaluated their fellow members more positively in terms of friendliness and contributions to group discussions. Cooperative groups were also better than competitive groups in terms of performance, as measured by the productivity, diversity, and quality of problem solutions offered (Deutsch, 1949).

These research findings have been supported in subsequent classroom research. Haines and McKeachie (1967) compared competitively and cooperatively oriented discussion groups and found that competitive groups experienced higher levels of tension that was associated with low cohesiveness and that disrupted individual performance. The researchers reported a higher level of learning in cooperative learning groups than in competitive learning groups. In a somewhat different setting, Blau (1954) found that cooperative work groups in a public employment agency produced more sharing of job information and more job placements than in competitively oriented work groups. Competitive work-group members tended to stick to themselves and to "sit on" job openings that might bring them more bonus points in the future.

In the next chapter, on intergroup relations, you will see how some researchers in the field of race relations have used these facts about cooperative value orientations to produce improvements in academic achievement and interpersonal relations in racially desegregated classrooms (Aronson et al., 1978; Weigel et al., 1975).

So it appears that members of groups with cooperative value orientations have significantly more behavior potential with respect to being able to satisfy intrinsic values having to do with both work and other people. It is not surprising that the institution of cooperative group values, as expressed in decision making, work structure, and personal adjustment, were also key factors in the experimental halfway house for ex-patients presented earlier. Consider the disorganized *individualistic* orientations of most of The Lodge members a few days following their transfer from the hospital:

During this early period at The Lodge, the general atmosphere was one of confusion and turmoil. There was an awareness that the real-life community was vastly different from the hospital and a feeling of freedom from incarceration prevailed among the men. "Each man should be independent" was a commonly heard phrase. If a man slept late, no one would get him up. . . . Although the leader complained that he and two others were doing all the work, he could not alter this. . . . Testing the limits of propriety often occurred. Excessive drinking, refusal to follow medication regimes, and emotional behavior were common (Fairweather et al., 1969, pp. 48–49).

Contrast this with the situation a year or so later, after ex-patients had helped develop and be responsible for *cooperative* group structures and behavior. Not only were all routine decisions made and work done by ex-patients, but they were learning to take care of problems as they arose:

On Saturday, I got a telephone call from Mr. March. He told me the telephone company had changed our (business) number. . . . I went to check . . . and found Mr. Parker, Mr. Spears, and Mr. March sitting in the office systematically going through our business cards and changing the numbers so that we could have the new cards ready the next week. They were also taking a whole series of realistic and appropriate actions to make sure the new telephone number was in the hands of "Information" sources in case potential customers should call to get it (Fairweather et al., 1969, p. 93).

While these ex-patients were coordinating their efforts to solve this common problem, many of their counterparts in the control group were being readmitted to the hospital. Such were the consequences of a group that specifically incorporated a cooperative value orientation into its life and structure. It enabled its members not only to survive in the community but to regain much of their former capability and status.

GROUP NORMS AND STANDARDS

Group values give meaning and coherence to the activities of group members. Values also provide the basis for evaluating the behavior of members. *Group norms are given by judgments that given behaviors do or do not violate shared group values.* Two features of group norms will be discussed: (1) norms are not particular behaviors but *judgments* about behavior, and (2) norms are *boundary conditions* for the expression of group values.

Group Norms as Value Judgments

Only under certain restrictive conditions do group norms specify particular behaviors as acceptable or unacceptable in the light of group values (see discussion of prescriptive rules below). Typically, group norms call for the exercise of judgment on the part of the group members, rather than the automatic application of rules specifying particular behaviors.

Even in the same group, over time, the same specific behavior may be seen on one occasion as expressing and at another time as violating group values, if these values are changing. Consider again the Robber's Cave research at the boys camp (Sherif et al., 1961). Harrassing other campers was a valued activity under the regime of competitive group values, but the same activity was judged to be inappropriate when the change was made to cooperative values.

Group Norms as Boundary Conditions

Normative group judgments typically indicate what are the limits on possible expressions of group values. Normative judgments rarely indicate what specific behaviors satisfy group values, since there are a very large number of ways a given group value can be expressed. Thus, norms are not typically rigidly specified behaviors, but are *boundary* markers for what is acceptable/unacceptable to the group.

It is also rare for the boundary condition to refer to a single unidimensional value. As we have already seen, most real-life groups have multiple values, so that the boundary condition for expression of group values is not a single point on a linear scale, but more like the solution to a complex simultaneous equation, where the values act as a set of constraints that must be satisfied for any given behavior.

The general concept of norms as boundary conditions has been well illustrated in research on informal work norms in industrial production settings. In the pioneering research of Roethlisberger and his colleagues (Roethlisberger & Dickson, 1939) at the Western Electric Company, it was observed that the workers in a mass-production "bank-wiring" section consistently produced below their capabilities and the goals set by management. Moreover, it was employees with the greatest seniority and experience who adhered most to the informal work norm (see Figure 15.3). The decision to limit production was based on a number of values that older workers saw as essential to group survival (for example, getting a fair return for their work, not being exploited, avoiding lay-offs due to overproduction). Note that in Figure 15.3 there is not one particular number on the production index that all workers had to meet, but a range of production that was acceptable and a range that was unacceptable. In this case, most attention was given to workers who violated the upper limit or boundary of production, since this most threatened the group values of fairness and job tenure. Violation of the upper limit was termed "rate busting" and sanctions were imposed in the form of "binging" (hitting the arm of the rate buster to indicate disapproval and to disrupt work) and psychological isolation in the group (not talking to the violator).

The use of communication within a group to either influence or isolate norm violators has been demonstrated experimentally by Schachter (1951). In this research several discussion groups were set up to decide on what should be done with a delinquency case. In each group, confederates of the experimenters performed three different roles: (1) the *mode,* who adopted the consensus of the group and maintained it throughout the discussion, (2) the *sli-*

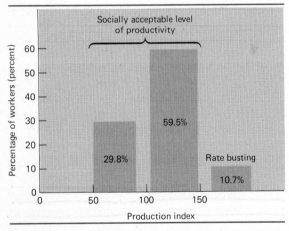

FIGURE 15.3
Worker norms can influence productivity. At the Western Electric Company, most men produced within a socially acceptable range (50 to 150 on the productivity scale). These men were perceived as putting in an "honest day's work." A few men's output exceeded 150 on the productivity scale. These men were called "rate busters" and subject to harassment ("binging") and social isolation.
Figure drawn from data reported in W. F. Whyte's (1955, pp. 40–41) *Money and motivation.*

der, who initially adopted an extreme position but moved toward the group consensus during discussion, and (3) the *deviate*, who chose an extreme position and stuck with it throughout.

The results showed that the initial group discussion was directed primarily to the two deviants (slider and deviate), but not after it became apparent that the *deviate* would not change. The group eventually excluded the deviate from the discussion (asked no questions, ignored contributions). These findings have been both replicated and added to in subsequent studies. Levine, Saxe, and Harris (1970) found that members' ratings of attraction were directly related to deviancy, although they did not support Schachter's communication patterns. Wahrman and Pugh (1974) found that in work groups, the earlier workers violated norms, the less influential and liked they were, and that even later conformity did not regain much of the status loss in the group.

Once the boundaries of normative judgments are set for a given group, they will remain that way until group values and/or circumstances change. Sherif and colleagues (see Sherif & Sherif, 1969) have formalized the concept of group normative judgment in terms of *latitudes* of *acceptance* or *rejection* and have demonstrated its use in group situations that range from group judgments of single physical stimuli (autokinetic effect) to group-member reactions to influence attempts affecting central values (prohibition on alcohol and the like). In the real-life groups, Sherif found that the more important the group values, the narrower the latitudes (boundaries) of acceptable behaviors and the broader the latitudes of unacceptable behavior.

Group Norms and Rules

Norms and rules often have similar functions. When rules refer to "rules of the game" (for example, in football, stock transactions, and so forth), they function as boundary conditions that make this particular game possible. For example, in football there is a rule that states that (with certain exceptions) only the quarterback can throw a forward pass. This rule does not tell the quarterback to whom specifically to pass (other rules may restrict this). It is simply one of the limits to be observed, if the game being played is to be U.S. football and not something else. Similarly, norms specify the limits on possible expressions of group values that are to be observed if a member is to remain in good standing with this group with its particular group values.

Unfortunately, groups and/or group leaders often try to reduce group norms to sets of **prescriptive rules** that specify what actions must be taken if the members are to remain in good standing in the group. This is similar to trying to make a football team run automatically by completely removing judgment calls by players or coaches. Of course this is impossible, but it does not stop some teams from trying. The major problem with the use of prescriptive rules in groups is that they *severely restrict the behavior potential of members to exercise judgment and choice with respect to group values and their own behavior*. Also, if a given prescriptive rule does not happen to fit a given set of group values in a particular situation, group members are faced with a conflict between external compliance to an arbitrary rule versus being able to act on values that are important to them and the group.

These facts about prescriptive rules also help us to understand how modern bureaucracies often go wrong. The misguided attempts in government and private agencies to reduce all judgments to a set of specific rules and regulations (cf. the overregulation issue) can make the day-to-day work of the agency impossible, and reduce bureaucratic workers to unthinking cogs in a machine. That is, they remove the exercise of worker judgment discretion and this in turn alienates the workers. They are deprived of intrinsic involvement in the work and tend to simply "go through the motions." This can lead at times to prescriptive rule-governed actions that are contrary to the expressed values of the agency and it can also facilitate worker "burn-out" (cf. Bush & Gordon, 1978).

A more limited case of the negative effects of prescriptive rules on member behavior potential is given in the following incident at The Lodge. An ex-patient, Mr. Steele, started a fire in his room by absentmindedly emptying his ashtray into a waste basket. The reaction of the staff coordinator illustrates an initial prescriptive-rule approach:

I did two things immediately. I had a large number of cans placed around the central space in The Lodge grounds and called a general meeting. At the meeting I announced a new rule . . . that all ashtrays must be emptied only in the cans then in place on the grounds (Fairweather et al., 1969, p. 76).

Note first that the new prescriptive rule limits the behavior potential *of all* responsible group members and not just the irresponsible member. Second, it does not do much to enhance the judgment of the irresponsible member, who will not have outside cans for his cigarettes when he is away from The Lodge in the community.

As it turned out, a later decision of the new Lodge executive committee, under the guidance of the staff coordinator, reversed this decision and placed a responsible roommate with the violator. This procedure made it much more likely that the offender could learn to take important group values like physical security into account in his judgments and actions.

Conformity to Group Norms

Most of the time, acting in conformity with group norms is no problem for members of voluntary groups (that is, they choose to be members and are not forced to be). Since conformity to norms is acting on shared intrinsic values, members are typically doing what they want to

do. Problems arise when members are pressured to comply with values and norms they do not share with other members of their own group or with the norms of other groups. Kelman (1958) has made some useful distinctions with respect to this problem. *Internalization* is the label given by Kelman to the condition in which members act on shared values that are also the member's own intrinsic values, *Identification* occurs when members conform to group norms because they really like and/or admire other members. This may be an intrinsic value or an instrumental motive or both. In a *compliance* situation, individuals are pressured to act in accordance with group values that they do not accept. In this case, conformity is entirely instrumental (in avoiding sanctions, and so on).

Much of the laboratory research on conformity to group norms has been presented in Chapter 14, where the research was described in terms of conformity as the expression of various power bases that may be thought of as related to group values. In general, however, the laboratory work has revealed some useful information about compliance, but very little about the other major types of conformity. One problem is that the subjects in the conformity experiments are strangers who meet together briefly and who do not share any common values and norms *as a small group*. They do, however, share certain cultural values about conformity and compliance.

That compliance behavior in laboratory research is at least partly a function of cultural group values has been shown in cross-cultural research using modified versions of the Asch paradigm for judging length of lines (see p. 362). Milgram (1977) found that Norwegian subjects showed much higher rates of compliance than French subjects and attributed this to differences in social values and worlds.

Frager (1970) discovered an effect with Japanese students that is almost never observed in U.S. studies. After being subjected to a few initial trials where the majority gave false judg-

SOCIAL FOCUS 15.2
Who Is Deceiving Whom in Conformity Experiments?

Beyond the central question of what group is represented in typical laboratory conformity studies, basic questions have been raised about the use and consequences of deception in these studies (for example, the unanimous false judgments by confederates in the Asch (1956) experiment).

The typical assumption is that the naive subject in a deception experiment will simply accept the deception at face value and react as if it were a real situation. Research has shown, however, a variety of subject responses to deception that are far from being passive reactions. Several studies have shown that subjects who become suspicious of the unanimous false majorities in conformity experiments do not replicate the usual results (Stricker, Messick, & Jackson, 1967). Other subjects may react negatively and do the opposite of what the experimenter communicates (Masling, 1966). Still others may go along with the deception and be cooperative (Orne, 1962), and yet others may react by seeking to present themselves in a favorable light (Sigall, Aronson, & Van Hoose, 1970).

In one deception study, where subjects were secretly informed before the experiment about what was really happening, subjects who confessed to this knowledge after the experiment did not replicate the "usual" results. Subjects who did not confess their secret knowledge did, however, produce the usual results (Golding & Lichtenstein, 1970). That is, they would have successfully deceived a naive experimenter by their role-playing efforts!

Because of inadequate concepts about groups and human behavior, we literally cannot interpret what behavior in deception experiments represents (Forward, Canter, & Kirsch, 1976). Alternative nondeception simulation methods are being developed, based on more appropriate conceptualizations about people and groups (Ginsburg, 1980; Ossorio, 1981; Mixon, 1972, 1974).

ments, some Japanese subjects reciprocated by giving deliberately incorrect judgments on trials where the majority was programmed to give correct answers! Frager attributes this to the value Japanese place on independence with respect to institutional pressures.

STATUS WITHIN GROUPS

We have seen how group norms can have more or less constrictive effects on group numbers' behavior potential (that is, the ability to act on shared intrinsic values). Another related set of constraints on the behavior potential of members are status limits. *Within-group status* is a summary term for a member's place or *standing* in the group. Status is tied directly to the actual set of member relationships that a given member engages in. In these relationships, members assign each other certain statuses (standings) with respect to (a) what kind of people they are, (b) what that kind of person can be expected to do, and (c) how they are to be treated in everyday interactions.

The personal characteristics attributed among members can be grouped into many different status typologies. The *power bases* of influence discussed in Chapter 14 is one useful typology. Some members may be <u>highly knowledgeable about things of importance to the group</u> (expert power). Some members may be granted leadership status because of their <u>sense of responsiblity for the group norms</u> (legitimate power). Others may <u>have certain abilities and competencies to help the group achieve its goals</u>*Being seen by other members as being competent in some area of group life not only enables members to do what they are good at, but simultaneously helps the whole group.*

A good example of this kind of nonarbitrary assignment of group statuses is seen in the way the janitorial work crews organized themselves at The Lodge:

The Lodge became a business-like organization. Individual specialization began occurring. Mr. Rich, for example, was officially designated as the "stove man" because he became expert in cleaning stoves. Mr. Black became good at cleaning rugs and he was often sent to jobs with rug-cleaning. And, of course, Mr. Sears, the member coordinator, had become the expert in administration (Fairweather et al., 1969, p. 66).

It is clear that groups in which member status assignments take into account the competencies of group members will be able to increase both individual behavior potential as well as group effectiveness. Unfortunately, this ideal is rarely realized since member status is frequently restricted by *prescriptive roles* rather than being based on member competence.

Status and Prescriptive Roles

Prescriptive roles <u>are specific expectations for behavior that are treated as "objective" and have little to do with member competencies and characteristics.</u> Take the problem of sex roles (traditional or otherwise). In groups that adhere to sex roles of some kind, members of either sex are expected to have certain dispositions and to engage in specified performances and not others (for example, be aggressive, suppress emotional expression, if male; be passive and nurturant, if female). These kinds of <u>prescribed roles severely limit members whose personal characteristics and competencies differ from the prescribed sex roles.</u>

To demonstrate the effects of status assignment versus sex-role stereotyping, Sapin (1979) devised a test to discriminate two kinds of people: those with a *performative orientation*, who <u>categorize specific performances in terms of prescribed roles</u>, and those with a *significance orientation, who judge any specific behavior in terms of what values and competencies it represents.* Both groups were given a series of situations in which either a male or a female faced certain problem situations (for example, a car breaking down, dealing with a high-pressure salesperson, sitting near a smoker in a restaurant). In each situation the central character in the story made one of two types of response: an *obvious* response (for example, telling the smoker to please stop) or a *nonobvious* response (such as coughing loudly or glaring at the smoker). Subjects were asked to rate the characters' behavior in terms of a series of adjectives that included the traditional sex-typed terms.

The results showed that <u>performative types displayed clear-cut sex-role stereotyping for the nonobvious situations and equally clear-cut counterstereotyping in obvious situations</u> (see Table 15.2). For example, in the nonobvious cases, the female coughing in the restaurant was rated passive, while the male coughing was rated aggressive. In the obvious case, telling the smoker to stop was rated aggressive for the female and more passive for the male (counterstereotype).

The seemingly nonsensical switch from stereotyping to counterstereotyping across different versions of the same situation highlights the concrete and "external" nature of the per-

TABLE 15.2				
Performative Group: Mean Ratings of Character Sex Differences for All Stories				
TYPE OF RESPONSE (SELECTED ITEMS ONLY)	ADJECTIVE	MALE CHARACTER	FEMALE CHARACTER	P<
Obvious	Feminine adjective total	34.60	24.29	.031
	Assertive	4.93	6.93	.053
	Soft-spoken	5.73	3.86	.053
	Warm	6.33	4.00	.036
Nonobvious	Masculine adjective total	40.43	25.06	.010
	Feminine adjective total	23.50	36.81	.002
	Assertive	7.00	4.56	.012
	Warm	4.00	7.44	.000
	Soft-spoken	3.35	6.63	.001

Source: Sapin (1979), p. 105.

formative criteria involved. In obvious situations where sex roles were easily attributed, performative people applied the new societal rule (it is "wrong" to stereotype). In the nonobvious settings, however, performative subjects returned to their typical stereotyping ways. This demonstrates that for these people, the new "liberated" norms are simply new prescribed rules; that is, they are reactions, not judgments.

By contrast, the significance subjects showed no stereotyping effects. Each situation was rated according to the appropriateness of responses, and these were not tied in any way to simple gender characteristics. They did not use irrelevant sex-role prescriptions (either traditional or androgynous).

The status-versus-role distinction is well illustrated in an incident at The Lodge, where one of the workers was reprimanded several times for calling his coworkers "patients." With their new Lodge status as independent, self-supporting citizens, the ex-patients no longer accepted the prescribed role of patient formerly ascribed to them in the hospital with its stereotyped assignment of personal characteristics, limited expectations for behavior, and degraded treatment from others (see the section on status degradation below).

Status Accreditation and Degradation

For members of The Lodge, the move from the hospital to The Lodge resulted in *status accreditation,* both within the Lodge group and society at large. In the Lodge business, members were able to act on shared values that were important to them and not just go through the motions, as they did in their hospital roles. *Status accreditation is an increase in behavior potential that results from a change in relationship(s).* Members gain a new "place" in the world—one that offers more possibilities for self-actualization. This was the major purpose of the Lodge experiment, as eloquently stated by the researchers:

For too long, the concept of "illness-and-cure" has restricted the imagination of those charged with . . . aiding chronic mental patients because it has linked the pessimism with which the patient has been viewed to his social marginality. . . . "Curing" chronic mental disorder [should] mean maintaining a person in the community in a participating social status. The strategy of building a new social institution which creates a new network of social relationships that represent more participative statuses may be the only alternative to continued residence in a mental hospital (Fairweather et al., 1969, p. 15).

Status as Finite Commodity

In groups with strong shared values of competition and power acquisition, within-group status is often treated as a fixed "commodity" that is divided among members according to their power ranking in the group (that is, their control over valued resources). Much of the laboratory research on group status has investigated this restricted version of status. For example, "ownership" of interpersonal space is usually assigned to the high-status person in such groups, and low-status persons must defer to such ownership by keeping their distance (Dean, Willis, & Hewitt, 1975). Communication is similarly divided unequally among the status hierarchy, with control being assigned to high-status high-power members (Kelley, 1951; Bradley, 1978). Attributions about relative skill and competence are distributed in the same way in hierarchically organized, competitive group situations (Zimmer & Sheposh, 1975).

The major difficulties with group members treating status as a commodity is that it tends to ignore the actual skills, knowledge, and competencies of members, and that it restricts status accreditation in the group to those at the top of the hierarchy (that is, status is gained only at the expense of other members). Groups operating on these concepts are inherently limited in terms of what they can provide in the way of positive behavior change for *all* group members.

Status Accreditation as Synergistic

It is not surprising that groups that do allow for an increase in status for all members tend to be more cohesive and effective. In these groups, status is treated as an expanding resource for all members. For example, as new members of The Lodge developed their own particular competencies and coordinated their efforts, the more effective the group became in being able to realize its shared intrinsic values and goals. The more effective the group became, the greater the potentials for individual status accreditation. Status was not a finite divisible resource in this group but was *synergistic*; that is, the more the members gained, the more there was to be gained. Everybody won.

An experimental demonstration of this was seen in the changed behavior of *low-need-achievement* individuals who were placed in positions of responsibility in a group (Zander & Forward, 1968; Forward, 1969). Typically, individuals who have weak motives for achievement and strong motives to avoid the consequences of failure set aspiration levels for themselves that are either very easy (success is ensured) or very difficult (can't be blamed for failure). While this behavior minimizes the consequences of failure, it does not allow for goals that challenge the individual's interest and competence. When low-need-achievement individuals are placed in positions of responsibility for group goals and tasks, however, they act more like *high-achievement* persons in setting challenging goals and behaving responsibly toward group outcomes.

This is similar to what happened when ex-patients created new statuses for each other at The Lodge. The very same people who a few

		GROUP RESPONSIBILITY	
		High	Low
Individual achievement orientation	High	.56*	.61
	Low	.62	1.14

TABLE 15.3
Aspirations for the Group for Achievement- and Failure-Oriented Individuals in Positions of High or Low Responsibility for Group

*The smaller the goal-deviation score, the better the aspiration for group achievement.
Source: Adapted from Zander and Forward (1968), p. 286.

weeks earlier acted like helpless patients began to act more like responsible citizens when assigned new statuses in the Lodge organization. The significance of their behavior had changed dramatically with their change in status.

The amount of status accreditation possible within a group is restricted only by the capacities, needs, and deficiencies of the members and how they are willing to treat each other. The ways in which this happens has been the subject of much small-group research.

People with strong needs for security and safety develop a fairly rigid hierarchical control structure in temporary experimental groups (Aronoff & Messe, 1971). In similar studies, Tuckman (1964) and Turney (1970) found that groups composed of highly categorical (concrete) types developed fairly closed, structural group systems. On the other hand, groups with more complex, differentiated thinkers (abstract) developed more open and flexible structures that allowed for more member participation.

It is of interest to note that in The Lodge, the initial group structure for decision making, norm enforcement, and work allocation was fairly rigid and structured. As members gained experience and granted each other enhanced status, the group structure became more flexible and open. This in turn provided more potential for behavior change on the part of group members.

Status Degradation

Status degradation is the opposite of accreditation in that it involves *a status reassignment that reduces a member's behavior potential*. Within-group status degradation most often follows a successful accusation that a group member has violated a group norm (Garfinkel, 1956; Ossorio, 1978). The degradation may range in severity from expulsion from the group (death, exile, termination of membership) to a mild reprimand that may affect the member's status only slightly. At The Lodge, the executive committee, elected by the members, was the main group charged with decisions concerning norm violations and sanctions. Following is an account of one of the more serious cases.

The following problems were presented to the committee by Mr. Edwards, the lay leader:

1. Mr. Ring startled a lady on the job by talking about knife injuries.

2. Mr. Ring has been going through people's bureau drawers on the job.

3. Mr. Ring has been undermining the entire organization before the public.

The executive committee's notes show that they took the following action . . . that Mr. March inform Mr. Ring of these charges and invite him to our meeting on March 6 to defend himself and give reasons why he should not leave The Lodge. . . . As a result of this meeting, a decision was reached—"Decision: we recommend by a vote of 4 to 3 that Mr. Ring be put on two weeks' probation and one week's fine. He is guilty of all three charges." At that point, Mr. Ring told another customer that the Janitorial Service was a "corrupt outfit." Another vote was held and Mr. Ring was requested to leave The Lodge by a 4 to 3 vote (Fairweather et al., 1969, p. 92).

Status degradation as a result of norm violation is not always as formal as this. We considered the case of violation of informal work norms earlier and saw that although no formal procedures of accusation, defense, and sentencing occurred, the sanction of "binging" and psychological isolation were just as explicit, in terms of status degradation.

Another form of status degradation noted earlier is that of restricting status to prescriptive roles that essentially remove choice and autonomy in the exercise of group status. In The Lodge, the status of worker was used to enhance status while the role of patient was used as a status degradation. Although little or no research has been done on the use of prescriptive role assignments as a means for status degradation within groups, extensive consideration has been given to the status degradation of groups as a whole within the larger social context.

One major research study by Rosenhan (1973) that we considered earlier (see Chapter 7) investigated the degradation of patients when admitted to mental hospitals. The most dramatic results noted by the pseudopatients after admission was that "normal" behaviors were treated quite differently, once the prescribed role of patient had been assigned. Taking notes was described by staff as "compulsive behavior." Asking questions was taken as a sign of resistance (patients are supposed to be passive) and so on. The assignment of the degraded-status role of patients completely changed the attribution of personal characteristics, expectations for behavior, and how the very same behaviors that are normal on the outside were treated by the staff. That is, the reassignment of status involved a change in the *significance* of the pseudopatients' behavior.

Unfortunately, the stigma and degraded status assigned to mental patients (and prisoners, the disabled, and so forth) tends to stay with them for life (Goffman, 1961). The ex-patients at The Lodge were constantly met with this kind of stereotyping and labeling in the community:

When the customer knew beforehand that the workers were ex-mental patients, they often indicated distrust of them. To compound this distrust, the men often worked in an unorthodox fashion and sometimes their work was careless . . . although such "errors" were always corrected upon final inspection. If the customer happened on a job . . . he was likely to see at least one of them cleaning himself into a corner, cleaning the lower (window) panes before the upper, or doing work not included in the job estimate. These "odd" work behaviors were so irritating to many customers that the final product—a clean house—was ignored (Fairweather et al., 1969, p. 54).

Even more unfortunate was the fact that among the customers who stereotyped the most were hospital staff, who of course knew of the workers' former status. It is to the credit of the Lodge experiment that many ex-patients were able to create new accredited statuses for themselves, even in the face of this pervasive degradation from the community.

Status Negotiation

In most groups, when members are accused of violating a group norm, there is an opportunity to defend themselves against the accusation (that is, negotiate their status). Kirsch (in press) has outlined, in order of increasing effectiveness, the kinds of negotiation moves possible for the accused: (a) mere acceptance or rejection of the accusation; (b) apology; (c) justifications and excuses; (d) challenges; and (e) contingency statements. Mere *acceptance* and *apology* indicate the member's agreement with the judgment of the group. Apology further indicates regret for the violation and will often lead to "forgiving the offense." *Justification* and *excuses* are negotiation moves where the behavior itself is not denied but a case is made that other values or circumstances took precedence over the norm that was violated. *Challenges* are directed not at the behavior in question but the right of the accuser(s) to make such accusations. *Contingency statements* are the most effective negotiation moves, since they preserve the accused's group status regardless of the outcome of the negotiation. An example might be, "Let's consider it and see what can be done." In this case, the accused takes charge of the proceedings and is treated as having that capacity even if subsequently shown to be in violation of a norm.

It is quite possible that the kinds of negotiation moves available to group members will vary as a function of their total within-group status. Members with high status are more

SOCIAL FOCUS 15.3
Status Degradation, Suicide, and Wife Battering

The status formulation presented here promises to cast new light on old problems. Formerly almost all the research on suicide focused on the internal psychological functioning of individuals or on broad social and demographic correlates of suicide. Kirsch (1982, in press) has reformulated suicide attempts as outcomes of status degradation in relationships and as negotiation moves in such relationships. Kirsch's focus is thus neither on the individual nor on the society. Rather, it is on the dynamics of people's relationships with one another.

Like suicide, the new wave of research on spouse battering and family violence (see Chapter 19; Steinmetz & Straus, 1974) focuses either on characteristics of the victims (learned helplessness) or broad social correlates. Since battering, by definition, takes place in a relationship, the status dynamic formulation may help account for the behavior of both the batterer and the battered. For example, the physical beating is only part of a whole pattern of status degradation on the part of the batterer, as seen in the following account by a victim of abuse:

He was very, very possessive and suspicious. I wasn't allowed to do anything. I was always scared of him. I tried to keep the peace, do anything to avoid a fight. It was like being in prison—I was completely dependent on him. He was always angry with me—he'd either verbally or physically abuse me all the time. He always went to the grocery store with me. He'd decide what to buy and what brand. It got to the point that if we were driving down the street, I'd look down in my lap so he wouldn't think I was looking at another man. He rarely let me go to my family, and if I did, he sat there so I couldn't talk.

The status degradation for the woman in this excerpt is clear. Her behavior potential in that relationship was close to zero; for example, not being able to look out the car window without its being treated as a "violation" of the relationship, resulting in further degradation. Although we don't know, it is quite likely that the battering male is responding to his own perceived status degradation—probably outside the relationship at work, with friends, or family. Successful long-term prevention and intervention must treat these status dynamics directly.

---

likely to be given the right to use challenges and contingency statements, whereas low-status members may be restricted to apologies, excuses, and justifications. This may be one function that contributes to the well-established finding that group leaders are given more leeway to violate group norms than lower-status members—a topic to which we now turn.

GROUP LEADERSHIP AND PERFORMANCE

Leaders and Group Values

¥ Group leadership is typically assigned to a member or subset of members who can best represent the shared values of the group and best facilitate the coordination of members in the expression of these values and the attainment of value-related goals.

That leaders are assigned this status on the basis of how well they represent central group values has been demonstrated in several research studies. Newcomb (1961), in a study of ongoing small-group leadership, found that the members who were elected leaders were those who could best articulate group values. In a study of leadership in farming communities, Wilkening (1952) found that leaders' attitudes were the same as those of the majority of farmers and also that they were perceived as the most competent persons in the group. In experimental groups, Hollander and Julian (1970) found that the perceived competence of the leaders and their motivation in solving group tasks were the major factors affecting member endorsement of leaders. Similar results were obtained by Michener and Lawler (1975). So leaders must not only be able to represent group values but be able to help the group realize them.

That group values anchor leadership status in a group was also seen at The Lodge. As The Lodge developed, the initial values of doing everything possible to help ex-patients remain in The Lodge (the rehabilitation values) gradually gave way to greater value being given to the survival of the janitorial business (the business values). At this point, several members, who had been allowed to stay at The Lodge despite having poor work histories, were put on probation or expelled. The leadership of the executive committee directly reflected these group value changes:

It's also apparent that there is a more balanced vote in the Executive Committee now. I'm referring to the rehabilitation-business struggle. . . . Apparently now the faction for business seems to be Mr. Smith and Mr. Porter and the faction for rehabilitation seems to be centered around Mr. March, who occasionally is able to bring in Mr. Miller and Mr. Kennedy (Fairweather et al., 1969, p. 90).

These conflicts over group values and leadership produced considerable difficulty for group decisions and problem solving (as is discussed later), but the business/work values finally became dominant and, in this marginal situation, ensured that the central Lodge values of independence and self-sufficiency would be realized.

Leadership and Group Norms

One of the interesting findings from the research literature on group norms is that once group values and norms are established, leaders are given more leniency for norm violation than members of lower group status (Sherif & Sherif, 1969; Harvey & Consalvi, 1960; Hollander, 1958; Wiggins, Dill, & Schwartz, 1965). Several reasons for this apparent contradiction have been explored.

A social exchange notion has been proposed by Hollander (1958, 1960). The reasoning is that since leaders are important to other group members in expressing values, attaining goals, and satisfying needs, they are granted in return more leeway in violations of group norms. Hollander used an economics analogy to capture this concept and proposed that leaders "accumulate" *idiosyncrasy credits* for helping the group, which can then be cashed in for leniency in deviant behavior. There is some indirect support for this concept in research using ad hoc experimental groups. In real-life groups it may work this way, if leaders and members are not intrinsically committed to group values as goals. Otherwise, it would be difficult to understand why leaders would want to violate the group norms and values in which they are intrinsically involved.

Another explanation that has been advanced in several studies is that leaders appear to violate group norms when they are actually either helping to change group values or are innovating changes in the way group values and goals are realized (Bales, 1953; Hollander,

1961). In this approach, leader violations of group norms are <u>viewed from the leader perspective as not just willful violations but as attempts to facilitate group change</u>.

One further consideration, as yet untested, is that because leaders have greater status in the group, they are better able to negotiate norm violations—especially of the innovative kind. That is, they are better able to justify behavior in the description of group significances and values, and if it comes down to a power struggle, to resort to challenges and contingency statements.

There are limits, however, on the exent to which leaders may violate established group norms. Wiggins, Dill, and Schwartz (1965) demonstrated experimentally that deviant actions by high-status members that clearly led to <u>group failure</u> were punished more severely than the same actions performed by medium-status members.

Even though leaders are granted greater leeway to innovate and change group norms, once the members perceive that they have ceased to take group values into account, they will withdraw their endorsement (see Figure 15.4).

Leadership Functions and Group Performance

Group values and norms set the basic constraints on group-leadership behavior. But within these constraints, many versions of group leadership are possible. The thinking and research on leadership was changed significantly when the focus shifted from the concept of a group having only one leader to the concept of *leadership function* as being any activity by any member that *facilitates group value expression, particularly in the form of goal attainment* (Cartwright & Zander, 1968). In this manner, leadership is directly tied to group performance.

Given the basic value orientation of any

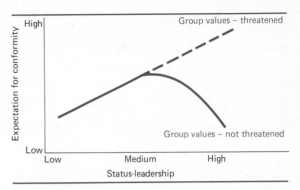

FIGURE 15.4
Group-member expectations for leader conformity when group members are threatened and when not threatened

group, successful leadership functioning will depend on two broad sets of constraints: member competencies and situation or group circumstances.

Leadership and member competencies. In a group that knows what it wants to do in what circumstances, leadership functions will fall to those members who either already have the appropriate competencies or are willing to acquire them. As we have seen, the Lodge members built a successful janitorial service, in part by making good use of the talents of members for such things as cleaning, public relations, finance, and administration. With this group it was not always easy to make use of these talents, since the years spent in the hospital had affected their self status assignments (self-concepts) in many areas. After some initial leadership from the staff coordinators, however, many of these problems were overcome:

Mr. Page . . . has been in training as a driver. . . . He shows initiative in alerting the crew chiefs for our steady gardening jobs to the fact that they are going out that day. He makes a point of coming in and looking at the board to see who is going to what job so that he knows who to go and speak to about getting the truck loaded. . . . But it was very necessary with Mr. Page to give him plenty of structure at the

While group leaders are typically strong supporters of group norms, they are often given more leeway to violate these norms and introduce changes in group practices. This apparent contradiction has been explained by Hollander's concept of idiosyncrasy credits.

beginning and to slowly relinquish the direct control over him as he showed enough confidence to take it. This is something that I was only able to do by just seeing how he responded. I wasn't able to put any particular plan or schedule into effect except the overall plan of giving him more autonomy (Fairweather et al., 1969, p. 79).

This is an excellent illustration of the difference between mere skill (which can be trained) and competence, which involves not only specific skills but the concept that "I can do this kind of work" (self status assignment). The staff coordinator showed exceptional sensitivity in helping the ex-patients regain some of the competencies that contributed to a successful Lodge business.

Unfortunately, the extensive research literature that has examined this issue has largely looked for personality traits of leaders across groups that differ greatly in terms of member values, competencies, and group circumstances. It is not surprising that reviews of this literature reveal no consistent patterns of leader traits, except for some very general cultural stereotypes such as physical size, sex, and intelligence (Gibb, 1969; Mann, 1959; Stogdill, 1948).

Other research in this area has established

the fact that✳when a collection of strangers meet for an hour or so as a group, the stranger nominated as leader at the end of the experimental session is the one who talks the most✗ (Ginter & Lindskold, 1975). In a real group, verbose talkers would need to demonstrate competencies beyond just talking in order to be granted leadership status in the group.

A more productive line of research has shown that member competencies can be classified broadly into two categories:✳those that contribute to group *task* and goal attainment, and those that serve the *relationship* needs of members✗(Bales & Slater, 1955; Cartwright & Zander, 1968). That group members tend to specialize in one or another of these categories of competence (at least in U.S. culture) has been demonstrated in experimental groups (Bales & Strodtbeck, 1951), families and clinic settings (Grusky, 1957), and in large factor-analytic studies of leadership in organizations (Fleishmann, Harris, & Burtt, 1955). More recently, Fiedler (1971) has incorporated this distinction into a more general model of leadership (see below).

Group situation. ✳The kind of leadership exercised by a group with a given set of shared values and member competencies will also be responsive to the circumstances the group faces.✗We saw a good example of this in the Robber's Cave research, where the Eagles and Rattlers chose more aggressive leaders as the rivalry between the two groups increased. Numerous investigators have demonstrated this effect—✳that groups call on more structured, authoritarian leadership when faced with threat or severe situational stress✗(Hamblin, 1958; Worchel, Andreoli, & Folger, 1977).

At The Lodge, a very clear change in leadership occurred when the survival of the janitorial business was threatened by "strange" behavior on the job and by customers' reactions to this (see the section on Leadership and Member competencies). The response to this was that those members with business compe-

tencies rose to positions of leadership on the executive committee, since they were best able to see the group through the crisis.

✳One approach that has attempted to take into account both member competencies and group circumstances is Fiedler's contingency theory of leadership (Fiedler, 1967, 1971). The measure of leader competency used was similar to the task-versus-relationship distinction presented above. Leaders were designated as *task oriented* if they gave unfavorable ratings to the group member they liked least (*low LPC*—that is, low rating for least preferred coworker). Leaders designated as *relationship oriented* gave more positive ratings to their least liked coworker (*high LPC*).

The measures used for group situation were (a) leader-follower relations (which ranged from very good to very poor), (b) task clarity (from task clearly defined to very ambiguous), and (c) leader power (which ranged from leaders with many resources to influence the group to leaders low on these). Fiedler combined these three measures into an overall measure labeled "situational favorableness," where the most favorable situation was one with good group relations, clear task structure, and high leader power.

Fiedler predicted that leader competence and group situation would interact to produce variations in group performance. In Figure 15.5 the prediction is that task-oriented leaders will facilitate group performance where the group situation is either very unfavorable or very favorable, and that relationship leaders will do best for the group when the situational factors are of intermediate favorableness.✗Fiedler has presented research data from numerous group studies that appear to provide some support for his model, but the adequacy of the data has been severely criticized (Ashour, 1973; Graen, Orris, & Alvares, 1971). Although the model is a step in the right direction, the measure of leader competency is far too general to fit specific situations with different group values. Also, the measures of group situation have

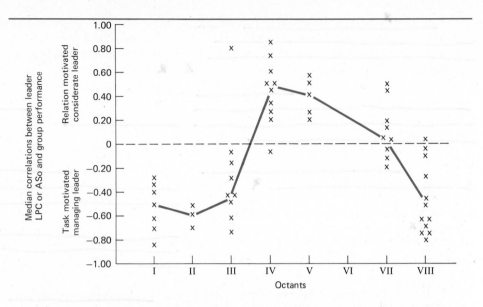

FIGURE 15.5
Correlations between leaders' LPC scores and group effectiveness (task performance). Plotted for each combination of leader-member relations, task structure, and leader position power. Each x on graph indicates the median correlation for a set of groups, and the curve marks the median for that set. In order to interpret the figure, look at the baseline. The three factors used to order the groups were not linearly related; therefore, the order on the baseline is by "octants." An octant is one cell in an 8-cell model (2 × 2 × 2) of three-dimensional space. The octants are arranged as "good" to "bad" with respect to leader-member relations. Task structure for the particular cell is indicated below, followed by leader position power as a subdivision under task structure. (LPC stands for "least preferred co-worker.")
Source: Fiedler (1968), p. 371.

more to do with the group itself than the circumstances the group faces.

As seen in our brief analysis of the Lodge group, some knowledge of group values, member competencies, and group situation are necessary for an understanding of what kind of leadership will best facilitate the expression of group values and achievement of group goals.

GROUP DECISIONS AND COMMITMENT

Group decision making is closely related to leadership functions as defined in the last section. Faced with a particular set of circumstances, group members (or their representatives) <u>will</u> *choose a course of action that (a) <u>best</u>* <u>*represents group values and norms and therefore (b)*</u> <u>*enhances the behavior potential of group members*</u>.

This concept of group decision making is illustrated in the decision made at The Lodge to expel Mr. Ring, whose talk of knife injuries and "bad-mouthing" of the organization had upset customers and threatened the livelihood of the janitorial service. This, however, was not a simple rule-governed decision. It was the outcome of a lengthy series of discussions over the central values of Lodge members and what was best for the future of the group. On the one hand, members would have preferred to be able to keep ex-patients like Mr. Ring at The Lodge in a nonjanitorial job. But this would constitute a financial burden on the already stressed budget. Putting rehabilitation values above business values at this point in Lodge development might have threatened the viabil-

ity of the whole project and greatly reduced the behavior potential of all other members.

That the final decision on Mr. Ring was the result of finding the best course of action in the light of conflicting group values and restrictive group circumstances is best illustrated in the remarks of Mr. March, one of the new business/work leaders:

Mr. March, who was again working overtime in the office to keep things ship-shape made a really extraordinary speech to me. . . . He was speaking specifically about the case of Mr. Ring . . . how much he regretted . . . that he would have to leave The Lodge. And how much he regretted this, especially because he saw the value of The Lodge to people like Mr. Ring and knew very well that he had very slim chances outside The Lodge. But still, how complicated this was by the fact that all the other men at The Lodge had to be protected also and that it was more important to save The Lodge as an institution for the benefit of a greater

Based on his analysis of historical documents, Janis believes that "groupthink" contributed to Kennedy's disastrous decision to invade Cuba's Bay of Pigs. In later policy decisions, Kennedy successfully avoided this tendency.

number of men than it was to risk it being harmed by keeping Mr. Ring (Fairweather et al., 1969, p. 92).

Group Decision Processes

The ways in which groups make decisions and the nature of the outcome will vary with the group value structure and the situation faced by the group. In general, where groups have one dominant value orientation, *consensus* and *value-extremity shifts* in the direction of group values are common processes. Where there are value conflicts in the group, or multiple values to satisfy, *majority rule, compromise,* or *redescriptions of significance* are more likely.

Consensus. In groups where members are highly committed to a single set of group values and goals, there is strong pressure to arrive at a **consensus** on issues rather than to engage in formal discussions and vote taking (Schachter, 1951; Davis, 1969). While this may avoid the expression of differences and conflict in the group, the dangers inherent in this process have been presented by Janis (1972), who coined the term **groupthink.** This process refers to groups that arrive at a premature decision consensus that overlooks or excludes important aspects of the group and its circumstances. Janis believed that the Kennedy cabinet decision to invade Cuba (Bay of Pigs) and its disastrous consequences were the product of groupthink. He outlined a number of conditions that produced it: (1) the Kennedy cabinet was highly **cohesive**—that is, strongly committed to the same values and to each other; (2) the cabinet *insulated* itself from other viewpoints; (3) the cabinet did not search out or appraise *alternative* courses of action; and (4) Kennedy used a *directive* form of leadership in these particular meetings that discouraged genuine discussion in the group. Although subsequent research and thinking does not fully support Janis's original analysis (Longley & Pruitt, 1980), the concept of groupthink does point out some potential dangers of premature consensus in group decision making.

Value-extremity shifts. Where problems are discussed in groups with dominant values, it has been observed that the group decision is even more extreme (in the direction of the value) than the average of individual decisions before discussion. This effect was first noted in decisions involving the value of risk (Stoner, 1968; Wallach, Kogan, & Bem, 1964). It has since been generalized to many kinds of groups with different values, attitudes, and opinions. For example, Moscovici and Zavalloni (1969) found that French students who were initially anti-American became even more so following group discussion.

From the extensive research on the topic, it appears that the extremity shift is in large part due to members' decisions moving in the direction of best expressing the group value (Brown, 1965). It has been reported that the value shift is typically in the direction that the majority of members lean toward initially (Andrews & Johnson, 1971). Burnstein, Vinokur, and Thope (1973) found the group shift related directly to the number of persuasive arguments made in favor of the group position. In other research, leadership in decision making is typically given to members who best represent group values (Newcomb, 1961). Although simply providing members with information of the initial position of other members produces a slight shift, group discussion produces a much stronger movement in the direction of the group value (Moscovici & Zavalloni, 1969).

Majority rule. Where groups have value conflicts in decision making (like The Lodge group), it is unlikely that either premature consensus or value-extremity shifts will occur. There is much more likely to be group debate and discussion over value priorities and often the issue will be settled by majority vote. This is what happened in the Lodge decision on Mr.

Ring, who was ousted on a 4–3 vote of the executive committee.

Even though there are many possible ways to vote on issues (Davis, 1973), majority decisions have been the focus of research. Much of the research has involved both simulated and real jury decisions, which strongly illustrate a majority-rule procedure (Davis, Bray, & Holt, 1977). Only in rare cases, where a minority argues strongly, persistently, and effectively for a nonmajority position, does a shift occur away from majority-rule decisions (Moscovici, 1974).

Compromise. The value of compromise when dealing with differences in values is so obvious that research on this process is either self-evident or unnecessary. There are some limits on the use of compromise, however. If the conflicting values lead to incompatible courses of actions (which, due to budget restrictions, was the case in The Lodge), a compromise is not possible. One value or another needs to be given priority in the group's decision. But even here, the Lodge group might have been able to compromise between work and rehabilitation values if they had had more resources; that is, they might have kept Mr. Ring at The Lodge in a nonjanitorial job, if they had the means to support him.

Redescription of significance. ✗At times group discussions of problems may lead to the creation of new versions of group values, or redescriptions of significance.✗Although the negotiation of multiple group values has not been investigated systematically by psychologists, it is possible to give an example of this more innovative type of decision making in the Lodge group. As part of setting up the janitorial business, it was necessary to lease a truck.

To lease the truck, two research staff members accompanied three Lodge members to a local automobile agency. All arrangements were soon made successfully by The Lodge members—with one exception. All three members quickly chose

the size and type of truck, the kind of gear shift, and so on. Then the salesman asked what color the truck should be. One member said "red," another "green," and the third "blue." Each member refused to change his opinion and the salesman began to show frustration as the debate continued. Finally, one member remarked that since they had just organized a new janitorial service, the choice was obvious: "White—for purity" (Fairweather et al., 1969, p. 50).

✗Colors are like values in the sense that you cannot simply compromise or average them, since that would produce an outcome no one liked✗(probably a murky grey in the case of colors). In this case a creative solution was called for and provided. The solution represented an ingenious use of a group value—that the business represented cleanliness or purity, and so white was an appropriate choice. Note also that the solution changed the significance of the truck color from mere decoration to a symbol of the group's enterprise.

Such creativity in group decision making is rare in any group, but was quite remarkable for people just recently released from a mental hospital. It is a further demonstration that changes in group values and statuses can produce great changes in member behaviors.

Participation in Decision Making and Commitment to Group

✗There is a long tradition of research in social psychology that shows that the more group members are involved in group decision making, the stronger their commitment to the group and the more effective the group in effecting changes. ✗

Kurt Lewin (1947), a pioneer in group research, demonstrated that housewives were much more likely to help the war effort and eat sweetmeats when they had participated in a group discussion and decision than when they simply heard a lecture. In a nicely controlled field experiment, Coch and French (1948) found that a group of workers in a manufacturing plant who participated either directly or through elected representatives in decisions about production changes showed much better postchange productivity and satisfaction than a nonparticipatory control group. Research in other industries has shown that where workers have an intrinsic interest in their jobs, greater participation in decision making through *job enlargement* enhances their productivity and satisfaction (Hackman, 1977). Moreover, a number of small-group research studies have demonstrated the synergistic effects of increased commitment and group effectiveness (cf. Shaw, 1981).

A final example must go back to the Lodge experiment, which provided ex-patients with maximum opportunity to participate in all phases of group development. This did a number of things for group members. It enabled them to develop shared intrinsic values, to contribute their unique competencies in realizing these values, and in the process, to create new statuses for each other as hard-working, self-sufficient, responsible members in the community in place of their former status of ex-and-soon-to-be-again mental patients.

After The Lodge had become an autonomous living-working organization and the research had been evaluated, the researchers made a specific proposal for broadening social experimentation:

It is most likely that . . . institutes for experimental social innovation need to be formed. Since marginal persons (ex-patients, ex-convicts, handicapped, racially and sexually oppressed) would need to be involved in all phases of such innovation . . . such institutes would bring together researchers, marginal members of society, and its decision-makers. Using them as common meeting ground for planning research and implementing results could make such institutes powerful instruments for creating needed social change (Fairweather et al., 1969, p. 342).

The Lodge experiment not only has shown us a lot about group dynamics and status change, but the participative program proposed for extending such efforts is right in line with the values and objectives of the Society for the Psychological Study of Social Issues as outlined in Chapter 1.

SUMMARY

In this chapter a group is defined as two or more people who share intrinsic values and who coordinate behavior in ways that allow them to act on group values. Value orientations are sets of related values that anchor group world; that is, everything the group is and does. Value orientations can greatly enhance or reduce the behavior potential of members. This was demonstrated by the research on the consequences of cooperation, competition, and rivalry for individual and group behavior.

Group norms are boundary conditions on the ways in which group values are expressed in behavior; that is, they are judgments as to whether a given behavior counts as an expression or a violation of group values. Group norms contrast with prescriptive rules, which have the effect of reducing behavior potential of members by restricting judgment, choice, and group participation.

Within-group status refers to a member's standing in the group. Members assign each other status with respect to (a) what kinds of people they are, (b) what can be expected of that kind of person, and (c) how they are to be treated. Status is directly tied to member behavior potential (being able to act on intrinsic values). Status accreditation is a status assignment that takes into account member competence and capacities and thus allows for greater participation and involvement. Status degradation is a status assignment that reduces status and therefore behavior potential. Prescriptive role assignment and associated stereotypes and labeling are forms of status degradation. Within-group status degradation most often follows an unsuccessful defense against accusations of group-norm violations.

Leadership functions in a group are a special case of status assignments that take into account who can best represent group values and best facilitate ways of expressing values—especially value-related goal attainment. Because of their special status as innovators, leaders can often appear to be given more freedom to violate norms than other group members. In general, leader functions are assigned to group members on the basis of what competencies they have and the nature of the group situation.

Group decisions are special cases of leadership functioning, in that they are judgments as to which courses of action best express group values and facilitate coordination. Where there are dominant group values, decision-making processes may involve consensus and/or value-extremity shifts. Where group values are in conflict, decision processes may include majority rule, compromise, or redescription of significance.

SUGGESTED READINGS

Berkowitz, L. (Ed.). *Group processes*. New York: Academic Press, 1978.

Cartwright, D., & Zander, A. (Eds.). *Group dynamics: Research and theory*, 3d ed. New York: Harper & Row, 1968.

Ossorio, P. G. Foundations of descriptive psychology. In K. E. Davis (Ed.), *Advances in descriptive psychology*, Vol. 1. Greenwich, Conn.: JAI Press, 1981.

Shaw, M. E. *Group dynamics: The psychology of small group behavior*, 3d ed. New York: McGraw-Hill, 1981.

Sherif, M., & Sherif, C. W. *Social psychology*. New York: Harper & Row, 1969.

16

INTERGROUP RELATIONS

INTRODUCTION

Like many of the other authors of this text, I was born at the time of the Second World War—a time when America was segregated. Black people could not attend school with whites or live in the same neighborhoods; they could not go to the same hotels, restaurants, or bars, use the same toilets, or drink from the same fountains. In many states, blacks could not vote and they were not even allowed to sit with whites in the gallery of the United States Senate. The Jim Crow laws that enforced this segregation were the most formal and visible examples of the prejudice and discrimination that was so prevalent in American life before World War II.

Since World War II, America has experienced a revolution in relations between the races. Beginning in 1948, when President Truman integrated the armed forces and the Supreme Court struck down the restrictions that were used to maintain residential segregation, the visible symbols of segregation began to fall. In *Brown* v. *Board of Education* (1954), the Supreme Court moved to eliminate school segregation. Rosa Parks refused to sit in the back of a Montgomery, Alabama, bus in 1955, leading to the first major civil-rights march of the postwar period. The civil-rights movement of the 1960s led to the enactment of the first Civil Rights Act (1964) since the years after the Civil War. Discrimination in accommodations, housing, and jobs became illegal. These changes in race relations were followed by others, especially during the decade of the 1960s. The ratio of the average income earned by black compared to white families improved from 53 percent in 1961 to 64 percent in 1970 (U.S. Census, 1970). In 1971 more blacks had been elected to office than at any time since the Civil War—

1500, 62 percent of them outside the South (Kilson, 1971). College attendance by blacks more than doubled in the period between 1964 and 1970 (Wilson, 1973). In 1964 fewer than 1 percent of the nation's black children attended schools where the majority was white; by 1974 this figure was 33 percent. The attitudes of whites toward blacks gradually became less prejudiced during this period. For instance, in a 1963 survey, nearly a third of the nation's whites regarded blacks as inferior to whites, but by 1976 this figure had dropped to 15 percent ("A New Racial Poll," 1979). In the early 1960s most white parents in the South opposed school integration, but by 1966 a majority favored it (Gallup, 1972).

This impressive array of statistics points to the strides American society has made toward racial equality. Lest this lead to complacency, read on. If the 1960s were a period of progress, they were also a period of turmoil. Blacks rioted in many cities during the summers of 1965–1967. The riots in Newark, Watts, and Detroit led to the loss of over one hundred lives and $350 million in property damage. In the 1970s progress toward racial equality came to a standstill. The income differential between blacks and whites did not change in that decade. In 1978, the median income for white families was $18,368, but for blacks it was only $10,879. The percentage of people earning incomes below the poverty line who were black actually increased from 22 percent in 1970 to 28 percent in 1978 (Dorn, 1979). Unemployment rates among black males, relative to white males, were greater in 1976 than in 1960. Black teenagers were eight times as likely as white teenagers to be unemployed in 1976 (U.S. Commission on Civil Rights, 1978). The degree of residential segregation in our cities is as great now as it was after World War II (Farley, 1975). Likewise, the gap between whites and

---

This chapter is written by Walter G. Stephan.

Up until World War II, visible examples of prejudice and discrimination were common in the United States. Beginning in 1948, when President Truman integrated the armed forces and the Supreme Court struck down restrictions that were used to maintain residential segregation, visible symbols of segregation began to fall.

blacks in rates of infant mortality has narrowed only slightly since 1950 (Christmas, 1977).

These grim statistics make it clear that America has not eliminated its race problems. I have focused on blacks because their experiences have been carefully documented. Much the same could be said of other minorities, such as Mexican Americans, Americans of oriental backgrounds, Native Americans, and women. This chapter will focus on the relations between these and other groups in our society. First, some of the basic terms in the area of intergroup relations will be defined. Differences between the terms "prejudice," "stereotype," and "discrimination" will be analyzed to elimi-

nate confusion later. After this, the origins and functions of stereotypes will be discussed. The questions that will be addressed here are, What causes prejudice? and What functions does prejudice serve? The next issue we will take up is the relationship of prejudicial attitudes to other attitudes and behavior. The basic question here is, What are the effects of prejudice? Finally, this theoretical and empirical material about prejudice will be applied to a specific issue, school desegregation. In the discussion of school desegregation several specific topics will be considered. The primary emphasis will be on what social psychologists thought the effects of desegregation would be and what the effects have been. The chapter ends with a discussion of how intergroup relations can be improved in desegregated schools.

In the course of presenting this material, three types of roles that social psychologists have played in intergroup relations will be discussed. First, they have been responsible for generating the theories that we will discuss in the first section of the chapter. Second, social psychologists have played an active role in influencing public policy, as we will see in the discussion of the school desegregation trials. Third, social psychologists have developed intervention strategies designed to create conditions conducive to improved intergroup relations.

Prejudice, Discrimination, and Stereotyping

What exactly is **prejudice?** We will define it as a negative attitude toward members of socially defined groups. This definition means that people can be prejudiced toward members of different religions, political parties, social classes, and even such groups as the mentally retarded and the elderly as well as toward racial and ethnic groups. Attitudes, as has been noted elsewhere in this book (Chapters 4 and 5), are overall evaluations based on beliefs about the attitude object and evaluative responses associated with those beliefs. In the case of prejudice, the overall evaluation is usually exclusively negative, but it may be positive as well. Thus, one person may have a favorable attitude toward New Yorkers and feel that all New Yorkers are "good," while another person may have an opposite, unfavorable attitude toward New Yorkers.

The relationship between prejudice, a type of attitude, and both behavioral intentions and actual discriminatory behaviors is a complex one. When a prejudicial attitude leads to overt negative behavior, this is individual **discrimination.** When an anti-Semitic owner of a small business refuses to hire a Jew, we have a situ-

Despite the impressive strides American society has made toward racial equality, on the average, blacks still have a lower standard of living than whites. Blacks are still more apt to face problems such as migrant work, poor pay, or unemployment.

ation in which prejudice leads to discrimination. This type of discrimination can be distinguished from institutionalized discrimination, which refers to institutional practices that result in discrimination, such as the practice by some real estate agencies of showing black clients only houses in black neighborhoods. Here the individual real estate agents may not be racially prejudiced, but their behavior is racist (Carmichael & Hamilton, 1967). On the other hand, consider the case of a sexist personnel director of a large corporation. He may not discriminate against women because of equal opportunity laws. In this instance a person who is prejudiced is not behaving in a discriminatory manner. The important point is that prejudice is an attitude and discrimination is a behavior, and that the two are not necessarily directly related. It is possible to have prejudice without discrimination and discrimination without prejudice.

SOCIAL FOCUS 16.1
Sex Role Stereotyping

Although they are a statistical majority in the United States, women must still fight against stereotypes and discrimination as if they were a minority group.

The majority of people in the United States are women and yet women are often labeled as a minority group. The reason is that women in America have suffered from prejudiced attitudes and discriminatory behavior. Sandra Bem (1974) has suggested that there is a nonconscious ideology according to which women are regarded as being less important and less valuable to society than men.

An index of the low opinion in which women are held is the stereotyping of men and women. In one study (Broverman, Vogel, Broverman, Clarkson, & Rosenkrantz, 1972) psychiatrists and psychologists were asked for their concepts of the healthy male and female. The results indicated that compared to men, healthy women were thought to be more submissive, emotional, excitable, conceited, and more easily influenced, while being less independent, adventurous, aggressive, competitive, and objective. The healthy woman was also thought to dislike math and science more than men and to have her feelings more easily hurt than a man.

The importance of these findings is that they suggest that these are the goals toward which therapists are striving in trying to make their women clients healthy. One could argue that possessing many of these traits would be adaptive for women, given the discrimination against them. From this perspective, psychological health means fitting into the prevailing stereotypes and discriminatory social norms. This might make it easier to accept the fact that in 1978, at a time when one-third of the full-time working force in the United States were women, on the average they were paid only 60 percent of what men earned (Dorn, 1979). While a variety of factors may contribute to the difference, one study found that 84 percent of the income differential between men and women was due to sex-based discrimination (Featherman & Hauser, 1976).

The sterile view that psychological health for women means accepting limits on self-expression is one many people find unacceptable. The battle for equal rights for women is an attempt to overcome the nonconscious ideology that oppresses them. The prejudice and discrimination that this movement is battling is deeply entrenched in our society, but some signs of progress are evident. Between 1970 and 1978 the number of women lawyers tripled, the proportion of women receiving medical degrees doubled, and in graduate studies as a whole, 380,000 women entered school between 1970 and 1978, while only 160,000 men did (Dorn, 1979).

Stereotypes are the perceptions or beliefs we hold of others; they consist of sets of traits attributed to socially defined groups. In some cases, stereotypes are associated with prejudicial attitudes and in other cases they are not. In some instances these sets of traits consist primarily of positive characteristics, such as the traits imputed to doctors or to the groups of which we are members. Most stereotypes, however, consist of a mixture of positive and negative traits, such as those associated with males and females. Thus, while prejudice toward a given group is usually associated with a stereotype for that group, stereotypes can also coexist with positive attitudes, or even with a mixture of positive and negative attitudes. We will find as we progress through this chapter that one of the hallmarks of attitudes toward socially defined groups is their complexity. It is often the case that feelings of sympathy toward members of a given group, such as the physically handicapped, exist side by side with feelings of discomfort and aversion (Katz & Glass, 1979).

ORIGINS AND FUNCTIONS OF PREJUDICE AND STEREOTYPES

Each of us acquires attitudes toward social groups in a variety of ways. The two most important ways are through socialization and through our contacts with members of other groups. During socialization we acquire information and attitudes from parents, other authority figures such as teachers and relatives, the mass media (especially television), and our peers about the existence of our own and other groups and the nature of members of these groups. Much of this information will be based on the relations that exist between the groups.

These intergroup relations may have a long history, as the relations between blacks and whites in America do, or they may be relatively recent, as in the case of the relationships between Vietnamese immigrants and American citizens. We will discuss three aspects of the historical relationship between blacks and whites in America to illustrate how the attitudes and stereotypes that are handed down through socialization processes evolved. The three aspects to be considered are the economic roles occupied by members of the two groups, their rural or urban place of origin, and their social-class membership.

Historical Intergroup Relations

✱ Campbell (1967) has noted that the roles played by members of two groups that coexist are especially important in determining how each group will perceive the other. By roles Campbell is referring primarily to the occupations that the members of each group typically hold. The master-slave relationship between blacks and whites in the South before the Civil War furnishes a clear example of a situation where two groups occupied specific economic roles. It was inevitable that the master-slave relationship would shape how each group viewed the other. Consider the working and living conditions of the slaves. They were forced to work under threat of punishment; their maintenance was provided for only in the most minimal ways; it was actually illegal to educate slaves before the Civil War; and blacks could be severely punished for any signs of rebellion. It shouldn't surprise us to find that whites viewed blacks as lazy, dirty, and ignorant, and that they often believed that the slaves were content with their lot. These perceptions are not unique to whites' views of blacks, however. Similar views are held in many societies toward groups that perform manual labor. People who perform these types of economic roles are usually seen as strong,

pleasure-loving, stupid, and as spendthrifts.

A second aspect of intergroup relations that contributes to stereotyping is place of residence. The fact that blacks have traditionally lived in rural areas has contributed to the view that urban dwellers have of them. It is generally true in all cultures that rural residents are viewed by urban dwellers as unsophisticated, guileless, gullible, and ignorant (LeVine & Campbell, 1972). (See Social Focus 16.2 for a discussion of racial differences in intelligence.) A third historical aspect that has been important in shaping whites' views of blacks is the fact that blacks have been predominantly lower class and lower-class people in all cultures tend to be viewed as ignorant, lazy, loud, dirty, and happy-go-lucky. What these universal tendencies toward stereotyping manual laborers, rural residents, and lower-class people make clear is that much of the historical stereotype of blacks in America has little to do with black people themselves, but rather is due to the roles they have occupied and the places they have lived.

Correspondingly, the views of whites held by blacks are largely due to the historical roles occupied by the whites with whom blacks interacted. Again relying on the work of LeVine and Campbell (1972), we can see that there are several universal tendencies that have shaped stereotypes of whites. Businessmen are seen by manual laborers as grasping, haughty, winning, and domineering, and upper-class people tend to be seen as ambitious, neat, progressive, and intelligent. In addition, rural residents perceive urban dwellers as dishonest, immoral, greedy, urbane, and sophisticated. The traits attributed to businessmen, the upper classes, and urban residents match blacks' stereotype of whites remarkably well. This stereotype consists of the traits deceitful, sly, intelligent, industrious, selfish, conceited, and cruel, among others (Stephan & Rosenfield, 1981). Again, this has little to do with the traits of whites per se, since people who occupy these roles tend to be viewed this way in all societies.

One of the most remarkable things about

the stereotypes of blacks and whites is that, despite the vast changes that have occurred in relations between the two groups during this century, these stereotypes have changed relatively little (Karlins, Coffman, & Walters, 1969). It is true that blacks are more often viewed as proud and militant now (Samuels, 1973), but many of the traits in both stereotypes endure. How can this possibly be the case? There are several answers to this question. The first is that in the absence of contact between the groups, it is these historically produced stereotypes that will be passed from one generation to the next. The second answer is that there are some fundamental psychological processes that operate to maintain stereotypes and prejudice, even in the face of changing intergroup relations. It is to these processes that we will turn next.

Social Categorization

If you have ever been in an international airport you have no doubt enjoyed the pastime of people-watching. The reason we all enjoy this game is that we can revel in the diversity of people who pass before us. At a glance we see foreigners, rich people, members of different ethnic groups, attractive women and men, the elderly, babies, unusual-looking people—a little bit of everything. It is almost impossible to avoid the temptation to fit labels to them, to categorize them into groups. We do this because the social world we live in would be utter chaos if we did not attempt to break it down and organize it into intelligible units. To bring order out of this chaos we all categorize the people we interact with, using categories like sex, age, nationality, ethnicity, and social class. One reason for categorization is that it facilitates interaction. Whenever we interact with another person we make certain assumptions. Typically, we assume that we share the same systems of verbal and nonverbal communication. Further, we assume that the other person will follow the same norms we have learned for how to behave in the setting we are in. When we go to a formal dinner party, for instance, we assume that the other guests won't behave abusively, shout at each other, eat with their fingers, put food in their hair, or take their clothes off. In other words, we know how we are expected to behave in this situation and we assume that others do too. But even with these assumptions, we will still feel a lot of uncertainty about how to behave. What do we say to people? How do we choose topics of conversation? How can we avoid venturing into sensitive topic areas? Categorizing other people helps us to reduce this uncertainty. We know not to advocate abortion when talking to a Catholic nun; we will probably avoid criticizing affirmative action in the presence of a black congressman; we can guess that a young lawyer might be interested in discussing law; and a homosexual would probably respond positively to support for gay rights, and so on. Making assumptions about other people on the basis of group membership facilitates interacting with them when the assumptions are correct. The problem is that the assumptions may be wrong. There are two psychological processes associated with categorization that increase the chances of our making invalid assumptions.

The first process is called **assimilation** and it occurs when the amount of variability within a group is ignored and members of that group are perceived as being more similar than they actually are. If a male regards nearly all women as being physically weak, he is guilty of assimilation, since he is ignoring the enormous variation in strength among women. The second psychological process that contributes to making mistaken assumptions about members of other groups is called **contrast.** In this case the differences between groups are perceived as being greater than they actually are. The male in the example above is likely to think that the difference between men and women in physical strength is greater than it actually is.

SOCIAL FOCUS 16.2
Racial Differences in IQ Scores: SPSSI's View on the Heredity vs. Environment Controversy

Blacks, on the average, score about 15 points lower on IQ tests than do whites. Given the numerous studies of this phenomenon, the results, per se, are generally accepted. What is at issue, however, is the importance and causes of this difference. Two main factors (heredity versus environment) have been used as explanatory concepts (see Wrightsman, 1977).

In championing a hereditarian (or genetic) explanation of racial differences in IQ, Arthur Jensen (1969) and others have made the following points.

1. Identical twins reared apart have very similar IQ scores, thus implying the great importance of heredity, and the lesser influence of environmental factors.
2. Blacks with lighter skin pigmentation (presumed to be a sign of racial mixing) score higher on IQ tests than do darker-skinned blacks.
3. Between the First and Second World Wars, the economic conditions of blacks improved. The test scores of black army recruits did not, however, improve in comparison to the test scores of white recruits.
4. Blacks score less well than whites on so-called "culture free" tests. Culture free tests are designed so that only ability—independent of the culture in which the test-taker lives—should influence performance.

The environmentalists have challenged many of these points and added further arguments of their own (see Wrightsman, 1977). With regard to the twins' studies, the environmentalists note that Jensen relied heavily on data reported by Sir Cyril Burt. Shortly after his death in 1971, serious flaws and inaccuracies in Burt's data came to light. It appears Burt fabricated his data on several occasions. More recent studies in the U.S. by Sandra Scarr and others show a lower correlation between the IQ scores of identical twins reared apart.

The relationship of skin color to IQ could, claim the environmentalists, actually be a function of environmental conditions. Most of the pigmentation studies were done during the first half of this century. At that time, it is likely that lighter-skinned blacks had more opportunities and were the target of less prejudice.

With regard to the hereditarians' third point, environmentalists have retorted as follows: Between the First and Second World Wars, the condition of blacks undoubtedly did improve. But, their relative economic status vis-a-vis whites remained fairly constant. Therefore, it is unreasonable to expect their IQ scores, relative to whites, to have increased. Finally, environmentatlists have questioned whether it is possible to construct truly "culture free" tests.

Having rebutted the genetic viewpoint, what do the environmentalists have to say in behalf of their own position? A classic study reported in 1922 found a correlation of $+.77$ between the money per capita allocated for education in each state and the average intelligence test score for army recruits from that state. More recently some environmental enrichment programs have been shown to have beneficial effects on the IQ scores of black children. Perhaps most convincing of all is a recent study (Scarr and Weinberg, 1976) of 130 black or interracial children adopted by well educated white families. Not only did these children score 15–20 points higher on IQ tests than the average American black child, but also, they scored higher than the average white child. Furthermore, the earlier in life these children were adopted, the better they did on the tests.

Besides the direct evidence for the importance of economic and social influences on IQ test scores, environmentalists have noted the importance of the test-taking situation itself. The test takers' previous experience with similar exams, the test takers' motivation, and the race of the examiner may influence performance. For instance, in some studies, blacks have done better when tested by a black experimenter. It appears likely that the testing situation generally favors the performance of whites. One can't help but wonder: Are the obtained differences really indicative of underlying differences in ability or are they merely differences in the scores on a flawed test?

In 1969, the Society for the Psychological Study of Social Issues formally spoke out on this controversy. It stated:

The evidence of four decades of research on this problem can be readily summarized. There are marked differences in intelligence test scores when one compares a random sample of whites and Negroes. What is equally clear is that little definitive evidence exists that leads to the conclusion that such differences are innate. The evidence points overwhelmingly to the fact that when one compares Negroes and whites of comparable cultural and educational background, differences in intelligence test scores diminish markedly; the more comparable the background, the less the difference. There is no direct evidence that supports the view that there is an innate difference between members of different racial groups.

We maintain that the racism and discrimination of our country impose an immeasurable burden upon the black person . . . We believe that a more accurate understanding of the contribution of heredity to intelligence will only be possible when social conditions for all races are equal and when this situation has existed for several generations (SPSSI Council, 1969, pp. 1–2).

Thus, when we make assumptions about the nature of members of other groups, we are apt to see them as being more similar to each other than they actually are and to perceive the differences between their group and ours as being greater than it actually is.

Ingroup-Outgroup Bias

A second problem stemming from categorization is the universal tendency toward **ethnocentrism.** We all tend to evaluate ingroup members more positively than outgroup members, partly because assimilation and contrast lead us to misperceive the degree of similarity that exists within and between groups. Instead of looking for similarities we focus on the dissimilarities between the groups. This **ingroup-outgroup bias** doesn't apply just to ethnic groups, as the term ethnocentrism implies. It appears to occur whenever people are categorized.

Ingroup-outgroup bias is so basic that it can

be elicited even when the distinctions between groups are arbitrary and trivial. A study by Tajfel (1970) on high school students in England illustrates this phenomenon. The students were asked to guess the number of dots they saw projected on a screen. After viewing a series of slides, the students were given false feedback, indicating that they had consistently overestimated or underestimated the number of dots in the slides. Later, the students played a game in which they could allocate rewards to two other students. One of the other students made the same type of errors they had made and the other differed in the errors made in dot guessing. The results showed that the students allocated more rewards to the student who made the same kind of errors they did in the dot-estimation task and discriminated against the one whose performance differed from theirs. Clearly, the distinction between overestimators and underestimators is unimportant, but it does serve to create an ingroup and an outgroup and this was sufficient to elicit ingroup-outgroup bias.

The reason ingroup-outgroup bias is an inevitable outcome of categorization is that most of us have a desire to maintain a positive self-image. One way we can bolster our views of ourselves is to positively evaluate the groups to which we belong. This tendency is so pervasive that we hardly ever think about it. Imagine for a moment all the groups of which you are a member. Isn't it true that in most cases you have a positive evaluation of your group and in fact can think of numerous ways in which it is better than other comparable groups? For instance, don't you have a higher opinion, on most dimensions that are important to you, of members of your sex and age groups than those of other groups? If you are like most people, you evaluate your school, your class in school, your sorority or fraternity, your intramural team, and your informal group of friends favorably when comparing them to the alternatives. Having these favorable evaluations allows you to take some pride in being a

member of these groups, which in turn serves to maintain and enhance self-esteem. An exception to this general pattern of high regard for ingroups can occur for very-low-status groups. When coupled with assimilation and contrast, the usual effect of ingroup-outgroup bias is that it leads to positive evaluations of the ingroup at the cost of rejecting outgroup members.

In the area of race and ethnic relations the consequences of assimilation and contrast and ingroup-outgroup bias have been carefully examined. Because of differences in language and cultural heritage there are ethnic-group differences in social norms, characteristic traits, and nonverbal behavior. When considering these differences, ingroup-outgroup bias leads members of ethnic ingroups to emphasize the traits that allow them to regard the ingroup as being superior to the outgroup (Brewer, 1979). In addition, the influence of assimilation and contrast effects will lead them to overestimate the amount of difference between the groups on these dimensions. Thus, the ingroup will choose a positive label when describing a trait possessed by the group and the contrasting trait of the outgroup will be described by a negative label. For instance, when Americans describe themselves they say they are friendly and outgoing. The English, describing these same traits, say that Americans are intrusive and forward. The English describe themselves as being reserved and respectful of the rights of others. Americans, however, think of the English as cold and snobbish (Campbell, 1967). This biased labeling process contributes to the formation of positive stereotypes for ingroups and negative stereotypes for outgroups.

Ethnocentric labeling is not restricted to the labeling of entire groups; it also occurs when individuals are interacting in specific situations. Several studies have shown that there is an ethnocentric bias in the attributions that are used to explain the behavior of ingroup and outgroup members. When an ingroup member does something good, it is explained in terms of some underlying personality trait. If an outgroup member does equally well, the performance tends to be explained in terms of situational factors. Just the opposite occurs for negative behaviors. Here it is the outgroup member's behavior that is explained by enduring traits, whereas the ingroup member's behavior is attributed to situational pressures. For instance, in one study it was found that when a black person did well on an extrasensory perception (ESP) task, ethnocentric white students believed that it was due to luck, but when a white did well, the ethnocentric white students believed it was because of ESP abilities. In contrast, when a black did poorly, white students said it was because of a lack of this ability, while when a white did poorly, it was seen as being due to bad luck (Greenberg & Rosenfield, 1979). This bias has been called the "ultimate attribution error" (Pettigrew, 1979). It implies that positive traits will be used to explain ingroup behavior, but negative traits will be used to explain the behavior of outgroups.

These ethnocentric biases in the perception and labeling of outgroup behavior, combined with the characteristic role relations between groups, account for much of the specific content of stereotypes. The consequence of the tendency to perceive outgroups as differing from ingroups and the tendency toward ingroup-outgroup bias is prejudice: negative attitudes toward members of other groups. The irony is that the categorization of others, which is originally undertaken in an attempt to understand them and interact with them more effectively, can ultimately lead to prejudice toward the people who are categorized.

Psychodynamic Factors

Up to this point in the discussion, cognitive processes that promote prejudice and stereotyping have been emphasized. Several biases that affect our thinking about other groups have been highlighted but they involve rather subtle shadings of reality. The two psychodynamic processes to be discussed next, projection and scapegoating, involve greater distortions of reality.

Projection occurs when individuals attribute to other individuals or groups traits that they themselves possess, but which they regard as undesirable. We may think it is wrong to bear hostile feelings toward other people or groups. We can avoid the dilemma posed by having such feelings by attributing them instead to members of the other group. It is they who are hostile, not we. Schofield (1980) has provided an example of this type of projection from interviews she did in a desegregated junior high school. One of the black students told her, "A whole lot of black kids think that everybody that's white hates them. So, they'll hate white people back" (p. 34). In this example the hostility toward whites is not denied, but its origins are presented in a way that justifies it. In another study white children were reported to believe that blacks were ignorant but that whites were intelligent (Brigham, 1974). It seems likely that these fourth- and fifth-grade students would prefer to believe that whites are not ignorant, in spite of the diversity that obviously exists within this group. It is easier to maintain this positive view of whites if ignorance is imputed to the other group. Thus, the white students believe that it isn't their own group that is ignorant but rather it is blacks who are ignorant.

Scapegoating is a process by which other individuals or groups are held to be the cause of one's own problems. Typically, it involves members of a higher-status group blaming a less powerful group for a particular problem. An unemployed white male may blame equal opportunity programs, affirmative action, and women's liberation for his lack of employment, using programs designed to help blacks and women as an excuse for his inability to find or keep a job. In this defensive maneuver the individual avoids blaming himself and redirects the blame toward others. To the extent that he blames these groups for his problems, he is likely to be prejudiced toward them. This process is thought to contribute to the high levels of prejudice that characterize members of the lower classes. The hostility generated by the frustrations of lower-class existence is apparently displaced outward, especially toward members of ethnic and religious outgroups.

A somewhat different instance in which the process of scapegoating is thought to occur is in the case of authoritarian individuals. The authoritarian personality was studied by a group of American investigators in the period after World War II (Adorno, Frenkel-Brunswik, Levinson, & Sanford, 1950). They were attempting to understand how the persecution of the Jews during World War II could have occurred in a country as civilized as Germany. They suggested that certain kinds of people, whom they labeled authoritarian personalities, were particularly susceptible to falling under the sway of powerful authority figures. The syndrome of traits that characterizes these people includes rigid adherence to conventional values, low tolerance for ambiguity, a preoccupation with dominance and submission, and a disposition to attribute evil motives to others (Sanford, 1971). Authoritarianism has also been found to be related to child-rearing practices in which parents emphasize obedience and instill fear in their children (Harris, Gough, & Martin, 1950). The frustration and hostility caused by these child-rearing practices cannot be directed toward the parents because of the punishment that would be likely to follow. Some children reared in this type of environment grow up with a need to displace hostility toward others, that is, with a need to be prejudiced. The most likely targets of this displaced aggression are downtrodden groups in society who cannot retaliate. These powerless groups are then blamed for the problems that the individual or the society is experiencing.

In several of my own experiments I have found that scapegoating can occur in face-to-face interactions with members of stigmatized groups. In one study, college students worked on a cooperative task of solving anagrams with another student. The second student was either handicapped or nonhandicapped. When the students were told that they had performed poorly, they disliked the handicapped partner more than the nonhandicapped partner. This study suggests that when the partner was different from the subject, the partner was blamed for their poor joint performance (Gibbons, Stephan, Stephenson, & Petty, 1980).

This type of scapegoating had a curious parallel when the team performed well. In this case, the handicapped person was liked better than the nonhandicapped person. Other studies have shown that when whites interact with blacks, similar paradoxical findings emerge (Katz & Glass, 1979). It appears that responses to outgroup members are amplified in comparison to responses to ingroup members. In positive situations we often evaluate outgroup members even more favorably than we would evaluate ingroup members, but in negative situations we tend to evaluate outgroup members more negatively than ingroup members. This **response amplification** effect illustrates the ambivalence of our attitudes toward many outgroups, which are often a mixture of sympathy and aversion. Which of these attitudes is likely to prevail over the other depends on the situation.

Race versus Belief Similarity

Due to the operation of ingroup-outgroup bias, assimilation and contrast, and psychodynamic processes, differences between groups tend to be exaggerated. The result is that ingroup members frequently assume that there are differences in beliefs, values, and traits between ingroup and outgroup members. This assumed dissimilarity is generally associated with negative attitudes toward outgroup members. Rokeach, Smith, and Evans (1960), pursuing this line of thought, asked whether the negative attitude we call racial prejudice might really be caused by this assumed dissimilarity rather than by race. To answer this question they conducted a study in which they varied belief similarity and race independently. That is, they presented subjects with information about other people who were either similar or dissimilar to them and who were either of the same or a different race. The subjects liked the similar other more than the dissimilar other, regardless of race. This led Rokeach et al. to conclude that what we call racial prejudice is really due to belief dissimilarity.

Rokeach et al.'s surprising conclusion was subsequently tested by other investigators. In these studies, one type of similarity (for example, beliefs, traits) was compared with race in one or more situations. The results of these studies are complex and contradictory. Sometimes belief appears to be more important than race and other times race appears to be more important. One generally accepted conclusion is that as the interracial contact situation becomes more intimate, the other person's race becomes a more important determinant of behavior (Triandis & Davis, 1965). Thus, this research suggests that in informal or work settings we tend to be more concerned with whether another person is similar to us, whereas in more intimate situations, like dating, race plays a greater role.

A study supporting this general thesis was conducted by Silverman (1974). The behavior he was concerned with was choice of college roommates. He provided students with information about prospective roommates who were either similar or dissimilar to them in beliefs and who were either from the same or a different ethnic group. When the choice was a purely hypothetical one, the students tended to select roommates who were similar to them in beliefs and disregarded race, but when the students thought they were choosing their actual roommates, race similarity became an important determinant of their choices. The re-

sults of this study indicate that both belief and race similarity can be important determinants of behavior, with the importance of race increasing as the consequences of the behavior have a greater impact on the individual. They also demonstrate that race prejudice cannot be reduced to belief prejudice, since both race and belief similarity affect behavior.

Attitudes, Behavior, and Self-Fulfilling Prophecies

The brief discussion of the race-versus-belief-similarity issue highlights an issue of fundamental importance for social psychology: the relationship between attitudes and behavior. As the research on response amplification indicates, situational factors play an important role in determining the manner in which attitudes are translated into behavior. A model of the attitude-behavior relationship that stresses the importance of situational factors (see Chapter 5) has been proposed by Fishbein and Ajzen (1975). They have analyzed the factors that influence people's intentions to carry out a specific act. These behavioral intentions are determined by: (1) the person's attitudes toward the specific act, (2) the person's perception of the social norms that govern behavior in this situation, and (3) the person's motivation to comply with the social norms. A study by Johnson (1980) applied Fishbein and Ajzen's model to prejudice and extended it to include not only behavioral intentions but actual behavior as well.

Johnson arranged to have both a white person and a black person call apartment managers who had apartments available for rent. When they called, they identified the section of Los Angeles they presently lived in to convey information about their own racial background. Then they asked to rent the apartments and the managers' responses were recorded. The responses to this question were used as an index of discriminatory behavior. In order to gather information on the managers' behavioral intentions, their perceptions of relevant social norms, and their attitudes toward renting to blacks, an interviewer called each manager three weeks later. As would be predicted by Fishbein and Ajzen's model, the results revealed that behavioral intentions were based to a substantial degree on attitudes toward the act and norms for the situation. More importantly, the apartment managers' behavioral intentions were significantly correlated with their actual decisions about whether or not to rent to blacks ($r = .43$).

Thus, this study and many others using Fishbein and Ajzen's model indicate that prejudicial attitudes can—and often do—lead to discrimination.

Of course, as was discussed in Chapter 5, our attitudes are sometimes different than our behaviors. Even if this is the case, our attitudes still have several other important consequences. The first is that our attitudes shape other people's attitudes and behavior. For example, the discriminatory behavior of the apartment managers in Johnson's study was found to correlate with the managers' perception of the racial attitudes of their families and friends. Several other studies have shown that parents' racial attitudes are correlated with their children's racial attitudes (Epstein & Komorita, 1966a, 1966b; Mosher & Scodel, 1960; Stephan & Rosenfield, 1978). The most obvious explanation for this finding is that children are learning prejudicial attitudes from their parents.

Our attitudes toward others also influence their attitudes toward us and toward themselves. An example of the first process (Group A's attitudes influencing Group B's attitudes toward members of Group A) can be found in a recent study of desegregation in Dallas, Texas. It was found that the prejudices of whites toward blacks was greatest in classrooms where blacks had the most negative attitudes toward whites (Rosenfield, Sheehan, Marcus, & Stephan, 1981). One interpretation

of this finding is that the negative attitudes of the blacks toward the whites in these newly desegregated schools caused the whites to be negative toward the blacks. An example of how the attitudes of one group can affect the attitudes of another group toward itself can be found in a legal brief written by a group of social scientists at the time that the Brown case was being argued before the Supreme Court (Allport et al., 1953).

> [When] minority group children learn the inferior status to which they are assigned . . . they often react with feelings of inferiority and a sense of humiliation. . . . Under these conditions, the minority group child is thrown into a conflict with regard to his feelings about himself and his group. He wonders whether his group and he himself are worthy of no more respect than they receive (pp. 429–430).

These examples suggest that a group that is the target of prejudice may react by adopting negative attitudes toward the other group or toward themselves or they may do both.

One of the most powerful consequences of our prejudices and stereotypes is that our attitudes affect the behavior of other group members in ways that may lead them to confirm the expectancies we hold about them (see Chapters 2 and 6). An example of this self-fulfilling prophecy directly related to race relations comes from Schofield's (1980) study of a recently desegregated school. In this school whites have a stereotyped view of blacks as aggressive. According to Schofield, "Many [of the white students] are so afraid of blacks that they do not stand up for themselves even in very unthreatening encounters. This lack of willingness to assert themselves and to protect their own rights when interacting with blacks makes whites attractive targets [for harassment by blacks] since their behavior also reinforces attempts to dominate them" (p. 40). Thus, the white students' expectancy that blacks will behave aggressively leads them to engage in behavior that makes the prophecy come true.

In this example, the expectancy leads ingroup members to behave in ways that cause outgroup members to confirm the expectancy. Two additional aspects of this self-fulfilling prophecy should be noted. First, there is a bias to perceive that others have acted in ways that confirm our expectancies, even when they have not (Cooper & Fazio, 1979). Again, Schofield's (1980) study provides us with an example. In the school she studied, blacks have a stereotype of whites as being prejudiced and conceited. In contrast, the whites feel that they are unprejudiced. The whites, acting on this self-perception, sometimes offer to help the black students. How do you suppose the black students interpret this behavior? Here is what Schofield reports: "Black students often see such offers of help as yet another indication of White feelings of superiority and conceit" (p. 37). The black students interpret this behavior as confirming their expectancies, even though the white students' intentions are just the opposite. A second bias that operates in situations where members of one group have expectancies concerning another group is that disconfirming evidence tends to be ignored, whereas confirming evidence tends to be remembered (Rothbart, Evans, & Fulero, 1979). Thus, prejudices and stereotypes bias our memory for events that we have seen, and this bias increases the chances that we will believe that our expectations are justified.

To summarize the self-fulfilling prophecy briefly, stereotypes set up expectancies concerning how members of other groups will behave. They may also influence the behavior of ingroup members. The ingroup member's behavior increases the chances that the outgroup member will confirm the expectancy. Even if the ingroup member's behavior is not affected by the expectancy, however, the fact that the ingroup members hold the expectancy will bias their perception of the outgroup member's behavior. These biases make it probable that the ingroup members will believe that the other person's behavior confirmed their expectan-

cies. The self-fulfilling prophecy is one of the most damaging effects of stereotyping. It creates a series of traps in the social-interaction process that are difficult to escape, due to their subtle nature. It is likely to affect relations between women and men, teachers and students, mental patients and doctors, members of different ethnic groups—and any other group for which a stereotype exists.

How do we overcome the negative effects of prejudice and stereotyping? The social scientists who participated in the Brown decision thought that educational institutions were one place where this could be accomplished. In the next section we will review what these social scientists thought would happen. Then we will examine what the effects of school desegregation have been and discuss the role of social scientists in the judicial process in the light of these results. The section will end with a discussion of some experimental techniques that are currently being used to reduce prejudice and stereotyping in desegregated schools.

SCHOOL DESEGREGATION AND INTERGROUP RELATIONS

For much of this century our education system has been one of the primary battlegrounds in the struggle for racial equality. The choice of educational institutions was a conscious one by the National Association for the Advancement of Colored People (NAACP), the organization that fought many of the legal battles. Educational institutions were chosen because inequality was clear, they were publicly controlled, and it was believed that they could be more easily changed than other institutions. Starting in 1935 the NAACP brought suits against institutions of higher education such as law schools. In the 1940s they brought suits against the public school system. The basic premise in these suits was that school segregation denied blacks equal educational opportunities because segregated facilities resulted in inferior education. In some of the cases leading up to the decision that mandated an end to segregation (*Brown* v. *Board of Education*, 1954), it was argued that the facilities provided for blacks were inferior to those for whites. In other cases it was argued that segregating blacks had negative effects on their self-esteem and achievement and that it caused them to be prejudiced toward whites. The argument that segregation caused these undesirable effects was presented by social scientists. In order to understand the nature of this argument, a few examples of their testimony will be presented.

Social Scientists' Testimony in *Brown* v. *Board of Education*

Social scientists made two types of contributions to the Brown decision. They testified in the trials leading up to Brown and they filed the Friend of the Court brief (*amicus curiae*) cited earlier. Below are some samples of their reasoning, taken from testimony given in the Brown trial. The first quote is from Kenneth Clark, a recent president of the American Psychological Association (APA).

I have reached the conclusion . . . that discrimination, prejudice, and segregation have definitely detrimental effects on the personality development of the Negro child. The essence of this detrimental effect is a confusion in the child's concept of his own self-esteem—basic feelings of inferiority, conflict, confusion in his self-image, resentment, hostility towards himself, [and] hostility towards whites (Kluger, 1976, p. 353).

Clark is suggesting that the self-esteem of blacks is low in segregated schools and that segregation leads black children to be prejudiced toward whites. This view is echoed by David Krech who testified:

Legal segregation, . . . because it is obvious to everyone, gives . . . environmental support for the belief that Negroes are in some way different from and inferior to white people, and in turn that

. . . supports and strengthens beliefs of racial differences, of racial inferiority (Kluger, 1976, pp. 361–362).

Krech's testimony indicates that he thought segregation led both blacks and whites to regard blacks as inferior. This perceived inferiority would be expected to lead to white prejudice against blacks and to low self-esteem among blacks.

Horace English testified that segregation had negative effects on achievement.

If we [communicate to] a person that he is incapable of learning, then he is less likely to be able to learn. . . . There is a tendency for us to live up to—or perhaps I should say down to— social expectations and to learn what people say we can learn, and legal segregation definitely depresses the Negro's expectancy and is therefore prejudicial to his learning (Kluger, 1976, p. 415).

English was referring to the self-fulfilling prophecy as an explanation for the low achievement levels of blacks. Because he believed that it was segregation that led to these low expectancies, we can also infer that he believed that ending legalized segregation would increase the achievement levels of blacks.

The ultimate consequences of the social scientists' testimony can be seen in the decision rendered by the Court. Below is a quote from Chief Justice Earl Warren's decision:

Does segregation of children in public schools, solely on the basis of race . . . deprive the children of the minority group of equal educational opportunities? We believe it does. . . . To separate Negro school children from others of similar age and qualifications, solely because of their race, generates a feeling of inferiority as to their status in the community that may affect their hearts and minds in a way unlikely ever to be undone.

From the testimony and the *amicus curiae* brief we can formulate a theory about why the social scientists believed segregation had negative effects. White prejudice was regarded as the cause of segregation, and segregation was believed to lead to low self-esteem among blacks. This in turn was thought to affect black students' motivation to learn, as well as their achievement. Low self-esteem and frustration over low achievement were then turned outward in the form of prejudice toward whites. The low self-esteem and low achievement of blacks and their hostility toward whites reinforced white prejudice and the vicious circle was complete (see Figure 16.1).

Because the plaintiffs in the Brown case were attempting to establish the ways in which school segregation violated the "equal protection under the laws" guaranteed by the Fourteenth Amendment to the Constitution, their testimony referred primarily to the damaging consequences of segregation (Cook, 1979). It is possible, however, to infer some of their thinking about the effects of desegregation. My synthesis of this reasoning is that they believed desegregation would break the vicious circle created by segregation, by eliminating an institutionalized sanction for white prejudice. If the behavior of whites was changed from attending segregated schools to attending desegregated schools (or allowing their children to attend them), the whites who were prejudiced would be faced with a dilemma. Their prejudiced attitudes would be inconsistent with their decision to attend desegregated schools. Apparently, the social scientists believed that the students and parents would resolve this in-

consistency by changing their attitudes so that they would be consistent with their behavior, that is, by becoming less prejudiced. The social scientists also believed that the self-esteem of blacks would increase in desegregated schools because blacks would no longer be stamped with the badge of inferiority represented by segregation. It was expected that these increases in self-esteem would be associated with increased achievement and reduced prejudice toward whites. The improved facilities in desegregated schools and the opportunity to interact with white students were also expected to contribute to improvements in black achievement. In addition, intergroup contact in desegregated schools was expected to reduce the prejudices of both groups.

To summarize this section, there are four hypotheses that can be derived from this testimony, which we will examine in the light of the empirical data that have been gathered in the quarter-century since the Brown decision: (1) desegregation should lead to reductions in the prejudice of whites toward blacks; (2) desegregation should raise black self-esteem; (3) desegregation should raise the achievement levels of blacks; and (4) desegregation should reduce the prejudices of blacks toward whites.

The Effects of School Desegregation

A few years ago the author reviewed over eighty studies of the effects of desegregation on prejudice, self-esteem and achievement (Stephan, 1978). The conclusions I reached are similar to those reached by other investigators (Crain & Mahard, 1978; St. John, 1975). Some of the studies I reviewed were published in journals, while others were doctoral dissertations or unpublished reports prepared by individual school districts. Unfortunately, these studies have a number of problems that make it difficult to draw firm conclusions about the effects of desegregation. Many of the studies used measures that cannot be easily compared

FIGURE 16.1
Causal model derived from social science testimony in *Brown* v. *Board of Education*

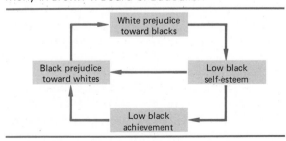

SOCIAL FOCUS 16.3
The Myth of Black Self-Rejection

One of the cornerstones of the social scientists' arguments in the Brown case was that segregation led to low self-esteem among black students. This argument was based on studies done by Clark and Clark (1947). In their studies they showed children a black doll and a white doll and asked them questions such as, "Which doll looks nice?" and "Which doll looks bad?" The results indicated that blacks more frequently chose the black doll as the bad one and the white doll as the nice one. This pattern of results was interpreted as an indication that black children reject themselves.

The inferential chain in this argument has three links: (1) it is assumed that the black and white dolls represent black and white people; (2) it is assumed that choosing the white doll implies a rejection of the black doll and consequently a rejection of black people; and (3) it is assumed that rejecting black people is associated with self-rejection among black children. Clearly, this is a very indirect measure of self-rejection. Subsequent investigators have frequently employed more direct measures of self-esteem in which children respond to questions about their feelings of self-worth or inadequacy. These studies show that blacks in segregated schools usually do not have lower self-esteem than whites (Edwards, 1974; Hodgkins & Stakenas, 1969; McDonald & Gynther, 1965; Powell & Fuller, 1970; Stephan & Kennedy, 1975; Stephan & Rosenfield, 1978), although a smaller number of studies have found that blacks sometimes do have lower self-esteem than whites (Deutsch, 1960b; Gerard & Miller, 1975; Williams & Byars, 1968).

How were the earlier researchers led astray? One possibility is that they correctly perceived that black children who reject blacks do tend to reject themselves (Stephan & Rosenfield, 1979; Ward & Braun, 1972). Considering this fact, together with the obvious prejudice toward blacks that existed in the 1940s and 1950s, they apparently concluded that black children would accept society's negative view of blacks and come to reject themselves as a consequence. It appears, however, that black children do not hold their group or themselves in low esteem. In fact, there is considerable evidence that blacks, like most other groups, display ingroup-outgroup bias (Gerard & Miller, 1975; Rosenberg & Simmons, 1972; Stephan & Rosenfield, 1978, 1979).

and some were poorly designed. Another limitation of the studies is that almost all of them deal only with the first year or two of desegregation. They often do not distinguish between different types of racial mixing in the schools, such as natural neighborhood integration, voluntary desegregation, and busing. This is a problem because students probably react differently, depending on whether they are participating in voluntary desegregation or a court-ordered busing program. Also, in an attempt to get an overall picture of the outcome of desegregation, important differences between the studies—such as when they were done, where they were done, and the age of the students—must be ignored. Bearing these reservations in mind, below are the tentative conclusions reached by the author on the basis of his review of the evidence:

(a) desegregation generally does not reduce the prejudices of Whites toward Blacks,
(b) the self-esteem of Blacks rarely increases in desegregated schools,
(c) the achievement level of Blacks sometimes increases and rarely decreases in desegregated schools, and
(d) desegregation leads to increases in Black prejudice toward Whites about as frequently as it leads to decreases (Stephan, p. 217).

It should be added that white achievement rarely decreases as a result of desegregation (Weinberg, 1975).

It appears that the short-term effects of desegregation offer only weak support for the high expectations that were proposed in the school segregation trials. This raises two important issues and we will consider each in turn. The first concerns the role played by social scientists in the judicial process. While the social scientists who testified in the Brown trial did not mislead the courts, neither were their predictions strongly confirmed. This raises the question of whether or not social scientists should play a role in judicial decision making. The second question we will consider is why the social scientists' predictions were not more strongly confirmed. After discussing each of these issues we will consider the conditions under which desegregation can lead to more favorable intergroup relations.

Social Science and the Judicial Process

Since the Brown decision, social scientists have continued to testify in desegregation trials and they also have become more active in other types of judicial cases, including testifying on the effectiveness of juries of different sizes (Tanke & Tanke, 1979) and the reliability of eyewitness reports (Fishman & Loftus, 1978),

aiding in the selection of juries (see Chapter 3), and giving opinions in competency hearings and commitment proceedings. The nature of the judicial system creates problems for the social scientists who choose to participate in it, because the issues on which the courts seek guidance are typically new issues that have not been subjected to careful empirical study.

An example of this problem is the Brown decision. Most of the social scientists who testified in this case were asked to present evidence on the harmful effects of segregation. Although we have reviewed the rather large number of studies done since 1954, at the time few studies of segregation existed and almost none of these had compared segregation with desegregation. A more recent illustration is provided by a case in which the author participated in Austin, Texas. The issue addressed in this case was the "incremental segregative effect" of school board policies. That is, how much do school board decisions contribute to residential segregation over and above the amount of segregation that would have existed in the absence of illegal segregative school policies? The Supreme Court made it clear in the *Washington* v. *Davis* (1976) case that the amount of remedial desegregation that would be required of a school district should be based on the magnitude of the board's role in creating segregation. This new way of determining the extent of desegregation that would be required raised a question that social scientists had never studied directly: Do school board decisions affect housing decisions?

In the deposition for this case the author stated:

The board's decisions provide the basis for members of the minority community to draw inferences about the attitudes of the board with respect to members of the minority community. . . . What happens is that over time there is a correspondence between the actions of the board and the inferred motives for those actions. . . . The question is what do members of

SOCIAL FOCUS 16.4
Social Scientists and the Adversary Role

A general problem that social scientists participating in the judicial system face is that witnesses are placed in an adversarial role. Typically, when social scientists agree to give expert testimony, they are enlisted by one party to the dispute. Loftus and Monahan (1980) have summarized the role of psychologists in the judicial process as follows:

At the root of many of the dilemmas of psychologists in the courtroom is a clash of traditions. Law is an adversary process. The truth is believed to emerge from a brawl in which each participant pulls no punches and gives no quarter. The judge is the referee who watches for rabbit punches and keeps things above the belt. The jury does the scoring. The best man or woman—the one with the most truth—wins, it is hoped. Psychology, on the other hand, likes to think it is above all this (p. 281).

In the role of advocate, the witness is asked to develop the arguments favoring one view of an issue. The exact nature of the presentation is usually worked out in advance between the witness and the legal representatives of that side of the dispute. The lawyers provide the social scientist with information on what type of evidence is legally relevant and on how to present the evidence in the strongest manner. For instance, after the author had given the testimony in the deposition cited in the text, the lawyers for the Justice Department informed him that the school board's actions in resisting desegregation were legally irrelevant to the effect of their decisions on residential segregation. The reason is that from a legal perspective the form their resistance took was to appeal previous decisions by the court, which is a right guaranteed by our judicial system. Thus, even though the board's resistance did foster the impression that they were hostile toward school desegregation, it was not germane to the case.

The shaping of what testimony to present and how to present it often has the consequence of eliminating the ambiguities and qualifications that social sci-

---

the minority groups think about the attitudes of the majority toward them on the basis of the board's behavior.

The principle I'd like to rely on here is called the covariance principle (Kelley, 1971). . . . When we see the same kind of behavior repeated across time, we use that as the basis for drawing inferences about the motives for the behavior. In the case of the policies of the school board, what this principle suggests is that members of the minority community infer that in the board's attempt to maintain segregation and to resist desegregation, there is a negative attitude being expressed toward Blacks and toward Mexican-

Americans, and I think the effect of this inference is to make members of the minority community more reluctant to move into segregated Anglo communities. It affects their housing decisions.

The author's testimony in this case was based on the general principles of attribution theory (Chapter 6). It was not possible to rely on specific studies relevant to this particular question, because apparently none had been done.

Reading the Social Focus 16.4 on the judicial process and the preceding discussion might lead you to ask, "Why do social scientists par-

entists are most comfortable with when making public pronouncements. On the stand, this tendency to present overly simplified conclusions is further promoted by the control that the attorneys exert over what questions will be asked on direct cross-examination. The power of attorneys to choose their questions means that they can often avoid eliciting contrary evidence and carefully qualified conclusions. The judge or jury for whose benefit the conversation between the attorney and the witness is being staged cannot ask questions to clarify issues that occur to them. This can potentially deprive them of the kind of complete understanding that comes from the open discussion to which social scientists are accustomed.

The dialectical process of building knowledge that characterizes the academic exchange of information in the classroom, in symposia, and in journal articles is incomplete in the courtroom. The process of cross-examination embodies some aspects of this dialectical process, but it is limited by the fact that the goal of the attorneys here is to undermine the impact of the direct testimony. Although this goal may at times be most effectively achieved by asking critical questions and requesting qualifications of previous testimony, lawyers are not restricted to these scholarly techniques. In the intense atmosphere of the courtroom, undermining the credibility of witnesses through character assassination and other stressful tactics is not unheard of. The highly critical nature of the cross-examination process also encourages witnesses to say things in ways that are difficult to refute. The statements that can be made in this way may or may not be the most useful ones for deciding the case. Finally, it is important to keep in mind that expert witnesses are paid for giving testimony and this too may compromise the objectivity of social scientists who serve as expert witnesses. Thus, the adversarial system is not an optimal one for generating neutral, objective analyses of complex social-science issues. A solution to these dilemmas that has been used with some success is to have the court appoint expert witnesses, so that they are not advocates for either side.

ticipate in the judicial process?" Although there are undoubtedly many factors involved, one primary reason is that the courts often need guidance to help them understand and resolve complicated disputes. Where there are empirical studies relevant to an issue, such as the visual-discrimination capabilities of eyewitnesses, who can better interpret the findings than experts in that field? Where the issues concern general aspects of human nature, social scientists may be better sources of opinion than others who have less expertise. When the option is that the courts will make less informed decisions in the absence of testimony by social scientists, social scientists often feel an obligation to provide testimony.

A second reason why social scientists choose to serve as expert witnesses is that it provides them with an opportunity to influence public policy in ways that are consistent with their own value systems. The majority of the social scientists who testified in the Brown decision deeply believed that segregation was wrong. For these people, testifying in the desegregation cases allowed them to speak out against the injustices of racial discrimination.

In addition to shaping social policy through their participation in the judicial system, social scientists also influence public policy by developing and testing intervention programs designed to address problems of social significance (see Chapter 19). During the last decade several different groups of social psychologists have attempted to develop techniques to improve intergroup relations in the schools. We will analyze one set of these techniques.

IMPROVING INTERGROUP RELATIONS IN DESEGREGATED SCHOOLS

Although we have reviewed evidence that suggests that school desegregation, at least initially, does not lead to general improvements in intergroup relations, recent research shows that it can. The primary reason that social scientists believed that desegregation would improve race relations is known as the contact hypothesis. One of the original statements of this hypothesis was offered by Allport (1954).

Prejudice . . . may be reduced by equal status contact between majority and minority groups in the pursuit of common goals. The effect is greatly enhanced if this contact is sanctioned by institutional supports (i.e., by law, custom or local atmosphere), and provided it is of a sort that leads to the perception of common interests and common humanity between members of the two groups (p. 281).

The problem, as Aronson and Bridgeman (1979) as well as others have pointed out, is that these conditions are rarely achieved in desegregated schools. First, the intergroup contact that occurs in desegregated schools is typically not between students of equal status. Most frequently, the minority-group students are from lower social-class backgrounds and are achieving at lower levels than the students of the majority group. Their status within the school may also be lowered if they are in the numerical minority. If teachers have prejudicial attitudes toward minority students, this will also lower their perceived status. Second, desegregation plans are often implemented after considerable community opposition from school boards, community leaders, administrators, and parents. This means that the intergroup contact that occurs in the schools does not have the enthusiastic support of these important authority figures. Third, competition prevails in the traditional classroom, rather than cooperation in pursuit of common goals. Taking into consideration the conditions under which contact generally occurs in desegregated schools, perhaps we should not be surprised that the outcomes are so mixed. It seems that the social scientists' predictions have not been adequately tested, because the conditions necessary for them to work have rarely existed.

Can desegregation lead to improved intergroup relations if these conditions are met? Until the last decade we did not have a clear answer to this question.

Social scientists have generally responded to the challenge of school desegregation in a reactive rather than an innovative fashion. Their role has been to evaluate the outcome of desegregation experiences as these have occurred. They have not, by contrast, proposed and studied alternative methods by which school desegregation might be carried out (Weigel, Wiser, & Cook, 1975, p. 432).

More recently, however, this trend has been reversed. In the last half-dozen years a number of researchers have designed and evaluated techniques to improve intergroup relations in desegregated schools. Before we discuss these techniques, it may be useful to trace their origins.

The foundations of most of these techniques are the classic studies of two investigators. One of these psychologists provided us with a basic theory of how cooperation and

Interracial contact can, under some conditions, contribute to improved intergroup relations. What aspects of these tennis lessons would (and would not) promote positive relationships?

competition affect behavior (Deutsch, 1949b) and the other did a seminal study that illustrates this theory (Sherif, Harvey, White, Hood, & Sherif, 1961). According to Deutsch, the hallmark of competition is that resources are allocated according to performance; the better you do the more you get and the less someone else gets. In competition, when one person gains another person loses. In contrast, the hallmark of cooperation is shared outcomes. When one person in a group does well, that improves everyone's outcomes. This encourages people to work together for the common good in comparison to competition, which can encourage selfishness. Cooperation increases liking for the people you are working with, whereas competition often decreases liking for

the people with whom you are competing.

The study by Sherif and his colleagues, previously discussed in Chapter 15, was conducted at a summer camp for boys. When they arrived at the camp, the boys were divided into two groups, and placed in competition with one another in such activities as football, tug-of-war, and cabin inspections. Gradually a considerable amount of hostility was generated. Later in the summer, the experimenters set out to try to create goodwill through cooperation between the groups. They created several "emergencies," such as having a vehicle break down, which required the cooperative efforts of all the boys. The hostile feelings between the groups slowly began to subside. The boys made friends with members of the other group and they began to cooperate spontaneously.

Armed with the knowledge acquired in this research and the principles of the contact theory, several groups of social psychologists have used cooperative groups in an attempt to improve race relations in desegregated schools. The majority of these techniques involve small groups of children from different ethnic backgrounds working together on school projects. One of these techniques is known as the *jigsaw classroom.* Here is how it works. (The material the students have been assigned is divided up into sections, with one section going to each student in the group. In one study biographies of famous people like Eleanor Roosevelt and Joseph Pulitzer were used. Each student in the group had to learn information about one period of the person's life and then present it to the other students.) What happens in these groups? In the words of one of the originators of this technique,

> When thrown on their own resources, the children eventually learned to teach each other and to listen to each other. The children came to learn that none of them could do well without the aid of each person in the group—and that each member had a unique and essential contribution to make. Suppose you and I are children in the same group. You've been dealt Joseph Pulitzer as a young man; I've been dealt Pulitzer as an old man. The only way I can learn about Joseph Pulitzer as a young man is to pay close attention to what you are saying. You are a very important resource for me. The teacher is no longer the sole resource—she isn't even an important resource; indeed, she isn't even in the group. Instead, every kid in the circle becomes important to me. I do well if I pay attention to other kids; I do poorly if I don't (Aronson, 1980, p. 230).

In this technique, the students must cooperate and learn from one another to acquire all the pieces of the jigsaw puzzle. The students are all equal in status. The high-status role of teacher is rotated among the members of the group. After all the pieces have been presented, the students are tested individually as they ordinarily would be, and they do as well or better than students taught in a traditional manner (Aronson, Blaney, Stephan, Sikes, & Snapp, 1978).

In this technique and several others the status of the students tends to be equalized, since they all play the same roles and are responsible for similar amounts of the material to be learned. The contact is cooperative and somewhat informal in nature, so the students have an opportunity to learn about one another. Typically, when these techniques are used, the teachers and administrators who select them do so because they wish to take steps to improve intergroup relations. This means that the contact that occurs in these cooperative groups usually has been approved by important authority figures. Thus, these groups appear to fulfill all of the criteria presented by Allport for optimal contact situations.

The research evidence from more than a dozen studies using cooperative learning groups indicates that they do lead to improved intergroup relations. Several studies have found that cross-ethnic helping and friendships increase (DeVries & Edwards, 1974; Slavin, 1977; Weigel, Wiser, & Cook, 1975), empathy and liking for other students increases (Blaney, Stephan, Rosenfield, Aronson, & Sikes, 1977; Bridgeman, 1977), self-esteem increases (Blaney et al., 1977), and there are increases in minority student achievement levels (Lucker, Rosenfield, Sikes, & Aronson, 1977). Thus, it appears that cooperative groups can accomplish all the goals that the social scientists hoped desegregation would fulfill: prejudice is decreased and self-esteem and minority achievement are increased. A variety of factors appear to be operating together to produce these favorable results.

Working in cooperative groups tends to undercut ethnocentrism. As you will recall, ethnocentrism is based on identification with the ingroup and rejection of outgroups. When students work together in teams, they come to identify with and favorably evaluate their own team, which contains members of different ethnic groups. Interaction with outgroup members in cooperative groups also provides the students with an opportunity to acquire information that is inconsistent with their stereotypes. Over time the students learn that outgroup members vary considerably, which undermines contrast and assimilation tendencies. Also, the realistic information they learn about outgroup members can eliminate the perception that the ingroup and the outgroup are highly dissimilar.

One problem that sometimes remains in these groups is that the white students are often higher in social class and achievement than the minority students. Under these circumstances cooperation could have the effect of confirming the negative expectancies of the white students. Cohen (1980) and her coworkers have found, however, that even these status inequalities can be overcome if minority students are pretrained on the tasks that will be used in the cooperative groups, so that their skills exceed those of the white members. Her technique has the effect of reversing stereotypes involving negative expectancies. Another approach to this problem has been developed by DeVries and Edwards (1974). In their cooperative groups each student's performance contributes to the team's overall standing. To avoid the possibility that low-achieving students will hinder the team, the students receive scores based on their performance with respect to their achievement division. In this way, low-achieving students can help their team as much as high-achieving students. These solutions to this problem have the added benefit of making it unlikely that students whose performance is low will necessarily be used as scapegoats on whom group failures can be blamed.

The results from the studies of cooperative groups are encouraging, but it is clear that the use of such groups will not solve all the problems of school desegregation. For instance, Cohen has found that it is difficult to obtain equal-status interactions between black and white students when the school administration and teaching staff do not have blacks in positions of authority. In another study it was found that whites tend to dominate blacks on collective work tasks to the degree that they outnumber blacks in the school (Iadicola, 1979). Since it is not likely that cooperation will replace competition or individual- and teacher-oriented learning techniques, the beneficial effects of cooperative groups may be limited. Fortunately, as Aronson and Bridgeman (1979) note, "The jigsaw method has proved effective even if it is employed for as little as 20% of a child's time in the classroom. Moreover, other techniques have produced beneficial results even when interdependent learning was purposely accompanied by competitive activities" (p. 445). While it is clear that cooperative techniques are not a panacea for the problems involved in desegregation, their development is a clear illustration of a successful intervention by social scientists in an issue of enormous significance.

The school, of course, is just one setting in our society in which people from different groups interact. It is an important one, because we all participate in these institutions and we enter them at an age when intergroup attitudes have not yet fully crystallized. If we are successful in producing intergroup tolerance in this situation, it is likely that it will have a significant effect on the future of intergroup relations within our society and between our society and others. Nonetheless, the schools represent only one institution in our society, and prejudice, stereotyping, and discrimination pervade nearly all of them. The fact that we cannot create intervention techniques as thorough as the cooperative learning tasks that have been used in the schools should not lead us to throw up our hands and give up. Some of the conditions conducive to improving intergroup relations can be introduced in work, religious, political, and recreational settings, but new techniques may have to be devised for these situations. This is the challenge for the future. At the very least, each of us can be aware of the principles covered in this chapter and attempt to overcome the influence of stereotypes, categorization, self-fulfilling prophecies, and prejudice in our relations with members of other groups.

SUMMARY

The focus in this chapter has been on intergroup relations, particularly on the concepts of prejudice, stereotyping, and discrimination. Prejudice is a special type of attitude consisting of negative evaluations of members of socially defined groups. Stereotypes are sets of traits attributed to the members of social groups, and discrimination is negative behavior toward the members of such groups. Prejudice and stereotypes have their origins in the history of relations between groups, basic categorization processes such as assimilation and contrast, ingroup-outgroup bias, and psychodynamic factors such as projection and scapegoating. The attitudes generated by these processes can result in discriminatory behavior. Whether or not they do depends on several factors. Fishbein and Ajzen (1974) suggest that behavioral intentions depend on peoples' attitude toward the specific act (discrimination against an outgroup member in this case), the social norms that govern behavior in this situation (that is, whether there is social support for discriminatory behavior), and the individual's motivation to comply with the social norms (that is, does the individual want to conform to or deviate from the social norms).

The prejudices and stereotypes we hold toward members of other groups can have a variety of other effects, even when they do not lead to discrimination. Stereotypes set up expectancies for outgroup behavior that may lead outgroup members to conform to them. They are also likely to lead ingroup members to perceive that outgroup members have confirmed their expectations, even when they have not. In addition, prejudice and stereotypes may also affect outgroup members' attitudes toward themselves.

In the second half of the chapter these theoretical considerations were applied to the issue of school desegregation. The arguments by social scientists that school segregation depressed the self-esteem and achievement of black students and promoted prejudice between whites and blacks were presented as a background for considering the effects of desegregation. The evidence indicates that the short-term effects of desegregation are that it does not generally lead to reductions in prejudice nor improve black self-esteem, although it sometimes does improve black achievement. Two issues raised by the modest support for the social scientists' predictions in the desegregation trials are whether social scientists should contribute to the judicial process, and why the social scientists' predictions in *Brown* v. *Board of Education* were not supported more strongly.

In response to the first issue it was suggested that the nature of the judicial system has usually placed social scientists in a role where they are forced to make predictions about school desegregation on the basis of little or no empirical data. Nonetheless, social scientists continue to testify in court. They do this because they are deeply committed to their own human values and because they perceive that they are in a position to shed some light on the complex issues that come before the courts.

The reason that the optimistic expectations concerning the effects of desegregation were not confirmed is that the conditions necessary to fulfill them are rarely present in desegregated schools. The contact occurring in these schools is usually not between group members of equal status, nor is it supported by major authority figures, and cooperative interactions in the pursuit of common goals are strikingly absent.

A remedy for these problems that has been investigated by several groups of investigators was considered in the final section of the chapter. Students working together in ethnically mixed cooperative teams come to like each other and school more, they tend to help each other more, and their self-esteem increases. These benefits are achieved without any apparent costs in performance. The success of these techniques seems to be due to the fact that ingroup-outgroup bias is undermined by equal-status cooperative interaction and stereotypes tend to be unlearned in the face of realistic disconfirming evidence.

The material presented in this chapter illustrates three roles that social psychologists have played in intergroup relations. Social psychologists have generated theories of intergroup relations, participated in the judicial process in an attempt to influence policy in accord with predictions derived from these theories, and they have developed and tested techniques to create conditions under which these predictions can be fulfilled.

SUGGESTED READINGS

Austin, W. G., & Worchel, S. (Eds.). *Social psychology of intergroup relations*. Monterey, Cal.: Brooks/Cole, 1979.

Billig, M. *Social psychology and intergroup relations*. London: Academic Press, 1976.

Franklin, J. H. *From slavery to freedom* (4th ed.). New York: Knopf, 1974.

LeVine, R. A., & Campbell, D. T. *Ethnocentrism*. New York: Wiley, 1972.

Miller, A. G. (Ed.). *In the eye of the beholder: Contemporary issues stereotyping*. New York: Praeger, 1982.

Stephan, W. G., & Feagin, J. R. *School desegregation: Past, present and future*. New York: Plenum Press, 1980.

Williams, J. E., & Morland, J. K. *Race, color and the young child*. Chapel Hill: University of North Carolina Press, 1976.

17

THE ENVIRONMENTAL
CONTEXT OF BEHAVIOR

- Introduction
- Organizing Principles
- Research Areas in Environmental Psychology
- Summary

INTRODUCTION

Future shock—the population bomb—limits to growth—small is beautiful—these terms summarize well the somber themes of the 1970s and early 1980s. During the past decade, the unprecedented technological advances of the Space Age were accompanied by a growing concern about the environmental constraints and uncertainties of the future—overpopulation, the depletion of natural resources, and pollution. Confronted by these uncertainties, psychologists have become increasingly involved in studying the behavioral and health implications of environmental problems. The resulting flurry of research has contributed to the rapid development of **environmental psychology**—the study of human behavior and well-being in relation to the large-scale sociophysical environment.

The term *large-scale environment* refers in this chapter to places such as homes, offices, neighborhoods, and whole communities that are occupied by individuals and groups. These places can be described in terms of several physical and social dimensions, including their geographical location, architectural design, and natural resources, as well as the membership, social organization, and activities of their occupants. The term *sociophysical environment* reflects the assumption that the physical and social dimensions of places are often closely intertwined. The architectural design of an apartment building, for example, can exert a subtle but substantial impact on the friendship patterns that develop among residents (Festinger, Schachter, & Back, 1950). Also, individuals and groups often develop strong emotional attachments to their home or work environments, and experience mental and physical trauma when forced to leave these places (Fried, 1963). Thus, the present chapter emphasizes the interdependence between physical and social aspects of places, rather than viewing these dimensions as separate and isolated.

Prior to the late 1960s and early 1970s very few psychologists expressed interest in the impact of the large-scale environment on people. Exceptions to this trend were Kurt Lewin (1935), whose research emphasized the importance of the "life space," or the psychological situation as perceived by the individual, and Roger Barker (1960), who launched a systematic study of "behavior settings"—places in which patterns of human activity recur on a regular, predictable basis. For the most part, however, psychologists defined the environment not in terms of geographical areas and complex situations, but rather in terms of discrete, separable units—*stimuli*—which were amenable to isolation and observation within the laboratory (cf. Underwood, 1957). Moreover, behavior was defined in terms of the *responses* of individuals to specific stimuli, rather than as the complex patterns of human activity that occur within naturalistic settings.

During the past decade, however, the "doomsday" predictions of demographers (for example, Ehrlich, 1968), the shrinkage of natural resources (Meadows, 1972), and the deterioration of environmental quality prompted widespread concern about the constraints of the ecological environment. Suddenly, psychologists "rediscovered" the large-scale environment and, in collaboration with other social scientists, architects, and planners, became increasingly involved in studying its impact on behavior. The appearance of numerous textbooks, the establishment of new journals, and the development of a formal division of the

---

This chapter is written by Daniel Stokols.

American Psychological Association (entitled Population and Environmental Psychology) all attest to the rapid growth of environmental psychology during the past decade (cf. Craik, 1977; Proshansky & Altman, 1979; Stokols, 1978).

It would be most convenient, perhaps, to portray environmental psychology during the 1980s as an area of applied research, involving primarily the application of psychological theory and methodology to the study of contemporary environmental problems. Clearly, societal concerns have influenced the course of research on environment and behavior, as is evident in recent applications of social psychological theories of attitude change, attribution, and group dynamics to the analysis of energy conservation (Stern & Gardner, in press), overcrowding (Baum & Epstein, 1978), and noise pollution (Cohen, Evans, Krantz, & Stokols, 1980).

Yet, the field of environmental psychology is more than an area of applied psychological research, in at least two respects. First, owing to the enormous complexity of contemporary environmental problems, much of the current research on environment and behavior is interdisciplinary in scope, involving the close collaboration of psychologists, sociologists, urban planners, architects, public health specialists, and other professionals, studying problems of mutual concern. Thus, environmental psychology is better characterized as part of an emerging interdisciplinary field of environment and behavior, or human-environment relations, than as a topic within applied social psychology or as a distinct subarea of psychology. The field of environment and behavior encompasses several diverse perspectives, such as urban sociology, architecture, planning, and behavioral geography (cf. Michelson, 1976; Zeisel, 1981). While closely related to these areas, environmental psychology diverges from them by placing relatively greater emphasis on basic psychological processes (such as cognition, personality, development, and learning), and

on individual and group (versus societal) levels of analysis.

Second, environmental psychology involves not only the application of existing psychological theories to the resolution of current community problems but also the development of new theoretical and methodological perspectives for understanding the complex interplay between people and their everyday environments. An analysis of the relationship between people and the large-scale environment suggests several theoretical issues that are especially germane to social psychology, yet few of these issues have been studied systematically. For example, in what ways do the physical arrangements of places (for example, homes, neighborhoods) influence observers' attributions about the occupants of those places? In what ways do physical environments convey social and cultural messages, thereby affecting the socialization and identity of occupants? These and the related issues that will be discussed in this chapter reflect the theoretical focus of environmental psychology: namely, the scientific study of the connections between people and places. Whereas the typical emphasis of social psychological research is on interpersonal processes, environmental psychology gives more explicit attention to people-place processes, or the nature of the links between individuals, groups, and the architectural-geographical environment.

In the preceding paragraphs, we have traced some of the societal and scientific origins of environmental psychology, and have outlined four major attributes of this relatively new field: (1) its emphasis on the large-scale environment and the interdependence between physical and social dimensions of places; (2) its interdisciplinary scope; (3) its community-problems orientation; and (4) its theoretical emphasis on the psychological processes reflected in the connections between people and places. The combination of a community-problems orientation with the systematic study of people-place processes exemplifies the Lewinian tradition of "action research"—the application of scientific knowledge to the resolution of societal problems, and the resulting derivation of new insights and information about human behavior from the analysis of those problems (Lewin, 1948).

In the ensuing discussion, the theoretical emphases of environmental psychology are considered in greater detail, and several of the major findings from recent research on environment and behavior are reviewed. Subsequently, we consider some of the unique dilemmas that are posed by efforts to utilize these findings as a basis for understanding and resolving community problems.

ORGANIZING PRINCIPLES

The present chapter is organized around certain basic principles or assumptions about the nature of human-environment relations. The first assumption is that the transactions between people and their surroundings involve at least four kinds of psychological processes. Specifically, people orient to and *interpret* their environment in terms of existing information, goals, and expectations. For example, a college student arriving on campus for the first time begins to develop a mental image of the environment incorporating the locations of relevant buildings, transportation routes, and commercial areas. People *operate* on the environment in an effort to achieve their goals and maintain desired levels of satisfaction. The entering student, in an effort to meet new people, may participate in orientation programs and join the staff of the student newspaper. While people often operate in an active fashion to control or modify their surroundings, they also are affected by and *respond* to environmental forces. After the first week on a new campus, entering students may feel profoundly fatigued from their encounters with so many new people and situations. Finally, people *evaluate* the quality

of their surroundings as a basis for future activity and goal attainment. The college student may decide to move into an apartment off campus if experiences with dormitory living (for example, monotonous food, noisy suitemates) have been unsatisfactory.

Two of the above-mentioned processes, interpretation and operation, reflect an active orientation toward the environment. In each case the individual brings certain goals and expectations to the situation which guide interpretations and actions within that setting. The processes of evaluation and response reflect a more passive orientation toward the environment, whereby people react emotionally, behaviorally, or physiologically to existing environmental conditions. Thus, the basic processes by which people relate to their surroundings reflect either *active* or *reactive phases of transaction* with the environment.

Whether people are actively or reactively involved with their surroundings, they exhibit both *cognitive* (symbolic or emotional) and *behavioral* (or physical) forms of transaction with the environment. The processes of interpretation and evaluation, for instance, reflect mental forms of interchange with the environment. Operation and response, on the other hand, involve behavioral forms of transaction whereby the individual physically influences, or is influenced by, the environment. Thus, by combining the phases and forms of interchange with the environment, four major modes of human-environment transaction are derived: (1) interpretive (active-cognitive); (2) evaluative (reactive-cognitive); (3) operative (active-behavioral); and (4) responsive (reactive-behavioral). The first mode involves individuals' cognitive representation of the environment; the second, their evaluation of the situation against predefined standards of quality; the third, their movement through or direct impact on the environment; and fourth, the environment's effects on their behavior and well-being.

The processes of human-environment transaction described above reflect some additional assumptions about the relationship between people and their surroundings:

1. The influence between people and the environment is reciprocal rather than one-sided. People shift between active and reactive orientations toward the environment, sometimes merely responding to existing conditions, while at other times designing and modifying their surroundings. Accordingly, the environment is viewed as both a product and a determinant of human behavior.

2. People's transactions with the environment are guided by personal goals and plans. While individuals are not always thinking about their goals or actively trying to achieve them (as, for example, when they are sleeping or daydreaming), most of their encounters with the sociophysical environment are implicitly or explicitly goal directed (for example, maintaining personal security and comfort, or completing specific tasks).

3. Human-environment transactions occur within specific places and settings. A **setting** is a place that has become associated with recurring patterns of human activity—for example, grocery stores, dorm lounges, classrooms (Barker, 1968). These places are associated with personal and collective goals, and they provide the organized contexts in which most of our daily activities occur.

4. The settings in which people participate can be described in terms of their scale or complexity. The scale of an environment ranges from the specific stimuli and situations that occur within a given setting (for example, a professor's favorable response to a student's question during class) to the **life domains** that are comprised of multiple situations and settings—a college campus, for example, in which individuals attend classes, reside in dorms or apartments, and socialize with friends on various occasions. The more complex the environmental context of behavior, the greater the range of factors—psychological, social, cultural, architectural—that affect people's relationships with their surroundings.

5. The degree of fit (or **congruence**) between people and their environments has an important bearing on their emotional and physical well-being. Person-environment fit is high to the extent that a situation or setting supports personal needs and goals, and low to the degree that these goals are blocked by environmental constraints. As a case in point, a large dormitory may afford an excellent living situation for the first-year college student, since it offers numerous opportunities for meeting people and becoming involved in activities on campus. For the senior student who prefers a quieter and more private living arrangement, however, dormitory residence could prove to be quite stressful due to a lack of fit between personal goals and environmental conditions. Thus, the personal goals and environmental conditions that jointly contribute to the individual's perception of fit are not static. Rather, the level of environmental congruence experienced by a particular individual within a given situation depends on the day-to-day accommodation between an ever-changing set of personal needs, activities, and environmental resources.

The preceding principles of human-environment transaction reflect certain distinctive emphases of environmental psychology. They thus provide a conceptual frame of reference for examining recent research on environment, behavior, and well-being. We turn now to a review of that research.

RESEARCH AREAS IN ENVIRONMENTAL PSYCHOLOGY

Currently, environmental psychology is comprised of several active research domains. In this section of the chapter, the various modes of human-environment transaction will be used to represent some of the major areas of environmental psychology in terms of their respective emphases and concerns—that is, the ways people interpret, evaluate, operate on, and respond to their surroundings (see Figure 17.1).

One implication of the proposed representation of environmental psychology is that most research in this field has focused on a single mode (in some cases two or three, but rarely all four) of human-environment transaction. Yet the processes by which people relate to the environment are highly interdependent, and the boundaries between the various modes of human-environment transaction are not always clear and distinct. Returning to our earlier example of the college student, the emotional and health consequences of living in a dormitory depend greatly on the student's interpretations and evaluations of the setting; the perceived friendliness of roommates, for

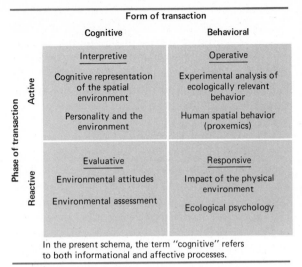

Form of transaction

	Cognitive	Behavioral
Active	Interpretive Cognitive representation of the spatial environment Personality and the environment	Operative Experimental analysis of ecologically relevant behavior Human spatial behavior (proxemics)
Reactive	Evaluative Environmental attitudes Environmental assessment	Responsive Impact of the physical environment Ecological psychology

Phase of transaction

In the present schema, the term "cognitive" refers to both informational and affective processes.

FIGURE 17.1
Modes of Human-Environment Transaction and Related Areas of Research.
Source: Stokols, 1978.

example. Likewise, the student's evaluation of those roommates will depend on how they have treated the student in the past. In view of the interdependence among interpretive, evaluative, operative, and responsive processes, an important direction for future research is to link the various research perspectives outlined in Figure 17.1 so as to provide a more adequate understanding of human-environment relations than presently exists. This issue is discussed further in the final section of the chapter. We will now turn to an overview of research findings that are relevant to each mode of human-environment transaction.

Interpreting the Environment

Five professors were hiking along a trail in the forest when one of them, a psychologist, stumbled over a rock. As the psychologist cursed the object of his frustration, his colleagues became involved in a lively discourse regarding the true nature of the rock. The art professor commented on the esthetic qualities of the rock and noted that it would complement his formal garden at home rather nicely. The engineer added that the rock would make an excellent paper weight for his desk at the office. After closely inspecting the rock's surface, the physicist speculated about its molecular structure, while the geographer offered some tentative conclusions about recent volcanic and seismic activity in the area. The psychologist, having recovered his composure, cited the advantages of interdisciplinary research and emphasized the importance of cognitive processes in mediating the relationship between environment and behavior; at which point several members of the group advised that they should press on with the hike.

People have an insatiable craving for knowledge. Without this craving, it is doubtful that the human species would have survived throughout the ages (Kaplan, 1976). One of the clearest indications of the human capacity for acquiring knowledge is the myriad of ways in which people describe and interpret their surroundings. In the preceding example a simple ordinary rock was interpreted from five distinctly different perspectives. These interpretive perspectives exemplify what psychologists have termed *cognitive schemas*—mental representations of the world about us (Bartlett, 1932; Kelly, 1955; Neisser, 1976). Cognitive schemas provide a set of symbolic categories with which we can make predictions about the environment and can evaluate alternative plans of action in terms of their probable consequences. Whether we conceive of a rock as a paperweight, a trail marker, or as radioactive material has direct implications for deciding what to do with the rock and for avoiding the potentially harmful consequences of inappropriate behavior.

Chapter 6 of this volume emphasized one type of cognitive schema, namely, *attributions* about the causal relationships among two or more entities. Upon observing an individual stumble over a stone, for example, we might attribute this event to the person's clumsiness (personal cause) or to the fact that the rock was concealed by a clump of grass (situational cause). In the present chapter we are concerned not so much with people's attempts to explain their own and others' behavior, or to understand the attributes of particular objects, but rather with the ways in which they describe and interpret the large-scale environment.

The tasks of perceiving and interpreting the large-scale environment are cognitively challenging and complex. Unlike discrete stimuli or objects, environments surround and engulf the individual. "One cannot be a subject of an environment, one can only be a participant" (Ittelson, 1973, p. 12). Ittelson delineates a number of other important aspects of environmental perception, including (1) the multimodal nature of environments—the fact that they convey information through several sense modalities; (2) the informational complexity of environments—the fact that environments contain more information than can be processed at any one time, and that certain parts of the environment always remain peripheral or outside of the individual's attentional focus; (3) the role of the environment in calling forth symbolic meanings, motivational messages, and patterns of activity; and (4) the ambiance of the environment—its unique esthetic, cultural, and historical qualities.

Confronted by the complexity of the large-scale environment and faced with the task of trying to understand it, people develop **cognitive maps.** A cognitive map is, essentially, a mental description of the spatial environment—a kind of schema that enables the individual to depict and remember a particular environment in terms of its important or outstanding features. Cognitive maps are similar to geographic maps in that they summarize information about the attributes and relative locations of elements within a given area. And like professional map makers, we develop representations of the spatial environment to help us understand, predict, and navigate through our surroundings. Thus, the metaphor of people as map makers is useful in emphasizing the human capacity for visual and symbolic representation of the environment, and the crucial importance of these skills for our survival and well-being.

Yet, our mental images of the environment are dissimilar in many ways from geographic maps or photographs. Most importantly, the content of mental maps does not necessarily correspond to the visible features and actual layout of the spatial environment. On the one hand, the information contained in cognitive maps may be less detailed than that reflected in photographs or actual maps, due to the selectivity of the individual's experience with the environment. Cognitive maps, therefore, are highly personalized and incomplete accounts of the environment. On the other hand, cognitive maps may contain an enormous amount of information that is not immediately apparent from the visible features and spatial layout of the environment. The representation of a rock as a chunk of radioactive material, or a seemingly serene mountain as a potentially explosive volcano, reflect complex and sophisticated views of the world.

Research on cognitive mapping. Recent studies have identified several factors that influence cognitive mapping—the processes by which people acquire and utilize information about the spatial environment. The architectural and geographical features of an environment, sociocultural variables, and personal psychological factors jointly affect people's interpretations of the large-scale environment. A consideration of these diverse factors may help to explain why people's cognitive maps are so personalized and incomplete, yet at the same time so complex and sophisticated.

Research on cognitive mapping has had to address a fundamental methodological question: how can people's mental images of the environment be *externalized*, or made public? As Milgram and Jodelet (1976) have noted, "The person's mental image of Paris is not like his driver's license, something he can pull out for inspection. Rather, we shall have to tease the information from the subject, using whatever means psychology can offer to inspect the contents of the mind" (p. 104). Numerous strategies have been employed by researchers to assess the content of cognitive maps—for example, asking people to draw free-hand sketch maps of an environment, observing how well they find their way in an actual setting, or assessing people's knowledge about places on the basis of their responses to photographs.

The use of sketch maps to assess people's representations of the environment was introduced by Kevin Lynch in his influential book, *The Image of the City* (1960). As an environmental designer, Lynch was especially interested in identifying the architectural and geographical attributes that render some places more *imageable*, or easier to remember, than others. According to Lynch, the likelihood that an environment will evoke a vivid image in an observer depends on its visual clarity or **legibility**—"the ease with which its parts can be recognized and organized into a coherent pattern" (1960, p. 3). Furthermore, Lynch posited that the legibility of an area is determined by the form and arrangement of five physical elements: namely, paths, edges, districts, nodes, and landmarks:

Paths are the channels along which the observer moves. They may be streets, walkways, transit lines, canals, railroads. . . . *Edges* are the linear elements not used or considered as paths by the observer. They are the boundaries between two phases . . . shores, railroad cuts, edges of development, walls. . . . *Districts* are the medium-to-large sections of the city, conceived of as having two-dimensional extent, which the observer mentally enters "inside of." . . . *Nodes* are points, the strategic spots in a city into which an observer can enter, and which are the intensive foci to and from which he is traveling. They may be primarily junctions, a crossing or convergence of paths, . . . a street-corner hangout or an enclosed square. . . . *Landmarks* are another type of point-reference but in this case the observer does not enter within them, they are external. . . . They are usually a rather simply defined physical object: building, sign, store, or mountain (1960, pp. 47–48).

To examine the relationship between these physical features of environments and their imageability, Lynch interviewed 60 residents in three American cities: Boston, Jersey City, and Los Angeles. The participants were asked to sketch the central portion of their cities on a blank piece of paper, to furnish directions for trips between various points in the city, and to describe those parts of the city that they considered to be most vivid and distinctive. The sketch maps and verbal responses were later compared with inventories of environmental features compiled by trained observers, aerial photographs, and actual maps of the area.

Lynch's data confirmed that the form and arrangement of the urban landscape are closely associated with residents' sketches and descriptions of their cities. For most participants in the study, paths were the most commonly represented elements, although persons with least knowledge of an area tended to describe it in terms of large regions rather than as a network of paths. Also, certain aspects of paths, such as unusual width or heavy usage by pedestrians and vehicles, increased the prominence of those elements in residents' sketch maps and descriptions. Clear boundaries between districts and the placement of landmarks at path intersections also enhanced the imageability of the area.

Subsequent studies have corroborated and elaborated upon Lynch's earlier findings. De Jonge (1962), focusing on the relationship between path structure and imageability, found that residents of cities with more regular street grid patterns compiled more accurate and detailed sketch maps. Also, several studies suggest that the presence of clear visible landmarks facilitates the learning and memory of an area, both among children and adults (for example, Acredolo, 1977; Evans, Marrero, & Butler, in press; Heft, 1979; Siegel & Schadler, 1977).

Physical features affecting the interior and exterior legibility of buildings have been delineated in a number of recent investigations. Evans and colleagues found that newcomers who were exposed to the interior of a color-coded building performed better on way-finding tasks, floor-plan recall, and target-sighting tasks (using a surveyor's transit) than did those who were exposed to the same building but without the color coding (Evans, Fellows, Zorn, & Doty, in press). The semantic labeling of buildings (for example, as library, student union) also was found to enhance their recall among participants in a model-reconstruction task (Pezdek & Evans, 1979). And Appleyard (1969, 1970) has identified several exterior features of buildings that increase their legibility, including the frequency of their use, their proximity to important road intersections, the distinctiveness of their shape, and their historic-symbolic significance.

The research on building legibility reflects the diverse methods that have been used to assess people's cognitive representation of the environment—sketch maps, way-finding tasks, model-reconstruction exercises, and sighting tasks, among others. The use of multiple measures is an important prerequisite for establishing the convergent validity of cognitive mapping processes—that is, the obtainment of corresponding or convergent results across several indexes of the same phenomenon (see Chapter 2). For instance, because the detail and accuracy of sketch maps may be significantly affected by an individual's drawing ability or previous experience with using maps, measures that are not distorted by these factors, such as photograph recognition and verbal descriptions of the city, can be used as supplemental probes of environmental knowledge.

Milgram and Jodelet's (1976) study of residents' images of Paris nicely illustrates the use of convergent measures to assess cognitive mapping. In their research, the sketch maps of 218 Parisians were examined individually and in conjunction with several aggregate measures derived from the collective responses of all participants. For example, the frequency with which various elements of Paris (for example, the Eiffel Tower) appeared in residents' sketch maps (see Figure 17.2), the order in which they were drawn, and the percentage of participants who did or did not recognize specific elements in a photograph-recognition task were among the group measures utilized in this study.

One of the most important findings of Milgram and Jodelet's research is that the imageability of urban elements depends not only on their architectural uniqueness, but also on the historic and symbolic significance attributed to them by city residents. Thus, certain elements strongly associated with the "heart and history" of Paris—for example, the Seine River, Notre Dame, the Eiffel Tower, and the Etoile—were included in most residents' maps, were usually among the first elements drawn, and were routinely recognized by participants. Numerous other places, however, remained unrecognized and unremembered by residents, in spite of their architectural uniqueness and great beauty. Thus, Milgram and Jodelet conclude that the imageability of cities depends as much on social factors as on physical attributes. "The perception of a city is a social fact, and as such needs to be studied in its collective as well as its individual aspect. It is not only what *exists* but also what is *highlighted* by the community that acquires salience in the mind of the person" (p. 108).

Variations in cognitive mapping relating to socioeconomic class have been observed in several studies. Orleans (1973) found that upper-class residents of Los Angeles drew broader and more accurate sketch maps than their middle- or lower-class counterparts (see Figure 17.3). A similar pattern was observed by Francescato and Mebane (1973) among residents of

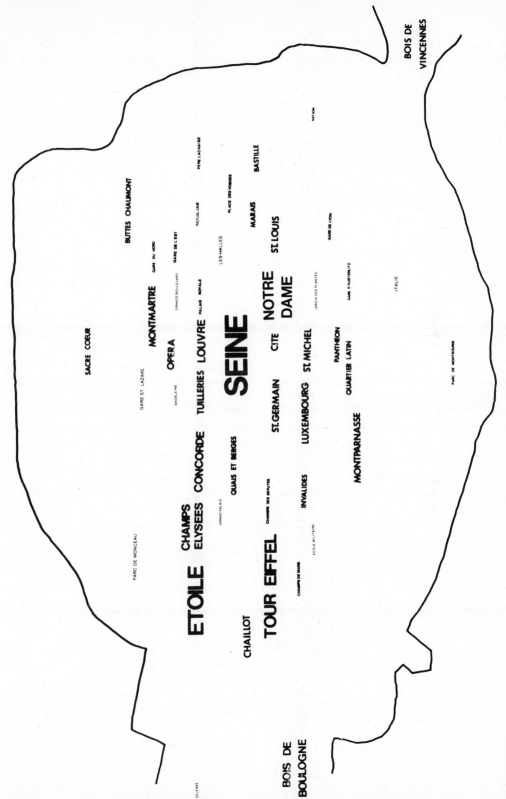

FIGURE 17.2
Sketch map of Paris. The relative size of each element is proportional to the frequency with which it was included in the sketch maps of Paris drawn by participants in Milgram and Jodelet's research.

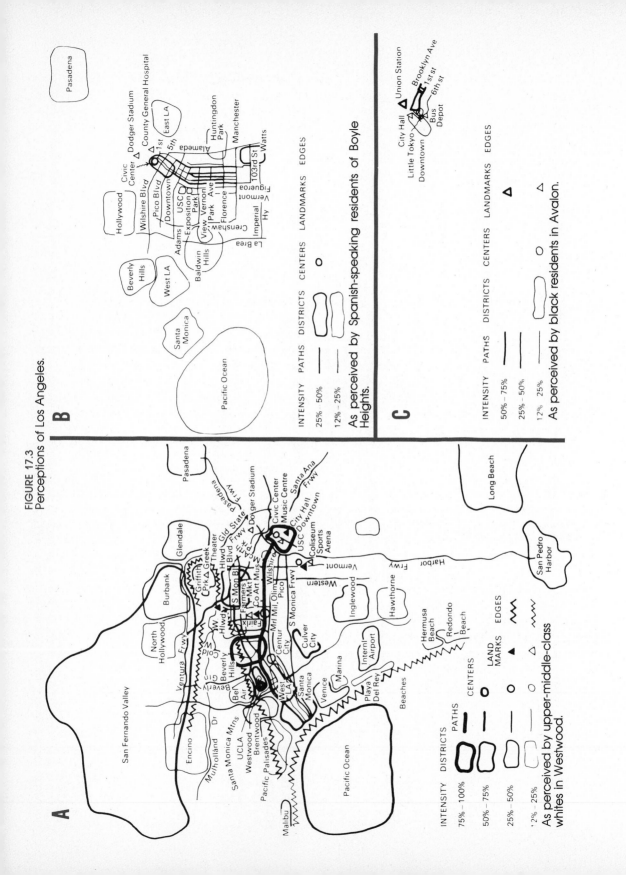

FIGURE 17.3
Perceptions of Los Angeles.

Milan and Italy. These researchers attributed the effects of social class on cognitive mapping to the greater mobility and broader social contacts of upper-class, professional residents. From an action research perspective, the studies by Orleans and by Francescato and Mebane raise important policy issues concerning the kinds of community programs that might be developed to enhance the range of environmental experience and knowledge among economically disadvantaged groups.

The relationship between people's familiarity with an area and their knowledge and recall of the area has been observed in several studies (for example, Appleyard, 1976; Bannerjee, 1971; Holahan, 1978; Milgram & Jodelet, 1976). Holahan, for example, found that students drew more detailed sketches of the campus areas they used most often. Bannerjee found that greater length of residence in Boston enhanced residents' ability to correctly identify and locate photographs of their city.

Other personal factors that have been found to affect environmental cognition are age, gender, and sense of direction. In general, older children and adults provide more accurate and detailed sketches of their environments than younger children, suggesting the possible role of the cognitive-developmental stage in environmental cognition (Herman & Siegel, 1978; Moore & Golledge, 1976). Where sex differences in cognitive mapping have been observed, they appear to reflect different mobility patterns among males and females (Appleyard, 1976; Hart, 1979). Hart, for example, found that girls in a New England town, whose activity ranges were more restricted than those of boys, drew smaller and less detailed maps than the boys. Finally, Kozlowski and Bryant (1977) observed that individuals with a good sense of direction exhibited greater learning of a novel environment than those with a poorer sense of direction.

Personality and environmental decision making. Individuals are often faced with the task of interpreting and planning for future environmental events. This task requires not only the capacity to mentally represent the characteristics of existing places but also the ability to predict and prepare for future situations. Research on the perception and prediction of environmental hazards reveals the difficulties that people face in their attempts to forecast future environments. It has frequently been observed that individuals living in hazardous areas (such as flood zones or volcanic areas) ignore experts' warnings about impending disasters and refuse to resettle in safer locations (Burton, Kates, & White, 1978).

Several personal factors have been found to influence individuals' comprehension of future environmental risks, including the amount of previous experience with similar hazards and the accuracy of one's beliefs about the likelihood of such events (Burton et al., 1978). Cognitive limitations, together with anxieties about environmental uncertainties, often result in the denial or underestimation of potential risks (cf. Slovic, Fischhoff, & Lichtenstein, 1979; Weinstein, 1978).

One dimension that may influence the ways in which people perceive and respond to environmental risks is personality. Internality of control—the belief that one can influence events occurring in one's life—has been found to be associated with more active responses to tornado warnings (Baumann & Sims, 1972). Moreover, the tendency to adopt a broad rather than restricted time perspective appears to promote a more realistic and vigilant orientation toward potential environmental hazards (Burton et al., 1978).

The dimension of future-time perspective also has been identified as a determinant of successful contraceptive behavior and family planning. In a prospective study of Planned Parenthood participants, individuals exhibiting future-time perspective were better able to avoid unwanted pregnancies than those whose time perspective was more restricted (Oskamp, Mindick, Berger, & Motta, 1978). Thus, the ten-

The Pruitt-Igoe Housing Project built in 1954 and demolished in 1972 illustrates the need for evaluation and assessment of environments prior to their construction.

dency to think about future events is directly relevant to the individual's environmental decision making and well-being.

Evaluating the Environment

To survive and thrive in a complex world, people must not only be capable of interpreting current and future environments—they must also *evaluate* the desirability of these situations and *act* accordingly. The present section focuses on *environmental evaluation*—the processes by which individuals and groups judge the quality of their surroundings. Whether it is an individual deciding upon which college to attend, a family contemplating the purchase of a new home, or a city council assessing alternative locations for a regional airport, their decisions will be guided by judgments about the

impact of immediate or imagined environments on personal and/or collective well-being. Social Focus 17.1 describes the activities of an environmental assessment team that operates on a university campus.

What factors influence people's evaluations of their environments? Do standardized, reliable procedures exist for measuring people's assessment of their milieu? Can such measures be utilized by environmental designers to improve existing settings or to create more desirable ones in the future? In an era of limited resources, these questions assume enormous practical importance, for communities can no longer afford to squander their resources by creating dysfunctional environments—those that obstruct rather than support the activities and needs of their occupants.

A rather dramatic example of dysfunctional architecture is the construction, and eventual

SOCIAL FOCUS 17.1
Action Research: The Campus Environmental Assessment Team

The Campus Environmental Assessment Team (CEAT) was established at the University of California, Irvine, in 1977. Development of CEAT was initiated by a group of undergraduates with advanced training in environmental psychology who were concerned about the lack of student input into the design of university environments. This group approached the Campus Planning Committee at the University of California, Irvine, and offered its environmental assessment skills to the committee on a project-by-project basis. The committee was receptive to CEAT's proposal and invited the group to undertake an extensive needs-assessment study of existing student housing on campus as an aid to developing future design proposals for university housing. The findings from this study were used as a basis for establishing behavioral criteria for the design of new residence halls at U.C.I.

Since its inception in 1977, CEAT has continued to provide environmental assessment data to various administrative and planning groups at U.C.I. Participation in CEAT is supervised by faculty in the Social Ecology Program at U.C.I. and enables students to earn full course credit while working on projects that involve the application of psychological theory and research to the development of environmental design solutions. Recent CEAT projects have included (1) an evaluation of social and study spaces on the U.C.I. campus, (2) a study of littering patterns at U.C.I., (3) the establishment of a new newsletter entitled *Human Environments*, and (4) the initiation of a "Creative Change Contest" at U.C.I. to solicit student proposals for improving the quality of the campus environment. Contest proposals are evaluated by CEAT members and by the Chancellor's Committee on the Quality of the Physical Environment. Annual funding for the implementation of winning proposals is provided by the U.C.I. administration. Funded projects have included the botanical tagging of trees in Campus Park, the design and construction of a garden-amphitheater area, and the construction of bus shelters on campus.

demolition, of the Pruitt Igoe housing project in St. Louis. Originally hailed as an innovative model of low-income housing, the project proved to be an architectural disaster. Constructed in 1954, only 16 of its 43 buildings were occupied by 1970. High rates of crime, vandalism, and vacancy eventually forced the destruction of Pruitt Igoe in 1972.

Less dramatic but more pervasive instances of dysfunctional design can be cited. College classrooms often are evaluated by students as being uncomfortable, cramped, impersonal, sterile, and bland (Sommer & Olsen, 1980). Yet few efforts have been made to assess and improve the physical features of institutional learning environments. Similarly, the design of dormitories, apartments, and offices rarely has been guided by empirical assessments of occupants' environmental preferences and needs.

In an effort to protect environmental quality and to promote more cost-effective design, federal and state governments have enacted legislation requiring the evaluation of proposed environmental changes in terms of their potential community impact. The National Environmental Policy Act of 1969 requires all agencies of the U.S. government to prepare detailed statements of the anticipated impacts of any proposed actions "which may significantly affect the quality of the human environment." Other examples of environmentally protective legislation are the 1971 Town and Country Planning Act in England and the 1970 California Environmental Quality Act.

Heightened public concern about environmental quality and the passage of relevant legislation have stimulated a great deal of research in the area of environmental assessment. Alternative methods for quantifying people's evaluations of the environment have been tested and these procedures have yielded much information about the determinants of environmental preference.

Before examining the findings from this research, it is important to distinguish between the terms **environmental attitude** and **environmental assessment.** An environmental attitude is the tendency to respond favorably or unfavorably toward one's surroundings (see Chapter 4). This response tendency can be measured in terms of the individual's emotional reactions (for example, negative feelings about air pollution), beliefs (for instance, about the health consequences of smog), and behavior (such as refraining from strenuous exercise on smoggy days). Research on environmental attitudes has focused on such issues as the extent of public knowledge about environmental problems (for example, the perceived severity of pollution and resource shortages) and the degree of consistency among people's attitudes, beliefs, and behavior relevant to the improvement of environmental conditions (for example, attitudes toward recycling and participation in community recycling programs). A comprehensive review of this work is provided by Lipsey (1977).

Research on environmental assessment is concerned not only with people's attitudes toward their present surroundings but also with their preferences concerning the shape of future environments. The basic goals of this research are to identify personal and collective preferences about the environment, and to utilize these preferences as a basis for community planning and architectural design.

Whereas environmental attitudes can refer broadly to national and global issues, such as the worldwide energy crisis, environmental assessments typically focus on people's judgments about specific places—their residential, recreational, and work environments, for example. Procedures have been developed to measure people's reactions to both the physical and social characteristics of places. Physical assessments have focused on the perceived quality of buildings and landscapes, while social assessments have emphasized the interpersonal "climate" in organizational and institutional settings.

Assessing the physical features of places. A major assumption of assessment research is that certain physical arrangements of places evoke consistently favorable responses, while others tend to be disliked and avoided. To identify which aspects of places elicit positive or negative evaluations, certain research strategies are required. First, it is necessary to specify the environmental unit of study—for instance, a particular campground in Yosemite National Park. Second, the campground must be presented to observers for their evaluation. This presentation may involve an on-site visit to the campground by the observers or, alternatively, their exposure to simulated versions of the setting (for example, photographs, movies, or scale models). Third, observers are asked to evaluate the campground on several dimensions. They may, for example, be requested to rate the aesthetic quality of the setting on several attitude scales or to compare the campground with several camping areas located elsewhere.

Ideally, ratings of the campground should be obtained from several observers, since environmental evaluations can be influenced as much by observer attributes as by the physical properties of the setting (cf. Craik, 1968). If different observers provide similar judgments about the campground across several response formats, we can be more confident that the evaluations are attributable to the physical features of the place.

Because it is not always convenient for observers to make on-site visits and evaluations, many assessment studies have employed environmental simulation procedures. The use of simulations to assess environmental quality rests on the assumption that observers' reactions to photographs and models of places correspond closely to their on-site responses. Recent research supports this assumption, indicating that people's responses to color photographs and scale models of buildings and places are predictive of their on-site reactions (cf. McKechnie, 1977; Shafer & Richards, 1974; Zube, Brush, & Fabos, 1975).

Environmental simulation studies have identified certain physical features that evoke favorable responses among observers. When presented with photographs of landscapes, people tend to prefer spacious scenes that afford panoramic views (Craik, 1972; Kaplan, 1977). High levels of naturalism (the predominance of natural versus man-made elements) and land-use compatibility (the perceived fit between a structure and its surrounding landscape) also have been found to be associated with favorable evaluations of landscapes (cf. Hendrix & Fabos, 1975; Kaplan, Kaplan, & Wendt, 1972; Zube et al., 1975).

One of the most ambitious simulation studies undertaken to date is being conducted at the University of California, Berkeley. The Berkeley Environmental Simulation Laboratory, developed by Appleyard and Craik (1978), features a computer-guided camera that provides simulated tours (via TV monitor and videotape) through a scale model representing a 1 $\frac{1}{2}$-square-mile section of Marin County. An important advantage of this research is that it permits a comparison of observers' reactions to both simulated video displays and actual automobile tours of the same environment. The preliminary data from this project indicate a high degree of correspondence between observers' evaluations of the simulated and actual tours.

The potential applications of simulation methodology to the realm of urban planning are numerous. Scale models of proposed buildings are currently used by many architects to assess the preferences of their clients prior to the construction process. At the community level, simulation procedures have been used less widely, but are potentially applicable to a diversity of urban planning problems. Because scale models can be altered to provide previews of alternative, future environments, they can be used to forecast residents' reactions to urban settings before they are built. Such procedures may enable planners to avoid the kinds of costly design "mistakes" that were made at Pruitt-Igoe.

Assessing the social properties of settings. The patterns of social interaction that occur within settings markedly affect occupants' overall evaluations of those places. Positive feelings about one's neighborhood, for example, are closely related to length of residence in the area and involvement in social relationships with neighbors (Fischer, 1976; Kasarda & Janowitz, 1974). Also, environments endowed with historic and social significance are more widely known and more favorably evaluated than others (Milgram & Jodelet, 1976). At the level of institutional and organizational environments, much effort has been devoted to the conceptualization and measurement of **social climate** (cf. Moos, 1976; Pace & Stern, 1958). Moos defines social climate in terms of three basic dimensions, on which all settings can be described and compared: the degree to which the setting fosters social relationships among its members, provides opportunities for personal development, and reflects an emphasis on organizational maintenance or change.

These dimensions have been derived through statistical analyses of occupants' responses to standardized questionnaires and are based on data obtained in a variety of settings (for example, hospitals, classrooms, and dormitories).

The questionnaires developed by Moos and his colleagues have been employed in a number of field studies to assess the impact of the physical environment on social climate. Wilcox and Holahan (1976), in a study of high-rise dormitories (10 to 13 stories) at the University of Texas, found that the residents of higher floors placed less emphasis on social relationships and group cohesion than did those living on the lower floors. Also, Holahan and Saegert (1973) found that the remodeling of a psychiatric ward (repainting the walls in bright colors, adding new furniture, and providing increased opportunities for privacy) led to greater social involvement among the patients and increased levels of interaction among patients and staff.

The preceding studies highlight an important principle mentioned earlier in the chapter—namely, the high degree of interdependence among physical, social, and psychological properties of settings. To obtain meaningful evaluations of the sociophysical environment, it is often necessary to employ multiple strategies of assessment. For instance, questionnaires and interviews pertaining to the physical and social features of settings can be supplemented by a variety of observational measures. One of the most useful techniques of environmental evaluation is *behavioral mapping*—the process of recording the physical location and temporal sequence of individuals' behavior (Ittelson, Rivlin, & Proshansky, 1976). Behavioral mapping can identify areas in settings that are over- or underused (for examples empty dorm lounges), and sources of conflict between architectural design and activity patterns (such as the placement of food-dispensing machines near a library study room). The joint use of behavioral and self-report measures provides a broader representation of occu-

pants' evaluations than can be obtained by using either strategy alone. Furthermore, by employing multiple assessment procedures, designers can more readily identify environmental problems and develop strategies for resolving them.

Although environmental assessment research can contribute to the solution of architectural and planning problems, the usefulness of this research is often tempered by political realities. More often than not, the data from assessment studies reveal conflicting opinions among different users of the setting (for example, staff versus clients, research consultants versus citizen groups), and potential trade-offs among opposing values and design criteria. Thus, certain members of a residential community may advocate the construction of an amusement park for children and adolescents as a means of reducing juvenile crime, while other residents oppose the project for fear that it will promote noise and traffic congestion. In such instances, assessment techniques can merely reveal the range of citizens' opinions and the level of support for each point of view. But the reconciliation of opposing viewpoints about the environment is largely a political matter involving participatory procedures such as town meetings and local referenda. The political context of environmental decision making is discussed further in the final section of the chapter.

Taking Action in the Environment

Each day we engage in activities that physically modify our surroundings. Driving to work in a gas-guzzling automobile, decorating our homes and work spaces, using the air conditioner on hot summer days, purchasing soft drinks in returnable bottles or disposable cans—all of these behaviors leave their mark on our immediate and more distant milieux.

Under what circumstances do people decide to take an active role in protecting or modifying their surroundings? Do people act in accord with their interpretations and evaluations of the environment? What kinds of policies and programs can be implemented at the community level to reduce environment-destroying behavior? These issues have been addressed in recent research on the behavioral underpinnings of environmental problems.

Determinants of environment-protection behavior. By now, most people in industrialized nations are aware of and concerned about the global energy crisis, yet many concerned citizens continue to engage in activities that waste energy and degrade the environment. The discrepancy between public awareness of ecological problems and the perpetuation of environment-damaging behavior has led several psychologists to apply an "operant" or reinforcement perspective to the analysis of environmental problems. In Skinnerian learning theory (Skinner, 1953), the term **operant** refers to any behavior by which an individual operates on the environment. A fundamental assumption of operant theory is that behavior is shaped (that is, reinforced or extinguished) by its consequences. If the consequences of a behavior are rewarding, it will be likely to recur in the future; if the consequences are punishing, the behavior will be less likely to recur. According to this perspective, environmentally relevant behavior can be predicted more adequately on the basis of its rewarding or punishing consequences than by individual's attitudes and knowledge about ecological problems.

Behavioral analyses of ecological problems have focused on two major issues: resource management and the protection of environmental quality. Studies of the first issue have focused largely on the determinants of energy conservation in households. It has been estimated that 47 percent of the energy consumed by American households is transportation related (especially the operation of automobiles). The remaining 53 percent of the energy consumed is associated with in-home uses, such as

air conditioning and water heating. These figures suggest that the modification of transportation behavior (for example, increased use of public transportation or the purchase of energy-efficient automobiles) could have a substantial impact on household energy consumption (cf. Stern & Gardner, in press).

Reinforcement strategies for the modification of travel behavior have been developed and tested by Peter Everett and his colleagues at Pennsylvania State University (Everett, 1981). According to Everett, travel behaviors such as driving one's car or taking the bus to work are associated with both pleasant and unpleasant consequences. The advantages of car driving, for example, include the privacy afforded by traveling alone in one's own vehicle, a high degree of choice over travel schedule and route, and the convenience of using credit cards to defer payment of travel expenses. The disadvantages of automobile commuting include exposure to traffic congestion and waiting in long lines to purchase gasoline. Similarly, the use of public transportation is associated with its own costs and rewards—limited choice of travel routes and inflexible schedules, increased travel time, and lack of privacy, versus freedom from the responsibilities of driving and parking and the avoidance of exorbitant fuel costs.

The reinforcement analysis of travel behavior suggests that people use the forms of transportation that are associated with the greatest benefits and the fewest costs. Moreover, the most effective strategy for modifying travel behavior is to alter the relative costs and benefits associated with alternative forms of transportation. This is precisely the strategy that has been employed by Everett and his colleagues in their experimental analyses of bus ridership.

In an effort to increase the rate of bus ridership on a university campus, Everett, Hayward, and Meyers (1974) instituted a token-reinforcement procedure for rewarding people who rode on a specially marked bus over a period of eight days. The effectiveness of their procedure was tested by recording the total number of daily riders on two campus buses over a 36-day period. During the first 16 days of the study (the baseline period), the two buses were not distinguished in any way. On the seventeenth day, however, a large red star was placed on the experimental bus and an experimenter was stationed behind the driver. The experimenter gave each person who boarded the Red Star bus a token redeemable for cash prizes and thanked the individual for riding the bus. The tokens could be exchanged in varying quantities for goods and services at local stores. For instance, one token would purchase a cup of coffee, a candy bar, or an additional bus ride. Two tokens would buy an ice-cream cone, three would buy a beer, and 28 would purchase a record album. During the final phase of the study, the token procedure was discontinued, but ridership counts on both buses continued (through the thirty-sixth day). Throughout all phases of the study, the riders on both buses paid the same standard fare of ten cents.

The results of this experiment were dramatic. Bus ridership increased by 150 percent on the Red Star bus (see Figure 17.4), while the level of ridership on the control bus stayed the same during all phases of the experiment. Moreover, ridership on the experimental (Red Star) bus returned to baseline levels immediately upon withdrawal of the token-reinforcement procedure. Subsequent studies have indicated that the effects of reinforcement strategies on bus ridership are even more pronounced when they are combined with newspaper advertisements announcing the details and scheduling of the experiment (Everett, 1981). These findings are being further evaluated by Everett in a series of field experiments designed to increase public use of mass transit in Spokane, Washington and St. Paul, Minnesota.

Reinforcement procedures have also proven to be effective in modifying patterns of energy consumption in the home, waste disposal, and

Attractive waste receptacles increase the likelihood that people will use them rather than litter.

newspaper recycling. The provision of cash rewards or special privileges (for example, rebates on monthly utility bills) appears to be the most potent means of encouraging household energy conservation (Cone & Hayes, 1980; Stern & Gardner, in press), whereas the mere dissemination of information (such as providing families with energy conservation manuals) has been the least effective strategy (Kohlenberg, Phillips, & Proctor, 1976). Moreover, in the absence of material contingencies, social praise and the provision of verbal or written

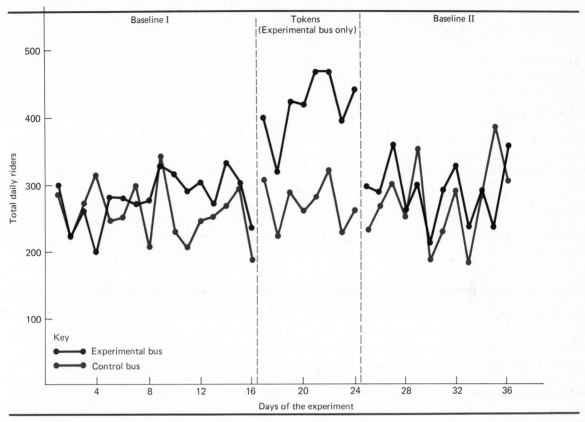

FIGURE 17.4
Ridership Rates for the Experimental and Control Buses during All Phases of the
Everett Study (1974)
Source: Everett, Hayward, and Meyers, 1974

feedback to families about their rate of electricity usage have been moderately effective in reducing levels of energy consumption (Seaver & Patterson, 1976; Seligman & Darley, 1978; Winett & Nietzel, 1975).

Littering has been decreased in various settings through the use of antilitter "prompts" (for example, printed messages on disposable materials) and by providing rewards for the proper disposal of trash (Geller, Witmer, & Orebaugh, 1976; Hayes, Johnson, & Cone, 1975). Also prompting and reward strategies have been implemented to promote recycling of various items (newspapers, food containers) and the reduction of waste (cf. Geller, 1979). Recent

studies indicate that the attractiveness and proximity of waste receptacles and recycling bins can substantially affect patterns of trash disposal and resource conservation (Geller, Brasted, & Mann, 1979; Luyben & Bailey, 1979).

The application of these findings to the development of community environmental protection programs will depend largely on the cost-effectiveness of the proposed procedures. Unlike short-term demonstration studies, community interventions must be economically feasible. The prospects for developing cost-effective programs to encourage environment-protection behavior are favorable, in view of the proven impact of social praise and feedback on conservation behavior, and recent evidence that intermittent levels of reinforcement are as effective as continuous reward schedules in promoting the use of public transit (Everett, 1981).

Aside from the economic feasibility of environmental protection programs, an additional criterion of their effectiveness should be considered: namely, their impact on community participation and cohesion. Recent research on community development suggests that active participation in group planning efforts is associated with psychological and social benefits (Wandersman, 1979). If reinforcement policies are designed and implemented by government planning agencies without community participation, public acceptance of these programs may be undermined. An advantage of the social praise and feedback strategies mentioned above is that they may increase individuals' sense of belonging to community groups. Regardless of whether monetary or social reinforcement strategies are utilized, however, the effectiveness of these programs may well be enhanced by ensuring grass-roots, community participation in their design and implementation.

Human spatial behavior.   Behavioral analyses of environmental problems have emphasized human activities that are directly relevant to resource conservation and the preservation of environmental quality. Yet the ways in which people influence and modify their surroundings extend far beyond the issues of energy consumption, trash disposal, and recycling. One of the most extensively researched topics in environmental psychology is *human spatial behavior,* or the ways in which people use the physical environment to regulate their social interaction. Edward Hall, an anthropologist, has coined the term **proxemics** to refer to this area of investigation (Hall, 1966).

Hall was one of the first researchers to systematically study the subtle uses of space in human social behavior. Hall postulated four different zones of interpersonal distance: *intimate distance* (ranging from direct touch to 18 inches), *personal distance* ($1^1/_2$ to 4 feet apart), *social distance* (4 to 7 feet), and *public distance* (12 to 25 feet). Hall found that the use of these interaction zones depends upon the nature of the relationship between participants and type of situation in which they are involved. In general, the first two zones are reserved for interactions among close friends and family in informal situations, whereas the latter two zones are typically exhibited among strangers or casual acquaintances interacting in more formal, public settings. Another important discovery of Hall's research was the variation in spatial behavior across different cultures, with the members of Northern European and American cultures generally exhibiting greater interpersonal distance (particularly in interactions among strangers) than those from Mediterranean and Latin cultures.

Recent proxemic research has emphasized two basic categories of human spatial behavior: **territoriality** and **personal space.** The concept of territoriality is closely tied to research on animal behavior and refers to the behavior by which individuals lay claim to a particular area and defend the area against members of their own species (Hall, 1967). Personal space refers to "an area with an invisible boundary surrounding the person's body into which intruders may not come" (Sommer, 1969, p. 26). Whereas territoriality involves the appropriation of specific places and objects, personal space is invisibly "attached" to the individual, and its dimensions fluctuate greatly in relation to the immediate situation.

Territoriality and distancing behavior have been observed in numerous species, and appear to be closely related to individual and collective well-being. One of the most comprehensive theories of territoriality was developed by Wynne-Edwards (1962), a population biologist who hypothesized that the foremost function of territoriality is to maintain a balance between population size and existing resources within an area. According to this analysis, all habitats have a "carrying capacity," or maximum number of animals that can be supported by the available food supply. When population size exceeds carrying capacity, the survival of all group members is endangered by the scarcity of food and other resources. In situations where resources are being consumed too rapidly, inhabitants of the area may not recognize the problem until it is too late, and mass starvation ensues.

Wynne-Edwards suggests that territoriality has evolved as a population-regulating mechanism, designed to prevent overexploitation of available resources, and the calamitous "population crashes" (mass die-offs) that result from starvation. In essence, territorial behavior creates a "mosaic" of breeding and feeding lots that regulates resource consumption and imposes a ceiling density on the group. The ceiling density, established through territoriality, is assumed to be lower than the actual carrying capacity of the habitat. When population size begins to increase, animals come into closer contact with each other and territorial infringements are more common. This intensified level of social contact prompts more frequent displays of ritualized aggression (for example, threatening or antagonistic behavior). Through such displays, animals are "notified" that population size has become too large for the existing level of resources.

Interestingly, the behavioral implications of aggressive displays depend on the relative dominance of group members. While the "property holders" cling to their territories more tenaciously, the "untenured" animals are forced either to emigrate to a new geographical region, or to suffer the consequences of increased vulnerability to predation and physiological stress arising from their lack of a home base. The fact that dominant animals (by virtue of their physical size and assertive behavior) have first access to territory, food, sexual partners, and other limited resources increases the

likelihood that the strongest and most fit members of the community will survive, even during periods of extreme resource shortages.

Subsequent analyses have noted several differences between territoriality in people and in nonhuman species, and have emphasized the psychological and social functions of territorial behavior rather than its biological origins (cf. Altman, 1975; Baldassare, 1978; Edney, 1976). Altman (1975), for example, points out that people, unlike most animals, are typically associated with multiple territories (such as one's home, office, and automobile), some of which are extremely large (for example, one's nation). Also, the personal activities and social roles performed in human territories extend beyond the biological functions of food gathering, mating, and reproduction usually emphasized in animal research. Moreover, people personalize and demarcate their territories with a variety of social and cultural symbols (for example, ethnic and religious symbols), and have developed a broader repertoire of behavior for dealing with territorial encroachments (such as property and copyright laws, social norms) than is typical of other species. Thus, territorial intrusions among people are less frequently accompanied by physical defense and aggressive displays than they are among animals.

Altman (1975) has proposed that a crucial function of human territoriality is the regulation of privacy. Privacy, or the level of contact between self and others, is viewed by Altman as a basic human need present in all cultures. By establishing personal territory, individuals are able to regulate their contact with others. The regulation of privacy through territoriality and distancing behavior is regarded as crucial for the development of individuality and the preservation of emotional well-being.

Empirical studies have documented the strong tendency of individuals to personalize their environments and the relationship between territoriality and well-being. Hansen and Altman (1976) studied the territorial behavior of dormitory residents at the University of

Utah. By taking photographs of dorm rooms at the beginning and end of the fall quarter, they were able to measure the amount and diversity of room decorations installed by residents during the quarter. They found that 88 percent of the participants in their study had done some form of decorating (for example, photographs, calendars, and posters) within the first two weeks of residence, and that virtually all residents (98%) had put something on the wall over their beds by the end of the quarter.

A subsequent study by Vinsel, Brown, Altman, and Foss (1980), also conducted at the University of Utah, found that college dropouts reported fewer and less effective privacy regulation mechanisms in their dormitory rooms (for example, using the dorm bathroom during quiet versus noisy times; opening or shutting the door to one's room) and were less active in various campus environments. Interestingly, dropouts tended to decorate their rooms more than "stayins," but their decorations showed less diversity and less commitment to the university setting. The room decorations of dropouts, for example, typically were associated with noncampus settings and interpersonal relationships, whereas those of the students who remained in school were more closely connected with various campus areas and activities. Taken together, the studies by Hansen and Altman and by Vinsel et al. suggest that people generally strive to personalize environments that are important to them, and that the content of room decorations (their diversity and environmental focus) may be a reliable index of personal commitment to the setting.

The importance of territoriality for personal and collective well-being is suggested by several studies. Fried (1963), in a study of residential movers, found that departure from highly valued living environments was accompanied by a syndrome of depression and psychosomatic symptoms. Also, Altman and Haythorn (1967) and Sundstrom and Altman (1974) observed that groups that established clear-cut norms for territorial regulation were more

likely to survive and to function effectively than those that failed to develop such norms. These findings reflect both the psychological and social regulating functions of human territoriality (cf. Edney, 1976).

The regulation of interpersonal distance is another strategy by which people maintain desired levels of contact with others. Much of the research on personal space has been guided by an equilibrium model of intimacy (Argyle & Dean, 1965). According to this theory, the level of interpersonal contact desired by a person in a given situation is determined through an interplay of approach and avoidance forces. In some situations, such as those involving interaction with close friends, approach forces prevail (for example, the desire for affection and feedback from others) and the preferred level of intimacy is high. In situations involving proximity to unpredictable strangers, however, avoidance tendencies (such as fear of being embarrassed or rejected) are more dominant and the desired level of contact is lower.

Equilibrium theory suggests that when a discrepancy arises between preferred and actual levels of intimacy, the individual will compensate by attempting to reestablish the desired level of interpersonal contact. For example, strangers approaching on a sidewalk often look away from each other as their proximity increases. In such instances, the aversion of eye contact compensates for increased levels of interpersonal proximity. Similarly, Argyle and Dean (1965) found that when participants in their study were seated close to an individual (2 feet away) during a discussion task, they spent significantly less time looking at that person than when they were seated farther away (6 or 10 feet). At close distances participants were also more likely to lean backwards in their chairs, presumably as a means of further reducing the existing level of intimacy.

Subsequent studies of personal space have provided additional support for equilibrium theory, although some have found that individuals sometimes reciprocate rather than compensate for others' attempts to approach them (Patterson, 1976). In an effort to explain these findings and to link the processes of reciprocity and compensation in a broader conceptual framework, Patterson proposed an arousal-attribution model of interpersonal distancing. According to this theory, physical proximity with another person invariably elevates physiological arousal. It is the interpretation of this arousal (for example, as anxiety, embarrassment, physical attraction) that determines whether the individual will reciprocate or compensate for the increased level of intimacy. The individual's attributions about the other's intentions and the source of heightened arousal are based on a combination of personal and situational factors—for example, whether the approaching individual is familiar or strange, and the apparent formality or informality of the situation. Thus, the mediating processes of physiological arousal and emotional labeling help to account for the situational variation in individuals' personal space needs and their alternative responses to increased intimacy in different settings.

The research on personal space and territoriality emphasizes people's active efforts to satisfy their needs for privacy, self-expression, and interpersonal contact. In some situations, however, these needs are thwarted by inflexible environmental conditions. It becomes quite difficult for example, to regulate acoustical and visual privacy in a noisy, overcrowded apartment building. And efforts to establish personal territory are defied by the inflexible conditions in certain institutional settings, such as hospitals or prisons.

Altman's (1975) model of spatial behavior suggests that when individuals are prevented from achieving desired levels of contact with others, at least two forms of emotional stress can occur: **isolation,** (where desired contact with others exceeds achieved contact) and **crowding** (where achieved contact exceeds desired contact). A large body of research suggests that these experiences, if prolonged, of-

ten lead to psychological, behavioral, and physiological problems (Baum & Epstein, 1978). In the following section, we turn to a consideration of the impact of environmental conditions on behavior and well-being.

Responding to the Environment

Imagine yourself as a decision maker in the following situations: (1) as the member of a campus planning committee that is drawing up plans for a new dormitory complex; (2) as a city council member considering a proposal for a high-density housing tract that has been submitted by a local land-development firm; (3) as the manager of an environmental-impact consulting firm who must assess the potential effects on the children attending a nearby elementary school of constructing a new airport; (4) as the president of a large company who is considering the cost-effectiveness of developing a commuter van-pooling program for employees; and (5) as a psychologist preparing to serve as an expert witness in a class-action suit filed by the inmates of a state prison, who are charging that they are being adversely affected by high density and noisy conditions in the prison.

Each of these situations raises several questions about the impact of the sociophysical environment on people. How are people affected by the design of their living environments? Under what conditions does population density exert negative effects on health and behavior? Are automobile commuters adversely affected by routine exposure to traffic congestion? What are the effects on children and adults of prolonged exposure to noise? Until recently, community planners arrived at their decisions on the basis of intuitive hunches about the answers to such questions. During the past decade, however, experimental research has produced a substantial amount of data relevant to the impact of the large-scale environment on behavior, and some of this information is finding its way into the environmental decision-making arena. The results from studies of the effects on children of airport noise *are* being made available to school administrators. Psychologists *are* serving as consultants to environmental design and assessment firms and as expert witnesses in court cases concerning the impact of high density on prison inmates.

The environment affects behavior and health in two major ways: it provides people with opportunities and it imposes constraints on them. Residents of midtown Manhattan, for example, enjoy ready access to numerous cultural and entertainment activities, yet they also experience high levels of population density, congestion, and noise. Most situations involve a combination of environmental opportunities and constraints. An individual's response to a particular setting is likely to depend on the relative number and importance of the opportunities it provides and the constraints it imposes.

The environment as a source of opportunities. The provision of opportunities for social contact and friendship is an important consequence of environmental design. As was noted in Chapter 8, Festinger, Schachter, and Back (1950) found that the physical distance between the front doors of apartments was a significant predictor of residents' friendship formation and attitudinal similarity. Neighbors were significantly more likely to develop lasting friendships and similar political attitudes than were residents who lived farther apart. Other features of the environment, such as the location of stairwells and mailboxes, also promoted informal social contact and enhanced friendship formation.

Research by Roger Barker and his colleagues (Barker & Associates, 1978; Wicker, 1979) on behavior settings provides additional evidence for the social consequences of environments. As noted earlier in the chapter, behavior settings are recurring patterns of human activity associated with particular places and

times (for example, a psychology class, a concert). Barker developed a theory of settings that emphasizes the behavioral and psychological consequences of **undermanning**—a condition in which available participants are fewer than the number normally required to maintain the setting at an optimal level (for instance, three rather than five persons on a basketball team). An important finding of Barker's research was that students attending small high schools (assumed to be more undermanned than large schools) were more likely to perform leadership roles in extracurricular activities and to experience feelings of responsibility and importance than were those enrolled in larger schools.

By providing opportunities for social involvement and the development of close relationships (thereby reducing loneliness), environments may exert a positive influence on the physical health of their occupants. A longitudinal study of 6928 randomly selected adults in Alameda County, California (discussed earlier in Chapter 9) found that the death rate during the nine year course of the investigation of people who lacked social and community ties (such as contact with friends and relatives, or church membership) was higher than that of those who participated in social networks (Berkman & Syme, 1979). The relationship between social ties and mortality was found to be independent of socioeconomic status and health practices such as smoking, alcohol consumption, and physical exercise.

Because people spend so much of their time in residential settings, interaction among neighbors serves as an important source of social support. One strategy that appears to be effective in promoting social involvement among neighbors is the implementation of community gardening programs. In 1963, the New York City Housing Authority established the Tenant Gardening Contest as a means of promoting better communication among the residents of low-income housing projects. Tenants wishing to enter the contest are assigned

Gardening programs in housing projects decrease vandalism and increase the social involvement of the residents.

a garden site on the grounds of their project and receive $35 for the purchase of seeds, tools, and fertilizer, plus a gardening manual. In a twelve-year study of the New York gardening contest and similar programs in Philadelphia and Chicago, Lewis (1976) found that participation in gardening was associated with reduced rates of vandalism and increased social involvement among building residents. These findings suggest that social planning as well as architectural design can promote increased interaction in residential settings.

The positive effects of gardening programs observed among apartment residents are consistent with Oscar Newman's (1973) concept of **defensible space**—those features of an environment that serve to bring it under the control of its occupants. By actively participating in gardening programs, residents become ac-

quainted with their neighbors and more concerned about their welfare. They are also more likely to be protective of their shared environment and more vigilant toward outsiders. Newman's research has focused on architectural features of residential environments that enhance defensible space—for example, visible territorial boundaries and markers, opportunities for surveillance over play areas and approaches to the building, and ample lighting of hallways and stairwells.

Two environmental variables that may interfere with the development of defensible space are building height and the number of apartments per building. In a study of crime rates in low-income housing projects in New York City, Newman categorized buildings according to their height (seven or more stories versus six or fewer) and their size (greater than or less than 1000 residential units). He also selected buildings that were comparable in terms of their racial, socioeconomic, and ethnic composition. Newman found the highest crime rates in buildings with seven or more stories and 1000 or more apartments. He concluded that large housing projects contain many more "anonymous," indefensible areas, due to the difficulties of recognizing fellow residents and of maintaining surveillance over common areas (for example, play areas that are beyond the view of occupants on the top floors). Thus, while the lack of defensible space offers ample opportunities for would-be criminals, it imposes definite constaints on the emotional and physical well-being of apartment residents.

The environment as a source of constraints. Because one person's opportunity may be another's constraint, the definition of environmental constraints depends greatly on the individual's interpretation and evaluation of the situation at hand. In general, when environmental conditions interfere with a wide range of personally important goals and activities—as when living in a noisy high-rise dormitory makes it difficult to study, sleep, and manage one's privacy—then the environment becomes a source of stress. **Stress** arises when there is an imbalance between environmental demands and our capacity to cope with them. The need for greater understanding of environmental stress is vividly illustrated in Social Focus 17.2.

The concept of stress was developed by Hans Selye (1956), a biomedical researcher who discovered that when animals were exposed to a variety of demanding conditions (for example, abrupt changes in temperature, injection with toxic material), they exhibited a common set of physiological symptoms: enlargement of the adrenal glands, shrinkage of the lymphatic (immune) system, and the formation of gastrointestinal ulcers. Selye referred to this triad of symptoms as the General Adaptation Syndrome and posited that it occurs in response to a diversity of **stressors**—environmental demands that tax or exceed the animal's adaptive capacity.

The importance of cognitive and emotional processes in stress was recognized by Lazarus (1966), who developed the concept of **psychological stress.** According to Lazarus, psychological stress arises whenever the individual appraises the environment as threatening—that is, as potentially uncontrollable and harmful. Psychological stress thus occurs when *perceived* environmental demands exceed the individual's *perceived* ability to cope. The experience of psychological stress triggers a variety of emotional, physiological, and behavioral reactions (such as anxiety, elevated blood pressure, impaired task performance), the severity of which depends on the degree of threat perceived by the individual. Some people, for example, may enjoy meeting strangers in crowded public settings, whereas more introverted individuals would prefer to avoid such situations. The latter group, therefore, would be expected to show greater symptoms of stress in situations involving exposure to large numbers of strangers than the former.

Several studies have demonstrated the importance of cognitive and psychological factors in mediating people's reactions to environmental stressors. In a series of laboratory experiments, Glass and Singer (1972) exposed individuals to fixed or random intervals of high-intensity noise (108 decibels) while they worked on a series of tasks. After 25 minutes, participants moved to a quiet room where they were asked to complete a proofreading task and a series of difficult puzzles. Those who had been exposed to the random, unpredictable noise evidenced more proofreading errors and less persistence on the puzzle task than those who had heard fixed-interval, predictable noise. And among participants in the random-noise condition, those who had been told that they could push a button to terminate the noise (but were asked by the experimenter to refrain from using the button if at all possible) made fewer proofreading errors and displayed greater persistence on the puzzle task than persons who were not given the option of turning off the noise. In these studies, no differences between experimental groups were found on the arithmetic tasks performed concurrently with the noise. But on postnoise tasks, individuals exposed to predictable and controllable noise performed better than those who had experienced random, uncontrollable noise.

Glass and Singer's studies demonstrate that while individuals are able to adapt (behaviorally and physiologically) to high-intensity noise in the short run, they frequently exhibit post-stressor aftereffects—particularly when the noise is unpredictable and uncontrollable. The relationship between environmental controllability and stress reactions has been demonstrated in numerous laboratory and field investigations. Sherrod (1974) found that under conditions of high density, individuals who believed they could leave a crowded room at any time showed fewer negative aftereffects on a postdensity task (that is, they persisted longer on the task) than did those who were instructed not to leave the room during the experimental session. And in a series of field experiments concerning residential density and

SOCIAL FOCUS 17.2
Environmental Stress and Aggression: "Piano Killer" Strikes a Responsive Chord in Noise-Filled Japan

Tokyo—Matsuzo Ohama had a thing about noise. When he was a young man, one of his neighbors complained that he was playing his phonograph too loudly. Chagrined by such criticism, he vowed to live as quietly as possible, and he came to believe that others should live the same way.

Sometimes he went to extremes. Sitting in his two-room apartment in one of the "danchi," or high-rise government housing developments that dot Tokyo and its suburbs, he would listen to his television and stereo sets through earphones so he wouldn't disturb his neighbors. He would sit perfectly still when taking a bath so no one would be offended by splashing water. He even complained that his wife's knitting made too much noise.

And then he murdered his neighbors, Yaeko Okummura and her two daughters, eight-year-old Mayumi and four-year-old Yoko.

The Okummura children, it seemed, played the piano—loudly and not very well. Every note pierced the paper-thin wall that separated Mr. Ohama's apartment from the Okummura family. Mayumi would usually begin to play at about 7 a.m., and little Yoko would join in a few minutes later.

Finally, the 46-year-old Mr. Ohama had had enough. He sent Mrs. Okummura a note complaining about the noise. "You should apologize to me, but you don't even acknowledge my presence as your neighbor," he wrote. But nothing changed. The next morning the children were at it again. Enraged, Mr. Ohama jumped from his bed, grabbed a knife from his kitchen table and stormed into Mrs. Okummura's apartment, where he stabbed her and the two children to death (*Wall Street Journal*, December 3, 1974).

social behavior, Baum and Valins (1977) found that the occupants of corridor-design dormitories were more likely to complain about crowding and forced interaction than were residents of suite-design dorms, presumably because the former design provides less shielding from unwanted social contacts. Furthermore, the residents of corridor-design dorms established greater interpersonal distance between themselves and strangers in laboratory settings, exhibited greater competitiveness on experimental tasks, and made more trips to the student health center for counseling services than did those of suite-design dorms.

Studies of train and automobile commuters provide further evidence that environmental controllability plays an important role in me-

diating stress reactions. Lundberg (1976) found higher ratings of perceived crowding and higher adrenalin levels among train commuters on a day when more passengers rode the train than on another when the train was occupied by fewer people, presumably because crowded conditions reduce travelers' feelings of control over the environment. Routine exposure to traffic congestion on the highway was also found to be associated with stress reactions in a recent study of automobile commuters (Stokols, Novaco, Stokols, & Campbell, 1978). The distance and duration of the commute between home and work was found to be significantly correlated with systolic and diastolic blood pressure. Moreover, among long-distance commuters traveling 18–50 miles each way in 30 to

75 minutes, those who reported having a greater choice in deciding where to live and higher levels of job involvement performed better on experimental tasks and had lower blood pressure than those reporting less residential choice and job involvement. These findings suggest that the aftereffects of chronic exposure to commuting constraints are mediated by perceptions of environmental controllability, and that the impact of environmental demands in one life domain (for example, transportation settings) may be offset by the opportunities available in other domains (such as residential amenities, job satisfaction).

At least two theoretical explanations have been offered to account for the negative aftereffects of environmental stressors. The first is based on the concept of **attentional overload**—a psychological state in which the quantity and rate of environmental stimulation exceeds the individual's ability to process the incoming information (Cohen, 1978; Milgram, 1970). Overload theory assumes that people's capacity for attention is limited and that uncontrollable or unpredictable stimuli require more attention (due to their novelty and complexity) than controllable events. The former are therefore more likely to deplete attentional capacity and to result in impaired task performance and social relations.

Empirical support for the propositions of overload theory has been found in several field investigations. In two such studies, pedestrians in noisy areas were observed to be less helpful to strangers than those in quieter areas (Korte, Ypma, & Toppen, 1975; Mathews & Canon, 1975). And a recent study of children attending elementary schools near Los Angeles International Airport documented the physiological, motivational, and behavioral effects of chronic exposure to aircraft noise (Cohen, Evans, Krantz, & Stokols, 1980). In this field experiment, third- and fourth-graders attending four noisy schools near the airport were compared with children of similar age and background at-

tending three quieter schools, located farther away from the airport. A total of 262 children were tested on two successive days in a noise-insulated trailer parked outside their schools. The results of the study indicated that children attending noisy schools had significantly higher blood pressure than those enrolled in the quieter schools, and that they were more likely to give up or fail on a difficult puzzle task. Moreover, as duration of exposure to the noise (the number of years enrolled in the school) increased, noisy-school children exhibited poorer performance on a proofreading task (crossing out all the e's from a paragraph while listening to the tape recording of a man reading a story) than quiet-school children.

The findings that noisy-school children are more likely to give up or become distracted on cognitive tasks are also consistent with the concept of **learned helplessness** (Seligman, 1975). Helplessness involves a syndrome of cognitive, motivational, and emotional disturbances stemming from repeated encounters with uncontrollable events. Through exposure to such events, individuals come to believe that personal outcomes are independent of their behavior, and consequently relinquish their attempts to influence the environment. Helplessness theory thus provides an additional explanation for the negative aftereffects of stressors.

Experimental evidence indicates that the severity of learned helplessness is related to the amount of earlier exposure to uncontrollable events and the psychological importance of those events to the individual (Krantz, Glass, & Snyder, 1974; Roth & Kubal, 1975; Wortman & Brehm, 1975). Two recent studies of the institutionalized aged further suggest that helplessness may be reduced and possibly reversed by providing persons with greater control over various aspects of their environment. In one study, residents who were visited by student volunteers on a predictable basis exhibited increased social participation and reduced medication rates relative to those who were visited on a random, unpredictable schedule (Schultz, 1976). And in another study, nursing-home residents who were assigned personal responsibility for taking care of plants and the sched-

uling of their activities displayed increased alertness and social involvement, compared to those who did not assume these responsibilities (Langer & Rodin, 1976).

SUMMARY

This chapter has examined some of the major research areas in environmental psychology. Each of these areas reflects a predominant emphasis on one of the four modes of human-environment transaction—interpretation, evaluation, action, and response. Although the research areas have been treated separately, it is important to recognize the interdependence among people's interpretations and evaluations of their surroundings, their behavior, and overall well-being. As a case in point, the research on environmental stress discussed in the preceding section highlights the role of cognitive appraisal and motivational processes in mediating people's reactions to stressors.

An important direction for future research in environmental psychology is to give greater attention to the inherent relationship among different modes of human-environment interchange, which may yield practical as well as scientific benefits. In the field of transportation planning, for example, the research paradigms of reinforcement theory and environmental cognition could be combined to establish comprehensive programs for encouraging increased use of public transit. Along these lines, Everett (1981) is presently examining alternative strategies for developing route maps of rapid transit systems, based on Lynch's (1960) notion of imageability, and possible advantages of combining these cognitive strategies with token-reinforcement procedures in promoting increased bus ridership. Also, information pertaining to the stressful consequences of automobile commuting (such as effects of traffic congestion on employee health, motivation, and morale) could be utilized by public and corporate planners to assess the cost-effectiveness of ride-sharing programs (Stokols et al., 1978).

At a theoretical level, the potential combination of existing research paradigms suggests several intriguing questions for future study. For instance, do imageable environments foster a sense of orderliness and personal control? What kinds of settings prompt people to think about and plan for the future? What kinds of social programs and architectural arrangements promote creativity? Under what circumstances do people shift from a passive stance toward the environment to a more active (for example, interpretive and operative) orientation?

These questions suggest an important priority for research in environmental psychology—namely, the development of a more complete understanding of situations and settings than presently exists. Virtually all of the research programs reviewed in the preceding sections indicate that human behavior and well-being must be understood in relation to specific environmental contexts. Whether we are attempting to predict people's preferences for solitude or affiliation, or their reactions to traffic congestion, residential density, and noise, a knowledge of contextual factors is crucial. We have seen, for example, that the effects of residential proximity on friendship formation depend on the socio-economic similarity of neighbors, and that people's reactions to uncontrollable events depend on the psychological importance of the settings in which they occur (Stokols, 1981; Stokols & Shumaker, 1981).

Barker's (1968) theory of behavior settings and Moos's (1976) research on social climate illustrate two alternative but complementary perspectives on settings. The integration of these and related conceptualizations of settings could provide a more comprehensive and eclectic science of settings than currently exists. The development of a broader conceptualization of environmental settings would serve both the scientific and social goals of action research (Lewin, 1948). First, the identification and measurement of important contextual processes would facilitate more accurate prediction of specific environment-behavior relations (for example, the consideration of density effects in relation to the overall controllability and desirability of the setting). Second, explicit consideration of contextual factors would enhance the effectiveness of social planning and environmental design. The potential utility of ride-sharing programs, conservation campaigns, and gardening contests, for example, all depend on a variety of political and sociocultural conditions—especially the receptivity of community decision makers and citizen groups toward the proposed programs. Thus the development of a more systematic and comprehensive analysis of the environmental context of action research would generate new theoretical insights as well as sound social policy.

SUGGESTED READING

Altman, I. *The environment and social behavior.* Monterey, Cal.: Brooks/Cole, 1975.

Bell, P. A., Fisher, J. D., & Loomis, R. J. *Environmental psychology.* Philadelphia: N. B. Saunders, 1978.

Cone, J., & Hayes, S. *Environmental problems/behavioral solutions.* Monterey, Cal.: Brooks/Cole, 1980.

Ittelson, W. H., Proshansky, H. M., Rivlin, L. G., & Winkel, G. H. *An introduction to environmental psychology.* New York: Holt, Rinehart and Winston, 1974.

Glass, D. C., & Singer, J. E. *Urban stress.* New York: Academic Press, 1972.

Lynch, K. *The image of the city.* Cambridge, Mass.: M.I.T. Press, 1960.

Michelson, W. *Man and his urban environment: A sociological approach* (2d ed.). Reading, Mass.: Addison-Wesley, 1976.

Stokols, D. *Perspectives on environment and behavior: Theory, research, and applications.* New York: Plenum, 1977.

Wicker, A. W. *An introduction to ecological psychology.* Monterey, Cal.: Brooks/Cole, 1979.

Zeisel, J. *Inquiry by design: Tools for environment-behavior research.* Monterey, Cal.: Brooks/Cole, 1981.

18

ORGANIZATIONAL EFFECTIVENESS

- Organizational Effectiveness
- Commitment Mechanisms
- Integrating Organizational Outsiders
- Positions in Complex Organizations and Their Impact on Behavior
- Organizational Change: Work Improvements in the Auto Factory
- Summary

ORGANIZATIONAL EFFECTIVENESS

"The middle of a hurricane is not a very good place to discuss long-term trends in weather and climatic conditions," wrote Marina Whitman, vice-president and chief economist of General Motors Corporation (*New York Times*, September 3, 1980). "The automotive industry is currently in the throes of an economic cyclone."

In 1980 U.S. auto companies were in deep financial trouble. Chrysler Corporation, one of the big three auto makers along with Ford and GM, was seeking massive federal loan guarantees to enable the company to stay in business and to save jobs. Ford was closing major plants. General Motors had massive layoffs. What had happened to the effectiveness of one of the most powerful sets of organizations in America?

Organizational effectiveness is a concept with a number of dimensions; indeed, it appears in different guises to different "stakeholder" groups—those with a stake in an organization's operations (Connolly, Conlon, & Deutsch, 1980). To auto company lenders and stockholders, effectiveness is probably a matter of profits. To plant managers it may mean the sheer number of cars turned out, while to customers it is a matter of the quality and utility of those cars. To consumer advocates like Ralph Nader, it is partly a matter of turning out a safe and nonpolluting product. For unions and the employees they represent, effectiveness might be judged by the number and adequacy of jobs and the level of pay they make possible. In fact, the definition of effectiveness that guides most of any organization's functioning is the outcome of a bargaining process in which key groups form a dominant coalition that can speak for the organization and define its oper-

ating goals. Usually top executives form this dominant coalition, but their own tenure in office is increasingly a matter of how well they listen and respond to the needs and demands of the other stakeholder groups in and around the organization, who form its environment.

During the late 1970s, the auto companies did not seem to be listening to their stakeholders very well, and so they were suffering in terms of nearly every classic social science definition of effectiveness (Goodman & Pennings, 1977). Traditional measures of "task effectiveness" or "goal attainment" include such matters as productivity (number of units of product turned out for each unit of labor), sales, market share, and resource acquisition (obtaining money and support from the environment). All of these indicators were down. Japanese auto makers were beginning to dominate the market because of shifting customer preference for smaller cars, but the U.S. auto makers had not read the signals fast enough to begin to produce the cars their customers suddenly wanted. The energy crisis and soaring gasoline prices, the success and savvy of the Japanese, and continued regulatory pressure to build safer cars with fewer social costs, were all affecting the ability of the auto companies to be as effective as they had been in the past.

But these goal-attainment and external-responsiveness measures are only one side of effectiveness, the side that economists and macrosociologists are most likely to consider. For social psychologists an equally important issue in organizational effectiveness concerns the organization's ability to harness human energy to get the internal work done—in an efficient way for the organization and a beneficial way for the person. The indicators of this kind of effectiveness are largely personal and interpersonal, although they also add up to productivity (get-

---

This chapter is written by Rosabeth Moss Kanter and Martha Glenn Cox.

During the late 1970s, American auto companies were faced with stiff competition from Japan, cars the public wasn't buying, and disgruntled workers. In short, these companies were suffering from organizational ineffectiveness. In this chapter, successful means for achieving organizational effectiveness will be discussed.

ting units of work of a given quality for X units of labor). They concern such matters as conflict and strain (strikes, labor grievances, sabotage), morale and satisfaction, motivation and effort, and impact on mental and physical health.

On these social-psychological indicators the auto industry was also in trouble in the 1970s. The big companies were not yet listening to a major group of internal stakeholders—employees on the shop floor of the auto factories, for whom effectiveness was a matter of the quality of their jobs. The following quotes from Lordstown, Ohio, auto assembly workers give a sense of what their jobs were like a decade ago:

"It's not the money."
"It pays good, but it's driving me crazy."
"I don't want more money. None of us do."
"My father worked in auto for thirty-five years,

and he never talked about the job. What's there to say? A car comes, I weld it. A car comes, I weld it. A car comes, I weld it. One hundred and one times an hour."

"There's a lot of variety in the paint shop. You clip on the color hose, bleed out the old color, and squirt. Clip, bleed, squirt, think; clip, bleed, squirt, yawn; clip, bleed, squirt, scratch your nose. Only now management has taken away the time to scratch your nose."

"Well, [it used to be] like all men when they used to work, they had a specific job to do. They told them to shovel 100 tons of coal within X amount of time, and that's what they did. And they left them alone."

"But like now they tell you, 'Put in 10 screws,' and you do it. Then a couple of weeks later they say, 'Put in 15' and next they say, 'Well, we don't need you no more, give it to the next man.' "

"From day to day, you don't know what your job's going to be. They always either add to your job or take a man off. I mean management's word is no good. They guarantee you—they write to the union—that this is the settlement on the job, this is the way it's going to run—103 cars an hour, and we're the only ones in the world could do that pace. Know what I mean?"

"They agree that so many men are going to do so many things, period! Fine, the union will buy that because they negotiated it. Two weeks later management comes down and says, 'Hey, listen, let's add something else to that guy.' They don't even tell the union. And management says, if you don't do it, they'll throw you out, which they do. No problem. Zap! away you go. . . ."

"A black guy worked next to me putting sealer into the cracks. He used to get cut all the time on sharp edges of metal. One day his finger really got stuck and he was bleeding all over the car. So I stopped the line [there's a button every so many feet.] Sure they rushed him to the hospital, but boy did they get down on me for stopping the line. That line runs no matter what the cost."

"Last week someone up the line put a stink bomb in a car. I do rear cushions, and the foreman says, 'You get in that car.' We said, 'If you can put your head in that car we'll do the job.' So the foreman says, 'I'm giving you a direct order.' So I hold my breath and do it. My job is every other car so I let the next one pass. He gets on me, and I say, 'It ain't my car. Please, I done your dirty work and the other one wasn't mine.' But he keeps at me, and I wind up with a week off. Now, I got a hot committeeman who really stuck up for me. So you know what? They sent him home too. Gave the committeeman a DLO!"

"Just like the Army. No, it's worse 'cause you're welded to the line."

"That ain't no joke. You raise your little hand if you want to go wee-wee. Then wait maybe half an hour till they find a relief man. And they write it down every time too. 'Cause you're supposed to do it on your own time, not theirs. Try it too often, and you'll get a week off."

"Sabotage is just a way of letting off steam. You can't keep up with the car so you scratch it on the way past. I once saw a hillbilly drop an ignition key down the gas tank. Last week I watched a guy light a glove and lock it in the trunk. We all waited to see how far down the line they'd discover it. . . . If you miss a car, they call that sabotage. They expect the sixty-second minute. Even a machine has to sneeze. Look how they call us in weekends, hold us extra, send us home early, give us layoffs. You'd think we were machines the way they turn us on and off." (Garson, 1979).

Clearly, this factory was failing a major test of effectiveness—it was not tapping the human energy of its workers. Instead, it was a highly alienated work place. The workers' words reflect all the dimensions of alienation: meaninglessness, powerlessness, isolation, and self-estrangement (Blauner, 1964). The workers felt little sense of commitment to their work; and workers in our age won't stand for such conditions for long, regardless of the pay. Clearly, something had to be done; but what? How can organizations change themselves to be more effective in their use of human energy? In seeking an answer to this question, this chapter will explore how organizations unlock the energy and talent of their members. We will look, first, at the general mechanisms of commitment that allow people to feel engaged with and concerned about an organization. Second, we will take a look at the special case of organizational outsiders, to understand how they are aided or blocked from becoming effective and committed. And finally we will explore aspects of organizational structures that affect *everyone* in organizations and that either turn the power on—fully engaging the energy of the people in them—or off. In closing, we will take a brief look at another automobile plant, this time in Tarrytown, New York, which has tried to put these ideas about organizational effectiveness into action by fundamentally altering life at work for auto workers and contributing to a new kind of management for General Motors.

COMMITMENT MECHANISMS

Individuals are routinely drawn toward and into organizations. Once they enter, they develop feelings of really "belonging" to it, and exert effort on its behalf. These are the key features of an elusive concept: **organizational commitment.** What is it about individuals and organizations that makes commitment possible?

Organizations vary widely in the kind of commitment they expect or demand from members. Commitments required of most employees are limited and pragmatic, since most corporations are "utilitarian," as Etzioni (1961) put it—they focus on a specific concrete outcome, such as making a profit. Religious organizations, political organizations, and educational organizations are likely to demand a more total commitment—all of the members' time and their ideological and economic commitment, rather than simply their energy while on the job. Yet even these lines are not hard and fast. Some corporations, for example, have sought fiercely devotional, almost total life commitment from senior executives, whereas some religious organizations are content with limited commitment from a shifting membership. So in thinking about the general process of commitment, we need to keep in mind the range of organizations in modern society and the variety of commitments they seek. Still, certain key mechanisms of commitment can be differentiated. Some of them have religious labels because they are most visible in religious organizations, but similar mechanisms operate in the corporate world as well.

Commitment to organizations has been studied recently in a wide variety of settings: among hospital employees (Steers, 1977), research scientists and engineers (Sheldon, 1971), school teachers (Alutto, Hrebiniak, & Alsonso, 1973), managers and executives (Grusky, 1966), industrial sales representatives (Kanter 1977a), low-level bank and phone company workers (Dubin, Champoux, & Porter, 1975), and Japanese industrial workers (Marsh & Mannari, 1977)—to name just a few. Commitment has also been heavily studied in religious organizations and social movements, where extremes of commitment may be required just to sustain the organization at all (Kanter, 1972b).

Whatever the setting, one question raised by researchers is whether commitment is the product of individual personalities. That is, are people simply born more or less inclined to commitment and do organizations simply respond to these innate differences? For certain religious organizations and social movements, there do seem to be commitment-prone people, whom Lofland (1966) and others have termed "seekers": people who are waiting to find something in which to fully invest themselves as a total life commitment. Most studies of commitment in work organizations, however, agree that characteristics of individuals play a minor role in explaining commitment (Hrebiniak & Alutto, 1972; Steers, 1977). Characteristics of the job and the organization turn out to be much more important in generating commitment.

One key feature is how much choice people have about whether to take the job in the first place. It is interesting to think about whether people are most likely to feel more committed to a relationship when they know they have chosen it above many others, or when they think they do not have any alternative other than that particular relationship. Is it more commitment producing, for example, to have many job offers and to have *chosen this* job, or to have no other offers and to *need this* job? Both factors seem to be important, up to a point. *Awareness of options foregone* helps stimulate commitment. But going to either extreme—of full choice or no choice—undermines commitment. On the one hand, having a large number of alternatives readily accessible—the extreme of "voluntariness" of the present choice—tends to make it too easy to avoid a full commitment. On the other hand, having no choice whatsoever—the extreme of "involuntariness," as for people in prison—also tends to destroy commitment potential. Commitment occupies a middle ground where people come to feel that they *want* to do what they *have* to do (Kanter, 1968, 1972a).

Commitment to work organizations often has much to do with people's sense that they are relatively successful, that they are "getting somewhere," and that they could not be doing better elsewhere. At least, this is a plausible way to interpret research that shows that commitment is positively related to skill level in the job, job prestige, earnings, and likelihood of promotion (Kanter, 1977a; Hrebiniak & Alutto, 1972). At the same time, commitment also tends to be associated with job satisfaction, job challenge, job achievement, and cohesiveness with fellow employees (Marsh & Mannari, 1977). Of all these factors, concrete material rewards like earnings tend to be less important than symbolic rewards that bolster people's sense of esteem and success and help form a valued social identity (Brown, 1969). We saw this clearly in the Lordstown case. Earnings were not the central issue. Workers' grievances stemmed from a total lack of satisfaction with the work—from the boring, repetitive tasks they had to perform at nerve-wracking speed. There was no chance to feel challenged or to experience achievement in the work.

Note that money is, of course, not entirely unrelated to commitment. Certainly people need money to survive, and pay rates may be very influential in initial attraction to the organization or for immediate motivation, particularly in lower-level jobs. But long-term feelings of connection and investment of self depend heavily on one's own feeling of accomplishment, recognition, and acceptance by others in the organization.

Age or seniority are also related to commitment. Age is not an individual factor (for example, that older people are more "mature" and able to "settle down") but an organizational one. With age in an organization, more benefits are accrued, more relationships are formed, more pieces of a person's identity such as reputation are associated with the organization, and more alternatives are foregone. Becker (1960) suggested that people invest in their organization or occupation by staking something they value in it—like placing side bets in a poker game. The more side bets at stake, the greater becomes the commitment to the organization. Time, reputation, learning are all side bets that help commit people. In a

sense, because the workers at Lordstown were all newcomers and were young, they had fewer side bets staked in the organization. They were perhaps willing to risk more than older workers would have been. The older workers may want or need the changes just as much, but may feel that they cannot risk what seniority and security they have managed to accrue.

Time does not always simply increase commitment, however. Instead, there tends to be an initial period of great enthusiasm and then a "mid-career slump" in which people evaluate whether they are moving in the right direction and whether the organization has lived up to its promises (Alutto et al., 1973). At that point, which may come after two to five years in the careers of industrial sales representatives for example (Kanter, 1977), people decide either to leave, if promises are not met, growth is not ahead, and alternatives exist; or to continue, in which case commitment is likely to grow with age and seniority.

But organizations often do not passively wait for new recruits to decide on their own whether they like the place or not; organizations may actively engage in processes of socialization. Organizational socialization functions not only to teach people what they will need to know to perform adequately in the organization but also to make them feel committed, by transforming their identities into those of organization members. Such attempted identity transformations operate through elevating the rewards and benefits of the organization (material, social, and symbolic) and denigrating other organizations such as "the competition." They may try to make people feel that their own personal sense of meaning, belonging, and value critically depend on involvement in this organization. In short, they may try to create a feeling of membership in a community quite beyond the obligation to perform a particular work role. (See the example in Social Focus 18.1 on McDonald's "Hamburger University.")

SOCIAL FOCUS 18.1
Commitment to a Hamburger

. . . The American company that has grown to annual sales of a billion dollars fastest, at least in modern times, is McDonald's, a franchise firm. But the problem of integrating new members, so that the overall culture and coherence as well as effectiveness of the organization is preserved, is still a problem for companies like McDonald's. It has partly solved this problem by creating "Hamburger University," a national training ground for new batches of managerial talent. Hamburger University, in Elk Grove, Illinois, not only trains managers in procedures that keep McDonald's uniform across the country, but it also indoctrinates them in a company culture to which it is hoped they will become committed. McDonald's is not the only fast food chain to have its own elaborate training facility (Quincy, Massachusetts, is the home of Dunkin Donuts University) but Hamburger University is perhaps the most elaborate and the fanciest. Though extreme and moderately amusing in many of their activities, the training programs offered at Hamburger University are not very different from the way many companies attempt to solve one of their "growing pains" by bringing new members up to speed quickly.

Hamburger University is dedicated to laying the foundations of success by passing on the founder's idea: to put the hamburger on the assembly line, the way Henry Ford did it with the Model T (Haden-Guest, 1973). The course lasts nine days, with audio-visual aids, closed circuit television systems, and units on such matters as the shake machine, [and] carbonation principles. . . . There are pep talks about ideal management and attempts to build pride in the company. "Wearables," such as ties and jackets with the McDonald golden arches on the pocket, are also geared toward promoting an ideal image and identification with the company. Tests are given on the subjects of the courses, with scores totalled: hamburgers, fries and fryers, store maintenance, ice machine, teenagers, shortening, and apple pie. Then there are snappy graduation ceremonies with cocktails, diplomas and the "Archie Award" to the top person in the class, consisting of a McDonald's shaped base on which rests a symbolic burger.

Anthony Haden-Guest, who visited Hamburger University, watched the rehearsal of a McDonald's musical spectacular to be produced in front of 2,000 McDonald's conventioneers in Hawaii, complete with song and dance routines, and actors playing such characters as the hamburger, the french fry, and the milkshake. One song was the "customers' song," with lines like "Everytime I look you sell a billion more. I never cease to wonder how they multiply. . . . I hope and trust you realize to put those billions in the air. It's guys like me that got you there, never mind the 8 billion, just the one in my hand." "This is big business nowadays," Haden-Guest observed. "General Motors spends a million dollars a year on theatrical industries, and more money is invested in live theatrical entertainment by industry than by all the Broadway backers put together" (Haden-Guest, 1973, p. 209).

Lavish productions and training programs are used especially for sales people, often to build company identification as well as to inspire people not to rest on past successes. It is interesting to note how training programs and sales conferences function to "artificially build in the kinds of commitment mechanisms that are a more "natural" part of a newer, smaller organization: relationships of trust, ceremonies and rituals, uniforms and identifying symbols, ideologies and traditions, chances for communal sharing (Kanter & Stein, 1979, pp. 263–265).

Kanter (1968, 1972a, b, 1976) studied nine-teenth-century utopian communities and twen-tieth-century communes in order to discover what commitment-building practices lay be-hind the strength of viable, long-term, alterna-tive communities that needed their members' full commitment in order to survive. This re-search found that stable organizations tended to have many examples of six ways of creating feelings of membership: sacrifice, investment, renunciation, communion, mortification, and transcendence.

Sacrifice

Sacrifice operates on the basis of a cognitive dissonance principle discussed in Chapter 5: the more it costs people to do something, the more valuable they will consider it. This justi-fies the psychic expense and helps them achieve cognitive consistency. For example, Festinger and Carlsmith's (1959) laboratory ex-periment demonstrated that when people work for very small rewards, they must justify their poorly compensated efforts by belief or com-mitment, and they become convinced of the worth of what they are doing. Ironically then, commitment is often unrelated to the rewards people get, even among managers in corpora-tions; it is more often related to the obstacles people have had to overcome to get those re-wards (Grusky, 1966).

Certain sacrifices are part of the general hardship of the early days of an organization, such as poor living or office quarters and the necessity of building from scratch. Others are part of "earning one's stripes," such as the long hours and high pressure placed on aspir-ing young managers. In the Lordstown plant, union rules required that newcomers be put in the frame-assembly part of the line, where the hottest, heaviest work was done. Workers had to stay there until they gained enough seniority to move elsewhere on the line.

Many observers have pointed out that radi-cal movements often define suffering and per-secution by the establishment as an integral part of growth in the movement. The early American labor movement, for example, stressed the persecution of its members by owners and management (Boyer & Morais, 1955). Members of many groups use the mar-tyrdom of themselves or their leaders as an aid to commitment. Sacrifice, then, welds mem-bers together in common suffering and com-mon denial. What has been sacrificed for has been invested with value and is thus hard to leave.

Investment

The process of **investment** provides the per-son with a stake in the organization's fate, like the side bets discussed earlier. Time, energy, money, property, and reputation all become bound up with the organization, so that leav-ing it means leaving behind all these resources. Through investment, individuals become inte-grated with the group, since their resources have become part of its *economy*. Members have, in fact, purchased a share in the pro-ceeds or results of the group and now have a stake in its continued good operation.

For example, this was true in nineteenth-century American utopian communities. More of the longer-lasting (or successful) groups than the short-lived (unsuccessful) ones asked the following of members: no membership without full-time involvement; financial contri-bution and sign-over of property to the group at admission; and sign-over of property re-ceived while a member. Moreoover, such in-vestments were often irreversible; defectors were sometimes not reimbursed when they left. In one community the book in which orig-inal contributions were recorded was even-tually burned as unneeded (Kanter, 1972a). Benefits packages and union pension funds may serve a similarly committing function today.

Renunciation

Committed membership in an organization often involves giving up any social ties that potentially compete with loyalty to the new group. **Renunciation** is common in communities, especially, but it can also characterize involvement in work organizations. Excessive demands for overwork in corporations can be a commitment mechanism for executives, as well as demands that they move to a new part of the country, and informal requirements that they dress or behave in a certain way or pursue particular leisure-time activities. All of these changes make the person more dependent on the employing organization, as other emotional ties are severed. Some religious organizations carry this even farther, reaching into people's lives to regulate even their sexual relationships, either in the direction of celibacy (the Shakers) or promiscuity (Oneida community). Either way, the quality of the individual's sexual or emotional intimacy is regulated by the organization.

Communion

The *we-feelings* of brotherhood (or sisterhood) and comradeship and the experience of communities encompassed by **communion** are essential to the determination to maintain the group, even in the face of obstacles and disagreements. People can be committed to what they do individually (their professions or tasks) or the rewards it will get them, without being committed to the *organization* in which they do it; it is social involvements that produce the latter commitment (Sheldon, 1971). Common activity and work help solidify ties among the members.

Beyond shared activities and space is the experience of shared ownership, both of property and work. These emphasize joint effort over individual achievement and common identity over private ambition; members' efforts are directed toward group rather than individual ends, and they share equally in group tasks and rewards. Job rotation helps move people toward organizational commitment.

Many groups develop a sense of communion by finding common endeavors in which all members can participate. Constructing a building is an important example, for it leaves the group with a permanent monument to their shared work. The end—the actual building—may not be as important for the group's identity as the means by which the building came about. Committee participation on a project may do the same thing.

Among the most important communion mechanisms are the very rituals that often give the organization part of its definition as a special place. Through ritual, members affirm their oneness and pay homage to the ties that bind them. Ritual provides symbols by which group loyalty is elevated, celebrated, and enhanced. Here Durkheim's classic proposition that religion is the worship of the immediate social group becomes clear. Organizations use Christmas parties or special office events or annual sales conferences as rituals of this kind. Even working late as a group to turn out an important report can build the sense of communion. The sharing of food and song are both experiences that, cross-culturally, are invested with meaning and help develop and sustain group solidarity. The key is to involve group members in a common, emotionally charged experience in which barriers among them are broken down.

In Lordstown, there was communion among workers, but none between workers and management. Clearly, a truly effective organization would have to structure work and communication so that a common sense of purpose could extend across levels and functions. Creating contexts where the formal and informal barriers between workers and management can be broken down, while preserving authority structures necessary to coordinated effort, is a key element of many organizational change efforts.

Mortification

An important aspect of strong commitment to a new organization or relationship is changing one's identity—the death of the old self and the birth of a new one. The identity change process is variously conceptualized and symbolized by social movements: taking a new name, as in many hippie communes and the Black Muslims; calculating a person's age from the date of joining or conversion, as in other communities. To borrow a term from religion, **mortification** processes attempt to convince people that true meaning and worth derive from allowing their self-concepts to be directed by the organization. They provide a new set of criteria for evaluating the self and choosing behavior; they reduce all people to their common human denominator, distinctions erased, and transmit the message that the self becomes whole and fulfilled when the person can finally live up to the new moral standards of the organization.

Mortification sometimes occurs during a defined period of resocialization, after which the person is considered reborn. But it may also be an ongoing process in which humility, brotherhood, and the meaning of the group are continually held before the person, while his prideful, separate ego is continually eroded. Systems of feedback, confession, self-criticism, and mutual criticism are ways of promoting mortification. Whereas most work organizations in the United States do not stress mortification, work organizations in other parts of the world do. In the People's Republic of China, for example, this kind of activity is integrated into work life as "self-criticism sessions" in which workers are to harshly evaluate how well they have lived up to the moral dictates of the Revolution.

Transcendence

Finally, commitment is built through **transcendence,** the experience of higher power and

For his followers, Reverend Moon provides charismatic leadership that gives his group a sense of higher power and meaning. This builds commitment through the process called transcendence.

meaning residing in the group, the felt connection with forces and events outside of and beyond the life of a single person. Transcendence provides the new sources of identity and meaning. It ties the group and its purpose to important events. It makes the self whole again. Of Kelman's (1958) three processes of attitude change (in Chapter 15), the most enduring are those that involve internalization—or taking in a set of values so that people fully believe in what they are doing.

Transcendence develops out of an organization's ideology, its leadership practices, and its connection with tradition. It develops to the extent that a group successfully captures and promotes awe and mystery and elevates its own importance in history, as many modern corporations try to do in their "institutional ads" that stress their important contributions to modern life rather than promote a product. These ads are often directed to employees, to make them feel part of something valuable, as much as to the public.

Among transcendence-inducing characteristics are elaborate ideologies that explain the essential nature of humanity and that account both for how things became as they are and how they will be in the future. Businesses often have philosophies or creeds as much as religious communities do.

A movement also gains power and meaning through charismatic figures who seem to possess special magical, superhuman properties. Even if leaders did not have these traits, it is likely, in some instances, that followers would invent them. It is also important that the charisma be somewhat removed from the life of the ordinary member—be, in effect, *larger than life*. Charismatic leaders have been found throughout the history of successful organizations, from great religious figures to the entrepreneurs who start companies.

The kinds of ideas and practices that promote transcendence imbue the organization and its demands with moral necessity, for the person's own internal sense of meaning becomes wedded to the organization's operations. This can be a danger. Subtle pressures may encourage members to focus on the organization's growth and survival as a moral aim, even to the detriment of employee or consumer health, as some exposés reveal. Ways must be found to promote commitment to the welfare of the society as a whole, even as commitment to particular institutions develops.

The six commitment-building processes just described give an organization a committed membership. It is not necessary to have all of them; indeed, no one actual group could have all the characteristics. But having a number of commitment mechanisms adds to the chances that an organization will arouse devotion and loyalty in its members. Even a pragmatic work organization like a fast-food chain may employ a large number of quasi-communal commitment mechanisms, as the McDonald's example in Social Focus 18.1 illustrated.

In general, then, these mechanisms allow the energy of an organization's members to be unlocked. People feel part of the organization and want to further its development. We have pointed out, however, a potential danger in a too narrow definition of commitment: people may become committed to restricted organizational goals and become oblivious to larger social goals. In the next section of this chapter we will look briefly at one of these larger social goals, a goal that will be important for any future organization—the integration of new kinds of people into the work force. We include this topic for two reasons: first, because it is a good example of the kind of overarching social good to which we feel commitment must be generated, even while members work to attain more immediate organizational goals; and second, because it illustrates important aspects of the general concern of this chapter with how peoples' energies can be effectively engaged by organizations.

INTEGRATING ORGANIZATIONAL OUTSIDERS

We have all, at some time in our lives, been in situations where we felt awkward and uncomfortable, as if we didn't belong. A wide variety of characteristics can make us feel "different"—being the only child at an adult get-together, the only American in a group of foreigners, or the only novice in a sport in which everyone else is proficient. Some of these characteristics can be changed over time. Others, such as sex, race, and religious affiliation, are not readily altered. It is these latter characteristics that have traditionally excluded women and minorities from the mainstream in business. This exclusion affects commitment. It is easy to recall from our own experience how difficult it is to feel part of or committed to a group when you are an outsider, regardless of how committed everyone else feels. How can groups that were traditionally outsiders be integrated into organizations? A key element in solving this problem is to understand the powerful effect a sheer difference in numbers can have on outsiders, regardless of the particular characteristics that make them different from the majority. Take a look at these recent news articles and note what they have in common.

TWO AT WEST POINT LEAVE CHARGING SEXIST HAZING

West Point, N.Y., Nov. 9—The United States Military Academy admitted today that female cadets had been ordered last summer during maneuvers to kill chickens "by biting them across the tendons of their necks" and that hazing antics were becoming malicious, degrading and, in some cases, sexist.

Lieut. Gen. Andrew J. Goodpaster, the superintendent, said that a two-month investigation of charges made by two cadets, a male and a female, who had left after being harassed and threatened, disclosed that a "significant number of incidents did occur." He said that punishment would be meted out and charges made. . . .

(*New York Times,* November 10, 1979)

PANIC BEFORE A DINNER PARTY: ALL THE MEN SENT REGRETS

Maybe it happens to everyone, but never before had it happened to me. A week earlier I had mailed out 18 dinner invitations. Now, on the day of the fateful night, yet another person had telephoned, to cancel his previous acceptance. He had sprained his thigh playing softball.

Head in hand I sat, considering the totality of the catastrophe. Nine out of nine women had accepted their invitations, promptly. But for a week the nine men had fussed around like debutantes with dance cards. One had accepted twice, and called back thrice to say he could not come, the last time only this afternoon.

One said he would surely come; the painters were sure to finish on time. The painters had not finished on time. Another said he would be delighted; the children were not coming this week. The children had come. And now, like the 10 little Indians, there was no man left but me.

For three days, as the sex ratio had deteriorated, then finally disappeared, I had been obsessed with the gender of those who accepted my invitation. Not once had I considered how lucky I was to have their company at all (Allman, 1979).

Situations such as these can range from mildly amusing, as when we contemplate the

For institutions like West Point, successfully integrating organizational outsiders is a major task for the 1980s.

dinner-party host surrounded by nine women guests, to awkward, to outright dangerous, as when the first female West Point cadets faced the hostility of some of the numerically dominant men who clearly resented women entering "their" territory. To be apparently out of place, because one is usually surrounded in a particular setting by people of a distinctly different kind, is discomforting, to say the least. Yet more and more organizations are facing or acknowledging these tensions, as we become more aware of our diversity as people, and as we seek to break down racial, sexual, cultural, or physical-capacity distinctions by introducing new kinds of people into places where they were previously rarely found—female managers in male-dominated corporations, male operators in telephone companies, black students in white-dominated schools, and so forth.

The Problem of Numbers

What happens when only a few of one kind of person are introduced into situations in which another kind is numerically dominant— or, for that matter, what happens to the **tokens** (the numerically rare outsiders) who are forced to operate among peers of a different social type? Social composition has an impact above and beyond the effects of attitudes or traditional cultural-role definitions. Numbers are a structural feature that have importance in and of themselves. Recent research shows that what appear to be prejudicial responses on the part of the numerically dominant group may turn out to have less to do with the inbred attitudes that are impervious to change (or at least require in-depth psychological work to change) than with the forces and dynamics set in motion by the group's skewed social composition. Similarly, what appear to be ineffective behaviors on the part of people in the token category may say much less about their capacities and abilities or the effect of their cultural heritage than about what they are forced to do because they are unusual or "out of place"—and treated as such by members of the dominant group. This is the rather universal experience of being the one "oddity"—the O in a group of otherwise all Xs.

These issues have been known in a general way for decades but not examined in particular detail until very recently. In the 1940s, watching the influx of blacks into white work groups in industry because of labor shortages during World War II, Everett Hughes (1946) described the tendency of the majority whites to force isolated blacks into stereotypical roles, such as jokers or comedians. Outsiders generally seemed to have a more difficult time being taken seriously and had to work harder to demonstrate their loyalty and value to the numerically dominant others.

Researchers in industry in the 1950s called this the problem of "status incongruence," when they examined the effects of being non-Irish-American in a mostly Irish-American work group (Zaleznik, Christensen, & Roethlisberger, 1958). That is, some personal characteristics seemed out of line with the expected fit or match with the people who usually occupied the statuses. In short, if people are too different from their peers, their status is ambiguous, and this creates anxiety for everyone involved. Thus, they found that when most of the work team was from one ethnic group, the people in that numerically dominant category were

- more certain of their standing in the eyes of others;
- more likely to interact frequently with others;
- more likely to participate with the group in non-work activities;
- more supportive of group norms;
- less likely to find it necessary to try to outperform workmates or demonstrate greater technical competence.

On the other hand, the outsider from another ethnic group was

- less certain of his standing in the eyes of others;
- more anxious;
- more likely to interact less often;
- more likely to restrict activities to more structured and formal social relationships;
- more likely to try to excel in technical performance, where skill, competence, and knowledge are important;
- less supportive of the group.

Furthermore, the reaction of those who fitted in to those who did not was often expressed in the form of jokes, ridicule, or blame, but the outsiders did not either take offense or joke about the dominant group (Zaleznik, Christensen, & Roethlisberger, 1958). Indeed, it is well known that people who differ from the rest of the group on some important dimension are likely to be "scapegoated"—blamed for the group's problems (see Chapter 16). It is also known that jokes and laughter tend to be directed by those of superior status (in this case, those who "belong") to those of inferior status (who do not "belong"), but are rarely permitted in the opposite direction (Coser, 1960).

Kanter's research on the entry of women into professional and managerial occupations draws similar conclusions (Kanter, 1977a, 1977b; Kanter & Stein, 1979). The problems of acceptance and effectiveness that many women encounter in new or nontraditional areas may derive primarily from their token status—the fact that there are, as yet, so few women in those positions. In general, people whose social type is represented in very small proportion tend to be more visible and "on display." In laboratory experiments, too, one black seen (in simulated group pictures) in a white group, compared with being one of three, received disproportionate attention (Taylor & Fiske, 1976).

These pressures are especially evident when we look at what happens to women and minorities as they move into formerly white-male management positions. Many minority executives, for example, describe the same experience of feeling constantly on stage, constantly in the spotlight. Every move they make—from where they eat lunch to the success of their new business plan—is scrutinized. Everyone knows who they are and what they are doing. Tokens, as a consequence, feel more pressure to conform, to make fewer mistakes. Sometimes tokens try to become socially invisible—to dress, talk, go to the same clubs, and tell the same jokes as white males do. Some try to signal their identification with the dominant group and win acceptance from them by leading the way in attacking other minorities— what has been called the "queen bee syndrome" in women. Sometimes it seems that such compromises are the price for success. But should it really be necessary for women or minorities to give up their femininity or cul-

tural identity in order to be successful in business? Surely this raises moral and pragmatic issues for majority as well as minority group members.

Outsiders also find it difficult to gain credibility and trust in their ability to do the job, particularly in situations involving risk. As one woman put it, "Everyone *assumes* a man is competent until he proves them wrong. A woman is assumed to be a scatterbrain until she pulls something off that's so striking no one can deny she has talent. But even after such a coup a woman has to go on proving her competence; it's like a daily negotiation. One slip, and she's back where she started."

It is certainly not easy to live with such pressures day in and day out. It helps somewhat to be able to talk with other tokens about the difficulties. For many it is a big relief to find out that they are not the only ones who feel the pressure. Indeed some tokens start to doubt their own abilities, until they find out that other newcomers are given the same competence-questioning messages that they receive. Then they realize that if everyone in their category is being given the same messages, the messages must have more to do with their role in the organization than with individual abilities.

So it helps for tokens to be able to exchange information. But they have to be careful. One minority executive who had a group of younger minority managers to his home found himself in trouble with the president for trying to organize the blacks and stirring up discontent, even though the meeting was quite innocuous. Perhaps because of their visibility, exclusive minority gatherings make the majority nervous; the majority tends to assume that the minority group is plotting against it.

In general, newcomers are isolated and peripheral. They are often given the "window-dressing" jobs—highly visible to the outside world but lacking any real power or significance in the organization. They may also be excluded from informal peer networks, often quite unintentionally. In a regional sales office of a major medical products company, for example, a new sales representative was hired who was female. When lunchtime rolled around, the male sales reps would go out to lunch with the male boss, whereas the female rep went out with the secretaries. In a way, this was the most socially comfortable solution for everybody. The men weren't sure the new rep would feel comfortable with an all-male group, and the new rep didn't want to seem to intrude on "the boys." But the outcome was that the new rep got systematically less of the kind of information and moral support one can only get from experienced peers or bosses— such as how to handle difficult customers, what product changes were in the works, or what kinds of political shake-ups were going on in the company. Lacking this informal information and support made it much harder for the woman rep to be effective.

A final difficulty newcomers face by virtue of their differentness is that they may have much less chance of being sponsored in an organization, since sponsorship often grows out of a sense of identification and social similarity. One young woman in a previously all-male company said, "Which of those men looks at me and sees himself twenty years earlier?!" So newcomers have fewer opportunities to get help along the way. In short, there is more personal and organizational stress for tokens or social outsiders. And the pressures operate in much the same way, whether the person is an outsider because of sex, race, religious, or even age differences from the majority.

Some outsiders or nontraditional organization members tend to do very well despite these pressures and stereotypes, but they are generally the exceptions. Indeed, Hughes (1946) pointed out that one way blacks could be accepted in white work groups was to allow themselves to be defined as "exceptional," and therefore as having more in common with the whites than with other blacks. Similarly, high-achieving women have been praised as "thinking like a man." The successful token, then, often succeeds by outperforming the dominants, something that is clearly impossible for most members of the token's group. This is the "superstar" problem: that an unusual kind of person can always succeed if extraordinarily talented, and that person's success can then be touted as demonstrating that the system as a whole is not biased. But the *average* member of the outsider group is more likely to suffer under the undue pressures put on tokens. One writer asked in an article title, "Must Black Executives Be Superstars?" (*America*, 1979). In short, is it fair, as some feminists wonder, for nontraditional people to have to either be overachievers in order to succeed, or face looking less effective than traditional organization members?

In general, then, cycles of advantage are set in motion for those in the majority category and cycles of disadvantage for those in the token category. Numbers emerge as important, as a condition that itself accounts for who is likely to look good in the organization and thus to get further opportunity. The social composition of work groups may shape performance as much as individual aptitude or skills.

The Problem of Communication

Tokens or newcomers are also at a disadvantage in another way besides sheer scarcity. This disadvantage arises because there are differences in forms of verbal and nonverbal communication across cultural and subcultural groups. Generally, majority-group members are unfamiliar with the styles used by minorities and women. This lack of familiarity can cause misperceptions and miscommunication on both sides. Two examples can illustrate the basic point: women's speech and Asian/Native American-Anglo interaction.

As a first example of how speech styles can affect perceptions, consider women's speech. Researchers have tried to ascertain whether men and women speak differently in American culture and in what ways. Lakoff (1973), for example, claimed that there are cultural norms requiring women to use more indirection in their speech, to avoid strong expressions of feeling, and to express uncertainty about their opinions. West (1979) reported that men interrupt women, but that women do not interrupt men in cross-sex conversation. Brend (1975) pointed out that women have four pitch levels, whereas men use only the three lower levels. Further, women tend to use the more polite, proper, or deferential intonation patterns. And Crosby and Nyquist (1977) found that women were significantly less assertive in their speech than men. In sum, it appears that women tend to use a more indirect and nonassertive style than men. If this is true, what effect does it have on others' perceptions?

It seems likely that women who use indirect and nonassertive styles will not be seen as good prospects for promotion into top management roles. American managers value people who express their opinions directly and clearly. They regard this style as a sign of self-confidence and an ability to take the initiative and act decisively, rather than waiting for someone else to take the lead. If women seem retiring and deferential, they will not be considered for managerial roles, because their style does not fit existing conceptions of what it takes to be a manager.

Yet the inference here that a difference in style somehow implies incompetence is not warranted. In fact, the speech styles attributed to women in these studies are remarkably similar to those used by Japanese businessmen (Pascale, 1973)—and certainly, given the current economic picture, one could hardly say the Japanese are not good managers! The important point here is that men may be unaccustomed to the more indirect interpersonal style used by many women. They may assume the style would not be appropriate to managerial functions. But this simply reflects a lack of experience, since such styles are effectively em-

Verbal and nonverbal communication patterns vary from culture to culture. These styles can put minority groups at a disadvantage in U.S. corporations, even though the same communication patterns work well in other societies.

ployed in management elsewhere in the world. Still, if men devalue the style, then women using that style will be treated as outsiders, regardless of the content of the contribution they make. In this way, lack of understanding of stylistic differences will inhibit effective incorporation of women.

The second example combines two groups, Asians and Native Americans. Clearly, these groups differ in many ways, yet they are similar, and distinct from Anglos, with respect to rules for making eye contact. If you observe people talking around you, you will see that the general Anglo pattern of eye contact while speaking is that the listener gazes continuously at the speaker. The speaker meanwhile looks away—at the floor, or ceiling, or off to the side—glancing every now and then at the listener. Only at the end of the statement does the speaker gaze steadily at the listener (Duncan, 1974). The pattern for Asians and Native Americans is different. Direct eye contact is considered very rude (Philips, 1972; Gearing, 1970), so the eyes of the listener are kept directed downward while the speaker gazes off into the distance, sometimes not even faced toward the addressee. Among Anglos, not looking at the speaker is taken as a sign of shyness or, if the speaker is reprimanding the addressee, of hostility or rebellion. We have all heard parents or teachers say "Look at me when I talk to you!" To an Asian or Native American *not* looking is the norm, or even a sign of respect, but this gesture is likely to be misunderstood by the Anglos with whom they interact. Indeed, this may be part of the reason Anglos perceive Native Americans as having a fierce reluctance to interact, attributed to "an 'instinctive dignity,' 'an impoverished language' or, perhaps worst of all, the Indians 'lack of personal warmth' " (Basso, 1972). This is not an accurate perception, but only a stereotype based on lack of familiarity. As long as the misperception persists, however, the minority member will be regarded as odd, shy, or hostile, any of which ensures that he or she will not be allowed to be an effective member of the group.

In two ways, then, tokens or minorities are placed at a disadvantage in organizations. The sheer smallness of their numbers sets up visibility and performance pressures that make it difficult to function. And lack of familiarity of majority-group members with minority culture creates misperception and exclusion.

But a hopeful note can also be struck by blaming unbalanced social composition and social unfamiliarity for some prejudicial or discriminatory behavior, rather than blaming individual attitudes. Social composition can yield to more balanced numbers, and unfamiliarity recedes with greater experience and education. As people gain more experience with outsiders in their group, the outsiders gradually come to seem more like insiders. The tokens themselves learn to feel comfortable and to manage as part of a group dominated by another kind of person. Look at how the one-man, nine-women dinner party turned out:

This story is characterized by an anticlimax. The dinner did not turn into a women's liberation rally, nor did my apartment become a seraglio. There were no echoes of "Suddenly Last Summer." It was the champagne that was devoured, not I. The evening, one of the pleasantest I can remember, marched to no melodramatic climax, only the gentle revelation at 3 A.M., after the last guest had left, that sexual chauvinism takes many forms.

Had the responses to the invitations come in the opposite way—had the men accepted, and all the women refused—it would not have caused me a moment's alarm, I realized. But when all the women had accepted, the implicit assumption—my assumption—had been, without even considering it, that there was something inferior in the female condition that made them incompetent to enjoy an evening if the sex ratio went askew (Allman, 1973).

It appears, then, that experience with new kinds of people can be educational and even enjoyable for the individuals involved. Moreover, as we enter the 1980s, changing economic, environmental, and labor-force trends demand new, innovative responses. More diversified management groups may well have a better chance of finding creative approaches to these problems. Integrating people who were once organizational outsiders may have benefits for both minority- and majority-group individuals, and for the health of the organization as a whole. In this sense, the integration of outsiders may well be a key to organizational effectiveness in navigating the complex currents that lie ahead.

POSITIONS IN COMPLEX ORGANIZATIONS AND THEIR IMPACT ON BEHAVIOR

Chapter 15 discussed status in groups. In this chapter, we want to examine upward mobility in organizations and its impact on organizational members' behavior.

Anyone who has worked in an organization knows that opportunity in them is structured. There are some kinds of jobs from which it is easy to move on—to gain formal advancement, or to have new responsibilities and chances to learn added to the existing job. Management-trainee positions are one example. Such jobs are often linked in what White (1970) called chains of opportunity, and people can travel along these organizational pathways rather easily. Other kinds of jobs do not provide opportunity for movement; they are the same now as they will be in the future, and there is no likelihood of promotion or change. The production-line jobs at Lordstown were of this latter kind. Wages could increase, but there was no room for the workers to advance through formal promotions, or for their jobs to grow or become more challenging over time.

Opportunity, when it has been studied, has been most often identified in terms of formal advancement prospects: promotion routes and rates (Rosenbaum, 1979); but this is not the only aspect of opportunity structures. Positions can also expand in importance or resources without formal advancement. For example, in the administrative ranks of universities, career paths have tended to be haphazard. A major source of opportunity came from the responsibility expansion inherent in organizational growth and new regulatory requirements, so that many functional areas nominally the same in title and level could expand in terms of staff, resources, and tasks (Scott, 1975; Kanter, 1979a). In this way, the job grows, and the person in it, even without formal promotion.

There is also a task and technology component of opportunity; that is, whether a sequence of more important problems or challenges lies ahead, again regardless of formal advancement. Such a sequence may characterize the work of professionals in organizations or of higher-ranking executives whose nominal position may not change but whose tasks may continually add accomplishments and importance to their portfolios. This explains why it can be said that those who occupy top positions may still be advantaged in terms of opportunity, even though they cannot by definition move up any more.

The opportunity sequence inherent in tasks with complexity or skills to be mastered can also differentiate between types of blue-collar jobs and provide understanding of what skill-level differences really mean. For example, in some organizations opportunity begins to decline with time in a position (after an initial period based on expected position occupancy), because those too far over the age mean or who occupy the position too long find the probability of moving out decreasing (Kanter, 1977); they get "stuck" with time, and this stuckness shows up in feelings of increased career vulnerability and in signs of weakened work attachments. When a research team investigated this in a computer assembly factory, however, it found that the relationship held for some work groups but not for others (Stein, 1979b). In the low-skill, routine assembly area, length of time in a position seemed to be associated with a *decrease* in promotion prospects (there was no union and thus no seniority rule) and an increase in feelings of career vulnerability. In a high-skill, custom assembly area, however, longer tenure was associated with *more* career security and perception of opportunity, because in a craft area people became more important to the organization over time and would thus be involved in ever more important tasks, even without promotion. So in high-skill blue-collar jobs, tenure is associated with opportunity—the opportunity to become ever more skilled in a valuable job. Very few of the

Lordstown jobs, however, were in the high-skill category.

Thus, opportunity in a formal sense is a function of at least three things: advancement and mobility prospects via routes connecting positions in intentional or traditional sequences; the potential for job expansion; and the potential for carrying out more important tasks over time. Two macro variables play a part in an organization's opportunity structure: the overall expansion or contraction of the organization, particularly as this affects staffing needs for specific functions; and the age distribution of its membership, both overall and as age groups are clustered in particular functions and levels—a salient issue for American industry today, as the baby-boom population bulge is at lower levels and is blocked from moving up (see Social Focus 18.2). Clearly, new ways of providing opportunity on the job must be found to meet these demographic pressures. Opportunity, then, describes the location of positions in terms of the ease with which personnel move from one position, or amount of responsibility and reward, to another; it refers to future potential of the job.

The structure of opportunity does not, however, merely describe the career chances of individuals; it also affects their behavior and relationships in any one position. People respond to the amount of opportunity available to them. Behavior is a function of past and future as well as present time—where people have been and where they and others think they are going. Thus, the structural task is to identify organizational locations by the degree and kind of opportunity they contain and for what kinds of people. To simplify the picture, we can say there are two kinds of jobs, those with high opportunity and those with low opportunity. These two kinds of jobs in turn create two kinds of people—the "moving" and the "stuck." These characters are at least informally recognized by everyone who works in an organization, and there are names for both kinds of persons. Movers are often referred to as fast-trackers, water-walkers, golden-haired boys (there are just beginning to be golden-haired girls), or high-pots, short for "high-potential candidates." Labels for the stuck are not so colorful; they are called deadwood, 9-to-5ers, retired on the job, or paycheck-oriented employees. Of course, not everyone fits these extremes, but they do illustrate a commonly perceived difference between employees. Often the difference is thought to reflect underlying attitudes of the employee. But it seems equally plausible that the amount of opportunity in a job actually shapes the behavior and attitudes of the person in it. This idea seems to hold up; opportunity tends to be concentrated in certain areas of the organization, and wherever opportunity is high or low, you see employees showing the characteristics of each group.

Being Upwardly Mobile versus Being Stuck

What, exactly, are these characteristics of stuckness or movingness? There are at least five different areas in which the differences appear.

First is aspirations. The moving dream big, they set their sights high, whereas the stuck have low aspirations (Bonjean, Grady, & Williams, 1967). This makes a great deal of sense upon reflection. People generally set their expectations in accord with what they can realistically expect to achieve. Why desire something you are absolutely certain not to be able to attain? So the moving look upward toward the goals they are enroute to; the stuck show no such dreams.

Belief in one's own abilities is another differentiator. People do not start out knowing whether they are competent or incompetent. We all rely on feedback from our environment in making this determination. The moving get a lot of messages from their organizations: "We have confidence in you, we think you have what it takes, and we expect you to go far."

SOCIAL FOCUS 18.2

Impact of Population and Value Changes on Career Prospects

The tension makes its way into conversations among friends and colleagues with assertions like these: "They gripe because they aren't moving faster, but they have no loyalty, dedication or discipline." Or, on the other side, "The job is stifling, I don't feel appreciated, and I'm getting out as soon as I find something better."

Those debating points—roughly, veteran managers versus employees 35 years old or younger—underscore the clashes arising from the arrival into the American work force of 40 million jobholders born in the baby boom after World War II.

In fact, the great surge of younger workers may be distorting the perceptions at both ends, according to labor and organization specialists. It is a wave of talent—ranging from marginal to exceptional—that most companies will have trouble assimilating "simply because the intake will be greater than the capacity," said Jerome M. Rosow, president of Work in America Institute Inc., of Scarsdale, N.Y.

By 1990, workers in the 25-to-44 age group are expected to make up 52 percent of the work force, compared with 42 percent today, while the 16-to-24 age group drops 6 percent.

The intraorganization, intergenerational clashes frequently are over how much time and effort the baby-bulge generation is willing to put into jobs, and, at the same time, slower pace of promotions compared with people further along the career track.

Barry A. Stein, a productivity specialist and president of Goodmeasure Inc., a Cambridge, Mass., management-consulting concern, added: "The opportunity gap is here right now, and it is going to get a lot worse."

"In a society that has defined success primarily in terms of advancement up the organizational ladder, this bottlenecking of would-be executives will cause friction, discontent and intense competition," said Mr. Rosow, a former personnel executive with the Exxon Corporation, who was Assistant Labor Secretary in the Administration of President Richard M. Nixon.

Most companies give managers little guidance for helping employees with career assessments. Most of them avoid the topic, because it frequently involves the questions of pay and logical next career steps—issues the manager may not be able to control.

Most executives, who grew up in the Depression and the patriotic World War

---

The stuck receive different messages. Located in low-growth jobs, they are expected to stay there. The implicit message is, "We don't really think you have the capacity to offer the organization much more than you are offering now." It is an unusual person who won't start to doubt his or her own abilities if given such messages consistently. Indeed, it might be mentioned in passing that this is a major problem with self-help or open-door programs for affirmative action. They leave all the initiative up to the individual. But people who have

ll era, according to career specialists, focus on what they regard as selfish attitudes among younger employees and find them hard to accept. As a result, few large organizations have attempted to adapt the ways they develop and promote people.

"I hear managers saying over and over that younger people have high career expectations but aren't willing to dedicate their lives to the business," said Stuart P. Scheingarten, who is 38, an independent psychologist and management consultant in Cincinnati. "Many have never had any responsibilities for anyone other than themselves. In a word, many are narcissistic."

Dr. Kanter acknowledged that the high commitment to work among the older generation appears to have waned among the younger workers. But, she added, that is partly because jobs have not been upgraded to match the more highly educated, under-35 group.

"It's true that we have a lot of new attitudes that are sometimes not helpful," she said. "Many in the young work force have unrealistic expectations and think they have more skills than they do. Even going to college doesn't guarantee that they can read and write."

"There are also a lot of virtues in the new work force," said Dr. Kanter. "People are willing to work autonomously and take responsibility if they are given it. It's also up to managers to communicate to their people what their limits are, so they can keep their expectations manageable."

Kevin O'Sullivan, the executive director of the American Society for Training and Development, who is 42, dismisses all the worry over the baby bulge and its blocks to career advancement.

"We will start to have a shortage of young workers in the mid-1980's," he said. "Over and above the baby-boom numbers, I've never seen a time when someone dedicated to teamwork and willing to cling to the organization's ideals has so much opportunity." Moreover, he said, it will be those companies that are able to identify and develop the ambitious, dedicated employees who will be most successful.

"That means younger executives today have a chance to find themselves at the top much more rapidly than in recent decades," Mr. Sullivan added. "It's not a numbers game at all: It's a values game." (From Thomas C. Hayes, "Logjam on Executive Track." *New York Times,* October 12, 1980).

been stuck for a long time doubt their abilities and are afraid to take risks (Kanter, 1977) and so do not take advantage of such do-it-yourself opportunities. Sadly, the lack of response is in turn interpreted as demonstrating a lack of desire for growth. The important point is that opportunity must be structured into people's existing jobs if it is to be effective, not left in totally free-standing programs.

Third, the moving show high work attachment (Hrebiniak & Alutto, 1972). They work long hours, show great interest in learning anything that might be useful in future job performance, and they talk about their work whether on or off the job. After all, people tend to invest their energy where they think it will pay off. For the moving, investment in work tends to be effective. For the stuck, no matter how hard they work they won't receive either advancement or new challenges. This may result in higher turnover among the stuck (Smith, 1979; Porter & Steers, 1973) or a plodding performance, combined with dreams of escape and "central life interests" outside the job (Dubin, Champoux, & Porter, 1975).

Interpersonal and group orientation differ widely between the moving and the stuck, too. The moving are task oriented, politically involved, and tend to form allegiances and alliances upward in the organization. After all, they expect to be up there one of these days themselves, so they'd better find out what is going on and what is expected at those levels. The stuck, meanwhile, are socially oriented and put much emphasis on relationships with peers (Pennings, 1970; Tichy, 1973). The work the stuck do is often boring; satisfaction comes from social interaction and intrigue on the job. Some of this attitude was in evidence among the Lordstown workers, where peer-group solidarity and allegiances were very important. Indeed, in some cases individuals who act to try to gain more opportunity on the job may find themselves ostracized by other members of the group.

Finally, the moving and stuck show very different reactions to problems. If the moving don't like the way something is being handled, they are likely to speak up about it in a constructive way. After all, their general experience is that the organization listens and responds to them, so it seems reasonable that action will result if the current problem is brought to light. The stuck, however, hold jobs that are low-level or peripheral, so that they feel no one cares about their problems or would listen to them anyway, if they voiced a grievance. Consequently, they tend toward passive griping, sullen resistance, or even outright sabotage. In the Lordstown case, the line workers first tried to get management to respond to their complaints, but they were unsuccessful. Afterwards, they resorted to the more destructive forms of protest, perhaps because that seemed the only way to provoke a response.

This picture of the behavioral consequences of opportunity is consistent with the expectancy theory of work motivation. In that theory, the perceived *payoff* to initiative is the crucial element in generating initiative to work (Vroom, 1964; Porter & Lawler, 1968). In our terms, of course, it is the opportunity structure that defines the payoff. Similarly, recent research using large-scale survey data shows an association between payoffs in labor-market situations (for both young and middle-aged men, and blacks and whites) and willingness to take initiative—independent of individual differences in skills, abilities, and demographic characteristics (Andrisani, 1977). In short, the amount of opportunity available to employees turns out to be very important in explaining whether their energies are hooked into the organization or not.

Being Powerful

A second major structural feature that accounts for work effectiveness is power. Power is used here in a generic sense, subsuming both authority (a formal side of power) and influence (an informal side). Power in organizations sometimes brings to mind only dominance, control, and oppression, but it can have a positive meaning, too. It can mean efficacy and capacity, analogous in simple terms to physical power: the ability to mobilize resources (human and material) to get things done. A true sign of power, then, is accomplishment—not fear, terror, or tyranny. Where the power is "on," the system can be productive; where the power is "off," the system bogs down (Kanter, 1979b).

The effectiveness that power brings evolves from two kinds of capacities: first, access to the resources, information, and support necessary to carry out a task; and second, ability to get cooperation in doing what is necessary.

Often (see Chapter 14) social-psychological treatments of power deal with it as a personal (McClelland, 1975) or interpersonal resource (French & Raven, 1959). But power can also be viewed as stemming from organizational location—in terms of both job definition and connection to other important people in the organization. Formal authority, then, may be a component of power, but it is not enough to create power. The uniquely organizational sources of power consists of three power "lines."

First are lines of supply. Influence outward, over the environment, means that leaders have the capacity to bring in the things that their own organizational domain needs—materials, money, resources to distribute as rewards, and perhaps even prestige. In a classic study, leader influence outward, over the environment, was shown to be more important than leader style in determining follower response (Pelz, 1952).

Second are lines of information. To be effective, leaders need to be "in the know" in both the formal and the informal sense; communication channels need to be open. A number of social-psychological studies have shown that location in formal communications structures have a great impact on behavior (Leavitt, 1951). The example of the woman sales rep described earlier makes clear that informal channels of information are important, too.

Third are lines of support. A leader's job parameters need to allow for nonordinary action, for a show of discretion or exercise of judgment. Thus, managers or other authorities need to know that they can assume innovative,

risk-taking activities without having to go through a stifling, multilayered approval process. And, informally, managers need the backing of other important figures in the organization, whose tacit approval becomes another resource they bring into their own work units, as well as a sign of the manager's being "in."

Productive power, then, comes through these lines of supply, information, and support from elsewhere in the organization. But how are these power lines tapped? How do people get access to them? There are really two fundamental sources of these kinds of power: job activities and political alliances. These are what connect people to the power centers. Below we examine the features of activities and alliances that engage and create power. Job activities allow the accumulation of power when they allow discretion, recognition, and relevance. Discretion means that the job is nonroutinized, but rather allows for flexible and creative contributions. Generally, organizations value and reward risk taking and innovation rather than a competent carrying out of a job someone else designed (Crozier, 1964). So if employees want to demonstrate their talents and gain access to organizational support, approval, and supplies, they should be in jobs where something new and innovative can be created, whether it is a new marketing strategy, or a better system for handling old problems, or a new product idea.

It won't make any difference how great the employee's innovation is, however, if nobody knows about it. Consequently, the second aspect of job activities that allows power accumulation is recognition and visibility. Some jobs provide contact with people at higher levels in the organization or in other functions. These connections become important channels through which others can learn of an employee's outstanding contributions. Visibility is important. In fact, examination of military officers' careers, for example, indicates that good performance is necessary to get an individual into the ranks of the "promotables," but as an officer's career progresses, visibility becomes the predominant influence on promotion (Moore & Trout, 1978). The final feature of power-generating job activities—relevance—refers to how central the activity is to the larger organizational picture. Organizations have different critical needs at different points in time (Hinings, Hickson, Pennings, & Scheck, 1974). In the early phases of industrialization, production functions were key. Once established, companies' capital investments had to be managed, and finance functions became crucial. Some theorists think that the changing composition and demands of the work force may make personnel the important function, beginning in the 1980s. In any event, certain functions in organizations receive a lion's share of attention. People who make visible, innovative contributions in these key functions stand a much better chance of gaining further resources and support, because their activities are perceived as critical to the life of the organization.

The second source of power, political alliances, extends in three directions: up, down, and sideways. Connections upward in the organization are connections with one's boss or other established powers in the hierarchy. These higher-ups help in a variety of ways: they can give advice on career planning and on the political realities of the organization, they may give one access to resources not usually available, they may suggest the employee for special tasks or promotions, and may even provide moral support and encouragement (Turner, 1960; Kanter, 1977).

Connections sideways, with peers, are also important: they, too, can give moral support. Old-timers can give newcomers tips on how to do the job. The peer grapevine can carry important messages faster than formal channels. And people can begin to build a reputation with peers for good work, which gains them recognition from elsewhere in the organization.

Connections downward with subordinates increase power by relieving the boss of many daily pressures, freeing him or her to concentrate on potentially more important or central tasks (Levenson, 1961). Indeed, empowered and innovative subordinates can create the most successful bosses (see Social Focus 18.3). They give the boss logistical support, represent his or her view to other factions or levels in the organization, and bring back important pieces of information. Meanwhile the boss continues to build the subordinates' skill, expertise, and visibility, sending them off to better positions elsewhere in the organization. Powerful bosses build powerful subordinates and vice versa. In this sense it is not simply an accident that in large corporations certain cohorts and managers' teams produce a disproportionate share of all top leaders in the corporation (Stein, 1979a).

As with opportunity, the amount of power a person has from job activities and alliances has effects on behavior. Powerful and powerless employees differ strikingly from one another. The difference can be seen, first, in their exercise of authority. There is a tendency for different leadership styles (or perceptions of leadership styles—it is often difficult to distinguish these in the research) to develop in more powerful versus less powerful locations. As was noted in Chapter 14, the more powerful seem to be associated with persuasive methods, the less powerful with more coercive methods. This has to do in part with degree of anticipated resistance (Goodstadt & Kipnis, 1970), which is much lower for the more powerful, especially because aggression and hostility tend to be expressed toward the more powerless and inhibited for the more powerful (Thibaut & Riecken, 1955).

Second, closeness of supervision tends to be inversely related to power; that is, it goes up as power decreases (Kanter, 1977). Similarly, the tendency to invoke rules and focus on procedures rather than results also seems to increase with decreasing power (Crozier, 1964; Dalton, 1959). Powerless bosses can drive their

SOCIAL FOCUS 18.3
Empowered Sales Teams Are More Effective

What type of management style leads to the most effective sales teams? This question was addressed in 1966 by three researchers at the University of Michigan, Jerald G. Bachman, Clagett G. Smith, and Jonathan A. Slesinger. Their answer (based on their research) was a bit surprising: managers who provide their salesmen with the opportunity to control their own jobs become the leaders of the most effective sales teams.

This conclusion was based on the results of a survey of 656 salesmen in 36 branch offices of a service organization. The survey found that the most effective offices—the ones with the highest levels of satisfaction and performance (sales)—were characterized by a "high control syndrome." This term describes a situation in which both the manager and the members of the sales force feel that they have a high degree of control over their jobs.

This finding seems to be a contradiction of terms. How can both boss and subordinates feel in control of the situation? The answer is simple. The bosses *empower* their employees; they give them the room to make decisions about how to carry out their jobs. Empowering means supporting, consulting, and giving advice to employees, not trying to control them. Instead of pulling rank, handing out punishment, or even withholding rewards, empowering managers rely on their expertise and high esteem in the office to motivate high performance from the sales force. And according to the study, this type of management style is associated with the most effective offices.

---

subordinates crazy by demanding perfection in picayune details and by constantly peering over their shoulders while they work.

Willingness to delegate also tends to rise with increasing power—in part, of course, as a function of the task overload often associated with more powerful positions. This is consistent with studies showing that there is a greater propensity for the use of participative methods at higher oganizational levels (Heller & Yukl, 1969; Jaco & Vroom, 1977). In short, powerless bosses don't feel they can trust their subordinates to do anything right, while powerful bosses turn over ever more challenging tasks to their people. And high-power bosses reward their people for excellence, whereas lower-power bosses reward mediocrity (Hetzler, 1955).

As a result, work-group morale is higher under higher-power bosses, and employees report active preferences for working for more powerful people (Roussell, 1974; Kanter, 1977). Thus powerful people can attract the most talented subordinates and a cycle of advantage for the powerful is set in motion.

It's easy to see why workers prefer powerful bosses; the picture of powerless bosses is hardly appealing. But it would be too simple to merely condemn them. After all, their behavior may also be a direct response to their situations. Chances are they are themselves in a "stuck" position and do not receive the kinds of contacts and support they need to be more effective. What may be needed, therefore, is an examination and redesign of the powerless person's job. Of course, this is not to say that changing the job can make everyone into a more powerful, desirable boss. There are individual abilities and inabilities at work, too; not everyone can be first-rate at every kind of job. But generally (as we saw in the section on commitment), organizational and structural features have a bigger impact on behavior than do individual traits or characteristics.

In Lordstown, for example, first-line supervisors (the people directly in charge of the line workers) were in powerless positions. On the one hand, they were supposed to tell the workers what to do, monitor their work, and issue reprimands if things went wrong. So the supervisors were supposed to exercise authority over the workers. But at the same time supervisors were given very little real authority to work with. They could not allocate resources or get new materials their people needed. They could not arrange the work schedules or control wages. They had little contact and no clout with higher management where decisions were made about the future of the plant or about how it was to be run. And when decisions or changes were made, the supervisors were often the last to know; the line workers heard about changes through the grapevine, which was very efficient, whereas the supervisors had to wait for the official communication channels to operate. In sum, the first-line supervisors were given orders, which they were in turn supposed to impose on the line workers, but they could not alter or affect the orders. It is little wonder the supervisors were regarded by line workers as impotent and treated with indifference or even hostility when they issued orders. The supervisors in turn would clamp down with harsh disciplinary measures—a classic response in powerless bosses and one that clearly exacerbated an already tense situation.

The effects of being in less powerful locations, then, cascade downward (Crozier, 1964). As one study put it, a superior's reinforcing behavior is a function of reinforcements received (Hinton & Barrow, 1975); a leader's own situation defines the situations the leader is likely to create for others. To some extent, then, these findings can lead to the conclusion that structural *powerlessness*, rather than power, can "corrupt" (Kanter, 1977, 1979b).

Thus, the lack of commitment of the Lordstown auto workers and their antagonistic feelings toward the company may have been associated with their lack of opportunity and power. There was no opportunity in their job. There was no possibility of formal advancement. There was also no possibility of the job growing over time—of its including "a sequence of more important problems or challenges." The workers, then, were in low-opportunity jobs and showed some of the classic responses—disengagement from work, peer orientation, and resistance, including sabotage. They also had no power—they had no control over how resources were to be allocated, they could not get access to the people who did have power, and they received no information about how or why decisions were made the way they were. And they were supervised by largely powerless bosses. But what could be done about it? Cars still have to be built, and no one has yet found a faster way to do that than the assembly line. Yet the people working on the line found it intolerable and the rift between management and labor was widening daily. It seemed a long way off to a more humanized work environment and a greater sense of commitment and community spanning across employees.

Yet in the 1970s General Motors did decide to learn the lessons of Lordstown and its own accumulated employee research (Dowling, 1975). The world's largest manufacturing company decided to improve its effectiveness by improving the quality of its work life. To a remarkable degree, at the Tarrytown, New York, auto plant, something *was* done that had a profound effect on everyone who worked there. In the next and final section of this chapter, we will take a look at the changes that made the auto plant more effective in its use of its human resources.

ORGANIZATIONAL CHANGE: WORK IMPROVEMENTS IN THE AUTO FACTORY

In the 1960s Tarrytown was much like Lordstown—angry workers, thousand of grievances on file, management feeling under attack and reacting by "clamping down" (Guest, 1979)—the same old story.

But in April 1971, Tarrytown faced a serious threat of being shut down. The plant manager decided things had to change. He approached the union to say he wanted to create a new style of management in the plant, and that if the union would work with him, he would see that his managers cooperated with the new way of doing things.

Suspicious at first, the union gradually came to believe that the manager meant what he said. In fact, when two departments, hard trim and soft trim, were about to be reorganized, the production supervisors—who knew top management was trying to create a new approach—suggested that the workers be involved in designing the new departments. The idea was a shock to many. Usually departments were designed by technical specialists and workers were supposed to just fit into place, once the jobs were designed for them. But this time supervisors, supported by the top, took the plans to the workers and asked for their input. And they got it. The workers made hundreds of suggestions, many of which were adopted.

This began an effort to expand communication between management and workers more broadly. People were specially trained to run courses for everyone in the plant. The purposes of the courses were to give everyone more information about the financial and other demands placed on the plant, and about projected plans to meet these demands; to invite feedback and suggestions from participants on all aspects of the plant's functioning; and to give everyone training and experience in problem solving in communicating constructively across groups.

It took a lot of time before people in both labor and management started to believe that there were no ulterior motives, but gradually the results began to speak for themselves. Countless valuable ideas were generated and put into action by employees. Problems that arose on the floor, which would have grown into major problems in the old days, were handled cooperatively on the spot. Absenteeism dropped from $7^{1}/_{4}$ percent to 2 percent; grievances fell from 2000 to 32. And the union reported that quality performance at Tarrytown went from one of the worst to one of the best among the 18 plants in the division. But the main payoff, as far as the people who worked there was concerned, was that workers had become involved in the process of controlling their own work.

It is important to realize that in this change effort the *process* was critical. The change efforts kept the means consistent with the ends. The goal was to empower line workers. Instead of management devising a scheme to empower workers—which would actually keep the controls firmly in management's hands—workers were involved in the change efforts from the beginning. This involvement has many important effects:

- It gives workers more information about the current state and long-range goals of the company.
- Workers can make expert input into the change efforts involving the areas they know best—the design of work on the line.
- It allows informal interaction between management and labor. (Recall the importance of communion discussed at the beginning of the chapter.)
- Workers are more fully informed about changes

long before they go into effect; start-up time and coordination problems are greatly decreased.

- Workers learn new skills as they research and design new options.
- Workers have a genuine voice in shaping their work; people have more interest and pride in seeing a system work that they have built themselves.
- Management acquires a new respect for rank-and-file workers; they are subsequently less likely to resort to punitive control and more likely to assume that if things are going wrong, there is a good reason, which needs to be found and corrected.

In all of these ways, then, the actions at Tarrytown created more opportunity, power, and commitment for labor and management alike, as they worked together to help the plant survive and grow.

These changes increased opportunity on the job. Workers had a chance to learn new skills, apply old skills in new ways, and tackle a sequence of problems and challenges. Their jobs were moving, and the workers began to show the signs of the moving: work attachment increased, confidence in their own ability rose, they had an active problem-solving orientation, and became interested in the functioning of the organization as a whole.

The changes also increased workers' power. They had access and control over resources, obtained vastly greater amounts of information about their functions and the company as a whole, and were given the full support of management in their efforts. The task facing them could not possibly have been more relevant, since it was nothing less than the survival of the plant that was at stake. Workers had full discretion; that is, no solutions were ruled out or preformulated. New ideas were what were sought; the old, routine ways of doing business had failed. And their action gained recognition, from peers, from management, and from the larger corporation. These lines of input and task characteristics all accord with what were outlined as sources of power in a job.

Finally, the shared information, the demands for some sacrifice in the form of wage restrictions, the camaraderies, the reality of shared purpose and effort—all of these features of the change process built commitment in a way not possible in the factory as it had been.

The story does not end here, of course. It is only the beginning. The changes made have to be carried on. The assembly line still remains a boring, if efficient, way to work; it is waiting for someone to come up with a better idea. The exciting aspect of Tarrytown is that now more people than ever before are willing and able to give creative thought to critical problems on the job, because they know their ideas will be heard and acted on.

Will these attempts spread to other plants and industries? Will they be successful? It is difficult to say. Good ideas are not always adopted, even when their benefits are clear, because of the nature of modern organizations (Walton, 1975).

Deliberate, planned organizational change is a complicated subject, matching the complexity of organizations themselves (Bennis, Benne, Chin, & Corey, 1976). Even the most powerful leaders can rarely dictate immediate change; there are too many parts and too many people, interwoven in complex ways and with material and psychic investments in past ways of operating to make planned change simple. Furthermore, organizations consist of both a formal, official, designed component (for example, the array of officials, tasks, and chains of command linking them) and an informal or spontaneous component (the relationships that spring up between people, their unofficial understandings about how they *really* operate, irrespective of the "rules"). Whatever is said officially, on the formal side, sufficient power may rest in the informal arrangements to permit resistance to change.

Or sometimes planned change in formal structures by decision makers, unaware of the importance of the members' own traditions of doing the tasks, can backfire, reducing effectiveness because of disruptions in the hidden structures that had produced success in the past. And if significant stakeholders are not included in change decisions, they sometimes undercut the effort.

The Tarrytown example, however, shows that the ideas about commitment, group composition, opportunity, and power presented here have a bearing on the process of organizational change in at least two ways. First, they can provide a normative model—a vision of a more ideal organization with enhanced opportunity and more empowered members. Second, they can offer some guideposts on the route to the ideal, by indicating that change will be facilitated when the *process* of introducing the change opens opportunities (thereby awakening motivation and commitment) and provides power to the people who have to accept or live with the change, so that they not only *feel* involved but also help design the change to take account of their own circumstances.

These lessons are being applied in more and more organizations concerned with improving their own effectiveness on both monetary and human indicators (Hackman & Suttle, 1977). As we have seen, the auto companies are among them. To its credit, General Motors not only learned from the experiences at Lords-

town, but as we saw in Tarrytown, has gone on to develop pioneering union-management organization change efforts resembling those at Volvo and Saab-Scania in Sweden (Gyllenhammer, 1977), Harman Industries in Tennessee (Zwerdling, 1980), and the Gaines Pet Food Plant (Zwerdling, 1980), and has also broken new ground in reducing worker alienation.

At least one "sleeping giant"—a troubled auto company—is waking up to new realities. For General Motors, quality of work life for employees is an essential part of its plan to improve effectiveness in the 1980s. And now these change efforts are models for other organizations. Creating more opportunity to grow on the job and empowering people by connecting them to other people, information, and resources—these are changes that allow people to become committed to their organizations and to channel their energy into affecting and improving them. Both individual members and the organization as a whole become more effective and creative in dealing with problems. Finding concrete ways to enlarge opportunity and increase power on the job is one of the great challenges for organizational specialists, social scientists, workers and management alike, as we move ahead toward a more productive, equitable, and meaningful vision of life at work.

SUMMARY

The focus of this chapter is on a key element of organizational effectiveness: unlocking the energy of the people who work in organizations. The auto industry is used as an example of one set of organizations which has tried to institute new human resource management techniques.

The first section of the chapter examines commitment mechanisms which draw people into organizations and hold them there. Organizational structures have more influence on commitment than individual personalities do. People are most likely to be attracted to and retained by organizations when they sense that they are "getting somewhere" within it. Organizations employ one or more of the following socialization processes in engendering commitment: sacrifice, investment, renunciation, communion, mortification, and transcendence.

The second section highlights the problems of people who historically have not been sought for powerful roles in organizations. Women and minorities are new on the scene. Some of the difficulties they experience are due solely to their scarcity. Skewed social composition produces certain effects, regardless of the particular features which make the numerically scarce group "different." Thus, the scarce experience increased status incongruence, scapegoating, visibility, isolation and less likelihood of sponsorship whether they are females in a male organization, males in a female organization, blacks in a white organization, whites in a black organization, and so on. There are also differences between groups in communication style which can unintentionally produce discomfort and miscommunication. Both scarcity and unfamiliarity can be overcome through balancing numbers and increasing knowledge of cultural differences. In these ways, historically excluded groups can also become active contributors to and shapers of organizations.

The next section explores the impact on behavior of two structural features of organizations: opportunity and power. Opportunity is defined as the chance for increased learning, challenge and impact on the job, as well as for formal advancement. Amount of opportunity in a job affects the people who hold it, high opportunity producing "movers" and low opportunity producing the "stuck." The moving and the stuck differ in aspirations, belief in their own ability, work attachment, allegiances, and response to difficulties. Each of these in turn affects the amount of energy the individual puts into his or her job. Power is the second structural feature. Power comes through job activities and alliances. The discretion, visibility, and relevance of job activities determine power, as do alliances up, down, and sidewise in the organization. As with opportunity, power shapes behavior. To have people contributing their most to the organization, their jobs must be structured to maximize opportunity and power.

Finally, the chapter closes with a close-up look at an attempt to change organizational structure in the auto industry. The Tarrytown project gives living proof of the tremendous impact a creative, sincere, and concerted effort to create change can have within even a very rough industry. It stands as a challenge to organizations' development in the future: to find innovative and effective means to promote rather than frustrate the energy of the millions of people who live and work in organizations every day.

SUGGESTED READINGS

Haas, A. Male and female spoken language differences: Stereotypes and evidence. *Psychological Bulletin*, 1979, *86*, 616–626.

Kanter, R. M. *Men and women of the corporation.* New York: Basic Books, 1977.

Mitchell, T. R. *People in organizations: Understanding their behavior.* New York: McGraw-Hill, 1978.

19

SOCIAL PROBLEM SOLVING AND SOCIAL CHANGE

- Introduction
- Stages in the Policy Process
- The Social-Engineering Approach to Social Change
- Utilizing Research in Policy Decisions: Assumptions versus Reality
- Recent Directions and Alternatives
- Summary

INTRODUCTION

Domestic violence is not a pleasant topic. The study of wife abuse and child abuse engenders in most people feelings of disgust and, occasionally, of strange fascination. The phenomenon of husbands beating their wives is so at variance with people's assumptions about appropriate behavior in the American family that it appears to demand some kind of explanation. In recent years, as the evidence on its incidence has grown, a number of explanations have been offered, ranging from those that essentially blame the beaten wife for her own problem to those that find the causes of such violence in outmoded and stereotyped sex roles and antiquated legal and institutional practices that condone such behavior.

What have social scientists had to say about this issue? How objective or selective have been their approaches to the problem? What role does social research and psychological theory play in the process of determining policies for dealing with such problems? What role should it play? These are some of the issues to be addressed.

This chapter differs from the others in at least two major respects: the scale of the problems considered to which social research may be applied, and the balance between enthusiasm and optimism for applying social research, on the one hand, and sobering considerations about the limits and constraints for responsible application, on the other. The chapter will deal with domestic violence as an illustration of several general points about large-scale social problems that receive attention on a national level. The emphasis will be not on the direct application of research on a local or immediate-case basis but rather on social problems as they occur on a nationwide basis. In the case of domestic violence, attention will concentrate not on the giving of help in individual cases but rather on how a society deals with the widespread occurrence of this problem.

This means looking at social problems at a different level of aggregation, as well as from a different level of analysis. This viewpoint is a movement away from the clinical origin of applied social psychology, as well as away from the interpersonal and small-group level of analysis that is social psychology's historic tradition. It involves looking at social problems from the level of the nation as a whole, as well as attempts to formulate national policies to treat those problems. This perspective is necessary—as a complement to, and not a replacement for, more traditional social-psychological perspectives—because as particular social problems increase in incidence, size, and scale, there usually also arise qualitatively different issues that are not relevant at the smaller group or local level. And because all psychologists—even social psychologists—are accustomed to looking at issues at the latter level, it is easy to overlook many of the national-level issues that have powerful effects on how successful social scientists can be in trying to alleviate particular social problems.

Just as engineering draws upon physics and medicine upon biology, social scientists concerned with application have relied upon basic theoretical concepts and proven methodological techniques. Many contributions of psychology and social research to the betterment of society can be cited—for example, consumer research, public-opinion polling, management consulting and organizational development, programmed learning instruction, and research on how humans interact with machines, to mention just a few. The promise that professional knowledge in social psychology would be useful in solving social problems has moti-

---

This chapter is written by Stephen D. Nelson and Nathan Caplan.

vated people to enter these professions, and has attracted large-scale investment in research by the government. In 1978 a National Academy of Sciences report estimated that the government spends $2–3 billion annually on social science research. That represents a considerable investment, which has until recently grown steadily. (As a journalist once observed, however, this amount is about the size of a cost overrun on a single major weapons system for the Department of Defense.) In 1974 the General Accounting Office found that the amount of money spent on federally funded program evaluations alone was $146 million. This amount represented a 500 percent increase in such expenditures over the period from 1969 to 1974. Estimates for the amount of federally funded evaluation studies in 1980 are in the $400–500 million range.

Yet spending such funds does not automatically bring about social science knowledge that is demonstrably usable in social problem solving. Indeed, the usefulness of social knowledge has emerged as an issue of considerable concern and controversy in recent years, largely because of this uncertain relation between advancements in the social sciences and progress in resolving social problems. A number of blue-ribbon committees and official study groups investigated the problem during the 1970s. In addition, research on social science utilization also emerged as a research area in its own right, and focused its attention on a broad range of application-related issues.

Consequently, given the current state of social scientists' understanding, it would be presumptuous to offer a set of prescriptive directions for transferring social knowledge into social action. Nevertheless, in view of the seriousness of the many problems facing the United States in the last two decades, the social and behavioral sciences have an obligation to try to bring their knowledge and expertise to bear upon the ills that beset society, if not out of a sense of duty and citizenship, then for a more pragmatic reason: in times of increasing demands upon tight governmental budgets, the society will not continue to provide resources to activities that are not seen as having some societal relevance and payoff. In addition, more is involved than a threat to the funding of application-oriented research—if even it cannot be linked to social progress, then basic research will appear even more artificial.

This chapter, divided into four main sections, will outline ways of using social science knowledge in the solution of large-scale social problems. It will emphasize the relationship between social science knowledge and governmental policy. The first segment of the chapter will discuss the stages involved in formulating and implementing government policies. As will be seen, the way problems are defined is a particularly important stage, yet problem definition is a highly political and only partially objective process. In the second section, the government's traditional way of implementing social change will be described. Called the "social engineering approach," this method operates from the top down and has fallen far short of complete success. The third section focuses on assumptions about (or conceptualizations of) when scientific knowledge is used. By implication, these conceptualizations offer important insights into why social science information has all too frequently been ignored.

Following this, a few of the more recent directions that social science knowledge about social problems has been taking will be discussed, including the following:

- A social systems approach, dealing with a social problem on its own terms, rather than attempting to impose one's disciplinary blinders on it
- Closely related to the above, the attempt to understand social problems in their entirety, from a more systemic, holistic viewpoint, rather than concentrating on only a single dimension of the problem and proposing piecemeal solutions
- A number of more directly policy-relevant roles and activities for the social sciences that are emerging, including program evaluation, social indicators, impact assessments, and futures research and forecasting

- A model problem-solving system for reducing domestic violence, the focal social problem considered throughout this chapter.

In order to understand these issues in perspective, it is necessary to review very briefly some of the historical background of social science's involvement in social-problem-related issues, especially in relation to government involvement with such issues.

Early Efforts at Applying Social Science Knowledge

During World Wars I and II extensive use was made of psychological findings, largely in the areas of testing and training. By World War II, the range of applications was broad and seemed to illustrate the potential usefulness of psychology. These applications and some of the research in prejudice, leadership, and specifically, the area of group dynamics, with its emphasis on small sets of individuals, appeared to fulfill the predictions of European psychologists such as Lazarsfeld and Lewin, who escaped to the United States before World War II.

The tight relation assumed to exist between scientific and social progress was exemplified by Lewin's well-known mandates: "No research without action and no action without research," and "Nothing is more practical than a good theory." Lewin's and his colleagues' work on the consequences of democratic, authoritarian, and laissez-faire leadership styles (Lippitt & White, 1947), and Adorno's and his colleagues' work on the authoritarian personality at the root of prejudice, appeared at the time to exemplify the usefulness of psychological research to social issues. (See also Social Focus 1.2 in Chapter 1.) Such work carried with it the message that reform-minded social scientists could merge their scientific and social concerns. For example, the social-action implications of sensitivity training (also called T-groups), which grew out of small-group research by Lewin's followers, were viewed by

practitioners as being equivalent in importance for the social sciences to the atomic bomb in physics (Back, 1978). In his study of the sensitivity training movement, Back concluded that the discoveries did not live up to these grandiose expectations. While there are undoubtedly some who would argue that sensitivity training was not given a real chance, few if any would today claim its importance was analogous to the development of the atomic bomb.

The need to reconsider assumptions about social change and the role of psychology came about largely as a result of increased awareness of the seriousness of social problems in the 1960s, and as a result of the lessons from the legislative outpourings of the mid-1960s Great Society programs initiated in the Johnson administration. Psychologists' concerns became more socially relevant, and at the same time, many large-scale programs were launched to deal with pressing social problems.

The actual relationship between the activities of reform-minded social scientists, on the one hand, and the success (or lack of it) of policies, programs, and treatment strategies designed to alleviate social problems, on the other, is not really clear. That is, it is not clear that professional knowledge of psychology or sociology was really implemented or actually tested. Nor is it really clear that the programs succeeded or failed. But people react to what they perceive, and one of the outcomes of the Great Society era was the belief that social science had been put to the test and had failed. (A mid-1970s joke went, "Did you hear about the outcome of the War on Poverty? Poverty won.") True or not, it would be fair to say that some commonsense notions of social change were experimented with and failed to produce positive results. Surely, the process of social change was not obvious and at a minimum was different from what one would deduce from theory or research. Apparently, good intentions combined with some social science advice were not a sufficient basis for national programs.

Regardless of how one interprets the outcome of the Great Society programs, there is no doubt that practitioners and applied researchers benefited from the experience. Several major lessons were learned: program evaluation (that is, the research-based evaluation of ameliorative programs) was essential as a tool for measuring effects, and more careful research planning and sophisticated evaluation techniques needed to be developed and applied; techniques needed to be developed to produce, disseminate, and increase the utilization of socially relevant information; and there was an urgent need to reconsider the assumptions underlying attempts at social change. The state of the art with respect to each of these related areas of concern is about the same: there is increasing awareness of difficulties that had not been considered in the overly simplified notions of change underlying the initial ideology that social science progress and social action should be linked. In short, the experiences of the 1960s and early 1970s provided a lesson in the realities of the social and political environments in which knowledge is used.

In order to begin to appreciate some of the ways in which earlier assumptions were either inadequate or misleading, it may be useful to turn next to a brief description of the public policy process and a discussion of the roles that social research plays in it.

STAGES IN THE POLICY PROCESS

Below is a figure depicting five stages in the process by which policies for social problems may be decided and acted upon. Although it is vastly oversimplified, and although there are a number of other ways of conceptualizing the sequences of events, this model is useful in discussing social research's role in the process.

Note that the point at which the policy intended to address the problem is decided upon is Stage 3, after which the intervention programs designed to alleviate the problem are implemented. This, in turn, is followed by some sort of evaluation or assessment, whether formal or informal, of the success of the program. Finally, there usually is some sort of feedback process by which the evaluation or assessment is then fed back into the previous stages to rethink the adequacy of the entire approach to the problem. (Actually, the feedback loops and mutual influences between the various stages are far more complex and interrelated, and this is indicated by the top set of arrows.) The policy process is iterative, meaning that the cycle of these stages is repeated over and over again in actual practice. The process may not loop all the way back to Stage 1, but may instead recycle again beginning only at Stage 2 or, more commonly, Stage 3.

Policy decisions, however, depend heavily on at least two prior stages: first, whether a set of conditions becomes identified as a social problem worthy of recognition and action at all, called *problem identification;* and second, the way in which that set of conditions becomes defined, or what is identified as the very nature of the problem, called *problem definition.* This discussion will concentrate primarily on the problem definition stage, because of its central role in determining the nature of the policy or program selected to address the social problem. Although problem identification precedes problem definition, both logically and in actual fact, discussion of it will be postponed until later, following the discussion of problem definition. The issue of domestic violence is used to illustrate a number of general points that apply to a wide range of social problems.

Domestic violence received little attention from writers or researchers prior to the 1970s.

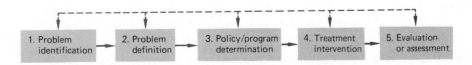

Traditionally psychiatrists and others blamed the victims of wife-abuse for their plight. More recently feminists have placed the blame on pornography and other factors external to the individual. Specifying the cause of the problem has important implications for how best to solve the problem.

In fact, the extent of the problem was largely unrecognized until brought to the attention of the public by members of the women's movement, particularly antirape activists.

The research to date on domestic violence can be divided for conceptual purposes into three categories: that which attempts to document the scope of the problem—that is, estimate its incidence in a community, a segment of society, or the population at large; that which attempts to explain it—that is, pinpoint its causes, usually by focusing on characteristics of the victim, the abuser, or one or more aspects of the social system; and that which attempts to develop or improve models for intervention and prevention through the development of therapeutic programs and improved services for victims, and so forth. (Notice that these three categories closely parallel the first

three stages of the policy process model described above.)

Domestic violence is frequently called "the hidden crime" because it takes place in the home and because it is vastly underreported to authorities. Most statistics on its incidence are preceded by the statement that the figures are almost certainly lower than the actual occurrence of abuse. A 1968 Harris poll of the attitudes of adult Americans toward violence was one of the early indications of the extent to which they approve the use of force on each other (Stark & McEvoy, 1970). (Twenty percent of those surveyed in the general population approved of hitting a spouse "on appropriate occasions"; among the college educated, the figure was 25 percent.) This survey, however, did not attempt to estimate the actual amount of violence among spouses. In a nationwide sample, Straus (1977) surveyed over 2000 families and discovered that among 3.8 percent of couples, violence severe enough to be considered a beating had occurred in the previous year. He estimates that for 60–70 percent of American couples at least one violent incident will occur during the course of marriage.

Problem Definition and Its Importance

Problem-defining activities are important because of their crucial role in the policy formulation process. As can be seen from the five stages above, problem definition largely determines the nature of the subsequent stages in the process—what is done about the problem, and what attempts will be made at remediation, or even whether such attempts will be made—by suggesting both the focuses and the techniques of intervention and by ruling out alternative possibilities.

Problem definitions are based on assumptions about the causes of the problem and where they lie. If the causes of delinquency, for example, are defined in person-centered terms (for example, inability to delay gratification, or incomplete sexual identity), then it would be logical to initiate person-change treatment techniques and intervention strategies to deal with the problem. Where person-centered interpretations provide the foundation on which corrective intervention is based, little need be done about external factors, since they would presumably be of lesser or no causal significance.

On the other hand, if explanations are situation-centered—for example, if delinquency is interpreted as the substitution of extralegal paths for already preempted, conventionally approved pathways for achieving socially valued goals, then efforts toward corrective treatment would logically have a system-change orientation. Efforts would be launched to create suitable opportunities for success and achievement along conventional lines; thus, existing physical, social, or economic arrangements, not individual psyches, would be the targets for change.

The importance of this distinction between personal and situational causation has been well documented in social-psychological research and theory on causal attribution (see Chapter 6), and its decisive role in determining public or official response to social problems has been well illustrated (Caplan & Nelson, 1973; Mills, 1959; Ryan, 1971; Warren, 1971; and Gregg, Preston, Geist, & Caplan, 1979.) Gregg and his colleagues (Gregg et al., 1979) have used the continuum depicted in Figure 19.1 below to illustrate the range of potential causal attributions for social problems.

The way a problem is defined determines not only what is done about it, but also what is not done—or what apparently need not be done. If matrifocal family structure is argued to be the basis for deviancy, nonachievement, and high unemployment, then opportunity structure, discriminatory hiring practices, and other system defects would appear less blameworthy as the causes of poverty. Likewise, if it is argued that the use of nonstandard speech interferes with the ability to mediate thought and consequently is the cause of poor performance on formal academic tasks, then such a person-centered explanation removes pressure for structural and institutional changes in the educational system to raise the educational levels of persons from "linguistically deficient" backgrounds.

FIGURE 19.1
Intrapsychic and Social Influences on Behavior.
From Gregg et al., 1979, p. 32

Psyche ◄───────		─────Person─────		─────► Society	
(Psycho-dynamic and physio-logical-level factors)	Cognitive and emotional processes	Traits and beliefs	Family, friends and work	Organi-zations and institutions	(Political and economic system level factors)

Whether the social problem to be attacked is delinquency, mental health, drug abuse, unemployment, ghetto riots, or whatever, the significance of the defining process is the same: the action (or lack of action) taken will depend largely on whether causes are seen as residing within individuals or in the environment.

The idea that the female victim of assault is somehow to blame for her situation appears in more or less subtle form throughout the literature on domestic violence. Ryan (1971) describes the process of blaming the victim, which focuses the source of a problem within the individual: although societal influences may be acknowledged, "the stigma, the defect, the fatal difference . . . is still located within the victim, inside his skin" (pp. 6–7). It is clear from the tiresome frequency with which advocates for battered women have found it necessary to answer the questions "Why does she stay, if she doesn't like it?" and "What did she do to provoke him?" that the tendency to blame the victim is widespread. It should therefore be no surprise to see theories that focus on personality traits of victims appearing in the domestic violence literature and research.

An early, almost classic example of victim blame occurs in "The Wifebeater's Wife" (Snell, Rosenwald, & Robey, 1964). In this study three psychiatrists, whose task was to do psychiatric evaluations of men charged with wife assault in a middle-class community, discovered that the wives were much more amenable to therapy than their husbands. Accordingly, the doctors decided to interview and study the women instead. The result of their investigation was a description of a family structure in which the woman was viewed as "castrating" and "masochistic," and the man "passive." Their "periodic role reversal," during which the husband assaulted the wife, was seen as a means of holding the family together, providing a way for the husband to assert himself as a male and alleviating the wife's feelings of guilt by punishing her for unfeminine behavior.

Social scientists who have turned their attention to family violence have often suggested that women's verbal behavior provokes assault (Gelles, 1972). Some have even asserted that women are in general more verbally skilled than men, and that physical assault may be the only recourse on the part of the beleaguered male (Goode, 1971; Steinmetz, 1978).

Problem definitions, once legitimated and acted upon, tend to become permanent, irrespective of their validity. Once in effect, they resist replacement by other definitions. Program administrators and professional change agents develop a vested interest in maintaining established definitions, since their very jobs, status, power, and the employment of subordinates may depend on those definitions being accepted as correct. If intervention fails, the problem definition and the delivery system are seldom held responsible. Instead, responsibility for failure may be avoided by locating blame in the target group and by interpreting that failure as a further sign of the seriousness of the "pathology" being dealt with.

Also, to the extent that a problem definition conforms to and reinforces dominant cultural myths and clichés (for example, Horatio Alger), as most definitions must do in order to become widely accepted, its change or replacement will be stubbornly resisted. Furthermore, people tend to conform to public definitions and expectations; even if there are doubts regarding their accuracy, they at least provide people with a publicly defined role and definite image of what they are and what is expected of them. Still further, of course, many groups have economic and political interests in seeing that certain definitions are accepted over others (for example, the business community with regard to the causes of unemployment). In the context of such pressures, an invalid person-centered problem definition often has its most pernicious effect: it can convince the target population of its blameworthiness as alleged.

Thus, problem definitions take on a life of their own; they set in motion a variety of social-psychological forces that give them important functional significance. Consequently, to question established definitions is to challenge important institutions and belief systems that have their origins in those definitions.

It is increasingly common for at least some attention to be given to the historic inequality between the sexes as a factor in domestic violence (Straus, 1977). It has remained for feminists both in and out of academia, however, to begin to delineate just how the cultural supports for traditional sex roles and other cherished institutions of society contribute to the problem of wife beating. Dobash and Dobash (1978) have pointed out that women's economic dependence on men requires constant negotiation for the necessities of everyday life. When such negotiation is not agreeable to the husband, it can be labeled "nagging" and may be considered to justify the use of violence. Their study of 109 battered women in Scotland examined the response of medical, legal, judicial, and social service agencies to the problem. They concluded that there was a strong victim-blame bias in these institutions, and that in many cases service providers either did not recognize the problem at all or were unresponsive to it. In this country, Pagelow (1977) surveyed numerous service providers in the state of California, from welfare workers to judges, and discovered similar attitudes. She cites "institutional response" as one of the three crucial variables that determine whether a battered woman remains in a violent marriage or escapes from it.

Intervention and Prevention

Beginning with Pizzey (1974), founder of the shelter movement in England, much of the literature on the treatment of domestic violence has been developed by grass-roots workers concerned with providing direct services to battered women. Consequently, there is a body of material—including training manuals on crisis intervention for abused women (Resnik, 1976;

Cooper, 1976) and guidelines for starting a local task force on spouse abuse—that is directed mainly at low-budget, nontraditional organizations interested in trying to provide women with alternatives to violence. These kinds of practical, "how-to" pamphlets and the growing number of accounts of the development of shelters for battered women in various communities represent the trial-and-error efforts of many dedicated workers who were committed to helping women before the issue of wife beating received much attention from the media.

Practitioner-scholars (for example, Walker, 1979) have contributed theories such as "learned helplessness" that have much practical importance for other workers in the field. Pointing to studies of animals that are physically restrained or punished in a dangerous situation until they learn not to respond even when nonresponse may be life threatening, she theorizes that battered women face a similar no-win situation. Therefore, the helping person may have to repeatedly "walk the victim through" the options available to her, until the battered woman begins to believe again that she can make choices.

Almost absent from the literature has been any consideration of treatment or intervention with the batterer. This is undoubtedly at least partially due to the general unwillingness of batterers to admit that they have a problem, much less seek treatment, as well as to the fact that therapists have only very recently begun to consider treatment modalities for violent men.

Prevention of domestic violence, although of the utmost importance, is another area that has received little consideration, no doubt due to the complexity of the subject and the priority of helping those in immediate danger. While many feminists and some social scientists have pointed to the necessity of eradicating sex-role stereotypes if battering is to end, such fundamental social change is more easily discussed than realized. Certainly at this stage of social science knowledge it must be noted that early intervention is the closest thing to prevention that is available.

Theorists and practitioners (Pagelow, 1977; Walker, 1979) are pointing increasingly to violence as learned behavior passed on from generation to generation; in this light, early intervention will probably assume increasing importance as a means of circumventing the learning of violent behavior by children who observe their parents.

The development of public policy toward domestic violence is currently at a critical stage. Facilitated by women's rights activists, research and theoretical attention to the problem are growing, and will undoubtedly produce strategies to deal with this increasingly visible problem. But unless the problem definitions advanced now are consonant with the real causes of the problem and the needs of victims, research and the interventions that flow from it may do more harm than good. "The Wifebeater's Wife," for instance, focusing on the personal pathology of the woman, suggests solutions that would alter the behavior of the victim, not the assailant, because it defines the problem as being victim precipitated. The traditional legal institution of marriage and women's relatively powerless economic and cultural position in it are ignored, as is the most elementary understanding of the differences in physical size and strength of most women and men. Even more recent studies that locate the problem within the psychodynamics of the marriage often fail to address the issue of whether battered women have economic alternatives to dependency on a violent husband. Causal attribution is thus sought in character traits of the victims themselves.

If domestic violence is studied in isolation from cultural and economic institutions that contribute to, excuse, and even condone it, victims will be twice traumatized—first within the home and second, when dealing with agencies or researchers whose purported goal is to help, but who in fact may unwittingly further humiliate by seeking individual pathology and untenable remedies.

A review of the literature on domestic violence indicates that the victim-blame perspective has been balanced by recent approaches to the problem that include an investigation of factors external to the individual. Certainly, feminists have advanced a new definition of the problem by placing it squarely within a culturally sanctioned continuum of oppressive behavior toward women. But activist literature often fails to shape policy agendas. The evolution of shelters for battered women, for example, did not derive from research on the problem or a concerted policy effort; rather, they grew out of grass-roots workers' understanding of the gravity of the problem.

As domestic violence rapidly gains attention from social scientists and policy makers, it is crucial that the problem definition be relevant and accurate, and that theory, research, policy, and practice be cohesively articulated and linked. Unless this is done, the interest in domestic violence will become simply another growth area for academically oriented research, rather than a force for change and alleviation of an insidious problem.

Attributional Biases in Explaining the Causes of Social Problems

The foregoing describes why problem definitions are crucial in determining what is done or not done about social problems and, more specifically, how person-centered definitions may deflect attention and energies away from important situational determinants, often to the detriment of those supposedly being helped. The significance of this is that regardless of the type of social problem and the intent of the investigator, the bulk of social science theory and research lends itself more easily to person-blame than to system-blame interpretations of the problem. Consequently, such research frequently plays an integral role in a chain of events that has the (probably unintended) effect of blaming people in difficult situations for their own predicament.

Psychologists are particularly vulnerable to this sort of causal attribution bias. Using data from articles on black Americans listed in *Psychological Abstracts,* it was possible to document a few years ago (Caplan & Nelson, 1973) the fact that as much as 82 percent of the classifiable psychological research reported in the half year of the *Abstracts* under study lent itself, either directly or by implication, to interpreting the difficulties of black Americans in terms of personal shortcomings. And more recently the authors found similar evidence of a person-centered preoccupation across 40 years of social-problem research in six different areas: alcohol and drug abuse, suicide, delinquency, job satisfaction, rape, and race relations (Gregg et al., 1979). (It is possible that social psychologists could be expected to be less prone than other kinds of psychologists to this kind of bias, since they are more inclined to look at situational influences on behavior. The literature on social problems, however, is not written by social psychologists only. Furthermore, it has been observed that most social psychologists are not immune from this causal attribution bias, and that the situational factors they consider tend to be in the immediate situation rather than larger, more pervasive forces.)

Such causal attribution bias seems to result from a number of different sources: first, the "Law of the Instrument," as described in Caplan and Nelson (1973, pp. 202–203):

When psychologists turn their attention to social problems, we see something akin to what Archibald (1970) called the "clinical orientation" to the utilization of social scientific knowledge, which she characterizes as assuming that "if the shoe doesn't fit, there's something wrong with your foot." The reasons for this parochial perspective are understandable. To begin with, it is an occupational expectancy that the psychologist would want to demonstrate the applicability of his skills and services. Kaplan (1964) called this widely observed tendency the Law of the Instrument: give a small boy a hammer, and suddenly he discovers that everything needs hammering. Train a person in psychological theory and research, and suddenly a world disastrously

out of tune with human needs is explained as a state of mind. As we shall see presently, the probability of locating cause in variables outside one's area of familiarity or expertise is not great. "It comes as no particular surprise to discover that a scientist formulates problems in a way which requires for their solution just those techniques in which he himself is especially skilled [Kaplan, 1964, p. 31]." The difficulty is that, as Kaplan says, "The price of training is always a certain 'trained incapacity': the more we know how to do something, the harder it is to learn to do it differently [p. 31]."

A second major reason for this preoccupation with person-centered variables pertains to career incentives. Social researchers' career rewards and chances for advancement are determined primarily by their colleagues in the scientific community, rather than persons outside it. It is the goodwill and approval of one's colleagues in the scientific community, not that of the target population members affected by one's work, that get researchers ahead. A social scientist's findings may provide or influence the underlying assumptions on which "corrective" programs affecting thousands or perhaps millions of persons will be predicated. It is ironic, then, that career gains will depend more on the contribution to the advancement of one's discipline from studying applied problems than on the success or failure of those programs.

What is good for science and the individual scientist, however, may not be good for those on whom the research is based. For example, to talk (see Social Focus 16.2) of hereditary and environmental effects on intelligence means one thing when discussed in terms of its relevance to psychological theory, but quite another—as Jensen learned from his critics—when applied to those in a problematic relationship to the rest of society.

Persons in all fields studying social problems have an obligation to consider a balanced approach in selecting which variables to study, for one elementary reason: namely, that any discipline-bound approach to any given social problem is at best only partially correct and at worst just plain wrong. In addition to this, however, psychology and closely related research areas have special reason to show caution: person-blame explanations of social problems, whether valid or not, hold the potential for reinforcing established stereotypes and thereby perpetuating the condition of the so-called problem group.

Further, it is usually considered disrespectful and unseemly to challenge authorities' definitions of the ways things really are. Thus, when authorities offer person-blame explanations for particular social problems and make research funds available, suddenly one's disciplinary outlook, career gains, and socially acceptable behavior all converge for the psychologist. By investigating a social problem in the given terms, a mutually beneficial exchange relationship is established: the researcher is rewarded both materially and in terms of prestige by using the tools of the trade; on the other side of the exchange, officialdom stands to have its preferred interpretation buttressed by the respectability of "scientific data."

Problem Identification: Objective Reality or Negotiated?

Even in the best of all political worlds of well-intentioned, responsible, and courageous political leaders, such causal attribution bias on the part of social scientists as was demonstrated above would be serious cause for concern. Under current conditions, however, this bias is mirrored in today's major social, politi-

These photos illustrate major problems such as poverty, unemployment, and pollution. Most major problems like these are political in nature. Problem identification is often done in a manner consistent with the values and interests of dominant groups in society.

cal, and economic institutions, often because it is advantageous to those institutions to define problems in person-centered terms.

One by-product of socialization is that people come to identify social problems as if they were independent, objective entities. Everyone knows what is meant by delinquency, crime, alcoholism, and so on. They are problems that one reads about daily, talks about, and comes to accept as "givens," and are viewed with just about the same level of concreteness as medical problems, tonsilitis, an inflamed appendix, and so forth—all about equal in the degree to which they are viewed as independent entities.

It may be well worthwhile to ask why it is that these particular problems have been singled out for special attention. These problems have not only been identified but have also been defined in a particular way, as requiring psychological attention. Why delinquency? Why not corporate crime? Why not some problem other than one that has been around for centuries and does not seem to change despite efforts to reduce it?

As Blumer (1971) and other have pointed out, most social problems are the result of collective definitions, rather than being objective realities that exist in their own right, independent of any particular observer. Furthermore, most serious problems—such as poverty, unemployment, environmental pollution—are highly political, in the sense that they involve conflicts of interest between those who benefit from particular definitions of the problem and those who do not, as well as the relative political effectiveness or power of the sets of opposing interests. Thus, when social scientists are called in to help solve a problem, they are not only actually participating in a process that helps to legitimate the problem as a real one but are also assisting in a process that has already defined the problem in a certain way.

For example, when most people talk about antisocial or criminal behavior, what kind of crime do they mean? White-collar crime? Corporate crime? No, teenage crime. And which

teenagers? Studies of undetected delinquency (for example, Williams & Gold, 1972) show that delinquent acts occur with almost equal frequency among youths in all socioeconomic levels. Most people, however, think of delinquency as existing only among young people who get arrested by the police—that is, those that fit the public stereotype. Thus, one function of this process, intentional or not, is to maintain and reinforce the common definition of juvenile delinquency. This definition is based on the characteristics of youths who commit crimes where there are police and who get caught—a combination of socioindividual qualities (that is, lower socioeconomic status) and unknown factors that distinguish those who get caught from those who do not.

The question, "Why is this a problem that demands attention?" often involves value issues and hidden agendas. "Why delinquency?" is a more difficult question than "Why job dissatisfaction?" or "Why poverty?" This is not to impugn the real motive of all social action; indeed, there is no doubt that most programs are derived from good intentions and represent an underlying set of values with which most persons would agree. The point here is that social action is usually aimed at those who are politically vulnerable to study and manipulation. What is left untouched are the social problems represented among those who are not vulnerable or amenable to help. Thus both the identification and definition of problems carry with them a strong note of morality in keeping with the values of those in society with the power and means to impose their social values and attendant punishment for misbehavior. Rendered vulnerable by this are those who lack the power or resources to defend themselves (Nelson, 1974, 1975). Why is it illegal to be a "wetback" but not illegal to hire one (Bustamente, 1972)? Why is alcoholism in the suburbs a medical problem (and called a disease), with Blue Cross willing to pay up to 13 weeks of hospital stay, while in the Bowery alcoholism is a moral problem? Why do we constantly study the poor rather than the non-poor in order to understand the causes of poverty?

Certain groups within society become continually stigmatized as problem groups (e.g., migratory workers, mental patients, blacks, the poor) because they are visible and accessible, but, most especially, because they are vulnerable to the social scientist for research purposes. In this sense the criteria by which social scientists select "problem" groups for study are not unlike the criteria by which the wider culture selects certain groups as scapegoats. Indeed, the former process often follows the lead of the latter. Nonachieving lower income children are more identifiable and accessible as a research population than are greedy "entrepreneurially motivated" slum landlords, for example, and they command far less countervailing power and resources than do landlords. Thus, there is much person-centered research data to justify initiating a program such as Head Start (all of the data suggesting, essentially, that it is the child who fails, rather than the school and the educational system). But, by contrast, there is a lack of data on landlords, bankers, and city officials who permit building code violations that would justify using them as targets for person-change treatment efforts (Caplan & Nelson, 1973, p. 207).

Thus social problems are not objective realities independent of values and interests. To take part in action to deal with such problems is to take part in a process that usually serves to perpetuate social myths and the status quo, by virtue of those in power making resources available to action agents to work with the politically vulnerable. Judge David Bazelon (1972, p. 6) made much the same point in a speech to correctional psychologists:

Why should we even consider fundamental social changes or massive income redistribution if the entire problem can be solved by having scientists teach the criminal class—like a group of laboratory rats—to march successfully through the maze of our society? In short, before you respond with enthusiasm to our pleas for help, you must ask yourselves whether your help is really needed, or whether you are merely engaged as magicians to perform an intriguing side-show so that the spectators will not notice the crisis in the center ring. In considering our motives for offering you a role, I think you would do well to consider how much less expensive it is to hire a thousand psychologists than to make even a minuscule change in the social and economic structure.

In the light of the foregoing, at least five latent functions of person-blame interpretations of social problems can be identified:

1. They offer a convenient apology for freeing the government and primary cultural institutions from blame for the problem.
2. Since those institutions are apparently not the cause of the problem, it may be legitimately contended that they cannot be held responsible for amelioration. If they do provide such help, they are credited with being exceedingly humane, while gaining control over those being helped, through the manipulation of problem definitions in exchange for treatment resources.
3. Such interpretations provide and legitimate the right to initiate person-change rather than system-change treatment programs. This in turn has the following functions: (a) it serves as a publicly acceptable device to control troublesome segments of the population, (b) it distracts attention from possible systemic causes, and (c) it discredits system-oriented criticism. . . .
4. The loyalty of large numbers of the well-educated, melioristic-minded nonneedy is cemented to the national structure by means of occupational involvement in "socially relevant" managerial, treatment, and custodial roles required to deal with those persons designated as needing person-centered correction.
5. Person-blame interpretations reinforce social myths about one's degree of control over his own fate, thus rewarding the members of the great middle class by flattering their self-esteem for having "made it on their own." This in turn increases public complacency about the plight of those who have not "made it on their own."

The major conclusion that can be drawn from the above is that *person-blame interpretations are in everyone's interests except those subjected to analysis* (Caplan & Nelson, 1973, p. 210).

Thus social scientists should be wary of accepting problems as given. They should actively examine potential hidden agendas, look for alternative interpretations of problems, and should stress problem areas where they could be useful, were the problems publicly recognized. Not questioning problem identification and definitions locks them into a situation as impossible as that of those whose behavior is the target of change—wittingly or unwittingly, consciously or unconsciously. One should constantly ask, "Action in whose interest?"

THE SOCIAL-ENGINEERING APPROACH TO SOCIAL CHANGE

Perhaps the most common set of assumptions about alleviating social problems—and certainly the most important in recent U.S. history—center around what has been called a social-engineering approach to social change. This approach gives the central role in the alleviation of large-scale social problems to government—at all levels, but primarily at the federal level. The assumptions underlying this approach are held implicitly by much of the populace, but quite explicitly by bureaucrats and many policy makers, including professional politicians. It remains to be seen whether the Reagan administration will back up its rhetorical attacks on this approach with a fundamentally different but genuine approach toward alleviating social problems, or whether its rhetoric will serve merely as a prelude to government abdicating its responsibilities in these areas.

The social-engineering approach to social problems and their alleviation has the following characteristics:

From the top down. It is presumed that the most appropriate locus for both decisions about solutions and action is within a governmental unit with responsibility for a given issue area, although opinions of persons at the grass-roots level may in some cases be solicited. Solutions arrived at are then imposed upon specific target areas (in the quasi-military imagery used by policy makers), usually in a uniform fashion across the entire political jurisdiction (nation or state). It is assumed that the problem cannot be adequately con-

ceptualized and acted upon at the local or grass-roots level.

Expert-dominated. The social-engineering approach assumes that the persons who know the most about a particular problem, who understand the situation best, and who know best what should be done, are "experts"—persons who are professionally engaged in studying, researching, or dealing administratively with a particular problem. If the indigenous population who are experiencing the problem are assumed to have knowledge of any value at all about it, they are also seen as being "stimulus-bound" in their views and not able to see "the big picture."

Bureaucratic. Because ameliorative programs are often very large in scope, involve massive expenditures of public funds, require the coordination of several different levels of government and types of functions, and necessitate uniformity of treatment in all locales, such programs are heavily—often overwhelmingly—bureaucratic. They involve massive amounts of paperwork to assess people's qualifications to receive assistance, to verify that funds were in fact spent in the ways intended, and to assess the effectiveness of the program. For all these reasons, target populations are often subjected to the mindlessness and inadvertent totalitarianism of bureaucratic thinking and procedures.

Controlling. In order to assure that public funds go for intended purposes, that appropriate persons receive assistance and inappropriate persons do not, and so forth, the dominant thinking and behavior of an intervention program is often concerned with control over the target population, or at least that portion of their lives relevant to the program. This might be contrasted with other alternative intentions toward persons experiencing problems, whereby efforts are made to enable or empower persons to use more effective action on their own behalf in the future, rather than controlling them.

Tunnel-visioned, or narrow in viewpoint. Because the agency assigned the responsibility of dealing with a particular problem is concerned primarily—or only—with that single issue, it is easiest to concentrate on it and the actions that presumably affect it, while giving little or no attention to either other factors contributing to the problem, or effects of the action program, other than the intended ones (referred to as "side effects").

When we think in terms of systems, we see that a fundamental misconception is embedded in the popular term "side-effects.". . . This phrase means roughly "effects which I hadn't foreseen, or don't want to think about." As concerns the basic mechanism, side-effects no more deserve the adjective "side" than does the "principal" effect. It is hard to think in terms of systems, and we eagerly warp our language to protect ourselves from the necessity of doing so (Hardin, 1969, p. 291).

Consequently, persons with this orientation have a crude understanding of the social/political/economic system, seeing it in an engineering sense as mechanistic, rather than dynamically homeostatic.

Service-delivery oriented. The social-engineering approach is oriented toward providing or "delivering" services of a presumably ameliorative nature to an essentially passive but needy target group. The orientation is toward treatment of a situation after something untoward has already occurred, rather than preventing its occurrence in the first place. Further, the services provided and the means by which they are provided often have the effect of continuing the dependence if not also the passivity of the recipient group.

It will probably not come as any crashing revelation to the reader that the social-engineering approach to alleviating social problems has not been spectacularly successful, despite decades of use and, at times, massive public expenditures. In addition to the various reasons implied in the above description, this may be in part because of the implicit assumptions about helping in such ameliorative programs.

Recent work in social psychology has been shedding new light on the nature of both giving and receiving help. For example, Brickman and his colleagues (Brickman, Karuza, Cohn, Rabinowitz, Coates, & Kidder, 1982, in press) have identified four qualitatively different models of (or sets of assumptions about) helping and coping, based upon their distinction between attribution of responsibility for a problem (that is, who is to blame for past events) and attribution of responsibility for a solution (that is, who is to control future events). Associated with these four models are different assumptions about human nature and the nature of the social order. (See Table 19.1 for a summary of these assumptions.) The ingeniousness of this formulation is that the authors are able to summarize a great deal of research on both the determinants and consequences of choosing one model rather than another.

Certainly one of the lessons from the past few decades is that ameliorative programs cannot routinely be mounted on the basis of intuitive notions about the helping process, and expect to be effective.

TABLE 19.1
Consequences of Attribution of Responsibility in Four Models of Helping and Coping

ATTRIBUTION TO SELF OF RESPONSIBILITY FOR PROBLEM	ATTRIBUTION TO SELF OF RESPONSIBILITY FOR SOLUTION	
	High	Low
High	**Moral Model**	**Enlightenment Model**
Perception of Self	Lazy	Guilty
Actions Expected of Self	Striving	Submission
Others Besides Self Who Must Act	Peers	Authorities
Actions Expected of Others	Exhortation	Discipline
Implicit View of Human Nature	Strong	Bad
Pathology	Loneliness	Fanaticism
Low	**Compensatory Model**	**Medical Model**
Perception of Self	Deprived	Ill
Actions Expected of Self	Assertion	Acceptance
Others Besides Self Who Must Act	Subordinates	Experts
Actions Expected of Others	Mobilization	Treatment
Implicit View of Human Nature	Good	Weak
Pathology	Alienation	Dependency

Source: Brickman et al., 1982 (in press).

UTILIZING RESEARCH IN POLICY DECISIONS: ASSUMPTIONS VERSUS REALITY

It has been an article of faith among social researchers for countless decades that social conditions could be improved if only those governmental units with responsibility for particular policy questions would pay attention to and actually use social research knowledge in their policy decision making. Assumptions about how this might be accomplished have only rarely been carefully examined or clearly stated, and for most researchers the clarity of just how their research is used, or could be used, fades out rapidly beyond the laboratory door.

Research Utilization Theories

Perhaps the oldest and still the most common conception of the research utilization process is what we call the "better-mousetrap" theory (Caplan, 1977). The name derives from a quote attributed to Ralph Waldo Emerson: "If a man can write a better book, preach a better sermon, or make a better mousetrap than his neighbor, though he builds his house in the woods, the world will make a beaten path to his door." This assumption, usually unexamined by those who hold it, presumes that the use of relevant social research by policy makers will result simply from more and better research. That is, the power of the "facts" to speak for themselves is so compelling that findings with social utility will be sought out, discovered, and put to appropriate use by persons in policy-making positions in government.

Unfortunately the process by which most government agencies acquire information (when they choose to acquire it at all) is not so open and outward reaching. Most social research information used by policy makers is either produced under contract or conducted in-house by the using agency, and for many agency personnel the control of such information is more important than its substantive content or its potential use. Under such conditions of direct control over its production, procurement, and use, the opportunity for outside information to enter into the utilization process is often effectively foreclosed. Thus, if research is to come to the attention of agency personnel, it will have to be by some means other than the "normal" processes of scientific investigation and communication.

One step above the better-mousetrap theory is a fairly sizable body of literature that focuses on the role of one or more factors thought to affect the use and nonuse of research knowledge. Some of this literature is armchair speculation, some of it is by researchers with some degree of contact with government agencies, some of it is written by experienced policy makers, and a few pieces have been contributed by researchers who have served a tour of duty in a government agency and returned to academia with battle stories. Most of this literature can be classified into one of three clusters:

Knowledge-specific theories, which see the nonuse (or underuse) of social science knowledge as resulting from the nature of the information itself, the research techniques employed, or the behaviors of social scientists. For example, it is argued that social scientists conceive complex problems only in the limited terms provided by their own discipline; that overreliance on quantitative methods limits the utility of the information; that there are often theoretical or methodological shortcomings, or both; that researchers take too long to research a problem and cannot deliver helpful information at the time it is needed; that social scientists are politically too far to the Left in their beliefs; that research is more oriented to merely understanding an issue than to providing the necessary action framework; and so forth.

Policy-maker constraint theories, which view the nonuse of social research as resulting primarily from the constraints under which the policy maker operates. It is argued, for example, that policy makers typically need concise information in a short period of time and that social scientists simply cannot be helpful under such circumstances. It is also argued that policy makers can deal only with malleable variables, those open to manipulation, and must often base their actions upon the course that appears politically most feasible. Therefore, the policy maker's capability to apply research is necessarily limited. These theories suggest that if utilization is to be increased, either the knowledge producers must tailor their activities to meet such constraints, or the constraints themselves will have to be removed.

Two-communities theories, which try to explain nonutilization in terms of the basic incompatibility of the research and the policy communities. The argument is similar to that which C. P. Snow (1959) makes in The Two Cultures to explain the gap between the humanities and the hard sciences. People holding this view argue that social scientists and policy makers live and operate in separate worlds with different and often conflicting values, different reward systems, and different skills and cognitive styles. Researchers are theory oriented, concerned with "pure" science and esoteric issues. By contrast, government policy makers are action oriented, practical persons concerned with obvious and immediate dilemmas. Some holding this position argue that the gap between the two communities is not simply due to different styles that might conceivably be bridged to some extent through closer personal relationships and greater trust or empathy. In addition, they argue, there are very real conflicts over who is to determine the ends of policy, with the specter of misuse of knowledge by power holders tending to widen the gap.

Much of the literature, especially that written by researchers, seems to assume that research utilization, where it occurs, is a highly rational process involving (to exaggerate only slightly, if at all) a single empirical study answering a specific, well-defined question of the policy maker or decision maker, resulting in an identifiable effect on a particular decision. Although something like this may happen in a few instances, as a general model this set of assumptions is questionable on almost every point. A handful of empirical studies on how fairly high-level federal executives actually use social science knowledge has revealed quite a different picture (Caplan, Morrison, & Stambaugh, 1975; Caplan, 1979).

To begin with, policy makers tend not to identify single, discrete studies but rather clusters of studies around a particular issue or question. Further, they often do not make a clear distinction between empirically grounded research and other types of social science knowledge. Upper-level policy makers appear to use social science knowledge in at least two different ways: instrumentally, as when specific information is used in documentable ways to answer relatively specific questions; and conceptually, as when the effect of the information is not to answer any particular question, but rather to change policy makers' understanding of the issue, to cause them to see things in a new light or from a different perspective. It happens that the latter kind of use is at least as common as the former among upper-level policy makers.

To return to a point made earlier, the information-seeking systems, or "inquiry systems," of most governmental agencies appear to be relatively closed, rather than open and actively searching for all relevant information. The information needs of the agency tend to be specified from the top down; the degree of utilization is roughly proportional to the degree of control the agency has over the production and dissemination of the information; and a surprisingly large proportion of uses (between one-third and one-half, according to one study) deal with internal administrative and management issues rather than the substantive policy issues related to the agency's mission.

A final point of some importance: researchers and academics, as well as most other persons, believe that knowledge reduces uncertainty. However true this may be for many contexts, in policy settings it is often the case that instead of reducing uncertainty, new knowledge in fact increases uncertainty for the organization. The introduction of new knowledge can, if acted upon, create turbulence and political costs for the agency. Consequently, nonuse of information may be seen as a way of avoiding risks because use may threaten organizational stability. Further, what may appear to be nonuse may in fact be a considerable lag in time from when the information is introduced to when it is actually used, this lag time allowing the organization opportunity to deal with the organizational difficulties that ensue when an idea, innovation, or new finding is first introduced.

It should be emphasized that these findings are general tendencies found to apply to the largest proportion of uses of social science knowledge. As with all generalizations, there are many exceptions and innumerable cases where things operate rather differently. The reader should not conclude that policy makers are completely sealed off from sources of information outside the regular channels of their agencies, or that all attempts by outside researchers to bring relevant research to the attention of policy makers are doomed to failure. For one thing, policy makers get a wide range of information from a wide variety of sources, and they report learning of a considerable amount of social science knowledge from the mass media, including newspapers, television, and magazines.

With this more realistic picture of research utilization as background, the argument is offered that utilization should not be considered *the* supreme goal by researchers. First, as should be obvious from the earlier section on *Stages in the Policy Process*, not all utilization of social research is necessarily good, and not all nonuse is necessarily undesirable. Second, even in cases where the social research knowledge is unimpeachable in its validity and its implications for responsible social action, the political process cannot be ignored or circumvented in coming to a policy decision. On many—perhaps most—occasions, policy decisions are best made on the basis of nonresearch information—for example, taking into account the values and interests held by the various stakeholders on a particular issue. Politics, after all, is the art of finding acceptable compromises between parties with differing interests, and public officials cannot proceed in a technocratic fashion directly from research findings to policy decisions, unmindful of the political situation in which that policy will have to be authorized, funded, implemented, and evaluated.

Joseph Coates (1977) makes essentially this point when he suggests that when it comes to public policy questions, the scientific/technical community habitually confuses issues with problems, and tries to convert the former into the latter. A problem, says Coates, is something that can be solved, by either scientific information or technical know-how. For problems, there is an answer or solution, and all one has to do is find it. Issues, on the other hand, are questions over which there is conflict between groups with opposing interests. In this sense, an issue cannot be solved, but rather must be *resolved*, whether by compromise, persuasion, coercion, or trickery. Coates asserts that the tendency of the scientific/technical community to mistake issues for problems is compounded by the fact that issues far outnumber problems. The relative inability of the scientific/technical community, in Coates's view, to appreciate this distinction—which comes across as political naivete—has often caused scientists to get caught in the cross fire between contending groups, when they thought they were contributing to the solution of a problem. As a result, many feel unappreciated or "burned," and retreat from the political arena.

Another respect in which research utilization, though necessary, is not the whole answer is expressed in the views of some high-level federal executives. Some of these people say that improving the utilization of scientific/technical information will not help them significantly, because what they need as decision makers is not just more or better information, but rather something that will improve the policy-making or decision-making process itself—in other words, something that will tell them how to make better decisions.

Donald Michael (1973) has argued for years that one cannot necessarily expect "better" or increased amounts of scientific information to make conventional decision making somehow better. More or better information, Michael argues, does not necessarily lead to better decisions, if the decision-making processes are so compromised that the end products are almost inevitably defective. Instead, he argues, the improved knowledge has to actually change the way decisions are made—change the very nature of decision making and the ways that people typically use information.

RECENT DIRECTIONS AND ALTERNATIVES

Perhaps before proceeding it will be useful to clarify the assumptions made in this chapter. The primary message thus far is one of caution in attempting to use social science knowledge for alleviating large-scale social problems. This should not be interpreted, however, as saying that social scientists and others should do nothing, or should not make efforts to put social science knowledge to good use. Inaction on this score is neither helpful nor responsible. There is no hidden hand that distributes social and economic rewards in a just fashion, or at least one cannot afford to behave as if there were. The intention here has been simply to point out the various risks and dangers of naive approaches to trying to be useful, so as to better equip all parties—policy makers, the public, social scientists, and so on—to make responsible uses of needed social science knowledge.

Nor should the comments in the preceding sections be interpreted as suggesting that activities or approaches discussed there should not be employed. In most cases, many of them have a perfectly appropriate role and should be undertaken. In no case, however, is any one of them sufficient, or *the* answer. Each should be carried out, if at all, with careful attention to its limitations and an awareness of the larger view of the social problem in question. For example, there is a great deal to be gained from a continued emphasis on the utilization of social science knowledge, but in its more recent and more sophisticated form, with due attention to what even the best utilization systems will and will not do for public policy making.

Consideration will now be given to some more recent directions and alternatives for the future that seem promising. Many of the comments in this section, but not all, have to do less with specific activities or approaches and are more on the order of guidelines that need to be kept in mind in deciding what to do.

The Social-Systems Approach to Problem Solving

In thinking about the ways in which social science can contribute responsibly to the solving of social problems, it seems useful to think more in terms of what we call social problem solving than in terms of applying social science to a particular problem. By this is meant an attempt to understand and deal with a particular problem on its own terms and in its fullest context. If this notion seems all too obvious and "motherhood and apple pie," then perhaps it can be better appreciated by contrasting it with the more usual law-of-the-instrument approach, whereby one tries to apply one's own expertise to situations, irrespective of its appropriateness. The latter orientation has been characterized, not unfairly, as "tools looking for a function," or "solutions looking for problems."

A social problem-solving approach emphasizes the connection and interdependence of issues that could go unrecognized if treated separately. One of the difficulties in dealing with social problems is that some can be dealt with only politically, and if intervention fails, it would appear that either the subjects are incurable or the social change agents do not know what they are doing. In fact, social action in such instances may have been doomed to disaster from the outset, for reasons that went unrecognized. The point here is that social intervention is part of a process, and to understand why it fails or succeeds requires some basic understanding of the context in which intervention occurs. It also requires a sense of historical events to identify external factors that may be unnoticed but that may play an overriding role in determining what is done, why it was done, and the outcome.

What the authors are essentially arguing for is an attempt to understand particular social problems in their entirety, with some appreciation for the larger situational and environmental forces that determine problem situations and behavior. Instead of approaching problems only through one's disciplinary blinders, one needs to adopt at least an interdisciplinary, or even better, a *human* view of the problem and its context. As has often been observed, the "real world" does not manifest itself along lines corresponding to the departmental breakdown in a university. One needs to acquire the habit of looking at social problems in the context of the entire system within which they are embedded, and to learn to recognize the systemic dynamics and forces to which all systems—from the individual cell to the society as a whole—are subject.

As an illustration of this point, consider briefly a phenomenon common to almost any action within any system: unintended consequences. One of the underlying principles of ecology and of all living systems is the fact that "you can't produce just one effect." Any action in a highly interrelated system will produce not only the intended result (perhaps) but also a number of other consequences not intended. For example, Sesame Street did increase the cognitive abilities of the disadvantaged children for whom it was intended. But it also improved the abilities of middle- and upper-class children even more, resulting in an even wider gap between the two groups than originally existed (Cook, Appleton, Conner, Shaffer, Tamkin, & Weber, 1975). As another example, it is fairly well known that some of the criteria established to qualify families for AFDC funds (Aid to Families with Dependent Children) had the net effect of destabilizing the family unit.

Social scientists need to develop the habit of looking for and anticipating such unintended effects *before* design and implementation of ameliorative programs. Learning to see the entire problem within its system will aid this process.

Another characteristic of systems is the interrelatedness of their various elements, or as ecologists have put it, "Everything is related to everything else." Similarly, particular social problems do not exist—nor can they be dealt with—in isolation from other problems. As a relatively simple example, take three social problems that are usually dealt with separately, in piecemeal fashion: education, housing, and income (or socioeconomic status). Programs are designed to attack each of these problems separately, but in fact they are closely interrelated. For example, a family's income level will determine the neighborhood it can afford to live in and the quality of housing it can afford. The neighborhood location will in turn determine which schools the children will attend, and in some measure the quality of education that they will receive in those schools. The quality of their education will in large part determine the type of occupation and hence the income level they will have when they grow up, thus perpetuating the cycle. Whether the cycle is vicious or benign depends upon whether one's income is low or high.

Daniel Patrick Moynihan, originally a political scientist and now a U.S. senator, argues that government in the United States has long relied upon disconnected, ad hoc programs to treat social problems, rather than policies from which specific programs would logically follow. In fact, he argues, most government officials in this country do not even have a good grasp of what the policy approach, as distinguished from the program approach, is all about. In Moynihan's view, the program approach is characterized by responses to surface-level symptoms, being reactive to problems once they have emerged, being present oriented (or very short-range future oriented), and being ameliorative, in the sense of trying to patch up supposedly minor system defects and returning the situation to a hypothetical status quo. By contrast, the policy approach attempts to deal with more basic root causes; to be anticipatory, formative, and guiding, rather than reactive; to be future oriented; and to be more "maximizing" than "satisfying" (March & Simon, 1958) in terms of correcting problems.

Still another system characteristic that one needs to learn to be attentive to is that events or conditions are usually multiply determined. That is, there usually is not just one cause of a particular event or condition but many. Thus, any ameliorative program that attempts to deal with a social problem by attacking what is thought to be *the* cause, is probably going to be less than effective. For example, job-training programs that proceed on the assumption that unemployment is primarily due to lack of motivation are almost certain to have limited success, if any.

Enlightenment Approaches

Highly congruent with this social systems approach is another cluster of approaches that promise a significant role for psychological and social research, although one that is more diffuse and long-term than is usually assumed. If the social-engineering approach to social problems and their alleviation is at one extreme of a continuum, standing at the other end is a cluster of loosely related approaches and assumptions that may be called "enlightenment" approaches to social change. These include such rubrics as consciousness raising, self-awareness, understanding of one's situation, demystification of traditional authorities and myths, and more recently, what has been called "personal transformation" (Harman, 1976; Ferguson, 1980). These approaches all share the assumption that responsible, effective action to eliminate or escape from problem

situations will result from a change in the way one views oneself and the situation one is in. This may come from education, from having access to information, or simply from reconceptualizing information already available.

By contrast with the social-engineering approach, these approaches have the following characteristics:

- There is an assumption that effective change occurs not from the top down, but from the bottom up.
- Emphasis is on the capacity and autonomy of the individual.
- They are noncontrolling and noncoercive, with the emphasis on decentralization of control.
- They are implicitly egalitarian, in the sense that they assume the validity of experience and the capacity for intelligent insight within each person. In this sense, these approaches are not expert oriented, although they recognize and value expertise (which may or may not be credentialed or licensed).

Often such approaches place great emphasis on self-awareness and self-fulfillment, and in this respect they have been attacked as being "selfish" and undermining of one's social conscience or commitment to changing social conditions. The two are not mutually exclusive, however; they are or can be complementary. According to Donald Michael, the original idea behind Socrates's admonition to "know thyself" was that this is a necessary precondition to being truly socially useful.

Policy-Relevant Types of Social Research

During the past decade and a half, a number of types of research using the methods of the social/behavioral sciences have been developed, which are designed to be much more directly relevant to policy issues than are the more traditional types of social research. Many of these are still at an early stage of development, almost more art than established scientific technique, and hardly any of them can be considered a polished set of methods. They have proven sufficiently useful to policy makers, however, and sufficiently intriguing to researchers, to deserve some mention here. A few of them will be briefly described and an attempt will be made to show their policy role in relation to the problem-solving system represented by government and science acting together.

Program evaluation. Program evaluation refers to the systematic, research-based assessment of the effectiveness of specific government programs in meeting their objectives. (See also the subsection on program evaluation in Chapter 2.) The usual purpose of program evaluations is to assist policy makers in planning, implementing, or redirecting particular programs. In this respect they are one aspect of the cycle of planning, implementation, and evaluation that occurs continuously in agencies. Evaluation requires a definition of program objectives, the development of measures of progress toward those objectives, and an assessment of what difference the program actually makes. Although the major purpose of an evaluation is primarily focused on output or impact variables (What was its effect? Did it make a difference?), it has also become accepted practice to give attention to input or process variables, in order to be able to tell whether the program being evaluated was in fact implemented as originally intended. Occasionally, there is an opportunity for an evaluation to be conducted with a fairly rigorous experimental research design (using random assignment of persons or groups to experimental and control conditions), but this is usually not possible for political, administrative, or ethical reasons. Evaluations have perhaps been most common in educational policy issues (for example, the Head Start program), although in other instances they have included income and welfare issues, health service delivery programs, and so forth. Evaluations may be not only *summative*, as discussed above, where the focus is on an overall evaluation of a program, but also *formative*, whereby the results of an evaluation are used throughout the course of a program to shape or improve its development.

The value of program evaluation research is in the feedback it provides regarding specific programs intended to deal with problem conditions. Of the various types of research discussed here, it is the clearest and most explicit about linking program interventions to effects in the problem condition. It is often, however, too tied to specific cases to test the validity of the policy assumptions from which a specific program evolved.

Social indicators. For decades the United States has had a system of economic indicators that systematically and regularly assess the nation's economic health. Everyone who reads the newspaper or listens to the radio or TV news is familiar with some of these measures. In the last two decades there has been an effort to develop a set of social indicators, analogous to economic indicators, to measure other important, noneconomic aspects of the nation's life. The United States still has no official set of social indicators per se, although federal agencies (including the Office of Management and Budget, located in the Executive Office of the president, and more recently the Bureau of the Census in the Commerce Department) have published a series of volumes containing a wide variety of such measures.

Social indicators may be thought of as noneconomic statistical indexes that measure progress toward important national goals. The recent government volumes mentioned above have focused on the following areas: health (long life, disability, access to medical care), public safety (safety of life and property from crime), education (including both basic education and higher and continuing education), employment (employment opportunities, quality of employment life), income (the level, distribution, and expenditure of income, and the low-income population), housing (both quantity and quality), leisure time and recreation, and population growth. Such indexes are usually presented as time-series data so that

SOCIAL FOCUS 19.1
The Sense of Well-being Among Americans

Self-reported happiness and sense of well-being are two important subjective social indicators. A series of national opinion polls dating back as far as 1957 show that the overwhelming majority (85–90%) of Americans report they are "very" or "pretty" happy (Campbell et al., 1976). Despite the saying "bad news travels fast," available research evidence suggests we have a positivity bias in what we see, remember, and report (Matlin & Stang, 1978).

Campbell and his associates (1976) conducted a comprehensive study of the well-being of Americans in the early 1970s. To assess well-being, over 2000 respondents were asked to evaluate their lives on ten bipolar scales (that is, boring–interesting) and to indicate their overall satisfaction in life. The respondents were also asked how satisfied they were with 17 different areas of their lives such as their work, their health, and so on.

The results showed that people who were satisfied with one area of their life were apt to be satisfied with other areas as well. Furthermore, people satisfied with the specific domains of their life reported a high general sense of well-being. Satisfaction with leisure activities, satisfaction with family life, and satisfaction with standard of living were three especially strong predictors of overall well-being.

Some groups were lower in overall sense of well-being than others. The unfortunate included the poor, the unemployed, blacks, people living in very large cities, and divorced persons. On the other hand, retired senior citizens, whites, people living in smaller communities, and married persons generally reported higher levels of well-being. There was no difference in the well-being of men and women.

The results from this study also provide several clues concerning what contributes to people's sense of well-being. First, there are one's persisting, objective circumstances. These contribute to one's on-going sense of well-being. Changes in one's circumstances alter one's sense of well-being, with positive events making us feel better and negative events making us feel worse.

But, objective conditions are not by any means the only determinant of people's evaluation of their situations. Personality attributes and cognitive processes play a role. For instance, respondents prone to giving socially desirable answers and those high in personal competence were higher in well-being. Social skills are also important: respondents with numerous friends were higher in well-being than those with few friends. Finally, people's frames of reference played a crucial role. People whose aspirations far exceeded their own circumstances were less satisfied. Similarly, people who felt their situation was below that of most other people's situation, were less happy.

changes in social conditions can be monitored over time. Ideally, such data would also be anticipatory and suitable for social forecasting in order to facilitate long-range social planning. Although most attention, including the government volumes, has centered on so-called objective social indicators (that is, objectively countable items or phenomena), there has also been considerable research on subjective or perceptual social indicators (Campbell, Converse, &

Rodgers, 1976; Andrews & Withey, 1976), which are basically people's feelings about life. Social Focus 19.1, which discusses the subjective well-being of Americans, illustrates this kind of research.

Social indicators can be analyzed at the national level or they can be disaggregated to detect unusual problems in particular regions or subgroups of the society. They are not, however, capable of providing information directly relevant to assessing the effectiveness of particular intervention programs, in the way that evaluation research can.

Impact assessments. Environmental impact assessments, technology assessments, and more recently, social impact assessments are specific types of this general class of research. The first two grew out of concerns about the likely consequences of either introducing a major development into a geographic region, or developing and introducing a new technology—for example, the environmental consequences of locating a new chemical plant in a particular place, or the many ramifications that could result from establishing electronic funds-transfer techniques in the banking industry, or from the development of lasers for commercial application in industry. A much more recent outgrowth has been risk/benefit assessment, which attempts to delineate and evaluate the net balance of risks and costs on the one hand, and benefits on the other, from the introduction of a new activity, product, or program. Psychologists have had a prominent role in this latter area, theoretically and methodologically, based upon research on how people make decisions and evaluate the probable consequences of alternative decisions.

Impact assessments of all types have in common the purpose of trying to anticipate in as complete and rigorous a fashion as possible all the potential consequences (not only direct consequences, but perhaps more importantly the unanticipated secondary and tertiary impacts as well) that might result from a particular development or intervention. In this sense they differ from traditional research (which is present or past oriented), in that they attempt to be anticipatory or future oriented, so that more intelligent choices and decisions can be made about activities or products before their effects are seen.

Futures research. This field—or more accurately, conglomeration of approaches—is related to impact assessments insofar as it is anticipatory and explicitly oriented toward the future. Its scope is even broader, however, since it is usually concerned not simply with the range of impacts from a single event, activity, or product, but with what an entire system may look like in the future under different sets of assumptions. A number of different specific techniques have been developed for trying to anticipate future conditions, including cross-impact analysis (how various events are likely to interact dynamically through time, usually performed by computer modeling) and the use of scenarios, or coherent pictures of qualitatively different alternative futures, each of which is to some degree plausible. These methods do not attempt to predict or forecast *the* future, since a primary tenet of futures research is that many alternative futures are possible, and which one eventuates depends heavily upon choices made in the present that make one or another alternative future more or less probable.

It should be obvious that in each of these types of research, the researcher is much more directly and intimately involved in the policy process than is the case in more traditional research approaches.

An Integrated Approach for Reducing Domestic Violence

Treatment of social problems such as domestic violence should be considered very broadly, in the sense of the variety of means employed to alleviate particular problems. Thus, treatment programs for domestic violence may include, but are not necessarily limited to, large-scale federal programs. They may also include policy planners and treatment delivery personnel at any level of government or even within nongovernmental settings such as self-employed professionals or privately operated concerns. Finally, combating domestic violence may involve volunteer action groups and grass-roots participants. These considerations follow from the perspective of seeing social problems and their treatment not just as the province of governmental activities, but rather seeing the society in toto as the problem-solving system, only one element of which is government and another of which is the social science community and the relevant knowledge it can offer.

As mentioned earlier, the primary approach of government toward social problems has been to provide services or treatment after the fact. Another approach, needed to balance this traditional emphasis would be get "upstream" from where the problem occurs and to act to prevent or minimize its occurrence, rather than try to treat it "downstream" once it has occurred. The obvious analogy that leaps to mind is the recent emphasis on prevention in the area of health. Treatment of health problems is increasingly costly, and some experts have even suggested that an approach to health based on after-the-fact treatment has reached a point of diminishing returns. There is increasing recognition that an approach that places considerably more emphasis on the prevention of health problems and the promotion of positive health practices can be far more efficient in terms of use of resources, as well as more effective in terms of maximizing people's health.

If one were to carry this analogy even further, one might imagine a rather different social problem-solving system. Below are some of the characteristics that such a system might have, followed by the implications that each feature might have for the specific problem of domestic violence.

1. Less reliance on after-the-fact treatment intervention, and more emphasis on prevention, by altering the environmental determinants of the problem, and by encouraging a sense of personal responsibility for those behaviors and life-styles—to the extent that they are under one's control—that can contribute to or attenuate the problem. In the area of domestic violence, two factors are particularly relevant to this feature. The first is the nature of the marriage contract itself as a legal set of arrangements, which will be discussed under number 5 below. The second is a cluster of related issues, including the popular culture's exploitation of sexual violence, the promotion of the view that the use of physical aggression and force as means of social control are to be seen as masculine (as examples from the movies, James Bond and the characters portrayed by John Wayne), and the macho ethos in the United States that makes violence, particularly against women, socially acceptable and virtually makes rape the Great American Crime. These themes are evident everywhere, and the public is bombarded with them in movies, television (both programs and advertisements), magazine ads, paperback books, and record albums (for example, the Rolling Stones' album "Black and Blue," in which one of the selections contains the line, "I'm black and blue, and I love it"). These themes, as was discussed in Chapter 10, powerfully condition personal values and expectations, and contribute to the predilection of males to engage in violence and females to be perhaps more accepting of it than they otherwise would be. Increasing sensitivity to these themes, together with promoting alternative models of behavior for both males and females, can help in lessening the incidence of violence.

2. Promotion of positive activities and behaviors, in part by enhancing the incentives for them. Domestic violence has been, and continues to be, largely a hidden crime. Anything that can increase the incentives for those women affected to come out and declare that they are being beaten will help to reduce the widespread ignorance on this issue, and enable everyone to realize that in fact there are large numbers of women in such conditions. Publicity of the issue helps, as do assault crisis centers, by providing a supportive environment as well as legal and medical assistance. Recent legislation to promote these ends will be described further under number 5 below.

3. An emphasis on education and personal capacity building, rather than passive dependence upon experts or outside sources. In addition it may be important to provide information to young

people, perhaps particularly at the junior high and high school level, about appropriate sex-role behaviors. It should be explained that macho behavior is not "manly"; rather, it is pathological—certainly in its consequences, if not necessarily in its origins. Similarly, it is important for girls of that age who may be entering into an arrangement with a boy to know that they do not have to remain passive or to stay in that arrangement if the male is inflicting violence on them. In short, some degree of consciousness raising is in order, to point out the unequal positions of women and men in the society, the limitations of traditional stereotyped views of both, and the availability of alternative models of behavior.

4. Analogous to preventive health's emphasis on allowing the physical body's natural healing mechanisms to play a larger role, an enhancement of (or at least noninterference with) those personal resources and capacities and social support systems that can aid in either preventing or minimizing problematic conditions or behavior. A comprehensive approach to avoiding domestic violence must provide conditions and opportunities for abused women to rebuild their sense of worth and feelings of personal efficacy—feelings that may have been shattered by the violence against them. Again, crisis centers can be helpful in this regard.

5. Reducing the incentives for being in a problematic condition, and enhancing the incentives for being autonomous and effective. A central feature here is the nature of the marriage contract itself as a legal set of arrangements. Many states' laws are such that not only is the marriage contract virtually a license for beating, but also the laws practically force the woman to stay in the household with the man who is beating her. In such states, if the woman leaves she forfeits her legal rights to the couple's property, children, or the nonsalary benefits accruing from the male's employment. Some laws are going to have to change in order to allow the woman to leave a dangerous situation without sacrificing her rights in these areas. Legislation in both England and the United States during the past decade is a modest beginning toward these ends. The U.S. legislation attempts to meet two broad sets of needs. The first provides criminal penalties for domestic violence and is designed to make the crime more public by increasing the willingness of women to report it and increasing the willingness of police and prosecutors to acknowledge the crime and take action on it, rather than treating it as a private domestic quarrel. The other major emphasis is on providing sanctuary for the woman. Three different stages or types of protection are provided for. The first, the crisis center, is a refuge where the woman can be safeguarded from her husband, and where her immediate needs for physical

safety and counseling can be met. The location of the center is kept secret. By entering the center the woman does not relinquish her rights to property or custody of the children. The second stage is more communal, intended to foster independence. This is designed for the woman to begin to be woven back into the community, still with protection from the husband. In the third stage the woman is rehoused somewhere other than her original home. The upshot of this legislation is that the criminal justice system cannot continue to adopt a laissez-faire attitude toward what were previously regarded as private quarrels.

In developing an integrated approach to reducing domestic violence, one point is clear. What is needed is the ability to see and appreciate social problems and conditions from both the macro or system view (as the social-engineering approach tries, crudely, to do), and the micro or individual-embedded-in-the-situation view: in short, a multilevel awareness. It has been said that the hallmark of true intelligence is not highly abstracted grand theories, but rather the ability to see all levels of abstraction/concreteness simultaneously, as well as the relationships among them. Like a zoom lens on a camera, this enables one easily to shift back and forth from one level to another and to focus on each level when appropriate. It combines a systems view with a strong empathic sense of how things look from the individual's viewpoint, especially those persons at the bottom—those who are experiencing the problem.

Finally, if this integrated approach to domestic violence (and other social problems) is to work, social scientists will have a new responsibility. Caplan and Nelson (1973, p. 209) have elaborated on this.

One of the most serious philosophical and psychological problems of our age may be to provide a view of man and his surroundings that recognizes the validity of situational causality without leaving the individual feeling helpless and unable to shape his fate. Part of that view will have to contain a more complex and sophisticated view of causality than the implicit constant-sum model that most people seem to hold (i.e., the more my environment is responsible for my outcomes, the less responsible I am, and vice versa). But until that state is reached, social scientists, especially those concerned with environmental determinants of behavior and thought, have a responsibility: we must recognize that much of our work holds the potential for further eroding an already changing social order and crumbling value system; and, therefore, it may be argued that we have an obligation to put something better in the place of that which we help destroy. It is in this spirit that Miller (1969) suggested that perhaps the most radical activity that psychology can undertake is to build a new image of man, more valid and hopeful than those of the past, and to freely dispense that image to anyone who will listen.

SUMMARY

This chapter deals with large-scale social problems, emphasizing the relationship between social science knowledge and governmental policies for alleviating such problems. Social problems are best understood not as being independent, objective entities but rather as being the products of political and social definitions of their nature.

The unadulterated optimism of two or three decades ago regarding social science's capacity to eliminate or reduce large-scale social problems has faded in the light of the nation's experience of the past 10 to 15 years. The promise of considerable impact still remains, however, if some of the misleading assumptions of the past can be replaced with a more realistic view of the public policy process and the ways in which and reasons for which social science can be used or misused in the public arena.

The policy process may be thought of, for present purposes, as consisting of five stages that comprise an iterative process: the identification of a particular social problem; the public definition of that problem; a decision about the nature of the policy or program designed to alleviate the problem; the implementation of that policy or program; and finally, an evaluation or assessment of the effectiveness of that policy or program in meeting its goals, with the results then being fed back into the process. How a problem is defined determines what is done or not done about it. Social problems typically involve considerable negotiation over blame for the problem and responsibility for doing something about it. The issue of domestic violence is used to illustrate several general points about how (or whether) particular situations become identified as problems per se, how problem definitions are negotiated, and whose interests are served (or ill served) by particular problem definitions becoming publicly accepted.

Efforts to deal with social problems have been dominated in the public policy sphere by the social-engineering approach, which gives government the central role for action, relies overwhelmingly on knowledge and opinions of experts, and bureaucratically imposes attempted solutions from the top down. This approach has been complemented in the social science community by relatively simplistic assumptions about the utilization of social science knowledge for the purpose of enlightening policy decisions. The chapter describes a number of misunderstandings about the utilization process and summarizes research findings on how this process actually takes place.

There are, however, more sophisticated approaches that hold the potential for enhancing responsible contributions from the social sciences. Accordingly, an argument is made in the chapter for what is called social problem solving. This involves the recognition of the complexity and interdependence of issues, and the willingness to try to understand particular problems on their own terms and in their context, rather than trying single-mindedly to apply one's particular expertise to problems, irrespective of its appropriateness. Four types of research specifically designed to be policy relevant, and thus encompassing a wider field of vision, are described: program evaluation, social indicators, impact assessments, and futures research. The case is made for seeing problems whole in the context of the social and political processes that define them—an approach that recognizes the realities of the situation, yet maximizes the payoff from research.

The chapter essentially describes a stance on the part of social researchers that is seen as necessary in making responsible contributions to improving the human condition by means of social research. Such contributions are not merely the products of substantive knowledge and technical expertise, although these are important. What is primarily needed is a sense of responsibility—a sense of really caring about a particular problem or issue—as well as a sensitivity to the implications and potential uses of research from the viewpoints of different actors in the public arena.

SUGGESTED READINGS

Sarason, S. B. *Psychology misdirected*. New York: Free Press, 1981.

Ryan, W. *Blaming the victim*. New York: Pantheon, 1971.

Miller, G. A. Psychology as a means of promoting human welfare. *American Psychologist*, 1969, 24, 1063–1075.

Gregg, G., Preston, T., Geist, A. & Caplan, N. The caravan rolls on: Forty years of social problem research. *Knowledge: Creation, Diffusion, Utilization*, 1979, 1(1), 31–61.

Mills, C. W. *The sociological imagination*. New York: Oxford, 1959.

GLOSSARY

Absolute standard model Defining normality by specifying what behaviors are considered normal and which are abnormal, regardless of the social or cultural context.

Achievement motivation A desire to do well in academic settings, choose achievement tasks, work hard, and persist in the face of failure.

Acquiescence The tendency to agree with some or all items in a questionnaire, regardless of their content.

Aggression Behaviors intended to harm others.

Altruism Unselfish concern for the welfare of others; altruism contrasts with egoism, the view that concern for others is based on self-concern.

Anger An emotion frequently resulting from insult- or attack-induced arousal. The use of the term "anger" to describe one's arousal is a product of learning and of inferences about the source of the arousal.

Assignment rule The procedure or rule that accounts for why different individuals receive or are exposed to different levels of the treatment variable. Different assignment rules define different research designs.

Assimilation Perceiving members of a given category to be more similar than they actually are.

Attack A physical or verbal assault.

Attentional overload A psychological state in which the quantity and rate of environmental stimulation exceeds the individual's ability to process the incoming information.

Attitude Evaluative (good/bad) feeling toward a particular object, person, issue, or any other identifiable target in the environment.

Awareness The second level in Levinger and Snoek's model of relationships, where knowledge of another person is gained through his or her observable characteristics.

Balance theory A consistency theory of attitude change, based on the assumption that people like (or should like) people who share their important opinions and dislike (or should dislike) people who hold different views on issues that are important. When this assumption is violated, people are motivated to reestablish it by changing their attitudes, either toward the other person or toward the relevant issue.

Behavior potential Being able to act on intrinsic values; that is, things that are important to the person and/or group.

Behavioral intention An individual's intention to perform a specific behavior. It is a subjective probability, that is, the person's estimate of how likely it is that he or she will perform the behavior.

Belief Cognitive link between an object and an attribute or characteristic. It is a subjective probability, that is, an estimate of the probability that the object possesses the attribute.

Blaming the victim Reacting to the victims of discrimination and oppression by blaming them for their plight.

Bogus pipeline Technique for measuring attitudes that involves convincing subjects that they are connected to a machine that accurately measures their attitudes. Subjects are asked to guess what the machine is revealing about their attitudes.

Catharsis Reductions in angry arousal (emotional catharsis) or in the tendency to aggress (behavioral catharsis) due to having engaged in aggression or having witnessed aggression.

Causal attribution A belief about why a particular event occurred.

Central trait In impression formation, a key characteristic that has a significant influence on the overall impression formed.

Classical conditioning Process by which a stimulus comes to evoke a response that it did not previously evoke by being paired with another stimulus that naturally evokes the response. The conditioned response can be emotional, behavioral, or both.

Coercive power Social power that derives from the ability to inflict punishment on the target as a consequence of noncompliance.

Cognitive map A mental description of the spatial environment that enables individuals to organize and remember the important or distinguishing features of their surroundings.

Cohesiveness The extent to which group members are committed to group values and each other.

Communion Rituals and activities that bring individuals into contact with the collective whole, so that "we feelings" develop; one of Kanter's six commitment mechanisms.

Comparison level (CL) Individuals' perception of the level of positive versus negative outcomes to which they are entitled in the present as a function of their past experience with similar relationships or their perception of the positive versus negative outcomes experienced by others in similar relationships. (See *Outcomes.*)

Complementarity Patterning of traits in a relationship so that the partners have traits that are opposite in character or fit well together.

Conformity A change in the behavior of an individual that results in the individual becoming more similar to others in a group.

Congruence The degree of fit between people and their environment.

Consensus Agreement among people that is arrived at by informal rather than formal decision procedures.

Consistency Whether a person's behavior toward a stimulus object is similar to how that person has behaved toward the object in the past.

Construct Phenomena of theoretical interest to social researchers, for example, prejudice, attraction, similarity, conflict. To conduct research, constructs must be operationally defined; that is, variables that represent them must be defined.

Construct validity A criterion for evaluating social research that concerns the extent to which the

variables used in the research adequately represent the constructs of theoretical interest.

Contrast Perceiving the differences between two groups to be greater than they actually are.

Control group A group of individuals in a research design who do not receive the treatment of theoretical interest and yet who are observed for purposes of comparison with the treatment group.

Controllability The degree to which behavior or events can be intentionally affected.

Conventional legal reasoning Thinking about legal matters in terms of fulfilling role expectations and conforming to social norms; Level II in the Tapp-Levine model.

Correlational design A research design to gather data on the relationship between variables, in which the assignment rule is unknown and data is gathered only after the treatment has been delivered.

Correspondent inferences Attributing an act to an intention of the actor produced by a disposition to act in this manner. Correspondence is greatest when the act is attributed to a single disposition not shared by others.

Covariation principle An event is attributed to the one of its possible causes that is present when the event occurs and absent when the event does not occur.

Crowding A situation in which achieved contact with others exceeds desired contact.

Defensible space Those features of an environment that serve to bring it under the control of its occupants.

Demand characteristics Characteristics of a research project perceived by those participating in the research to be what the researcher expects. The participants may then attempt to give responses that seem to be expected; such responses are responses to the demand characteristics of the research.

Dependent or outcome variable The variable that the treatment is expected to affect.

Descriptive intimacy The disclosure of otherwise unavailable factual information about one's self (for example, detailed account of one's sex life or a car accident).

Diffusion of responsibility The tendency of people in a crowd to feel less personal responsibility because others are present.

Disclosure reciprocity Phenomenon in which individuals tend to match one another in their levels of communication intimacy.

Discrimination Overt negative behavior toward members of socially defined groups.

Disinhibition (of aggression) A reduction in the internalized societal constraints (inhibitions) against overt aggressive behavior.

Dissonance theory A consistency theory of attitude change, which postulates that awareness of inconsistencies among individuals' beliefs, attitudes, and behaviors produces an aversive state of tension or discomfort. To reduce this discomfort, they may change their attitudes.

Distinctiveness Whether a person's behavior toward a stimulus object is different from how that person behaves toward other (relevant) objects.

Double standard Believing that members of one gender (males) are entitled to a greater sexual freedom than members of the other gender (females).

Ego In Freud's theory, the component of the personality structure that mediates between the id impulses and the demands of the superego.

Egoism An early principle for explaining behavior, stressing that people act to obtain personal power.

Empathic concern Sympathetic, compassionate feelings toward another person or persons.

Environmental assessment People's judgments about the quality of specific places, for example, their residences or work environments.

Environmental attitudes The tendency to respond favorably or unfavorably toward one's surroundings.

Environmental psychology The study of human behavior and well-being in relation to the large-scale sociophysical environment.

Equality A hypothesized cultural value that states that all participants to an exchange situation should receive equal shares of its positive or negative outcomes. (See *Outcomes; Social exchange.*)

Equity A hypothesized cultural value that states that people should receive positive or negative outcomes in direct proportion to their deservingness or investments. (See *Outcomes; Social exchange.*)

Ethnocentrism Using the ingroup as a standard against which outgroups are judged. It is usually associated with a positive evaluation of ingroups and a negative evaluation of outgroups.

Evaluative intimacy The disclosure of personal feelings or judgments (for example, an intense expression of love, anger, or shame).

Excitation transfer Cognitively reassigning arousal to a category that may increase a tendency to label arousal as anger; such reassignment can result in increased aggression.

Expert power Social power that derives from the target's belief that the influencer has superior knowledge.

External validity A criterion for evaluating social research that concerns the extent to which generalizations can be made from the research to populations of interest.

Eye contact Mutual gaze, a significant element of intimacy.

False consensus A general belief that other people possess the same attitudes and behaviors as oneself.

Feminist A person who believes that men and women should have equal opportunities for individual development and power.

Frustration Blocking ongoing goal-directed behavior or the omission of an expected reinforcer.

Frustration-aggression hypothesis A theory proposed in 1939 that asserted that frustration always leads to aggression and aggression always results from frustration.

Functional approach A theory that postulates that attitudes fulfill important needs or functions for the individual and that to change attitudes one must provide alternative ways of satisfying these needs. Four types of functions have been suggested: *instrumental, knowledge, ego-defensive,* and *value-expressive.*

Functional model Defining normality on the basis of whether an act contributes to the welfare and survival of the species or group.

Groupthink A condition in which a highly cohesive group with directive leadership leads to uncritical consensus or decisions.

Group world The total perspective of a group, including its shared values, norms, beliefs, practices, customs, and so forth.

Halo effect In impression formation, the tendency to form a global positive impression that may subsequently exert illogical influences on judgment.

Hedonic relevance The extent to which an actor's behavior has positive or negative consequences for the perceiver.

Hedonism An early principle for explaining behavior, stressing that people act to obtain pleasure.

Identification In psychoanalytic theory, this refers to the process by which one individual (for example, the child) takes on or incorporates the beliefs and behaviors of another individual (for example, the parent).

Id In Freud's theory, the part of the personality that houses instinctual desires and seeks immediate gratification of its needs and desires.

Idiosyncracy credits Credits a leader builds up by following group norms that then permit him or her to lead the group in new, unfamiliar directions.

Imageability The ease with which a place is remembered.

Impact assessment Efforts to specify in a rigorous, complete manner all the consequences that might result from a particular development or intervention.

Impression management theory A theory of attitude change, which postulates that individuals are socialized to want to appear consistent to others. Consequently, they may report attitude change in order to appear consistent with past behaviors, when in fact they have not really changed their at-

titudes. The theory is suggested as an alternative explanation to dissonance theory for experiments on induced compliance.

Independent or treatment variable The variable in social research that represents the causal construct of the research hypothesis. It is expected to affect the dependent or outcome variable.

Induced compliance Paradigm for testing the effects of counterattitudinal behavior on attitude change. Subjects are induced to behave in some way that goes against their attitudes. Dissonance, impression management, and self-perception theories provide different explanations for the effects of induced compliance.

Information overload Having more incoming information than one can process; according to Milgram, this is a characteristic of urban life and reduces prosocial behavior.

Informational power Social power that derives from the persuasive content of a message.

Ingroup-outgroup bias The combination of favorable attitudes toward the ingroup and hostile attitudes toward the outgroup.

Inhibition (of aggression) Internalized societal constraints against overt aggressive behavior.

Inputs The positive or negative personal characteristics that a participant contributes to social relationships with others. (See *Investments.*)

Instinctive theory of aggression The view that aggression stems from species-wide unlearned behavior tendencies.

Instrumental aggression Aggression primarily motivated by a calculated desire to gain something (for example, money or property).

Interaction matrix A simplified representation of social relationships in which each participant's behavior is classified into a limited number of categories. (See *Prisoner's Dilemma.*)

Internal-external attributions The degree to which an attributed cause is in the person rather than in the environment.

Internal validity A criterion for evaluating social research that concerns the extent to which the observed relationship between the independent and dependent variables is a causal one.

Interpersonal attraction Attraction for another person, such as friendship or liking.

Intrinsic Valued and engaged in for its own sake and not as a means to something else.

Intrinsic-extrinsic motivation The degree to which behavior is enjoyable or an end in itself rather than instrumental or a means to an end.

Investment Putting one's time, money, or other resources into an organization, so that one has an interest in the organization's continued successful operation; one of Kanter's commitment mechanisms.

Isolation A situation in which desired contact with others exceeds achieved contact.

Just world A belief that people who receive rewards must be good while those who receive undesirable outcomes must be bad.

Latitudes Concept from social judgment theory of attitude change. Regions that can be located along an attitude dimension, which differ in their acceptability to the individual. The *latitude of acceptance* is the range of positions on the attitude issue that the person finds acceptable. The *latitude of rejection* is the range of positions that the person finds unacceptable. The *latitude of noncommitment* constitutes those positions that the person finds neither acceptable nor unacceptable.

Law of the Instrument Kaplan's notion that scientists (including social scientists) use the skills or techniques they have acquired via training to solve particular problems (including social problems), regardless of the relevance of these skills.

Learned helplessness A syndrome of cognitive, motivational, and emotional disturbances stemming from repeated encounters with uncontrollable events.

Legal socialization The process by which people develop a sense of legal consciousness and a sense of justice.

Legibility The ease with which the parts of an environment can be recognized and organized into a coherent pattern.

Legitimate power Power stemming from the target person's acceptance of the notion that a particular individual, by virtue of role or position, has the right to tell the target person what to do.

Likert's method of summated ratings Technique for measuring attitudes that involves asking subjects to indicate the extent of their agreement with a large number of statements on an issue. An *item analysis* identifies ambiguous and irrelevant statements. Attitude scores are obtained by summing respondents' ratings of the statements that remain after the item analysis.

LPC Least Preferred Coworker measure of leader orientation; high LPC ratings indicate a relationship orientation; low LPC ratings indicate a task-oriented leader.

Machiavellianism A personality trait that leads the individual to seek to achieve his or her self-interested goals regardless of the ethicality of the means employed in doing so.

Matching principle The tendency of people to choose partners who are approximately equal to themselves in attractiveness.

Mere exposure Mere repeated exposure to a stimulus increases liking for the stimulus (that is, familiarity leads to liking).

Mortification Exchanging a former identity for a new one as part of becoming a group member; one of Kanter's six commitment mechanisms.

Multiple act behavioral criterion Measure of behavior that includes a large number of actions toward an object. It assesses the overall class of actions that are relevant to the object.

Mutuality The fourth level in Levinger and Snoek's model of relationships in which deeper and more intimate information is exchanged between friends.

Noncommon effects Consequences of an action that would not occur if alternative actions were chosen.

Nonverbal communication Communication through such channels as facial expression, vocal cues, and body movements. Important to the communication of emotion and subtle interpersonal expectations.

Nonverbal sensitivity Ability to detect or "read" the nonverbal cues of others.

Norm of reciprocity Norm that people should treat others in a similar fashion to the way they are treated by others.

Norm of social responsibility Norm that an individual should help a person in need who is dependent upon that individual.

Normative social influence Influence stemming from a person's desire to adhere to what is perceived as the group norm.

Norms Socially accepted rules for appropriate behavior that regulate a person's overt behavior in various social situations.

Obedience A change in the behavior of an individual in the direction intended by a higher-status person.

Observational learning Learning by watching the behavior of a model.

Operant Adjective referring to any behavior by which an individual operates on the environment.

Organizational commitment People's sense of loyalty and allegiance to a group or organization.

Outcomes Pleasurable or unpleasurable consequences that result from one's social relationships with others.

Overjustification effect A reduction in the enjoyment of some activity produced by perceiving that the activity is a means to an end rather than an enjoyable end in itself.

Personal space An area with an invisible boundary surrounding the person's body into which intruders may not come.

Personalism The extent to which the perceiver believes that an actor intended to benefit or harm the perceiver.

Physical attractiveness Physical features of others that affect perception of and actions toward them; often expressed as a stereotypical tendency to believe that attractive people possess desirable characteristics.

Placebo A therapy that does not have a specific effect on the condition being treated; it may be a sugar pill or other treatment regimen.

Postconventional (principled) legal reasoning Thinking about legal matters in terms of ethical principles and choices distinct from concrete laws or social conventions; Level III in the Tapp-Levine model.

Preconventional legal reasoning Thinking about legal matters in terms of fear of punishment and/or deferring to authority; Level I in the Tapp-Levine model.

Prejudice Negative attitudes toward socially defined groups.

Prescriptive rule/role The reduction of group rules and roles to specific performative expectation that exclude judgment and choice on the part of group members.

Presentation of self In impression formation, the control exercised over the information people reveal about themselves, usually to present themselves in a favorable light.

Prevention Any strategy for coping with social problems by taking steps so that the problems do not develop.

Primacy-recency effects In impression formation, a primacy effect occurs when first impressions have a greater impact on overall impressions than later information. A recency effect occurs when more recent information has greater influence on social perception than initial information.

Prisoner's Dilemma An interaction matrix used to study bargaining and conflict resolution in which each participant's behavior is restricted to either a cooperative or a competitive choice. (See *Interaction matrix.*)

Privacy Process by which a person regulates interactions with others. It includes the individual's right to decide whether to disclose personal information and who will receive it.

Problem definition The process in which the nature of a social problem and its causes are identified. Two common ways of defining problems are those that focus on the person (person-centered) and those that focus on the situation (situation-centered).

Problem identification The process in which a particular set of conditions becomes identified as a social problem.

Program evaluation The systematic, research-based assessment of the effectiveness of programs in meeting their objectives.

Projection The perception that members of out-groups possess traits that are negatively evaluated by the ingroup.

Propinquity Proximity or geographical closeness. Propinquity is an important factor in interpersonal attraction.

Prototype A specific example that represents a category.

Provocation-motivated aggression Aggression when angry motives predominate, and the actor's primary purpose is retaliation.

Proxemics The study of human spatial behavior and the ways in which people use the physical environment to regulate their social interaction.

Psychological stress A psychological state that occurs when perceived environmental demands exceed the individual's perceived ability to cope.

Punishment Delivering a noxious stimulus to a person contingent upon his or her performance of an undesired behavior.

Quasi-experimental research design A research design in which the assignment rule is not random and in which the dependent variable is measured both before and after individuals receive the treatment.

Randomized experimental research design A research design in which a random assignment rule is used. Such a rule usually implies a great deal of control over the independent variable.

Recidivism A measure of institutional failure in rehabilitation programs; for example, the rate at which ex-mental patients return to the hospital, ex-cons to prison, and so forth.

Referent power Social power that derives from the target's desire to be similar to the influencer.

Relative deprivation A feeling of dissatisfaction experienced by people who, in the course of comparing their own lot in life with that of others with whom they sense a social or psychological affinity, come off second best.

Reliability The extent to which variables in research are free of error. Reliable variables are variables that contain relatively little measurement error.

Renunciation Enhancing one's loyalty to a group by giving up competing relationships outside the group; one of Kanter's six commitment mechanisms.

Response amplification Stigmatized others are evaluated more positively or more negatively than comparable members of nonstigmatized groups.

Reward power Social power that derives from the ability to provide the target of influence with a desired commodity in exchange for compliance.

Role taking Viewing the world from another person's perspective.

Roles Behavior patterns associated with or defined by norms.

Scapegoating Blaming outgroup members for one's own problems and frustrations.

Script A cognitive representation of events that organizes information about situations, roles, and behaviors.

Selective exposure Prediction from dissonance theory that people actively seek information that is consistent with their beliefs, attitudes, and behaviors, and actively avoid information that is inconsistent with their beliefs, attitudes, and behaviors.

Self-disclosure One important class of verbal communication; defined as what individuals tell others about themselves.

Self-focused attention Thinking primarily about oneself and one's own needs.

Self-fulfilling prophecy A belief that something is true that in turn leads to behavior that confirms the belief.

Self-monitoring An individual's concern with ascertaining what behaviors are appropriate in a given situation and success at managing his or her impressions accordingly.

Self-perception theory A theory of attitude change that postulates that individuals infer their attitudes from their previous, voluntary actions toward the attitude object; suggested as an alternative explanation to dissonance theory for experiments on induced compliance.

Self-rating technique Technique for measuring attitudes that involves only one general question on the issue. Subjects rate the favorability of their attitudes on a response scale.

Self-reward A process in which people reinforce their own behaviors by seeing themselves as good, and so on.

Semantic differential technique Technique for assessing the general meaning of a concept, often used to measure attitudes. Subjects rate the concept on bipolar, adjective dimensions. When the technique is used to measure attitudes, only dimensions that reflect evaluative feelings are used.

Sensitivity training groups (or T-groups) Groups in which people interact and receive feedback from others about themselves and their interpersonal behavior.

Setting A place that has become associated with recurring patterns of human activity (for example, grocery stores, dorm lounges, classrooms).

Sex guilt The extent to which a person feels guilty for violating a set of standards for sexual conduct.

Sex-role socialization The process by which children acquire the behaviors that their culture deems appropriate for their sex.

Situational thresholds Pressures of a situation that affect the probability of particular behaviors. When attitudes are used to predict behaviors, the attitudinal and behavioral measures must be equated in terms of situational thresholds.

Sleeper effect Finding that attitude change following exposure to a message from a low credibility source increases over time.

Social climate The degree to which a setting fosters social relationships among its members, provides opportunities for personal development, and reflects an emphasis on organizational maintenance or change.

Social control The process by which existing power and status relationships are maintained.

Social desirability The effect produced when individuals who participate in research attempt to "put their best foot forward."

Social-engineering approach An approach, often employed by the government, in which experts' solutions to social problems are bureaucratically imposed from the top down.

Social exchange A reciprocal transfer of goods, services, or sometimes even ideas and feelings among the various parties to a relationship.

Social facilitation The tendency of people to perform faster on some tasks when they are in the presence of others than when they are alone.

Social indicators Social measures that reflect on the quality of life in a society and that can be used to assess a country's progress toward national goals.

Social influence A change in behavior, perception, or attitude in the direction intended by another.

Social judgment theory A theory of attitude change that distinguishes between regions on an attitude dimension and postulates that messages that advocate positions within these various regions will be differentially successful in producing attitude change; particularly useful for understanding the effect of ego-involvement with an issue on susceptibility to persuasion.

Social power The potential for bringing about change in the behavior, perceptions, or attitudes of another.

Social problem solving An approach to social problems that emphasizes the connection and interdependence of issues, and that attempts to deal with given problems in context on their own terms.

Social psychology The study of how people affect and are affected by one another.

Socialization The process by which people come to learn and internalize the rules of their society.

Stable-unstable attributions The degree to which an attributed cause is permanent or unchanging, versus temporary or changing.

Statistical model Defining normality according to the frequency of an act within a particular culture or group. If the behavior is engaged in by a substantial percentage of the group, it is considered normal. If it is statistically infrequent, it is considered abnormal.

Status The extent to which a person possesses valued traits.

Stereotypes Beliefs and expectations held about some category of people such that all members of the category are assumed to possess the same traits.

Stigma A characteristic of a person that is perceived by others to be discrediting and usually as indicating something bad about the moral status of the individual.

Stress An imbalance between environmental demands and a person's capacity to cope with them.

Stressors Environmental demands that tax or exceed the individual's adaptive capacity.

Superego In Freud's theory, the part of personality that most closely corresponds to the conscience or internalized moral values.

Surface contact The third level in Levinger and Snoek's model of relationships, where knowledge of another person is gained through casual, face-to-face interaction.

Sympathy An early principle for explaining behavior, stressing that people imitate others.

Territoriality The behavior by which individuals lay claim to a particular area and defend the area against members of their own species.

Time out A disciplinary procedure in which a child is seated alone for a period of time after engaging in an undesirable behavior.

Tokens Numerically rare people belonging to a group whose membership is predominantly of some other kind of person (for example, a "token" female). Tokenism refers to relatively insignificant positive actions for members of a group that are used to relieve responsibility for taking more important actions.

Tolerance limit model Defining normality based on whether an act sufficiently annoys or bothers others in a position to do something about it, such as report it to the police.

Transcendence A process whereby an individual, feeling that a higher power or meaning resides in the group, lets the group make decisions for that individual.

Treatment group A group of individuals in a research design who receive the treatment of theoretical interest. Their responses on the dependent variable are compared with responses from a control group to infer the effects of the treatment variable.

Undermanning A condition in which available participants are fewer than the number normally required to maintain the setting at an optimal level.

Value confrontation Technique designed to induce people to change the importance they place on certain values and thereby to affect their behavior; involves convincing subjects that the priorities they assign to certain values reflect uncomplimentary truths about themselves.

Weapons effect A tendency for angered persons who strongly associate weapons with aggression to be more aggressive in the presence of weapons than when no weapons are present.

Yale communication research program Program of research on attitude change initiated at Yale University in the 1940s, which investigated the characteristics (source, message, audience) that affect the success of a persuasive message.

Zero contact The first level in Levinger and Snoek's model of relationships, where there is no contact or awareness between persons.

A new racial poll. *Newsweek,* February 26, 1979, pp. 48–53.

Abel, G. G., Barlow, D. H., Blanchard, E., & Guild, D. The components of rapists' sexual arousal. *Archives of General Psychiatry,* 1977, 34, 395–403.

Abelson, R. P. Script processing in attitude formation and decision-making. In J. S. Carroll & J. W. Payne (Eds.), *Cognition and social behavior.* Hillsdale, N.J.: Lawrence Erlbaum Associates, 1976.

Abramson, L. Y., Seligman, M. E. P., & Teasdale, J. D. Learned helplessness in humans: Critique and reformulation. *Journal of Abnormal Psychology,* 1978, 87, 49–74.

Abramson, P. R. Ethical requirements for research on human sexual behavior: From the perspective of participating subjects. *Journal of Social Issues,* 1977, 33(2), 184–192.

Abramson, P. R. Implications of the sexual system for the contraceptive process. In D. Byrne & W. Fisher (Eds.), *Adolescents, sex and contraception.* New York: McGraw-Hill, 1980.

Abramson, P. R. *The sexual system: A theory of human sexual behavior.* New York: Academic Press, 1981.

Acredolo, L. P. Frames of reference used by children for orientation in unfamiliar spaces. In G. Moore & R. Golledge (Eds.), *Environmental knowing.* Stroudsburg, Penn.: Dowden, Hutchinson & Ross, 1976.

Adair, J. G. Psychology at the turn of a century: Crises, challenges, promises. *Canadian Psychology,* 1980, 21, 165–178.

Adams, J. S. Inequity in social exchange. In L. Berkowitz (Ed.), *Advances in experimental social psychology* (Vol. 2). New York: Academic Press, 1965.

Adelson, J. The development of ideology in adolescence. In S. E. Dragastin & G. H. Elder, Jr. (Eds.), *Adolescence in the life cycle.* Washington, D.C.: Hemisphere, 1975.

Aderman, D., Brehm, S. S., & Katz, L. B. Empathic observation of an innocent victim: The just world revisited. *Journal of Personality and Social Psychology,* 1974, 29, 342–347.

Adorno, T. W., Frenkel-Brunswik, E., Levinson, D. J., & Sanford, N. R. *The authoritarian personality.* New York: Harper & Row, 1950.

Ahlgren, A., & Johnson, D. N. Sex differences in cooperative and competitive attitudes for the 2nd through 12th grades. *Developmental Psychology,* 1979, 15, 45–49.

Ajzen, I., & Fishbein, M. Attitudinal and normative variables as predictors of specific behaviors. *Journal of Personality and Social Psychology,* 1973, 27, 41–57.

Ajzen, I., & Fishbein, M. *Understanding attitudes and predicting social behavior.* Englewood Cliffs, N.J.: Prentice-Hall, 1980.

Alan Guttmacher Institute. *11 million teenagers.* New York: Alan Guttmacher Institute, 1976.

Aliotta, J., & Tapp, J. L. *Developmental, legal, and social aspects of rights-consciousness.* Unpublished manuscript, University of Minnesota, 1981.

Allen, V. L. Social support for nonconformity. In L. Berkowitz (Ed.), *Advances in experimental social psychology* (Vol. 8). New York: Academic Press, 1975.

Allman, T. D. "Panic before a dinner party: All men send regrets." *New York Times,* May 23, 1979, Section C, 1 & 3.

Allport, F. H. *Social psychology.* Boston: Houghton-Mifflin, 1924.

Allport, F. H. The effects of segregation and the consequences of desegregation: A social science statement. *Minnesota Law Review,* 1953, 37, 429–440.

Allport, G. The historical background of modern social psychology. In G. Lindzey & E. Aronson (Eds.), *The handbook of social psychology* (Vol. 1, 2d ed.). Reading, Mass.: Addison-Wesley, 1968.

Allport, G. W. Attitudes. In C. Murchison (Ed.), *Handbook of social psychology.* Worcester, Mass.: Clark University Press, 1935.

Allport, G. W. *The nature of prejudice.* Reading, Mass.: Addison-Wesley, 1954.

Allport, G. W. *Pattern and growth in personality.* New York: Holt, Rinehart and Winston, 1963.

Allport, G. W., & Vernon, P. E. *Studies in expressive movement.* New York: Macmillan, 1933.

Altman, I. Reciprocity of interpersonal exchange. *Journal for the Theory of Social Behavior,* 1973, 3, 249–261.

Altman, I. *The environment and social behavior: Privacy, personal space, territoriality, crowding.* Monterey, Cal.: Brooks/Cole, 1975.

Altman, I. Privacy regulation: Culturally universal or culturally specific? *Journal of Social Issues*, 1977, *33*(3), 66–84.

Altman, I. & Haythorn, W. W. Interpersonal exchange in isolation. *Sociometry*, 1965, *23*, 411–426.

Altman, I., & Haythorn, W. W. The ecology of isolated groups. *Behavioral Science*, 1967, *12*, 169–182.

Altman, I., & Taylor, D. A. *Social penetration: The development of interpersonal relationships.* New York: Holt, Rinehart and Winston, 1973.

Alutto, J. A., Hrebriniak, L. G., & Alsonso, R. C. On operationalizing the concept of commitment. *Social Forces*, 1973, *51*, 448–454.

Amabile, T. M., De Jong, W., & Lepper, M. R. Effects of externally imposed deadlines on subsequent intrinsic motivation. *Journal of Personality and Social Psychology*, 1976, *34*, 92–98.

American Friends Service Committee. *In place of war: An inquiry into non-violent national defense.* New York: Grossman, 1967.

Anderson, R., Manoogian, S. T., & Reznick, J. S. The undermining and enhancing of intrinsic motivation in preschool children. *Journal of Personality and Social Psychology*, 1976, *34*, 915–922.

Andreoli, V., & Worchel, S. Facilitation of social interaction through deindividuation of the target. *Journal of Personality and Social Psychology*, 1978, *36*, 549–556.

Andrews, F., & Withey, S. *Social indicators of well-being.* New York: Plenum, 1976.

Andrews, I. R., & Johnson, D. L. Small group polarization of judgments. *Psychonomic Science*, 1971, *24*, 191–192.

Andrews, G. R., & Debus, R. L. Persistence and causal perception of failure: Modifying cognitive attributions. *Journal of Educational Psychology*, 1978, *70*, 154–166.

Andrisani, P. J. Internal-external attitudes, personal initiative, and the labor market experiences of Black and White men. *Journal of Human Resources*, 1977, *12*, 308–328.

Antonovsky, A. *Health, stress, and coping.* San Francisco: Jossey-Bass, 1979.

Anyon, J. Ideology and United States history textbooks. *Harvard Educational Review*, 1979, *49*, 361–386.

Apple, W., Streeter, L. A., & Krauss, R. M. Effects of pitch and speech rate on personal attributions. *Journal of Personality and Social Psychology*, 1979, *37*, 715–727.

Appleyard, D. A. Why buildings are known. *Environment and Behavior*, 1969, *1*, 131–156.

Appleyard, D. A. Styles and methods of structuring a city. *Environment and Behavior*, 1970, *2*, 100–116.

Appleyard, D. A. *Planning a pluralistic city.* Cambridge, Mass.: M.I.T. Press, 1976.

Appleyard, D. A., & Craik, K. H. The Berkeley Environmental Simulation Laboratory and its research programme. *International Review of Applied Psychology*, 1978, *27*, 53–55.

Archer, R. L., & Berg, J. H. Disclosure reciprocity and its limits: A reactance analysis. *Journal of Experimental Social Psychology*, 1978, *14*, 527–540.

Archibald, K. Alternative orientations to social utilization. *Social Science Information*, 1970, *9*(2), 7–34.

Arend, R., Gove, F., & Sroufe, L. A. Continuity of individual adaptation from infancy to kindergarten: A predictive study of ego-resiliency and curiosity in preschoolers. *Child Development*, 1979, *50*, 950–959.

Argyle, M., & Dean, J. Eye-contact, distance, and affiliation. *Sociometry*, 1965, *28*, 289–304.

Aristotle. In W. R. Roberts (Ed. & trans.), *Aristotle, rhetoric and poetics.* New York: Modern Library, 1954.

Arms, R. L., Russell, G. W., & Sandilands, M. L. Effects on the hostility of spectators of viewing aggressive sports. *Social Psychology Quarterly*, 1979, *42*, 275–279.

Aronfreed, J. The socialization of altruistic and sympathetic behavior: Some theoretical and experimental analyses. In J. Macaulay & L. Berkowitz (Eds.), *Altruism and helping behavior.* New York: Academic Press, 1970.

Aronoff, J., & Messe, L. A. Motivational determinants of small group structure. *Journal of Personality and Social Psychology*, 1971, *17*, 319–324.

Aronson, E., *The social animal.* San Francisco: W. H. Freeman, 1980.

Aronson, E., & Bridgeman, D. Jigsaw groups and the desegregated classroom: In pursuit of common goals. *Journal of Personality and Social Psychology*, 1979, *5*, 438–446.

Aronson, E., Blaney, N., Stephan, C., Sikes, J., & Snapp, M. *The jigsaw classroom.* Beverly Hills, Cal.: Sage, 1978.

Asch, S. Forming impressions of personality. *Journal of Abnormal and Social Psychology*, 1946, *41*, 258–290.

Asch, S. Effects of group pressure upon the modification and distortion of judgment. In H. Guetzkow (Ed.), *Groups, leadership and men.* Pittsburgh, Pa.: Carnegie Press, 1951.

Asch, S. *Social psychology.* New York: Prentice-Hall, 1952.

Asch, S. Opinions and social pressure. *Scientific American,* 1955, *11,* 32.

Asch, S. Studies of independence and conformity: A minority of one against a unanimous majority. *Psychological Monographs,* 1956, *70,* No. 9.

Ashley, J. A. *Hospitals, paternalism, and the role of the nurse.* New York: Teachers College Press, 1976.

Ashour, A. S. Further discussion of Fiedler's contingency model of leadership effectiveness. *Organizational Behavior and Human Performance,* 1973, *9,* 369–376.

Austin, W., & Walster, E. Reactions to confirmations and disconfirmations of expectancies of equity and inequity. *Journal of Personality and Social Psychology,* 1974, *30,* 208–216.

Axelrod, R. Effective choice in the Prisoner's Dilemma. *Journal of Conflict Resolution,* 1980, *24,* 3–26. (a)

Axelrod, R. More effective choice in the Prisoner's Dilemma. *Journal of Conflict Resolution,* 1980, *24,* 379–404. (b)

Bachman, J. G., Smith, C. G., & Slesinger, J. A. Control, performance and satisfaction: An analysis of structural and individual effects. *Journal of Personality and Social Psychology,* 1966, *4*(2), 127–136.

Back, K. (Ed.). *In search for community: Encounter groups and social change.* Boulder, Colo.: Westview Press, 1978.

Bakan, D. *The quality of human existence.* Chicago: Rand McNally, 1966.

Baldassare, M. Human spatial behavior. *Annual Reveiw of Sociology,* 1978, *4,* 29–56.

Baldwin, A. L. *Theories of child development.* New York: Wiley, 1968.

Bales, R. F., & Cohen, S. P. *SYMLOG: A system for the multiple level observation of groups.* New York: The Free Press, 1979.

Bales, R. F., & Slater, P. Role differentiation in small decision-making groups. In T. Parsons & R. F. Bales (Eds.), *Family, socialization and interaction processes.* Glencoe, Ill.: Free Press, 1955.

Bales, R. F., & Strodtbeck, F. L. Phases in group problem-solving. *Journal of Abnormal and Social Psychology,* 1951, *46,* 485–495.

Bales, R. F. The equilibrium problem in small groups. In T. Parsons, R. F. Bales, & E. A. Shils (Eds.), *Working papers in the theory of action.* Glencoe, Ill.: Free Press, 1953.

Ball, S., & Bogatz, G. A. *The first year of Sesame Street: An evaluation.* Princeton, N. J.: Educational Testing Service, 1970.

Bandura, A. *Aggression: A social learning analysis.* Englewood Cliffs, N.J.: Prentice-Hall, 1973.

Bandura, A. *Social learning theory.* Englewood Cliffs, N.J.: Prentice-Hall, 1977.

Bandura, A., & McDonald, F. J. Influence of social reinforcement and the behavior of models in shaping children's moral judgments. *Journal of Abnormal and Social Psychology,* 1963, *67,* 274–281.

Bandura, A., Ross, D., & Ross, S. A. Vicarious reinforcement and imitative learning. *Journal of Abnormal and Social Psychology,* 1963, *67,* 601–607.

Bandura, A., & Walters, R. *Adolescent aggression.* New York: Ronald Press, 1959.

Bane, M. J. Marital disruption and the lives of children. *Journal of Social Issues,* 1976, *32*(1), 103–117.

Bannerjee, T. K. *Urban experience and the development of city image: A study in environmental perception and learning.* Unpublished doctoral dissertation, M.I.T., 1971.

Barker, R. G. Ecology and motivation. *Nebraska Symposium on Motivation,* 1960, *8,* 1–48.

Barker, R. G. *Ecological psychology: Concepts and methods for studying the environment of human behavior.* Stanford, Cal.: Stanford University Press, 1968.

Barker, R. G. & Associates. *Habitats, environments, and human behavior.* San Francisco: Jossey-Bass, 1978.

Barker, W. J., & Perlman, D. Volunteer bias and personality traits in sexual standards research. *Archives of Sexual Behavior,* 1975, *4,* 161–171.

Baron, R. A. Exposure to an aggressive model and apparent probability of retaliation as determinants of adult aggressive behavior. *Journal of Experimental Social Psychology,* 1971, *7,* 343–355.

Baron, R. A. *Human aggression.* New York: Plenum Press, 1977.

Baron, R. A., & Bell, P. A. Sexual arousal and aggression by males: Effects of type of erotic stimulation and prior provocation. *Journal of Personality and Social Psychology,* 1977, *35,* 79–87.

Baron, R. A., & Kepner, C. R. Model's behavior and attraction toward the model as determinants of adult aggressive behavior. *Journal of Personality and Social Psychology,* 1970, *14,* 340–344.

Barry, H., Bacon, M., & Child, I. L. A cross-cultural survey of some sex differences in socialization. *Journal of Abnormal and Social Psychology*, 1957, *55*, 327–332.

Bar-Tal, D., & Guttman, J. A comparison of teachers', pupils', and parents' attributions regarding pupils' academic achievements. *Contemporary Educational Psychology*, in press.

Bartlett, F. C. *Remembering*. Cambridge: Cambridge University Press, 1932.

Basso, K. H. "To give up on words": Silence in Western Apache culture. In P. Giglioloi (Ed.), *Language and social context*. London: Penguin, 1972.

Batson, C. D., & Coke, J. S. Empathy: A source of altruistic motivation for helping? In J. P. Rushton & R. M. Sorrentino (Eds.), *Altruism and helping behavior*. Hillsdale, N.J.: Lawrence Erlbaum Associates, 1981.

Batson, C. D., Coke, J. S., Jasnoski, M. L., & Hanson, M. Buying kindness: Effect of an extrinsic incentive for helping on perceived altruism. *Journal of Personality and Social Psychology*, 1978, *4*, 86–91.

Batson, C. D., Duncan, B., Ackerman, P., Buckley, T., & Birch, K. Is empathic emotion a source of altruistic motivation? *Journal of Personality and Social Psychology*, 1981, *40*, 290–302.

Batson, C. D., Harris, A. C., McCaul, K. D., Davis, M., & Schmidt, T. Compassion or compliance: Alternative dispositional attributions for one's helping behavior. *Social Psychology Quarterly*, 1979, *42*, 405–409.

Baum, A., & Epstein, Y. (Eds.). *Human response to crowding*. Hillsdale, N.J.: Lawrence Erlbaum Associates, 1978.

Baum, A., & Valins, S. (Eds.). *The social psychology of crowding: Studies of the effects of residential group size*. Hillsdale, N.J.: Lawrence Erlbaum Associates, 1977.

Baumann, D. D., & Sims, J. H. The tornado threat: Coping styles of the north and south. *Science*, 1972, *176*, 1386–1392.

Bazelon, D. L. Untitled. Address to the American Association of Correctional Psychologists' Conference on "Psychology's Roles and Contributions in Problems of Crime, Delinquency and Corrections." Lake Wales, Florida, January 20, 1972. (Mimeo).

Beach, F. A. (Ed.). *Sex and behavior*. New York: Wiley, 1965.

Beaman, A. L., Barnes, P. J., Klentz, B., & McQuirk, B. Increasing helping rates through information dissemination: Teaching pays. *Personality and Social Psychology Bulletin*, 1978, *4*, 406–411.

Becker, H. S. Notes on the concept of commitment. *American Journal of Sociology*, 1960, *66*, 32–40.

Becker, M. H., Drachman, R. H., & Kirscht, J. P. Predicting mothers' compliance with pediatric medical regimens. *Journal of Pediatrics*, 1972, *81*, 843–854.

Bell, P. A., Fisher, J. D., & Loomis, R. J. *Environmental psychology*. Philadelphia: Saunders, 1978.

Belsky, J. Child maltreatment : An ecological integration. *American Psychologist*, 1980, *35*, 320–335.

Bem, D. Self-perception: An alternative interpretation of cognitive dissonance phenomena. *Psychological Review*, 1967, *74*, 183–200.

Bem, D. J. *Beliefs, attitudes, and human affairs*. Belmont, Cal.: Brooks/Cole, 1970.

Bem, D. Self-perception theory. In L. Berkowitz (Ed.), *Advances in experimental social psychology* (Vol. 6). New York: Academic Press, 1972.

Bem, S. L. The measurement of psychological androgyny. *Journal of Consulting and Clinical Psychology*, 1974, *42*, 155–162.

Bennis, W. G., Benne, K. D., Chin, R., & Corey, K. E. (Eds.). *The planning of change*. New York: Holt, Rinehart and Winston, 1976.

Bentler, P. M., Jackson, D. N., & Messick, S. Identification of content and style: A two-dimensional interpretation of acquiescence. *Psychological Bulletin*, 1971, *76*, 186–204.

Berg, J. H., & Archer, R. L. Disclosure or concern: A second look at liking for the norm breaker. *Journal of Personality*, 1980, *48*, 245–257.

Berglas, S., & Jones, E. E. Drug choice as a self-handicapping strategy in response to noncontingent success. *Journal of Personality and Social Psychology*, 1978, *36*, 405–417.

Berkman, L. F., & Syme, S. L. Social networks, host resistance, and mortality: A nine-year follow-up study of Alameda County residents. *American Journal of Epidemiology*, 1979, *109*, 186–203.

Berkowitz, L. The frustration-aggression hypothesis revisited. In L. Berkowitz (Ed.), *Roots of aggression*. New York: Atherton, 1969.

Berkowitz, L. Social norms, feelings, and other factors affecting helping and altruism. In L. Berkowitz (Ed.), *Advances in experimental social psychology* (Vol. 6). New York: Academic Press, 1972.

Berkowitz, L. Some determinants of impulsive aggression: The role of mediated associations with reinforcements for aggression. *Psychological Review*, 1974, *81*, 165–176.

Berkowitz, L., & Daniels, L. Responsibility and dependency. *Journal of Abnormal and Social Psychology*, 1963, *66*, 429–436.

Berkowitz, L., & LePage, A. Weapons as aggression eliciting stimuli. *Journal of Personality and Social Psychology*, 1967, *7*, 202–207.

Berkowitz, L., & Powers, P. Effects of timing and justification of witnessed aggression on observers' punitiveness. *Journal of Research in Personality*, 1979, *13*, 71–80.

Bernardez-Bonesatti, T. Women and anger. *The Sciences*, 1978, *18*(9), 20–22.

Bernstein, I. S., & Mason, W. A. Group formation by rhesus monkeys. *Animal Behavior*, 1963, *11*, 28–31.

Berscheid, E., Dion, K., Walster, E., & Walster, G. W. Physical attractiveness and dating choice: A test of the matching hypothesis. *Journal of Experimental Social Psychology*, 1971, *7*, 173–189.

Berscheid, E., & Walster, E. When does a harmdoer compensate a victim? *Journal of Personality and Social Psychology*, 1967, *6*, 435–441.

Berscheid, E., & Walster, E. Physical attractiveness. In L. Berkowitz (Ed.), *Advances in experimental social psychology* (Vol. 7). New York: Academic Press, 1974.

Berscheid, E., & Walster, E. *Interpersonal attraction* (2d ed.). Reading, Mass.: Addison-Wesley, 1978.

Bickman, L. Social influence and diffusion of responsibility in an emergency. *Journal of Experimental Social Psychology*, 1972, *8*, 438–445.

Biener, L. *The effect of message repetition on attitude change: A model of informational social influence.* Unpublished doctoral dissertation, Columbia University, 1972.

Black, T. E., & Higbee, K. L. Effects of power, threat, and sex on exploitation. *Journal of Personality and Social Psychology*, 1973, *27*, 382–388.

Blaney, N., Stephan, C., Rosenfield, D., Aronson, E., & Sikes, J. Interdependence in the classroom: A field study. *Journal of Educational Psychology*, 1977, *69*, 121–128.

Blau, P. Cooperation and competition in a bureaucracy. *American Journal of Sociology*, 1954, *59*, 530–535.

Blau, P. M. *Exchange and power in social life.* New York: Wiley, 1964.

Blauner, R. *Alienation and freedom.* Chicago: University of Chicago Press, 1964.

Block, J. H. Conceptions of sex role: Some cross-cultural and longitudinal perspectives. *American Psychologist*, 1973, *28*, 512–526.

Block, J. H., Haan, N., & Smith, M. B. Socialization correlates of student activism. *Journal of Social Issues*, 1969, *25*(4), 143–177.

Blumenthal, M., Kahn, R. L., Andrews, F. M., & Head, K. B. *Justifying violence: Attitudes of American men.* Ann Arbor: Institute for Social Research, 1972.

Blumer, H. *Symbolic interactionism.* Englewood Cliffs, N.J.: Prentice-Hall, 1969.

Blumer, H. Social problems as collective behavior. *Social Problems*, 1971, *18*, 298–306.

Bock, E. W., & Webber, I. L. Suicide among the elderly: Isolating widowhood and mitigating alternatives. *Journal of Marriage and the Family*, 1972, *34*, 24–31.

Bogardus, E. S. Measuring social distance. *Journal of Applied Sociology*, 1925, *9*, 299–308.

Boice, R. In the shadow of Darwin. In R. G. Geen & E. C. O'Neal (Eds.), *Perspectives on aggression.* New York: Academic Press, 1976.

Bonjean, C. M., Grady, B. D., & Williams, J. A., Jr. Social morality and job satisfaction: A replication and extension. *Social Forces*, 1967, *46*, 492–501.

Bowlby, J. *Attachment.* New York: Basic Books, 1969.

Bowlby, J. *Separation.* New York: Basic Books, 1973.

Bowles, S., & Gintis, H. *Schooling in capitalist America.* New York: Basic Books, 1976.

Bowman, C. H., & Fishbein, M. Understanding public reaction to energy proposals: An application of the Fishbein model. *Journal of Applied Social Psychology*, 1978, *8*, 319–340.

Boyer, R. O., & Morais, H. M. *Labor's untold story.* New York: United Electrical, Radio & Machine Workers of America, 1955.

Bradburn, N. *The structure of psychological well-being.* Chicago: Aldine, 1969.

Bradley, P. H. Power, status, and upward communication in small decision-making groups. *Communication Monographs*, 1978, *45*, 33–43.

Bramel, D., Taub, B., & Blum, B. An observer's reaction to the suffering of his enemy. *Journal of Personality and Social Psychology*, 1968, *8*, 384–392.

Brehm, J. W. Post-decision changes in desirability of alternatives. *Journal of Abnormal and Social Psychology*, 1956, *52*, 384–389.

Brehm, J. W. *A theory of psychological reactance.* New York: Academic Press, 1966.

Brehm, J. W. Responses to loss of freedom: A theory of psychological reactance. In J. W. Thibaut,

J. T. Spence, & R. C. Carson (Eds.), *Contemporary topics in social psychology.* Morristown, N.J.: General Learning Press, 1976.

Brehm, J. W., & Cohen, A. R. Re-evaluation of choice alternatives as a function of their number and qualitative similarity. *Journal of Abnormal and Social Psychology,* 1959, *58,* 373–378.

Brehm, J. W., & Cole, H. Effects of a favor which reduces freedom. *Journal of Personality and Social Psychology,* 1966, *3,* 420–426.

Bremer, A. H. *An assassin's diary.* New York: Harper & Row, 1972.

Brend, R. M. Male-female intonation patterns in American English. In B. Thorne & N. Henley (Eds.), *Language and sex: Difference and dominance.* Rowley, Mass.: Newbury House, 1975.

Brewer, M. The role of ethnocentrism in intergroup conflict. In W. G. Austin & S. Worchel (Eds.), *The social psychology of intergroup relations.* Monterey, Cal.: Brooks/Cole, 1979.

Brickman, P., & Bryan, J. H. Equity versus equality as factors in children's moral judgments of thefts, charity, and third-party transfers. *Journal of Personality and Social Psychology,* 1976, *34,* 757–761.

Brickman, P., Karuza, J., Cohn, E., Rabinowitz, V. C., Coates, D., & Kidder, L. Models of helping and coping. *American Psychologist,* in press.

Brickman, P., Redfield, J., Harrison, A. A., & Crandall, R. Drive and predisposition as factors in the attitudinal effects of mere exposure. *Journal of Experimental Social Psychology,* 1972, *8,* 31–44.

Bridgeman, D. L. *The influence of cooperative interdependent learning on role taking and moral reasoning: A theoretical and empirical field study with fifth grade students.* Unpublished doctoral dissertation, University of California, Santa Cruz, 1977.

Brigham, J. C. Views of Black and White children concerning the distribution of personality characteristics. *Journal of Personality,* 1974, *42,* 144–158.

Brim, O. G., Jr., & Wheeler, S. *Socializations after childhood.* New York: Wiley, 1966.

Brock, T. C. Implications of commodity theory for value change. In A. G. Greenwald, T. C. Brock, & T. M. Ostrom (Eds.), *Psychological foundations of attitudes.* New York: Academic Press, 1968.

Brock, T. C., & Balloun, J. L. Behavioral receptivity to dissonant information. *Journal of Personality and Social Psychology,* 1967, *6,* 413–428.

Brookmire, D. A., & Sistrunk, F. The effects of perceived ability and impartiality of mediators and time pressure on negotiation. *Journal of Conflict Resolution,* 1980, *24,* 311–327.

Brophy, J., & Good, T. *Teacher-student relationships: Causes and consequences.* New York: Holt, Rinehart and Winston, 1974.

Broverman, I. K., Vogel, S. R., Broverman, D., Clarkson, F. E., & Rosenkrantz, P. S. Sex-role stereotypes: Current appraisal. *Journal of Social Issues,* 1972, *28*(2), 59–78.

Brown, C. A., Feldberg, R., Fox, E. M., & Kohen, J. Divorce: Chance of a new lifetime. *Journal of Social Issues,* 1976, *32*(1), 119–133.

Brown, M. E. Identification and some conditions of organizational involvement. *Administrative Science Quarterly,* 1969, *14,* 346–355.

Brown, P., & Elliott, R. Control of aggression in a nursery school class. *Journal of Experimental Child Psychology,* 1965, *2,* 103–107.

Brown, R. *Social psychology.* New York: Free Press, 1965.

Brownmiller, S. *Against our will: Men, women and rape.* New York: Simon & Schuster, 1975.

Bryan, J. H., & Test, M. A. Models and helping. *Journal of Personality and Social Psychology,* 1967, *6,* 400–407.

Bryant, J., & Zillmann, D. Effects of intensification of annoyance through unrelated residual excitation on substantially delayed hostile behavior. *Journal of Experimental Social Psychology,* 1979, *15,* 470–480.

Buck, R. Nonverbal communication of affect in children. *Journal of Personality and Social Psychology,* 1975, *31,* 644–653.

Buck, R. Individual differences in nonverbal sending accuracy and electrodermal responding: The externalizing-internalizing dimension. In R. Rosenthal (Ed.), *Skill in nonverbal communication: Individual differences.* Cambridge, Mass.: Oelgeschlager, Gunn, & Hain, 1979.

Bugental, D. E., Kaswan, J. W., & Love, L. R. Perception of contradictory meaning conveyed by verbal and nonverbal channels. *Journal of Personality and Social Psychology,* 1970, *16,* 647–655.

Burnstein, E., & Worchel, P. Arbitrariness of frustration and its consequences for aggression in a social situation. *Journal of Personality,* 1962, *30,* 528–540.

Burnstein, E., Vinokur, A., & Trope, Y. Interpersonal comparison versus persuasive argumentation: A more direct test of alternative explanations for group-induced shifts in individual choice. *Journal of Experimental Social Psychology,* 1973, *9,* 236–245.

Burton, I., Kates, R. W., & White, G. F. *The environment as hazard.* New York: Oxford University Press, 1978.

Bush, M., & Gordon, A. C. Bureaucracies and people. *Journal of Social Issues,* 1978, 34(4), 1–5.

Buss, A. H. *The psychology of aggression.* New York: Wiley, 1961.

Buss, A. H. Aggression pays. In J. L. Singer (Ed.), *The control of aggression and violence.* New York: Academic Press, 1971.

Bustamente, J. A. The "wetback" as deviant: An application of labelling theory. *American Journal of Sociology,* 1972, 77, 706–718.

Byrne, D. The influence of propinquity and opportunities for interaction on classroom relationships. *Journal of Abnormal and Social Psychology,* 1961, 67, 1–7.

Byrne, D. Attitudes and attraction. In L. Berkowitz (Ed.), *Advances in experimental social psychology* (Vol. 4). New York: Academic Press, 1969.

Byrne, D. *The attraction paradigm.* New York: Academic Press, 1971.

Byrne, D. Social psychology and the study of sexual behavior. *Personality and Social Psychology Bulletin,* 1977, 3, 3–30.

Byrne, D. Determinants of contraceptive values and practices. In M. Cook & G. Wilson (Eds.), *Love and attraction.* New York: Pergamon Press, 1979.

Byrne, D., & Clore, G. L. A reinforcement model of evaluative responses. *Personality: An International Journal,* 1970, 1, 103–128.

Byrne, D., Ervin, C. R., & Lamberth, J. Continuity between the experimental study of attraction and real-life computer dating. *Journal of Personality and Social Psychology,* 1970, 16, 157–165.

Byrne, D., Miller, C., Fisher, W. A., & White, L. A. *Affective and attributional responses to communicating a sexual message.* Paper presented at the meeting of the Psychnomic Society, St. Louis, November 1976.

Byrne, D., & Nelson, D. Attraction as a linear function of proportion of positive reinforcements. *Journal of Personality and Social Psychology,* 1965, 1, 659–663.

Byrne, D., & Rhamey, R. Magnitude of positive and negative reinforcements as a determinant of attraction. *Journal of Personality and Social Psychology,* 1965, 2, 884–889.

Cairns, R. B. *Social development: The origins and plasticity of interchanges.* San Francisco: W. H. Freeman, 1979.

Calder, B. J., & Ross, M. *Attitudes and behavior.* Morristown, N.J.: General Learning Press, 1973.

California's waiting game. *Newsweek,* May 21, 1979, pp. 26–27.

Cameron, C., Oskamp, S., & Sparks, W. Courtship American style: Newspaper ads. *Family Coordinator,* 1977, 26, 27–30.

Campbell, A., Converse, P., & Rodgers, W. *The quality of American life.* New York: Russell Sage, 1976.

Campbell, D. T. Factors relevant to the validity of experiments in social settings. *Psychological Bulletin,* 1957, 54, 297–312.

Campbell, D. T. Social attitudes and other acquired behavioral dispositions. In S. Koch (Ed.), *Psychology: A study of a science* (Vol. 6). New York: McGraw-Hill, 1963.

Campbell, D. T. Stereotypes and the perception of group differences. *American Psychologist,* 1967, 22, 817–829.

Campbell, D. T. Reforms as experiments. *American Psychologist,* 1969, 24, 409–429.

Campbell, D. T. On the conflicts between biological and social evolution and between psychology and moral tradition. *American Psychologist,* 1975, 30, 1103–1126.

Campbell, D. T., & Fiske, D. W. Convergent and discriminant validation by the multitrait-multimethod matrix. *Psychological Bulletin,* 1959, 56, 81–105.

Campbell, D. T., & Stanley, J. C. *Experimental and quasi-experimental designs for research.* Chicago: Rand McNally, 1963.

Cantor, N., & Mischel, W. Prototypes in person perception. In L. Berkowitz (Ed.), *Advances in experimental social psychology* (Vol. 12). New York: Academic Press, 1979.

Cantor, R. C. *And a time to live: Toward emotional well-being during the crisis of cancer.* New York: Harper & Row, 1978.

Caplan, N. Utilization and the better mousetrap theory. *APA Monitor,* December, 1977, p. 2.

Caplan, N. The two-communities theory and knowledge utilization. *American Behavioral Scientist,* 1979, 22, 459–470.

Caplan, N., Morrison A., & Stambaugh, R. *The use of social science knowledge in policy decisions at the national level: A report to respondents.* Ann Arbor, Mich.: Institute for Social Research, University of Michigan, 1975.

Caplan, N., & Nelson, S. On being useful: The nature and consequences of psychological research on social problems. *American Psychologist,* 1973, 28, 199–211.

Caplan, N., & Nelson, S. Who's to Blame? *Psychology Today,* November, 1974, 8, 99–104.

Carmichael, S., & Hamilton, C. V. *Black power: The politics of liberation in America*. New York: Random House, 1967.

Carnevale, P. J. D., Pruitt, D. G., & Britton, S. D. Looking tough: The negotiator under constituent surveillance. *Bulletin of Personality and Social Psychology*, 1979, 5, 118–121.

Carroll, J. S. Causal attributions in expert parole decisions. *Journal of Personality and Social Psychology*, 1978, 36, 1501–1511.

Carroll, J. S., & Payne, J. W. The psychology of the parole decision process: A joint application of attribution theory and information-processing psychology. In J. S. Carroll & J. W. Payne (Eds.), *Cognition and social behavior*. Hillsdale, N.J.: Lawrence Erlbaum Associates, 1976.

Carroll, J. S., & Payne, J. W. Judgments about crime and the criminal: A model and a method for investigating parole decision. In B. D. Sales (Ed.), *Perspectives in law and psychology* (Vol. 1). New York: Plenum Press, 1977.

Carroll, J. S., & Weiner, R. L. Cognitive social psychology in court and beyond. In A. Hastorf & A. Isen (Eds.), *Cognitive social psychology*. New York: Elsevier, in press.

Cartwright, D. P. Social psychology in the United States during the Second World War. *Human Relations*, 1948, 1, 333–352.

Cartwright, D. P. Contemporary social psychology in historical perspective. *Social Psychology Quarterly*, 1979, 42, 82–93.

Cartwright, D. P., & Zander, A. *Group dynamics, research and theory* (3rd ed.). New York: Harper & Row, 1968.

Carver, C. S. The facilitation of aggression as a function of objective self-awareness and attitudes toward punishment. *Journal of Experimental Social Psychology*, 1975, 11, 510–519.

Cash, T. F., & Derlega, V. J. The matching hypothesis: Physical attractiveness among same-sexed friends. *Personality and Social Psychology Bulletin*, 1978, 4, 240–243.

Cash, T. F., Kehr, J. A., Polyson, J., & Freeman, V. Role of physical attractiveness in peer attribution of psychological disturbance. *Journal of Consulting and Clinical Psychology*, 1977, 45, 987–993.

Cassileth, B. R. (Ed.). *The cancer patient: Social and medical aspects of care*. Philadelphia: Lea & Febiger, 1979.

Cauter, S. Personality traits in twins. In G. Claridge, S. Canter, & W. Hume (Eds.), *Personality differences and biological variations*. New York: Pergamon Press, 1973.

Chaiken, S. Heuristic versus systematic information processing and the use of source versus message cues in persuasion. *Journal of Personality and Social Psychology*, 1980, 39, 752–766.

Chaikin, A. L., & Derlega, V. J. Liking for the norm-breaker in self-disclosure. *Journal of Personality*, 1974, 42, 117–129. (a)

Chaikin, A. L., & Derlega, V. J. Variables affecting the appropriateness of self-disclosure. *Journal of Consulting and Clinical Psychology*, 1974, 42, 588–593. (b)

Chase, A. *The legacy of Malthus: The social costs of the new scientific racism*. New York: Knopf, 1976.

Chelune, G. J. Reactions to male and female disclosure at two levels. *Journal of Personality and Social Psychology*, 1976, 34, 1000–1003.

Cherry, F., Byrne, D., & Mitchell, H. E. Clogs in the bogus pipeline: Demand characteristics and social desirability. *Journal of Research in Personality*, 1976, 10, 69–75.

Chertkoff, J. M., & Conley, M. Opening offer and frequency of concession as bargaining strategies. *Journal of Personality and Social Psychology*, 1967, 7, 181–185.

Christie, R., & Geis, F. L. (Eds.). *Studies in Machiavellianism*. New York: Academic Press, 1970.

Christmas, J. J. How our health system fails minorities. *Civil Rights Digest*, 1977, 10, 4.

Cialdini, R. B., Darby, B. L., & Vincent, J. E. Transgression and altruism: A case for hedonism. *Journal of Experimental Social Psychology*, 1973, 9, 502–516.

Cialdini, R. B., & Kenrick, D. T. Altruism as hedonism: A social development perspective on the relationship of negative mood state and helping. *Journal of Personality and Social Psychology*, 1976, 34, 907–914.

Cialdini, R. B., Kenrick, D. T., & Hoerig, J. H. Victim derogation in the Lerner paradigm: Just world or just justification? *Journal of Personality and Social Psychology*, 1976, 33, 719–724.

Cialdini, R. B., Petty, R. E., & Cacioppo, J. T. Attitude and attitude change. *Annual Review of Psychology*, 1981, 32, 357–404.

Cicone, M. V., & Ruble, D. N. Beliefs about males. *Journal of Social Issues*, 1978, 34(1), 5–16.

Clark, K. Empathy: A neglected topic in psychological research. *American Psychologist*, 1980, 35, 187–190.

Clark, K. B., & Clark, M. P. Racial identification and preference in Negro children. In T. M. Newcomb & E. L. Hartley (Eds.), *Readings in social psy-*

chology. New York: Holt, Rinehart and Winston, 1947.

Clark, L., & Lewis, D. *Rape: The price of coercive sexuality.* Toronto: The Women's Press, 1977.

Clark, M. S., & Mills, J. Interpersonal attraction in exchange and communal relationships. *Journal of Personality and Social Psychology,* 1979, *37,* 12–24.

Clark, R. D., & Word, L. E. Why don't bystanders help? Because of ambiguity? *Journal of Personality and Social Psychology,* 1972, *24,* 392–401.

Clark, R. D., & Word, L. E. Where is the apathetic bystander? Situational characteristics of the emergency. *Journal of Personality and Social Psychology,* 1974, *29,* 279–288.

Clifford, M., & Walster, E. The effect of physical attractiveness on teacher expectation. *Sociology of Education,* 1973, *46,* 248–258.

Cline, V. B., Croft, R. G., & Courrier, S. Desensitization of children to television violence. *Journal of Personality and Social Psychology,* 1973, *27,* 360–365.

Coates, J. F. *What is a public policy issue?* Paper presented at the Annual Meeting of the American Association for the Advancement of Science, Denver, February, 1977.

Coch, L., & French, J. R. P., Jr. Overcoming resistance to change. *Human Relations,* 1948, *1,* 512–532.

Cohen, E. G. Design and redesign of the desegregated school. In W. G. Stephan & J. R. Feagin (Eds.), *School desegregation: Past, present and future.* New York: Plenum Press, 1980.

Cohen, M. *Recent advances in our understanding of school effects research.* Paper presented at the meeting of the American Association of Colleges of Teacher Education, Chicago, March 1979.

Cohen, R. L. On the distinction between individual deserving and distributive justice. *Journal for the Theory of Social Behavior,* 1979, *9,* 167–186.

Cohen, S. Environmental load and the allocation of attention. In A. Baum, J. E. Singer, & S. Valins (Eds.), *Advances in environmental psychology.* New York: Lawrence Erlbaum Associates, 1978.

Cohen, S., Evans, G. W., Krantz D. S., & Stokols, D. Physiological, motivational, and cognitive effects of aircraft noise on children. *American Psychologist,* 1980, *35,* 231–243.

Coke, J. S., Batson, C. D., & McDavis, K. Empathic meditation of helping: A two-stage model. *Journal of Personality and Social Psychology,* 1978, *36,* 752–766.

Coleman, J. C. Friendship and the peer group in adolescence. In J. Adelson (Ed.), *Handbook of adolescent psychology.* New York: Wiley, 1980.

Coleman, J. S. *The adolescent society.* New York: Free Press, 1961.

Cone, J., & Hayes, S. *Environmental problems/Behavioral solutions.* Monterey, Cal.: Brooks/Cole, 1980.

Conger, J. J. *Adolescence and youth* (3rd ed.). New York: Harper & Row, 1977.

Connolly, T., Conlon, E., & Deutsch, S. Organizational effectiveness: A multiple-constituency approach. *Academy of Management Review,* 1980, *5*(2).

Cook, S. W. Social science and school desegregation: Did we mislead the Supreme Court? *Personality and Social Psychology Bulletin,* 1979, *5,* 420–437.

Cook, T. D., Appleton, H., Conner, R. F., Shaffer, A., Tamkin, G., & Weber, S. J. *"Sesame Street" Revisited.* New York. Russell Sage Foundation, 1975.

Cook, T. D., & Campbell, D. W. *Quasi-experimentation: Design and analysis issues for field settings.* Chicago: Rand McNally, 1979.

Cooper, B. *Wife Beating: Counselor Training Manual #2.* Ann Arbor, Mich.: Domestic Violence Project, Inc., 1976.

Cooper, H. M. Controlling personal rewards: Professional teachers' differential use of feedback and the effects of feedback on the students' motivation to perform. *Journal of Educational Psychology,* 1977, *69,* 419–427.

Cooper, H. M. Pygmalion grows up: A model for teacher expectation communication and performance influence. *Review of Educational Research,* 1979, *49,* 389–410.

Cooper, J., & Fazio, R. H. The formation and persistence of attitudes that support intergroup conflict. In W. G. Austin & S. Worchel (Eds.), *The social psychology of intergroup relations.* Monterey, Cal.: Brooks/Cole, 1979.

Corea, G. *The hidden malpractice.* New York: Jove, 1977.

Coser, R. L. Laughter among colleagues: A study of the social functions of humor among the staff of a mental hospital. *Psychiatry,* 1960, *23,* 81–95.

Court, J. H. Pornography and sex crimes: A reevaluation in the light of recent trends around the world. *International Journal of Criminology and Penology,* 1976, *5,* 129–157.

Court, J. H. Sex and violence: A ripple effect. In N. Malamuth & E. Donnerstein (Eds.), *Pornography and sexual aggression.* New York: Academic Press, in press.

Covington, M. V., & Omelich, C. L. Effort: The double-edged sword in school achievement. *Journal of Educational Psychology,* 1979, *71,* 169–182. (a)

Covington, M. V., & Omelich, C. L. It's best to be able and virtuous too: Student and teacher evaluative responses to successful effort. *Journal of Educational Psychology,* 1979, *71,* 688–700. (b)

Cozby, P. C. Self-disclosure, reciprocity, and liking. *Sociometry,* 1972, *35,* 151–160.

Cozby, P. C. Self-disclosure: A literature review. *Psychological Bulletin,* 1973, *79,* 73–91.

Cozby P. C., & Jebousek, S. *Courtship via newspaper advertisements.* Unpublished manuscript, California State University, Fullerton, 1977.

Craik, K. H. The comprehension of the everyday physical environment. *Journal of the American Institute of Planners,* 1968, *34,* 646–658.

Craik, K. H. Appraising the objectivity of landscape dimensions. In J. V. Krutilla (Ed.), *Natural environments: Studies in theoretical and applied analysis.* Baltimore, Md.: The Johns Hopkins University Press, 1972.

Craik, K. H. Multiple scientific paradigms in environmental psychology. *International Journal of Psychology,* 1977, *12,* 147–157.

Crain, R. L., & Mahard, R. E. Desegregation and Black achievement: A review of the research. *Law and Contemporary Problems,* 1978, *42,* 17–56.

Crandall, V. C. *Expecting sex differences and sex differences in expectancies: A developmental analysis.* Paper presented at the annual meeting of the American Psychological Association, Toronto, September 1978.

Crano, W. D., & Brewer, M. B. *Principles of research in social psychology.* New York: McGraw-Hill, 1973.

Cronbach, L. J., & Meehl, P. E. Construct validity in psychological tests. *Psychological Bulletin,* 1955, *52,* 281–302.

Crosbie, P. V. (Ed.). *Interaction in small groups.* New York: Macmillan, 1975.

Crosby, F. A model of egoistic relative deprivation. *Psychological Review,* 1976, *83,* 85–113.

Crosby, F., & Nyquist, L. The female register: An empirical study of Lakoff's hypothesis. *Language in Society,* 1977, *6,* 313–322.

Crozier, M. *The bureaucratic phenomenon.* Chicago: University of Chicago Press, 1964.

Crutchfield, R. S. Conformity and character. *American Psychologist,* 1955, *10,* 191–198.

Crutchfield, R. S., & Krech, D. Some guides to the understanding of the history of psychology. In L. Postman (Ed.), *Psychology in the making.* New York: Knopf, 1962.

Curran, J. P. Skills training as an approach to the treatment of heterosexual-social anxiety: A review. *Psychological Bulletin,* 1977, *84,* 140–157.

Curran, J. P., & Lippold, S. The effects of physical attraction and attitude similarity on attraction in dating dyads. *Journal of Personality,* 1975, *43,* 528–539.

Cutrona, C. E. Transition to college: Loneliness and the process of social adjustment. In L. A. Peplau and D. Perlman (Eds.), *Loneliness: A sourcebook of current theory, research and therapy.* New York: Wiley-Interscience, 1982.

Dalton, M. *Men who manage.* New York: Wiley, 1959.

D'Andrade, R. G. Sex differences and cultural institutions. In E. E. Maccoby (Ed.), *The development of sex differences.* Stanford, Cal.: Stanford University Press, 1966.

Darley, J. M., & Batson, C. D. From Jerusalem to Jericho: A study of situational and dispositional variables in helping behavior. *Journal of Personality and Social Psychology,* 1973, *27,* 100–108.

Darley, J. M., & Berscheid, E. Increased liking as a result of the anticipation of personal contact. *Human Relations,* 1967, *20,* 29–39.

Darley, J. M., & Latané, B. Bystander intervention in emergencies: Diffusion of responsibility. *Journal of Personality and Social Psychology,* 1968, *10,* 202–214.

Darley, J. M., & Latané, B. Norms and normative behavior: Field studies of social interdependence. In J. Macaulay & L. Berkowitz (Eds.), *Altruism and helping behavior.* New York: Academic Press, 1970.

Darley, J. M., Teger, A., & Lewis, L. Do groups always inhibit individuals' responses to potential emergencies? *Journal of Personality and Social Psychology,* 1973, *26,* 395–399.

Davis, D. Implications for interaction versus effectance and mediators of the similarity-attraction relationship. *Journal of Experimental Social Psychology,* 1981, *17,* 96–116.

Davis, J. H. *Group performance.* Reading, Mass.: Addison-Wesley, 1969.

Davis, J. H. Group decision and social interaction. *Psychological Review,* 1973, *80,* 97–125.

Davis, J. H., Bray, R., & Holt, R. The empirical study of decision processes in juries. In J. L. Tapp & F. J. Levine (Eds.), *Law, justice, and the individual* *in society: Psychological and legal issues.* New York: Holt, Rinehart and Winston, 1977.

De Carufel, A. Factors affecting the evaluation of improvement: The role of normative standards and allocator resources. *Journal of Personality and Social Psychology,* 1979, *37,* 847–857.

De Carufel, A., & Schopler, J. Evaluation of outcome improvement resulting from threats and appeals. *Journal of Personality and Social Psychology,* 1979, *37,* 662–673.

de Jonge, D. Images of urban areas: Their structure and psychological foundations. *Journal of the American Institute of Planners,* 1962, *28,* 266–276.

de Tocqueville, A. *Democracy in America* (Vol. 1). New York: Schocken Books, 1961.

Dean, L. M., Willis, F. N., & Hewitt, J. Initial interaction distance among individuals equal and unequal in military rank. *Journal of Personality and Social Psychology,* 1975, *32,* 294–299.

Delgado, J. M. R. Offensive-defensive behavior in free monkeys and chimpanzees induced by radio stimulation of the brain. In S. Garattini & E. G. Sigg (Eds.), *Aggressive behavior.* New York: Wiley, 1969.

Dengerink, H. A., & Myers, A. The effects of failure and depression on subsequent aggression. *Journal of Personality and Social Psychology,* 1977, *35,* 88–96.

DePaulo, B. M., & Rosenthal, R. Ambivalence, discrepancy, and deception in nonverbal communication. In R. Rosenthal (Ed.), *Skill in nonverbal communication.* Cambridge, Mass.: Oelgeschlager, Gunn, & Hain, 1979.

Derlega, V. J., & Chaikin, A. L. Norms affecting self-disclosure in men and women. *Journal of Consulting and Clinical Psychology,* 1976, *44,* 376–380.

Derlega, V. J., & Chaikin, A. L. Privacy and self-disclosure in social relationships. *Journal of Social Issues,* 1977, *33*(3), 102–115.

Derlega, V. J., Durham, B., Gockel, B., & Sholis, D. Sex differences in self-disclosure: Effects of topic content, friendship, and partner's sex. *Sex Roles,* 1981, *7,* 433–448.

Derlega, V. J., & Grzelak, A. L. Appropriateness of self-disclosure. In G. J. Chelune (Ed.), *Self-disclosure: Origins, patterns, and implications of openness in interpersonal relationships.* San Francisco: Jossey-Bass, 1979.

Derlega, V. J., Harris, M. S., & Chaikin, A. L. Self-disclosure reciprocity, liking and the deviant. *Journal of Experimental Social Psychology,* 1973, *9,* 277–284.

Derlega, V. J., & Margulis, S. T. Why loneliness occurs: The interrelationship of social-psychological and privacy concepts. In L. A. Peplau & D. Perlman (Eds.), *Loneliness.* New York: Wiley-Interscience, 1982.

Derlega, V. J., Wilson, M., & Chaikin, A. L. Friendship and disclosure reciprocity. *Journal of Personality and Social Psychology,* 1976, *34,* 578–582.

Dermer, M., & Pyszczynski, T. A. Effects of erotica upon men's loving and liking responses for the women they love. *Journal of Personality and Social Psychology,* 1978, *36,* 1302–1309.

Dermer, M., & Thiel, D. L. When beauty may fail. *Journal of Personality and Social Psychology,* 1975, *31,* 1168–1176.

Deur, J. D., & Parke, R. Effects of inconsistent punishment on aggression in children. *Developmental Psychology,* 1970, *2,* 403–411.

Deutsch, M. An experimental study of the effects of cooperation and competition upon group process. *Human Relations,* 1949, *2,* 199–231. (a)

Deutsch, M. A theory of cooperation and competition. *Human Relations,* 1949, *2,* 129–152. (b)

Deutsch, M. The effect of motivational orientation upon trust and suspicion. *Human Relations,* 1960, *13,* 123–129. (a)

Deutsch, M. Minority group and class status as related to social and personality factors in scholastic achievement. *Society for Applied Anthropology Monographs,* 1960, No. 2. (b)

Deutsch, M. *The resolution of conflict.* New Haven, Conn.: Yale University Press, 1973.

Deutsch, M. Equity, equality and need: What determines which value will be used as the basis of distributive justice? *Journal of Social Issues,* 1975, *31*(3), 137–149.

Deutsch, M., & Collins, M. *Interracial housing: A psychological evaluation of a social experiment.* Minneapolis: University of Minnesota Press, 1951.

Deutsch, M., & Gerard, H. B. A study of normative and informational social influence upon individual judgment. *Journal of Abnormal and Social Psychology,* 1955, *51,* 629–636.

Deutsch, M., & Krauss, R. M. The effect of threat upon interpersonal bargaining. *Journal of Abnormal and Social Psychology,* 1960, *61,* 181–189.

Deutsch, M., & Krauss, R. M. Studies of interpersonal bargaining. *Journal of Conflict Resolution,* 1962, *6,* 52–76.

DeVries, D. L., & Edwards, K. J. Student teams and learning games: Their effects on cross-race and cross-sex interaction. *Journal of Educational Psychology*, 1974, *66*, 741–749.

Dickens, W., & Perlman, D. Friendship over the life cycle. In S. Duck & R. Gilmour (Eds.), *Personal Relationships 2: Developing personal relationships*. London: Academic Press, 1981.

Diener, E. Effects of prior destructive behavior, anonymity and group presence on deindividuation and aggression. *Journal of Personality and Social Psychology*, 1976, *33*, 497–507.

Dillehay, R. C. On the irrelevance of the classic negative evidence concerning the effect of attitudes on behavior. *American Psychologist*, 1973, *28*, 887–891.

DiMatteo, M. R. A social-psychological analysis of physician-patient rapport: Toward a science of the art of medicine. *Journal of Social Issues*, 1979, *35*(1), 12–33.

DiMatteo, M. R., Friedman, H. S., & Taranta, A. Sensitivity to bodily nonverbal communication as a factor in practioner-patient rapport. *Journal of Nonverbal Behavior*, 1979, *4*(1), 18–26.

Dion, K. K. Physical attractiveness and evaluation of children's transgressions. *Journal of Personality and Social Psychology*, 1972, *24*, 207–213.

Dion, K. K. The incentive value of physical attractiveness for young children. *Personality and Social Psychology Bulletin*, 1977, *3*, 67–70.

Dion, K. K. Physical attractiveness, sex roles and heterosexual attraction. In M. Cook (Ed.), *The bases of human sexual attraction*. London: Academic Press, 1980.

Dion, K. K., Berscheid, E., & Walster, E. What is beautiful is good. *Journal of Personality and Social Psychology*, 1972, *24*, 285–290.

Dipboye, R. L., Arvey, R. D., & Terpstra, D. E. Sex and physical attractiveness of raters and applicants as determinants of resume evaluations. *Journal of Applied Psychology*, 1977, *62*, 288–294.

Dipboye, R. L., Fromkin, H. L., & Wiback, K. Relative importance of applicant sex, attractiveness, and scholastic standing in evaluation of job applicant resumes. *Journal of Applied Psychology*, 1975, *60*, 39–45.

Dittes, J., & Kelley, H. H. Effects of different conditions of acceptance upon conformity to group norms. *Journal of Abnormal and Social Psychology*, 1956, *53*, 100–107.

Dobash, R. E., & Dobash, R. P. Wives: The "appropriate" victims of marital violence. *Victimology*, 1978, *2*, 426–442.

Dollard, J., Doob, L. W., Miller, N. E., Mowrer, O. H., & Sears, R. R. *Frustration and aggression*. New Haven: Yale University Press, 1939.

Donnerstein, E. Aggressive-erotica and violence against women. *Journal of Personality and Social Psychology*, 1980, *39*, 269–277.

Donnerstein, E., & Berkowitz, L. Victim reactions in aggressive erotic films as a factor in violence against women. *Journal of Personality and Social Psychology*, 1981, *41*, 710–724.

Donnerstein, E., Donnerstein, M., & Evans, P. Erotic stimuli and aggression: Facilitation or inhibition? *Journal of Personality and Social Psychology*, 1975, *32*, 237–244.

Donnerstein, M., & Donnerstein, E. Modeling in the control of interracial aggression: The problem of generality. *Journal of Personality*, 1977, *45*, 100–116.

Donovan, M., & Pierce, S. *Cancer care nursing*. New York: Appleton-Century-Crofts, 1976.

Doob, A. N., & MacDonald, G. E. Television viewing and fear of victimization: Is the relationship causal? *Journal of Personality and Social Psychology*, 1979, *37*, 170–179.

Doob, A. N., & Wood, L. Catharsis and aggression: The effects of annoyance and retaliation on aggressive behavior. *Journal of Personality and Social Psychology*, 1972, *22*, 156–162.

Dorn, E. *Rules and racial equality*. New Haven, Conn.: Yale University Press, 1979.

Dowling, W. F. At General Motors: System 4 builds performance and profits. *Organizational Dynamics*, 1975, *3*, 23–38.

Drabman, R. S., & Thomas, M. H. Does media violence increase children's tolerance of real-life aggression? *Developmental Psychology*, 1974, *10*, 418–421.

Driscoll, R., Davis, K. E., & Lipetz, M. E. Parental interference and romantic love: The Romeo and Juliet effect. *Journal of Personality and Social Psychology*, 1972, *24*, 1–10.

Dubin, R., Champoux, J. E., & Porter, L. W. Central life interests and organizational commitments of blue-collar and clerical workers. *Administrative Science Quarterly*, 1975, *20*, 411–421.

Duncan, S., Jr. Some signals and rules for taking speaking turns in conversations. In S. Weitz (Ed.), *Nonverbal communication*. New York: Oxford University Press, 1974.

Dunphy, D. C. The social structure of urban adolescent peer groups. *Sociometry*, 1963, *26*, 230–246.

Dutton, D., & Aron, A. Some evidence for heightened sexual attraction under conditions of high anxiety. *Journal of Personality and Social Psychology*, 1974, 30, 510–517.

Duval, S., & Wicklund, R. A. *A theory of objective self-awareness.* New York: Academic Press, 1972.

Dweck, C. S. The role of expectations and attributions in the alleviation of learned helplessness. *Journal of Personality and Social Psychology*, 1975, 31, 647–685.

Dyck, R. J., & Rule, B. G. Effect on retaliation of causal attributions concerning attack. *Journal of Personality and Social Psychology*, 1978, 36, 521–529.

Eagly, A. H. Sex differences in influenceability. *Psychological Bulletin*, 1978, 85, 86–116.

Eagly, A. H., Wood, W., & Chaiken, S. Causal inferences about communications and their effect on opinion change. *Journal of Personality and Social Psychology*, 1978, 36, 424–435.

Edney, J. J. Human territories: Comment on functional properties. *Environment and Behavior*, 1976, 8, 31–48.

Edwards, D. W. Black versus whites: When is race a relevant variable? *Journal of Personality and Social Psychology*, 1974, 29, 39–49.

Efran, M. G. The effect of physical appearance on the judgment of guilt, interpersonal attraction, and severity of recommended punishment in a simulated jury task. *Journal of Research in Personality*, 1974, 8, 45–54.

Ehrlich, P. *The population bomb.* New York: Ballantine Books, 1968.

Eibl-Eibesfeldt, I. Phylogenetic adaptation as determinant of aggressive behavior in man. In J. deWit & W. W. Hartup (Eds.), *Determinants and origins of aggressive behavior.* Paris: Mouton, 1974.

Eibl-Eibesfeldt, I. *Ethology: The biology of behavior* (2d ed.). New York: Holt, Rinehart and Winston, 1975.

Ekman, P. (Ed.). *Darwin and facial expression.* New York: Academic Press, 1973.

Ekman, P., & Friesen, W. V. Nonverbal leakage and clues to deception. *Psychiatry*, 1969, 32, 88–106.

Ekman, P., & Friesen, W. V. Detecting deception from body or face. *Journal of Personality and Social Psychology*, 1974, 29, 288–298.

Ekman, P., & Friesen, W. V. *Unmasking the face.* Englewood Cliffs, N.J.: Prentice-Hall, 1975.

Elder, G. H., Jr. Adolescence in historical perspective. In J. Adelson (Ed.), *Handbook of adolescent psychology.* New York: Wiley, 1980.

Ellis, D. P., Weiner, P., & Miller, L. Does the trigger pull the finger? An experimental test of

weapons as aggression-eliciting stimuli. *Sociometry*, 1971, 34, 435–465.

Ellsworth, P. Direct gaze as a social stimulus: The example of aggression. In P. Pliner, L. Krames, & T. Alloway (Eds.), *Nonverbal communication of aggression.* New York: Plenum Press, 1975.

Ellsworth, P. C., & Langer, E. J. Staring and approach: An interpretation of the stare as a nonspecific activator. *Journal of Personality and Social Psychology*, 1976, 33, 117–122.

Elms, A. C., & Milgram, S. Personality characteristics associated with obedience and defiance toward authoritative command. *Journal of Experimental Research in Personality*, 1966, 1, 282–289.

Endler, N. S., Wiesenthal, D. L., & Geller, S. H. The generalization of the effects of agreement and correctness on relative competence mediating conformity. *Canadian Journal of Behavioural Science*, 1972, 4, 322–329.

Engle, T. L. Personality adjustments of children belonging to two minority groups. *Journal of Educational Psychology*, 1948, 36, 443–460.

English, D. The politics of pornography. *Mother Jones*, 1980, 5, 20–23; 43–47.

Entwisle, D. *Modeling young children's performance expectancies.* Paper presented at the LRDC Conference: Teacher and Student Perceptions of Success and Failure, Pittsburgh, 1979.

Enzle, M. E., Hansen, R. D., & Lowe, C. A. Causal attribution in the mixed-motive game: Effects of facilitory and inhibitory environmental forces. *Journal of Personality and Social Psychology*, 1975, 31, 50–54.

Enzle, M. E., & Shopflocher, D. Instigation of attribution processes by attributional questions. *Personality and Social Psychology Bulletin*, 1978, 4, 595–599.

Epstein, R., & Komorita, S. S. Childhood prejudice as a function of parental ethnocentrism, punitiveness, and outgroup characteristics. *Journal of Personality and Social Psychology*, 1966, 3, 259–264. (a)

Epstein, R., & Komorita, S. S. Prejudice among Negro children as related to parental ethnocentrism and punitiveness. *Journal of Personality and Social Psychology*, 1966, 4, 643–647. (b)

Epstein, S. The stability of behavior: I. On predicting most of the people much of the time. *Journal of Personality and Social Psychology*, 1979, 37, 1097–1126.

Epstein, S., & Taylor, S. P. Instigation to aggression as a function of the degree of defeat and the perceived aggressive intent of the opponent. *Journal of Personality*, 1967, 38, 313–328.

Erickson, F. Talking down: Some cultural sources of miscommunication in interracial interviews. In A. Wolfgang (Ed.), *Nonverbal behavior*. New York: Academic Press, 1979.

Ericsson, K. A., & Simon, H. A. Verbal reports as data. *Psychological Review*, 1980, *87*, 215–251.

Erikson, E. H. *Identity: Youth and crisis*. New York: Norton, 1968.

Eron, L. D., Huesmann, L. R., Lefkowitz, M. M., & Walder, L. O. Does television violence cause aggression? *American Psychologist*, 1972, *27*, 253–263.

Etzioni, A. *A comparative analysis of complex organizations: On power, involvement, and their correlates*. New York: Free Press, 1961.

Evan, W. M., & Simmons, R. G. Organizational effects of inequitable rewards: Two experiments in status inconsistency. *Administrative Science Quarterly*, 1969, *14*, 224–237.

Evans, G. W., Fellows, J., Zorn, M., & Doty, K. Cognitive mapping and architecture. *Journal of Applied Psychology*, 1980, *65*, 474–478.

Evans, G. W., Marrero, D., & Butler, P. Environmental learning and cognitive mapping. *Environment and Behavior*, 1981, *13*, 83–104.

Evans, R. B. Childhood parental relationships of homosexual men. *Journal of Consulting and Clinical Psychology*, 1969, *33*, 129–135.

Everett, P. B. Reinforcement theory strategies for modifying transit ridership. In I. Altman, J. Wohlwill, & P. B. Everett (Eds.), *Human behavior and the environment: Transportation*. New York: Plenum Press, 1981.

Everett, P. B., Hayward, S. C., & Meyers, A. W. The effects of a token reinforcement procedure on bus ridership. *Journal of Applied Behavioral Analysis*, 1974, *7*, 1–10.

Fairweather, G. W., Sanders, D. H., Maynard, H., Cressler, D. L., & Bleck, D. S. *Community life for the mentally ill: An alternative to institutional care*. Chicago: Aldine, 1969.

Falbo, T., & Peplau, L. A. Power strategies in intimate relationships. *Journal of Personality and Social Psychology*, 1980, *38*, 618–628.

Fanon, F. *The wretched of the earth*. New York: Grove Press, 1963.

Farina, A., Fischer, E. H., Sherman, S., Smith, W. T., Groh, T., & Mermin, P. Physical attractiveness and mental illness. *Journal of Abnormal Psychology*, 1977, *86*, 510–517.

Farley, F. Residential segregation and its implications for school integration. *Law and Contemporary Problems*, 1975, *39*, 164–193.

Fazio, R. H., & Zanna, M. P. Attitudinal qualities relating to the strength of the attitude-behavior relationship. *Journal of Experimental Social Psychology*, 1978, *14*, 398–408.

Fazio, R. H., & Zanna, M. P. Direct experience and attitude-behavior consistency. In L. Berkowitz (Ed.), *Advances in experimental social psychology* (Vol. 14). New York: Academic Press, 1981.

Fazio, R. H., Zanna, M. P., & Cooper, J. Dissonance and self-perception: An integrative view of each theory's proper domain of application. *Journal of Experimental Social Psychology*, 1977, *13*, 464–479.

Feather, N. T. A structural balance approach to the analysis of communication effects. In L. Berkowitz (Ed.), *Advances in experimental social psychology* (Vol. 3). New York: Academic Press, 1967.

Feather, N. T. Values in adolescence. In J. Adelson (Ed.), *Handbook of adolescent psychology*. New York: Wiley, 1980.

Featherman, D., & Hauser, R. Sexual inequalities and socioeconomic achievement in the U.S., 1962–1973. *American Sociological Review*, 1976, *41*, 462–483.

Feldman, J. M. Stimulus characteristics and subject prejudice as determinants of stereotype attribution. *Journal of Personality and Social Psychology*, 1972, *21*, 333–340.

Feldman-Summers, S., & Kiesler, S. B. Those who are number two try harder: The effect of sex on attribution of causality, *Journal of Personality and Social Psychology*, 1974, *30*, 846–855.

Fenigstein, A. Does aggression cause a preference for viewing media violence? *Journal of Personality and Social Psychology*, 1979, *37*, 2307–2317.

Fennell, M. L., Barchas, P. R., Cohen, E. G., McMahon, A. M., & Hildebrand, P. An alternative perspective on sex differences in organizational settings. *Sex Roles*, 1978, *4*, 589–604.

Ferguson, M. *The Aquarian conspiracy: Personal and social transformation in the 1980's*. Los Angeles: J. P. Tarcher, 1980.

Festinger, L. Architecture and group membership. *Journal of Social Issues*, 1951, *7*, 152–163.

Festinger, L. A theory of social comparison processes. *Human Relations*, 1954, *7*, 117–140.

Festinger, L. *A theory of cognitive dissonance*. Stanford, Cal.: Stanford University Press, 1957.

Festinger, L. Behavioral support for opinion change. *Public Opinion Quarterly*, 1964, *28*, 404–417.

Festinger, L., & Carlsmith, J. M. Cognitive consequences of forced compliance. *Journal of Abnormal and Social Psychology*, 1959, *58*, 203–211.

Festinger, L., Pepitone, A., & Newcomb, T. Some consequences of deindividuation in a group. *Journal of Abnormal and Social Psychology*, 1952, *47*, 283–289.

Festinger, L., Schachter, S., & Back, K. *Social pressures in informal groups: A study of a housing community.* New York: Harper & Row, 1950.

Fiedler, F. E. *A theory of leadership effectiveness.* New York: McGraw-Hill, 1967.

Fiedler, F. E. Validation and extension of the contingency model of leadership effectiveness: A review of empirical findings. *Psychological Bulletin*, 1971, *76*, 128–148.

Finison, L. J. Unemployment, politics, and the history of organized psychology. *American Psychologist*, 1976, *31*, 747–753.

Finison, L. J. An aspect of the early history of the Society for the Psychological Study of Social Issues: Psychologists and labor. *Journal of the History of the Behavioral Sciences*, 1979, *15*, 29–37.

Fischer, C. S. *The urban experience.* New York: Harcourt, Brace, Jovanovich, 1976.

Fischer, C. S., & Phillips, S. L. Who is alone? Social characteristics of people with small networks. In L. A. Peplau & D. Perlman (Eds.), *Loneliness: A sourcebook of current theory, research and therapy.* New York: Wiley-Interscience, 1982.

Fischer, W. F. Sharing in preschool children as a function of amount and type of reinforcement. *Genetic Psychology Monographs*, 1963, *68*, 215–245.

Fischhoff, B. Attribution theory and judgment under uncertainty. In J. H. Harvey, W. J. Ickes, & R. F. Kidd (Eds.), *New directions in attribution research* (Vol. 1). Hillsdale, N.J.: Lawrence Erlbaum Associates, 1976.

Fischoff, S. "Recipe for a jury" revisited: A balance theory prediction. *Journal of Applied Social Psychology*, 1979, *9*, 335–349.

Fishbein, M. An investigation of the relationships between beliefs about an object and the attitude toward that object. *Human Relations*, 1963, *16*, 233–240.

Fishbein, M., & Ajzen, I. Attitudes toward objects as predictors of single and multiple behavioral criteria. *Psychological Review*, 1974, *81*, 59–74.

Fishbein, M., & Ajzen, I. *Belief, attitude, intention and behavior: An introduction to theory and research.* Reading, Mass.: Addison-Wesley, 1975.

Fishbein, M., & Coombs, F. S. Basis for decision: An attitudinal analysis of voting behavior. *Journal of Applied Social Psychology*, 1974, *4*, 95–124.

Fisher, J. D., & Nadler, A. The effects of similarity between donor and recipient on recipient's reactions to aid. *Journal of Applied Social Psychology*, 1974, *4*, 230–243.

Fisher, W. A., & Byrne, D. Sex differences in response to erotica? Love versus lust. *Journal of Personality and Social Psychology*, 1978, *36*, 117–125.

Fisher, W. A., & Byrne, D. Emotional barriers to contraception. In D. Byrne & W. A. Fisher (Eds.), *Adolescents, sex, and contraception.* New York: McGraw-Hill, in press.

Fisher, W. A., Byrne, D., Edmunds, M., Miller, C. T., Kelley, K., & White, L. A. Psychological and situation-specific correlates of contraceptive behavior among university women. *The Journal of Sex Research*, 1979, *15*, 38–55.

Fisher, W. F. Sharing in preschool children as a function of amount and type of reinforcement. *Genetic Psychology Monographs*, 1963, *68*, 215–245.

Fishman, D. B., & Loftus, E. F. Expert testimony on eyewitness identification. *Law and Psychology Review*, 1978, *4*, 87–103.

Fitzgerald, F. *America revisited.* Boston: Atlantic/Little, Brown, 1979.

Flavell, J., Botkin, P. T., & Fry, C. L. *The development of role-taking and communication skills in children.* New York: Wiley, 1968.

Flavell, J. H. *Cognitive development.* Englewood Cliffs, N.J.: Prentice-Hall, 1977.

Fleischman, E. A., Harris, E. F., & Burtt, H. E. *Leadership and supervision in industry.* Columbus, Ohio: Ohio State University Press, 1955.

Fling, S., & Manosevitz, M. Sex typing in nursery school children's play interests. *Developmental Psychology*, 1972, *7*, 146–152

Foa, E. B., & Foa, U. G. Resource theory of social exchange. In J. W. Thibaut, J. T. Spence, & R. C. Carson (Eds.), *Contemporary topics in social psychology.* Morristown, N.J.: General Learning Press, 1976.

Foa, E. B., Turner, J. L., & Foa, U. G. Response generalization in aggression. *Human Relations*, 1972, *25*, 337–350.

Foa, U. G., & Foa, E. B. *Societal structures of the mind.* Springfield, Ill.: Charles C. Thomas, 1974.

Fontana, V. J. *Somewhere a child is crying.* New York: Macmillan, 1973.

Ford, C. S., & Beach, F. A. *Patterns of sexual behavior.* New York: Harper & Row, 1951.

Forward, J. R. Group achievement motivation and individual motives to achieve success and to avoid failure. *Journal of Personality*, 1969, *37*, 297–309.

Forward, J. R., Canter, R., & Kirsch, N. Role-enactment and deception methodologies: Alternative paradigms? *American Psychologist*, 1976, *31*, 595–604.

Fox, L. H. Sex differences in mathematical precocity: Bridging the gap. In D. P. Keating (Ed.), *Intellectual talent: Research and development*. Baltimore, Md.: The Johns Hopkins University Press, 1976.

Frager, R. Conformity and anticonformity in Japan. *Journal of Personality and Social Psychology*, 1970, *15*, 203–210.

Francescato, D., & Mebane, W. How citizens view two great cities: Milan and Rome. In R. Downs & D. Stea (Eds.), *Image and environment*. Chicago: Aldine, 1973.

Freedman, J. L. Involvement, discrepancy, and change. *Journal of Abnormal and Social Psychology*, 1964, *69*, 290–295.

Freeman, J. The women's liberation movement: Its origins, organizations, activities and ideas. In J. Freeman (Ed.), *Women: A feminist perspective*. Palo Alto, Cal.: Mayfield, 1979.

Freidson, E. *Professional dominance: The social structure of medical care*. Chicago: Aldine, 1970.

French, J. R. P., & Raven, B. The bases of social power. In D. Cartwright (Ed.), *Studies in social power*. Ann Arbor: University of Michigan Press, 1959.

Frey, D., & Wicklund, R. A. A clarification of selective exposure: The impact of choice. *Journal of Experimental Social Psychology*, 1978, *14*, 132–140.

Fried, M. Grieving for a lost home. In L. J. Duhl (Ed.), *The urban condition*. New York: Basic Books, 1963.

Friedman, H. S. The interactive effects of facial expressions of emotion and verbal messages on perceptions of affective meaning. *Journal of Experimental Social Psychology*, 1979, *15*(1), 453–469. (a)

Friedman, H. S. Nonverbal communication between patients and medical practitioners. *Journal of Social Issues*, 1979, *35*, 82–99. (b)

Friedman, H. S., DiMatteo, M. R., & Taranta, A. A study of the relationship between individual differences in nonverbal expressiveness and factors of personality and social interaction. *Journal of Research in Personality*, 1980, *14*, 351–364.

Friedman, H. S., Prince, L. M., Riggio, R. E., & DiMatteo, M. R. Understanding and assessing nonverbal expressiveness: The ACT. *Journal of Personality and Social Psychology*, 1980, *39*, 333–351.

Frieze, I. H. The role of information processing in making causal attributions for success and failure. In J. S. Carroll & J. W. Payne (Eds.), *Cognition and social behavior*. Hillsdale, N.J.: Lawrence Erlbaum Associates, 1976.

Frieze, I. H. Perceptions of battered wives. In I. H. Frieze, D. Bar-Tal, & J. S. Carroll (Eds.), *New approaches to social problems: Applications of attribution theory*. San Francisco: Jossey-Bass, 1979.

Frieze, I. H., Fisher, J., Hanusa, B., McHugh, M. C., & Valle, V. A. Attributions of the causes of success and failure as internal and external barriers to achievement in women. In J. Sherman & F. Denmark (Eds.), *Psychology of women: Future directions of research*. New York: Psychological Dimensions, 1978.

Frieze, I. H., McHugh, M., & Duquin, M. *Causal attributions for women and men and sports participation*. Paper presented at the annual meeting of the American Psychological Association, Washington, D.C., September 1976.

Frieze, I. H., Parson, J. E., Johnson, P. B., Ruble, D. N., & Zellman, G. L. *Women and sex roles*. New York: Norton, 1978.

Frieze, I. H., & Snyder, H. N. Children's beliefs about the causes of success and failure in school settings. *Journal of Educational Psychology*, 1980, *72*, 186–196.

Frieze, I. H., & Weiner, B. Cue utilization and attributional judgments for success and failure. *Journal of Personality*, 1971, *39*, 591–606.

Frieze, I. H., Whitley, B. E., Hanusa, B. H., & McHugh, M. C. Assessing the theoretical models for sex differences in causal attributions for success and failure. *Sex Roles* (in press).

Frodi, A., Macaulay, J., & Thome, P. R. Are women always less aggressive than men? A review of the experimental literature. *Psychological Bulletin*, 1977, *84*, 634–660.

Fuller, L. L. Human interaction and the law. *The American Journal of Jurisprudence*, 1969, *14*, 1–36.

Furstenberg, F. F. Premarital pregnancy and marital stability. *Journal of Social Issues*, 1976, *32*(1), 67–86.

Fyans, L. J. *Cultural variation in the meaning of achievement*. Paper presented at the annual meeting of the American Educational Research Association, Boston, April 1980.

Fyans, L. J., & Maehr, M. L. Attributional style, task selection and achievement. *Journal of Educational Psychology*, 1979, *71*, 499–507.

Gaertner, S. L., & Bickman. L. Effects of race on the elicitation of helping behavior: The wrong number technique. *Journal of Personality and Social Psychology*, 1971, *20*, 218–222.

Gaertner, S. L., & Dovidio, J. F. The subtlety of white racism, arousal, and helping behavior. *Journal of Personality and Social Psychology*, 1977, 35, 691–708.

Gaes, G. G., Kalle, R. J., & Tedeschi, J. T. Impression management in the forced compliance situation: Two studies using the bogus pipeline. *Journal of Experimental Social Psychology*, 1978, 14, 493–510.

Gager, N. & Schurr, C. *Sexual assault: Confronting rape in America*. New York: Grosset & Dunlap, 1976.

Gagnon, J., & Simon, W. *Sexual conduct: The social sources of human sexuality*. Chicago: Aldine, 1973.

Gallatin, J. Political thinking in adolescence. In J. Adelson (Ed.), *Handbook of adolescent psychology*. New York: Wiley, 1980.

Gallo, P. S. Effects of increased incentives upon the use of threat in bargaining. *Journal of Personality and Social Psychology*, 1966, 4, 14–20.

Gallup, G. H. *The Gallup poll: Public opinion, 1935–1971*. New York: Random House, 1972.

Gamson, W. A. *Power and discontent*. Homewood, Ill.: Dorsey Press, 1968.

Gamson, W. A. *The strategy of social protest*. Homewood, Ill.: Dorsey Press, 1975.

Garfinkel, H. Conditions of successful degradation ceremonies. *American Journal of Sociology*, 1956, 61, 420–424.

Garson, B. Luddites in Lordstown. In R. Kanter & B. Stein (Eds.), *Life in organizations*. New York: Basic Books, 1979.

Gearing, F. O. *The face of the fox*. Chicago: Aldine, 1970.

Geen, R. G. The meaning of observed violence and its consequent effects on aggression. *Journal of Research in Personality*, 1975, 9, 270–281.

Geen, R. G. Some effects of observing violence upon the behavior of the observer. In B. A. Maher (Ed.), *Progress in experimental personality research* (Vol. 8). New York: Academic Press, 1978.

Geen, R. G., & Donnerstein, E. *Human aggression: Theoretical and empirical reviews*. New York: Academic Press, 1981.

Geen, R. G., & O'Neal, E. C. Activation of cue-elicited aggression by general arousal. *Journal of Personality and Social Psychology*, 1969, 11, 289–292.

Geen, R. G., & O'Neal, E. C. (Eds.). *Perspectives on aggression*. New York: Academic Press, 1976.

Geen, R. G., & Quanty, M. B. The catharsis of aggression. In L. Berkowitz (Ed.), *Advances in experimental social psychology* (Vol. 10). New York: Academic Press, 1977.

Geen, R. G., Rakosky, J., & O'Neal, E. C. Methodological study of the measurement of aggression. *Psychological Reports*, 1968, 23, 5–62.

Geen, R. G., Stonner, D., & Shope, G. L. The facilitation of aggression by aggression: A study in response inhibition and disinhibition. *Journal of Personality and Social Psychology*, 1975, 31, 721–726.

Gelfand, D. M., Hartmann, D. P., Cromer, C. C., Smith, C. L., & Page, B. C. The effects of instructional prompts and praise on children's donation rates. *Child Development*, 1975, 46, 980–983.

Geller, E. S. Saving environmental resources through waste reduction and recycling: How the behavioral community psychologist can help. In G. L. Martin & J. G. Osborne (Eds.), *Helping in the community: Behavior applications*. New York: Plenum Press, 1979.

Geller, E. S., Brasted, W. S., & Mann, M. F. Waste receptacle designs as interventions for litter control. *Journal of Environmental Systems*, 1979, 9, 145–160.

Geller, E. S., Witmer, J. F., & Orebaugh, A. L. Instructions as a determinant of paper-disposal behaviors. *Environment and Behavior*, 1976, 8, 417–439.

Gelles, R. *The violent home*. Beverly Hills, Cal.: Sage Publication, 1972.

Gelles, R. J., & Straus, M. A. Determinants of violence in the family: Toward a theoretical integration. In W. R. Burr, R. Hall, F. I. Nye, & I. L. Reiss (Eds.), *Contemporary theories about the family*. New York: Free Press, 1979.

Gerard, H. B. The anchorage of opinion in face-to-face groups. *Human Relations*, 1954, 7, 313–326.

Gerard, H. B., & Miller, N. *School desegregation*. New York: Plenum Press, 1975.

Gerbner, G., & Gross, L. Living with television: The violence profile. *Journal of Communication*, 1976, 26, 173–199.

Gerbner, G., & Gross, L. The scary world of TV's heavy viewer. *Psychology Today*, April 1976, pp. 41–45.

Gergen, K. J. Social psychology as history. *Journal of Personality and Social Psychology*, 1973, 26, 309–320.

Gergen, K. J., Ellsworth, P., Maslach, C., & Seipel, M. Obligation, donor resources, and reactions to aid in 3 cultures. *Journal of Personality and Social Psychology*, 1975, 31, 390–400.

Gerrard, M. Sex guilt in abortion patients. *Journal of Consulting and Clinical Psychology*, 1977, 45, 708.

Giarusso, R., Johnson, P., Goodchilds, J., & Zellman, G. *Adolescents' cues and signals: Sex and assault*. Paper presented at the annual meeting of the

Western Psychological Association, San Diego, April 1979.

Gibb, C. A. Leadership. In G. Lindzey & E. Aronson (Eds.), *Handbook of social psychology* (Vol. 4). Reading, Mass.: Addison-Wesley, 1969.

Gibbons, F. X., Stephan, W. G., Stephenson, B., & Petty, C. R. Reactions to stigmatized others: Response amplification vs. sympathy. *Journal of Experimental Social Psychology,* 1980, *16,* 591–605.

Gibbons, F. X., Wicklund, R. A., & Rosenfield, D. I. *Self-focused attention and other-directed behavior.* Unpublished manuscript, Iowa State University, 1980.

Gillan, P. Therapeutic uses of obscenity. In R. Dhavan & C. Davies (Eds.), *Censorship and obscenity.* Totowa, N.J.: Rowman & Littlefield, 1978.

Gillig, P. M., & Greenwald, A. G. Is it time to lay the sleeper effect to rest? *Journal of Personality and Social Psychology,* 1974, *29,* 132–139.

Ginsburg, G. P. Situated action: An emerging paradigm. In L. Wheeler (Ed.), *Review of Personality and Social Psychology,* 1980, *1,* 295–325.

Ginter, G., & Lindskold, S. Rate of participation and expertise as factors influencing leader choice. *Journal of Personality and Social Psychology,* 1975, *32,* 1085–1089.

Glass, D. C., & Singer, J. E. *Urban stress.* New York: Academic Press, 1972.

Glenn, N. D., & Weaver, C. N. Attitudes toward premarital, extramarital, and homosexual relations in the U.S. in the 1970s. *The Journal of Sex Research,* 1979, *15,* 108–118.

Goethals, G., & Darley, J. Social comparison theory: An attributional approach. In J. M. Suls & R. L. Miller (Eds.), *Social comparison processes: Theoretical and empirical perspectives.* Washington, D.C.: Halstead-Wiley, 1977.

Goffman, E. *The presentation of self in everyday life.* Garden City: Doubleday Anchor Books, 1959.

Goffman, E. *Asylums: Essays on the social situation of mental patients and other inmates.* Garden City, N.Y.: Doubleday, 1961.

Goffman, E. *Stigma: Notes on the management of spoiled identity.* Englewood Cliffs, N.J.: Prentice-Hall, 1963.

Goffman, E. *Interaction ritual.* New York: Doubleday Anchor Books, 1967.

Gold, M. W., & Ryan, K. M. Vocational training for the mentally retarded. In I. H. Frieze, D. Bar-Tal, & J. S. Carroll (Eds.), *New approaches to social problems: Applications of attribution theory.* San Francisco: Jossey-Bass, 1979.

Goldberg, H. *The hazards of being male: Surviving the myth of masculine privilege.* New York: New American Library, 1976.

Golding S. L., & Lichtenstein E. Confession of awareness and prior knowledge of deception as a function of interview set and approval motivation. *Journal of Personality and Social Psychology,* 1970, *14,* 213–223.

Goldman, W., & Lewis, P. Beautiful is good: Evidence that the physically attractive are more socially skillful. *Journal of Experimental Social Psychology,* 1977, *13,* 125–130.

Goode, W. Force and violence in the family. *Journal of Marriage and the Family,* 1971, *33,* 624–636.

Goodman, P. S., & Pennings, J. M. *New perspectives on organizational effectiveness.* San Francisco: Jossey-Bass, 1977.

Goodstadt, B., & Kipnis, D. Situational influences on the use of power. *Journal of Applied Psychology,* 1970, *54,* 210–207.

Gouldner, A. W. The norm of reciprocity: A preliminary statement. *American Sociological Review,* 1960, *25,* 161–179.

Graen, G., Orris, J., & Alvares, K. Contingency model of leadership effectiveness: Some methodological issues. *Journal of Applied Psychology,* 1971, *55,* 205–210.

Graziano, W., Brothen, T., & Berscheid, E. Height and attraction: Do men and women see eye-to-eye? *Journal of Personality,* 1978, *46,* 128–145.

Green, D. Dissonance and self-perception analyses of "forced compliance": When two theories make competing predictions. *Journal of Personality and Social Psychology,* 1974, *29,* 819–828.

Green, R. G. Effects of frustration attack and prior training in aggressiveness upon aggressive behavior. *Journal of Personality and Social Psychology,* 1968, *9,* 316–321.

Green, R. G., & Pigg, R. Acquistion of an aggressive response and its generalization to verbal behavior. *Journal of Personality and Social Psychology,* 1970, *15,* 165–170.

Greenberg. J. Equity, motivation, and effects of past reward on allocation decision. *Personality and Social Psychology Bulletin,* 1978, *4,* 131–134.

Greenberg, J. Groups vs. individual equity judgments: Is there a polarization effect? *Journal of Experimental Social Psychology,* 1979, *15,* 504–512.

Greenberg. J., & Leventhal, G. S. Equity and the use of overreward to motivate performance. *Journal of Personality and Social Psychology,* 1976, *34,* 179–190.

Greenberg, J., & Rosenfield, D. Whites' ethnocentrism and their attributions for the behavior of

Blacks: A motivational bias. *Journal of Personality*, 1979, 47, 643–657.

Greenberg. M. S., & Shapiro, S. P. Indebtedness: An adverse aspect of asking for and receiving help. *Sociometry*, 1971, 34, 290–301.

Greene, D., Sternberg, B., & Lepper, M. R. Overjustification in a token economy. *Journal of Personality and Social Psychology*, 1976, 34, 1219–1234.

Greenwell, J., & Dengerink, H. A. The role of perceived versus actual attack in human physical aggression. *Journal of Personality and Social Psychology*, 1973, 26, 66–71.

Gregg, G., Preston, T., Geist, A., & Caplan, N. The caravan rolls on: Forty years of social problem research. *Knowledge: Creation, Diffusion, Utilization*, 1979, 1, 31–61.

Grier, W., & Cobbs, P. *Black rage.* New York: Basic Books, 1968.

Griffitt, W. Response to erotica and the projection of response to erotica in the opposite sex. *Journal of Experimental Research in Personality*, 1973, 6, 330–338.

Griffitt, W., & Veitch, R. Hot and crowded: Influence of population density and temperature on interpersonal affective behavior. *Journal of Personality and Social Psychology*, 1971, 17, 92–98.

Grim, P. F., Kohlberg, L., & White, S. H. Some relationships between conscience and attentional processes. *Journal of Personality and Social Psychology*, 1968, 8, 239–252.

Gross, A. E. The male role and heterosexual behavior. *Journal of Social Issues*, 1978, 34(1), 87–107.

Gross, A. E., & Bellew-Smith, M. Social interaction and pregnancy risk in adolescence. In D. Byrne & W. Fisher (Eds.), *Adolescent sexuality.* New York: McGraw-Hill, in press.

Gruder, C. L., & Cook, T. D. Sex, dependency, and helping. *Journal of Personality and Social Psychology*, 1971, 19, 290–294.

Gruder, C. L., Cook, T. D., Hennigan, K. M., Flay, B. R., Alessis, C., & Halamaj, J. Empirical tests of the absolute sleeper effect predicted from the discounting cue hypothesis. *Journal of Personality and Social Psychology*, 1978, 36, 1061–1074.

Grusec, J. E. Socialization processes in the development of altruism. In J. P. Rushton & R. M. Sorrentino (Eds.), *Altruism and helping behavior.* Hillsdale, N.J.: Lawrence Erlbaum Associates, 1981.

Grusky, O. A case for the theory of familial role differentiation in small groups. *Social Forces*, 1957, 35, 209–217.

Grusky, O. Career mobility and organizational commitment. *Administrative Science Quarterly*, 1966, 10, 488–503.

Guest, R. H. Quality of work life—Learning from Tarrytown. *Harvard Business Review*, 1979, 57(4), 76–87.

Guilford, J. P. *Psychometric methods*, (2d ed.). New York: McGraw-Hill, 1954.

Gunnar, M. *Sex-of-child differences in father's discipline and play with his one-year-old.* Paper presented at the annual meeting of the Western Psychological Association, Sacramento, April 1975.

Gyllenhammer, P. *People at work.* Reading, Mass.: Addison-Wesley, 1977.

Haan, N., Smith, M. B., & Block, J. The moral reasoning of young adults: Political-social behavior, family background, and personality correlates. *Journal of Personality and Social Psychology*, 1968, 10, 183–201.

Haas-Hawkings, G. Intimacy as a moderating influence on the stress of loneliness in widowhood. *Essence*, 1978, 2, 249–258.

Hackman, J. R. Designing work for individuals and groups. In J. Hackman, E. Lawler, & L. Porter (Eds.), *Perspectives in organizations.* New York: McGraw-Hill, 1977.

Hackman, J. R., & Suttle, J. L. *Improving life at work: Behavioral science approaches to organizational change.* Santa Monica, Cal.: Goodyear, 1977.

Haden-Guest, A. *The paradise program.* New York: William Morrow, 1973.

Haines, D. B., & McKeachie, W. J. Cooperative versus competitive discussion methods in teaching introductory psychology. *Journal of Educational Psychology*, 1967, 58, 386–390.

Haines, H., & Vaughan, G. M. Was 1898 a "Great Date" in the history of experimental social psychology? *Journal of the History of the Behavioral Sciences*, 1979, 15, 323–332.

Haise, J. Parents confide in Fred Rogers. *TV Magazine: Santa Ana Register.* Feb. 15, 1981, pp. 4–6.

Hall, E. T. *The silent language.* New York: Fawcett, 1959.

Hall, E. T. *The hidden dimension.* New York: Doubleday, 1966.

Hall, J. A. Gender effects in decoding nonverbal cues. *Psychological Bulletin*, 1978, 85, 845–857.

Hall, J. A. Gender, gender roles, and nonverbal communication skills. In R. Rosenthal (Ed.), *Skill in nonverbal communication.* Cambridge, Mass.: Oelgeschlager, Gunn, & Hain, 1979.

Halloway, R. L. *Primate aggression, territoriality, and xenophobia.* New York: Academic Press, 1974.

Hamblin, R. L. Leadership and crisis. *Sociometry*, 1958, 21, 322–335.

Hamilton, V. L. Intuitive psychologist or intuitive lawyer? Alternative models of the attribution process. *Journal of Personality and Social Psychology*, 1980, *39*, 767–772.

Hamner, W. C., & Harnett, D. L. Goal setting, performance, and satisfaction in an interdependent task. *Organizational Behavior and Human Performance*, 1974, *12*, 217–230.

Hanratty, M., O'Neal, E. C., & Sulzer, J. L. The effect of frustration upon the imitation of aggression. *Journal of Personality and Social Psychology*, 1972, *21*, 30–35.

Hansen, R. D. Commonsense attributions. *Journal of Personality and Social Psychology*, 1980, *39*, 996–1009.

Hansen, R. D., & Donoghue, J. M. The power of consensus: Information derived from one's own and others' behavior. *Journal of Personality and Social Psychology*, 1977, *35*, 294–302.

Hansen, W. S., & Altman, I. Decorating personal places: A descriptive analysis. *Environment and Behavior*, 1976, *8*, 491–504.

Hardin, G. The cybernetics of competition: A biologist's view of society. In P. Shepard & D. McKinley (Eds.), *The subversive science: Essays toward an ecology of man.* Boston: Houghton-Mifflin, 1969.

Harman, W. W. *An incomplete guide to the future.* San Francisco: The Stanford, 1976.

Harris, D. B., Gough, H. G., & Martin, W. E. Children's ethnic attitudes related to methods of child rearing. *Child Development*, 1950, *21*, 169–181.

Harrison, A. A., & Saeed, L. Let's make a deal: An analysis of revelations and stipulations in lonely hearts advertisements. *Journal of Personality and Social Psychology*, 1977, *35*, 257–264.

Harrison, J. Warning: The male sex role may be dangerous to your health. *Journal of Social Issues*, 1978, *34*(1), 65–86.

Hart, H. L. A., & Honore, A. M. *Causation in the law.* Oxford, England: Clarendon, 1959.

Hart, R. *Children's experience of place.* New York: Irvington, 1979.

Hartup, W. W. Nurturance and nurturance withdrawal in relation to the dependency behavior of young children. *Child Development*, 1958, *29*, 191–201.

Harvey, O. J., & Consalvi, C. Status and conformity to pressures in informal groups. *Journal of Abnormal and Social Psychology*, 1960, *60*, 182–187.

Hass, J. W., Bagley, G. S., & Rogers, R. A. Coping with the energy crisis: Effects of fear appeals upon attitudes toward energy consumption. *Journal of Applied Psychology*, 1975, *60*, 754–756.

Hayes, S. C., Johnson, V. S., & Cone, J. D. The marked item technique: A practical procedure for litter control. *Journal of Applied Behavior Analysis*, 1975, *8*, 381–386.

Haynes, R. B. A critical review of the determinants of patient compliance with therapeutic regimens. In D. L. Sackett & R. B. Haynes (Eds.), *Compliance with therapeutic regimens.* Baltimore, Md.: The Johns Hopkins University Press, 1976.

Heft, H. The role of environmental features on route-learning: Two exploratory studies of way-finding. *Environmental Psychology and Nonverbal Behavior*, 1979, *3*, 172–185.

Heider, F. Social perception and phenomenal causality. *Psychological Review*, 1944, *51*, 358–374.

Heider, F. *The psychology of interpersonal relations.* New York: Wiley, 1958.

Heiman, J. R. Women's sexual arousal. *Psychology Today*, 1975, *8*, 91–94.

Heller, F. A., & Yukl, G. Participation, managerial decision-making and situational variables. *Organizational Behavior and Human Behavior*, 1969, *4*, 227–241.

Heller, M. S., & Polsky, S. *Studies in violence and television.* New York: American Broadcasting Companies, 1975.

Henderson, J. B., Hall, S. M., & Lipton, H. L. Changing self-destructive behaviors. In G. C. Stone, F. Cohen, & N. E. Adler (Eds.), *Health psychology: A handbook.* San Francisco: Jossey-Bass, 1979.

Hendrick, C., & Shaffer, D. Murder: Effects of number of killers and victim mutilations on simulated jurors' judgments. *Bulletin of the Psychonomic Society*, 1975, *6*, 313–316.

Hendrix, W. G., & Fabos, J. G. Visual land use compatibility as a significant contributor to visual resource quality. *International Journal of Environmental Studies*, 1975, *8*, 21–28.

Henley, N. M. *Body politics: Power, sex and nonverbal communication.* Englewood Cliffs, N.J.: Prentice-Hall, 1977.

Herman, J., & Siegel, A. The development of spatial representations of large-scale environments. *Journal of Experimental Child Psychology*, 1978, *26*, 389–406.

Hernon, P. *A terrible thunder.* Garden City: Doubleday, 1978.

Hess, R. D., & Tapp, J. L. *Authority, rules, and aggression: A cross-national study of the socialization of children into compliance systems: Part I.* Washington,

D.C.: United States Department of Health, Education and Welfare, 1969.

Hetherington, E. M. A developmental study of the effects of sex of the dominant parent on sex-role preference, identification and imitation in children. *Journal of Personality and Social Psychology*, 1965, 2, 188–194.

Hetherington, E. M. The effects of familial variables on sex typing, on parent-child similarity and on imitation in children. In J. P. Hill (Ed.), *Minnesota Symposia on Child Psychology* (Vol. 1). Minneapolis: University of Minnesota Press, 1967.

Hetherington, E. M. Effects of father absence on personality development in adolescent daughters. *Developmental Psychology*, 1972, 7, 313–326.

Hetherington, E. M., Cox, M., & Cox, R. Play and social interaction in children following divorce. *Journal of Social Issues*, 1979, 35(4), 26–49.

Hetherington, E. M., & Parke, R. D. *Child psychology: A contemporary viewpoint* (2d ed.). New York: McGraw-Hill, 1979.

Hetzler, S. A. Variations in role-playing patterns among different echelons of bureaucratic leaders. *American Sociological Review*, 1955, 20, 700–706.

Heyman, S. R. *Relationship of sexual fantasies to sexual behavior and personality patterns in females and males.* Paper presented at the 87th annual meeting of the American Psychological Association, New York, September 1979.

Hicks, D. Imitation and retention of film-mediated aggressive peer and adult models. *Journal of Personality and Social Psychology*, 1965, 2, 97–100.

Higbee, K. L. Fifteen years of fear arousal: Research on threat appeals. *Psychological Bulletin*, 1969, 72, 426–444.

Hilgard, E. Propositions for the future. *APA Monitor*, 1980, 11(11), 3.

Hill, C. T., Rubin, Z., & Peplau, L. A. Breakups before marriage: The end of 103 affairs. *Journal of Social Issues*, 1976, 32(1), 147–168.

Hinde, R. A. *Animal behavior: A synthesis of ethology and comparative psychology* (2d ed.). New York: McGraw-Hill, 1970.

Hinings, C. R., Hickson, D. J., Pennings, J. M., & Scheck, R. E. Structural conditions of intraorganizational power. *Administrative Science Quarterly*, 1974, 19, 22–44.

Hinton, B. L., & Barrow, J. C. The superior's reinforcing behavior as a function of reinforcements received. *Organizational Behavior and Human Performance*, 1975, 14, 123–143.

Hodgkins, B. J., & Stakenas, R. G. A study of self-concepts of Negro and white youths in segregated environments. *Journal of Negro Education*, 1969, 38, 370–377.

Hoffman, M. L. Moral development. In P. H. Mussen (Ed.), *Carmichael's Manual of Child Psychology* (Vol. 2). New York: Wiley, 1970.

Hoffman, M. L. Moral internalization: Current theory and research. In L. Berkowitz (Ed.), *Advances in experimental social psychology* (Vol. 10). New York: Academic Press, 1977. (a)

Hoffman, M. L. Sex differences in empathy and related behaviors. *Psychological Bulletin*, 1977, 84, 712–722. (b)

Hoffman, M. L. Empathy, its development and prosocial implications. In C. S. Keasey (Ed.) *Nebraska Symposium on Motivation* (Vol. 25). Lincoln: University of Nebraska Press, 1978.

Hoffman, M. L. Development of moral thought, feeling and behavior. *American Psychologist*, 1979, 34(10), 958–966.

Hoffman, M. L., & Saltzstein, H. D. Parent discipline and the child's moral development. *Journal of Personality and Social Psychology*, 1967, 5, 45–57.

Hofling, C. K., Brotzman, E., Dalrymple, D., Graves, N., & Pierce, C. M. An experimental study in nurse-physician relationships. *Journal of Nervous and Mental Disease*, 1966, 143(2), 171–180.

Hokanson, J. E., & Shetler, S. The effect of overt aggression on level of physiological arousal. *Journal of Abnormal and Social Psychology*, 1961, 63, 446–448.

Hokanson, J. E., Willers, K. R., & Koropsak, E. The modification of autonomic responses during aggressive interchanges. *Journal of Personality*, 1968, 36, 386–404.

Holahan, C. *Environment and behavior.* New York: Plenum Press, 1978.

Holahan, C., & Saegert, S. Behavioral and attitudinal effects of large-scale variation in the physical environment of psychiatric wards. *Journal of Abnormal Psychology*, 1973, 82, 454–462.

Hollander, E. P. Conformity, status, and idiosyncracy credit. *Psychological Review*, 1958, 64, 117–127.

Hollander, E. P. Competence and conformity in the acceptance of influence. *Journal of Abnormal and Social Psychology*, 1960, 61, 365–370.

Hollander, E. P. Some effects of perceived status on responses to innovative behavior. *Journal of Abnormal and Social Psychology*, 1961, 63, 247–250.

Hollander, E. P., & Julian, J. W. A further look at leader legitimacy, influence, and innovation. In L. Berkowitz (Ed.), *Advances in experimental social psychology* (Vol. 5). New York: Academic Press, 1970.

Holmes, D. S. Effects of overt aggression on level of physiological arousal. *Journal of Personality and Social Psychology*, 1966, 4, 189–194.

Holmes, D. S. Compensation for ego threat: Two experiments. *Journal of Personality and Social Psychology*, 1971, 18, 234–237.

Homans, G. C. *The human group.* New York: Harcourt, Brace, Jovanovich, 1950.

Homans, G. C. *Social behavior: Its elementary forms.* New York: Harcourt, Brace, & World, 1961.

Homans, G. C. *Social behavior: Its elementary forms* (Rev. ed.). New York: Harcourt, Brace, Jovanovich, 1974.

Hook, J. G., & Cook, T. D. Equity theory and the cognitive ability of children. *Psychological Bulletin,* 1979, 86, 429–445.

Hope, D. J., & Cozby, P. C. *Relationships between environmental attitudes and behaviors.* Unpublished manuscript, California State University, Fullerton, 1981.

Hopkins, J. R. Sexual behavior in adolescence. *Journal of Social Issues,* 1977, 33(2), 67–85.

Hoppe, C. M. Interpersonal aggression as a function of subject's sex, subject's sex role identification, opponent's sex, and degree of provocation. *Journal of Personality,* 1979, 47, 317–329.

Hornstein, H. A. *Cruelty and kindness: A new look at aggression and altruism.* Englewood Cliffs, N.J.: Prentice-Hall, 1976.

Hornstein, H. A., Fisch, E., & Holmes, M. Influence of a model's feeling about his behavior and his relevance as a comparison other on observer's helping behavior. *Journal of Personality and Social Psychology,* 1968, 10, 222–226.

House, J. S. The three faces of social psychology. *Sociometry,* 1977, 40, 161–177.

Hovland, C. I., & Janis, I. L. (Eds.). *Personality and persuasibility.* New Haven, Conn.: Yale University Press, 1959.

Hovland, C. I., Janis, I. L., & Kelley, H. H. *Communication and persuasion.* New Haven, Conn.: Yale University Press, 1953.

Hovland, C. I., Lumsdaine, A. A., & Sheffield, F. D. *Experiments on mass communication.* Princeton, N.J.: Princeton University Press, 1949.

Hovland, C. I., & Weiss, W. The influence of source credibility on communication effectiveness. *Public Opinion Quarterly,* 1951, 15, 635–650.

Howard, J. L., Reifler, C. B., & Liptzin, M. B. *Effects of exposure to pornography* (Technical Reports of the Commission on Obscenity and Pornography, Vol. 8). Washington, D.C.: U.S. Government Printing Office, 1970.

Howard, J. W., & Dawes, R. M. Linear prediction of marital happiness. *Journal of Personality and Social Psychology,* 1976, 2, 478–480.

Hrebiniak, L. G., & Alutto, J. A. Personal and role-related factors in the development of organizational commitment. *Administrative Science Quarterly,* 1972, 17, 555–573.

Hughes, E. Race relations in industry. In W. F. Whyte (Ed.), *Industry and society.* New York: McGraw-Hill, 1946.

Hulka, B. S., Cassel, J. C., & Kupper, L. Disparities between medications prescribed and consumed among chronic disease patients. In L. Lasagna (Ed.), *Patient compliance.* Mt. Kisco, N. Y.: Futura, 1976.

Hunt, M. *Sexual behavior in the 1970's.* Chicago: Playboy Press, 1974.

Hurry, my children, hurry. *Time,* March 26, 1979, pp. 27–28.

Iadicola, P. *Schooling and social power: A presentation of a Weberian conflict model of the school.* Unpublished doctoral dissertation, University of California, Riverside, 1979.

Inhelder, B., & Piaget, J. *The growth of logical thinking from childhood to adolescence.* New York: Basic Books, 1958.

Isen, A. M. Success, failure, attention and reaction to others: The warm glow of success. *Journal of Personality and Social Psychology,* 1970, 15, 294–301.

Isen, A. M., & Levin, P. F. Effect of feeling good on helping: Cookies and kindness. *Journal of Personality and Social Psychology,* 1972, 21, 344–348.

Isen, A. M., Shalker, T. E., Clark, M., & Karp, L. Affect, accessibility of material in memory, and behavior: A cognitive loop? *Journal of Personality and Social Psychology,* 1978, 36, 1–13.

Ittelson, W. H. (Ed.). *Environment and cognition.* New York: Seminar Press, 1973.

Ittelson, W. H., Proshansky, H. M., Rivlin, L. G., & Winkel, G. H. *An introduction to environmental psychology.* New York: Holt, Rinehart and Winston, 1974.

Ittelson, W. H., Rivlin, L. G., & Proshansky, H. M. The use of behavioral maps in environmental psychology. In H. M. Proshansky, W. H. Ittelson, & L. G. Rivlin (Eds.), *Environmental psychology: People and their physical settings* (2d ed.). New York: Holt, Rinehart and Winston, 1976.

Jaccard, J. J., & Davidson, A. R. Toward an understanding of family planning behaviors: An initial investigation. *Journal of Applied Social Psychology,* 1972, *2,* 228–235.

Jaccard, J. J., Weber, J., & Lundmark, J. A multitrait-multimethod analysis of four attitude assessment procedures. *Journal of Experimental Social Psychology,* 1975, *11,* 149–154.

Jackson, D. J., & Huston, T. L. Physical attractiveness and assertiveness. *Journal of Social Psychology,* 1975, *96,* 79–84.

Jaco, A., & Vroom, V. H. Hierarchical level and leadership style. *Organizational Behavior and Human Performance,* 1977, *18,* 131–145.

Jacobs, P. A., Brunton, M., Melville, M. M., Brittain, R. P., & McClement, W. F. Aggressive behavior, mental subnormality, and the XYY male. *Nature,* 1965, *208,* 1351–1352.

Jacobson, M. B., Antonelli, J., Winning, P. U., & Opeil, D. Women as authority figures: The use and nonuse of authority. *Sex Roles,* 1977, *4,* 365–376.

Jakobovitz, L. A. Effects of mere exposure: A comment. *Journal of Personality and Social Psychology,* 1968, *9,* 30–32.

Janis, I. L. *Victims of groupthink.* Boston: Houghton-Mifflin, 1972.

Janis, I. L., & Feshbach, S. Effects of fear-arousing communications. *Journal of Abnormal and Social Psychology,* 1953, *48,* 78–92.

Janis, I. L., & Field, P. B. Sex differences and personality factors related to persuasibility. In C. I. Hovland & I. L. Janis (Eds.), *Personality and persuasibility.* New Haven, Conn.: Yale University Press, 1959.

Jellison, J. M., Jackson-White, R., Bruder, R. A., & Martyna, W. Achievement behavior: A situational behavior. *Sex Roles,* 1975, *1,* 375–390.

Jemail, J. A., & Geer, J. Sexual scripts. In R. Gemme & C. Wheeler (Eds.), *Progress in sexology.* New York: Plenum Press, 1978.

Jennings, M. K., & Niemi, R. G. The transmission of political values from parent to child. *American Political Science Review,* 1968, *62,* 169–184.

Jensen, A. R. How much can we boost IQ and scholastic achievement? *Harvard Educational Review,* 1969, *39,* 1–123.

Johnson, D. A. *Racial discrimination and attitude-behavior consistency.* Unpublished manuscript, Interaction Research Corporation, Stanton, California, 1980.

Johnson, E. J., Greene, D., & Carroll, J. S. *Reasons and overjustification: A test of the means-end hypothesis.* Unpublished manuscript, Carnegie-Mellon University, 1978.

Johnson, P. B. *Social power and sex role stereotyping.* Unpublished doctoral dissertation, University of California, Los Angeles, 1974.

Johnson, P. B. Women and interpersonal power. In I. H. Frieze, J. E. Parsons, P. B. Johnson, D. N. Ruble, & G. L. Zellman, *Women and sex roles.* New York: Norton, 1978.

Johnson, P. B., & Goodchilds, J. D. Pornography, sexuality, and social psychology. *Journal of Social Issues,* 1973, *29*(3), 231–238.

Jones, B., Steele, M., Gahagan, J., & Tedeschi, J. Matrix values and cooperative behavior in the prisoner's dilemma game. *Journal of Personality and Social Psychology,* 1968, *8,* 148–153.

Jones, E. E. *Ingratiation: A social psychological analysis.* New York: Appleton-Century-Crofts, 1964.

Jones, E. E., & Archer, R. L. Are there special effects of personalistic self-disclosure? *Journal of Experimental Social Psychology,* 1976, *12,* 180–193.

Jones, E. E., & Davis, K. E. From acts to dispositions: The attribution process in person perception. In L. Berkowitz (Ed.), *Advances in experimental social psychology* (Vol. 2). New York: Academic Press, 1965.

Jones E. E., & Gerard, H. B. *Foundations of social psychology.* New York: Wiley, 1967.

Jones, E. E., & Harris, V. A. The attribution of attitudes. *Journal of Experimental Social Psychology,* 1967, *3,* 1–24.

Jones, E. E., & McGillis, D. Correspondent inferences and the attribution cube: A comparative reappraisal. In J. H. Harvey, W. J. Ickes, & R. F. Kidd (Eds.), *New directions in attribution research* (Vol. 1). Hillsdale, N.J.: Lawrence Erlbaum Associates, 1976.

Jones, E. E., & Nisbett, R. E. *The actor and observer: Divergent perceptions of the causes of behavior.* Morristown, N.J.: General Learning Press, 1971.

Jones, E. E., & Sigall, H. The bogus pipeline: A new paradigm for measuring affect and attitude. *Psychological Bulletin,* 1971, *76,* 349–364.

Jones, K. E., Epstein, J., & O'Neal, E. C. *Experience with firearms mitigates the weapons effect.* Unpublished manuscript, Tulane University, 1981.

Jones, R. A. Volunteering to help: The effects of choice, dependence and anticipated dependence. *Journal of Personality and Social Psychology,* 1970, *14,* 121–129.

Jones, R. A. *Self-fulfilling prophecies.* Hillsdale, N.J.: Lawrence Erlbaum Associates, 1977.

Jones, R. A., & Brehm, J. W. Persuasiveness of one- and two-sided communications as a function of awareness there are two sides. *Journal of Experimental Social Psychology,* 1970, *6,* 47–56.

Jones, W. H. Loneliness and social behavior. In L. A. Peplau and D. Perlman (Eds.), *Loneliness: A sourcebook of current theory, research and therapy.* New York: Wiley-Interscience, 1982.

Jourard, S. M. *The transparent self* (Rev. ed.). New York: Van Nostrand Reinhold, 1971.

Judd, C. M., & Kenny, D. A. *Estimating the effects of social interventions.* New York: Cambridge University Press, 1981.

Julty, S. A case of sexual dysfunction. In J. H. Pleck & J. Sawyer (Eds.), *Men and masculinity.* Englewood Cliffs, N.J.: Prentice-Hall, 1974.

Kagan, S., & Madsen, M. C. Rivalry in Anglo-American and Mexican-American children of two ages. *Journal of Personality and Social Psychology,* 1972, *24,* 214–220.

Kahn, A., Lamm, H., & Nelson, R. E. Preferences for an equal or equitable allocator. *Journal of Personality and Social Psychology,* 1977, *35,* 837–844.

Kanin, E. An examination of sexual aggression as a response to sexual frustration. *Journal of Marriage and the Family,* 1967, *29,* 428–433.

Kanin, E., & Parcell, S. Sexual aggression: A second look at the offended female. *Archives of Sexual Behavior,* 1977, *6,* 67–76.

Kanouse, D. E., Gumpert, P., & Canavan-Gumpert, D. The semantics of praise. In J. H. Harvey, W. J. Ickes, & R. F. Kidd (Eds.), *New directions in attribution theory* (Vol. 3). Hillsdale, N.J.: Lawrence Erlbaum Associates, 1981.

Kanter, R. M. Commitment and social organization: A study of commitment mechanisms in utopian communities. *American Sociological Review,* 1968, *35,* 499–517.

Kanter, R. M. *Commitment and community: Communes and utopias in sociological perspective.* Cambridge, Mass.: Harvard University Press, 1972. (a)

Kanter, R. M. Commitment and the internal organization of millenial movements. *American Behavioral Scientist,* 1972, *16,* 219–243. (b)

Kanter, R. M. The romance of community: Communes as intensive group experiences. In M. Rosenbaum & A. Snadowsky (Eds.), *The intensive group experience.* New York: Free Press, 1976.

Kanter, R. M. *Men and women of the corporation.* New York: Basic Books, 1977. (a)

Kanter, R. M. Some effects of proportions on group life: Skewed sex ratios and responses to token women. *American Journal of Sociology,* 1977, *82,* 965–990. (b)

Kanter, R. M. Differential access to opportunity and power. In R. Alvarez & K. G. Lutterman (Eds.), *Discrimination in organizations.* San Francisco: Jossey-Bass, 1979. (a)

Kanter, R. M. Power failure in management circuits. *Harvard Business Review,* 1979, *57,* 65–75. (b)

Kanter, R. M., & Stein, B. A. Growing pains. In R. M. Kanter & B. A. Stein (Eds.), *Life in organizations: Workplaces as people experience them.* New York: Basic Books, 1979.

Kaplan, A. *The conduct of inquiry.* San Francisco: Chandler, 1964.

Kaplan, R. Preference and everyday nature: Method and application. In D. Stokols (Ed.), *Perspectives on environment and behavior.* New York: Plenum Press, 1977.

Kaplan, S. Adaptation, structure, and knowledge. In G. Moore & R. Gollege (Eds.), *Environmental knowing.* Stroudsburg, Pa.: Dowden, Hutchinson, & Ross, 1976.

Kaplan, S., Kaplan, R., & Wendt, J. S. Rated preference and complexity for natural and urban visual material. *Perception and Psychophysics,* 1972, *12,* 354–356.

Karlins, M., Coffman, T., & Walters, G. On the fading of social stereotypes: Studies in three generations of college students. *Journal of Personality and Social Psychology,* 1969, *13,* 1–16.

Karylowski, J. Self-focused attention, prosocial norms and prosocial behavior. *Polish Psychological Bulletin,* 1979, *10,* 57–66.

Kasarda, J. D., & Janowitz, M. Community attachment in mass society. *American Sociological Review,* 1974, *39,* 328–339.

Katz, D. The functional approach to the study of attitudes. *Public Opinion Quarterly,* 1960, *24.* 163–204.

Katz, D., & Braly, K. Racial stereotypes of one hundred college students. *Journal of Abnormal and Social Psychology,* 1933, *28,* 280–290.

Katz, I., Cohen, S., & Glass, D. Some determinants of cross-racial helping. *Journal of Personality and Social Psychology,* 1975, *32,* 964–970.

Katz, I., & Glass, D. C. An ambivalence-amplification theory of behavior toward the stigmatized. In W. G. Austin & S. Worchel (Eds.), *The social psychology of intergroup relations.* Monterey, Cal.: Brooks/Cole, 1979.

Keating, D. P. (Ed.). *Intellectual talent: Research and development.* Baltimore, Md.: The Johns Hopkins University Press, 1976.

Keating, D. P. Secondary school programs. In *The gifted and the talented: 78th Yearbook of the National Society for the Study of Education,* 1979.

Keating, D. P. Thinking processes in adolescence. In J. Adelson (Ed.), *Handbook of adolescent psychology.* New York: Wiley, 1980.

Kelley, H. H. The warm-cold variable in first impressions of persons. *Journal of Personality,* 1950, *18,* 431–439.

Kelley, H. H. Communications in experimentally created hierarchies. *Human Relations,* 1951, *4,* 39–56.

Kelley, H. H. Attribution theory in social psychology. In D. Levine (Ed.), *Nebraska Symposium on Motivation* (Vol. 15). Lincoln: University of Nebraska Press, 1967.

Kelley, H. H. *Attribution in social interaction.* Morristown, N.J.: General Learning Press, 1971.

Kelley, H. H. *Causal schemata and the attribution process.* Morristown, N.J.: General Learning Press, 1972.

Kelley, H. H., & Stahelski, A. J. Social interaction basis of cooperators' and competitors' beliefs about others. *Journal of Personality and Social Psychology,* 1970, *16,* 66–91.

Kelley, H. H., & Thibaut, J. W. *Interpersonal relations: A theory of interdependence.* New York: Wiley, 1978.

Kelley, K. Socialization factors in contraceptive attitudes: Roles of affective responses, parental attitudes, and sexual experience. *The Journal of Sex Research,* 1979, *15,* 6–20.

Kelly, G. *The psychology of personal contructs* (2 vols.). New York: Norton, 1955.

Kelman, H. Compliance, identification, and internalization: Three processes of attitude change. *Journal of Conflict Resolution,* 1958, *2,* 51–60.

Kelman, H. C., & Hovland, C. I. "Reinstatement" of the communicator in delayed measurement of opinion change. *Journal of Abnormal and Social Psychology,* 1953, *48,* 327–335.

Kendon, A. Some functions of gaze direction in social interaction. *Acta Psychologica,* 1967, *26,* 22–47.

Kenrick, D. T., & Cialdini, R. B. Romantic attraction: Misattribution versus reinforcement explanations. *Journal of Personality and Social Psychology,* 1977, *35,* 381–391.

Kenrick, D. T., Cialdini, R. B., & Linder, D. E. Misattribution under fear-producing circumstances: Four failures to replicate. *Personality and Social Psychology Bulletin,* 1979, *5,* 329–334.

Kenrick, D. T., Reich, J. W., & Cialdini, R. B. Justification and compensation: Rosier skies for the devalued victim. *Journal of Personality and Social Psychology,* 1976, *34,* 654–657.

Kenrick, D. T., Stringfield, D. O., Wagenhals, W. L., Dahl, R. H., & Ransdell, H. J. Sex differences, androgyny, and approach responses to erotica: A new variation on the old volunteer problem. *Journal of Personality and Social Psychology,* 1980, *38,* 517–524.

Kerckhoff, A. C., & Davis, K. E. Value consensus and need complementarity in mate selection. *American Sociological Review,* 1962, *27,* 295–303.

Kessler, J. J., & Wiener, Y. Self-consistency and inequity dissonance as factors in undercompensation. *Organizational Behavior and Human Performance,* 1972, *8,* 456–466.

Kett, J. F. *Rites of passage.* New York: Basic Books, 1977.

Kiesler, C. A., Collins, B. E., & Miller, N. *Attitude change: A critical analysis of theoretical approaches.* New York: Wiley, 1969.

Kiesler, C. A., & Kiesler, S. B. *Conformity.* Reading, Mass.: Addison-Wesley, 1969.

Kiesler, C. A., & Pallak, M. S. Minority influence: The effect of majority reactionaries and defectors, and minority and majority compromisers, upon majority opinion and attraction. *European Journal of Social Psychology,* 1975, *5,* 237–256.

Kilson, M. Black politicians: A new power. *Dissent,* August 1971, pp. 333–345.

Kinsey, A. C., Pomeroy, W. B., & Martin, C. E. *Sexual behavior in the human male.* Philadelphia: Saunders, 1948.

Kipnis, D. The powerholder. In J. T. Tedeschi (Ed.), *Perspectives on social power.* Chicago: Aldine, 1974.

Kipnis, D., Silverman, A., & Copeland, C. Effects of emotional arousal on the use of supervised coercion with black and union employees. *Journal of Applied Psychology,* 1973, *57,* 38–43.

Kirsch, N. L. Attempted suicide and restrictions in the eligibility to negotiate personal characteristics. In K. Davis (Ed.), *Advances in descriptive psychology* (Vol. 2). Greenwich, Conn.: JAI Press, in press.

Kirscht, J. P., & Rosenstock, I. M. Patients' problems in following recommendations of health experts. In G. C. Stone, F. Cohen, & N. E. Adler, (Eds.), *Health psychology: A handbook.* San Francisco: Jossey-Bass, 1979.

Kitano, H. H. L. *Race relations* (2d ed.). Englewood Cliffs, N.J.: Prentice-Hall, 1980.

Kleinke, C. L. Effects of personal evaluations. In G. J. Chelune (Ed.), *Self-disclosure: Origins, patterns, and implications of openness in interpersonal relationships.* San Francisco: Jossey-Bass, 1979.

Kleinke, C. L., Staneski, R. A., & Berger, D. E. Evaluation of an interviewer as a function of interviewer gaze, reinforcement of subject gaze, and interviewer attractiveness. *Journal of Personality and Social Psychology*, 1975, *31*, 115–122.

Kluger, R. *Simple justice.* New York: Knopf, 1976.

Kogan, N., & Wallach, M. A. *Risk taking: A study in cognition and personality.* New York: Holt, Rinehart and Winston, 1964.

Kohlberg, L. Stage and sequence: The cognitive-developmental approach to socialization. In D. A. Goslin (Ed.), *Handbook of socialization theory and research.* Chicago: Rand McNally, 1969.

Kohlenberg, R., Phillips, T., & Proctor, W. A behavioral analysis of peaking in residential electrical energy consumers. *Journal of Applied Behavioral Analysis*, 1976, *9*, 13–18.

Komarovsky, M. Cultural contradictions and sex roles. *American Journal of Sociology*, 1946, *52*, 184–189.

Komarovsky, M. Cultural contradictions and sex roles: The masculine case. *American Journal of Sociology*, 1974, *78*, 873–884.

Komarovsky, M. *Dilemmas of masculinity: A study of college youth.* New York: Norton, 1976.

Komorita, S. S., & Brenner, A. R. Bargaining and concession making under bilateral monopoly. *Journal of Personality and Social Psychology*, 1968, *9*, 15–20.

Komorita, S. S., & Mechling, J. Betrayal and conciliation in a two-person game. *Journal of Personality and Social Psychology*, 1967, *6*, 349–353.

Komorita, S. S., Sheposh, J. P., & Braver, S. L. Power, the use of power, and cooperative choice in a two-person game. *Journal of Personality and Social Psychology*, 1968, *8*, 134–142.

Konecni, V., & Ebbesen, E. B. Disinhibition versus the cathartic effect: Artifact and substance. *Journal of Personality and Social Psychology*, 1976, *34*, 352–365.

Korsch, B. M., & Negrete, V. F. Doctor-patient communication. *Scientific American*, 1972, *227*(2), 66–74.

Korte, C., & Kerr, N. Response to altruistic opportunities under urban and rural conditions. *Journal of Social Psychology*, 1975, *95*, 183–184.

Korte, C., Ypma, I., & Toppen, A. Helpfulness in Dutch society as a function of urbanization and environmental input level. *Journal of Personality and Social Psychology*, 1975, *32*, 996–1003.

Kozlowski, L. T., & Bryant, K. J. Sense of direction, spatial orientation and cognitive maps. *Journal of Experimental Psychology: Human Perception and Performance*, 1977, *3*, 590–598.

Kramer, C. Women's speech: Separate but unequal? In B. Thorne & N. Henley (Eds.), *Language and sex: Difference and dominance.* Rowley, Mass.: Newbury House, 1975.

Kramer, E. Judgment of personal characteristics and emotions from nonverbal properties. *Psychological Bulletin*, 1963, *60*, 408–420.

Krant, M. J. Problems of the physician in presenting the patient with the diagnosis. In J. W. Cullen, B. Fox, & R. Isom (Eds.), *Cancer: The behavioral dimensions.* New York: Raven Press, 1976.

Krantz, D. S., Glass, D. C., & Snyder, M. L. Helplessness, stress level and the coronary-prone behavior pattern. *Journal of Experimental Social Psychology*, 1974, *10*, 284–300.

Krauss, R. M., Geller, V., & Olson, C. *Modalities and cues in the detection of deception.* Paper presented at the annual meeting of the American Psychological Association, Washington, D.C., September 1976.

Krebs, D., & Adinolfi, A. A. Physical attractiveness, social relations, and personality style. *Journal of Personality and Social Psychology*, 1975, *31*, 245–253.

Krebs, D. L. Empathy and altruism. *Journal of Personality and Social Psychology*, 1975, *32*, 1134–1146.

Kruglanski, A. W., Hamel, I. Z., Maides, S. A., & Schwartz, J. M. Attribution theory as a special case of lay epistemology. In J. H. Harvey, W. J. Ickes, & R. F. Kidd (Eds.), *New directions in attribution research* (Vol. 2). Hillsdale, N.J.: Lawrence Erlbaum Associates, 1978.

Kubler-Ross, E. What is it like to be dying? *American Journal of Nursing*, 1971, *71*, 54–61.

Kuhlman, D. M., & Marshello, A. F. J. Individual differences in game motivation as moderators of preprogrammed strategy effects in prisoner's dilemma. *Journal of Personality and Social Psychology*, 1975, *32*, 922–931.

Kuhlman, D. M., & Wimberley, D. L. Expectations of choice behavior held by cooperators, competitors, and individualists across four classes of experimental game. *Journal of Personality and Social Psychology*, 1976, *34*, 69–81.

Kuhn, D. Z., Madsen, C. H., & Becker, W. C. Effects of exposure to an aggressive model and "frustration" on children's aggressive behavior. *Child Development*, 1967, *38*, 739–745.

Kuhn, T. S. *The structure of scientific revolution.* Chicago: University of Chicago Press, 1962.

Kulka, R. A., & Weingarten, H. The long-term effects of divorce in childhood on adult adjustment. *Journal of Social Issues*, 1979, *35*(4), 50–78.

Kuo, Z. Y. *The dynamics of behavior development.* New York: Random House, 1967.

Kutchinsky, B. *The effect of pornography: An experiment on perception* (Technical Report of the Commission on Obscenity and Pornography, Vol. 8). Washington, D.C.: U.S. Government Printing Office. 1970.

Kutchinsky, B. The effect of pornography. A pilot experiment on perception, behavior and attitudes. In *Technical Report of the Commission on Obscenity and Pornography* (Vol. 8). Washington, D.C.: U.S. Government Printing Office. 1971.

Lagerspetz, K. M. J., & Westman, W. Moral approval of aggression: A preliminary investigation. *Aggressive Behavior,* 1980, *6,* 119–130.

Lakoff, R. Language and woman's place. *Language in Society,* 1973, *2,* 45–79.

Lamb, M. E. Influence of the child on marital quality and family interaction during the prenatal, perinatal and infancy periods. In R. M. Lerner & G. D. Spanier (Eds.), *Contribution of the child to marital quality and family interaction through the life-span.* New York: Academic Press, in press.

Lang, A. R., Searles, J., Lauerman, R., & Adesso, V. Expectancy, alcohol, and sex guilt as determinants of interest in and reaction to sexual stimuli. *Journal of Abnormal Psychology,* 1980, *89,* 644–653.

Lang, K., & Lang, G. E. The mass media and voting. In E. Burdick & A. J. Brodbeck (Eds.), *American voting behavior.* Glencoe, Ill.: Free Press, 1959.

Langer, E. J. Rethinking the role of thought in social interaction. In J. H. Harvey, W. J. Ickes, & R. F. Kidd (Eds.), *New directions in attribution research* (Vol. 2). Hillsdale, N.J.: Lawrence Erlbaum Associates, 1979.

Langer, E. J., & Rodin, J. The effects of choice and enhanced personal responsibility for the aged: A field experiment in an institutional setting. *Journal of Personality and Social Psychology,* 1976, *34,* 191–198.

Lansky, L. M. The family structure also affects the model: Sex-role attitudes in parents of preschool children. *Merrill-Palmer Quarterly,* 1967, *13,* 139–150.

LaPiere, R. T. Attitudes vs. actions. *Social Forces,* 1934, *13,* 230–237.

Larsen, K. D., Coleman, D., Forbes, J., & Johnson, R. Is the subject's personality or the experimental situation a better predictor of a subject's willingness to administer shock to a victim? *Journal of Personality and Social Psychology,* 1972, *22,* 287–295.

Larwood, L., O'Neal, E. C., & Brennan, P. Increasing the physical aggressiveness of women. *Journal of Social Psychology,* 1977, *101,* 97–101.

Lasagna, L. Physician's behavior toward the dying patient. In O. Brim, H. Freeman, S. Levine, & N. Scotch (Eds.), *The dying patient.* New York: Russell Sage Foundation, 1970.

Latané, B., & Darley, J. M. Group inhibition of bystander intervention in emergencies. *Journal of Personality and Social Psychology,* 1968, *10,* 215–221.

Latané, B., & Darley, J. M. *The unresponsive bystander: Why doesn't he help?* New York: Appleton-Century-Crofts, 1970.

Latané, B., & Rodin, J. A. A lady in distress: Inhibiting effects of friends and strangers on bystander intervention. *Journal of Experimental Social Psychology,* 1969, *5,* 189–202.

Lavrakas, P. J. Female preferences for male physiques. *Journal of Research in Personality,* 1975, *9,* 324–334.

Laws, J. L., & Schwartz, P. *Sexual scripts: The social construction of female sexuality.* Hinsdale, Ill.: Dryden Press, 1977,

Lazare, A., Eisenthal, S., Frank, A., & Stoeckle, J. D. Studies on a negotiated approach to patienthood. In E. B. Gallagher (Ed.), *The doctor-patient relationship in the changing health scene.* Washington, D.C.: U.S. Department of Health, Education, and Welfare, 1978.

Lazarus, R. S. *Psychological stress and the coping process.* New York: McGraw-Hill, 1966.

Leavitt, H J. Some effects of certain communication patterns on group performance. *Journal of Abnormal and Social Psychology,* 1951, *46,* 38–50.

Lepper, M. R., & Greene, D. Turning play into work: Effects of adult surveillance and extrinsic rewards on children's intrinsic motivation. *Journal of Personality and Social Psychology,* 1975, *31,* 479–486.

Lepper, M. R., Greene, D., & Nisbett, R. E. Undermining children's intrinsic interest with extrinsic reward. *Journal of Personality and Social Psychology,* 1973, *28,* 129–137.

Lerner, M. The effect of responsibility and choice on a partner's attractiveness following failure. *Journal of Personality,* 1965, *33,* 178–187.

Lerner, M. J. The desire for justice and reactions to victims. In J. Macaulay & L. Berkowitz (Eds.), *Altruism and helping behavior.* New York: Academic Press, 1970.

Lerner, M. J. Observer's evaluation of a victim: Justice, guilt, and veridical perception. *Journal of Personality and Social Psychology,* 1971, *20,* 127–135.

Lerner, M. J. The justice motive: "Equity" and "parity" among children. *Journal of Personality and Social Psychology,* 1974, *29,* 539–550.

Lerner, M. J., Miller, D. T., & Holmes, J. G. Deserving and the emergence of forms of justice. In L. Berkowitz & E. Walster (Eds.), *Advances in experimental social psychology* (Vol. 9). New York: Academic Press, 1976.

Lerner, M. J., & Simmons, C. H. Observer's reaction to the "innocent victim": Compassion or rejection? *Journal of Personality and Social Psychology*, 1966, *4*, 203–210.

Lerner, R. M., & Gellert, E. Body build identification, preference, and aversion in children. *Developmental Psychology*, 1969, *1*, 456–462.

Levenson, B. Bureaucratic succession. In A. Etzioni (Ed.), *Complex organizations: A sociological reader*. New York: Holt, Rinehart and Winston, 1961.

Leventhal, G. S. Fairness in social relationships. In J. W. Thibaut, J. T. Spence, & R. C. Carson (Eds.), *Contemporary topics in social psychology*. Morristown, N.J.: General Learning Press, 1976.

Leventhal, G. S., Michaels, J. W., & Sanford, C. Inequity and interpersonal conflict: Reward allocation and secrecy about rewards as methods of preventing conflict. *Journal of Personality and Social Psychology*, 1972, *23*, 88–102.

Leventhal, H., & Singer, R. Affect arousal and positioning of recommendations in persuasive communications. *Journal of Personality and Social Psychology*, 1966, *4*, 137–146.

Leventhal, H., Singer, R., & Jones, S. The effects of fear and specificity of recommendation upon attitudes and behavior. *Journal of Personality and Social Psychology*, 1965, *2*, 20–29.

Levine, J. M., Saxe, L., & Harris, H. J. Reaction to attitudinal deviance: Impact of deviate's direction and distance of movement. *Sociometry*, 1970, *33*, 427–443.

LeVine, R. A., & Campbell, D. T. *Ethnocentrism*. New York: Wiley, 1972.

Levinger, G. Note on need complementarity in marriage. *Psychological Bulletin*, 1964, *61*, 153–157.

Levinger, G. A social psychological perspective on marital dissolution. *Journal of Social Issues*, 1976, *32*(1), 21–47.

Levinger, G., Senn, D. J., & Jorgensen, B. W. Progress toward permanence in courtship: A test of the Kerckhoff-Davis hypothesis. *Sociometry*, 1970, *33*, 427–433.

Levinger, G., & Snoek, J. D. *Attraction in relationship: A new look at interpersonal attraction*. Morristown, N.J.: General Learning Press, 1972.

Levitin, T. E. (Ed.). Children of divorce. *Journal of Social Issues*, 1979, *35*(4), 1–186.

Lewin, K. *A dynamic theory of personality*. New York: McGraw-Hill, 1935.

Lewin, K. Group decision and social change. In T. M. Newcomb & E. L. Hartley (Eds.), *Readings in social psychology*. New York: Holt, Rinehart and Winston, 1947.

Lewin, K. *Resolving social conflicts*. New York: Harper & Row, 1948.

Lewin, K. *Field theory in social science*. New York: Harper & Row, 1951.

Lewin, K., Lippitt, R., & White, R. K. Patterns of aggressive behavior in experimentally created "social climates." *Journal of Social Psychology*, 1939, *10*, 271–299.

Lewis, C. A. People/plant proxemics: A concept for human design. In P. Suedfeld & J. Russell (Eds.), *The behavioral basis of design: Proceedings of the 7th International Environmental Design Research Association Conference*. Stroudsburg, Pa.: Dowden, Hutchinson, & Ross, 1976.

Lewis, R. A. Emotional intimacy among men. *Journal of Social Issues*, 1978, *34*(1), 108–121.

Liebert, R. M., Cohen, L. A., Joyce, C., Murrel, S., Nisonoff, L., & Sonnenschein, S. Predispositions revisited. *Journal of Communications*, 1977, *27*, 217–221.

Liebert, R. M., Neale, J. M., & Davidson, E. S. *The early window: Effects of television on children and youth*. New York: Pergamon Press, 1973.

Liebert, R. M., & Poulos, R. W. Television and personality development: The socializing effects of an entertainment medium. In A. Davids (Ed.), *Child personality and psychopathology*. New York: Wiley, 1975.

Likert, R. A technique for the measurement of attitudes. *Archives of Psychology*, 1932, No. 140.

Lindemann, C. *Birth control and unmarried young women*. New York: Springer-Verlag, 1974.

Linder, D. E., Cooper, J., & Jones, E. E. Decision freedom as a determinant of the role of incentive magnitude in attitude change. *Journal of Personality and Social Psychology*, 1967, *6*, 245–254.

Lindquist, C. U., Kramer, J. A., Rhyne, L. D., MacDonald, M. L., & McGrath, R. A. Manual for systematic behavior rehearsal training program for male social skills. *JSAS Catalog of Selected Documents in Psychology*, 1975.

Lindskold, S. Trust development, the GRIT proposal, and the effects of conciliatory acts on conflict and cooperation. *Psychological Bulletin*, 1978, *85*, 772–793.

Linton, H., & Graham, E. Personality correlates of persuasibility. In C. I. Hovland & I. L. Janis (Eds.), *Personality and persuasibility.* New Haven, Conn.: Yale University Press, 1959.

Lippa, R. Expressive control, expressive consistency, and the correspondence between expressive behavior and personality. *Journal of Personality,* 1978, *46,* 438–461. (a)

Lippa, R. The naive perception of masculinity-femininity on the basis of expressive cues. *Journal of Research in Personality,* 1978, *12,* 1–14. (b)

Lippitt, R., & White, R. K. An experimental study of leadership and group life. In T. M. Newcomb & E. L. Hartley (Eds.), *Readings in Social Psychology.* New York: Henry Holt, 1947.

Lipsey, M. W. Attitudes toward the environment and pollution. In S. Oskamp, *Attitudes and opinions.* Englewood Cliffs, N.J.: Prentice-Hall, 1977.

Litman-Adizes, F., Fontaine, G., & Raven, B. Consequences of social power and causal attribution for compliance as seen by powerholder and target. *Personality and Social Psychology Bulletin,* 1978, *4,* 260–264.

Lockheed, M. E., & Hall, K. P. Conceptualizing sex as a status characteristic. *Journal of Social Issues,* 1976, *32*(3), 111–124.

Lofland, J. *Doomsday cult.* Englewood Cliffs, N.J.: Prentice-Hall, 1966.

Loftus, E., & Monahan, J. Trial by data: Psychological research as legal evidence. *American Psychologist,* 1980, *35,* 270–283.

London, P. The rescuers: Motivational hypotheses about Christians who saved Jews from the Nazis. In J. Macaulay & L. Berkowitz (Eds.), *Altruism and helping behavior.* New York: Academic Press, 1970.

Long, G. T., & Lerner, M. J. Deserving, the "personal contract," and altruistic behavior by children. *Journal of Personality and Social Psychology,* 1974, *29,* 551–556.

Longley, J., & Pruitt, D. G. Groupthink: A critique of Janis' theory. In L. Wheeler (Ed.), *Review of Personality and Social Psychology* (Vol. 1). Beverly Hills, Cal.: Sage, 1980.

Lord, R. G., & Hohenfeld, J. A. Longitudinal field assessment of equity effects on the performance of major league baseball players. *Journal of Applied Psychology,* 1979, *64,* 19–26.

Lorenz, K. *On aggression.* New York: Harcourt, Brace & World, 1966.

Lott, A. J., & Lott, B. E. The role of reward in the formation of positive interpersonal attitudes. In T. L. Huston (Ed.), *Foundations of interpersonal attraction.* New York: Academic Press, 1974.

Lowenthal, M. F., & Haven, C. Interaction and adaptation: Intimacy as a critical variable. *American Sociological Review,* 1968, *33,* 20–30.

Lucker, G. W., Rosenfield, D., Sikes, J., & Aronson, E. Performance in the interdependent classroom. *American Educational Research Journal,* 1977, *13,* 115–123.

Ludwig, D. J., & Maehr, M. J. Changes in self concept and stated behavioral preferences. *Child Development,* 1967, *38,* 453–467.

Luft, J. *Of human interaction.* Palo Alto, Cal.: National Press Books, 1969.

Lundberg, U. Urban commuting: Crowdedness and catecholamine excretion. *Journal of Human Stress,* 1976, *2,* 26–34.

Luyben, P. D., & Bailey, J. S. *Newspaper recycling behaviors: The effects of reinforcement versus proximity of containers.* Paper presented at the annual convention of the Midwest Association of Behavior Analysis, Chicago, 1979.

Lykken, D. Psychology and the lie detector industry. *American Psychologist,* 1974, *28,* 725–739.

Lynch, K. *The image of the city.* Cambridge, Mass.: M.I.T. Press, 1960.

Lynn, S. J. Three theories of self-disclosure exchange. *Journal of Experimental Social Psychology,* 1978, *5,* 466–479.

Maccoby, E. E. *Social development: Psychological growth and the parent-child relationship.* New York: Harcourt, Brace, Jovanovich, 1980.

Maccoby, E. E. The development of moral values and behavior in childhood. In J. A. Clausen (Ed.) *Socialization and society.* Boston: Little, Brown, 1968.

Maddi, S. R. Meaning, novelty, and affect: Comments on Zajonc's paper. *Journal of Personality and Social Psychology,* 1968, *9,* 28–29.

Maehr, M. L. *Culture and achievement motivation: Beyond Weber and McClelland.* Paper presented at the annual meeting of the American Educational Research Association, Boston, April 1980.

Maehr, M. L., & Nicholls, J. G. *Studies in cross-cultural psychology* (Vol. 3). New York: Academic Press, 1980.

Main, M. *Play, exploration and competence as related to child-adult attachment.* Unpublished doctoral dissertation, The Johns Hopkins University, 1973.

Maisel, R. *Report of the continuing audit of public attitudes and concerns.* Unpublished manuscript, Harvard Medical School, 1969.

Malamuth, N. *Erotica, aggression and perceived appropriateness.* Paper presented at the annual meeting of the American Psychological Association, Toronto, September 1978.

Malamuth, N. Rape fantasies as a function of exposure to violent sexual stimuli. *Archives of Sexual Behavior*, 1981, *10*, 33–47.

Malamuth, N. Rape proclivity among males. *Journal of Social Issues*, 1981, *37*(4), 138–154.

Malamuth, N., & Check, J. V. P. *The effects of mass media exposure on acceptance of violence against women: A field study.* Paper presented at the annual meeting of the American Psychological Association, Montreal, September 1980.

Malamuth, N., & Check, J. V. P. The effects of mass media exposure on acceptance of violence against women: A field experiment. *Journal of Research in Personality*, 1981, *15*, 436–446.

Malamuth, N., & Check, J. V. P. Penile tumescence and perceptual responses to rape as a function of victim's perceived reactions. *Journal of Applied Social Psychology*, 1980, *10*, 528–547.

Malamuth, N., Feshbach, S., & Jaffe, Y. Sexual arousal and aggression: Recent experiments and theoretical issues. *Journal of Social Issues*, 1977, *33*(2), 110–133.

Malamuth, N., Hager, S., & Feshbach, S. Testing hypotheses regarding rape: Exposure to sexual violence, sex differences, and the "normality" of rapists. *Journal of Research in Personality*, 1980, *14*, 121–137.

Malamuth, N., Heim, M., & Feshbach, S. The sexual responsiveness of college students to rape depiction: Inhibitory and disinhibitory effects. *Journal of Personality and Social Psychology*, 1980, *38*, 399–408.

Malamuth, N., Reisin, I., & Spinner, B. *Exposure to pornography and reactions to rape.* Paper presented at the annual meeting of the American Psychological Association, New York, September 1979.

Malamuth, N., & Spinner, B. A longitudinal content analysis of sexual violence in the best-selling erotic magazines. *Journal of Sex Research*, 1980, *16*, 226–237.

Malinowski, B. *Magic, science and religion and other essays.* New York: Doubleday Anchor Books, 1948.

Manis, M. Social psychology and history: A symposium. *Personality and Social Psychology Bulletin*, 1976, *2*, 371–372.

Mann, R. D. A review of relationships between personality and performance in small groups. *Psychological Bulletin*, 1959, *56*, 241–270.

March, J. G., & Simon, H. A. *Organizations.* New York: Wiley, 1958.

Marcia, J. E. Identity in adolescence. In J. Adelson (Ed.), *Handbook of adolescent psychology.* New York: Wiley, 1980.

Margulis, S. T. *Privacy as information management: A social, psychological and environmental framework.* Washington, D.C.: National Bureau of Standards, 1979.

Mark, V. H., & Ervin, F. R. *Violence and the brain.* New York: Harper & Row, 1970.

Marlowe, D., & Gergen, K. J. Personality and social behavior. In K. J. Gergen & D. Marlowe (Eds.), *Personality and social behavior.* Reading, Mass.: Addison-Wesley, 1970.

Marsh, R. M., & Mannari, H. Organizational commitment and turnover: A prediction study. *Administrative Science Quarterly*, 1977, *22*, 57–75.

Martin, J. Relative deprivation: A theory of distributive injustice for an era of shrinking resources. In B. M. Shaw & L. L. Cummings (Eds.), *Research in organizational behavior* (Vol. 3). Greenwich, Conn.: JAI Press, 1980.

Masling, J. Role-related behaviors of subject and psychological data. In D. Levine (Ed.), *Nebraska Symposium on Motivation* (Vol. 14). Lincoln: University of Nebraska Press, 1966.

Masters, W. H., & Johnson, V. E. *Human sexual response.* Boston: Little, Brown, 1966.

Masters, W. H., & Johnson, V. E. *Human sexual inadequacy.* Boston: Little, Brown, 1970.

Masters, W. H., & Johnson, V. E. *Homosexuality in perspective.* Boston: Little, Brown, 1979.

Mathews, K. E., & Canon, L. K. Environmental noise level as a determinant of helping behavior. *Journal of Personality and Social Psychology*, 1975, *32*, 571–577.

Matlin, M. W., & Stang, D. J. *The Pollyanna principle: Selectivity in language, memory, and thought.* Cambridge, Mass.: Schenkman, 1978.

Mayo, E. *The human problems of an industrial civilization.* New York: Macmillan, 1933.

McArthur, L. The how and what of why: Some determinants of consequences of causal attribution. *Journal of Personality and Social Psychology*, 1972, *22*, 171–193.

McArthur, L. Z., & Solomon, L. K. Perceptions of an aggressive encounter as a function of victim's salience and the perceiver's arousal. *Journal of Personality and Social Psychology*, 1978, *36*, 1278–1290.

McCary, J. L. *Human sexuality: Physiological, psychological, and sociological factors* (2d ed.). New York: Van Nostrand, 1973.

McCauley, C., & Jacques, S. The popularity of conspiracy theories of Presidential assassination: A Bayesian analysis. *Journal of Personality and Social Psychology*, 1979, 37, 637–644.

McClelland, D. *Power: The inner experience.* New York: Irvington, 1975.

McClintock, C. G. Development of social motives in Anglo-American and Mexican-American children. *Journal of Personality and Social Psychology*, 1974, 29, 348–354.

McClintock, C. G. Social values: Their definition, measurement and development. *Journal of Research and Development in Education*, 1978, 12, 121–136.

McClintock, C. G., & Keil, L. J. Equity and social exchange. In J. Greenberg & L. Cohen (Eds.), *Equity and justice in social behavior.* New York: Academic Press, 1981.

McCormick, N. B. *Gender role and expected social power behavior in sexual decision-making.* Unpublished doctoral dissertation, University of California, Los Angeles, 1976.

McDaniel, J., O'Neal, E. C., & Fox, E. Magnitude of retaliation as a function of similarity of available responses to those employed by the attacker. *Psychonomic Science*, 1971, 21, 30–35.

McDonald, R. L., & Gynther, M. D. Relationship of self and ideal-self descriptions with sex, race, and class in Southern adolescents. *Journal of Personality and Social Psychology*, 1965, 1, 85–88.

McDougall, W. *Introduction to social psychology.* London: Methuen, 1908.

McGinley, H., McGinley, P., & Nicholas, K. Smiling, body position, and interpersonal attraction. *Bulletin of the Psychonomic Society*, 1978, 12, 21–24.

McGrath, J. E. The first thirty-six years: The Journal of Social Issues in historical perspective. *Journal of Social Issues*, 1980, 36(4), 98–124.

McGuire, W. J. Personality and susceptibility to social influence. In E. F. Borgatta & W. W. Lambert (Eds.), *Handbook of personality theory and research.* Chicago: Rand McNally, 1960.

McGuire, W. J. Personality and attitude change: An information-processing theory. In A. G. Greenwald, T. C. Brock, & T. M. Ostrom (Eds.), *Psychological foundations of attitudes.* New York: Academic Press, 1968.

McGuire, W. J. The nature of attitudes and attitude change. In G. Lindzey & E. Aronson (Eds.), *The handbook of social psychology,* (Vol. 3, 2d ed.). Reading, Mass.: Addison-Wesley, 1969.

McKechnie, G. E. Stimulation techniques in environmental psychology. In D. Stokols (Ed.), *Perspectives on environment and behavior: Theory, research, and applications.* New York: Plenum Press, 1977.

McKinlay, J. Who is really ignorant—physician or patient? *Journal of Health and Social Behavior*, 1975, 16, 3–11.

Meadows, D. H. *The limits to growth.* New York: Universe Books, 1972.

Meeker, R. J., & Shure, G. H. Pacifist bargaining tactics: Some "outsider" influences. *Journal of Conflict Resolution*, 1969, 13, 487–493.

Mehrabian, A. Nonverbal betrayal of feeling. *Journal of Experimental Research in Personality*, 1971, 5, 64–73.

Mehrabian, A. *Nonverbal communication.* Chicago: Aldine, 1972.

Meyer, J. P., & Pepper, S. Need compatibility and marital adjustment in young married couples. *Journal of Personality and Social Psychology*, 1977, 35, 331–342.

Michael, D. N. *On learning to plan—And planning to learn.* San Francisco: Jossey-Bass, 1973.

Michelson, W. *Man and his urban environment: A sociological approach* (2d ed.). Reading Mass.: Addison-Wesley, 1976.

Michener, H. A., & Lawler, E. J. The endorsement of formal leaders: An integrative model. *Journal of Personality and Social Psychology*, 1975, 31, 216–223.

Michotte, A. *Perception of causality.* New York: Basic Books, 1963.

Midlarsky, E., & Midlarsky, M. Some determinants of aiding under experimentally induced stress. *Journal of Personality*, 1973, 41, 305–327.

Mikula, G. On the role of justice in allocation decisions. In G. Mikula (Ed.), *Justice and social interaction.* New York: Springer-Verlag, 1980.

Milgram, S. Behavioral study of obedience. *Journal of Abnormal and Social Psychology*, 1963, 67, 371–378.

Milgram, S. Some conditions of obedience and disobedience to authority. In I. D. Steiner & M. Fishbein (Eds.), *Current studies in social psychology.* New York: Holt, Rinehart and Winston, 1965.

Milgram, S. The experience of living in cities: A psychological analysis. *Science*, 1970, 167, 1461–1468.

Milgram, S. *Obedience to authority: An experimental view.* New York: Harper & Row, 1974.

Milgram, S. *The individual in a social world.* Reading, Mass.: Addison-Wesley, 1977.

Milgram, S., & Jodelet, D. Psychological maps of Paris. In H. M. Proshansky, W. H. Ittelson, & L. G. Rivkin (Eds.), *Environmental psychology: People and their physical settings* (2d ed.). New York: Holt, Rinehart and Winston, 1976.

Miller, D. T. Ego involvement and attributions for success and failure. *Journal of Personality and Social Psychology,* 1976, *34,* 901–906.

Miller, D. T., & Ross, M. Self-serving biases in the attribution of causality: Fact or fiction? *Psychological Bulletin,* 1975, *82,* 213–225.

Miller, F. D., Smith, E. R., & Uleman, J. Measurement and interpretation of situational and dispositional attributions. *Journal of Experimental Social Psychology,* 1981, *17,* 80–95.

Miller, G. A. Psychology as a means of promoting human welfare. *American Psychologist,* 1969, *24,* 1063–1075.

Miller, N. Involvement and dogmatism as inhibitors of attitude change. *Journal of Experimental Social Psychology,* 1965, *1,* 121–132.

Miller, N. E. The frustration-aggression hypothesis. *Psychological Review,* 1941, *48,* 337–342.

Miller, N. E. Theory and experiment relating psychoanalytic displacement to stimulus-response generalization. *Journal of Abnormal and Social Psychology,* 1948, *43,* 155–178.

Millet, K. The shame is over. *Ms. Magazine,* January 1975.

Mills, C. W. *The sociological imagination.* New York: Oxford, 1959.

Mills, J. Avoidance of dissonant information. *Journal of Personality and Social Psychology,* 1965, *2,* 589–593.

Mills, J., & Egger, R. Effect on derogation of a victim of choosing to reduce his distress. *Journal of Personality and Social Psychology,* 1972, *23,* 405–408.

Mischel, W. A social learning view of sex differences in behavior. In E. E. Maccoby (Ed.), *The development of sex differences.* Stanford, Cal.: Stanford University Press, 1966.

Mita, T. H., Dermer, M., & Knight, J. Reversed facial images and the mere-exposure hypothesis. *Journal of Personality and Social Psychology,* 1977, *35,* 597–601.

Mixon, D. Instead of deception. *Journal of the Theory of Social Behavior,* 1972, *2,* 146–177.

Mixon, D. If you don't deceive, what can you do? In N. Armistead (Ed.), *Reconstructing social psychology.* London: Penguin, 1974.

Moles, O. C., & Levinger, G. (Eds.). Divorce and separation. *Journal of Social Issues,* 1976, *32*(1), 1–223.

Molotch, H. The radicalization of everyone? In P. Orleans & W. R. Ellis, Jr. (Eds.), *Race, change, and urban society.* Beverly Hills, Cal.: Sage, 1971.

Monson, T. C., & Snyder, M. Actors, observers, and the attribution process: Toward a reconceptualization. *Journal of Experimental Social Psychology,* 1977, *13,* 89–111.

Montagu, A. Chromosomes and crime. *Psychology Today,* October 1968, pp. 42–49. (a)

Montagu, A. *Man and aggression.* New York: Oxford, 1968. (b)

Montagu, A. *Learning to be nonaggressive.* London: Oxford, 1978.

Moore, D. W., & Trout, B. T. Military advancement: The visibility theory of promotion. *American Political Science Review,* 1978, *72,* 452–468.

Moore, G. T., & Golledge, R. G. (Eds.). *Environmental knowing.* Stroudsburg, Pa.: Dowden, Hutchinson, & Ross, 1976.

Moos, R. H. *The human context.* New York: Wiley, 1976.

Morelock, J. C. Sex differences in susceptibility to social influence. *Sex Roles,* 1980, *6,* 537–548.

Morse, S. J., Gruzen, J., & Reis, H. T. The "eye of the beholder": A neglected variable in the study of physical attractiveness? *Journal of Personality,* 1976, *44,* 209–225. (a)

Morse, S. J., Gruzen, J., & Reis, H. T. The nature of equity-restoration: Some approval-seeking considerations. *Journal of Experimental Social Psychology,* 1976, *12,* 1–8. (b)

Morton, T. L. Intimacy and reciprocity of exchange: A comprison of spouses and strangers. *Journal of Personality and Social Psychology,* 1978, *36,* 72–81.

Moscovici, S. Social influence I: Conformity and social control. In C. Nemeth (Ed.), *Social psychology: Classic and contemporary integrations.* Chicago: Aldine, 1974.

Moscovici, S. *Social influence and social change.* London: Academic Press, 1976.

Moscovici, S., Lage, E., & Naffrechoux, M. Influence of a consistent minority on the responses of a majority in a color perception task. *Sociometry,* 1969, *32,* 365–380.

Moscovici, S., & Nemeth, C. Social influence II: Minority influence. In C. Nemeth (Ed.), *Social psychology: Classic and contemporary contributions.* Chicago: Rand McNally, 1974.

Moscovici, S., & Zavalloni, M. The group as a polarizer of attitudes. *Journal of Personality and Social Psychology*, 1969, *12*, 125–135.

Mosher, D. L. The development and multitrait-multimethod matrix analysis of three measures of three aspects of guilt. *Journal of Consulting Psychology*, 1966, *30*, 25–29.

Mosher, D. L. Sex differences, sex experience, sex guilt, and explicitly sexual films. *Journal of Social Issues*, 1973, *29*(3), 95–112.

Mosher, D. L. The meaning and measurement of guilt. In C. E. Izard (Ed.), *Emotions in personality and psychopathology*. New York: Plenum Press, 1979.

Mosher, D., & Scodel, A. Relationships between ethnocentrism in children and the ethnocentrism and authoritarian rearing practices of their mothers. *Child Development*, 1960, *31*, 369–376.

Moss, M. K., & Page, R. A. Reinforcement and helping behavior. *Journal of Applied Psychology*, 1972, *2*, 360–371.

Mower-White, C. J. Factors affecting balance, agreement, and positivity biases in POQ and POX triads. *European Journal of Social Psychology*, 1979, *9*, 129–148.

Moyer, K. E. Kinds of aggression and their physiological basis. *Communications in behavioral biology*, 1968, *2*(A), 65–87.

Mueller, D., & Donnerstein, E. The effects of humor-induced arousal upon aggressive behavior. *Journal of Research in Personality*, 1977, *11*, 73–82.

Murphy, G., & Murphy, L. B. *Experimental social psychology*. New York: Harper & Row, 1931.

Murphy, G., Murphy, L. B., & Newcomb, T. M. *Experimental social psychology* (Rev. ed.). New York: Harper & Row, 1937.

Murray, S. R., & Mednick, M. T. S. Perceiving the causes of success and failure in achievement: Sex, race and motivational comparisons. *Journal of Consulting and Clinical Psychology*, 1975, *43*, 881–885.

Murstein, B. I. Physical attractiveness and marital choice. *Journal of Personality and Social Psychology*, 1972, *22*, 8–12.

Mussen, P., & Eisenberg-Berg, N. *Roots of caring, sharing, and helping*. San Francisco: W. H. Freeman, 1977.

Nader, R., & Johnson, N. *Television violence survey* (Report of the National Citizens Committee for Broadcasting). Washington, D.C.: July 1979.

Neisser, U. *Cognition and reality: Principles and implications of cognitive psychology*. San Francisco: W. H. Freeman, 1976.

Nelson, P. A. *A sexual functions inventory*. Unpublished doctoral dissertation, University of Florida, 1979.

Nelson, S. D. Nature-nurture revisited I: A review of the biological bases of conflict. *Journal of Conflict Resolution*, 1974, *18*, 285–335.

Nelson, S. D. Nature-nurture revisited II: Social, political, and technological implications of biological approaches to human conflict. *Journal of Conflict Resolution*, 1975, *19*, 734–761.

Newcomb, T. M. *Personality and social change*. New York: Dryden, 1943.

Newcomb, T. M. The prediction of interpersonal attraction. *American Psychologist*, 1956, *11*, 575–586.

Newcomb, T. M. *The acquaintance process*. New York: Holt, Rinehart and Winston, 1961.

Newcomb, T. M. Persistence and regression of changed attitudes: Long range studies. *Journal of Social Issues*, 1963, *19*, 3–14.

Newcomb, T. M., Koenig, K., Flacks, R., & Warwick, D. *Persistence and change: Bennington College and its students after 25 years*. New York: Wiley, 1967.

Newman, O. *Defensible space*. New York: Macmillan, 1973.

Newtson, D. Dispositional inference from effects of actions: Effects chosen and effects foregone. *Journal of Experimental Social Psychology*, 1974, *10*, 489–496.

Nicholls, J. G. Quality and equality in intellectual development: The role of motivation in education. *American Psychologist*, 1979, *34*, 1071–1084.

Nisbett, R. E., & Borgida, E. Attribution and the psychology of prediction. *Journal of Personality and Social Psychology*, 1975, *32*, 932–943.

Nisbett, R. E., & Ross, L. *Human inference: Strategies and shortcomings of social judgment*. Englewood Cliffs, N.J.: Prentice-Hall, 1980.

Nisbett, R. E., & Schachter, S. Cognitive manipulation of pain. *Journal of Experimental Social Psychology*, 1966, *2*, 227–236.

Norton, A. J., & Glick, P. C. Marital instability: Past, present, and future. *Journal of Social Issues*, 1976, *32*(1), 5–20.

Nunnally, J. C. *Psychometric theory*. New York: McGraw-Hill, 1978.

O'Leary, V. E., & Hansen, R. D. *Sex-determining attributions*. Paper presented at the annual meeting of the Eastern Psychological Association, Philadelphia, April 1979.

Oliver, P. Selective incentives in an Apex game. *Journal of Conflict Resolution*, 1980, *24*, 113–141.

Olsen, M. E. Consumers' attitudes toward energy conservation. *Journal of Social Issues*, 1981, *37*(2), 108–131.

Olson, J. M., & Zanna, M. P. A new look at selective exposure. *Journal of Experimental Social Psychology*, 1979, *15*, 1–15.

Olweus, D. *Aggression in the schools.* New York: Wiley, 1978.

O'Neal, E. C. Environment and aggression. In R. G. Geen & E. Donnerstein (Eds.), *Human aggression: Theoretical and empirical reviews.* New York: Academic Press, 1981.

O'Neal, E. C., Brunault, M., Carifio, M., Troutwine, R., & Epstein, J. Insult and personal space preferences. *Journal of Nonverbal Behavior*, 1980, *5*, 56–62.

O'Neal, E. C., Brunault, M., Marquis, J., & Carifio, M. Anger and the body buffer zone. *Journal of Social Psychology*, 1979, *108*, 135–136.

O'Neal, E. C., Caldwell, C., & Gallup, G. G., Jr. Territorial invasion and aggression in young children. *Environmental Psychology and Nonverbal Behavior*, 1977, *2*, 14–25.

O'Neal, E. C., & McDonald, P. J. The environmental psychology of aggression. In R. G. Geen & E. C. O'Neal (Eds.), *Perspectives on aggression.* New York: Academic Press, 1976.

O'Neal, E. C., McDonald, P. J., Hori, R., & McClinton, B Arousal and initation of aggression. *Motivation and Emotion*, 1977, *1*, 93–100.

Orleans, P. Differential cognition of urban residents: Effects of social scale on mapping. In R. Downs & D. Stea (Eds.), *Image and environment.* Chicago: Aldine, 1973.

Orne, M. T. On the social psychology of the psychological experiment: With particular reference to demand characteristics and their implications. *American Psychologist*, 1962, *17*, 776–783.

Orne, M. T. Demand characteristics and the concept of quasi-controls. In R. Rosenthal & R. L. Rosnow (Eds.), *Artifact in behavioral research.* New York: Academic Press, 1969.

Orvis, B. R., Cunningham, J. D., & Kelley, H. H. A closer examination of causal inference: The role of consensus, distinctiveness and consistency information. *Journal of Personality and Social Psychology*, 1975, *32*, 605–616.

Orvis, B. R., Kelley, H. H., & Butler, D. Attributional conflicts in couples. In J. H. Harvey, W. J. Ickes, & R. F. Kidd (Eds.), *New directions in attribution research* (Vol. 1). Hillsdale, N.J.: Lawrence Erlbaum Associates, 1976.

Osgood, C. E. *An alternative to war or surrender.* Urbana: University of Illinois Press, 1962.

Osgood, C. E., Suci, G. J., & Tannenbaum, P. H. *The measurement of meaning.* Urbana: University of Illinois Press, 1957.

Oskamp, S. *Attitudes and opinions.* Englewood Cliffs, N.J.: Prentice-Hall, 1977.

Oskamp, S., Mindick, B., Berger, D., & Motta, E. A longitudinal study of success versus failure in contraceptive planning. *Journal of Population*, 1978, *1*, 69–83.

Ossorio, P. G. *Persons* (LRI Report 3). Los Angeles, Cal., and Boulder, Col.: Linguistic Research Institute, 1966.

Ossorio, P. G. *What actually happens.* Columbia: University of South Carolina Press, 1978.

Ossorio, P. G. Foundations of descriptive psychology. In K. Davis (Ed.), *Advances in descriptive psychology* (Vol. 1). Greenwich, Conn.: JAI Press, 1981.

Ostrom, T. M. The bogus pipeline: A new ignis fatuus? *Psychological Bulletin*, 1973, *79*, 252–259.

Pace, C. R., & Stern, G. G. An approach to the measurement of psychological characteristics of college environments. *Journal of Educational Psychology*, 1958, *49*, 209–277.

Page, D., & O'Neal, E. C. Weapons effect without demand characteristics. *Psychological Reports*, 1977, *41*, 29–30.

Page, M. M., & Scheidt, R. J. The elusive weapons effect: Demand awareness, evaluation apprehension and slightly sophisticated subjects. *Journal of Personality and Social Psychology*, 1971, *20*, 304–318.

Pagelow, M. *A secondary battering: Breaking the cycle of domestic violence.* Paper presented at the meeting of the American Sociological Association, 1977.

Pallak, M. S., & Cummings, W. Commitment and voluntary energy conservation. *Personality and Social Psychology Bulletin*, 1976, *2*, 27–30.

Parke, R. D. Rules, roles and resistance to deviation: Recent advances in punishment, discipline and self-control. In A. D. Pick (Ed.), *Minnesota Symposia on Child Psychology* (Vol. 8). Minneapolis: University of Minnesota Press, 1974.

Parke, R. D., Berkowitz, L., Leyens, J. P., West, S. G., & Sebastian, R. J. Some effects of violent and nonviolent movies on the behaviors of juvenile delinquents. In L. Berkowitz (Ed.), *Advances in experimental social psychology* (Vol. 10). New York: Academic Press, 1977.

Parsons, J. E., & Goff, S. B. Achievement motivation and values: An alternative perspective. In L.

J. Fyans (Ed.), *Achievement motivation: Recent trends in theory and research.* New York: Plenum Press, 1980.

Parsons, T. *The social system.* New York: Free Press, 1951.

Pascale, R. T. Zen and the art of management. *Harvard Business Review,* 1973, *51,* 153–162.

Pastore, N. The role of arbitrariness in the frustration-aggression hypothesis. *Journal of Abnormal and Social Psychology,* 1952, *47,* 728–731.

Patterson, G. R. The aggressive child: Victim and architect of a coercive system. In E. J. Mash, L. A. Hamerlynck, & L. C. Handy (Eds.), *Behavior modification and families. I: Theory and research.* New York: Brunner-Mazel, 1976.

Patterson, M. L. An arousal model of intimacy. *Psychological Review,* 1976, *83,* 235–245.

Payne, J. W., Braunstein, M. L., & Carroll, J. S. Exploring predecisional behavior: An alternative approach to decision research. *Organizational Behavior and Human Performance,* 1978, *22,* 17–44.

Peak, D. The elderly who face dying and death. In D. Barton (Ed.), *Dying and death.* Baltimore, Md.: Williams & Wilkins, 1977.

Pelz, D. C. Influence: A key to effective leadership in the first-line supervisor. *Personnel,* 1952, *29,* 3–11.

Pennings, J. M. Work-value systems of white collar workers. *Administrative Science Quarterly,* 1970, *15,* 397–405.

Peplau, L. A., & Perlman, D. (Eds.) *Loneliness: A sourcebook of current theory, research and therapy.* New York: Wiley, 1982.

Peplau, L., Rubin, Z., & Hill, C. Sexual intimacy in dating relationships. *Journal of Social Issues,* 1977, *33*(2), 86–109.

Percy, W. *Love in the ruins.* New York: Farrar, Straus & Giroux, 1971.

Perlman, D. Rear end analysis: The uses of social psychology textbook citation data. *Teaching of Psychology,* 1976, *6,* 101–104.

Perlman, D. The premarital sexual standards of Canadians. In K. Ishwaran (Ed.), *Marriage and divorce in Canada.* Toronto: McGraw-Hill, in press.

Perlman, D., & Oskamp, S. The effects of picture content and exposure frequency on evaluations of Negroes and Whites. *Journal of Experimental Social Psychology,* 1971, *7,* 503–514.

Pettigrew, T. F. The ultimate attribution error: Extending Allport's cognitive analysis of prejudice. *Personality and Social Psychology Bulletin,* 1979, *5,* 461–476.

Petty, R. E., & Cacioppo, J. T. Issue-involvement can increase or decrease persuasion by enhancing message-relevant cognitive responses. *Journal of Personality and Social Psychology,* 1979, *37,* 1915–1926.

Petty, R. E., & Cacioppo, J. T. *Attitudes and persuasion: Classic and contemporary approaches.* Dubuque, Iowa: Wm. C. Brown, 1981.

Pezdek, K., & Evans, G. W. Visual and verbal memory for objects and their spatial location. *Journal of Experimental Psychology: Human Learning and Memory,* 1979, *5,* 360–373.

Pfungst, O. *Clever Hans (The horse of Mr. von Osten)* (R. Rosenthal, Ed.). New York: Holt, Rinehart and Winston, 1965.

Phelps, L. Female sexual alienation. In J. Freeman (Ed.), *Women: A feminist perspective.* Palo Alto, Cal.: Mayfield, 1979.

Philips, S. Participant structure and communicative competence: Warm Springs children in community and classroom. In C. Cazden, V. John, & D. Hymes (Eds.), *Function of language in the classroom.* New York: Teachers College Press, 1972.

Piaget, J. *The moral judgment of the child.* New York: Free Press, 1965. (Originally published, 1932.)

Piaget, J. *Science of education and the psychology of the child.* New York: Orion Press, 1970.

Piaget, J., & Inhelder, B. *The psychology of the child.* New York: Basic Books, 1969.

Piliavin, I. M., Piliavin, J. A., & Rodin, J. Costs, diffusion and the stigmatized victim. *Journal of Personality and Social Psychology,* 1975, *32,* 429–438.

Piliavin, I. M., Rodin, J., & Piliavin, J. A. Good Samaritanism: An underground phenomenon. *Journal of Personality and Social Psychology,* 1969, *13,* 289–299.

Piliavin, J. A., & Piliavin, I. M. Effect of blood on reactions to a victim. *Journal of Personality and Social Psychology,* 1972, *23,* 353–362.

Piliavin, J. A., & Piliavin, I. M. *The Good Samaritan: Why does he help?* Unpublished manuscript, University of Wisconsin, 1973.

Pittman, T. S., Cooper, E. E., & Smith, T. W. Attribution of causality and the overjustification effect. *Personality and Social Psychology Bulletin,* 1977, *3,* 280–283.

Pizzey, E. *Scream quietly or the neighbors will hear.* Harmondswort, Eng.: Penguin, 1974.

Pleck, J. H. The male sex role: Definitions, problems, and sources of change. *Journal of Social Issues,* 1976, *32*(3), 155–164.

Polyson, J. A. Sexism and sexual problems: Societal censure of the sexually troubled male. *Psychological Reports,* 1978, *42,* 843–850.

Pope, H., & Mueller, C. W. The intergenerational transmission of marital instability: Comparisons by race and sex. *Journal of Social Issues*, 1976, 32(1), 49–66.

Popper, K. R. *The logic of scientific discovery*. London: Hutchinson, 1959.

Porter, L., & Lawler, E. *Managerial attitudes and performance*. Homewood, Ill.: Irvin-Dorsey, 1968.

Porter, L., & Steers, R. M. Organizational, work, and personal factors in employee turnover and absenteeism. *Psychological Bulletin*, 1973, 80, 151–176.

Porter, L. W., Steers, R. M., Mowday, R. T., & Boulian, P. V. Organizational commitment, job satisfaction, and turnover among psychiatric technicians. *Journal of Applied Psychology*, 1974, 59, 603–609.

Poulos, R. W., Harvery, S. E., & Liebert, R. M. Saturday morning television: A profile of the 1974–1975 children's season. *Psychological Reports*, 1976, 39, 1047–1057.

Pound, R. The theory of judicial decision. *Harvard Law Review*, 1923, 36, 940–962.

Powell, G. J., & Fuller, M. Self-concept and school desegregation. *American Journal of Orthopsychiatry*, 1970, 40, 303–304.

Prentice-Dunn, S., & Rogers, R. Effects of deindividuating situational cues and aggressive models on subjective deindividuation and aggression. *Journal of Personality and Social Psychology*, 1980, 39, 104–113.

Price, R. A., & Vandenberg, S. G. Matching for physical attractiveness in married couples. *Personality and Social Psychology Bulletin*, 1979, 5, 398–400.

Price, W. H., & Whatmore, P. B. Behavior disorders and crime among XYY males at a maximum security hospital. *British Medical Journal*, 1967, 1, 533–536.

Pritchard, R. D., Dunnette, M. D., & Jorgenson, D. O. Effects of perceptions of equity and inequity on worker performance and satisfaction. *Journal of Applied Psychology*, 1972, 56, 75–94.

Proshansky, H., & Altman, I. Overview of the field. In W. P. White (Ed.), *Resources in environment and behavior*. Washington, D.C.: American Psychological Association, 1979.

Pruitt, D. G. Reciprocity and credit building in a laboratory dyad. *Journal of Personality and Social Psychology*, 1968, 8, 143–147.

Pruitt, D. G., & Gleason, J. M. Threat capacity and the choice between independence and interdependence. *Personality and Social Psychology Bulletin*, 1978, 4, 252–255.

Pruitt, D. G., & Johnson, D. F. Mediation as an aid to face saving in negotiation. *Journal of Personality and Social Psychology*, 1970, 14, 239–246.

Quanty, M. B. Aggression catharsis: Experimental investigations and implications. In R. G. Geen & E. C. O'Neal (Eds.), *Perspectives on aggression*. New York: Academic Press, 1976.

Quigley-Fernandez, B., & Tedeschi, J. T. The bogus pipeline as lie detector: Two validity studies. *Journal of Personality and Social Psychology*, 1978, 36, 247–256.

Radecki, C., & Jennings, J. Sex as a status variable in work settings: Female and male reports of dominance behaviors. *Journal of Applied Psychology*, 1980, 10, 71–85.

Rank, S. G., & Jacobson, C. K. Hospital nurses' compliance with medication overdose orders: A failure to replicate. *Journal of Health and Social Behavior*, 1977, 18, 188–193.

Raush, H. L., Barry, W. A., Hertel, R. K., & Swain, M. A. *Communication, conflict, and marriage*. San Francisco: Jossey-Bass, 1974.

Raven, B. H. *Interpersonal relations and behavior in groups*. New York: Basic Books, 1965.

Raven, B. H., & Haley, R. W. Social influence in a medical context. In L. Bickman (Ed.), *Applied Social Psychology Annual* (Vol. 1). Beverly Hills, Cal.: Sage, 1980.

Raven, B. H., & Kruglanski, A. Conflict and power. In P. Swingle (Ed.), *The structure of conflict*. New York: Academic Press, 1970.

Rawls, J. *A theory of justice*. Cambridge, Mass.: Belknap Press, 1971.

Redfearn, D. *Individual-level and group-level determinants of nurses' compliance with physicians' inappropriate medical orders*. Paper presented at the annual meeting of the American Psychological Association, New York, September 1979.

Reeder, G. D., & Brewer, M. B. A schematic model of dispositional attribution in interpersonal perception. *Psychological Review*, 1979, 86, 61–79.

Regan, D. T., & Fazio, R. H. On the consistency between attitudes and behavior: Look to the method of attitude formation. *Journal of Experimental Social Psychology*, 1977, 13, 38–45.

Regan, D. T., & Totten, J. Empathy and attribution: Turning observers into actors. *Journal of Personality and Social Psychology*, 1975, 32, 850–856.

Reis, H. T., & Gruzen, J. On mediating equity, equality, and self-interest: The role of self-presentation in social exchange. *Journal of Experimental Social Psychology*, 1976, 12, 487–503.

Reizenstein, J. E., & Zimring, C. M. Evaluating occupied environments. *Environment and Behavior,* 1980, *12,* 427–468.

Report of the National Advisory Commission on Civil Disorders. New York: Bantam Books, 1968.

Resnick, M. *Wife Beating: Counselor Training Manual #1.* Ann Arbor, Mich.: Domestic Violence Project, Inc. 1976.

Rest, J. R. The hierarchical nature of moral judgment: A study of the patterns of comprehension and preference of moral stages. *Journal of Personality,* 1973, *41,* 86–109.

Rest, J. R. *Development of judging moral issues.* Minneapolis: University of Minnesota Press, 1979.

Rhine, R. J., & Severance, L. J. Ego-involvement, discrepancy, source credibility, and attitude change. *Journal of Personality and Social Psychology,* 1970, *16,* 175–190.

Richardson, D. C., Bernstein, S., & Taylor, S. P. The effect of situational contingencies on female retaliative behavior. *Journal of Personality and Social Psychology,* 1979, *37,* 2044–2048.

Ridgeway, C. L., & Jacobson, C. K. Sources of status and influence in all female and mixed sex groups. *Sociological Quarterly,* 1977, *18,* 413–425.

Ring, K. Experimental social psychology: Some sober questions about some frivolous values. *Journal of Experimental Psychology,* 1967, *3,* 113–123.

Rivera, A. N., & Tedeschi, J. T. Public versus private reactions to positive inequity. *Journal of Personality and Social Psychology,* 1976, *34,* 895–900.

Roberts, L. Female teenagers and contraception. In B. Schlesinger (Ed.), *Sexual behavior in Canada: Patterns and problems.* Toronto: University of Toronto Press, 1977.

Rodin, J., & Janis, I. L. The social power of health care practitioners as agents of change. *Journal of Social Issues,* 1979, *35*(1), 60–81.

Roethlisberger, F. J., & Dickson, W. J. *Management and the worker: An account of a research program conducted by the Western Electric Company, Hawthorne Works, Chicago.* Cambridge, Mass.: Harvard University Press, 1939.

Rogers, R. W., & Mewborn, C. R. Fear appeals and attitude change: Effects of a threat's noxiousness, probability of occurrence, and the efficacy of coping responses. *Journal of Personality and Social Psychology,* 1976, *34,* 54–61.

Rokeach, M. *Beliefs, attitudes, and values: A theory of organization and change.* San Francisco: Jossey-Bass, 1968.

Rokeach, M. *The nature of human values.* New York: Free Press, 1973.

Rokeach, M., Smith, P. W., & Evans, R. Two kinds of prejudice or one? In M. Rokeach (Ed.), *The open and closed mind.* New York: Basic Books, 1960.

Romer, D. Limitations in the equity-theory approach: Toward a resolution of the "negative-inputs" controversy. *Personality and Social Psychology Bulletin,* 1977, *3,* 228–231.

Rosen, S. Post-decision affinity for incompatible information. *Journal of Abnormal and Social Psychology,* 1961, *63,* 188–190.

Rosenbaum, J. Career paths and opportunities for advancement. In R. Alvarez & K. G. Luterman (Eds.), *Discrimination in organizations.* San Francisco: Jossey-Bass, 1979.

Rosenberg, B. O., & Sutton-Smith, B. Ordinal position and sex-role identification. *Genetic Psychology Monographs,* 1964, *70,* 297–328.

Rosenberg, M. Group size, prior experience and conformity. *Journal of Abnormal and Social Psychology,* 1961, *63,* 436–437.

Rosenberg, M., & Simmons, R. G. *Black and White self-esteem: The urban school child.* Washington, D.C.: American Sociological Association, 1972.

Rosenblatt, P. C. Cross-cultural perspectives on attraction. In T. L. Huston (Ed.), *Foundations of interpersonal attraction.* New York: Academic Press, 1974.

Rosenfield, D., Sheehan, D. S., Marcus, M. M., & Stephan, W. G. Classroom structure and prejudice in desegregated schools. *Journal of Educational Psychology,* 1981, *73,* 17–26.

Rosenhan, D. L. The natural socialization of altruistic autonomy. In J. Macaulay & L. Berkowitz (Eds.), *Altruism and helping behavior.* New York: Academic Press, 1970.

Rosenhan, D. L. On being sane in insane places. *Science,* 1973, *179,* 250–258.

Rosenhan, D. L., Moore, B. S., & Underwood, B. The social psychology of moral behavior. In T. Lickona (Ed.), *Moral development and behavior.* New York: Holt, Rinehart and Winston, 1976.

Rosenthal, R. The effect of the experimenter on the results of psychological research. In B. A. Maher (Ed.), *Progress in experimental personality research* (Vol. 1). New York: Academic Press, 1964.

Rosenthal, R. *Experimenter effects in behavioral research.* New York: Appleton-Century-Crofts, 1966.

Rosenthal, R. Interpersonal expectations: Effects of the experimenter's hypothesis. In R. Rosenthal & R. L. Rosnow (Eds.), *Artifact in behavioral research.* New York: Academic Press, 1969.

Rosenthal, R., & DePaulo, B. M. Sex differences in accommodation in nonverbal communication. In R. Rosenthal (Ed.), *Skill in nonverbal communication.* Cambridge, Mass.: Oelgeschlager, Gunn, & Hain, 1979.

Rosenthal, R., Hall, J. A., DiMatteo, M. R., Rogers, P. L., & Archer, D. *Sensitivity to nonverbal communication: The PONS test.* Baltimore: The Johns Hopkins University Press, 1979.

Rosenthal, R., & Jacobson, L. *Pygmalion in the classroom.* New York: Holt, Rinehart and Winston, 1968.

Ross, A. S., & Braband, J. Effect of increased responsibility on bystander intervention II: The cue value of a blind person. *Journal of Personality and Social Psychology,* 1973, *25,* 254–258.

Ross, E. A. *Social psychology.* New York: Macmillan, 1908.

Ross, L. D. The intuitive psychologist and his shortcomings: Distortions in the attribution process. In L. Berkowitz (Ed.), *Advances in experimental social psychology* (Vol. 10). New York: Academic Press, 1977.

Ross, L. D., Amabile, T. M., & Steinmetz, J. L. Social roles, social control and biases in social-perception processes. *Journal of Personality and Social Psychology,* 1977, *35,* 485–494.

Ross, L. D., Greene, D., & House, P. The "false consensus effect": An egocentric bias in social perception and attribution processes. *Journal of Experimental Social Psychology,* 1977, *13,* 279–301.

Ross, L. D., Lepper, M. R., & Hubbard, M. Perseverance in self-perception and social perception: Biased attributional processes in the debriefing paradigm. *Journal of Personality and Social Psychology,* 1975, *32,* 880–892.

Ross, M. Salience of reward and intrinsic motivation. *Journal of Personality and Social Psychology,* 1975, *32,* 245–254.

Ross, M., & Shulman, R. Increasing the salience of initial attitudes: Dissonance versus self-perception theory. *Journal of Personality and Social Psychology,* 1973, *28,* 138–144.

Roth, S., & Kubal, L. Effects of noncontingent reinforcement on tasks of differing importance: Facilitation and learned helplessness. *Journal of Personality and Social Psychology,* 1975, *32,* 680–691.

Rothbart, M., Evans, M., & Fulero, S. Recall for confirming events: Memory processes and the maintenance of social stereotypes. *Journal of Experimental Social Psychology,* 1979, *15,* 343–355.

Rotter, J. B. Interpersonal trust, trustworthiness, and gullibility. *American Psychologist,* 1980, *35,* 1–7.

Roussell, C. Relationship of sex of department head to department climate. *Administrative Science Quarterly,* 1974, *19,* 211–220.

Rubin, B. Prediction of dangerousness. In S. A. Pasternak (Ed.), *Violence and victims.* New York: Halsted, 1975.

Rubin, J. Z., & Brown, B. R. *The social psychology of bargaining and negotiation.* New York: Academic Press, 1975.

Rubin, J. Z., Provenzano, F. J., & Luria, Z. The eye of the beholder: Parents' view on sex of newborns. *American Journal of Orthopsychiatry,* 1974, *44,* 512–519.

Rubin, Z. Measurement of romantic love. *Journal of Personality and Social Psychology,* 1970, *16,* 265–273.

Rubin, Z. *Liking and loving: An invitation to social psychology.* New York: Holt, Rinehart and Winston, 1973.

Rubin, Z. Lovers and other strangers: The development of intimacy in encounters and relationships. *American Scientist,* 1974, *62,* 182–190.

Rubin, Z., Hill, C. T., Peplau, L. A., & Dunkel-Schetter, C. Self-disclosure in dating couples: Sex roles and the ethic of openness. *Journal of Marriage and the Family,* 1980, *42,* 305–317.

Rule, B. G, & Renner, J. Involvement and group effects on opinion change. *Journal of Social Psychology,* 1968, *76,* 189–198.

Rushton, J. P. Effects of prosocial television and film material on the behavior of viewers. In L. Berkowitz (Ed.), *Advances in experimental social psychology* (Vol. 12). New York: Academic Press, 1979.

Rushton, J. P. *Altruism, socialization and society.* Englewood Cliffs, N.J.: Prentice-Hall, 1980.

Ruth, D. Prison movies: Captive audiences view violent films. *Tampa Tribune,* September 9, 1978, pp. 1D; 7D; 10D.

Rutter, M. *Maternal deprivation reassessed.* Harmondsworth, England: Penguin, 1972.

Ryan, W. *Blaming the victim.* New York: Random House, 1971.

Sackett, D. L. The magnitude of compliance and noncompliance. In D. L. Sackett & R. B. Haynes (Eds.), *Compliance with therapeutic regimens.* Baltimore, Md.: The Johns Hopkins University Press, 1976.

Sackett, D. L., Haynes, R. B., Gibson, E. S., Hackett, B. C., Taylor, D. W., Roberts, R. S., & Johnson, A. L. Randomized clinical trial of strategies for improving medication compliance in primary hypertension. *Lancet*, 1975, *1*, 1205–1207.

Saegert, S. C., Swap, W., & Zajonc, R. B. Exposure, context, and interpersonal attraction. *Journal of Personality and Social Psychology*, 1973, *25*, 234–242.

Sampson, E. E. On justice as equality. *Journal of Social Issues*, 1975, *31*, 45–64.

Sampson, E. E. Psychology and the American ideal. *Journal of Personality and Social Psychology*, 1977, *35*, 767–782.

Sampson, E. E. Scientific paradigms and social values: Wanted—a scientific revolution. *Journal of Personality and Social Psychology*, 1978, *36*, 1332–1343.

Samuel, W. On clarifying some interpretations of social comparison theory. *Journal of Experimental Social Psychology*, 1973, *9*, 450–465.

Samuel, W. *Comtemporary social psychology: An introduction.* Englewood Cliffs, N.J.: Prentice-Hall, 1975.

Samuel, W. In further support of the Adams ratio: A reply to Dr. G. William Walster. *Personality and Social Psychology Bulletin*, 1976, *2*, 45–46. (a)

Samuel, W. Suggested amendments to "New directions in equity research." *Personality and Social Psychology Bulletin*, 1976, *2*, 36–39. (b)

Samuel, W. Toward a simple but useful equity theory: A comment on the Romer article. *Personality and Social Psychology Bulletin*, 1978, *4*, 135–138.

Samuels, F. *Group images.* New Haven, Conn.: College & University Press, 1973.

Sandberg, E. C. Psychological aspects of contraception. In B. J. Sadack, H. I. Kaplan, & A. M. Freedman (Eds.), *The sexual experience.* Baltimore, Md.: Williams & Wilkins, 1976.

Sanford, N. Authoritarianism and social destructiveness. In N. Sanford & C. Comstock (Eds.), *Sanction for evil.* San Francisco: Jossey-Bass, 1971.

Sapin, C. R. *A status formulation of sex differences.* Unpublished doctoral dissertation, University of Colorado, 1979.

Scarpetti, W. L. Autonomic concomitants of aggressive behavior in repressors and sensitizers: A social learning approach. *Journal of Personality and Social Psychology*, 1974, *30*, 772–781.

Scarr, S., & Weinberg, R. A. IQ test performance of black children adopted by white families. *American Psychologist*, 1976, *31*, 726–739.

Schachter, S. Deviation, rejection, and communication. *Journal of Abnormal and Social Psychology*, 1951, *46*, 190–207.

Schachter, S. The interaction of cognitive and physiological determinants of emotional state. In L. Berkowitz (Ed.), *Advances in experimental social psychology* (Vol. 1). New York: Academic Press, 1964.

Schachter, S., & Singer, J. E. Cognitive, social and physiological determinants of emotional state. *Psychological Review*, 1962, *69*, 379–399.

Schaps, E. Cost, dependency, and helping. *Journal of Personality and Social Psychology*, 1972, *21*, 74–78.

Scheier, M. F. Self-awareness, self-consciousness, and angry aggression. *Journal of Personality*, 1976, *44*, 627–643.

Scheier, M., Fenigstein, A., & Buss, A. Self-awareness and physical aggression. *Journal of Experimental Social Psychology*, 1974, *10*, 264–273.

Schmidt, G. Male-female differences in sexual arousal and behavior during and after exposure to sexually explicit stimuli. *Archives of Sexual Behavior*, 1975, *4*, 353–365.

Schneider, D. J., Hastorf, A. H., & Ellsworth, P. C. *Person perception* (2d ed.). Reading, Mass.: Addison-Wesley, 1979.

Schofield, J. W. Complementary and conflicting identities: Images and interaction in an interracial school. In S. Asher & J. Gottman (Eds.), *The development of friendship: Description and intervention.* Cambridge: Cambridge University Press, 1981.

Schonemann, P. H., Byrne, D., & Bell, P. A. Statistical aspects of a model for interpersonal attraction. *Bulletin of the Psychonomic Society*, 1977, *9*, 243–246.

Schopler, J., & Bateson, N. The power of dependence. *Journal of Personality and Social Psychology*, 1965, *2*, 247–254.

Schopler, J., & Matthews, M. The influence of the perceived causal locus of partner's dependence on the use of interpersonal power. *Journal of Personality and Social Psychology*, 1965, *2*, 609–612.

Schopler, J., & Thompson, V. Role of attribution processes in mediating amount of reciprocity for a favor. *Journal of Personality and Social Psychology*, 1968, *10*, 243–250.

Schultz, R. Effects of control and predictability on the physical and psychological well-being of the institutionalized aged. *Journal of Personality and Psychology*, 1976, *33*, 563–573.

Schumacher, E. F. *Small is beautiful: Economics as if people mattered.* New York: Harper & Row, 1973.

Schuman, H., & Johnson, M. P. Attitudes and behavior. *Annual Review of Sociology*, 1976, *2*, 161–207.

Schwartz, S. H. Normative influences on altruism. In L. Berkowitz (Ed.), *Advances in experimental social psychology* (Vol. 10). New York: Academic Press, 1977.

Schwartz, S. H., & Clausen, G. T. Responsibility, norms and helping in an emergency. *Journal of Personality and Social Psychology*, 1970, *16*, 299–310.

Schwartz, S. H., Feldman, K. A., Brown, M. E., & Heingartner, A. Some personality correlates of conduct in two situations of moral conflict. *Journal of Personality*, 1969, *37*, 41–57.

Scott, J. P. Biology and human aggression. *American Journal of Orthopsychiatry*, 1970, *40*, 568–576.

Scott, W. R. Organizational structure. *Annual Review of Sociology*, 1975, *1*, 1–20.

Sears, D. O. Biased indoctrination and selectivity of exposure to new information. *Sociometry*, 1965, *28*, 363–376.

Sears, R. R., Maccoby, E. E., & Levin, H. *Patterns of child rearing*. New York: Harper & Row, 1957.

Seaver, W. B., & Patterson, A. H. Decreasing fuel-oil consumption through feedback and social commendation. *Journal of Applied Behavior Analysis*, 1976, *9*, 147–152.

Seeley, T. T., Abramson, P. R., Perry, L. B., Rothblatt, A. B., & Seeley, D. M. Thermagraphic measurement of sexual arousal: A methodological note. *Archives of Sexual Behavior*, 1980, *9*, 77–85.

Segal, M. W. Alphabet and attraction: An unobtrusive measure of the effect of propinquity in a field setting. *Journal of Personality and Social Psychology*, 1974, *30*, 654–657.

Seligman, C., & Darley, J. M. Feedback as a means of decreasing residential energy consumption. *Journal of Applied Psychology*, 1978, *62*, 363–368.

Seligman, C., Kriss, M., Darley, J. M., Fazio, R. H., Becker, L. J., & Pryor, J. B. Predicting summer energy consumption from homeowners' attitudes. *Journal of Applied Psychology*, 1979, *9*, 70–90.

Seligman, M. E. P. *Helplessness: On depression, development, and death*. San Francisco: W. H. Freeman, 1975.

Selltiz, C., Wrightsman, L. S., & Cook, S. W. *Research methods in social relations*, (3rd ed.). New York: Holt, Rinehart and Winston, 1976.

Selye, H. *The stress of life*. New York: McGraw-Hill, 1956.

Sermat, V. The effects of an initial cooperative or competitive treatment upon a subject's response to conditional cooperation. *Behavioral Science*, 1967, *12*, 301–313.

Shafer, E. L., & Richards, T. A. A comparison of viewed reactions to outdoor scenes and photographs of those scenes. In D. Canter & T. Lee (Eds.), *Psychology and the built environment*. New York: Halsted Press, 1974.

Shaffer, D. R. The effects of cognitive style upon the inconsistency process. *JSAS Catalog of Selected Documents in Psychology*, 1975, *5*, 283.

Shaffer, D. R. *Social and personality development*. Monterey, Cal.: Brooks/Cole, 1979.

Shanteau, J., & Nagy, G. F. Probability of acceptance in dating choice. *Journal of Personality and Social Psychology*, 1979, *37*, 522–533.

Shapiro, A. K. Placebo effects in medicine, psychotherapy, and psychoanalysis. In A. Bergin & S. Garfield (Eds.), *Handbook of psychotherapy and behavior change*. New York: Wiley, 1971.

Shapiro, E. G. Effect of expectations of future interaction on reward allocations in dyads: Equity or equality. *Journal of Personality and Social Psychology*, 1975, *31*, 873–880.

Shaw, M. E. *Group dynamics: The psychology of small group behavior* (3rd ed.). New York: McGraw-Hill, 1981.

Sheldon, M. W. Investments and involvements as mechanisms producing commitment to the organization. *Administrative Science Quarterly*, 1971, *16*, 142–150.

Sherif, C. W., Sherif, M., & Nebergall, R. E. *Attitude and attitude change: The social judgment-involvement approach*. Philadelphia: Saunders, 1965.

Sherif, M. *The psychology of social norms*. New York: Harper & Row, 1936.

Sherif, M., Harvey, O. J., White, B. J., Hood, W. R., & Sherif, C. W. *Intergroup conflict and cooperation: The Robber's Cave experiment*. Norman: University of Oklahoma, Institute of Group Relations, 1961.

Sherif, M., & Hovland, C. I. *Social judgment: Assimilation and contrast effects in communication and attitude change*. New Haven, Conn.: Yale University Press, 1961.

Sherif, M., & Sherif, C. W. *Social psychology*. New York: Harper & Row, 1969.

Sherrod, D. R. Crowding, perceived control, and behavioral aftereffects. *Journal of Applied Social Psychology*, 1974, *4*, 171–186.

Shomer, R. W., Davis, A. H., & Kelley, H. H. Threats and the development of coordination: Further studies of the Deutsch and Krauss trucking game. *Journal of Personality and Social Psychology*, 1966, *4*, 119–126.

Shortell, J., Epstein, S., & Taylor, S. P. Instigation to aggression as a function of the degree of defeat and capacity for massive retaliation. *Journal of Personality,* 1970, *38,* 313–328.

Shure, G., Meeker, R., & Hansford, E. The effectiveness of pacifist strategies in bargaining games. *Journal of Conflict Resolution,* 1965, *9,* 106–117.

Siegel, A. W., & Schadler, M. Young children's cognitive maps of their classroom. *Child Development,* 1977, *48,* 388–394.

Siegler, R. S., & Liebert, R. M. Effects of contiguity, regularity, and age on children's causal inferences. *Developmental Psychology,* 1974, *10,* 574–579.

Sigall, H., Aronson, E., & Van Hoose, T. The cooperative subject: Myth or reality? *Journal of Experimental Social Psychology,* 1970, *6,* 1–10.

Sigall, H., & Ostrove, N. Beautiful but dangerous: Effects of offender attractiveness and nature of the crime on juridic judgments. *Journal of Personality and Social Psychology,* 1975, *31,* 410–414.

Sigall, H., & Page, R. Current stereotypes: A little fading, a little faking. *Journal of Personality and Social Psychology,* 1971, *18,* 247–255.

Silberman, C. E. *Crisis in the classroom: The remaking of American education.* New York: Random House, 1970.

Silverman, B. I. Consequences, racial discrimination, and the principle of belief incongruence. *Journal of Personality and Social Psychology,* 1974, *29,* 497–508.

Simons, C. W., & Piliavin, J. A. Effect of deception on reactions to a victim. *Journal of Personality and Social Psychology,* 1972, *21,* 56–60.

Simonton, O. C., Matthews-Simonton, S., & Creighton, J. *Getting well again.* Los Angeles: J. P. Tarcher, 1978.

Sistrunk, F., & McDavid, J. W. Sex variable in conforming behavior. *Journal of Personality and Social Psychology,* 1971, *17,* 200–207.

Skinner, B. F. *Science and human behavior.* New York: Macmillan, 1953.

Slavin, R. *Student teams and achievement divisions: Effects on academic performance, mutual attraction and attitudes* (Report No. 233). Baltimore, Md.: The Johns Hopkins University, Center for the Social Organization of Schools, August 1977.

Slobin, D. I., Miller, S. H., & Porter, L. W. Forms of address and social relations in a business organization. *Journal of Personality and Social Psychology,* 1968, *8,* 289–293.

Slovic, P., Fischhoff, B., & Lichtenstein, S. Rating the risks. *Environment,* 1979, *21,* 14–20; 36–39.

Smith, C. B. Influence of internal opportunity structure and sex of worker on turnover patterns. *Administrative Science Quarterly,* 1979, *24,* 362–381.

Smith, D. D. The social content of pornography. *Journal of Communication,* 1976, *26,* 16–33.

Smith, J. J. *When I say no, I feel guilty.* New York: Bantam, 1975.

Smith, W., & Anderson, A. Threats, communication, and bargaining. *Journal of Personality and Social Psychology,* 1975, *32,* 76–82.

Smith-Lovin, L., & Tickamyer, A. R. Nonrecursive models of labor force participation, fertility behavior, and sex role attitudes. *American Sociological Review,* 1978, *43,* 541–557.

Snell, J. D., Rosenwald, R. J., & Robey, A. The wifebeater's wife: A study of family interaction. *Archives of General Psychiatry,* 1964, *11,* 107–113.

Snow, C. P. *The two cultures and the scientific revolution.* New York: Cambridge University Press, 1959.

Snyder, M. The self-monitoring of expressive behavior. *Journal of Personality and Social Psychology,* 1974, *30,* 526–537.

Snyder, M. Cognitive, behavioral, and interpersonal consequences of self-monitoring. In P. Pliner et al. (Eds.), *Advances in the study of communication and affect* (Vol. 5). New York: Plenum Press, 1979.

Snyder, M., & Cantor, N. Testing hypotheses about other people: The use of historical knowledge. *Journal of Experimental Social Psychology,* 1979, *15,* 330–342.

Snyder, M., & Ebbesen, E. Dissonance awareness: A test of dissonance theory versus self-perception theory. *Journal of Experimental Social Psychology,* 1972, *8,* 502–517.

Snyder, M., & Swann, W. B., Jr. When actions reflect attitudes: The politics of impression management. *Journal of Personality and Social Psychology,* 1976, *34,* 1034–1042.

Snyder, M., & Tanke, E. D. Behavior and attitude: Some people are more consistent than others. *Journal of Personality,* 1976, *44,* 501–517.

Snyder, M., Tanke, E. D., & Berscheid, E. Social perception and interpersonal behavior: On the self-fulfilling nature of social stereotypes. *Journal of Personality and Social Psychology,* 1977, *35,* 656–666.

Snyder, M. L., Stephan, W. G., & Rosenfield, D. Egotism and attributions. *Journal of Personality and Social Psychology,* 1976, *33,* 435–441.

Snyder, M. L., Stephan, W. G., & Rosenfield, D. Attributional egotism. In J. H. Harvey, W. J. Ickes, & R. F. Kidd (Eds.), *New directions in attribution research* (Vol. 2). Hillsdale, N.J.: Lawrence Erlbaum Associates, 1979.

Sommer, R. *Personal space.* Englewood Cliffs, N.J.: Prentice-Hall, 1969.

Sommer, R., & Olsen, H. The soft classroom. *Environment and Behavior,* 1980, *12,* 3–16.

Spence, J. T., & Helmreich, R. The attitudes toward women scale: An objective instrument to measure attitudes toward the rights and roles of women in contemporary society. JSAS *Catalog of Selected Documents in Psychology,* 1972, *2,* 66 (Ms. No. 153)

SPSSI Council. Statement on race and intelligence. *Journal of Social Issues,* 1969, 25(3), 1–3.

Spence, J. T., & Helmreich, R. L. *Masculinity and femininity: Their psychological dimensions, correlates, and antecedents.* Austin: University of Texas Press, 1978.

Sprafkin, J. N., Liebert, R. M., & Poulos, R. W. Effects of a prosocial televised example on children's helping. *Journal of Experimental Child Psychology,* 1975, *20,* 119–126.

St. John, N. H. *School desegregation: Outcomes for children.* New York: Wiley, 1975.

Stang, D. J. Conformity, ability, and self-esteem. *Representative Research in Social Psychology,* 1972, *3*(2), 97–103.

Stark, R., & McEvoy, J. Middle class violence. *Psychology Today,* November, 1970, 52–65.

Staub, E. Helping a person in distress: The influence of implicit and explicit "rules" of conduct on children and adults. *Journal of Personality and Social Psychology,* 1971, *17,* 137–145.

Staub, E. Helping a distressed person: Social, personality, and stimulus determinants. In L. Berkowitz (Ed.), *Advances in experimental social psychology* (Vol. 7). New York: Academic Press, 1974.

Staub, E., & Baer, R. S., Jr. Stimulus characteristics of a sufferer and difficulty of escape as determinants of helping. *Journal of Personality and Social Psychology,* 1974, *30,* 279–285.

Steers, R. M. Antecedents and outcomes of organizational commitment. *Administrative Science Quarterly,* 1977, *22,* 46–56.

Stein, B. A. *Patterns in managerial success.* Cambridge, Mass.: Goodmeasure, 1979. (a)

Stein, B. A. Presentation to the 1979 conference on the Ecology of Work, Boston, July 1979. Cambridge, Mass.: Goodmeasure, 1979. (b)

Stein, L. The doctor-nurse game. *Archives of General Psychiatry,* 1967, *16,* 699–703.

Stein, W. The myth of the transparent self. *Journal of Humanistic Psychology,* 1975, *15,* 71–77.

Steinem, G. Erotica and pornography: A clear and present difference. In L. Lederer (Ed.), *Take back the night: Women on pornography.* New York: William Morrow, 1980.

Steinmetz, S. The battered husband syndrome. *Victimology,* 1978, *2,* 449–509.

Steinmetz, S. K., & Straus, M. A. *Violence in the family.* New York: Dodd Mead, 1974.

Stephan, W. G. School desegregation: An evaluation of predictions made in *Brown v. the Board of Education. Psychological Bulletin,* 1978, *85,* 217–238.

Stephan, W. G., & Kennedy, J. C. An experimental study of interethnic competition in segregated schools. *Journal of Social Psychology,* 1975, *13,* 234–247.

Stephan, W. G., & Rosenfield, D. Effects of desegregation on racial attitudes. *Journal of Personality and Social Psychology,* 1978, *36,* 795–804.

Stephan, W. G., & Rosenfield, D. Black self-rejection: Another look. *Journal of Educational Psychology,* 1979, *71,* 708–716.

Stephan, W. G., & Rosenfield, D. Racial and ethnic stereotypes. In A. Miller (Ed.), *In the eye of the beholder: Contemporary issues in stereotyping.* New York: Holt, Rinehart and Winston, 1981.

Stern, P. C., & Gardner, G. T. Psychological research and energy policy. *American Psychologist,* 1981, *36,* 329–342.

Stetson, D. M., & Wright, G. C., Jr. The effects of laws on divorce in American states. *Journal of Marriage and the Family,* 1975, *37,* 537–548.

Stewart, A. J., & Rubin, Z. The power motive in dating couples. *Journal of Personality and Social Psychology,* 1976, *34,* 305–309.

Stogdill, R. M. Personal factors associated with leadership: A survey of the literature. *Journal of Psychology,* 1948, *25,* 35–71.

Stokols, D. (Ed.). *Perspectives on environment and behavior: Theory, research, and applications.* New York: Plenum Press, 1977.

Stokols, D. Environmental psychology. *Annual Review of Psychology,* 1978, *29,* 253–295.

Stokols, D. Group x place transactions: Some neglected issues in psychological research on settings. In D. Magnusson (Ed.), *Toward a psychology of situations: An interactional perspective.* Hillsdale, N.J.: Lawrence Erlbaum Associates, 1981.

Stokols, D., Novaco, R. W., Stokols, J., & Campbell, J. Traffic congestion, type-A behavior, and stress. *Journal of Applied Psychology,* 1978, *63,* 467–480.

Stokols, D., & Schumaker, S. People in places: A transactional view of settings. In J. Harvey (Ed.),

Cognition, social behavior, and the environment. Hillsdale, N.J.: Lawrence Erlbaum Associates, 1981.

Stoner, J. A. F. Risky and cautious shifts in group decisions: The influence of widely held values. *Journal of Experimental Social Psychology,* 1968, *4,* 442–459.

Storms, M. D. Videotape and the attribution process: Reversing actors' and observers' points of view. *Journal of Personality and Social Psychology,* 1973, *27,* 165–175.

Storms, M. D., Denney, D. R., McCaul, K. D., & Lowery, C. A. Treating insomnia. In I. H. Frieze, D. Bar-Tal, & J. S. Carroll (Eds.), *New approaches to social problems: Applications of attribution theory.* San Francisco: Jossey-Bass, 1979.

Storms, M. D., & Nisbett, R. E. Insomnia and the attribution process. *Journal of Personality and Social Psychology,* 1970, *16,* 319–328.

Stotland, E. Exploratory studies of empathy. In L. Berkowitz (Ed.), *Advances in experimental social psychology* (Vol. 4). New York: Academic Press, 1969.

Straus, M. A sociological perspective on the prevention and treatment of wife beating. In M. Roy, (Ed.), *Battered women.* New York: Van Nostrand Reinhold, 1977.

Straus, M. Wife beating: How common and why? *Victimology,* 1978, *2,* 443–458.

Straus, M. A., Gelles, R. J., & Steinmetz, S. K. *Behind closed doors: Violence in the American family.* New York: Doubleday, 1979.

Stricker, L. J., Messick, S., & Jackson, D. N. Suspicion of deception: Implications for conformity research. *Journal of Personality and Social Psychology,* 1967, *5,* 379–389.

Stryker, S. Developments in "Two social psychologies." *Sociometry,* 1977, *40,* 145–160.

Suls, J., Gastorf, J., & Lawhon, J. Social comparison choices for evaluating a sex- and age-related ability. *Personality and Social Psychology Bulletin,* 1978, *4,* 102–105.

Sundstrom, E., & Altman, I. Field study of dominance and territorial behavior. *Journal of Personality and Social Psychology,* 1974, *30,* 155–175.

Sutton-Smith, B., & Rosenberg, B. G. *The sibling.* New York: Holt, Rinehart and Winston, 1970.

Tagliacozzo, D., & Ima, K. Knowledge of illness as a predictor of patient behavior. *Journal of Chronic Diseases,* 1970, *22,* 765–775.

Tajfel, H. Experiments in intergroup discrimination. *Scientific American,* 1970, *223,* 96–102.

Tanke, E. D., & Tanke, T. J. Getting off a slippery slope: Social science in the judicial process. *American Psychologist,* 1979, *34,* 1130–1138.

Tannahill, R. *Sex in history.* Briarcliff, N.Y.: Stein & Day, 1980.

Tapp, J. L. The psychological limits of legality. In J. R. Pennock & J. W. Chapman (Eds.), *The limits of law: Nomos XV.* New York: Lieber-Atherton, 1974.

Tapp, J. L. Psychology and the law: An overture. *Annual Review of Psychology,* 1976, *27,* 359–404.

Tapp, J. L., & Keniston, A. *Wounded Knee—Advocate or expert: Recipe for a fair juror?* Paper presented at the annual meeting of the American Psychological Association, Washington, D.C., September 1976.

Tapp, J. L., & Kohlberg, L. Developing senses of law and legal justice. In J. L. Tapp & F. J. Levine (Eds.), *Law, justice, and the individual in society: Psychological and legal issues.* New York: Holt, Rinehart and Winston, 1977.

Tapp, J. L., & Levine, F. J. Persuasion to virtue: A preliminary statement. *Law and Society Review,* 1970, *4,* 565–582.

Tapp, J. L., & Levine,·F. J. Legal socialization: Strategies for an ethical legality. *Stanford Law Review,* 1974, *24,* 1–72.

Tapp, J. L., & Levine, F. J. (Eds.). *Law, justice, and the individual in society: Psychological and legal issues.* New York: Holt, Rinehart and Winston, 1977.

Tapp, J. L., & Smolka, P. *Legal levels and socialization.* Unpublished manuscript, University of Minnesota, 1975.

Tapp, J. L., Kolman, A., Richardson, R. M., Vopava, J., & Drozdal, J. *Rights-consciousness and child-care.* Unpublished manuscript, University of Minnesota, 1981.

Taylor, D. A. The development of interpersonal relationships: Social penetration processes. *Journal of Social Psychology,* 1968, *75,* 79–90.

Taylor, D. A., & Altman, I. *Intimacy-scaled stimuli for use in research on interpersonal exchange.* Naval Medical Research Institute, May 1966.

Taylor, J. B., & Parker, H. A. Graphic ratings and attitude measurement: A comparison of research tactics. *Journal of Applied Psychology,* 1964, *48,* 37–42.

Taylor, S. E. Hospital patient behavior: Reactance, helplessness, or control? *Journal of Social Issues,* 1979, *35*(1), 156–184.

Taylor, S. E., & Fiske, S. T. Point of view and perceptions of causality. *Journal of Personality and Social Psychology,* 1975, *32,* 439–445.

Taylor, S. E., & Fiske, S. T. The token in a small group: Research findings and theoretical implications. In J. Sweeney (Ed.), *Psychology and politics: Collected papers*. New Haven, Conn.: Yale University Press, 1976.

Taylor, S. E., & Fiske, S. T. Salience, attention, and attribution: Top of the head phenomena. In L. Berkowitz (Ed.), *Advances in experimental social psychology* (Vol. 11). New York: Academic Press, 1978.

Taylor, S. P., & Gammon, C. B. Effects of type and dose of alcohol on human physical aggression. *Journal of Personality and Social Psychology*, 1975, *32*, 169–175.

Taylor, S. P., Gammon, C. B., & Capasso, D. R. Aggression as a function of the interaction of alcohol and threat. *Journal of Personality and Social Psychology*, 1976, *34*, 938–941.

Tedeschi, J. T., Schlenker, B. R., & Bonoma, T. V. Cognitive dissonance: Private rationalization or public spectacle? *American Psychologist*, 1971, *26*, 685–695.

Tedeschi, J. T., Schlenker, B. R., & Lindskold, S. The exercise of power and influence: The source of influence. In J. T. Tedeschi (Ed.), *The social influence process*. Chicago: Aldine, 1972.

Tedeschi, J. T., Smith, R. B., & Brown, R. C. A reinterpretation of research on aggression. *Psychological Bulletin*, 1974, *81*, 540–563.

Terhune, K. W. The effects of personality in cooperation and conflict. In P. Swingle (Ed.), *The structure of conflict*. New York: Academic Press, 1970.

Thayer, S. Lend me your ears: Racial and sexual factors in helping the deaf. *Journal of Personality and Social Psychology*, 1973, *28*, 8–11.

Thibaut, J. W., & Kelley, H. H. *The social psychology of groups*. New York: Wiley 1959.

Thibaut, J. W., & Riecken, H. W. Authoritarianism, status, and the communication of aggression. *Human Relations*, 1955, *8*, 95–120.

Thibaut, J. W., & Walker, L. *Procedural justice: A psychological analysis*. Hillsdale, N.J.: Lawrence Erlbaum Associates, 1975.

Thomas, G. C., & Batson, C. D. Effect of helping under normative pressure on self-perceived altruism. *Social Psychology Quarterly*, 1981, *44*, 127–131.

Thomas, G. C., Batson, C. D., & Coke, J. S. Do Good Samaritans discourage helpfulness? Self-perceived altruism after exposure to highly helpful others. *Journal of Personality and Social Psychology*, 1981, *40*, 194–200.

Thomas, M. H., Horton, R. W., Lippincott, E. C., & Drabman, R. S. Desensitization to portrayals of real-life aggression as a function of exposure to television violence. *Journal of Personality and Social Psychology*, 1977, *35*, 450–458.

Thomas, M. H., & Tell, P. Effects of viewing real vs. fantasy violence upon interpersonal aggression. *Journal of Research in Personality*, 1974, *8*, 153–160.

Thompson, W. C., Cowan, C. L., & Rosenhan, D. L. Focus of attention mediates the impact of negative affect on altruism. *Journal of Personality and Social Psychology*, 1980, *38*, 291–300.

Thornton, B. Linear prediction of marital happiness: A replication. *Personality and Social Psychology Bulletin*, 1977, *3*, 674–676.

Thurstone, L. L. Attitudes can be measured. *American Journal of Sociology*, 1928, *33*, 529–554.

Tichy, N. An analysis of clique formation and structure in organizations. *Administrative Science Quarterly*, 1973, *18*, 194–207.

Tieger, T. Self-rated likelihood of raping and the social perception of rape. *Journal of Research in Personality*, 1981, *15*, 147–158.

Tinbergen, N. *The animal in its world: Explorations of an ethologist*. London: Allen & Unwin, 1972.

Toch, H. *Violent men*. Chicago: Aldine, 1969.

Toffler, A. *Future shock*. New York: Random House, 1970.

Tolley, H. *Children and war: Political socialization to international conflict*. New York: Teachers College Press, 1973.

Totman, R. *Social causes of illness*. London: Souvenir Press, 1979.

Triandis, H. C., & Davis, E. Race and belief as determinants of behavioral intention. *Journal of Personality and Social Psychology*, 1965, *2*, 715–725.

Triplett, N. The dynamogenic factors in pacemaking and competition. *American Journal of Psychology*, 1898, *9*, 507–533.

Tuckman, B. W. Personality structure, group composition, and group functioning. *Sociometry*, 1964, *27*, 469–487.

Turner, C. W., & Simons, L. S. Effects of subject sophistication and evaluation apprehension on aggressive responses to weapons. *Journal of Personality and Social Psychology*, 1974, *30*, 341–348.

Turner, C. W., Layton, J. F., & Simons, L. S. Naturalistic studies of aggressive behavior: Aggressive stimuli, victim visibility, and horn honking. *Journal of Personality and Social Psychology*, 1975, *31*, 1098–1107.

Turner, R. H. Sponsored and contest mobility and the school system. *American Sociological Review*, 1960, *25*, 855–867.

Turney, J. R. The cognitive complexity of group members, group structure, and group effectiveness. *Cornell Journal of Social Relations*, 1970, *5*, 152–165.

Tyler, T. R., & Sears, D. O. Coming to like obnoxious people when we must live with them. *Journal of Personality and Social Psychology*, 1977, *35*, 200–211.

Underwood, B. *Psychological research*. New York: Appleton-Century-Crofts, 1957.

U. S. Commission on Civil Rights, 1978, cited in Kitano, H. H. L. *Race Relations* (2d ed.). Englewood Cliffs, N.J., Prentice-Hall, 1980.

U. S. Riot Commission. *Report of the National Advisory Commission on Civil Disorders*. New York: Bantam Books, 1968.

Valenstein, E. S. *Brain control*. New York: Wiley, 1973.

Valins, S. Cognitive effects of false heart-rate feedback. *Journal of Personality and Social Psychology*, 1966, *4*, 400–408.

Valle, V. A., & Frieze, I. H. The stability of causal attribution as a mediator in changing expectations for success. *Journal of Personality and Social Psychology*, 1976, *33*, 579–587.

Van Avermaet, E., McClintock, C., & Moskowitz, J. Alternative approaches to equity: Dissonance-reduction, pro-social motivation, and strategic accommodation. *European Journal of Social Psychology*, 1978, *8*, 419–437.

Van Egeren, L. F. Cardiovascular changes during social competition in a mixed-motive game. *Journal of Personality and Social Psychology*, 1979, *37*, 858–864.

Varela, J. A. *Psychological solutions to social problems: An introduction to social technology*. New York: Academic Press, 1971.

Vinacke, W. E., & Arkoff, A. An experimental study of coalitions in the triad. *American Sociological Review*, 1957, *22*, 406–414.

Vinsel, A., Brown, B. B., Altman, I., & Foss, C. Privacy regulation, territorial displays, and effectiveness of individual functioning. *Journal of Personality and Social Psychology*, 1980, *39*, 1104–1115.

Voss, H. L., & Hepburn, J. R. Patterns in criminal homicide in Chicago. *Journal of Criminal Law, Criminology and Police Science*, 1968, *59*, 499–508.

Vroom, V. *Work and motivation*. New York: Wiley, 1964.

Wagner, C., & Wheeler, L. Model, need and cost effects in helping behavior. *Journal of Personality and Social Psychology*, 1969, *12*, 111–116.

Wahrman, R., & Pugh, M. D. Competence and conformity: Another look at Hollander's study. *Sociometry*, 1972, *35*, 376–386.

Wahrman, R., & Pugh, M. D. Sex, nonconformity and influence. *Sociometry*, 1974, *34*, 137–147.

Waitzkin, H., & Waterman, B. *The exploitation of illness in capitalist society*. Indianapolis: Bobbs-Merrill, 1974.

Wall, J. A. The effects of mediator rewards and suggestions upon negotiations. *Journal of Personality and Social Psychology*, 1979, *37*, 1554–1560.

Wallach, M. A., Kogan, N., & Bem, D. J. Diffusion of responsibility and level of risk taking in groups. *Journal of Abnormal and Social Psychology*, 1964, *68*, 263–274.

Walker, L. *The battered woman*. New York: Harper & Row, 1979.

Walster, E., Aronson, V., Abrahams, D., & Rottman, L. Importance of physical attractiveness in dating behavior. *Journal of Personality and Social Psychology*, 1966, *4*, 508–516.

Walster, E., & Berscheid, E. A little bit about love. In T. L. Huston (Ed.), *Foundations of interpersonal attraction*. New York: Academic Press, 1974.

Walster, E., Berscheid, E., & Walster, G. W. New directions in equity research. *Journal of Personality and Social Psychology*, 1973, *25*, 151–176.

Walster, E., Walster, G. W., & Berscheid, E. *Equity: Theory and research*. Boston: Allyn & Bacon, 1978.

Walster, E., Walster, G. .W., Piliavin, J., & Schmidt, L. "Playing hard to get": Understanding an elusive phenomenon. *Journal of Personality and Social Psychology*, 1973, *26*, 113–121.

Walster, E., Walster, G. W., & Traupmann, J. Equity and premarital sex. *Journal of Personality and Social Psychology*, 1978, *36*, 82–92.

Walster, G. W. Reply to Dr. William Samuel: Suggested amendments to new directions in equity research. *Personality and Social Psychology Bulletin*, 1976, *2*, 40–44.

Walton, R. E. The diffusion of new work structures: Explaining why success didn't take. *Organizational Dynamics*, 1975, *3*, 21–22.

Wandersman, A. User participation: A study of types of participation, effects, mediators, and individual differences. *Environment and Behavior*, 1979, *11*, 185–208.

Ward, S. H., & Braun, J. Self-esteem and racial preference in Black children. *American Journal of Orthopsychiatry*, 1972, *42*, 644–647.

Ware, J., Davies-Avery, A., & Steward, A. The measurement and meaning of patient satisfaction. *Health and Medical Care Services Review*, 1978, *1*, 1–18.

Warren, R. L. The sociology of knowledge and the problems of the inner cities. *Social Science Quarterly*, 1971, *52*, 469–491.

Webb, E. J., Campbell, D. T., Schwartz, R. D., & Sechrest, L. *Unobtrusive measures: Nonreactive research in the social sciences.* Chicago: Rand McNally, 1966.

Wegner, D. M., & Crano, W. D. Racial factors in helping behavior: An unobtrusive field experiment. *Journal of Personality and Social Psychology*, 1975, *32*, 901–905.

Weigel, R. H., & Newman, L. S. Increasing attitude-behavior correspondence by broadening the scope of the behavioral measure. *Journal of Personality and Social Psychology*, 1976, *33*, 793–802.

Weigel, R. H., Wiser, P. L., & Cook, S. W. The impact of cooperative learning experiences on cross-ethnic relations and attitudes. *Journal of Social Issues*, 1975, *31*(1), 219–244.

Weinberg, M. The relationship between school desegregation and academic achievement: A review of the research. *Law and Contemporary Problems*, 1975, *39*, 240–270.

Weiner, B. *Theories of motivation: From mechanism to cognition.* Chicago: Rand McNally, 1972.

Weiner, B. A theory of motivation for some classroom experiences. *Journal of Educational Psychology*, 1979, *71*, 3–25.

Weiner, B. May I borrow your class notes? An attributional analysis of judgments of help giving in an achievement-related context. *Journal of Educational Psychology*, 1980, *72*, 676–681. (a)

Weiner, B. *The role of affect in rational (attributional) approaches to human motivation.* Paper presented at the annual meeting of the American Educational Research Association, Boston, April 1980. (b)

Weiner, B., Frieze, I., Kukla, A., Reed, L., Rest, S., & Rosenbaum, R. M. *Perceiving the causes of success and failure.* New York: General Learning Press, 1971.

Weiner, B., & Kukla, A. An attributional analysis of achievement motivation. *Journal of Personality and Social Psychology*, 1970, *15*, 1–20.

Weiner, B., Nierenberg, R., & Goldstein, M. Social learning (locus of control) versus attributional (causal stability) interpretations of expectancy of success. *Journal of Personality*, 1976, *61*, 144–151.

Weiner, B., Russell, D., & Lerman, D. Affective consequences of causal ascriptions. In J. H. Harvey, W. J. Ickes, & R. F. Kidd (Eds.), *New directions in attribution research* (Vol. 2). Hillsdale, N.J.: Lawrence Erlbaum Associates, 1978.

Weiner, F. H. Altruism, ambiance, and action: The effects of rural and urban rearing on helping behavior. *Journal of Personality and Social Psychology*, 1976, *34*, 112–124.

Weinstein, N. D. Cognitive processes and information seeking concerning an environmental health threat. *Journal of Human Stress*, 1978, *4*, 32–41.

Weiss, R. F., Buchanan, W., Altstatt, L., & Lombardo, J. P. Altruism is rewarding. *Science*, 1971, *171*, 1262–1263.

Weiss, R. S. The emotional impact of marital separation. *Journal of Social Issues*, 1976, *32*(1), 135–145.

Weitz, S. Sex differences in nonverbal communications. *Sex Roles*, 1976, *2*, 175–184.

West, C. Against our will: Male interruptions of females in cross-sex conversation. In J. Orasanu, M. K. Slater, & L. L. Adler (Eds.), *Language, sex and gender: Does la difference make a difference?* New York: New York Academy of Sciences, 1979.

West, S. G., Whitney, G., & Schnedler, R. Helping a motorist in distress: The effects of sex, race, and neighborhood. *Journal of Personality and Social Psychology*, 1975, *31*, 691–698.

Weyant, J. M. Effects of mood states, costs, and benefits on helping. *Journal of Personality and Social Psychology*, 1978, *36*, 1169–1176.

Wheeler, L., & Caggiula, A. R. The contagion of violence. *Journal of Personality and Social Psychology*, 1966, *2*, 1–10.

White, G. L. Physical attractiveness and courtship progress. *Journal of Personality and Social Psychology*, 1980, *39*, 660–668.

White, H. *Chains of opportunity.* Cambridge, Mass.: Harvard University Press, 1970.

Whyte, W. F. *Money and motivation.* New York: Harper, 1955.

Wichman, H. Effects of isolation and communication on cooperation in a two-person game. *Journal of Personality and Social Psychology*, 1970, *16*, 114–120.

Wicker, A. W. Attitudes versus actions: The relationship of verbal and overt behavioral responses to attitude objects. *Journal of Social Issues*, 1969, *25*(4), 41–78.

Wicker, A. W. *An introduction to ecological psychology.* Monterey, Cal.: Brooks/Cole, 1979.

Wicklund, R. A. Objective self-awareness. In L. Berkowitz (Ed.), *Advances in experimental social psychology* (Vol. 8). New York: Academic Press, 1975.

Wicklund, R. A. The influence of self-awareness on human behavior. *American Scientist,* 1979, *67,* 187–192.

Wicklund, R. A., & Brehm, J. W. *Perspectives on cognitive dissonance.* Hillsdale, N.J.: Lawrence Erlbaum Associates, 1976.

Wiggins, J. A., Dill, F., & Schwartz, R. D. On status-liability. *Sociometry,* 1965, *28,* 197–209.

Wiggins, J. S., Wiggins, N., & Conger, J. C. Correlates of heterosexual somatic preferences. *Journal of Personality and Social Psychology,* 1968, *10,* 82–90.

Wilcox, B. L., & Holahan, C. J. Social ecology of the megadorm in university student housing. *Journal of Educational Psychology,* 1976, *68,* 453–458.

Wilder, D. Perception of groups, size of opposition and social influence. *Journal of Experimental Social Psychology,* 1977, *13,* 253–268.

Wilke, H., & Lanzetta, J. T. The obligation to help: The effects of amount of prior help on subsequent helping behavior. *Journal of Experimental Social Psychology,* 1970, *6,* 483–493.

Wilkening, E. Informal leaders and innovators in farm practices. *Rural Sociology,* 1952, *17,* 272–275.

Williams, J. R., & Gold, M. From delinquency behavior to official delinquency. *Social Problems,* 1972, *20,* 209–229.

Williams, R. L., & Byars, H. Negro self-esteem in a transitional society. *Personnel and Guidance Journal,* 1968, *47,* 120–125.

Wilson, D. W., & Schafer, R. B. Is social psychology interdisciplinary? *Personality and Social Psychology Bulletin,* 1978, *4,* 548–552.

Wilson, E. O. *Sociobiology: The new synthesis.* Cambridge, Mass.: Harvard University Press, 1975.

Wilson J. P. Motivation, modeling and altruism: A Person X Situation analysis. *Journal of Personality and Social Psychology,* 1976, *34,* 1078–1086.

Wilson, W. C. Can pornography contribute to the prevention of sexual problems? In C. B. Qualls, J. P. Wineze, & D. H. Barlow (Eds.), *The prevention of sexual disorders: Issues and approaches.* New York: Plenum Press, 1978.

Wilson, W. J. *Power, racism and privilege.* New York: Free Press, 1973.

Winch, R. F. *Mate selection: A study of complementary needs.* New York: Harper & Row, 1958.

Winett, R. A., & Nietzel, M. T. Behavioral ecology: Contingency managememt of consumer energy use. *American Journal of Community Psychology,* 1975, *3,* 123–133.

Winfrey, C. Why 900 died. *New York Times Magazine,* February 25, 1979, pp. 39–41.

Wishnoff, R. Modeling effects of explicit and non-explicit sexual stimuli on the sexual anxiety and behavior of women. *Archives of Sexual Behavior,* 1978, *7,* 455–461.

Wispé, L., & Freshley, H. Race, sex, and sympathetic helping behavior: The broken bag caper. *Journal of Personality and Social Psychology,* 1971, *17,* 59–65.

Withey, J. B., & Abeles, R. P. *Television and social behavior: Beyond violence and children.* Hillsdale, N.J.: Lawrence Erlbaum Associates, 1980.

Witkin, H. A., Mednick, S. A., Schulsinger, F., Bakkestrom, E., Christiansen, K. O., Goodenough, D. R., Hirschhorn, K., Lundsteen, C., Owen, D. R., Phillip, J., Ruben, D. B., & Stocking, M. Criminality in XYY and XXY men. *Science,* 1976, *193,* 547–555.

Wolfe, J., & Baker, V. Characteristics of imprisoned rapists and circumstances of the rape. In C. G. Warner (Ed.), *Rape and sexual assault.* Germantown, Md.: Aspen Systems Co., 1980.

Wolfgang, M. *Patterns in criminal homicide.* Philadelphia: University of Pennsylvania Press, 1958.

Won-Doornink, M. J. On getting to know you: The association between the stage of a relationship and reciprocity of self-disclosure. *Journal of Experimental Social Psychology,* 1979, *15,* 229–241.

Wong, P. J. P., & Weiner, B. When people ask why questions and the heuristics of attributional search. *Journal of Personality and Social Psychology,* 1981, *40,* 650–653.

Worchel, S. The effects of three types of arbitrary thwarting on instigation to aggression. *Journal of Personality,* 1974, *42,* 300–318.

Worchel, S., Andreoli, V. A., & Folger, R. Intergroup cooperation and intergroup attraction. *Journal of Experimental Social Psychology,* 1977, *13,* 131–140.

Worthy, M., Gary, A., & Kahn, G. Self-disclosure as an exchange process. *Journal of Personality and Social Psychology,* 1969, *13,* 59–64.

Wortman, C. B., Adesman, P., Herman, E., & Greenberg, R. Self-disclosure: An attributional perspective. *Journal of Personality and Social Psychology,* 1976, *33,* 184–191.

Wortman, C. B., & Brehm, J. W. Responses to uncontrollable outcomes: An integration of reactance theory and the learned helplessness model. In L. Berkowitz (Ed.), *Advances in experimental social psychology* (Vol. 8). New York: Academic Press, 1975.

Wortman, C. B., & Dunkel-Schetter, C. Interpersonal relationships and cancer: A theoretical analysis. *Journal of Social Issues,* 1979, *35*(1), 120–155.

Wright, N. F. *Recording and analyzing child behavior.* New York: Harper & Row, 1967.

Wrightsman, L. S. *Social psychology in the seventies.* Belmont, Cal.: Brooks/Cole, 1972.

Wrightsman, L. S. *Social psychology* (2d ed.). Monterey, Cal.: Brooks/Cole, 1977.

Wynne-Edwards, V. C. Self-regulating systems in populations of animals. *Science,* 1962, *147,* 1543–1548.

Younger, J., & Doob, A. N. Attribution and aggression: The misattribution of anger. *Journal of Research in Personality,* 1978, *12,* 164–178.

Younger, J. C., Walker, L., & Arrowood, A. J. Post-decision dissonance at the fair. *Personality and Social Psychology Bulletin,* 1977, *3,* 247–287.

Yukl, G. A. Effects of situational variables and opponent concessions on a bargainer's perception, aspiration, and concessions. *Journal of Personality and Social Psychology,* 1974, *29,* 227–236.

Zajonc, R. B. Social facilitation. *Science,* 1965, *149,* 269–274.

Zajonc, R. B. Attitudinal effects of mere exposure. *Journal of Personality and Social Psychology Monograph Supplement,* 1968, *9,* 1–27. (a)

Zajonc, R. B. Cognitive theories in social psychology. In G. Lindzey & E. Aronson (Eds.), *The handbook of social psychology,* (Vol. 1, 2d ed.). Reading, Mass.: Addison-Wesley, 1968. (b)

Zajonc, R. B. Feeling and thinking: Preferences need no inferences. *American Psychologist,* 1980, *35,* 151–175.

Zaleznik, A., Christensen, C. R., & Roethlisberger, F. J. *The motivation, productivity and satisfaction of workers: A prediction study.* Boston: Harvard Business School, Division of Research, 1958.

Zander, A., & Forward, J. Position in group achievement motivation and group aspirations. *Journal of Personality and Social Psychology,* 1968, *8,* 282–288.

Zanna, M. P., & Cooper, J. Dissonance and the attribution process. In J. H. Harvey, W. J. Ickes, & R. F. Kidd (Eds.), *New directions in attribution research* (Vol. 1). Hillsdale, N.J.: Lawrence Erlbaum Associates, 1976.

Zanna, M. P., Olson, J. M., & Fazio, R. H. Attitude-behavior consistency: An individual difference perspective. *Journal of Personality and Social Psychology,* 1980, *38,* 432–440.

Zanna, M. P., & Pack, S. J. On the self-fulfilling nature of apparent sex differences in behavior. *Journal of Experimental Social Psychology,* 1975, *11,* 583–591.

Zeisel, J. *Inquiry by design: Tools for environment-behavior research.* Monterey, Cal.: Brooks/Cole, 1981.

Zellman, G. L., & Sears, D. O. Childhood origins of tolerance for dissent. *Journal of Social Issues,* 1971, *27*(2), 109–136.

Zillmann, D. *Hostility and aggression.* Hillsdale, N.J.: Lawrence Erlbaum Associates, 1979.

Zillmann, D., & Bryant, J. Viewer's moral sanctions of retribution in the appreciation of dramatic presentations. *Journal of Experimental Social Psychology,* 1975, *11,* 572–582.

Zillmann, D., Bryant, J., Cantor, J., & Day, K. Irrelevance of mitigating circumstances in retaliatory behavior at high levels of arousal. *Journal of Research in Personality,* 1975, *9,* 282–293.

Zillmann, D., & Cantor, J. Effects of timing of information about mitigating circumstances on emotional responses to provocation and retaliatory behavior. *Journal of Experimental Social Psychology,* 1976, *12,* 38–55.

Zillmann, D., & Johnson, R. Motivated aggressiveness perpetuated by exposure to aggressive films and reduced by exposure to nonaggressive films. *Journal of Research in Personality,* 1973, *7,* 261–276.

Zimbardo, P. The human choice: Individuation, reason and order versus deindividuation, impulse, and chaos. In W. J. Arnold & D. Levine (Eds.), *Nebraska Symposium on Motivation.* (Vol. 17). Lincoln: University of Nebraska Press, 1969.

Zimbardo, P. G. *Shyness.* Reading, Mass.: Addison-Wesley, 1977.

Zimbardo, P. G., & Newton, J. W. *Instructor's resource book to accompany Psychology and Life.* Glenview, Ill.: Scott, Foresman & Co., 1976.

Zimmer, J. L., & Sheposh, J. P. Effects of high status and low status actors' performance on observers' attributions of causality and behavioral intentions. *Sociometry,* 1975, *38,* 395–407.

Zube, E. H., Brush, R. O., & Fabos, J. G. (Eds.). *Landscape assessment: Values, perceptions and resources.* Stroudsburg, Pa.: Dowden, Hutchinson, & Ross, 1975.

Zuckerman, M. Belief in a just world and altruistic behavior. *Journal of Personality and Social Psychology,* 1975, *31,* 972–976.

Zuckerman, M., & Reis, H. T. Comparison of three models for predicting altruistic behavior. *Journal of Personality and Social Psychology,* 1978, *36,* 498–510.

Zwerdling, D. *Workplace democracy.* New York: Harper & Row, 1980.

NAME INDEX

SUBJECT INDEX

CREDITS

PHOTO ACKNOWLEDGMENTS

Part I Opener: p. 1, Sherry Suris/Photo Researchers.

Chapter 1: p. 6, Beryl Goldberg; p. 12, Daniel S. Brody/Editorial Photocolor Archives, Inc.; p. 13, Andrew McKeever/Editorial Photocolor Archives, Inc.

Chapter 2: p. 21, Erika Stone/Photo Researchers, Inc.; p. 22, Steve Kagan/Photo Researchers, Inc.; p. 36, Beryl Goldberg.

Part II Opener: p. 41, Herb Taylor/Editorial Photocolor Archives, Inc.

Chapter 3: p. 48, Michael Heron/Woodfin Camp & Associates; p. 51, Beryl Goldberg; p. 53, Rita Nannini; p. 63, Rita Nannini.

Chapter 4: p. 77, Rita Nannini; p. 94, Herman Emmet/Photo Researchers, Inc.

Chapter 5: p. 103, Wide World Photos, Inc.; p. 108, Beryl Goldberg; p. 114, Shell Oil Company; p. 119, Alice Kandall/Photo Researchers, Inc.

Chapter 6: p. 129, Paolo Koch/Photo Researchers, Inc.; p. 137, Beryl Goldberg; p. 145, Michael Uffer/Photo Researchers, Inc.

Chapter 7: p. 162, courtesy of the Bettman Archive; p. 163, Michael Meadows/Editorial Photocolor Archives, Inc.; p. 167, Elizabeth Wilcox/Photo Researchers, Inc.; p. 172, Peter Angelo Simon/Photo Researchers, Inc.

Part III Opener: p. 183, Beryl Goldberg.

Chapter 8: p. 190, Jan Halaska/Photo Researchers, Inc.; p. 191, Ray Ellis/Photo Researchers, Inc.; p. 199, Gamma/Liason Agency.

Chapter 9: p. 209, Michael Uffer/Photo Researchers, Inc.; p. 212, Michael Hayman/Photo Researchers, Inc.; p. 223, Anne Chwatsky/Editorial Photocolor Archives.

Chapter 10: p. 232, Jim Anderson/Woodfin Camp & Associates; p. 235, Steve Kagan/Photo Researchers, Inc.; p. 248, Tom McHugh/Photo Researchers, Inc.; p. 252, Arthur Tress/Woodfin Camp & Associates.

Chapter 11: U.S. Department of Justice; p. 261, Animals, Animals/Leonard Lee Rue III; p. 269, Beryl Goldberg; p. 270, Alon Reininger/Contact Press Images.

Chapter 12: p. 286, Beryl Goldberg; p. 290, Christina Thompson/Woodfin Camp & Associates; p. 294, Jan Lukas/Editorial Photocolor Archives, Inc.

Chapter 13: p. 314, Sepp Seitz/Woodfin Camp & Associates, Inc.; p. 317, Wide World Photos; p. 322, Catherine Noren/Photo Researchers, Inc.; p. 334, Linda Farrer/Woodfin Camp & Associates.

Chapter 14: p. 343, Lois Biener; p. 357, Frank Johnston, *Washington Post* Woodfin Camp & Associates; p. 363, Beryl Goldberg; p. 371, John Blaustein/Woodfin Camp & Associates.

Part Opener IV: p. 381, Christa Armstrong/Photo Researchers, Inc.

Chapter 15: p. 390, Sylvia Johnston/Woodfin Camp & Associates; p. 406, Catherine Ursillo/Photo Researchers, Inc.; p. 409, Wide World Photos.

Chapter 16: p. 416, Bruce Roberts/Photo Researchers, Inc.; p. 417, Robert M. Smith/Editorial Photocolor Archives; p. 418, Beryl Goldberg; p. 437, Katrina Thomas/Photo Researchers.

Chapter 17: p. 454, courtesy of UPI; p. 460, courtesy of Dan Stokols; p. 467, John Blaustein/Woodfin Camp.

Chapter 18: p. 475, Sam Pierson/Photo Researchers, Inc.; p. 482, Liason Photo Agency; p. 484, Bettye Lane/Photo Researchers, Inc.; p. 488, M.E. Warren/Photo Researchers, Inc.

Chapter 19: p. 508, Bettye Lane/Photo Researchers, Inc.; p. 514, Charles Gatewood; p. 515 (top), Ray Ellis/Photo Researchers, Inc.; p. 515 (bottom), Anne Meuer/Photo Researchers, Inc.

TEXT AND FIGURE ACKNOWLEDGMENTS

Chapter 3

Excerpts, pages 64 and 65, from Jean Anyon. Ideology and United States history textbooks. *Harvard Educational Review*, 1979, 49, 361–386. Reprinted by permission.

Social Focus 3.4, page 66, adapted from J. L. Tapp, & L. Kohlberg. Developing senses of law and legal justice. In J. L. Tapp and F. J. Levine (Eds.), *Law, justice, and the individual in society: Psychological and legal issues*. New York: Holt, Rinehart, and Winston, 1977. Reprinted by permission.

Classification schema, page 68, adapted from J. L. Tapp, & F. J. Levine. Legal socialization: Strategies for an ethical legality. *Stanford Law Review*, 1974, 24, 1–72. Reprinted by permission.

Chapter 4

Figure 4.2, p. 88, Fishbein & Ajzen. BELIEF, ATTITUDE, INTENTION & BEHAVIOR, © 1975 Addison-Wesley, Reading, MA. Figure 1.1 reprinted with permission.

Chapter 5

Figure 5.2, p. 109, reprinted by permission of John Wiley & Sons, Inc.

Chapter 6

Table 6.1, page 134, prepared and included by permission of Irene H. Frieze.

Table 6.2, page 136, adapted from D. J. Schneider, A. H. Hastorf, and P. C. Ellsworth. *Person perception* (2d ed.). Reading, Mass: Addison-Wesley, 1979. Reprinted by permission.

Figure 6.2, page 139, from B. R. Orvis, J. D. Cunningham, and H. H. Kelley. A closer examination of causal inference: The role of concensus, distinctiveness and consistency information. *Journal of Personality and Social Psychology*, 1975, 32, 605–616. Reprinted by permission.

Figure 6.3, page 144, from V. A. Valle, and I. H. Frieze. The stability of causal attribution as a mediator in changing expectations for success. *Journal of Personality and Social Psychology*, 1976, 33, 579–587. Reprinted by permission.

Excerpts, pages 132–33, from J. S. Carroll and J. W. Payne. Judgments about crime and the criminal: A model and a method for investigating parole decision. In B. D. Sales (Ed.), *Perspectives in law and psychology* (Vol. 1). New York: Plenum Press, 1977. Reprinted by permission.

Chapter 7

Quote, p. 158, from Aleksandr I. Solzhenitsyn, *Cancer Ward*, tr. by Rebecca Frank, reprinted by permission of Dial Press. Photos, p. 166, courtesy of Dr. Paul Ekman.

Chapter 8

Quote, p. 185, courtesy of the Orange County Register.

Figure 8.1, p. 186, copyright George Levinger and J. Diedrick Snoek, used by permission.

Quote, p. 188, reprinted by permission of Dr. Carol U. Lindquist.

Figure 8.2, p. 194, reprinted by permission of Edna B. Foa and Uriel G. Foa.

Quote, p. 204, from "The Emotional Impact of Marital Separation" by Robert S. Weiss in DIVORCE AND SEPARATION: CONTEXT, CAUSES, AND CONSEQUENCES by George Levinger and Oliver C. Moles (eds.). Copyright © 1979 by the Society for the Psychological Study of Social Issues, by permission of Basic Books, Inc., Publishers, New York.

Chapter 9

Quote, p. 210, from *Environment and Social Behavior* by I. Altman. Copyright © 1975 by Wadsworth Publishing, Inc. Reprinted by permission of Brooks/Cole Publishing Company, Monterey, California.

Figure 9.2, p. 216, reprinted by permission of the American Sociological Association.

Quote, pp. 218–219, from Taylor, D. A. & Altman, I. "Intimacy-Scaled Stimuli for Use in Research on Interpersonal Exchange." N.M.R.I., May, 1966, reprinted by permission.

Quote, p. 222, from DILEMMAS OF MASCULINITY, A Study of College Youth, by Mirra Komarovsky. W. W. Norton & Company, Inc. Copyright © 1976 by W. W. Norton & Company, Inc., reprinted by permission.

Chapter 10

Excerpts, page 233, from J. T. Spence, & R. Helmreich. The attitudes toward women scale: An objective instrument to measure attitudes toward the rights and roles of women in contemporary society. *JSAS Catalog of Selected Documents in Psychology*, 1972, 2, 66 (Ms. No. 153). Reprinted by permission of J. T. Spence and R. Helmreich.

Figure 10.1, page 240, from J. H. Court. Sex and violence: A ripple effect. In Neil Malamuth and E.

Donnerstein (Eds.) *Pornography and Sexual Aggression*. New York: Academic Press, in press. Reprinted by permission of J. H. Court.

Figure 10.2, page 241, adapted from J. L. Howard, C. B. Reifler, and M. B. Liptzin. Effects of exposure to pornography. *(Technical Reports of the Commission on Obscenity and Pornography, Vol. 8)*. Washington, D.C.: U.S. Government Printing Office, 1970. Reprinted by permission of J. L. Howard.

Figure 10.3, page 244, from E. Donnerstein, & L. Berkowitz. Victim reactions in aggressive erotic films as a factor in violence against women. *Journal of Personality and Social Psychology*, 1981, 41, 710–724. Reprinted by permission.

Figure 10.4, page 244, from N. Malamuth, and J. V. P. Check. The effects of mass media exposure on acceptance of violence against women: A field experiment. *Journal of Research in Personality*, 1981, 15, 436–446. Reprinted by permission.

Figure 10.5, page 250, adapted from Morton Hunt. *Sexual behavior in the 1970's*. Chicago: Playboy Press, 1974. Reprinted by permission.

Table 10.1, page 243, from D. T. Kenrich, D. O. Stringfield, W. J. Wagenhals, R. H. Dahl, and H. J. Ransdell. Sex differences, androgyny, and approach responses to erotica: A new variation on the old volunteer problem. *Journal of Personality and Social Psychology*, 1980, 38, 517–524. Copyright 1980 by the American Psychological Association and reprinted by permission.

Chapter 11

Table 11.1, p. 259, adapted from "Aggression Pays" by A. H. Buss in J. L. Singer (ed.), *The Control of Aggression and Violence*, Academic Press, 1971, reprinted by permission.

Photo, p. 260, reprinted by permission of the Federal Bureau of Investigation.

Chapter 12

Table 12.1, page 298, adapted from C. D. Batson, B. Duncan, P. Ackerman, T. Buckley, and K. Birch. Is emphatic emotion a source of altruistic motivation? *Journal of Personality and Social Psychology*, 1981, 40, 290–302. Reprinted by permission.

News paper article, page 284, reprinted by permission of Associated Press. Copyright Associated Press, 1976.

Chapter 13

Figure 13.2, p. 331, from Deutsch, M., & Krauss, R. M. The effect of threat upon interpersonal bargaining. *Journal of Abnormal and Social Psychology*, 1960, *61*, 181–189. Copyright © 1960 by the American Psychological Association. Reprinted by permission of the publisher and authors.

Chapter 14

Table 14.2, page 355, adapted from Stanley Milgram. *Obedience to Authority*. New York: Harper and Row, 1974. Reprinted by permission.

Table 14.3, page 367, adapted from A. H. Eagly. Sex differences in influenceability. *Psychological Bulletin*, 1978, 85, 86–116. Reprinted by permission.

Social Focus 14–4, page 374, "In Search of Right Rights Style", by Ellen Goodman. Reprinted by permission of Ellen Goodman.

Figure 14.1, page 362, from S. Asch. *Social Psychology*. New York: Prentice-Hall, 1952. Reprinted by permission.

Chapter 15

Figure 15.1, page 386, from G. W. Fairweather, D. H. Saunders, H. Maynard, D. L. Cressler, and D. S. Bleck. *Community life for the mentally ill: An alternative to institutional care*. Chicago: Aldine, 1969. Reprinted by permission.

Figure 15.2, page 392, from S. Kagan, and M. C. Madsen. Rivalry in Anglo-American and Mexican-American children of two ages. *Journal of Personality and Social Psychology*, 1972, 24, 214–220. Reprinted by permission.

Table 15.2, page 399, from C. R. Sapin. *A status formulation of sex differences*. Unpublished dissertation, University of Colorado, 1979. Reprinted by permission.

Table 15.3, page 400, adapted from A. Zander, and J. Forward. Position in group achievement motivation and group aspirations. *Journal of Personality and Social Psychology*, 1968, 8, 282–288. Reprinted by permission.

Figure 15.3, page 394, drawn from data reported in W. F. Whyte. *Money and motivation*. New York: Harper, 1955. Reprinted by permission.

Figure 15.5, page 408, from F. Fiedler, Personality and situation determinants. In D. Cartwright and A. Zander, (Eds.). *Group Dynamics*. New York: Harper and Row, 1968. Reprinted by permission.

Social Focus 15.3, page 403, quote from personal correspondence to the author. Reprinted by permission of the author.

Quotes, page 386, 388, 393, 396, 397, 398, 401, 402, 405, 406, 409, 410, 411, 412 from Fairweather et al. *Community life for the mentally ill. An alternative to institutional care*. Chicago: Aldine, 1969. Reprinted by permission.

Chapter 17

Figure 17.1, p. 447, adapted from Stokols, D. Environmental Psychology. *Annual Review of Psychology*, 1978, *29*, 253–295, reprinted by permission.

Quote, p. 448, reprinted by permission of the MIT Press.

Figure 17.2, p. 451, copyright © by Stanley Milgram, reprinted by permission.

Figure 17.3, p. 452, from "Differential cognition of urban residents: Effects of social scale on mapping" by P. Orleans in R. Downs & D. Stea (eds.), *Image and Environment*, Aldine, 1973, reprinted by permission.

Figure 17.4, p. 461, from "Reinforcement theory strategies for modifying transit ridership" by P. B. Everett in I. Altman, J. Wohlwill, & P. B. Everett (eds.), *Human Behavior and the Environment: Transportation*, Plenum Press, 1981, reprinted by permission.

Chapter 18

"Two at Westpoint Leave", page 484, copyright The New York Times, 1979. Reprinted by permission.

"Panic Before a Dinner Party", pages 484, and 489, T. D. Allman. Copyright The New York Times, 1979. Section C, 1 & 3. Reprinted by permission.

"Logjam on Executive Track", pages 492–493. T. C. Hayes. Copyright The New York Times, 1980. Reprinted by permission.

Social Focus 18.1, page 479, from LIFE IN ORGANIZATIONS: WORKPLACES AS PEOPLE EXPERIENCE THEM by Rosabeth Moss Kanter and Barry A. Stein, Editors. Copyright © 1979 by Rosabeth Moss Kanter and Barry A. Stein. By permission of Basic Books, Inc.

Excerpt, page 475–6, from "Lordstown" from ALL THE LIVELONG DAY by Barbara Garson. Copyright © 1972, 1980 by Barbara Garson. Reprinted by permission of Doubleday & Company, Inc.

Chapter 19

Figure 19–1, page 509, is redrawn from Gary Gregg and associates, "The caravan rolls on: Forty years of social problem research." *Knowledge: Creation, Diffusion, Utilization*, Vol. 1, No. 1 (Sept. 1979) p. 32, Copyright 1979 Sage Publications, Inc., with permission.

Table 19.1, page 519, from P. Brickman, J. Karuza, E. Cohn, V. C. Rabinowitz, D. Coates, and L. Kidder. Models of helping and coping. To appear in *American Psychologist*, 1982. Reprinted by permission.

Excerpt, page 513, from N. Caplan and S. Nelson. On being useful: The nature and consequences of psychological research on social problems. *American Psychologist*, 1973, 28, (3), 199–211. Copyright 1973 by the American Psychological Association, and reprinted by permission.

Excerpt, page 517, from N. Caplan and S. Nelson. On being useful: The nature and consequences of psychological research on social problems. *American Psychologist*, 1973, 28, (3), 199–211. Copyright 1973 by the American Psychological Association, and reprinted by permission.

Excerpt, page 530–531, from N. Caplan and S. Nelson. On being useful: The nature and consequences of psychological research on social problems. *American Psychologist*, 1973, 28, (3), 199–211. Copyright 1973 by the American Psychologist Association, and reprinted by permission.